THE AMERICAN LEGAL SYSTEM

the american legal system

SECOND EDITION

BLAIR J. KOLASA

Ph.D., University of Pittsburgh
J.D., Duquesne University
Dean Emeritus and Professor of Behavioral Science
School of Business and Administration
Duquesne University

BERNADINE MEYER

Ed.D., Columbia University
J.D., Duquesne University
Assistant Dean and Professor of Law Administration
School of Business and Administration
Duquesne University

Prentice-Hall, Inc., Englewood Cliffs, New Jersey 07632

Library of Congress Cataloging-in-Publication Data

Kolasa, Blair J. (Blair John)
  The American legal system.

  Rev. ed. of: Legal systems. c1978.
  Includes index.
    1. Justice, Administration of—United States.
2. Procedure (Law)—United States. I. Meyer.
Bernadine (date)   . II. Kolasa, Blair J. (Blair
John) (date)   . Legal systems. III. Title.
KF8700.K64 1987   347.73   86-9418
ISBN 0-13-027962-5   347.307

Previously published under the title of LEGAL SYSTEMS.

© 1987, 1978 by Prentice-Hall, Inc.
A division of Simon & Schuster
Englewood Cliffs, New Jersey 07632

Printed in the United States of America

10 9 8 7 6 5

Cover design: Edsal Enterprises
Manufacturing buyer: Carol Bystrom

ISBN 0-13-027962-5 01

Prentice-Hall International (UK) Limited, *London*
Prentice-Hall of Australia Pty. Limited, *Sydney*
Prentice-Hall Canada Inc., *Toronto*
Prentice-Hall Hispanoamericana, S.A., *Mexico*
Prentice-Hall of India Private Limited, *New Delhi*
Prentice-Hall of Japan, Inc., *Tokyo*
Prentice-Hall of Southeast Asia Pte. Ltd., *Singapore*
Editora Prentice-Hall do Brasil, Ltda., *Rio de Janeiro*

contents

TWO

the legal system

THREE

legal substance and procedure

FOUR

entry into the system:
a case arises

SEVEN

post-verdict motions
and appeal

EIGHT

entry into the system:
control subsystem and entry
into the court subsystem

NINE

initial processing phase: court subsystem

TWELVE

administrative process: occupational safety and health

THIRTEEN

torts

FOURTEEN

contracts

cases

preface

The impact of law upon the daily lives of individuals today is of such significance that men and women not only accept its pervasiveness but look to the law when seeking means to improve the quality of their lives. So influential is the law that persons who seek to understand their society, its institutions, and governance must have a basic understanding of the nature and functions of law, as well as of the legal system and the legal process. For this reason, study of law is essential in everyone's general education, not just for those intending to enter the legal profession. To meet this need, legal studies programs have become an increasingly important element in the offerings of universities and colleges.

This text has been prepared for use in undergraduate or graduate courses in law, primarily those offered outside the law school. Its objective is to help the student understand the legal process as well as such substantive areas of the law as contracts, torts, crimes, organizations, and commercial transactions. It is equally suitable for use in legal studies in liberal arts programs and in law courses offered in professional schools, notably the business school. For programs in law enforcement or the administration of legal systems, it is supportive of the objectives of the course work.

The approach is analytical. Law is viewed as much more than a set of rules. It is seen as a dynamic system and process, one in which human beings interact and influence not only one another but also the law and the legal system. Thus, law is considered not as an isolated discipline, but as one influenced by and influencing such other spheres of life as the economy, politics, ethics, social life, and business.

Rather than merely explain to the student what law, the legal system, and the legal process are, the text draws the student into examination of them through analysis of the decision making that takes place within the civil, criminal, and administrative agency processes. Decisions and procedures are shown in flow charts so the student can visualize not only the steps in the process, but also the outcomes of decision making. It is this decision analysis which is the unique contribution of the text.

The book begins with the study of law in a basic and fundamental manner, in order to provide a brief overview of the area and a foundation for later, more in-depth study. In this first part of the book, discussion of legal concepts and systems and their implementation is intended to serve *only as an introduction to the field,* not *as a complete and comprehensive survey of the law.* Greater awareness should come through the repetition and elaboration of legal concepts and their use in realistically portrayed incidents in subsequent chapters.

Chapters Four through Twelve deal with the civil, criminal, and administrative law processes. In each of these chapters students are presented with a situation that occurs in the lives of hypothetical people and eventually involves them in the legal system. Students follow these fictional people step by step, as they go all the way through the legal process. In doing so, the student finds that knowledge of substantive law is as important as knowledge of procedural law to resolution of the matter. Thus, the student realizes the significance of substantive law, and the final chapters provide some basic elements of selected substantive areas of law.

As in any complex area of disciplinary activity, one small volume will not contain all (or even most) of the material. Neither this book nor any one of similar length will satisfy those with a desire to delve more deeply into the discipline. Further professional pursuit of law will take the student so inclined to texts and courses in a law program beyond the scope of this work.

The text is recommended for use in such courses as introduction to law, legal process, legal systems, law and society, legal environment, business law, and survey of law. In introducing the student to law, the text provides a base for learning through the use of a systems format to delineate steps in the legal process. It has been the aim of the authors that it might serve to increase public understanding and appreciation of the law.

The increased focus on the international in the personal and business lives of Americans is recognized in this second edition, which incorporates a look at law on a global basis. There is added treatment in this edition of the legal aspects of technology, including the impact of computers upon personal privacy and the law. The areas of socioeconomic regulation and the law of employment have been expanded, while matters ordinarily taught in advanced business law courses have been eliminated. The total emphasis is upon the American legal environment. Another feature of the second edition is the use of more cases and judicial decisions in each chapter to enhance the specific topic being discussed. In the preparation of this edition, the student's use of the text has been the central concern of the authors. It is their hope that the student will enjoy the study of *The American Legal System* and find the textbook understandable, relevant, and exciting.

NOTE TO READERS

The hypothetical cases in this book refer to fictional persons, organizations, and places. If the names of persons or companies bear any similarity to those of actual persons or companies, the similarity is purely fortuitous.

Legal requirements vary among the different jurisdictions. The legal procedures, forms, and documents in this text are illustrative of those generally in use. They have been incorporated in the text solely for educational purposes in acquainting the student with the nature of the legal process. They may not meet specific legal requirements of particular states. *Under no circumstances* should procedures, forms, or documents be used or adapted for self-help purposes by persons not admitted to the bar. Readers with specific legal problems should consult an attorney.

ACKNOWLEDGMENT

The aid and advice of members of the Prentice-Hall community, especially Mr. David Boelio and his staff, has helped in great measure to shape this work and to reduce the burdens associated with it. For this they have the warm gratitude of the authors. We wish also to thank the reviewers who gave generously of their time and demonstrated a positive and professional approach to the discipline.

Blair J. Kolasa

Bernadine Meyer

THE AMERICAN LEGAL SYSTEM

law
and legal
questions

ONE

Law is a form of order.
> —*Aristotle*

The welfare of the people is the highest law.
> —*Cicero*

The Law, which is perfection of reason . . .
> —*Sir Edward Coke*

Law is what the judge says it is.
> —*Anonymous*

What then is law? The learned discussions in the past on this topic would probably fill more space than is available in many college libraries and still not provide answers to satisfy everyone. The various opinions and the problems connected with them have undoubtedly been responsible for the omission of definitions of law in many texts that have been written to outline "The Law." With the feeling that such scant attention is improper, the authors venture to provide a starting point for the systematic analysis of the law.

DEFINITION

When faced with the need for understanding the meaning of a word, people often open a dictionary and get the definition. While this approach may raise more questions than answers, it may be a good place to start.

Webster's *New Collegiate Dictionary,* for instance, defines law as:

> the binding custom or practice of a community; rules of conduct enforced by a controlling authority; also, any single rule of conduct so enforced . . . a rule of conduct or action prescribed by the supreme governing authority and enforced by a sanction, as any whole body of such rules; also the control or regulation, or state of society, brought about by the existence and enforcement of such rules.

Several aspects can be seen in this definition. It includes the concepts of:

1. Rules;
2. Conduct;
3. Sanctions;
4. Control.

There is no direct statement of the ultimate reason for the existence of law, however, and yet the answer to the question *why* may be the most important of all.

The notion that law is a set of rules that governs the actions of people in a community is probably the most common. This view sees law as a set of fixed principles known to lawyers and judges (ignorance of which excuses no one, not even the less knowledgeable or less affluent members of society). The approach seeks out the specific precepts that must be followed by citizens and that, if not followed, give rise to a cause of action in the courts. It is also the view of law that may be reinforced by a course in law or business law in which the student may feel a need to memorize all the rules and regurgitate them during a later examination. Not that memorization is unnecessary, but memorization is detrimental if it excludes analyzing the basic factors involved in the development of law and the reasons, if any, for the continuation of legal rules.

This approach to law as a logical set of rules by which behavior is to be governed has been responsible for most of the traditional classifications or distinctions as well as implementations made today in the legal order. When a famous early English jurist, Sir Edward Coke, stated, "Law . . . is perfection of reason," he was only one in a long series of legal scholars who focused on the basis for law in reason and pointed to its logical arrangement (but who seemed sometimes unaware when its "logic" broke down).

In a more extensive analysis, a student of law could identify still other functions or purposes of law. Clearly a legal system expresses specific values and its functioning fulfills certain needs. Individual rights may be fostered through actions of agents of government, but so too might there be a preservation of group consensus that may be perceived by individuals as an infringement upon their rights. That same preservation of group consensus may be considered as serving common interests and strengthening social solidarity.

Another view of law is that it is a means of social control or a method of establishing order by maintaining authority of a ruler over those governed. Older discussions of law often defined the field in that manner; the concept can be identified in some treatises to this day. Aristotle, in the "golden age" of Greece believed law to be a form of order. More recently, a well respected view holds that law begins only when a coercive apparatus comes into existence to maintain control through enforcement of social norms.[1] (Norms are guidelines developed by a society to provide leads to proper behavior of members of that society.) The same observer adds that the control group need not be agents of a political entity, but may be labor, business, or church organizations, and that the coercion can be psychological as well as physical.

Most observers, however, believe that law exists only in a formal setting that involves the legislative, judicial, and executive arms of a political body and its system. "What these officials do about disputes is . . . the law itself."[2] Although rules are certainly an important part of the process, the emphasis is upon actions for the purpose of adherence to those rules. Law is thus defined as "the formal means of social control that involves the use of rules that are interpreted, and are enforceable, by the courts of a political community."[3] In somewhat the same way, authority is an aspect of a legal system that some other observers focus upon as being the key element. The hallmark of law is viewed as the obligation to act in line with norms authoritatively determined.[4]

A complementary definition of law comes from the sociological approach of Parsons, who views the legal system as a web of interaction or a structuring of relations between actors.[5] Roles and relationships are significant for an understanding of the law; interactions between employer and employee, seller and buyer, husband and wife, or landlord and tenant are the bases for action and decision-making in this area of human activity.

More comprehensive views of law take various positions into account and combine them. Many observers insist that an adequate theory of law must include aspects such as:

1. the distinctive work done by law and society;
2. the resources of law;
3. the characteristic mechanisms brought into play.[6]

This outline serves as a good basis for a systems approach to the study of legal systems.

After all of the above discussion, perhaps we can finally focus upon a comprehensive definition that seems to cover all the aspects discussed.

> Law is . . . a body of binding obligations regarded as a right by one party and acknowledged as a duty by the other which has been reinstitutionalized within the legal institution so that society can continue to function in an orderly manner on the basis of rules so maintained.[7]

Note that not only elements are present, but processes as well; the interpersonal bases in law are included with an analysis of how the framework is developed (institutionalization), and the purpose for which it functions.

GLOBAL CLASSIFICATION OF SYSTEMS

Cultural and historical factors have played a decisive role in the emergence of legal systems in various parts of the world. Variations in patterns of behavior under law are evident in societies that differ in values and beliefs that have been transmitted through contact or control over the years.

Basic Western Systems

Law in Western societies has developed along two lines. In the countries of continental Europe and those areas influenced by them, the governing law dates back to Roman law and is known as the *Civil law system.* The law with which U.S. citizens are more familiar is known as the *common law,* the system that developed in English-speaking countries. For many purposes, however, some differences between the two systems are more historical than real at the present time.

The major difference between the two systems lies in the operation of judicial processes. Adjudication under the Civil law is made by the judge following principles established by the earliest developments of Roman law as embodied at present under an extensive code of law in effect in that particular country. The judge must apply the appropriate section of the code to the case in court. The common law develops more through the decisions of judges applying prior decisions of courts to the new facts at hand. When Mr. Justice Holmes stated "the life of the law has not been logic; it has been experience," he was writing the first sentence of his treatise on the common law.[8] This emphasis upon case-by-case decisions has been kept in order to maintain the flexibility that comes with continuing challenges to the validity of certain legal positions that can be made through the participation of a greater number of individuals. Again, it must be stated that there may not be much difference between the two great systems of law, especially these days when legislation in the common law countries is proceeding more rapidly than before.

A few more words might be said here about the common law, since it is the system under which we in America function. It has been stated that, in deciding a particular case, the prior decisions of judges in similar cases are noted. This adherence to precedent is known by the Latin term *stare decisis.* It would seem at first glance that this obedience to precedent makes common law more rigid than it is flexible. Actually, however, the judge can distinguish between the different facts of the cases or find some other reason for going the new way. The outstanding characteristic of the system still remains the great opportunity for judicial decision-making without discarding the experience built up from prior court decisions.

Although many observers from the outside (as well as some lawyers) perceive that courts are more prone to focus upon statutes or administrative rules than upon the common experience, the fact that judges review past cases before making a decision shows the strength of the common law concept.

There are a few more aspects of the general legal process in common law countries that might be mentioned here briefly, in order to avoid confusion over some distinctions that occur later in the text. At present, little reason exists to differentiate concepts of equity or principles of business law from the rest of the large body of common law. These concepts are based, however, upon early developments outside the common law, and their use of form at this time may bear some vague relationship to that historical fact. In early feudal times common law courts were very rigid and limiting in the kinds of cases that would be entertained. Very frequently many persons could obtain no relief in the courts and had to petition the king for redress. The king's chancellor concerned himself with meting out justice in a court system that became known as the *courts of equity*. Present-day courts (because equity courts were absorbed into the common law courts) enforce equitable remedies which include:

1. Injunction—a direction to persons to refrain from committing a particular act;
2. Specific performance—compelling the party to perform, usually under a contract;
3. Reformation—the alteration of a contract or other instrument where errors were made;
4. Enforcement of a trust—directing performance of duties owed benefiting someone else.

Rules of evidence are not as strict in equity cases, and the judge ordinarily sits as the court without a jury.

Most of the elements of commercial or business law have their origin in the Middle Ages in the body of laws known as the law merchant. As with equity matters, the courts of common law either could not or were not interested in settling problems arising between merchants, and therefore the merchants themselves had to do so. By the time of the settlement of America, however, most of these merchant courts had been absorbed into the general legal system, so that all cases in controversy were being handled by the same set of judges.

Non-Western Legal Systems

Systems of legal functioning in countries other than those functioning under the common or Civil law system deserve mention in the light of increased social and economic interaction in a shrinking world. Some of the systems of law in the non-Western world have been influenced by concepts developed under common law or Civil law or both. In other parts of the world resemblances to common law or Civil law may be more apparent than real.

A casual observer viewing the laws of one-party states, for instance, may notice concepts not foreign to those encompassed by law in Western countries. However, closer scrutiny may show that the resemblance is casual and superficial.

The laws of the Soviet Union are formulated and upheld in a manner that perpetuates the pre-existing conditions of the one-party state. As one close observer of that system has commented, the prime purpose of Soviet law is:

> To regulate all aspects of economic and social life, including the circulation of thought, while leaving the critical questions of political power to be decided by informal, secret procedures beyond the scrutiny of control of legislative or judicial bodies . . . [and] whose primary function is to discipline, guide, train, and educate Soviet citizens to be dedicated members of a collectivized and mobilized social order.[9]

The author of that review did perceive some changes taking place at the time he wrote the comments, but subsequent events have seemed to reinforce the control aspects of the Soviet legal system.

Other countries within the Soviet bloc have had their legal systems altered in the post-World War II era to conform to the model of the bloc leader, whereas prior to conflict and occupation these countries' codes were based upon the Civil law of continental Europe.

In Asia the pre-eminent country in political and economic terms is Japan. Although criminal law in Japan was influenced by American concepts introduced in the postwar occupation of the country, the earlier influences of French and German processes have been retained. In the governance of private interactions, the statutes and procedures are based upon Civil law as well. The concepts of greatest interest to foreign commercial entities are, of course, those that regulate trade and industry. "The private international law of Japan is one founded entirely upon Civil law models, both as to legislation and judicial law making."[10]

The People's Republic of China, both in terms of present size and potential for growth, represents the likeliest political entity in Asia to gain the interest of other entities, political or commercial. During the period of the so-called "Cultural Revolution" of the 1970s, legal concepts and lawyers were attacked, along with other intellectual areas and participants, with the argument that they were accretions foreign to the country and dangerous for the spirit of the type of socialism espoused by its communist leaders. By the beginning of the 1980s, however, a substantial reversal of these limiting concepts had taken place, and China moved to a more open stance of interaction with others, particularly in the Western world. Use of legal concepts and forms, even in commercial interactions, has come slowly and grudgingly. There is still a strong thrust toward avoidance of fixed forms, as in contracts, and a preference for informal adjustments of any differences that might arise, but Western business methods are slowly being incorporated into transactions with the Chinese, and law studies are being given a greater role in mainland universities. Legal changes are proceeding along the lines of Civil law models as codification is being expanded, primarily to meet the needs of foreign trade. The constraints of social and political forces still resemble those of the Soviet bloc, however.

The Islamic countries, those of the Middle East in particular, have come to play a greater role in the economy and political affairs of the world and are of increasing importance to those whose commercial interests are involved. Islamic law is based upon the concept of *Shari'a,* sacred law stemming from the Koran and other writings by the prophet Mohammed or reasoning based on these sources by Islamic interpreters. There is some variation among countries, however, as many have introduced elements based upon British and Civil law codes. In certain countries of the Moslem world, Shari'a has been limited to matters of family law.[11]

In the remaining countries of the Third World, common and Civil law patterns can be seen as remnants of colonial or commercial influences. However, moves toward centralized authoritarian regimes in some jurisdictions are bringing the functioning of the legal system in those countries closer to the pattern of the one-party states.

The following excerpt from a criminal code can provide an awareness of the philosophical or ideological foundations of that legal system.

Criminal Code of the People's Republic of China

Adopted July 1, 1979, effective January 1, 1980

Article 1

The Criminal Law of the People's Republic of China adopts Marxism-Leninism-Mao Zedong thought as its guide and the constitution as its basis. It has been drawn up according to the policy of combining punishment with leniency, and integrates the concrete experiences and actual conditions of the various nationalities in our country, in their practice of the people's democratic dictatorships led by the proletariat and based on the alliance of workers and peasants, and in their carrying out the socialist revolution and socialist construction.

Article 2

The task of the Criminal Code of the People's Republic of China is to combat all counterrevolutionary and other crimes by inflicting punishment, thus defending the dictatorship of the proletariat; protecting socialist property of all the people and the property collectively owned by the working masses; protecting legitimate property privately owned by the citizens; protecting citizen's rights of person, democratic rights and other rights; maintaining social order, order in production, order in work, order in education and scientific research, and order in the life of the masses; and guaranteeing the smooth progress of the socialist revolution and socialist construction. . . .

Chin Kim, trans., *The Criminal Code of the People's Republic of China* (Littleton, Colorado: Fred B. Rothman & Co., 1982).

FUNDAMENTAL CLASSIFICATIONS
IN LAW

The study of law, particularly in Western societies, can be approached in ways that are based upon certain distinctions. There may be a focus upon the importance to society of maintaining behaviors or the interest may be in form as opposed to function. These differentiations must be recognized and included in a comprehensive survey of the discipline.

Degree of Societal Interest

The magnitude of society's concern about the relationships of its members determines the extent to which the officials of that society play a role. Various kinds of controversies are handled by the courts, but selected officials of the legal system step in to actively prosecute a case in which the seriousness of the cause is deemed sufficient for the political unit to take over. This is the distinction between *civil* law and *criminal* law. In civil law problems the authorities are concerned primarily with providing a forum for the resolution of controversies between individuals or groups. In criminal law there is a concern for public safety and order or "morals." A criminal is one who violates those portions of the statutes which were set up to ensure the public welfare and stability of the society. When the public interest becomes threatened, the public officials must move to protect the interests of society.

It must be noted that the use of the term civil law in this context is quite different from the use of that term to refer to the continental European legal systems stemming from Roman law. To differentiate between the two, the word *civil* used in this way will not be capitalized.

Content Versus Process

A focus upon the specific kinds of rights and duties created among individuals is a concentration upon the substance of the law, or, as the domain is most often called, *substantive* law. The ways in which these rights and duties are maintained or enforced is the area of *procedural* law. In a specific case or controversy the lawyer will be interested in both aspects. He may want to know, for instance, whether the elements for a valid case of law are present; on the other hand, he will be concerned with how to proceed to secure a remedy. Both areas can be quite complex, but as the areas of substantive law are more easily distinguishable, we shall concentrate on them.

Substance   Substantive law itself can be divided into *public* law and *private* law. The public law category concerns broader questions covering activity under the governmental system such as *constitutional* law. In addition to this, *administrative* law covers those areas dealing with the activities of governmental agencies acting in implementation of broader social and political policy.

The area of private law has a greater number of differentiations; the major areas are:

1. *Contracts*—including various relationships under agreements, such as agreements to buy or sell, *negotiable instruments, secured transactions,* and *bailments.*

2. *Property*—laws relating to the ownership or use of whatever may be claimed or controlled by someone. *Real property* is land and anything permanently attached to it, whereas *personal property* covers all other objects or interests owned.

3. *Persons*—legal precepts covering the interrelationships among individuals. These can be of a personal nature, such as *family law* or *domestic relations,* or they can be of a business nature, such as those relationships encompassed under *agency, partnerships,* and *corporations.*

4. *Torts*—this substantive area of law refers to wrongs or injuries of a noncriminal nature. These can be physical, such as in *assault* and *battery,* or they can be verbal, as in *libel* or *slander.* By far the greatest number of tort cases arise when individuals are physically injured through the action of another, as in an automobile accident or an injury caused by a defective product.

Each of the substantive areas can be subdivided further for analysis.

Process   Legal procedure is a more cohesive topic than substantive law from the standpoint of logical distinctions as this application of substantive law focuses more upon steps in a sequence. Process will be a prime orienting concept in the development of this book.

LAW IN ACTION

Definitions or theories of law, no matter how complete, must be followed by a closer look into how the law is actually put into operation. How the legal system works is a function of the society that contains it. Analyzing actual behavior in a social setting adds to the conceptual base of law to provide a better understanding of the field. Law and society cannot be considered independently of each other.

A formal system of law may have certain aspects put down permanently in writing. Closer inspection of actual events, however, sometimes shows a much different picture. Totalitarian societies may have a written constitution or codes of law that state various freedoms for individuals and groups in that society. In actual practice those freedoms may be circumscribed by powers granted to police or other government officials. Freedom of religion, assembly, or speech, granted on paper, is often restricted or prevented altogether by agents of that government. Countries that consistently show a disregard for individual rights may even add to the irony by calling themselves a "people's democracy."

A truly democratic society possesses safeguards in the actual implementation of basic governing documents. Enforcement of civil rights proceeds on the strength of built-in checks and balances in the legal system. In addition, the presence of methods of free inquiry into governmental proceedings aids in the preservation of such rights.

A pure democracy exists when individuals determine each aspect of governmental functioning directly through a vote on the issues raised. However, in a large and complex society such direct participation in government is not always possible. In large societies, therefore, the democratic process is in the form of a *representative* democracy whereby the members of the political entity select representatives by popular vote to carry out governmental functions in their name.

Even in those countries where individual and property rights are preserved, there are social forces that must be taken into account because they continue to affect the functioning of the legal system. This is most true for those societies that are undergoing rapid technological change. According to one commentator on the American social scene, for example, the present legal order is challenged by three main thrusts:

1. a "drift toward mass society marked by high rates of mobility, fragmented social experience, rising demands for short run gratification, and more active participation";
2. "the emergence of the large scale organization as the representative institution of modern society";
3. "the ascendance of social interest over parochial interests."[12]

All three are viewed as emerging from the weakening of social controls based upon close kinship and community ties.

The following case in the Supreme Court of the United States illustrates some of the social dilemmas that can occur. In this instance a private plan for achieving racial equality on the job was challenged by a white worker who was not chosen for the program. He alleged that there was illegal discrimination.

Steelworkers v. *Weber*
443 U.S. 193 (1979)

MR. JUSTICE BRENNAN delivered the opinion of the Court.

. . .

Before 1964, blacks were largely relegated to "unskilled and semi-skilled jobs."

. . .

Because of automation the number of such jobs was rapidly decreasing.

. . .

As a consequence, "the relative position of the Negro worker [was] steadily worsening. In 1947 the nonwhite unemployment rate was only 64 percent higher than the white rate; in 1962 it was 124 percent higher." . . .

Congress feared that the goals of the Civil Rights Act—the integration of blacks into the mainstream of American society—could not be achieved unless this trend were reversed. And Congress recognized that that would not be possible unless blacks were able to secure jobs "which have a future."

. . .

Accordingly, it was clear to Congress that

"[t]he crux of the problem [was] to open employment opportunities for Negroes in occupations which have been traditionally closed to them," 110 Cong. Rec. 6548 (1964) (remarks of Sen. Humphrey), and it was to this problem that Title VII's prohibition against racial discrimination in employment was primarily addressed.

It plainly appears from the House Report accompanying the Civil Rights Act that Congress did not intend wholly to prohibit private and voluntary affirmative action efforts as one method of solving this problem. The Report provides:

> "No bill can or should lay claim to eliminating all of the causes and consequences of racial and other types of discrimination against minorities. There is reason to believe, however, that national leadership provided by the enactment of Federal legislation dealing with the most troublesome problems *will create an atmosphere conducive to voluntary or local resolution of other forms of discrimination.*" H. R. Rep. No. 914, 88th Cong., 1st Sess., pt. 1, p. 18 (1963). (Emphasis supplied).

Given this legislative history, we cannot agree with respondent that Congress intended to prohibit the private sector from taking effective steps to accomplish the goal that Congress designed Title VII to achieve. . . .

Our conclusion is further reinforced by examination of the language and legislative history of § 703 (j) of Title VII. Opponents of Title VII raised two related arguments against the bill. First, they argued that the Act would be interpreted to *require* employers with racially imbalanced work forces to grant preferential treatment to racial minorities in order to integrate. Second, they argued that employers with racially imbalanced work forces would grant preferential

treatment to racial minorities, even if not required to do so by the Act. See 110 Cong. Rec. 8618–8619 (1964) (remarks of Sen. Sparkman). Had Congress meant to prohibit all race-conscious affirmative action, as respondent urges, it easily could have answered both objections by providing that Title VII would not require or *permit* racially preferential integration efforts. But Congress did not choose such a course. Rather, Congress added § 703(j) which addresses only the first objection. The section provides that nothing contained in Title VII "shall be interpreted to *require* any employer . . . to grant preferential treatment . . . to any group because of the race . . . of such . . . group on account of" a *de facto* racial imbalance in the employer's work force. The section does *not* state that "nothing in Title VII shall be interpreted to *permit*" voluntary affirmative efforts to correct racial imbalances. The natural inference is that Congress chose not to forbid all voluntary race-conscious affirmative action.

The reasons for this choice are evident from the legislative record. Title VII could not have been enacted into law without substantial support from legislators in both Houses who traditionally resisted federal regulation of private business. Those legislators demanded as a price for their support that "management prerogatives, and union freedoms . . . be left undisturbed to the greatest extent possible." H. R. Rep. No. 914, 88th Cong., 1st Sess., pt. 2, p. 29 (1963). Section 703 (j) was proposed by Senator Dirksen to allay any fears that the Act might be interpreted in such a way as to upset this compromise. The section was designed to prevent § 703 of Title VII from being interpreted in such a way as to lead to undue "Federal Government interference

with private businesses because of some Federal employee's ideas about racial balance or racial imbalance." 110 Cong. Rec. 14314 (1964) (remarks of Sen. Miller). . . .
We therefore hold that Title VII's prohibition in §§ 703(a) and (d) against racial discrimination does not condemn all private, voluntary, race-conscious affirmative action plans.

. . .

The Empirical Basis of Law

A good scientist tries to get data in a specific area of inquiry so that some definite conclusions can be made with respect to relationships between events. Like the fictional detective in a pioneering TV series, the scientist states, "just give me the facts, Ma'm," and proceeds from there. It is not enough to assume relationships between a legal rule and the behavior that the rule is intended to influence. All too often legislation or decision-making in the legal system is based upon an intuitive feeling that certain consequences will result from a particular type of action. In many cases the law that was enacted on this basis proves to be ineffective, or to have unforeseen consequences. What is needed is a closer and more thorough analysis of individual and social behavior as it affects and is affected by the operation of the legal system.

To take a fundamental problem area in the law, for instance, consider the question "Does punishment deter?" Even casual examination would reveal that punishment (and reward) do influence behavior in some way. What is needed are more precise questions and deeper research into and analysis of behavioral events. The sorts of questions that should be considered and researched might include: what sort of punishment deters or causes adherence to norms? How often is punishment needed? Who is influenced by punishment, and who is not, and why?

There may be basic philosophical beliefs that underlie our reactions to such questions. A desire for retribution at one end of the spectrum and a hope for re-education at the other may mask a basic need for control in social activity. Or the emphasis might be upon enforcement on the one hand and correction on the other.

Control may be the question in the regulation of activity in the social area, an issue that might be stated in terms of a philosophy of control. Very often clearly antithetical positions may be recognized early. In a particular case there may be either a demand for punishment or simply a hope for the re-education of individuals who have violated the prescriptions of the legal order. These orientations are evident in emphases on enforcement on the one hand or for correction on the other. This might be referred to as the difference between a *laissez-faire* approach and a more paternal view of the forces of authority. In the former instance people are considered more on their own and are responsible for their actions in the world. In the paternal approach governmental agents may take the position that they are acting as concerned parents in prescribing particular procedures which will make better students, better workers, and, therefore, better citizens of the community. Instead of taking a punitive approach, the more humanitarian approach of society would seek to help the offender, young or old, intelligent or not.

Education might be regarded as the best approach for moving violators of society's norms toward acceptance of the proper guidelines for behavior. Although many would agree with this general proposition, there is an inherent danger in practice. Often what may be called "reeducation" or "treatment" in a correctional facility is far-removed from those concepts. The "treatment" may actually be punitive or, worse, it may contribute to further criminal behavior inside and out of prison.

There is the paramount question of individual rights in this and other settings. At the present time if one is adjudged responsible and guilty, one is faced with a specified penalty of certain maximum duration. Critics of the less formal approaches with an educational or paternal flavor are concerned that the treatment is very often worse in terms of separation from society than the ordinary punishment for the crime. Also, this determination might be reached without procedures which are intended to protect the rights of individuals, as in juvenile or commitment cases. This concern has been stated well by a long time professional researcher in the field of correction, the late Paul Tappan.

> There is one telling argument against wholesale abandonment of legal rule and procedural form to accomplish social objectives: wholly to free the law from the "dead hand of the past" one must entrust unlimited discretion to judge, reformer, or clinician and his personal views of expedience. Unless he be circumscribed in some degree by established instrumental or traditional rule and form, the fate of the defendant, the interest of society, the social objectives themselves must hang by the tenuous thread of the wisdom and personality of the particular administrator.[13]

This is another repetition of the oft-quoted maxim that we live under a rule of laws and not of man.

Law and Morals

Another area containing issues for contemporary society lies in the province that may be described as the overlap between law and morality. The relationship between law and morals has been hotly debated for centuries with little consensus on major points. At the present time controversy still exists in the concern about pornography, whether it be in books, in the movies, or some other form. Constitutional lawyers consider the issue in terms of the provisions of the First Amendment relating to free speech and free expression. It has been suggested, however, that a better understanding of the problems involved might come about if these are treated in the light of more fundamental aspects, namely, those involving the relationships between the enactments of a legislature and the prevailing moral sentiments of the community. Other issues that may be placed in the same category are those arising from the laws regulating all types of sexual activities and those concerned with drug addiction or abortion. All these problems not only have their medical bases but their behavioral ones as well; sometimes neither of these aspects is looked at sufficiently in the development of laws regulating this broad area. At times only the moral sentiments of single individuals or those of small groups in limited areas of the country are brought into the determination.

This interrelationship between law and morality was addressed by the Supreme Court in the following case.

Fed. Tr. Comm'n. v. *Keppel & Bro.*
291 U.S. 304 (1933)

MR. JUSTICE STONE delivered the opinion of the Court.

This case comes here on certiorari to review a decree of the Court of Appeals for the Third Circuit, which set aside an order of the Federal Trade Commission forbidding certain trade practices of respondent as an unfair method of competition. 63 F. (2d) 81; § 5, Federal Trade Commission Act, 38 Stat. 717, 719.

The Commission found that respondent, one of numerous candy manufacturers similarly engaged, manufactures, sells and distributes, in interstate commerce, package assortments of candies known to the trade as "break and take" packages, in competition with manufacturers of assortments known as "straight goods" packages. Both types are assortments of candies in packages in convenient arrangement for sale by the piece at a small price in retail stores in what is known as the penny candy trade. The break and take assortments are so arranged and offered for sale to consumers as to avail of the element of chance as an inducement to the retail purchasers. . . . Each assortment is accompanied by a display card, attractive to children, prepared by respondent for exhibition and use by the dealer in selling the candy, explaining the plan by which either the price or the amount of candy or other merchandise which the purchaser receives is affected by chance. The pieces of candy in the break and take packages are either smaller than those of the competing straight goods packages, which are sold at a comparable price without the aid of any chance feature, or they are of inferior quality. Much of the candy assembled in the break and take packages is sold by retailers, located in the vicinity of schools, to school children.

The Commission found that the use of the break and take package in the retail trade involves the sale or distribution of the candy by lot or chance; that it is a lottery or gambling device which encourages gambling among children; that children, enticed by the element of chance, purchase candy so sold in preference to straight goods candy; and that the competition between the two types of package results in a substantial diversion of trade from the manufacturers of the straight goods package to those distributing the break and take type. It found further that in some states lotteries and gaming devices are penal offenses; that the sale or distribution of candy by lot or chance is against public policy; that many manufacturers of competing candies refuse to engage in the distribution of the break and take type of package because they regard it as a reprehensible encouragement of gambling among children; and that such manufacturers are placed at a disadvantage in competition. The evidence shows that others have reluctantly yielded to the practice in order to avoid loss of trade to their competitors.

The court below held, as the respondent argues here, that respondent's practice does not hinder competition or injure its competitors, since they are free to resort to the same sales method; that the practice does not tend to create a monopoly or involve any deception to consumers or the public, and hence is not an unfair method of competition within the meaning of the statute.

. . .

Neither the language nor the history of

the Act suggests that Congress intended to confine the forbidden methods to fixed and unyielding categories. The common law afforded a definition of unfair competition and, before the enactment of the Federal Trade Commission Act, the Sherman Act had laid its inhibition upon combinations to restrain or monopolize interstate commerce which the courts had construed to include restraints upon competition in interstate commerce. It would not have been a difficult feat of draftsmanship to have restricted the operation of the Trade Commission Act to those methods of competition in interstate commerce which are forbidden at common law or which are likely to grow into violations of the Sherman Act, if that had been the purpose of the legislation. . . .

It is true that the statute does not authorize regulation which has no purpose other than that of relieving merchants from troublesome competition or of censoring the morals of business men. But here the competitive method is shown to exploit consumers, children, who are unable to protect themselves. It employs a device whereby the amount of the return they receive from the expenditure of money is made to depend upon chance. Such devices have met with condemnation throughout the community. Without inquiring whether, as respondent contends, the criminal statutes imposing

penalties on gambling, lotteries and the like, fail to reach this particular practice in most or any of the states, it is clear that the practice is of the sort which the common law and criminal statutes have long deemed contrary to public policy. For these reasons a large share of the industry holds out against the device, despite ensuing loss in trade, or bows reluctantly to what it brands unscrupulous. It would seem a gross perversion of the normal meaning of the word, which is the first criterion of statutory construction, to hold that the method is not "unfair." . . .

We hold that the Commission correctly concluded that the practice was an unfair method of competition within the meaning of the statute. It is unnecessary to attempt a comprehensive definition of the unfair methods which are banned, even if it were possible to do so. We do not intimate either that the statute does not authorize the prohibition of other and hitherto unknown methods of competition or, on the other hand, that the Commission may prohibit every unethical competitive practice regardless of its particular character or consequences. New or different practices must be considered as they arise in the light of the circumstances in which they are employed.

Reversed.

Mass Society

The administration of justice, never an easy task, becomes even more difficult in a complex and changing society. There is much concern that the legal system is unable to function efficiently in an era of "mass society." With technological change, greater mobility, and a growing population, the challenges to a system based upon earlier demographic and social conditions have increased significantly. The increase in numbers alone causes difficulty in using procedures that were tailored for the smaller and more cohesive society of this nation's past centuries.

Certain steps were taken, often informally at first, and then eventually incorporated into the formal system. One prime example in the criminal justice system is the phenomenon of *plea bargaining*. Faced with a serious backlog of cases that must be taken to trial, a prosecutor is often willing to accept a guilty plea for a lesser offense from someone accused of a more serious crime. There is a greater emphasis by the defense counsel and the prosecutor in getting a "deal" than in following a more arduous path through the formal steps in the criminal court system.

In this and other legal matters, concern has been expressed about the proper and adequate representation of accused parties, or even of those in a civil controversy. It is important to remember that the common law system, like some others, is an adversary one; to be able to have someone to "fight one's legal battles" is crucial in the process. Proper representation of individuals is of concern to a society sympathetic to personal rights and freedom. This is most important in the sphere of criminal justice, and recent court decisions have emphasized the need for assistance for defendants who have been unable to obtain legal aid. This assistance has been extended to entire groups—tenants, consumers, or citizens in a community.

As a result of the problems raised in "mass society," the traditional close personal relationship between lawyer and client is undergoing change. It may well be that the entire complexion of legal practice (and, therefore, the legal profession itself) will change. The deluge of accident and personal injury cases before the courts accounts for most of the backlog of cases; in some jurisdictions this backlog runs to three years and more. Whether this and other factors will lead to different procedures such as no-fault insurance in automobile claims is one of the prime topics of discussion. A radically different approach worries some practitioners, yet there have been some departures from the traditional advocacy-in-court system in the area of injury at work. Workmen's compensation superimposed an almost completely new system upon the traditional pattern, without, apparently, any serious denial of traditional rights. In much the same way, no-fault concepts have been introduced in divorce and auto insurance cases and, despite the departure from past procedures and philosophy, these moves have been accepted.

A further area of concern involves problems related to differential enforcement of the law along socio-economic lines. Arrest and incarceration are more likely to happen to those who are at the lower end of the social scale. The basis for this does not lie completely in the fact that more crime occurs as the result of unfavorable economic conditions, but in the more subtle variation in law enforcement influenced by the attitudes and values of law officials. Prosecution is more likely to take place for an activity that violates the sensitivities of the prosecutor. What at one level of society can be regarded as inoffensive behavior may be looked upon by persons at other levels, because of their different set of values and attitudes, as an undesirable or even immoral act. Middle-class values of lawyers will influence official activity in the community.

Organizations and Law

One of the most obvious aspects of mass society is the continuing growth in size and number of organizations of all types—economic, educational, social, religious, and those in mass media. This has led to the designation of these organizations as "private government."[14] Each of these organizations has some power to influence the lives of individuals, and some may exercise that power more than does government. Such influence may be out of proportion to the numbers involved; a few decision-makers may establish a policy with an impact upon hundreds within the organization and thousands outside it. The actions of large corporations affect not only their employees, but also consumers, suppliers and other business persons, as well as the community at large.

Is private government too strong or public influence too weak? That may not be the point. Instead, the question lies in whether the same basic checks on the power of the group over the individual that are preserved in the area of public government should not be transferred as well to private organizations. In this view, due process of law, judicial review, and other constitutional rights deserve a place in the procedures that could confront a single individual in a corporation, labor union, or even in an educational institution. Dismissal from a company has long been referred to as "industrial capital punishment." A union member who may not completely agree with a particular union policy may be thus cut off from the opportunity to earn a living (or be barred from employment in the first place). Dismissal of students from a university can be a matter that affects their future more than many sentences or punishments by a civil or criminal court acting as an agent of public government. Safeguards similar to those available to the individual under a public legal system may be desirable in the private organization.

Quality of Life

Much attention at the present centers upon issues that relate to individual and group welfare in existence in a modern environment. Perhaps this final section is the culmination of all concerns expressed above, in that the beneficial condition of man, physically and psychologically, should be the ultimate measure of success of legal efforts.

Invasion of a human being's physical life space has been a concern of law for centuries; tort and trespass actions have been a traditional and usually effective legal recourse. Protection against psychological intrusions such as the invasion of privacy, however, have a short history. Not yet a century old, the legal relief of individuals from having personal information bandied about has been hastened by reactions to the greater effectiveness (not necessarily accuracy) of collecting and storing large amounts of data. Technological advancements have gone hand-in-hand with commercial expansion and changes in social views. Huge data banks with mountains of information now serve business and governmental units in the rush to a credit-conscious society and the expansion of public services. How much others need to know in all this is a growing personal concern.

Concern for the environment is an even more recent phenomenon; only in the past decade has there been any serious movement toward the alleviation of physical conditions that are detrimental to human functioning. Previous attitudes fostered economic growth or furthered individual rights at the expense of efforts to preserve environmental balance. Ecology has become a prime topic overnight, and the growing awareness of others beyond a small band of "environmentalists" has been responsible for the enactment of a long series of statutes and the revival of long-dormant and little-used laws to conserve resources and protect health. One of the most significant of the statutes, the National Environmental Policy Act of 1969, states the intent of Congress to assure "for all Americans safe, healthful, productive, and esthetically and culturally pleasing surroundings."[15] The thrust of this act and others goes beyond dealing with air and water pollution as it also encompasses the preservation of natural resources and valuable elements of the national heritage.

There is little serious disagreement over the general goals in the environmental crusade; controversy comes when implementation of policy takes place. Economic costs must be allocated and various painful trade-offs made. Law has long served to settle controversies, and its extensive role in these matters extends well into the future.

"Quality of life" may be considered a broad area, as the following excerpt from a judicial opinion demonstrates.

People Against Nuclear Energy v. *U.S. Nuclear Reg.*
   678 F.2d 222 (1982)

J. SKELLY WRIGHT, Circuit Judge:

On March 28, 1979 Three Mile Island Unit 2, a nuclear reactor operated by Metropolitan Edison Company, was seriously damaged in the worst nuclear accident Americans have yet experienced. The incident precipitated widespread alarm and led to the evacuation of many neighboring residents from their homes. At the time of the event, Three Mile Island Unit 1 (TMI-1), another Metropolitan Edison nuclear reactor of similar design which shared some common facilities with Unit 2 (TMI-2) was not in operation. The Nuclear Regulatory Commission (Commission) ordered that it remain in a cold shutdown condition pending further investigation of whether it could be operated safely. Since then the Commission has held extensive hearings on technical, managerial, and operational issues related to the proposed restart of TMI-1. The Commission has refused, however, to consider whether renewed operation of TMI-1 might cause severe psychological harm to neighboring residents and serious economic and social deterioration in nearby communities.

People Against Nuclear Energy (PANE), one of the intervenors in the restart proceeding, is composed primarily of neighbors of TMI. It seeks judicial review of the Commission's decision to limit the scope of its inquiry in this manner. PANE contends that,

under the National Environmental Policy Act (NEPA), 42 U.S.C. § 4321 *et seq.* (1976), and the Atomic Energy Act, 42 U.S.C. § 2133 (1976), the Commission must take into account potential harms to psychological health and community well-being. We hold that these environmental impacts are cognizable under NEPA. Therefore, the Commission must make a threshold determination, based on adequate study, whether the potential psychological health effects of renewed operation of TMI-1 are sufficiently significant that NEPA requires preparation of a supplemental environmental impact statement.

. . .

In the National Environmental Policy Act, Congress accorded prominence to the effects of government actions on health and safety. NEPA was designed to "promote efforts which will prevent or eliminate damage to the environment and biosphere and stimulate the health and welfare of man." 42 U.S.C. § 4321 (1976). The Act declared a national environmental policy of "encourag[ing] productive and enjoyable harmony between man and his environment," *id.,* and explicitly recognized that each person "should enjoy a healthful environment," *id.* § 4331(c). In its regulations implementing NEPA's procedural requirements, the Council on Environmental Quality required agencies to consider "[t]he degree to which the proposed action affects public health and safety" as a factor in deciding whether a federal action "significantly" affected the human environment. 40 C.F.R. § 1508.27(b)(2) (1981). In short, "[n]o subject to be covered by an EIS can be more important than the potential effects of a federal program upon the health of human beings." *Citizens Against Toxic Sprays, Inc. v. Bergland,* 428 F.Supp. 908, 927 (D.Or.1977).

We conclude that, in the context of NEPA, health encompasses psychological health. To implement a national policy based on "the critical importance of restoring and maintaining environmental quality to the overall welfare and development of man," 42 U.S.C. § 4331(a) (1976), Congress required each federal agency to utilize a "systematic, interdisciplinary approach which will insure the integrated use of the natural and social sciences and the environmental design arts." . . .

The National Environmental Policy Act is designed to assure that governmental agencies take a "hard look" at the environmental consequences of major proposed actions, and that they adjust ongoing programs in light of new information or changed circumstances. PANE urges us to hold that NEPA requires the Commission to prepare a new or supplemental environmental impact statement (EIS) on the psychological health effects and community deterioration that might result from restart of TMI-1. We agree with PANE that these environmental effects fall within the scope of NEPA, and that the Commission has a continuing responsibility to comply with NEPA's procedural requirements in its supervision of licensed nuclear facilities, including TMI-1. At the same time, we recognize the agency's role in making a threshold determination of whether changed circumstances and new information regarding environmental effects require a supplemental EIS. We therefore remand the record to the Commission for a decision on the EIS question. . . .

. . .

We have concluded that psychological health is cognizable under NEPA and that the Commission's statutory responsibilities over licensed nuclear facilities create a continuing obligation to comply with the requirements of the statute. We therefore remand the record in this case to the Commission for study of potential psychological health effects and for a decision whether a supplemental EIS is necessary.

. . .

So ordered.

Further Development

The issues and problems mentioned above may point to the need for a review of the traditional concepts in legal and social activity. In his book *Ancient Law*, in the last century Sir Henry Maine outlined a pattern of legal development characterized as a move from status to contract.[16] Maine outlined a relationship between individuals in primitive societies based on roles determined by their placement in that society and their interaction with others. As societies increased in complexity, a concern with status changed to a focus upon relationships developed on a contractual basis. In a position based on status, an individual receives what is given under the social rules of the group; whereas in a contract situation, the person receives what was bargained for. It may well be that now in many respects there is a reversal in the direction of the changes, and developed societies are moving back from contract to status. Welfare benefits or other forms of governmental services cannot be bargained for by the parties receiving them; instead, it is a particular position (poverty, motherhood, neglected child) which is the determining factor for the individual's participation. Even in the area of business, where one might expect a contractual basis for action. some recent evidence indicates that businessmen frequently avoid legal sanctions available under contract law, and settle their differences in ways that are based on other considerations.[17] Researchers increasingly have begun to treat these problem areas not in traditional terms, but in ways that may better represent the issues involved.

One example of such responses is the position that decisions regarding procedure and the protection of individual rights should be based on whether they will affect social position, safety, comfort, or rectitude, rather than on whether the case fits into traditional legal categories.[18]

QUESTIONS

1. What are the basic differences between the common and Civil law systems? Are there any similarities?
2. How can law represent the basic ideology of a society? Give examples.
3. Describe the ways in which the functioning of a legal system is affected by "mass society."
4. Under what circumstances might law and morals intersect?
5. Are any elements forming the law more significant than others? Which are they, and why are they more significant?

NOTES

[1] Max Weber, *Law in Economy and Society,* ed. M. Rheinstein (Cambridge, Massachusetts: Harvard Univ. Press, 1954), p. 13.

[2] Karl Llewellyn, *The Bramble Bush* (New York: Oceana Publications, 1960), p. 12.

[3] F. James Davis, "Law as a Type of Social Control," in *Society and the Law,* F. James Davis et al. (New York: Free Press, 1962), p. 41.

[4] Philip Selznick, "The Sociology of Law," in *International Encyclopedia of the Social Sciences,* Vol. 9, ed. D. Sills (New York: Macmillan Co. and Free Press, 1968), p. 51.

[5] Talcott Parsons, *The Social System* (Glencoe, Illinois: Free Press, 1951).

[6] Selznick, "The Sociology of Law," p. 51.

[7] Paul Bohannon, "Law and Legal Institutions," in *International Encyclopedia of the Social Sciences,* Vol. 9, ed. D. Sills (New York: Macmillan Co. and Free Press, 1968), p. 33.

[8] Oliver Wendell Holmes, *The Common Law* (Boston: Little, Brown & Co., 1881), p. 1.

[9] Harold J. Berman, "The Dilemma of Soviet Law Reform," *Harvard Law Review,* 76 (1962-63), pp. 930-31.

[10] Albert A. Ehrenzweig, Sueo Ikahara, and Norman Jensen, *American–Japanese Private International Law* (Dobbs Ferry, NY: Oceana Publ., 1964), p. 13.

[11] William Ballantyne, *Legal Development in Arabia* (London: Graham and Trotman, Ltd., 1980).

[12] Selznick, "The Sociology of Law," p. 57.

[13] Paul Tappan, *Delinquent Girls in Court* (New York: Columbia Univ. Press, 1947), p. 22.

[14] Selznick, "The Sociology of Law," p. 57.

[15] The National Environmental Policy Act, Pub.L. 91–190, 83 Stat. 852.

[16] Henry J.S. Maine, *Ancient Law* (London: Oxford University Press, 1931). (First published in 1861).

[17] S. Macauley, "Non-Contractual Relations in Business: A Preliminary Study," *American Sociological Review,* 28 (1963), 55–67.

[18] Charles Reich, "The New Property," *Yale L.J.* 73 (April, 1964), pp. 733–87.

the legal
system

TWO

The term "system" is one of the most common labels used today, but it tends to represent many different things. Individuals may praise or blame "the system," using the term to mean either a general, unstructured set of factors in the social environment, or specific processes in an organizational setting. More structured is the term's use by students and practitioners of law when they speak of "the legal system," the entire conglomerate of concepts and processes of the law.

A SCIENTIFIC SYSTEMS APPROACH

A more scientific use of the term "system" involves an approach that analyzes and defines a set of elements becoming interrelated through pursuit of a goal. While definitions may vary according to a focus upon structure or function, the overall picture is that of a complex conglomerate of activities, actions and channels. A focus upon structure provides a definition such as "system is an organized or complex whole; an assemblage or combination of things or parts forming a complex or unitary whole."[1] Another view focuses upon "co-alignment, not merely of people (in coalition) but of institutionalized action—of technology and task environment into a viable domain, and of organizational design and structure appropriate to it."[2] This precise use of concepts relating to systems should be applied to discussions of legal systems, in order to appreciate how various elements affect the final social picture. Studies of legal systems offer the best results when the following factors are included:

1. Systematic working from a data base;
2. Integration from the collation of all information and operations;
3. Interdisciplinary combination of diverse techniques and skills;
4. Decision orientation;
5. Holistic concern with the interaction of the human elements with all other parts of an organized system;
6. Pursuit of a goal.

The outcome of the systems approach then will be an outcome that has taken into account all or virtually all aspects affecting the activity of the group or organization. This is important for law as well as for other social institutions.

A word of caution is required, however, in this attempt to grasp the total components and activities of a system. In real life many important situations are too complex for us to comprehend all their aspects easily. Yet this should not deter attempts in that direction. Rather, this fact should spur greater recognition of the desirability of interdisciplinary efforts, in which theoreticians and practitioners of varied disciplines interact to provide a better picture of the dynamics of society.

This brief introduction to the concepts of the scientific systems approach does not serve as a complete discussion of the topic, of course. A preliminary recognition of the highlights of the approach does serve, however, to provide a general orientation to the field and its usefulness in the study of law and its administration. This introduction serves also as a base for the use of certain specific conventions that attempt to describe the salient elements, channels, and decision points in a process. Models of a system aid in an analysis and understanding of that process.

A model is a representation of reality that helps viewers to see that reality more clearly by presenting key features of the situation and cutting through complexity. The picture may be, as the ancient Chinese maxim has it, worth a thousand words. A model may be either a *static* one, which shows structure, or a *dynamic* one, which shows changes in its state or structure. An example of a static model is the organization chart that outlines a simplified state court system in Figure 2–1. A dynamic model, on the other hand, shows steps in an ongoing process. Figure 2–2 illustrates the movement of criminal cases through a total system. The model shows the relative number of cases going through the process by the size of the shaded areas; the lines lead to specific outcomes.

We can make a more detailed representation of the steps in a process with the decisions necessary at each point by adopting the concepts of systems analysis. Figure 2–3 illustrates basic flow chart conventions which may be adopted in the analysis of legal process. A flow chart shows the value of tracing a legal issue step by step and identifying questions at each stage of the process. An example of the application of this technique in an initial phase of a criminal process is presented in Figure 2-4. This approach, which we have labelled the *analysis of decision systems,* will serve as an orientation basic to this text with the intent that it aid in the assimilation of substance and procedure in the area of law.

The United States Constitution established three branches of government at the federal level—the legislative, the judicial, and the executive. These three entities may also be referred to as subsystems of the United States legal system. In discussions in this book, however, that overall system will be divided in somewhat different ways at times in order to illustrate actual interrelationships more clearly. Keep in mind that views from different vantage points help in understanding the total picture of a system.

The functioning of law can be charted within the systems framework just sketched. In the criminal system one can further subdivide that total complex into three rather well-known subsystems—control, court, and correctional.

Control subsystems comprise the law enforcement area; the judicial and penal subsystems comprise the *courts* and *correctional* units of the legal system.

The descriptions that follow will focus upon the three subsystems individually, and each may be referred to as a system in itself. It should be remembered, however, that the three areas are subsystems of the entire system and the use of the term system is for the reader's convenience.

Figure 2-1. A State Judicial System, Adapted from Pennsylvania Code (Harrisburg, Pa.: Legislative Reference Series)

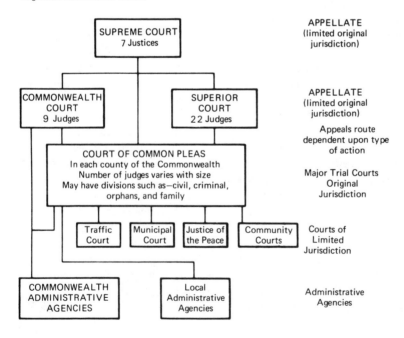

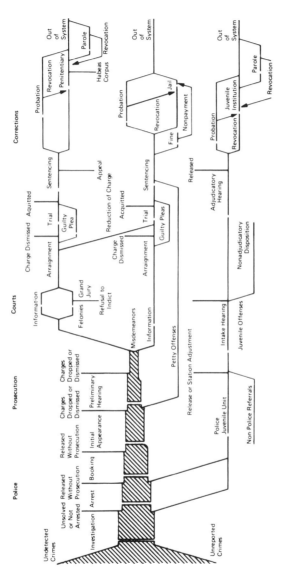

Figure 2-2. A Model of a Legal System, From *Challenge of Crime in a Free Society* (Washington, D.C.: President's Commission on Law Enforcement and Administration of Justice, 1967)

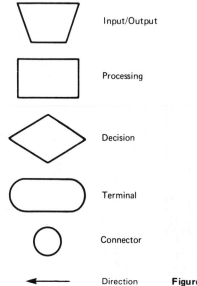

Input/Output

Processing

Decision

Terminal

Connector

Direction　　**Figure 2-3.** Basic Flow Chart Conventions

Figure 2-4. Flow Chart of Trial Subsystem

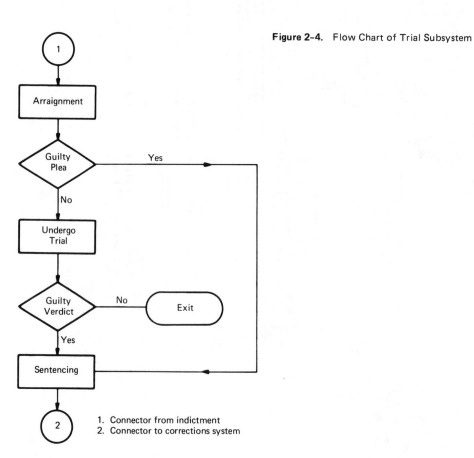

1. Connector from indictment
2. Connector to corrections system

CONTROL SYSTEMS

The usual initial phase of the criminal system is the area referred to as law enforcement. While these control units most often come into action in connection with an individual infraction, there are many opportunities for state and federal regulatory agencies to perform similar control operations in organizational activity. Their functioning occurs almost exclusively in a criminal law context, of course.

Federal Control Systems

The wide diversity of federal law enforcement agencies can be determined to a great extent from viewing Tables 2-1 and 2-2. These agencies all perform the functions of maintaining security of individuals and organizations in the specific duties entrusted to them by the Constitution, statutes, and perhaps agency regulation. Table 2-1 outlines

TABLE 2-1. Federal Agencies with Extensive Control Functions

AGENCY	MISSION	PERSONNEL
Department of Justice		
Federal Bureau of Investigation	Detection and apprehension of violators of federal laws; protecting security of U.S.	Special agents; technical specialists
Immigration and Naturalization Service	Prevention of entry of illegal persons into the country	Immigration inspectors Border patrolmen
Drug Enforcement Administration	Control under drug laws through inspection and detection	Compliance investigators and undercover agents
Bureau of Prisons	Administration of Federal Penal Institutions	Correctional officers, counselors and treatment specialists
Criminal Division	Supervision of enforcement of Federal criminal laws	Attorneys, investigators, scientific technicians
U.S. Marshals	Support court activities—serving summons, protecting courts	U.S. Marshals in all judicial districts
Law Enforcement Assistance Administration	Improvement of Criminal Justice System (created by the Omnibus Crime Control Safe Streets Act of 1968)	Expert consultants, researchers, government grants personnel
Department of the Treasury		
Internal Revenue Service	Detection of evasion of income, alcohol, tobacco, and other taxes	Internal revenue agents (accountants, examiners, technicians); intelligence agents; alcohol, firearms, and tobacco tax investigators
Bureau of Customs	Prevention of illegal entry of goods into the country	Customs inspectors, security officers, patrolmen
Secret Service	Protection of the President and other officials; prevention of counterfeiting	Special agents, analysts, investigators; scientific personnel in Bureau of Engraving and Printing

TABLE 2-2. Federal Agencies with Limited Control Activities

AGENCY	MISSION	PERSONNEL
Department of Defense		
Department of the Air Force, Army, and Navy	Promoting efficient armed services in support of national security	Investigators, security police, special investigators, military police, correctional officers, and criminal investigators
Department of State		
Office of Security	Providing security in department and installations abroad	Special agents
Agency for International Development	Assistance for law administration in developing countries	Investigators and public safety advisors
Department of the Interior		
National Park Service	Providing effective police services in national parks	U.S. Park Police
Bureau of Sport, Fisheries, and Wildlife	Enforcement of U.S. wildlife conservation statutes	U.S. game management agents
Department of Health, Education, and Welfare		
Internal Security Office	Investigations to maintain effectiveness of agency	Investigative officers
Public Health Service, Food and Drug Commission	Enforcement of laws protecting consumers	Consumer safety officers
Department of Transportation	*United States Courts*	*Federal Trade Commission*
Department of Agriculture	*Civil Service Commission*	*Federal Maritime Commission*
Department of Commerce	*General Services Administration*	*United States Postal Services*

the divisions and activities of the two federal departments most active in the investigative and control area. Other agencies, as illustrated in Table 2-2, have more limited external activities but all have an internal audit function for self-policing. The tables do not include still other organizations that may be considered a part of the overall structure of law enforcement. The CIA, the National Security Agency, and various branches of military intelligence, for instance, have certain enforcement activities, but their primary thrust is the protection of our society by gaining information on external threats to the continuing existence of the country.

Federal agencies are able to act only when there is a specific statute or agency regulation that invokes their involvement. A specific federal law enables the federal agencies to exist and perform their duties. Where there is no such statute, the offenses come under the jurisdiction of state agencies. When a federal agency is called in, either there is evidence that state lines have been crossed, or it is presumed that because of a lapse of time, state lines have been crossed in the commission of the crime. In addition to this establishment of jurisdiction, states can, of course, request the assistance of federal agencies.

State Control Systems

State police forces operate under the statutes of their particular state and their jurisdiction extends, at least theoretically, across the entire state. In reality most state police forces leave much of the work to local units at the municipal or county level. There is a dearth of coverage in thinly populated rural areas by local forces, but even here the state police are seldom very active because they are understaffed. Most of the activity of the state police takes the form of highway patrol and accident investigation. Occasional serious crimes in rural areas will be investigated, however, and special task force programs hitting a specific crime target also take place. Apart from these activities, most enforcement activity takes place at the local level.

Local Control Systems

By far the most common control system of which the average citizen is aware is that represented by the police, a sheriff, a constable, or, on rarer occasions, the county police. At this level there are over 30,000 separate police units all over the country, ranging in size from the one-man police force in a village or township to the more than 37,000 members of the police force of New York City. It can be expected that large municipal departments are complexly structured, and Figure 2–5 illustrates a model organizational arrangement of a larger city police department.

Variation in duties of officials with the same title may be somewhat confusing. A sheriff in many states, particularly those in the Southwest, may have extensive law enforcement duties, while the sheriff in an urban county in the East is often limited to activity such as service of court summons upon defendants in court actions. In Massachusetts, for instance, the sheriff maintains the peace and dignity of the courts and administers the jail and house of correction, in addition to serving writs of the court. There, as well as in most organized urban areas, local police units have taken over most of the criminal work that the movie-stereotyped sheriff may still perform in more open areas of the country.

County police also may show variation in duties. Some are truly investigative and active detective agencies; others are restricted to patrolling county parks and directing traffic at airports and other facilities.

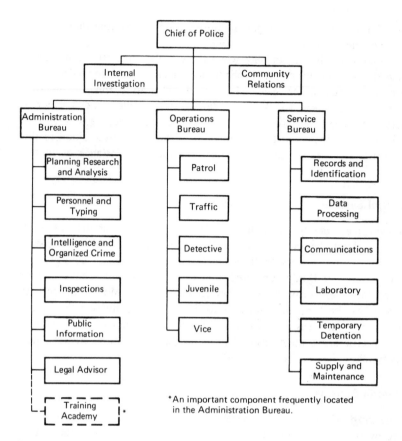

Figure 2-5. A Model Organizational Chart of A Municipal Police Department, From George T. Felkenes, *The Criminal System* (Englewood Cliffs, N.J.: Prentice-Hall, Inc., 1973), p. 22

COURT SYSTEMS

A court is a political entity organized for the purpose of administering justice. From a basic legal viewpoint the court consists of a judge and a jury, but a discussion about court systems must include many other personnel, since a court system needs a large number of support personnel in order to administer the activities that surround the cases.

Judicial activity in the United States takes place within two separate systems—the federal and the state courts. Each system has many tiers or levels, from the inferior magistrate's court to the ultimate court of appeals. In the federal system that final apellate body is the Supreme Court of the United States, which, however, has limited original jurisdiction. The cases that reach it upon appeal started out much earlier, either at the federal district court located within one of the judicial districts of the United States, or at a trial court in a particular state.

Some confusion may arise because of the apparent overlapping of state and federal courts and the number of special courts in the federal system. Even more confusing, however, is the variation in names of courts at the state level. An observer hearing the terms *superior* or *supreme* court used in different states must be very careful to recognize at which level the court is operating.

The Federal Court System

The Constitution of the United States established only one court by name, the Supreme Court, but also provided that inferior courts could be established by Congress. There is no limit on the number and types of federal courts that Congress may establish. The Constitution also established that the jurisdiction of federal courts would extend to all cases arising under the Constitution and laws of the United States, and controversies in which citizens of different states or different states themselves were involved—in short, all matters that could not be handled or considered within the boundaries of the single state. There is the added statutory provision that, at present, controversies between citizens of different states must amount to individual claims of more than $10,000.

There is a large number of different courts in the federal judicial system, as shown in Figure 2-6. It must be remembered, however, that the actual structure and functioning of the federal system is much more complex than is pictured. It will be sufficient to note here that the usual activity begins with an original case in one of the federal

Figure 2-6. The Federal Court System

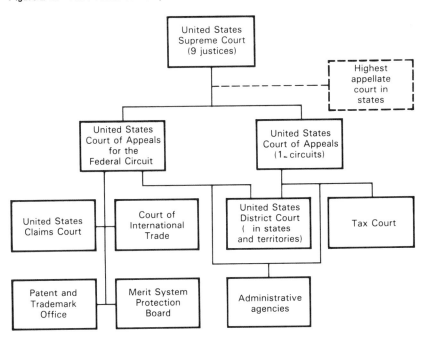

district courts in the fifty states and territories (populous states have more than one district). Appeals go to the United States Court of Appeals covering the larger area in which that district fits geographically. Further appeals from those decisions go to the United States Supreme Court.

State Courts

Designations of the courts in different states can be misleading at times. Usually the term *Supreme Court* refers to the court of last resort in the state system. As Table 2-3 shows, however, the highest court can be called by some other name. Even more confusing is the situation in New York where the Supreme Court is the basic trial court. In California that basic court is called the Superior Court, whereas in Pennsylvania the court by that name is a statewide intermediate (and sometimes final) court of appeal.

The inferior tribunals also carry a variety of titles. Most familiar are the terms *municipal* and *traffic* courts, or *justices of the peace.* Recently housing courts have been added to the list of other lower-level courts. Other courts, such as probate, surrogate, family, and juvenile courts, are considered to be more important and, therefore, handled at the basic trial level, the court of original jurisdiction. That basic court may have divisions incorporating those functions. In Pennsylvania, for example, the Court of Common Pleas (the basic trial court) has juvenile and family divisions, as well as the criminal and civil trial divisions.

Judges

The administration of justice in the court system is fundamentally in the hands of the judge. As a matter of fact, the judge has so critical a role in the process that he or she is often referred to as the court. The title "judge" may also have a more specific term attached to it, such as *District, Presiding,* or *Juvenile Court,* to designate the jurisdiction or assignment; often the judge may be called a justice (as on the U.S. Supreme Court) or chancellor. The justice of the peace or magistrate, however, is the lowest office in the

TABLE 2-3. A Comparison of State Court Systems

LEVEL OF COURT	SELECTED STATES		
	New York	*Pennsylvania*	*Minnesota*
Court of Last Resort	Court of Appeals	Supreme Court	Supreme Court
Intermediate Appeals Court	Appellate Division of Supreme Court	Superior Court Commonwealth Court	None
Major Trial Court	Supreme Court	Court of Common Pleas	District Court
How Elected	All elected by partisan ballot, except Governor appoints Judge of Court of Appeals and members of appellate division of Supreme Court. Mayor appoints judges of some local courts.	All elected by partisan ballot to serve for 10 years, nonpartisan retention thereafter.	All elected by ballot.

judicial system and the holder of that post is seldom regarded in the same way as a higher judge.

Judges are chosen in various ways. In the federal judicial system, the President of the United States, with the advice and consent of the Senate, appoints judges who serve for life.

Prior to making the appointment, the President consults with the Senators from the state where the vacancy exists; in addition, steps are usually taken to assure that the nominee is competent. Both approaches keep the number of rejections by the Senate at a minimum.

At the state level various ways exist for selection of judges. In over half the states judges are elected by popular vote. In some states nomination at a political primary pits two candidates in a partisan campaign; in other states the voting occurs on a non-partisan basis. In half a dozen states the legislature selects the judges, and in a few others the governors choose from a slate on the basis of merit determined by a panel or non-partisan group. The candidate must then be approved or rejected by the electorate after a period of judicial service. This procedure is often called the Missouri Plan after its first use in that state.

The Legal Profession

A fact often forgotten is that a legal system is, to a great extent, an adversary one. Without lawyers to protect the rights of individuals in the process, it may be ventured, justice would be more difficult to attain. While defendants in criminal matters need the protection of knowledgeable counsel, the prosecution must also discharge its responsibilities. In civil cases, as well, both sides need help. Thus there is no doubt that any discussion of legal systems must include a description of the legal profession and the role it plays in the system of justice.

Development of the legal profession proceeded slowly under English Common Law. At first, when trial by ordeal was abolished, judges permitted anyone to appear as counsel for the parties. Gradually it became evident that, for better representation of persons and for better control by the court, a program of training and selection was necessary. Educational development of lawyers was still somewhat casual, however, as prospective lawyers were tutored in the offices of practitioners; only at the end of the past century did law schools take over a significant role in the preparation of lawyers. Most states today require graduation from law school as a prerequisite for admission to the bar (and law schools generally require graduation from college). Admission to the bar means that the lawyer may represent litigants in court and, at the same time, submits to regulation by the court and peers, and accepts the provisions of the code of ethics of the profession.

In addition to their professional activity as advocates in a specific cause, lawyers are seen to play a significant role in shaping statutes and governmental processes. Their influence, as Mayer and other observers have pointed out, may be all out of proportion to their numbers in society (although the United States has more lawyers per capita than any other major nation in the world).[3]

Public Lawyers

Attorneys general and other prosecuting officers occupy so important a segment of the legal system that some descriptions of the system set them apart from the courts. Their major role is in the administration of justice through the judicial system, and they are known as officers of the court (as all lawyers are), but they are elected or appointed in actions separate from those initiated by the courts. Nevertheless, they are part of the court system more than any other subdivision, and therefore they are treated here.

The position of attorney general developed early in England, where the king appointed an attorney to represent him in all legal actions. The post was adopted in America in colonial times, and carried over into cabinet status in the federal government, as well as in the states one by one. Over this time span the role of the attorney general in all jurisdictions was remarkably similar to the role known today.

The Attorney General of the United States, in addition to advising the President on points of law, provides legal services to other departments of the government. In addition, this officer supervises the functioning of the most extensive legally-related federal department (Table 2-1). The Attorney General appoints the U.S. attorney in each judicial district of the United States. At that level the U.S. attorney presents evidence to and advises the grand jury. He or she is also in charge of all litigation and helps to conduct all those activities in that district for which the Attorney General of the United States is responsible.

The attorney general at the state level performs much the same function, except that providing legal opinions to the legislature as well as to the chief executive may be part of the duties of office. In 42 states the attorney general is an elected official, while in most of the remaining eight states he or she is selected by and reports to the governor. The opinions of the attorney general are quasi judicial in nature as those advisory opinions are often regarded as representing the status of the law.

At the local level, usually for a county unit, the enforcement of criminal law in the judicial system is in the hands of an officer of the court who is usually referred to as the county prosecutor or district attorney. In this discussion the local prosecutor is included in the court subsystem, but may be considered by some as an entity separate from it. He is elected or appointed as provided by statute and acts as any other public servant. At the federal and state level the attorney general operates more in the executive area, but the independence of the district attorney from the judicial and executive branches is almost complete at the local county or district level.

Attorneys For the Defense

Counsel for defendants have traditionally been selected in the course of the direct contacts that exist in the usual attorney-client relationships of both civil and criminal law. This is still a significant aspect of the functioning of the judical system, but recent greater concern for adequate representation has put the focus on publicly supported counsel. Courts appoint attorneys for indigent defendants, usually on a random basis from the general panel of local lawyers. Legal Aid Societies may also assist individuals in securing the assistance of counsel. Some limitation in this system has led to more formal arrangements through a permanently established office of a public defender. With increased workloads, particularly in large metropolitan areas, an organized system is needed to operate more efficiently than the more casual ad hoc appointment system. A public defender's office is, with luck, as well staffed as the local prosecutor's office, with public revenues supporting investigators and clerks, as well as lawyers. Even by the late 1960s, however, public defenders' offices were handling about one third of the indigent cases, while assigned counsel still took care of the majority of cases.[4]

The Jury

The strength of the jury, especially in criminal trials, comes from a strong tradition in Anglo-American common law. Probably as the result of arbitrary acts of the king's judges during colonial times, the founding fathers were determined that a panel of their peers would function to check the possible arbitrariness of a single judicial officer. The U.S. Constitution established the right of trial by jury in Article III, while two amendments in the Bill of Rights confirmed the right to speedy and public trial by jury (Sixth Amendment) and a right to jury trial in suits at common law where the value exceeds twenty dollars (Seventh Amendment). Each state followed with somewhat similar guarantees in state courts, and subsequent federal court decisions have extended the federal level of rights in criminal cases to those states with fewer safeguards (invoking the Fourteenth Amendment).

The jury has traditionally consisted of twelve persons selected from a larger list of candidates. While the number twelve has a long history, the trend today is toward juries of six persons. The U.S. Supreme Court has ruled that this size does not violate one's constitutional rights.[5]

In selecting the jury, prosecution and defense can exercise a set number of challenges, either for a specific reason involving possible bias (challenge for cause) or for no reason (peremptory challenge). Jurors, once selected, are to determine the facts under the guidance of the judge who instructs them in the law. The verdict reached by the jury stands unless the judge believes that he or she must set aside the verdict because of valid legal reasons. That verdict may be reached by less than a unanimous decision if the law permits. Moreover, a jury trial may even be waived by a defendant and the judge sits as trier of both fact and law.

The best-known type of jury is the *petit jury,* which hears the criminal or civil case at first resort. There are other juries, also determining factual situations, such as the *coroner's jury* or a *grand jury.* The grand jury (the name comes from the greater number of persons on it) inquires into matters brought before it by district attorney, sheriff, or other officer, to determine whether a basis exists for bringing the matter to trial. The grand jury also can be called to investigate other general matters such as corruption or related concerns in government or society. Many states are in the process of eliminating the grand jury and relying upon an *information* presented to the court by the prosecutor.

ADMINISTRATIVE AGENCIES

Because of the increasing complexity of society, particularly that of an industrially developed one, there are many matters that cannot be handled by the limited facilities of the existing three branches of government—the legislative, the executive, and the judicial. Matters that arise every day are often so involved that many legal functions are transferred to a governmental agency established for the purpose of investigating, monitoring, or regulating the activities of individuals or corporate entities. Administrative agencies have grown from nothing almost 100 years ago to their present regulation of atomic energy, radio and television, labor relations, the securities market, and countless other areas. The number and extent of federal agencies (Table 2-4) is to a great extent parallelled by agencies at the state level. Almost all states have a Public Utility Commission to regulate rates of utilities operating within the state, a Human Relations Commission, and myriad additional agencies that can even include a Liquor Control Board.

Administrative agencies are established by specific act of either the executive or legislative branch. There is no provision in the Constitution for them. The act of legislature or executive order, which establishes the agency, may also prescribe the policies

TABLE 2-4. Selected Federal Agencies

Action	Inter-American Foundation
Administrative Conference of the United States	Interstate Commerce Commission
American Battle Monuments Commission	National Aeronautics and Space Administration
Appalachian Regional Commission	National Credit Union Administration
Atomic Energy Commission	National Foundation of the Arts and Humanities
Canal Zone Government	National Labor Relations Board
Commission of Fine Arts	National Mediation Board
Commission on Civil Rights	National Science Foundation
Consumer Product Safety Commission	Occupational Safety and Health Review Commission
Delaware River Basin Commission	Overseas Private Investment Corporation
District of Columbia	Panama Canal Company
Economic Stabilization Program	Postal Rate Commission
Environmental Protection Agency	Railroad Retirement Board
Equal Employment Opportunity Commission	Renegotiation Board
Export-Import Bank of the United States	Securities and Exchange Commission
Farm Credit Administration	Selective Service System
Federal Communications Commission	Small Business Administration
Federal Deposit Insurance Corporation	Smithsonian Institution
Federal Home Loan Bank Board	Susquehanna River Basin Commission
Federal Maritime Commission	Tennessee Valley Authority
Federal Mediation and Conciliation Service	U.S. Arms Control & Disarmament Agency
Federal Reserve System	U.S. Civil Service Commission
Federal Trade Commission	U.S. Information Agency
Foreign Claims Settlement Commission	U.S. Postal Service
of the United States	U.S. Tariff Commission
General Services Administration	Veterans Administration
Indian Claims Commission	

for it and outline the general procedures that are to be followed. An agency may be placed within one of the three branches of government—executive, legislative, judicial— or it may be classified as an "independent" agency. The independent agency has more latitude than those in the branches, as its members generally enjoy a specific term of office. Some agencies have received the power to act in a quasi-judicial capacity and, therefore, are often significant adjuncts to the judicial system. Needless to say, their decisions are subject to appeal in the regularly established channels in the court system. If the agency has no judicial powers, the ability to establish specific rules and procedures governing its actions is a lawmaking function. In the final instance, however, both functions are under the ultimate control of the legislature—which determines its existence and continuing budget—and of the courts, which review administrative decisions.

Administrative Conference of the United States

A means of assembling representatives of federal agencies for the study of mutual problems was the objective of the act establishing the Administrative Conference of the U.S. The conference consists of not more than 91 and not less than 75 members who represent virtually all federal units active in the administrative sector. The ultimate goal is the expeditious functioning of federal agencies in the public interest.

THE CORRECTIONS SYSTEM

As much as our present-day correctional institutions are in need of improvement, there is no doubt that we have come a long way from the barbaric means of retribution that passed for correction of a transgression. Little useful purpose will be served by cataloging the cruel and unusual punishments that have been imposed in the past or perhaps even exist today in some parts of the world. What is important to keep in mind is that current practice in correctional institutions may lean more toward retribution than positive rehabilitation.

Penal Institutions

Jails and prisons have existed for centuries, but their expansion to a system that encompassed the totality of a political unit came as recently as the rise of the industrial revolution.[6] Earlier the care and feeding of prisoners was a nuisance to the community; when the rapid development of industry called for more labor, the jail population could supply that in quantity and at low cost. The rise in penal legislation and capacity of prisons began to match the industrial needs of the day. No longer was the local jailer dependent upon the meager fees for food and services that could be squeezed from prisoners—the political unit could pay jailers a wage and hire out convicts profitably. While today the practice of chain gangs on farms and road building has almost completely disappeared as a result of actions by concerned citizens, the financial support necessary to maintain the prison population in a semblance of humaneness is not being met. Reluctance to pay the costs of proper incarceration has hampered prison reform.

City and county units are the base of the correctional system. There are over 4000 municipal or county jails in the country, a majority of them very old and inadequate. They get more than two million commitments a year, most of them for such misdemeanors as drunkenness or motor vehicle charges.[7] Some may be held for trial for a longer period than they would serve if convicted, and many are eventually found not guilty after the long wait for trial.

Local jails are under the control of municipal police or county officers such as the sheriff. Standards of care and operation either do not exist or are very difficult to meet because of the usual limitations of funding of correctional facilities at any level; local facilities are especially subject to these conditions. The resulting shortage of trained personnel, poor physical and health conditions, and slack supervision encourage demeaning or even brutal responses on the part of guards and prisoners.

State correctional facilities sometimes show more professional planning and implementation of goals than local jails. Development of facilities has been matched by changes in attitudes to the point where positive correctional re-education has been introduced. Punitive actions by officials may not have been completely eliminated, but general civic concern has stimulated improvements upon past conditions, as the following case illustrates.

James v. Wallace

406 F. Supp. 318 (1976)

JOHNSON, CHIEF JUDGE . . . this Court has a clear duty to require the defendants in these cases to remedy the massive constitutional infirmities which plague Alabama's prisons. It is with great reluctance that federal courts intervene in the day-to-day operation of state penal systems, . . . a function they are increasingly required to perform. While this Court continues to recognize the broad discretion required for prison officials to maintain orderly and secure institutions, . . . constitutional deprivations of the magnitude presented here simply cannot be countenanced, and this Court is under a duty to, and will, intervene to protect incarcerated citizens from such wholesale infringements of their constitutional rights. . . .

. . . There has been growing recognition by the courts that prisoners retain all rights enjoyed by free citizens except those necessarily lost as an incident of confinement. . . . The Supreme Court recently identified three legitimate functions of a correctional system: deterrence, both specific and general; rehabilitation; and institutional security. . . . *Pell v. Procunier*, 417 U.S. 817 (1974). . . .

Prisoners are entitled to be free of conditions which constitute cruel and unusual punishment in violation of the Eighth and Fourteenth Amendments. The content of the Eighth Amendment is not static but "must draw its meaning from the evolving standards of decency that mark the progress of a maturing society." . . .

The conditions in which Alabama prisoners must live, as established by the evidence in these cases, bear no reasonable relationship to legitimate institutional goals. As a whole they create an atmosphere in which inmates are compelled to live in constant fear of violence, in imminent danger to their physical well-being, and without opportunity to seek a more promising future.

The living conditions in Alabama prisons constitute cruel and unusual punishment. Specifically, lack of sanitation throughout the institutions in living areas, infirmaries, and food service presents an imminent danger to the health of each and every inmate. Prisoners suffer from further physical deterioration because there are no opportunities for exercise and recreation. Treatment for prisoners with physical or emotional problems is totally inadequate. This Court has previously ordered that the penal system provide reasonable medical care for inmates in these institutions. . . .

Prison officials are under a duty to provide inmates reasonable protection from constant threat of violence. . . .

Not only is it cruel and unusual punishment to confine a person in an institution under circumstances which increase the likelihood of future confinement, but these same conditions defeat the goal of rehabilitation which prison officials have set for their institutions. . . .

Prisoners are protected by the Due Process and Equal Protection Clauses of the Fourteenth Amendment; therefore, they must be free from arbitrary and capricious treatment by prison officials. . . .

. . . However, a state is not at liberty to afford its citizens only those constitutional rights which fit comfortably within its budget. . . .

Probation and Parole

The correctional system includes activity that does not involve confinement. *Probation* is a program selected by the court to rehabilitate the offender outside of prison under the supervision of a court case worker. The judge's decision leaves the offender at liberty during a period of testing and proving of worthiness. *Parole* is the conditional release from a correctional institution of a person who has served part of the sentence. Release into the custody of a parole officer is based upon the assumption that he or she is ready to be received in society and has, in a sense, given one's word that behavior will be above reproach (*parole* comes from the French term or word for "promise").

Probation is based upon the power of the court to suspend a sentence or impose conditions other than incarceration. While a sentence may be suspended unconditionally (in which case the defendant is discharged), probation is a period of observation of a person under a suspended sentence in which certain conditions are imposed. The offender is then required to meet the conditions imposed by the court and is monitored by the probation officer to see that he or she does so. If not, the probationer can be sent to a correctional institution to serve the term appropriate for the offense when the court revokes the suspension.

Parole is determined by a board selected or appointed for that purpose. The members of the board meet to set policy and procedure, fix appropriate periods of trial before eligibility for parole, study individual cases, and decide whether the offender merits release on parole. As with probation, the parolee must report to an officer maintaining contact who also provides counseling and guidance in the period of parole. Violation of the conditions under which parole is granted will put the parolee back in prison.

Probation offices are also attached to the juvenile court where young offenders (who are a growing social problem on the basis of numbers alone) are directed. The realization that an adolescent should receive more attention has caused courts to treat juveniles with greater care than adults receive. Juvenile probation officers, therefore, often may be selected with more deliberation and followed more closely by the court and community.

Probation and parole officers have more to do than counsel and supervise the offenders. At the very outset, the court or parole board needs to know as much as possible about the offender so that it can arrive at a better decision about the treatment most likely to be effective in the individual case. Extensive investigation prior to sentencing may also be the job of the probation officer. Gathering the life history of the inmate as well as testing and evaluating is the task of the case workers in the parole office. The parole officer in the field must, in some way, investigate and file reports on the parolees under supervision.

Continuing concern about recurring deficiencies in the correctional process has generated attempts to approach the old problems in newer ways. Variations of long-standing probation and parole techniques, as well as completely innovative approaches, have been suggested to supplement or supplant the one-to-one relationship that has existed between the offender and the agency officer.

Work Release is a program developed in the federal corrections system, as well as in many states, which is intended to release inmates so that they can be productively and gainfully employed under previously set conditions. Either a complete exit or release during working hours prepares the inmate for return to society and reduces the financial strain on the corrections system when the inmate reimburses it and pays taxes.

External treatment centers, usually in the home area, are intended to reintroduce the offender gradually to the community. The centers can be either governmental units or those developed with the participation of private organizations. The Federal Bureau of Prisons has initiated community treatment centers and some states may follow suit. Halfway houses are set up for the same reasons by local governmental units or community agencies. These may have numerous volunteers involved or the services can be carried out in many supporting ways in the community, either in group projects or in the individual type of counseling that the probation or parole officer traditionally has provided.

Probation may not always be a simple matter, however, as the following case indicates.

United States of America v. Restor, et al.

130 Pittsburgh Legal Journal 198 (1982)

DIAMOND, J., January 13, 1982.—The defendants entered pleas of guilty to criminal contempt in violation of 18 U.S.C. §401(3) (1966), and each was sentenced to the custody of the United States Attorney General for a term of imprisonment of six months and to pay a fine of $1,000. Execution of the terms of imprisonment was suspended and the defendants were placed on probation for a period of three years. In addition to the usual conditions of probation, each defendant was ordered to perform eight hours per week of court-approved community service work for fifty weeks of each year of the probation term. The defendants appealed the sentences and have moved to stay execution thereof pending the appeals. For reasons set forth below, the motions will be denied.

Background

The defendants were employed by the United States Government as air traffic controllers and were officers of local unions of the Professional Air Traffic Controllers Organization (PATCO). As a result of their participation in a work stoppage in August, 1981, the defendants were indicted for violating 18 U.S.C. §1918 (1970), which prohibits employees of the Government of the United States from engaging in a strike, this court entered a temporary restraining order enjoining continuation of the work stoppage, and the defendants violated that order.

Motions by the defendants which, inter alia, challenged the legality of the indictment on the grounds that the government engaged in impermissibly selective prosecution, asserted that 18 U.S.C. § 1918 (1970) was vague and did not charge a crime, and contended that the President had granted amnesty to the defendants when he had issued them an ultimatum to return to work by August 5, 1981, or be discharged, were denied by the court, and the cases set down for trials.

In the meantime counsel advised the court that they had arrived at a plea agreement, and on November 9, 1981, the defendants appeared in court to enter pleas in accordance therewith. The proposed agreement provided that the defendants would plead guilty under 18 U.S.C. § 401(3) (1966) to a charge of contempt for the willful violation of the August 4, 1981, TRO, and would receive sentences limited solely to a fine of $500 after which the 18 U.S.C. §1918 (1970) felony charge would be dismissed. However, that agreement was rejected by the court pursuant to Rule 11(c), Fed. R. Crim. P., and the cases were rescheduled for trial with the understanding that the plea procedure was recessed and would be resumed if a plea bargain acceptable to the court was reached.

Later in the day on November 9, 1981, counsel advised the court that they had arrived at another plea agreement and the plea hearing was reconvened the following day. At the time the parties proposed a plea bargain under which the defendants would plead guilty to contempt of court in violation of 18 U.S.C. §401(3) (1970) and agree to the imposition of a sentence not to exceed imprisonment for six months or a fine of $1,000 or both. In return the government would recommend that the sentences not exceed a fine of $500 each and would agree to a dismissal of the felony indictments after the imposition of sentences on the contempt charges. This was accepted by the court. The defendants entered pleas accordingly, and each subsequently was sentenced as previously indicated.

We believe that the sentences were legal in substance, form, and manner of imposition. The authority of the district court to place a defendant on probation is governed by 18 U.S.C. §3651 (1981 Supp.). That statute provides that in cases such as those sub judice a court "when satisfied that the ends of justice and the best interests of the public as well as the defendant will be served thereby, may suspend the imposition or execution of sentence and place the defendant on probation for such period and upon such terms and conditions as the court deems best." id. Execution of the prison sentences in the cases at bar was suspended and the defendants were placed on probation for a term within the maximum permitted by 18 U.S.C. §3651 (1981 Supp.).

The sentences imposed by the court were within the limits of the plea agreement entered into among the parties. Indeed, we believe that the suspended sentences are more lenient than those bargained for by the defendants.

Of course, the conditions of probation must be legally permissible. The conditions imposed here appear to be legal since (1) the imposition of community service as a condition of probation appears to be within the broad discretion vested in the court by 18 U.S.C. §3651 (1981 Supp.) and has received appellate court approval, (2) the community service work is reasonably related to the purposes of probation as applied to the cases at bar, (3) the probation conditions are clear and specific, and (4) they do not constitute unduly harsh restrictions on the defendants' liberty.

We believe that in the instant cases community service is particularly appropriate. The defendants were officers of a labor organization consisting of individuals whose job it was to assist in air traffic control to promote the safety and efficiency of air commerce. They were employees of the government and hence paid by all taxpayers. When defendants became dissatisfied with the status of the contract negotiations through which they were seeking improved working conditions and higher wages, they attempted to force the government to accede to their demands by engaging in what was patently an illegal work stoppage. Not only was the strike a violation of their oath, their contract and the civil laws, but it was also in violation of the criminal code and a direct order of this court. Defendants were attempting through illegal means to extract from their fellow citizens employment benefits including wage increases, which defendants were unable to obtain through lawful collective bargaining.

The court takes judicial notice that the strike has resulted in hardship and inconvenience to the public, increased unemployment of innocent people, and the loss of millions of dollars in the airline and related industries. The defendants' conduct was, thus, uniquely antisocial. In our judgment it was necessary, therefore, to reinstate the defendants in society, and thus to promote their rehabilitation, by requiring that they perform community service work, designed "to restore [their] self-esteem, integrate [them] in a working environment, and inculcate in [them] a sense of social responsibility. . . ." Higdon, [v. United States, 627 F. 2d 893 (1980)].

Conclusion

The defendants entered into the plea bargain with their eyes open. They were concerned primarily with avoiding felony convictions under 18 U.S.C. §1918 (1970) and, inter alia, the adverse effect that would have on their hoped-for reinstatement as air controllers. In addition, they realized from statements made by the court to defense counsel when the TRO was entered that they also faced contempt of court charges. They attempted to negotiate a plea bargain by which they not only would have avoided the felony conviction, but also would have limited the total penalty of each defendant to a fine of $500. When this was rejected by the court as wholly inappropriate, they settled for what they could get rather than go to trial and to risk what they perceived to be virtually certain felony convictions and the consequences thereof. That the defendants were disappointed in sentences which they received is immaterial. In our opinion those sentences were legal and at least as good as those for which the defendants bargained.

Indeed, were it not for the mitigating factors which the court recognized at the sentencing, the cost savings *and* the viable alternative to incarceration as a vehicle of rehabilitation which the court perceived in the community service condition of probation, the defendants would have been sentenced to incarceration in the first instance.

For the foregoing reasons, we are unable to find sufficient apparent merit in the defendants' appeals to justify delay in the commencement of their sentences. . . .

ACCORDINGLY, each of the motions to stay will be denied. The terms of the probation, which commenced on December 10, 1982, will continue uninterrupted. Rule 38(a) (4) Fed. R. Crim. P.

QUESTIONS

1. What are the basic elements of the systems approach? How do they apply to the study of law?
2. How do static and dynamic models of a system differ? What are the specific applications to the legal system?
3. Identify control systems at various levels. Which are the most numerous?
4. What are the major differences between federal and state court systems of organization?
5. Describe the various roles that lawyers may play in the legal system and their accession to these positions.
6. What is the basis for the existence of administrative agencies?

NOTES

[1] Fremont Kast and James Rosenzweig, *Organization and Management: A Systems Approach* (New York: McGraw-Hill, 1967), p. 110.

[2] James D. Thompson, *Organizations in Action* (New York: McGraw-Hill, 1967), p. 157.

[3] Martin Mayer, *The Lawyers* (New York: Harper and Row, 1971), p. 13.

[4] The President's Commission on Law Enforcement and Administration of Justice, *The Challenge of Crime in a Free Society* (Washington, D.C.: Government Printing Office, 1967), p. 72.

[5] *Williams* v. *Florida,* 399 U.S. 78 (1970).

[6] George T. Felkenes, *The Criminal Justice System: Its Function and Personnel* (Englewood Cliffs, N.J.: Prentice-Hall, 1973), pp. 261–63.

[7] President's Commission, *The Challenge of Crime,* p. 72.

legal
substance
and procedure

THREE

Substantive law represents the foundation upon which the actors in the legal system base their solutions to treatable social problems. Various elements are brought into play as the system swings into action in the described legal process. Factors of substance and process are intertwined in this phase of societal activity, just as they are in other human events.

Certain fundamental legal concepts underlie the law of the United States and, to a great extent, that of other countries under the Anglo-American common law system. These concepts represent a basic philosophical approach toward maintaining a well-ordered society while preserving individual and group freedoms. Underlying the American common law system is the Constitution, a broad document that contains concepts such as due process, right to trial by jury, and other fundamental legacies of the system. A further source of law is the legislation that arises in conformity with this basic document.

CONSTITUTIONAL LAW

The Constitution of the United States was the first such document to be adopted by a people, and is still one of a limited number of broad, published fundamentals of a legal system. Theoretically, the Constitution is the basis for all legal decisions in the country. It is a source of all the freedoms possessed and a regulation for the common welfare of the society.

Powers

The Constitution outlines the basic interrelationships under which this nation must function. In its *enumeration of powers,* it states the powers granted to the federal government and those left to the states, as well as identifying rights held by individual citizens. A subsidiary concept is the *separation of powers:* that is, in addition to a structuring of the federal-state relationships, the roles of the three separate branches of government (legislative, executive, and judicial) are sketched. The purpose of the separation is to maintain a balance of power among the three branches and to limit each to its proper activity.

In the separation of powers there was no more important designation of role than that of the judicial branch. The founding fathers recognized the need for an independent judiciary. Article III, Section I of the Constitution states that:

> The judicial power of the United States shall be rested in one Supreme Court and in such inferior courts as the Congress may from time to time ordain and establish.

The article further states that this judicial power is to extend to all cases arising under the Constitution as well as under the laws and treaties made under this authority. It was left to later court decisions to buttress the concept of *judicial review,* the position that the courts are bound by the Constitution to declare, when called upon, whether or not a particular act of legislature or of the executive branch conforms to the Constitution. Justice John Marshall, early in the life of the republic, declared for the Supreme Court that the Court had the power of review.[1]

The doctrine of enumeration of powers and their separation did not continue without some controversy, however. An early president was said to have remarked that John Marshall had made his decision, let him enforce it. In this century, President Franklin D. Roosevelt, disturbed by Court decisions that hindered the development of social programs under the "New Deal," proposed to add justices to the Supreme Court. The attempts received little support but resulted in subsequent decisions that generally supported the programs of economic recovery. In more recent events, a president who claimed executive privilege to keep recorded conversations from being turned over to the Court was eventually convinced to make them available.[2] Similar restrictions exist in the relationships between legislative and executive branches. There is, for instance, no basis for the legislature to impose a veto upon action that is clearly in the domain of the executive.

How the Supreme Court views the powers of the three branches of the government is the crux of the following case.

Youngstown Co. v. *Sawyer*
343 U.S. 579 (1951)

MR. JUSTICE BLACK delivered the opinion of the Court.

We are asked to decide whether the President was acting within his constitutional power when he issued an order directing the Secretary of Commerce to take possession of and operate most of the Nation's steel mills. The mill owners argue that the President's order amounts to lawmaking, a legislative function which the Constitution has expressly confided to the Congress and not to the President. The Government's position is that his order was made on findings of the President that his action was necessary to avert a national catastrophe which would inevitably result from a stoppage of steel production, and that in meeting this grave emergency the President was acting within the aggregate of his constitutional powers as the Nation's Chief Executive and the Commander in Chief of the Armed Forces of the United States. The issue emerges here from the following series of events:

In the latter part of 1951, a dispute arose between the steel companies and their employees over terms and conditions that should be included in new collective bargaining agreements. Long-continued conferences failed to resolve the dispute. On December 18, 1951, the employees' representative, United Steelworkers of America, C.I.O., gave notice of an intention to strike when the existing bargaining agreements expired on December 31. The Federal Mediation and Conciliation Service then intervened in an effort to get labor and management to agree. This failing, the President on December 22, 1951, referred the dispute to the Federal Wage Stabilization Board to investigate and make recommendations for fair and equit-

able terms of settlement. This Board's report resulted in no settlement. On April 4, 1952, the Union gave notice of a nation-wide strike called to begin at 12:01 a.m. April 9. The indispensability of steel as a component of substantially all weapons and other war materials led the President to believe that the proposed work stoppage would immediately jeopardize our national defense and that governmental seizure of the steel mills was necessary in order to assure the continued availability of steel. Reciting these considerations for his action, the President, a few hours before the strike was to begin, issued Executive Order 10340, a copy of which is attached as an appendix, *post,* p. 589. The order directed the Secretary of Commerce to take possession of most of the steel mills and keep them running. The Secretary immediately issued his own possessory orders, calling upon the presidents of the various seized companies to serve as operating managers for the United States. They were directed to carry on their activities in accordance with regulations and directions of the Secretary. The next morning the President sent a message to Congress reporting his action. Cong. Rec., April 9, 1952, p. 3962. Twelve days later he sent a second message. Cong. Rec., April 21, 1952, p. 4192. Congress has taken no action.

Obeying the Secretary's orders under protest, the companies brought proceedings against him in the District Court. Their complaints charged that the seizure was not authorized by an act of Congress or by any constitutional provisions. The District Court was asked to declare the orders of the President and the Secretary invalid and to issue preliminary and permanent injunctions restraining their enforcement. Opposing the motion for preliminary injunction, the United States asserted that a strike disrupting steel production for even a brief period would so endanger the well-being and safety of the Nation that the President had "inherent power" to do what he had done— power "supported by the Constitution, by historical precedent, and by court decisions." The Government also contended that in any event no preliminary injunction should be issued because the companies had made no showing that their available legal remedies were inadequate or that their injuries from seizure would be irreparable. Holding against the Government on all points, the District Court on April 30 issued a preliminary injunction restraining the Secretary from "continuing the seizure and possession of the plants . . . and from acting under the purported authority of Executive Order No. 10340." 103 F. Supp. 569. On the same day the Court of Appeals stayed the District Court's injunction. 90 U.S. App. D.C.——, 197 F. 2d 582. Deeming it best that the issues raised be promptly decided by this Court, we granted certiorari on May 3 and set the cause for argument on May 12. 343 U.S. 937.

. . .

II.

The President's power, if any, to issue the order must stem either from an act of Congress or from the Constitution itself. There is no statute that expressly authorizes the President to take possession of property as he did here. Nor is there any act of Congress to which our attention has been directed from which such a power can fairly be implied. Indeed, we do not understand the Government to rely on statutory authorization for this seizure. There are two statutes which do authorize the President to take both personal and real property under certain conditions. However, the Government admits that these conditions were not met and that the President's order was not rooted in either of the statutes. The Government refers to the seizure provisions of one of these statutes (§ 201(b) of the Defense Production Act) as "much too cumbersome, involved, and time-consuming for the crisis which was at hand."

Moreover, the use of the seizure technique to solve labor disputes in order to prevent work stoppages was not only unauthorized by any congressional enactment; prior to this controversy, Congress had refused to adopt that method of settling labor disputes. When the Taft-Hartley Act was under consideration in 1947, Congress rejected an amendment which would have authorized such governmental seizures in cases of emergency. Apparently it was thought that the technique of seizure, like that of compulsory arbitration, would interfere with the process of collective bargaining. Consequently, the plan Congress adopted in that Act did not provide for seizure under any circumstances. Instead, the plan sought to bring about settlements by use of the customary devices of mediation, conciliation, investigation by boards of inquiry, and public reports. In some instances temporary injunctions were authorized to provide cooling-off periods. All this failing, unions were left free to strike after a secret vote by employees as to whether they wished to accept their employers' final settlement offer.

It is clear that if the President had authority to issue the order he did, it must be found in some provision of the Constitution. And it is not claimed that express constitutional language grants this power to the

President. The contention is that presidential power should be implied from the aggregate of his powers under the Constitution. Particular reliance is placed on provisions in Article II which say that "The executive Power shall be vested in a President . . ."; that "he shall take Care that the Laws be faithfully executed"; and that he "shall be Commander in Chief of the Army and Navy of the United States."

The order cannot properly be sustained as an exercise of the President's military power as Commander in Chief of the Armed Forces. The Government attempts to do so by citing a number of cases upholding broad powers in military commanders engaged in day-to-day fighting in a theater of war. Such cases need not concern us here. Even though "theater of war" be an expanding concept, we cannot with faithfulness to our constitutional system hold that the Commander in Chief of the Armed Forces has the ultimate power as such to take possession of private property in order to keep labor disputes from stopping production. This is a job for the Nation's lawmakers, not for its military authorities.

Nor can the seizure order be sustained because of the several constitutional provisions that grant executive power to the President. In the framework of our Constitution, the President's power to see that the laws are faithfully executed refutes the idea that he is to be a lawmaker. The Constitution limits his functions in the lawmaking process to the recommending of laws he thinks wise and the vetoing of laws he thinks bad. And the Constitution is neither silent nor equivocal about who shall make laws which the President is to execute. The first section of the first article says that "All legislative Powers herein granted shall be vested in a Congress of the United States. . . ." After granting many powers to the Congress, Ar-

ticle I goes on to provide that Congress may "make all Laws which shall be necessary and proper for carrying into Execution the foregoing Powers, and all other Powers vested by this Constitution in the Government of the United States, or in any Department or Officer thereof."

The President's order does not direct that a congressional policy be executed in a manner prescribed by Congress—it directs that a presidential policy be executed in a manner prescribed by the President. The preamble of the order itself, like that of many statutes, sets out reasons why the President believes certain policies should be adopted, proclaims these policies as rules of conduct to be followed, and again, like a statute, authorizes a government official to promulgate additional rules and regulations consistent with the policy proclaimed and needed to carry that policy into execution. The power of Congress to adopt such public policies as those proclaimed by the order is beyond question. It can authorize the taking of private property for public use. It can make laws regulating the relationships between employers and employees, prescribing rules designed to settle labor disputes, and fixing wages and working conditions in certain fields in our economy. The Constitution does not subject this lawmaking power of Congress to presidential or military supervision or control.

It is said that other Presidents without congressional authority have taken possession of private business enterprises in order to settle labor disputes. But even if this be true, Congress has not thereby lost its exclusive constitutional authority to make laws necessary and proper to carry out the powers vested by the Constitution "in the Government of the United States, or any Department or Officer thereof."

The Founders of this Nation entrusted

the lawmaking power to the Congress alone in both good and bad times. It would do no good to recall the historical events, the fears of power and the hopes for freedom that lay behind their choice. Such a review would but confirm our holding that this seizure order cannot stand.

The judgment of the District Court is

Affirmed.

MR. JUSTICE FRANKFURTER

Although the considerations relevant to the legal enforcement of the principle of separation of powers seem to me more complicated and flexible than may appear from what MR. JUSTICE BLACK has written, I join his opinion because I thoroughly agree with the application of the principle to the circumstances of this case. Even though such differences in attitude toward this principle may be merely differences in emphasis and nuance, they can hardly be reflected by a single opinion for the Court. Individual expression of views in reaching a common result is therefore important.

The Bill of Rights

At the time of the adoption of the Constitution, there was some reluctance to ratify the document, partly because many thought it had serious omissions, primarily in the area of individual and states' rights. There was consensus, however, that amendments to fill the gap were to be passed in short order. Those first ten amendments came to be known as the *Bill of Rights*. The highlights of each of the ten amendments are:

First—No establishment of religion or prohibition in its exercise as well as the right of free speech and press.

Second—The right to bear arms.

Third—No quartering of soldiers in private dwellings except by law.

Fourth—Prohibition against unreasonable search and seizures.

Fifth—Presentment or indictment required to hold for capital crime; no double jeopardy; no compulsion to be a witness against self; no deprivation of life, liberty, or property without due process.

Sixth—One accused of crime is to have a speedy trial, the right of confrontation of witnesses, and assistance of counsel.

Seventh—The right of trial by jury in civil matters when value in controversy exceeds twenty dollars.

Eighth—No excessive bail or cruel and unusual punishment.

Ninth—Enumeration of rights in Constitution does not deny others retained by people.

Tenth—Powers not delegated to the federal government are reserved to the states or the people.

Out of all these statements of rights, two words appear more significantly than others. *Due process* may represent the basis of our individual rights and freedoms. When some limits developed in practice, the Fourteenth Amendment came into existence in order to assure that due process and other rights would be provided by the states as well as by the federal government. At both levels, however, implementation of the concept of due process may provide some difficulty, as the term itself is somewhat ambiguous. Social and economic factors, as well as individual ones, influence outcomes of legal actions in this area as in other areas. Due process in matters of deprivation of life and liberty are of major concern to society and is more likely to be observed to an extent agreed upon by a majority of inhabitants. Cases of legally altering property rights are more difficult. Restriction of use of personal or real property, or even outright taking (even though for a public purpose), does not occur without controversy as to whether rights have been duly observed. *Zoning laws* or use of *eminent domain* to take property for some community benefit raise questions of due process. Similarly, restrictions on conditions of work also affects the property rights of employers.

The following case is one of many that consider the question of a possible violation of rights guaranteed by the Constitution.

Lake Butler Apparel Co. v. Secretary of Labor

In the United States Court of Appeals for the Fifth Circuit. No. 73-3518(1975)

A compliance officer on a routine inspection found several minor violations for which the employer was not assessed any nonabatement penalties. The employer, a clothing manufacturer employing over 100 sewing machine operators contested the citations on the ground that the provisions were unconstitutional in that they had a "chilling" effect on the right to seek review. The employer further contended that OSHA inspections and constitute illegal searches, violated the Fourth Amendment. Finally, the requirement to post a notice of the citation was alleged to be a violation of the employer's rights to freedom of speech under the First Amendment.

Before Brown, Chief Judge, and Thornberry and Ainsworth, Circuit Judges.

In [Atlas Roofing Co. v. Brennan (5 Cir. 75)] we analyzed and rejected two of the Lake Butler arguments: (i) the due process issue—penalties that become final absent employer initiated review are in violation of due process, citing *Snidach* v. *Family Finance Corp.,* 1969, 395 U.S. 337, 89 S. Ct. 1820, 23 L.Ed. 2d 349; and (ii) the Sixth Amendment argument—civil penalties under OSHA are essentially criminal in nature invoking the protections of the Sixth Amendment. There remains to be considered Lake Butler's arguments that (iii) the OSHA provisions for nonabatement penalties have the effect of "chilling" the employer's right to seek review; (iv) the Fourth Amendment is violated by the OSHA provisions allowing warrantless administrative searches without probable cause; (v) the authority vested in the Secretary of Labor to assess penalties usurps the powers of the judiciary under Article III. . .

Although we noted the importance of this argument in *Atlas,* we concluded there that the petitioner lacked standing to raise the point because the abatement date was stayed by the Commission and no nonabatement penalties were therefore possible. Unlike Atlas Roofing Company, Lake Butler has not received such a plenary stay. Instead, OSHRECOM ordered only the penalties assessed be stayed. According to Lake Butler, such a selective stay leaves the company vulnerable to a later determination by OSHRE-COM that the review proceeding was not initiated in "good faith" after which the abatement period could be considered to have retroactively commenced on the date originally specified in the citation. Thus, if such a determination were made, Lake Butler might be assessed a nonabatement per day penalty running retroactively from the original abatement deadline. Although no Court has yet so held, Lake Butler argues that such a possible penalty operates to "chill" the exercise of the employer's right to seek review proceedings. *Lance Roofing Company* v. *Hodgson,* N.D. Ga., 1972, 343 F. Supp. 685, 689-90, aff'd, 409 U.S. 1070, 93 S. Ct. 679, 34 L.Ed. 2d 659.

However, in order to challenge these specific provisions, Lake Butler must present this Court with a realistic case or controversy. *U.S. Const. Art. III* §2. We do not judge the hypothetical. To put those statutory provisions at issue Petitioner must show a demonstrable threat of future citations by the Secretary and that an employer would reasonably be dissuaded from invoking the elaborate review procedures of the Act by the possibility of cumulative fines. By our consideration at length of this case the Secretary could not possibly conclude this to be a bad faith appeal. The record contains no indication that the Secretary would intend to exercise these nonabatement sanctions. In any event, the possibility does not exist until after our affirmation of this case. If then the Secretary sought to invoke these retroactive penalties, they would—as we read the statute—be subject to the same administrative proceedings as might any original violation. 29 U.S.C.A. §666 (d). However, if there is any question that these employers would have a right of review in the Court of Appeals over such nonabatement penalties, it certainly is a sanction as to which the APA 5 U.S.C.A. §704 affords judicial review. We would not hold the provisions unconstitutional "in advance of its immediate adverse effect in the context of a concrete case." . . .

Lake Butler contends that OSHA authorizes warrantless inspections by its compliance officers in violation of the Fourth Amendment. Lake Butler would have this Court void the administrative hearing because the violations were discovered pursuant to an illegal search. In response, the government argues that business enterprises subject to OSHA inspections should fall under the "implied consent" exception to the Fourth Amendment. *United States* v. *Biswell,* 1972, 406 U.S. 311, 92 S. Ct. 1593, 32 L.Ed. 2d 87. In the past this exception has been limited to businesses the government has had "historically broad authority" to regulate, e.g., the liquor industry, and any attempt to expand the concept must be cautiously analyzed.

But here we need not reach the issue because, looking at the total circumstances of the search, we find that it was purely consensual. In fact, Lake Butler has never contended that the compliance officer did not have the fullest permission of the President of Lake Butler. The OSHA officer, on a routine inspection of plants in the Lake Butler area, presented himself to Stephenson who then accompanied him through the plant. The violations that were discovered during that walking tour—ungrounded machines, lack of color [coding] coating on the fire extinguishers, etc.—were in plain, obvious view. There was no search here of drawers or other sequestered areas. For that reason Lake Butler may not rely on the *Camara/See* precedent. In each of those instances appellants sought to avoid criminal punishment for the assertion of their Fourth Amendment rights. Lake

Butler cannot obtain a ruling on constitutionality when it did not assert its rights at the time of the inspection. . . .

Lake Butler argues that the provision of OSHA that permits the Commission to assess civil penalties for violation of the Act, 29 U.S.C.A. §666, usurps the powers of the judiciary under Article III by making the compliance officer "investigator, legislator, factfinder, prosecutor and judge." 29 CFR §§1903.7 and 1903.14. This argument is closely akin to an argument raised by the appellant in *Atlas*—that the absence of a jury in OSHA proceedings makes it violative of the Seventh Amendment. We reject the argument now for similar reasons.

It has long been recognized that it is well within the powers of Congress to entrust the enforcement of statutory rights to an administrative process and limit the participation of the Courts by the substantial evidence standard. *NLRB* v. *Jones & Laughlin Steel Corp.*; 1937, 301 U.S. 1, 57 S. Ct. 615, 81 L.Ed. 893. Most recently, the Supreme Court reiterated this in *Curtis* v. *Loether,* 1974, 415 U.S. 189, 94 S.Ct. 1005, 39 L.Ed. 2d 260. The administrative proceedings under OSHA present no unusual features that would cause us to deviate from this rule. . . .

Lastly, Lake Butler argues that the OSHA requirement that the information sign be posted at its clothing factory violates its First Amendment rights to freedom of speech. 29 CFR §1903.2(a). However, Lake Butler does not cite us to any cases on the issue and we are hard put to find any. The argument is seemingly nonsensical for if the government has a right to promulgate these regulations it seems obvious that they have a right to statutorily require that they be posted in a place that would be obvious to the intended beneficiaries of the statute—Lake Butler's employees. The posting of the notice does not by any stretch of the imagination reflect one way or the other on the views of the employer. It merely states what the law requires. The employer may differ with the wisdom of the law and this requirement even to the point as done here, of challenging its validity. He may as we once said, "take his views to a McGahey marked grave." *NLRB* v. *McGahey,* 5 Cir., 1956, 233 F. 2d 406, 409. But the First Amendment which gives him the full right to contest validity to the bitter end cannot justify his refusal to post a notice Congress thought to be essential.

Affirmed.

LEGAL PRECEDENTS

The adherence by judges to a settled pattern of decisions has been one of the hallmarks of the common law system. Precedents are important in determining aspects of litigation in several ways, but most notably to assist in making expectations of outcomes more predictable and realistic. This doctrine, known as *stare decisis*, provides more stability in a legal system and avoids the necessity of the judicial branch having to begin developing the law anew in each case presented.

There is a limitation on *stare decisis*, however, in that judges are constrained to follow only decisions set in the affected jurisdiction, although opinions from other common law areas may serve as guides. In addition, the court may determine that the elements of the controversy differ from those in cases adjudicated earlier, and that therefore the case calls for a different outcome.

HABEAS CORPUS

The writ of *habeas corpus* has been called the "stable bulwark of our liberties" by an English legal scholar, even though it may not be as visible as other fundamental elements of the common law.[3] Its importance lies in the protection of individual liberty through the prohibition of detention without a lawful basis. Although allegations of unlawful restraint arise most often in instances of imprisonment for crimes, the concept of *habeas corpus* covers a broad range of events. The writ is appropriate, for instance, in domestic matters such as child custody where legal awards affect the liberties of those involved.

STATUS IN LITIGATION

A further buttress of individual liberty under the common law and in most parts of the Western world is the idea that a person is innocent until proven guilty. This emphasis upon individual freedom is not a feature of systems under which authoritarian governments function. Their attempts at complete social control include approaches that favor official prosecutors.

A related element of the common law system is the recognition that action in the judicial system most often requires proper representation of the parties to the litigation. Advocacy is especially important in criminal matters, a fact that was recognized recently by the Supreme Court in its mandating appointment of legal counsel in criminal trials on serious grounds when the defendant could not afford to do so personally.[4] Many localities have a specific office, usually called that of the Public Defender, to staff cases for indigent defendants. In the absence of such office, the court will designate counsel from the local Bar. Representation in civil matters is not mandated, but is strongly recommended. An individual might appear before the court *in propria persona,* that is, conducting the case by oneself, but this is usually a risky venture. Considerable knowledge of the system and its underpinnings is required to proceed effectively before the court.

CONSTITUTIONAL LAW DECISIONS

It must be emphasized that a constitution is a broadly worded document that provides general outlines to follow. It differs from a code in that a code is more detailed, containing specific coverage. A constitution requires extensive interpretation by the judiciary, and there is considerable room for variation of opinion as to the correct determination of meaning.

As has been noted, court decisions have been influenced by social and economic variables, despite the expectation by some that such factors would play little or no role in legal outcomes. Basic philosophical positions also have played a significant role in court decisions. Indeed, one occupation of court watchers, especially those following the highly visible U.S. Supreme Court, has been to attempt to predict decisions based upon the supposed attitudes and values of individual justices.

Up until the depression years of the 1930s, the Supreme Court adhered strongly to the concept of economic *laissez-faire,* tying it to the principles inherent in individual rights. For example, in *Lochner* v. *New York,* the Court held that a state statute limiting a work week to 60 hours was unconstitutional because it restricted the employer and employee to contract to work longer hours.[5] At the time of the Depression, the Court had invalidated many of the industrial recovery acts of the Roosevelt Administration. Reaction to these legal outcomes was swift and sharp, so that the Court recognized the social and economic factors present in the situation, and in most subsequent cases new legislation was deemed to be in conformity with constitutional dictates. It was then possible to implement new responses to difficult economic problems in order to hasten recovery of the economy.

Similar developments occurred in connection with regulation by state and federal authorities. Although the Supreme Court declared early in its existence that interstate commerce was more than mere transportation, Court decisions did not apply that idea to activity that centered within a state. In the 1930s a significant departure was made when the Court noted that intrastate activities came under federal regulation when "they have a close and substantial relation to interstate commerce."[6] More recently, the basis for federal control was extended to the conduct of a motel business, because accommodations were open to interstate travelers and the Civil Rights Act of 1964 (prohibiting discrimination) applied.[7]

Recent concern about environmental quality has caused further movement away from extensive protection of individual circumstances. The taking of property or limiting of its use has been increasingly fostered by a concentration on the property's impact upon public welfare. Such taking has also been justified as a proper exercise of police power.

There is some opportunity for state regulation even if it affects interstate commerce, but there are limits. If interstate commerce is unreasonably hampered, the state regulation is struck down. Thus, a state statute limiting the length of tractor trailers below that of neighboring states was declared unconstitutional.[8] The Supreme Court does make the determination whether federal control is exclusive. When there is conflict between State and Federal controls, the federal regulation prevails, and in some cases only federal regulation is permitted.

STATUTORY LAW

In addition to being formed under constitutionally influenced processes, law may come into existence by legislation. Laws are enacted at all legislative levels from the federal to the local municipal. Congress, state legislatures, and local officials all pass statutory provisions, although at the municipal level these are referred to as ordinances.

The federal legislative body, the Congress, is composed of the Senate (100 members) and the House of Representatives (435 members). There are two senators from each state elected every six years, but members of the House are elected every two years from districts that are roughly of equal size in terms of population.

The course of enacting legislation starts with a *bill* presented by a senator and a representative. Bills are numbered consecutively; in the Senate the numbers start with S-1 while in the House the designation would be H-1. Introduced bills are sent to a committee of that body for consideration. After deliberation, perhaps including meetings and hearings by subcommittees, the bill may be amended or redrafted. The chairman of the committee or its members decide whether to report out the bill for consideration by the entire body. If they decide not to report out the bill, it is very difficult to get it on the floor. The Rules Committee determines the time for debate on the bill. If the bill is passed, whether amended or not, in each chamber and there are no differences, the legislation goes to the President. If there are differences, it goes to a conference committee of members of both House and Senate for resolution. The bill may be signed by the President, or he may let it become law after an interval without signing, or he may veto it. The veto may be overridden by a two-thirds vote in each chamber.

In the states, the composition and procedures of legislatures is similar to that at the federal level, except that Nebraska has one chamber rather than two.

Rule-making that has the practical force and effect of legislation emerges from administrative agencies. The agencies operate under powers delegated to them to regulate more directly the myriad social and economic activities that grew beyond the power of legislators or executives to monitor efficiently. These rulings often have more impact upon society or, more particularly, business, than does the legislation emerging from Congress or state legislatures. The Securities Exchange Commission (SEC), the Federal Trade Commission (FTC), and the Interstate Commerce Commission (ICC) are only a few of the many agencies at the federal level that have regulatory functions. Each state may also have many agencies performing related functions.

FINDING THE LAW

A statement that a specific position is *the* law is misleading. Given the dynamic nature of the legal process, it is more accurate to say that there are multiple sources of information that may aid in determining the probable outcome of a legal question.

Constitution and Statutes

The Constitution of the United States is printed by the Government Printing Office in a volume under that name. Federal statutes, most of them known as Public Laws, are numbered in sequence for each designated session of Congress. P.L. 94-580, for instance, is the 580th in a series of laws passed by the 94th Congress. Federal laws are officially published by the Government Printing Office in the *United States Code.*

Regulations promulgated by federal agencies are published in the *Federal Register* as they appear. These are assembled in the *Code of Federal Regulations* (C.F.R.).

Most states pattern their publications of constitutions and statutes in ways similar to the federal system, although the titles may vary.

Judicial Decisions

Decisions of courts have impact beyond the specific cases being decided. Under the doctrine of *stare decisis,* the opinions provide a basis for the continuation of a stable system of law. Searching prior opinions and using them for basing and predicting outcomes is a formidable task for judges and lawyers. About 50,000 opinions are published yearly (and not all court opinions are published). When published, the cases generally follow a set format.

In a trial court, the judgment will be for either the plaintiff or the defendant, and the opinion will so state. At the appellate level, the court will either *affirm* the lower court decision, *reverse* it, or *remand* the case to the original court for action commensurate with the appellate court opinion.

Publication of court opinions is through official and private commercial sources. The official edition for the U.S. Supreme Court is the *United States Reports* published by the Government Printing Office; other similar reports are printed privately.[9] Reports for lower federal courts are made by the West Publishing Co. in the *Federal Reporter* (now cited as F.2d) for the Court of Appeals, and the *Federal Supplement* (F.Supp.) for selected cases from district courts. Most states do not publish case opinions from their courts, but the West Publishing Co. collates cases on a regional basis in seven regional volumes, such as the *Atlantic Reporter* (A.2d) covering the States of Pennsylvania, New Jersey, Maryland, Delaware, and six others. New York and California have their own separate volumes.

Administrative agency decisions are published under various titles. These *Reports, Decisions,* or *Orders* are published by private firms that focus upon specific areas such as tax, labor law, or environmental law, and usually publish in loose-leaf format to accommodate changes.

Secondary Sources

Some general and specific insights into law may be gained from treatises that outline the common fundamentals and particulars of substantive areas. Law texts, encylopedias, and periodicals are commonly used sources for background. *American Jurisprudence* (Am. Jur. 2d) and *Corpus Juris Secundum* (C.J.S.) are well-known and often-used treatises. In addition, the *Restatement of the Law* has a significant place in legal research. This is a statement of legal principles in areas of law such as torts or contracts, which was assembled by the American Law Institute in response to an expressed need for a more precise and commonly accepted set of conceptual guidelines. These do not have the force of law, of course, but are often scrutinized in specific legal determinations.

CRIMES

One of the basic distinctions made in Chapter 1 was between criminal and civil law. This differentiation applies to the matter of how a particular act affects society. When society considers an act to be a wrong committed against society, the commission of that act is a crime. An injury done as a private wrong to a person is considered a tort, a civil injury, and one to be redressed in a civil action.

The same set of circumstances can be the basis for both a criminal and civil action. If, for instance, Smith strikes Jones, Jones may sign a complaint and have Smith prosecuted for assault and battery in a criminal court. Jones also may file a separate tort action in civil court for monetary damages. In the criminal case the state proceeds against Smith:

> *Commonwealth* v. *Smith;*
> *State* v. *Smith;*
> *People* v. *Smith.*

(The exact caption varies from state to state.) In a civil case the matter carries the caption "*Jones* v. *Smith,*" identifying the plaintiff and the defendant, in that order.

Crimes themselves can be distinguished on the basis of severity—some are more shocking to society than others. A basic twofold distinction in common law has been made between a *felony* and a *misdemeanor.* Under old English law a felony was an act punishable by forfeiture of life and property; all other, lesser offenses were misdemeanors. (There was also treason, an even more serious offense against the Crown.)

At the present time the criminal statutes differentiate between a felony and a misdemeanor on the basis of the penalty imposed:

1. Length of term, and
2. Place of incarceration.

The level of crime is specified in the statute or is recognized as *existing at common law.* Place of imprisonment and term vary accordingly. Some states have now extended the two classes and refer to felonies and misdemeanors of the first, second, and third degree, in that order of severity.

There are some general factors that must be considered. For a crime to have been committed, two elements must be present:

1. *Act* and
2. *Intent.*

Both must be considered; there is no crime if either is absent.

The various acts that constitute crimes are cataloged in a criminal code enacted by the legislature of that particular state and in federal statutes. Such codes are usually very specific in describing the prohibited acts and the penalties associated with them. The codes are also quite comprehensive, and the student with specific questions is directed to the code for his or her jurisdiction or to the more general substantive supplement available as chapters 13 to 18 of this text.

THE CRIMINAL PROCESS

Those serious acts against society that are called crimes involve the individual charged with the act and various agents of government assigned the task of maintaining law and order. The major steps taken in this activity are sketched in Figure 3-1.

The legal process in criminal matters begins with the police and community reaction to the initial incident. A crime may be observed by a police officer or instituted by a complainant—a witness to or victim of the criminal act. Investigation and the apprehension of the purported criminal can employ a series of witnesses, leads, or "tips" from informants or continuous surveillance.

Arrest and Booking

Arrest occurs when a person is taken into custody by law officers in order to charge him with a crime. A search may take place (a reasonable search without a warrant, or a search with a warrant or with the consent of the suspect). Most encounters of police with those questioned do not end in arrest; interrogation on the street or in the home may be the only contact a person has with the criminal process.

Booking takes place immediately after the arrest. This is merely a clerical process where the basic information is placed on the police record or *blotter*. In serious offenses the suspect will be fingerprinted and photographed. In minor matters the officer at the desk may decide that the best approach lies in taking care of the problem in an informal process in the station and releasing the person detained. Even more often, the officer in charge may determine, after hearing the evidence, that no basis exists for further detention.

The booking is reported to the prosecutor's office, where the decision is made as to whether the defendant should be charged with the crime and continued in the system. Deciding not to prosecute may happen as often as half the time. Charging the defendant means that the prosecutor prepares the complaint identifying the person and specifying the charge.

Appearance

Arrested persons in most jurisdictions are to be taken before a magistrate without unreasonable delay. For many reasons (e.g., numbers or time of day) the time span may be longer than would ordinarily be thought reasonable. In some states this appearance before a magistrate is known as a *presentment* but may be called a *preliminary arraignment*. In federal court it would be called an *appearance*. The defendant is advised of the charges, of the right to a preliminary hearing, and the right to assigned or retained

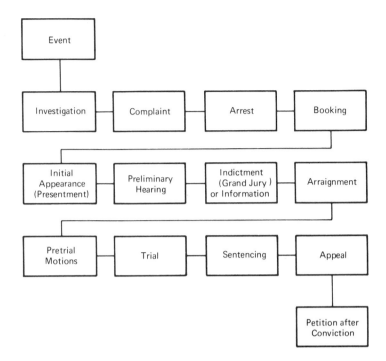

Figure 3-1. General Overview of the Criminal Law Process

counsel. The magistrate sets bail at a figure that matches the severity of the crime charged or, more rarely, makes use of new plans to provide release without regular bail, that is, release on recognizance, or nominal bail. If money bail is required, a nearby bondsman is usually ready to provide it at a cost that ordinarily runs to ten percent of the bail set. About half the defendants cannot afford this and are sent to jail for further processing.

The Preliminary Hearing

Further action on the case does not proceed until the magistrate is convinced by the prosecutor that there is probable cause that a crime was committed by the defendant. Cross-examination is available to the defendant, but very few go to this length; a vast majority of accused persons waive their right to a preliminary hearing. The magistrate usually finds probable cause and *binds over* or holds the defendant for trial.

Indictment by Grand Jury or by Information

In many jurisdictions the grand jury serves as an additional screening device through which the case passes before it comes to a full trial. This body is chosen from a larger panel of citizens to make a group of at least twelve, but seldom more than twenty-four, to decide whether the prosecutor has established probable cause. If more than half vote to indict, the defendant will stand trial. Those states that have eliminated the grand jury have substituted the process of *information,* a procedure whereby the court receives a statement prepared by the prosecutor showing wrongdoing by a party.

The Arraignment

This is the step in the process in which the defendant is brought to the trial court and receives information on the charges. The defendant is also informed of the possible pleas—guilty, not guilty, or *nolo contendere* (noncontesting). At this point as many as three-fourths of the defendants plead guilty. This comes about as the result of several factors. First of all, many individuals have been diverted out of the criminal justice system at one point or another, and most of the cases remaining are those that the prosecution feels with some degree of certainty should go to trial. In addition there is often *plea bargaining,* in which the defendant's attorney may be able to obtain a reduction of the charge to a lesser offense in return for a plea of guilty by the defendant.

Pretrial Motions

Objections of various kinds, if they have not been raised before, are made at this time before trial. A motion to suppress illegally obtained evidence is perhaps the most common. This motion is frequently seen in narcotics cases and, when the motion is successful, the case is often dismissed for lack of evidence. When defendants feel that too much publicity in the area has been prejudicial to the case, they may move to have a change in venue. Various other motions, such as sufficiency of indictment, prior jeopardy, or improper procedures of the grand jury, are more likely to have been raised earlier.

The Trial

Defendants in felony cases have a right to a trial by jury but they often waive the right and have the judge sit as judge and jury. There does not seem to be much difference in the percentage of acquittals; in either case the percentage seldom goes above one-third of the cases. A criminal trial has more rigorous standards than a civil trial in some respects. The defendant is presumed innocent; the defendant has a right not to take the stand and such action is not to be detrimental; evidence obtained illegally is not admitted; and proof beyond a reasonable doubt is required for conviction.

Sentencing

In most situations the judge has widespread discretion as to the sentence to be imposed. The judge may consign the defendant to prison or on probation. The sentence to imprisonment may be for a specific span of time or for an indeterminate period. Both are usually bound by a minimum and a maximum period of imprisonment, terms that vary by statute from state to state. In some jurisdictions the judge will delay sentencing until receiving advice from a behavior clinic or a similar group of professional evaluators, if there is some doubt in the judge's mind as to the kind of sentence that will best achieve the goals of the criminal justice system. It is not unusual for about one-half of the convicted defendants to be sent to prison while the other half receive a probation or suspended sentence.

Appeal

Defendants who are found guilty may appeal to a higher court, and about a fourth of them do. If an appeal is successful (and less than one-fourth of them are) the appellate court reverses the conviction; but in many cases the defendant may be retried and convicted.

Petitions After Conviction

Incarceration does not end the possibilities for the convicted prisoner's matter to come to the attention of the courts. Petitions for collateral relief from prison can be simply framed and presented to the courts, but they are rarely successful. Apparently prisoners are becoming more sophisticated in this area, however, or there is a greater recognition of availability of the right to petition, since the number of such petitions has increased considerably over the past few years.

CIVIL LAW

A wrong that is not considered by society to be an offense against that entity to a degree that would seriously damage it is placed in the category of civil law rather than criminal law. In the civil area, government agents play a lesser role in the process. Even on the civil side, however, there must be a source in law for the remedy or right residing in the plaintiff before the wrong can be taken to the judicial agents of the society for settlement.

As mentioned earlier, the legal source for civil remedies in the United States is found in remote beginnings in early English history. The two main streams of Anglo-American jurisprudence date from the twelfth century, when equity concepts developed under the chancellor in a reaction against the rigidity of common law mechanisms. Major common law remedies were recovery of possession (*replevin* for objects or *ejectment* for land) or *damages* (compensation for injury). Because pleas to common law courts had to be specifically addressed in proper language in a limited number of forms, there were many petitions for special relief that were not covered by common law. With a great increase in petitions the lord chancellor was given the task of dispensing justice in these cases in the name of the king. Equity, too, has its specific remedies, however. The major ones are rescission (cancelling the contract), injunction (order to cease an act), and specific performance (order to do something).

These two thrusts can still be identified in civil law even though they have merged in the court system. There is still an emphasis on form of action and the reliance on past decisions (*stare decisis*) in common law, whereas equity actions are more flexible, as in the beginning, in order to obtain justice that cannot be fitted easily into common law concepts. It may be due to this feature of flexibility that equity actions are expanding in our legal system.

To these two basic sources of contemporary law must be added the third significant area of civil law, the law merchant. The customary rules of dealing in the market-place have entered the law and enriched it, primarily in the extensive codifications of the Uniform Commercial Code.

A party seeking a remedy for a wrong, once it is determined that the requirements for entry are present, can use the court system to attempt to settle the dispute. The question at this point is which specific court can be used. A case in controversy can be brought to a court if that court has:

1. Jurisdiction over
   (a) subject matter,
   (b) parties;
2. Venue.

Jurisdiction refers to authority or power of a court to act; venue is a matter of physical location.

One division of a state court of original jurisdiction will generally hear a case arising within the borders of that state. A federal court has more requirements to be met before entry into the system. There must be:

1. A federal question—one arising under the Constitution or the laws of the United States, and amount over $10,000, or
2. Diversity of citizenship—citizens of different states or foreign states, and amount in controversy exceeding $10,000, or
3. Matter restricted by statute to federal courts.

If an action is brought in a state court it may be removed to a federal court by the defendant if the action is based on a federal question or if there is diversity of citizenship and the over $10,000 requisite is satisfied.

Jurisdiction over the parties extends to the persons (*in personam*) or their property (*in rem*). For a state court to have jurisdiction over the person it must be able to provide a copy of the summons and a complaint to the defendant who is present or domiciled in the state. This is known as personal service of process. Jurisdiction *in rem* (of the object or thing) exists for a state court if the object is within the boundaries of the state. Land, physical objects, or even such status as marriage can be the subject of court action not only when there is personal service on the defendant but also when there is substitute service such as publication in a newspaper if personal service cannot be obtained.

Venue refers to the location where the court can act. Usually the plaintiff can bring an action in the county where the cause of action arose or where the defendant resides. A court might have jurisdiction but not have venue, in which case the action may be challenged.

The two major classes of cases in controversy in civil disputes are those relating to contracts and torts. A contract is a promise to do something in the future; it gives rise to rights in the parties to the promise and grants remedies if the promises are breached. A tort is a breach of a duty imposed by society upon individuals to refrain from doing a specific sort of harm to others intentionally or unintentionally through lack of due care.

If a contract meets all the requirements that are set forth in the law of contracts or a statute, the courts will consider it a valid contract and will proceed to enforce it if asked to do so. The fundamental principles of contract law form the basis for court action when disputes arise. Some variations have been introduced under the *Uniform Commercial Code*, which has been adopted relatively recently by all states except Louisiana, which has adopted only a part. One provision, for instance, requires that contracts for the sale of goods in excess of $500 must ordinarily be in writing.

In a well-regulated society each individual has a duty not to damage the person or property of others in that society. A breach of that duty is a tort. Torts may be classified in the following way:

1. Intentional:
   (a) Interference with the person,
   (b) Interference with property,
2. Nonintentional.

Intentional torts on the person may consist of such physical acts as assault, battery, and false imprisonment or they may consist of words or acts that defame a person, invade his privacy, or place him in mental distress. Interference with property rights include the interference of possession of both real and personal property (trespass) as well as any action where economic advantage is gained over another through wrongful means. The injured party may recover actual, nominal, or punitive damages in some or all of the above situations.

Nonintentional torts are based primarily upon the concept of negligence, the failure to use due care in an injury to another that might have been avoided had due care been exercised. There are four elements that must be demonstrated before a tort action alleging negligence can be the subject of recovery:

1. Duty of care,
2. Breach of duty,
3. Proximate cause,
4. Injury or damage.

The actions of a reasonable and prudent person represent the standards by which courts will judge whether the duty of due care was breached. In addition the injury in the incident must be judged to have been the probable result of the plaintiff's actions. Defenses in actions of negligence include *contributory negligence* and *assumption of the risk*. Contributory negligence defenses allege that the plaintiff alone failed to exercise due care while assumption of the risk alleges that the injured party was aware of the risks faced and deliberately proceeded in spite of the foreseeable danger. In some special cases courts have gone further than failure to exercise due care and have imposed a standard of *strict liability* for actions. This makes a person liable even if one exercised all possible due care. This doctrine is applied when hazardous situations exist and the courts have decided that there is some social utility in protecting others through this rigorous interpretation. Mounting a spring gun in one's home to foil intruders or keeping vicious wild animals on the premises fall into this category. In the commercial area this concept is being applied more and more with respect to products when the item is placed upon the market in a defective condition which would make it more dangerous than the consumer would reasonably expect.

It is important to determine whether the elements for an action in tort or on a contract exist. It may be more beneficial, however, to determine the relative strengths of means of proof and the defenses available in the development of a case. This is because in many cases a cause of action may be brought in tort or on the contract. An injury received from using an allegedly defective product may be recoverable in a tort action showing negligence or strict liability, as well as in a contract action showing a breach of contract exemplified by the warranty which expressly or by law accompanies the product.

THE CIVIL PROCESS

A civil proceeding arises when a dispute occurs in an area of law that is not criminal in nature. One party feels wronged by another, whether this arises under a contract or through a tort or other actions, and recourse to the court of law appears to be the only remedy available to the plaintiff. A flow chart of the general process appears in Figure 3-2.

The plaintiff must now select the proper court to hear the case and initiate a civil action by filing a complaint in that court. The exact form and timing of the complaint, as with other steps of the civil proceeding subsequently described, will vary according to the procedural law of that jurisdiction. Complaints can be quite simple, alleging the nature of the dispute with the defendant, or the format can be somewhat complex. Whatever the form, a copy of the complaint must not only be presented to the court, but also to the defendant, along with the *summons,* a statement of the court calling the defendant to appear in the proceeding. This presentation of the summons of the court is known as *service* upon the defendant.

It is now the turn of the defendant to take action. In answering the complaint the defendant has several options available (sketched in Figure 3-3). The defendant can file preliminary objections stating that the complaint is defective in some way, that the court has no jurisdiction or does not have venue, or that the statute of limitations has been tolled (the time set for bringing the action has passed). The defendant may deny the allegations of the complaint in general or may do so with regard to any specific allegations. The defendant may also make a counterclaim by alleging a cause of action and ask for relief on the complaint. The defendant may admit the facts in the complaint but bring

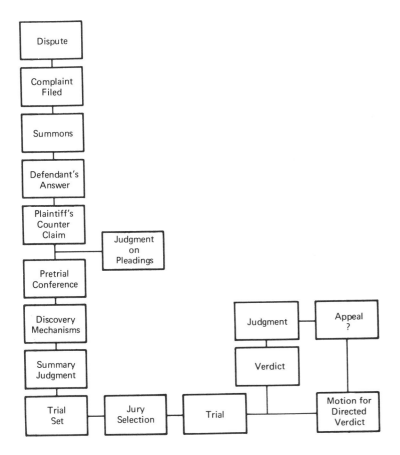

Figure 3-2. General Overview of the Civil Law Process

out additional facts which serve as a defense to the allegations of the plaintiff. In a similar response a defendant may file a *demurrer,* which claims that the complaint does not sufficiently state the cause of action, or that no legal wrong has been alleged.

Finally, the defendant can choose not to respond. In this case the court may consider that this lack of response means that the defendant acquiesces and a default judgment by the court may be made.

The plaintiff may file a response to the defendant's answers by objecting to any counterclaims or by adding to the original pleas.

Once the responses have been made, it may be argued by either party that there are no questions of fact to be decided by either judge or jury and that the only question is a matter of law. In this case either party may ask the judge for a judgment on the pleadings, a motion that claims a trial is not needed.

If the judgment on the pleadings is not requested or is denied by the judge, the next step is for the two sides to enter into pretrial procedures in which all elements of both parties' cases are extensively aired. The intent here is to improve the litigation

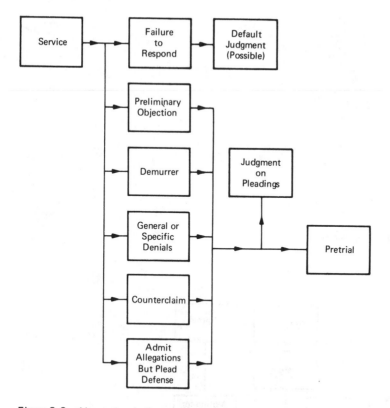

Figure 3-3. Alternatives in Responding to a Complaint

process by providing as much information as possible to prevent any surprises at the later trial.

Discovery mechanisms of various kinds provide further pretrial information to improve adjudication. *Depositions,* oral or written statements under oath by witnesses in the case, may be taken if such witnesses are likely to be unavailable for the trial. These are sometimes confused with written interrogatories, which are questions framed to the opposing party that must be answered before the trial. Similar requests may be made for admissions when the opposing party is asked to state whether a particular matter or document is true. Documents or other tangible materials that may be pertinent in the controversy may be produced under a motion for the production of real evidence. The physical or mental condition of a party may also be determined through a motion to require a physical or mental examination if those factors may be part of the matter.

The case is now ready to go on trial and is placed on the court calendar to be tried on a set date. If the case is to be tried before a jury the first order of business is the selection of the jurors (a process known as *voir-dire*). Without doubt, each attorney would like to obtain sympathetic jurors. How to achieve this has been the subject of some fascinating folklore and more recent attempts to apply behavioral science to help in the selection process. Jurors may be challenged for cause when there is clear reason for believing that a bias exists; or the challenge may be peremptory, and no reason need be given. Peremptory challenges are limited in number, but challenges for cause are unlimited.

The trial itself begins when attorneys for both sides make their opening statements, in which they may outline their case and state what they intend to prove in the trial. The first witness for the plaintiff is then called and questioned by the plaintiff's attorney in a procedure known as direct examination. The defendant's attorney is then allowed to cross-examine the witness on the earlier direct examination, as well as to test the witness' credibility. Questioning by the plaintiff's attorney of the same witness (redirect examination) and recross-examination by the defendant's attorney are usually sufficient. The plaintiff's attorney does this with each witness and then rests the case. The attorney for the defendant follows the same procedure in questioning witnesses for the defendant and, when all the witnesses have testified, rests the case for the defendant. At this point each attorney makes a summation of the case.

After the summation by both attorneys, either of them may make a motion for a directed verdict, in which the judge is asked to direct the jury to render a verdict for either party. Under such motion the plaintiff or defendant states that even if the facts are as the opponent has stated them, there is no legal basis for the complaint or defense.

If a motion for a directed verdict is denied, the judge then charges the jury, which means summarizing the evidence and explaining the law. The jury then leaves the courtroom to deliberate and decide on the facts and to apply the law. Upon return to the courtroom the jury informs the judge of its verdict.

After the verdict is rendered, the judge will pronounce judgment. If the verdict is for the plaintiff and the wrong is to be righted, the end result is an award for damages and/or suffering, both usually expressed in monetary terms. If the defendant prevails the defendant is exonerated, and an action for the same act can never be brought (*res judicata*).

ADMINISTRATIVE LAW

The wide range of activity of governmental agencies has been discussed in Chapter 2. No matter what the charge to the agency may be, however, the fundamental principles of the legal system apply to its functioning.

The fact that administrative agencies can seemingly exercise the powers of the traditional three branches of government would indicate a violation of the traditions of separation of powers, a basic conceptual approach that is looked to as the strength of the democratic form of government exemplified by the United States. The concerns of many observers in this area are met by responses that point out that the legislature really is not delegating its powers to make laws, it is merely allowing administrative officials to fill in any gaps in the laws, although some courts have permitted limited delegation under a grant of authority that contains sufficient standards for the action of the administrative agency. Further review by the legislature is possible through providing legislation that would alter the rules of the administrative agency or, as a final resort, abolish the agency entirely. Executive control over the administrative agencies comes through the appointment by the President or a governor of the members of the agency. The judiciary exercises a control over administrative agency functioning through a review of the activities of the agencies itself. This covers the judicial review of the rules and regulations under which the agency operates but can extend to the actual results of the operations of the agency. In the latter kind of review, however, courts will not disturb the findings of fact by the agency unless it is clear that no reasonable person would find as the agency personnel did.

The extensive number of agencies at both the federal and the state levels may raise further problems, in that areas of activity of the various agencies may begin to overlap. Various agencies in the past may have been called upon—or have taken upon themselves—to address various problems, and frequently several act concurrently. In addition, there are so many agencies and, therefore, so many rules and regulations, that no single individual could ever hope to keep up with all of them. The publication *The Federal Register* prints all the rules and regulations of administrative agencies, but the output over a short period of time makes extensive reading.

The Administrative Procedure Act

The activity of federal agencies is governed by the Administrative Procedure Act (APA), first passed in 1946 and subsequently amended.[10] Extensive and specific provisions affect all aspects of agency functioning, with the primary emphasis upon informing and protecting citizens who may be affected by the agencies' decision-making.

Information to the public is mandated with respect to agency rules, records, opinions, orders, and proceedings. All such information is to be published in the *Federal Register.* Meetings are required to be open, and no action may be taken by fewer than the prescribed number of members of the agency's decision-making body. Rule-making is strictly circumscribed, and any proposed substantive rule must be published at least 30 days before it is to take effect. People have the opportunity to participate in rule-making by submitting written statements or making oral presentations and the agency must give interested persons the right to petition for the issuance, amendment, or repeal of a rule.

Records maintained on individuals are restricted and disclosure is limited to preserve their privacy. In addition, a separate statute established the Privacy Protection Study Commission in order to foster the preservation of privacy of individuals in interaction with governmental agencies.[11] Seven members appointed by the President, the President of the Senate, and the Speaker of the House constitute the Commission.

Hearings are conducted under rules similar to those required in proceedings in court. Subpoenas may be issued, depositions taken, and a record made. Rules of evidence and the burden of proof requirements are generally the same as those in other judicial activity. Adjudications are determined on the record after the hearing.

Agencies are generally empowered to impose sanctions and determine licenses and their suspension or revocation. Judicial review of agency decisions is a right, but is limited to certain actions.

ADMINISTRATIVE PROCESS

The nature of the administrative process has been described and contrasted with pure judicial process as:

> a means by which a Governmental agency clothed with delegated legislative authority or performing a quasi judicial function, regulates activities of groups of persons within specified channels. In its operation the judicial process contemplates a proceeding in which each party is represented in person or by counsel, with the tribunal acting as an arbiter. The Administrative process envisages a proceeding in which the regulatory body may be represented before itself by its own counsel, who presents evidence in support of an action which he suggests that the agency should take, while parties who may be affected by the proposed action may be heard in person or by counsel. In one case, there is a determination of controversy by an impartial tribunal, while in the other instance, the regulatory agency or officer is in part an interested party and in part a trier of the respective contentions advanced by its counsel and the counsel for other parties represented at the hearing.[12]

In an appeal, the difference between the two—administrative and judicial processes—is more pronounced, as the administrative agent is a defendant or respondent in the review process and seeks to sustain the original action. A trial court has no more interest or role in the appeal.

Attempts by the bar to provide some guidance for the development and activity of administrative agencies, particularly at the state level, have led to the drafting of a Model State Act. The Act attempts to provide uniformity in that all state administrative procedures would show the following:

1. Uniformity in procedure for defining agencies in inclusive terms;
2. Adoption of well defined rules of procedure;
3. Proceedings to be publicly known;
4. That interested parties have a hand in establishing agency rules;
5. Prompt publication of agency rules;
6. Speedy determination of questions through declaratory judgment;
7. Cases decided speedily and fairly with an accurate record of proceedings;
8. Limits on deprivation of licenses;
9. Speedy and simple judicial review of decisions.

These reasonable guides to effective and fair administrative action should help to relieve concern over the validity of procedures and outcomes.

The case of *Morgan* v. *United States,* following, provides some understanding of the requirements for proper administrative agency action.

Morgan v. United States
304 U.S. 1 (1937)

Mr. CHIEF JUSTICE HUGHES delivered the opinion of the court.

This case presents the question of the validity of an order of the Secretary of Agriculture fixing maximum rates to be charged by market agencies at the Kansas City Stock Yards. Packers and Stockyards Act, 1921, 42 Stat. 159; 7 U.S.C. 181–229. The District Court of three judges dismissed the bills of complaint in fifty suits (consolidated for hearing) challenging the validity of the rates, and the plaintiffs bring this direct appeal. 7 U.S.C. 217; 28 U.S.C. 47.

The case comes here for the second time. On the former appeal we met, at the threshold of the controversy, the contention that the plaintiffs had not been accorded the hearing which the statute made a prerequisite to a valid order. The District Court had struck from plaintiffs' bills the allegations that the Secretary had made the order without having heard or read the evidence and without having heard or considered the arguments submitted, and that his sole information with respect to the proceeding was derived from consultation with employees in the Department of Agriculture. We held that it was error to strike these allegations, that the defendant should be required to answer them, and that the question whether plaintiffs had a proper hearing should be determined. *Morgan v. United States,* 298 U.S. 468.

. . .

The first question goes to the very foundation of the action of administrative agencies entrusted by the Congress with broad control over activities which in their detail cannot be dealt with directly by the legislature. The vast expansion of this field of administrative regulation in response to the pressure of social needs is made possible under our system by adherence to the basic principles that the legislature shall appropriately determine the standards of administrative action and that in administrative proceedings of a quasi-judicial character the liberty and property of the citizen shall be protected by the rudimentary requirements of fair play. These demand "a fair and open hearing,"—essential alike to the legal validity of the administrative regulation and to the maintenance of public confidence in the value and soundness of this important governmental process. Such a hearing has been described as an "inexorable safeguard."

. . .

In the light of this testimony there is no occasion to discuss the extent to which the Secretary examined the evidence, and we agree with the Government's contention that it was not the function of the court to probe the mental processes of the Secretary in reaching his conclusions if he gave the hearing which the law required. The Secretary read the summary presented by appellants' briefs and he conferred with his subordinates who had sifted and analyzed the evidence. We assume that the Secretary sufficiently understood its purport. But a "full hearing" —a fair and open hearing—requires more than that. The right to a hearing embraces not only the right to present evidence but also a reasonable opportunity to know the claims of the opposing party and to meet them. The right to submit argument implies that opportunity; otherwise the right may be but a barren one. Those who are brought into contest with the Government in a quasi-judicial proceeding aimed at the control of their activities are entitled to be fairly advised of what the Government proposes and to be heard upon its proposals before it issues its final command.

. . .

The maintenance of proper standards on the part of administrative agencies in the performance of their quasi-judicial functions is of the highest importance and in no way cripples or embarrasses the exercise of their appropriate authority. On the contrary, it is in their manifest interest. For, as we said at the outset, if these multiplying agencies deemed to be necessary in our complex society are to serve the purposes for which they are created and endowed with vast powers, they must accredit themselves by acting in accordance with the cherished judicial tradition embodying the basic concepts of fair play.

As the hearing was fatally defective, the order of the Secretary was invalid. In this view, we express no opinion upon the merits. The decree of the District Court is

Reversed.

QUESTIONS

1. In what ways does the Constitution of the United States shape the functioning of the legal system?
2. What is the critical concept underlying the Bill of Rights?
3. Explain how judicial decisions under the Constitution have reflected the common law tradition.
4. Identify the major sources of information regarding legislation and court decisions at the federal and state level.
5. The text identifies steps in the criminal process leading up to a trial. What purposes do the steps in the sequence serve? Would it be possible to streamline the process?
6. How does civil process reflect its ancient roots and what developments have taken place since?
7. What defense can be made to criticism that administrative agencies may usurp powers more properly vested in other governmental units?

NOTES

[1] *Marbury* v. *Madison,* 5V.S. (1 Cranch) 137 (1803).

[2] *United States* v. *Nixon,* 94 S.Ct. 3090 (1974).

[3] William Blackstone, *Commentaries on the Laws of England,* Book I, Chapter 1, S190. W. C. Jones (ed.) (San Francisco: Bancroft-Whitney, 1916), p. 238.

[4] *Gideon* v. *Wainright,* 372 U.S. 335 (1963).

[5] 198 U.S. 45 (1905).

[6] *N.L.R.B.* v. *Jones & Laughlin Steel Corp.,* 301 U.S. 1 (1937).

[7] *Heart of Atlanta Motel, Inc.* v. *United States,* 379 U.S. 241 (1964).

[8] *Kassel* v. *Consolidated Freightways Corp.,* 450 U.S. 662 (1981).

[9] *Supreme Court Reporter* (S. Ct.) and *United States Supreme Court Reports* (L.Ed.) are published by the West Publishing Co.; *United States Supreme Court Bulletin,* by Commerce Clearing House; *United States Law Week* by the Bureau of National Affairs.

[10] Pub. L. 89–554, 80 Stat. 392.

[11] Pub. L. 93–579, 88 Stat. 1896.

[12] Edwin W. Tucker, *Text—Cases—Problems on Administrative Law, Regulation of Enterprise and Individual Liberties* (St. Paul, Minnesota: West Publishing Co., 1975), p. 5.

entry
into
the system:
a case arises

FOUR

August 26 is a date Mary (Mrs. John Q.) Worker will always remember. It was that day when unexpected tragedy struck, with such rippling effects that the John Q. Worker incident became legal history and eventually came to be as well known to lawyers and law students as the name of Shakespeare is to students of English literature.

The newspapers in Big City on August 26 reported merely that John Q. Worker, at age 42, was dead as a result of an accident that occurred while he operated a cypres machine at The Firm, Inc., where he had been employed for 23 years.

Peter Superior, John's foreman, as well as his close friend and neighbor for many years, had difficulty reading the newspaper that evening. His thoughts kept returning to events of that afternoon when a new zagger on a cypres machine John Q. Worker had been operating had shattered while spinning at 2600 revolutions per minute. One of the pieces struck John Q. in the stomach with such force that it pierced his abdomen, causing instantaneous death. Within minutes every machine operator in the cypres department walked off the job, leaving Peter to describe what had happened to Tom Newboy, the firm's personnel manager, and to Fred Famous himself, president and son of the founder of The Firm.

Newspaper accounts of the accident were read avidly that same evening in the

United Cypres Operators of America Building, where John Q.'s co-workers congregated after leaving their jobs. Robert Leader, president of Local 135 and operator of the machine next to John Q.'s, held several pieces of the shattered zagger in his hand as he recounted what happened.

Because of his experience and recognized skill, John Q. had been the first man assigned to work on the initial production of a new type of chattel, which the firm had announced it would be placing on the market soon. Regular zaggers could not be used for this job, and a specially designed zagger had been manufactured by the company's usual zagger supplier. John Q. had just returned from the supplies department with a box of the new zaggers, opened it, put one on his machine, and started it up when the accident occurred. Neither Robert nor any of the other men had ever seen a zagger shatter with such explosive force and violence.

There was a general consensus that the new zaggers must not be safe. Members of the union safety committee were asked to check whether the new zaggers met the Safety Code for Zaggers promulgated by the Occupational Safety and Health Administration. Some of the cypres operators suspected that short cuts that disregarded safety standards may have been taken with the new zaggers, in order to get the new chattels into early production.

As the group disbanded, a number of the men left with Robert Leader to visit Mary Worker.

At home that evening, Mary Worker read the newspaper account of the accident and reflected on the drastic change that had occurred in her life in just one day. Married to John Q. Worker for twenty-one years, she was the mother of five children: a son, age 19, a 16-year-old daughter, another daughter, age 10, and four-year-old twins.

What would she do now? The death of John Q. was not only a great personal loss to her and the children, but it would create even more serious financial problems for the family. John Q.'s income as a cypres operator had sustained them in a modest way of life, but they had no substantial savings. She had not been employed outside the home since she resigned her secretarial job almost twenty years ago. She didn't know if she could find a job today, and—even if she did—who would care for the children? The twins were still preschoolers. She hoped her son would not have to leave the university. Long ago she and John Q. had determined to give their children a college education, something which neither of them had had. Her thoughts were interrupted by the arrival of members of Local 135, who spent some time talking with her about the accident. As they left, Robert Leader, holding several fragments of the zagger in his outstretched palm, said: "Remember, Mary, if there's anything we can do for you, be sure to call."

The next day engineers who had worked on development of the new zaggers were brought in from Zagger Supply, Inc. to consult with Sam Scott, chief plant safety engineer at The Firm. They attributed the accident to human error: improper placement or clamping of the zagger on the cypres machine or a momentary lapse of care by John Q. when he first brought the chattel form into contact with the zagger. The union safety committee was not satisfied with this explanation, and said so.

"It's a whitewash," they claimed, "nobody tested the new zaggers while they were revolving on the cypres machines."

When Peter Superior asked Timothy O'Goode to take over work on the new chattels, Timothy balked. He relented, however, after both Peter Superior and Sam Scott operated cypres machines using the new zaggers to demonstrate their safety and after Jim Boss, the plant manager, told him he must either work on the new chattels or lose his job.

At last, production of the new chattels began. Jim Boss breathed a sigh of relief. He knew the company had a deadline to meet in getting the new chattels on the market. Fred Famous had made a large loan to the firm from his personal funds to develop the new product. He had done so in the hope that this would give the firm a much-needed boost and help it to recover a sizable share of the market, which had been lost to competitors in recent years. Jim knew Fred would have been furious with any delay, even one resulting from something so tragic as John Q.'s death.

THE FIRM'S LIABILITY

Little did Jim know that at that very moment Fred was involved in a long, serious conference dealing with the company's legal liability arising from the death of John Q. Worker. Tom Newboy and Leo Lex, the firm's legal counsel, were the other participants.

Leo Lex was explaining that under the Workmen's Compensation Law of Great State an employer was responsible for injury or death that occurred to an employee during the course of his employment, regardless of fault. There were two exceptions, neither of which was applicable in this case. They were in cases of employee intoxication or self-inflicted injury. He went on to say that the statute limited the liability of employers, even in cases where the company was negligent, to the benefits specified in the act. These consisted of weekly payments to the widow for 700 weeks plus an additional sum for minor children. (In Great State a person reached legal majority at age 18.) Payments were determined by reference to a schedule in the act and were based upon the deceased employee's average weekly earnings.

After a series of calculations, all three agreed that the payments required for the Worker family were minimal and did not begin to approach John Q.'s take-home pay. Leo Lex noted that many persons had criticized workmen's compensation laws because they believed the payments required were inadequate, while others had raised concerns about the funding needed for increased payments.

That, however, did not change the fact that present Great State law applied to the matter at hand. Therefore, the one and exclusive remedy the John Q. Worker family had against The Firm was workmen's compensation benefits. The reason for such a provision in the statute, Leo said, was to place a uniform and definite limit on an employer's liability in cases of injury and death. It would be entirely discretionary with The Firm, he added, to make any additional payments.

Tom Newboy pointed out that the widow would receive the proceeds from a life insurance policy, which the firm carried on each of its employees as a fringe benefit. This would provide an immediate, large, lump sum payment to her. He added that he would also assist her in applying for social security benefits. These would supplement her benefits under workmen's compensation, and he believed his assistance would serve as a goodwill gesture to the family.

It was Fred Famous who made the decision regarding discretionary payments. Although he was sympathetic to the Worker family needs, he decided that company policy should limit payments to those required by law. His reasons were: (1) the strained financial position of the company; (2) the precedent that would be established for the future; (3) his conviction that the company had in no way contributed toward the employee's death by negligence or willful lack of care. Fred believed that The Firm, after payment to the Worker family of workmen's compensation benefits, would have discharged its legal, social, and moral obligations, in spite of Fred's understanding that discharging a legal obligation does not necessarily automatically discharge one's social and moral obligations.

MARY'S REACTION

Mary Worker was dismayed when she learned of the financial arrangements. Even when the social security and workmen's compensation benefits were added together, her family's standard of living would be lowered considerably. It might even mean that her oldest son would have to leave the university. She felt the company was responsible for her husband's death and should make arrangements to put her and her children in at least the same financial condition as they had enjoyed prior to John Q.'s death. She asked the company to reconsider. It was to no avail.

Mary went to see Robert Leader. It was he who first suggested that John Q.'s death might have been caused by an unsafe zagger. Since the accident, several of the new zaggers had shattered. No one had been seriously injured. However, the frequency with which this was occurring caused him to suspect that the zaggers were not sufficiently strong. Robert told her that the union safety committee had lodged a complaint with the local office of the Occupational Safety and Health Administration, alleging violation of the safety standards for zaggers at The Firm.

"Remember, Mary, I still have zagger fragments from the accident, if you or your attorney ever need them," he said in parting.

The germ of an idea had been planted.

"Why not?" she thought. "I really should talk with a lawyer. John Q. didn't have a will, and I have questions about what to do about the house and the car, anyway."

FINDING A LAWYER

Having made up her mind, Mary discovered that her first problem was that she did not know a lawyer. Nor did she know how to choose one from the hundreds listed in the yellow pages of the Big City telephone directory or advertised in the local papers or on the local television stations. Because she was also concerned about cost, she followed the

advice of a neighbor who told her that the Neighborhood Legal Services Association provided free legal assistance. Mary visited the nearest office, where she learned a great deal
about legal services programs available in Big City.

Legal Services Programs

Originally established under the Equal Opportunity Act to provide legal assistance for persons living in poverty, the NLSA office she visited now operated under the
Legal Services Corporation Act.[1] The latter was enacted to provide for a private, non-
membership, nonprofit corporation, which would be funded through Congressional appropriation as well as private grants. Its purpose was to continue to provide legal services
to the poor but through a nongovernmental agency. It was hoped that this would remove
the program from political pressures. The act authorized legal aid in civil matters (and in
exceptional instances, in criminal matters) to persons who were financially unable to afford it. The Corporation was authorized to develop guidelines for different parts of the
country for determining eligibility for assistance, using such criteria as income, total
assets, and other available resources.

Mary discovered that she could not qualify for assistance. She learned that she
would be ineligible, too, for legal services provided by the Legal Aid Society. This was a
public service organization funded by the United Way in Big City. It also rendered legal
help in civil matters to the needy.

Prepaid Legal Services

Searching for some way to aid Mary, the young woman in the NLSA office
asked if John Q. had been a member of a prepaid legal services plan. She explained that
many employers and unions in the Big City area sponsored such plans, which were similar
to medical and health care plans. Members and their families were eligible for legal advice
and services covered by the plan. The cost was covered through payments which were
either absorbed entirely by the employer, or shared with employees as a fringe benefit.
Some of these plans provided for selection of an attorney of one's choice, others for
selection from a specific list of attorneys. Often these plans were developed in association
with the local bar, and sometimes by insurance companies. Mary was skeptical about
John Q.'s membership in any such plan. Before leaving the NLSA office, she was given
the address and telephone number of the lawyer referral service of the local bar association. She continued her search for legal aid there.

Lawyer Referral Service

At bar association headquarters, Mary learned that lawyers who were members
of the referral panel agreed to provide one-half hour of consultation at a very minimal
fee. During that time, she could explain her situation to an attorney, learn what legal
action—if any—would be possible, be given an explanation of the costs and fees for any
such undertaking, and then decide for herself whether she wished to retain the particular
lawyer and proceed with any action. Mary decided to pay the minimum fee for a thirty-
minute consultation.

CONSULTATION

She was referred to attorney Henry Law who, after asking question upon question about her husband's accident, finally said:

"Do I understand correctly that your husband's death occurred during the course of his employment and as a result of an accident which you allege was due to a zagger which shattered while he operated a cypres machine?"

"That's right," Mary replied.

"And The Firm has made you an offer for financial settlement which you do not believe is adequate."

"Yes," said Mary.

"Do you know—or do you have any indication—that the zagger your husband was using at the time of his death was defective?" he asked.

Mary told him about the fragments in Robert Leader's possession and the complaint filed by the union with OSHA.

"Because of the limited liability of employers under the state's workmen's compensation act, the only hope I can hold out for you, Mrs. Worker, is to seek damages from the supplier or manufacturer of the zagger—provided, that is, it can be proved the zagger was defective and that this was the cause of your husband's death."

"But I don't even know who they are." Mary was skeptical.

"That would be my job—to learn that as well as a great many more facts." Henry Law explained that one could not charge another party with liability upon mere supposition; a factual basis was needed. Therefore, before he could render an intelligent opinion about any legal claim she might have against the zagger manufacturer or supplier, he would have to gather more information. For instance, he would want to talk with Robert Leader and possibly other witnesses to the accident; he would have the zagger fragments tested for defects; he would inquire into what action, if any, OSHA had taken with regard to the union's complaint.

Henry explained that he was not seeking enough evidence to prove a case in a court of law, but rather sufficient factual data to enable him to make an informed judgment about whether she had grounds or the basis for instituting legal proceedings—and what the expectations for success might be. Sometimes, he said, it becomes necessary for lawyers to inform their clients that they have no cause which can be pursued at law. Sometimes, he added, they must tell their clients that while there is a basis for legal action, it would not be worth pursuing for any number of reasons, such as lack of means of proof or costs that would far outstrip any possible recovery.

Therefore, he said, it would be necessary for him to undertake some fundamental investigative work about the cause of her husband's death. Once he possessed sufficient factual information, he would research the relevant law. Because this involved a civil matter, the requirements in litigation would be proof by a preponderance of the evidence. *Preponderance of the evidence,* he explained, does not mean the greater number of witnesses. It does mean evidence that is more credible and convincing than that offered by the opposing party; in other words, the evidence that meshes best with reason and probability. Therefore, Henry continued, he would assess the facts along with the appropriate law, in order to arrive at a judgment as to whether the preponderance of the evidence and the law were in her favor.

If he believed she had no legal claim, he would tell her so and remove himself from the case. However, he would have to bill her for the costs incurred in connection with his investigative work. On the other hand, if he believed that there was a basis for legal action, he would so inform her, explain the courses of action open to her together with possible outcomes, and then ask her to indicate her wishes as to future action.

Form 4-1. Agreement with Lawyer

Henry Law

Attorney-at-Law

Big City, Great State

I, the undersigned client, hereby retain and employ Henry Law as my attorney to represent me in my claim for damages against the supplier and/or manufacturer of zaggers to The Firm, Inc. and/or any other persons, firms or corporations liable therefor, resulting from an accident that occurred on August 26, 19XX, in which John Q. Worker, my late husband, was killed as he was engaged in the course of his employment at The Firm, Inc.

As compensation for said services, I agree to pay for the costs of investigation and court costs, if necessary, and to pay my attorney from the proceeds of recovery, the following fees:

33-1/3% if settled without suit
40%   if suit is filed
50%   if an appeal is taken by either side.

It is agreed that this employment is on a contingent fee basis, so that if no recovery is made, I will not owe my attorney any amount for attorney's fees.

Dated this _____ day of _____ 19 ____ .

_____ (SEAL)
                Client

I hereby accept the above employment.

_____ (SEAL)
        Henry Law, Attorney

ENGAGING LEGAL COUNSEL

If she wished to retain him to do this, he added, he would require a small down payment —a retainer—now. He would also ask that she sign a contract providing for legal fees to be paid on a contingent fee basis. He read through the contract form with her (see preceding page).

When Mary said she was not sure she understood the contingent fee system, he asked her to assume the following: jury verdict for $100; court costs of $20; contingent fee according to the contract. The amount Mary would receive would be determined as follows:

Jury verdict	$100
LESS 40% contingent fee payable to attorney	− 40
	$ 60
LESS court costs payable by client	− 20
Actual amount client would take home	$ 40

While that didn't leave much for the client to take home, Mary felt she would have everything to gain and nothing to lose by such an arrangement. Henry Law also explained that if she recovered nothing, he would receive no fee and she would pay only the $20 court costs.

In answer to Mary's question, Henry Law explained that the courts of Great State had always held that a client has an implied right to discharge an attorney if the client so wishes, even when there is a written agreement. However, the client must pay for all costs and fees earned by the attorney up to that point. On the other hand, an attorney could only withdraw for a good reason (for example, discovering his client had an unjust or immoral cause), and then only in such a way as to be sure that the client was fully protected at all times.

Positive that it was what she wanted to do, Mary signed the contract. Before leaving the office, she was asked by Henry Law to be sure not to get in touch with, talk with, or in any other way communicate with any persons who might be or might represent the other party. In order to be positive she would not jeopardize her case in any way, she should refer all such persons to him. Mary replied that she would be happy to do this. She felt good that at last someone would be taking action in her behalf.

INVESTIGATION

Henry Law proceeded to do just that. The turning point for him came in the report of the tests made on the zagger fragments by Professor Ira Learned at Great Scientific University. One of the outstanding zagger experts in the nation, Professor Learned examined the fragments under a microscope. He discovered a flaw "consisting of a pocket—or collection of crystals which are not bonded—within the composition of the zagger." Such imperfections, his report stated, would cause a zagger to shatter even when it was re-volved at a relatively low speed, and definitely at 2600 rpm. Neither visual inspection nor tapping for sound would reveal these flaws. Had the zaggers been subjected to a test approximating actual use of zaggers in motion at 2600 rpm, they would have disinte-grated or shattered, thus indicating the presence of a defect. Professor Learned's report concluded that such "in-motion" testing was required by the safety code for zaggers promulgated by the Occupational Safety and Health Administration.

From the local OSHA office, Henry secured a copy of the zagger safety require-ments. He learned, too, that action had not yet been taken on the union's complaint. Robert Leader also supplied Henry with information.

LEGAL RESEARCH

With this information at hand, Henry Law began his research of the law to determine if there was a legal cause of action arising out of the facts he now had. He knew that in cases of defective products, the law of torts regarding negligence and strict liability was applicable. It was the common law to which he would have to refer. Therefore, he checked the *Restatement of the Law of Torts 2d,* with annotations for Great State. Henry knew that in a recent decision the Supreme Court of Great State had adopted as the law of the state §402A of that Restatement.

Because the common law is "unwritten," that is, not codified, it is found in judicial decisions. In order to facilitate research, these decisions have been compiled into what is referred to as the *Restatement of the Law.* This is a reiteration of judicial hold-ings arranged according to subject matter and categories, with appropriate references to the cases in which the decisions were handed down. There is a separate Restatement for each of the major substantive areas of the law, including torts, contracts, and agency. *Annotations* are relevant comments from specific decisions, provided as an aid in under-standing the delimitations of the decisions.

The court opinions themselves are collected as handed down. Those from state trial courts are not always printed and bound in volumes. Instead, they may be found in the appropriate clerk of courts office. Federal district court opinions are printed in the *Federal Supplement,* those of the federal circuit courts of appeals in the *Federal Re-porter,* and those of the United States Supreme Court in the *United States Reports,* as well as in the *Supreme Court Reporter* and the *United States Supreme Court Reports, Lawyer's Edition.* State appellate decisions can be found in state reporters or in regional reporters.

To facilitate research the citation for each case includes the location, with vol-ume number preceding and page number following identification of the reporter in which a case is to be found. For example, the citation for the appellate decision excerpted later in this chapter reads as follows: *Webb* v. *Zern,* 422 Pa. 424, 220 A2d 853 (1966). This in-dicates that the case, decided in 1966, can be found in two places: volume 422, page 424 of the *Pennsylvania State Reports* (the reporter for the supreme court of that state) and in volume 220, page 853 of the *Atlantic Reporter, Second Series* (the regional reporter). That decision is an excellent example of the use of the *Restatement of the Law of Torts* by the courts.

Precedent

Henry Law also checked the most recent decisions of Great State's supreme court in defective products cases. He did so because of the doctrine of *stare decisis,* or the determining role of precedent in the common law. Precedent refers to the common law as it has been judicially declared in previously adjudicated cases involving the same or substantially the same issues and facts. Henry checked the supreme court's decisions because, as the highest court in Great State, its decisions were controlling and binding upon the lower courts of the state. He found no cases involving defective zaggers. In that respect, this would be a case of "first impression" in the state. For this reason he checked other states for defective zagger cases. He knew those decisions would not be controlling in Great State since they were "foreign" law. However, courts often refer to decisions of other states as a guide when they are faced with a case of first impression. Again, he found none.

He did, however, find in Great State a number of other cases involving defective products. From them he selected those similar in basic characteristics and concepts to the Worker case—employee injury, product used on the job, recovery from the manufacturer, for example. Once he found such comparability, Henry checked for the legal principle emerging from the case. He looked for the court's *holding,* that is, the rule of law that the court decided applied in the case at hand and determined its outcome. He did not want *dictum,* that is, an extraneous remark or additional pronouncement made by the court not essential to the determination of the case. In other words, he was looking for rules of law he could abstract from prior cases. Having found appropriate holdings of law, he could then quote them to the judge as precedent for the Mary Worker case. Given sufficient similarity in the fact situation, the judge would undoubtedly follow that precedent.

Thus it is that the common law evolves. A rule of law is set in one case, is followed in similar cases, and becomes fixed as the law. Predictability of outcome is possible. However, that does not mean the common law is stagnant. It may in later decisions be overruled or slowly eroded as social conditions, technological knowledge, and times, in general, change. Thus, there is also a flexibility, adaptability, and a dynamic quality to the common law. It is important to note that decisions are made on an *ad hoc* basis; that is, they are applied to a particular set of facts at a given period of time. If one can distinguish, differentiate, or find important differences in fact, then the court can be expected to decide differently. "Once you change the facts, you change the law," is a very old but true saying.

This kind of reasoning by analogy, from particular to general and back to particular again, is sometimes referred to as legal reasoning. It consists of finding from the specifics of prior cases generalizations that will fit the specifics of the present case. That was what Henry Law was engaged in doing.

The *Webb* v. *Zern* decision which follows exemplifies matters just discussed, including reference to decisions of other states in a case of first impression, evolution of the common law through judicial decisions, the role of *stare decisis* and its effect upon the stability and flexibility of the common law. It is a sample, also, of the kind of decision Henry would find in his research.

Webb v. *Zern*
422 Pa. 424, 220 A.2d 853 (1966)

MR. JUSTICE COHEN: This appeal is from the dismissal of a suit in trespass seeking damages for injuries resulting from the explosion of a beer keg purchased by the plaintiff's father.

Charles Webb purchased a quarter-keg of beer from a distributor, John Zern. That same day, plaintiff's brother tapped the keg and about a gallon of beer was drawn from it. Later that evening, when plaintiff entered the room in which the keg had been placed, the keg exploded, severely injuring plaintiff. . . .

[The issue determinative of this appeal] is the nature and scope of the liability in trespass of the one who produces or markets a defective product for use or consumption. . . . [M]odern case law and commentaries . . . extend and recommend the extension of the law of strict liability in tort for defective products. The new Restatement of Torts reflects this modern attitude. Section 402A thereof states:

"(1) One who sells any product in a defective condition unreasonably dangerous to the user or consumer or to his property is subject to liability for physical harm thereby caused to the ultimate user or consumer, or to his property, if (a) the seller is engaged in the business of selling such a product, and (b) it is expected to and does reach the user or consumer without substantial change in the condition in which it is sold."

"(2) The rule stated in Subsection (1) applies although (a) the seller has exercised all possible care in the preparation and sale of his product, and (b) the user or consumer has not bought the product from or entered into any contractual relation with the seller." Restatement 2d, Torts, §402A (1965).

We hereby adopt the foregoing language as the law of Pennsylvania.

The plaintiff in this litigation, therefore, must be given an opportunity to plead and prove his case. Since the plaintiff has broadly pleaded those facts necessary to a cause of action for defective products liability, plaintiff will be permitted to amend his complaint to explicitly state a cause of action in trespass for defective products liability. . . .

DISSENTING OPINION BY MR. CHIEF JUSTICE BELL:

I very emphatically dissent.

If such a drastic change in the field of tort *liability without fault* is to be made in our law—even the majority admit that "we are today adopting a new basis of liability"—it is difficult to imagine a more unlawyerlike judicial Opinion than the majority Opinion. . . .

The new role adopted by the majority so completely changes, not by legislative action but by judicial ukase, the law with respect to trespass actions for injuries resulting from noninherently dangerous products that are either manufactured or bottled or sold by any vendor—even a retail druggist—that in my opinion it is not only very unfair but absolutely *unjustifiable* in Justice or in Law. . . .

Today, no one knows from month to month or whenever the Supreme Court of Pennsylvania or the Supreme Court of the United States meets, what the law will be tomorrow—or, by retrospectivity, what the Court will now say it always should have been—or what anyone's rights, privileges, liabilities and duties are. The net result is uncertainty, confusion, dismay, and constantly diminishing respect for Law and for our Courts—and, of course, is one of the major causes of the constantly and rapidly increasing litigation which is literally swamping our Courts.

In a Constitutional form of government such as ours, which is based upon Law and Order, *certainty and stability are essential.* Unless the Courts establish and maintain *certainty and stability* in the Law, (1) public officials will not know from week to week or from month to month the powers and limitations of the Government, (2) Government cannot adequately protect law-abiding citizens or peaceful communities against criminals, (3) private citizens will not know their rights and obligations, (4) the meaning of wills, bonds, contracts, deeds, leases and other written agreements will fluctuate and change with each change in the personnel of a Court or their individual ideas of what the writing should and would have said if the present situation had been visualized in the light of today's conditions, (5) property interests will be jeopardized and frequently changed or lost, (6) businessmen cannot safely and wisely make agreements with each other or with their employees.

The basic need for certainty and stability in the law has been recognized for centuries by English-speaking peoples. LORD COKE, Chief Justice of England, thus wisely expressed (circa 1600) these truths: "The knowne certaintie of the law is the safetie of all." Until very recently, this has been a beacon light for Anglo-American Courts, for text authorities, and for law-abiding Americans ever since the foundation of our Country. In the realm of the Law it is usually expressed in the principle known as Stare Decisis. Stare Decisis is one of the bedrocks upon which the House of Law has been built and maintained.

If such a radical change in the Law is to be made—as is now made in the majority Opinion—it should be made and must be made only by the Legislature. It appears to be completely forgotten that we are not a super or Supreme Legislature or indeed a Legislature at all, desirable as that sometimes would be; or, as Mr. Justice FRANKFURTER politely reminded the Supreme Court of the United States in his concurring Opinion in *Green* v. *United States,* 356 U.S. 165, "Decision-making is not a mechanical process, but neither is this Court an originating lawmaker. The admonition of Mr. Justice BRANDEIS that we are not a third branch of the Legislature should never be disregarded" (page 193).

Too many appellate Judges envision themselves, not as interpreters of the Constitution and the laws, which is the role and province assigned and limited to them by the Constitution, but as possessing the right, the power and the duty to change and, if necessary, rewrite the Constitution and any and every Law, in order to bring it in accord with what they believe is or will be best for the social, political or economic interests of our State or Country.

I can never approve or condone such a Judge-made revolutionary and unfair rule as the majority promulgate.

I very vigorously dissent.

Tort Actions

Henry found that in recent years more cases involving defective products had been brought as strict liability cases than as negligence cases. After considering the elements of the two torts, one readily understands why. Elements are those ingredients of which the tort consists. They are the matters that have to be proved to a court to establish a *prima facie* case, that is, one sufficiently strong for the opposing party to be required to answer the charges or defend against it.

Since Mary Worker was the plaintiff, she would have the *burden of proof.* That meant she would have to go forward with the evidence to prove that a *prima facie* case existed. If that was not done, the judge would grant a defendant's motion for either a dismissal or for a directed verdict. This would mean the defendant would not even be required to "put in his case," that is, to call any witnesses or enter any testimony on his behalf. It would be similar to saying that Mary Worker did not have a sufficiently good case to be able to go forward with or continue the trial. Therefore, Henry Law understood the importance of the plaintiff's being able to establish each of the elements of the cause of action under which he was proceeding. He contemplated the proof that would be necessary in a negligence action.[2]

Negligence is the failure to exercise the degree of care that a reasonably prudent person would use under the circumstances, such conduct being the proximate cause of harm or injury to a person or property. One test of whether action is negligent involves *foreseeability*. This means the individual could reasonably have anticipated and foreseen the likelihood of harm resulting from his conduct. The elements which the plaintiff must establish to prove negligence are:

1. Duty of care;
2. Breach of that duty;
3. Proximate cause;
4. Injury or damage.

As for the duty of reasonable care owed to the plaintiff, Henry thought there would be little problem proving there was such a duty. The OSHA standards, having the force of law, would establish that zaggers must be manufactured according to certain stated requirements. Reasonable care, that of the ordinary, prudent person under similar circumstances, did not mean perfection. Henry Law would have to show there was a lack of reasonable care in the manufacture of the zagger involved. To do this, he would have to seek the manufacturer's records regarding quality control, inspection, production, and even records regarding complaints from other customers and return of unsatisfactory goods.

On the other hand, strict liability created legal liability regardless of the care exercised. That eliminated the need for all the proof necessary in establishing negligence. It would be easier, less expensive, require less fact finding. The evidence would have to establish that the product was unreasonably and dangerously defective at the time of sale and that this condition was still true at the time of use.

Both torts required proof of causation, of proximate cause. In other words,

Henry would have to prove that the defective zagger was the cause of the accident. Both torts also required a showing of injury or damage. With John Q.'s death following the injury, that would be no problem.

Different defenses were available under each tort action. In negligence, a showing that the plaintiff by his own negligence had contributed to the injury—contributory negligence—would be a complete defense in Great State. Other states, following a doctrine of comparative negligence, make it a partial or proportionate defense. However, in strict liability, the defendant would have to show that John Q. had voluntarily assumed a known risk. This means that of his own will and with knowledge of the risk involved, he undertook to do what he did. Henry Law believed that John Q. could not be said to have assumed a known risk with a latent defect.

Since both negligence and strict liability were tort actions, both had the same time requirements for bringing suit. Henry decided there was a legal cause of action in tort under either negligence or strict liability, but the advantages of strict liability far outweighed those of negligence.

Contract Actions

Before he made a final decision, however, Henry checked contract law to investigate the possibilities of a contract cause of action. There is a common law of contracts, but Henry Law knew that all states following the common (as distinguished from the civil) law have adopted the Uniform Commercial Code (UCC). As statutory law, it takes precedence over the common law. Its provisions cover contracts involving the sale of goods. *Goods* are personal or movable property as distinguished from real or fixed property. Since the sale of zaggers would be a contract for the sale of goods, he consulted both the UCC as enacted in Great State and annotations of Great State decisions involving the breach of warranty provisions of the UCC.

While statutory law is enacted by legislators, interpretation of that law is a function of the courts. It is true that the judiciary looks for legislative intent when the meaning of a statute is not clear. They also check the law's stated purpose, and study statements made at hearings and in committee before the law is passed. However, in the end, it is they who decide what the words mean. In this sense, they can be said to "make law."

Henry found examples of just this very thing in Great State. Contract cases had been brought involving defective products on grounds of breach of warranty. Breach of warranty occurs when there is failure or falsehood of a promise or statement that is part of the basis of the bargain in the sale of goods, unless there is a disclaimer. One such warranty is that goods shall be merchantable.[3] That includes being fit for the ordinary purposes for which such goods are used. Another implied warranty is that of fitness for a particular purpose when goods are purchased in reliance on the seller's knowledge of that purpose and expertise regarding the product.[4] These warranties are breached when the goods do not meet the standards of the warranties; in other words, when the goods are defective with respect to the qualities covered by the warranty.

Henry knew that in a contract action he would have to prove there was a contract of sale between the manufacturer and John Q.'s employer, that there were no disclaimers to eliminate warranties, and that the zagger was defective. To prove the contract would mean getting records of both The Firm and Zagger Supply.

In some states there would have been an added problem since John Q. was not the purchaser of the goods. That meant there existed no privity between him and the seller. In other words, there was lacking the close relationship that exists between contracting parties. When he checked the Great State decisions, Henry found that the state's supreme court had permitted recovery by a buyer's employees even when privity did not exist. The court stated that this was done to make it possible to achieve the same result when the case is brought in contract as when it is brought in tort. This was a good example of judicial interpretation of statutory meaning, Henry Law thought to himself. The reason for his so thinking was that the UCC is not explicit about recovery by persons lacking privity in industrial situations.[5]

One advantage of the contract action was that it allowed for twice the time for bringing suit—four years—as did tort. However, additional time was not one of Henry's concerns.

Causes of Action Compared

Comparison of the elements of each of these causes of action—negligence, strict liability, and contract—appears in Table 4-1, along with the time requirements for bringing action and the disadvantages associated with each. As Henry reflected upon these matters, he realized that three different possible causes of action existed in the Mary Worker case. He felt he was fortunate, for it is not often that lawyers find three different possible actions. The more usual situation is to find just one.

Having weighed the advantages and disadvantages of each of the three actions, Henry decided that his first preference was strict liability. Having decided that, he made a list of the items he would have to prove and his sources of proof. His list looked like this:

FACTS TO BE PROVED	SOURCES OF PROOF
1. Death of John Q.	1. Death certificate.
2. Death caused by defective zagger manufactured by Zagger Supply (he had learned their identity through Leader and Learned).	2. Testimony of Leader and other union members who witnessed the accident, or purchasing and production personnel at The Firm.
3. Death occurred because the zagger was defective—unreasonably and dangerously so.	3. Testimony of OSHA personnel and Professor Learned; offering of zagger fragment test results and OSHA standards into evidence.
4. Defect present when zagger was sold by Zagger Supply, and zagger substantially unchanged at time of accident.	4. Testimony of Leader, Superior, supplies room personnel who witnessed John Q. remove zagger from shipping box and place on machine to use.
5. Zagger Supply engaged in the business of selling zaggers.	5. Testimony of corporate personnel, if necessary. (Would probably be admitted by Zagger Supply.)

TABLE 4-1. Comparison of Negligence, Strict Liability, and Contract Actions

	TORT		CONTRACT
Elements of Tort Negligence	*Elements of Tort Under § 402A—Strict Liability*		*Elements of Action Under UCC— Breach of Warranty*

1. Duty of care
2. Breach of duty
3. Proximate cause
4. Injury or damage
	1. Defective product
	  a. Unreasonably dangerous
	  b. Defective at time of sale
	  c. Substantially unchanged
	    from condition at sale
	  d. Sold by seller engaged in
	    business of selling
	2. Proximate cause
	3. Injury or damage
			1. Valid contract for sale of goods
			2. Warranty—express or implied
			3. Breach of warranty
			4. Injury or damage
			5. Privity—in some states

Defense	*Defense*		*Defense*
Contributory negligence	Voluntary assumption of a known risk		Lack of valid contract Lack of warranty Lack of privity—in some states
Time Limitations	*Time Limitations*		*Time Limitations*
2 years from date of injury*	2 years from date of injury*		4 years from date of delivery of goods
Disadvantage	*Disadvantage*		*Disadvantage*

Need to prove lack of due care in
  manufacturing special product,
  resulting in defective product—
  records with defendant
	Need to prove defect existed
	  at time of sale and continued
	  to exist
			Need to prove contract and existence
			  of warranties between third party and
			  defendant—records with third party
			  and defendant

*May vary from state to state

It would be up to the defense to rebut the plaintiff's case. Aware that a good lawyer not only attempts to predict his adversary's position but also plans how to refute it, Henry made another list. In one column, he noted possible defenses. In the second, he listed his means of refutation.

DEFENSES	REFUTATION
1. Zagger was not defective.	1. Testimony of Professor Learned; offering of zagger fragment test results and OSHA standards into evidence.
2. Death was due to improper use of the zagger or actions of John Q., and not to a defective zagger.	2. Testimony of Leader, other cypres operators, Superior as to John's skill, his safety record; perhaps testimony of Professor Learned as to effect of improper use on machine.

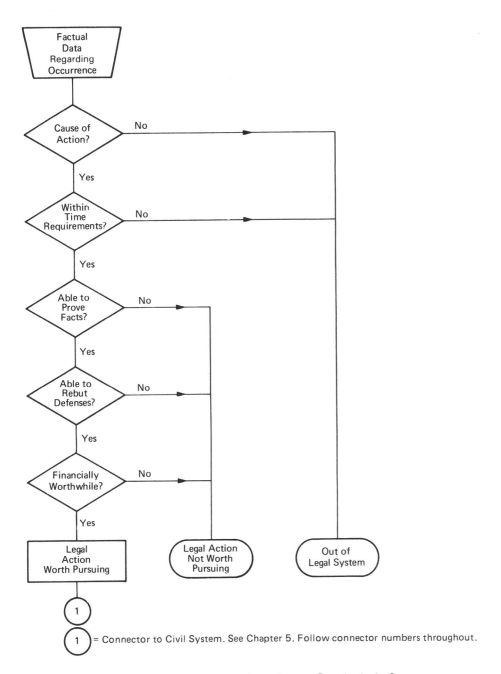

Figure 4-1. Henry Law's Decision that Mary's Cause Warrants Pursuing in the System

He wondered, would the defendant attempt to disclaim responsibility for any defects by charging that The Firm had the duty to inspect the zaggers before using them and had failed in this duty? If so, he believed he could answer that by referring to the fact that OSHA standards have the force and effect of law.[6] Therefore, zaggers which do not meet those standards cannot legally be used. Would Zagger Supply want to admit they sold zaggers that were not legally usable? He would ask the Zagger Supply witnesses if it were not the normal expectation of anyone purchasing zaggers to expect to receive and pay for zaggers which could be used. That should place the onus of inspection for OSHA standards on the manufacturer—and that would be all he would need. However, he would also refer to normal practice in the cypres industry: boxes of zaggers were opened and put on machines for use, not tested first. And since John Q. was starting a production run—not a trial run—normal expectations would be that testing processes were finished and usual operating procedures were in order.

After all this, Henry was finally satisfied that Mary had a worthy cause of action. He had completed the decision-making summarized in Figure 4-1, except for the financial considerations. Therefore, he set about determining the amount of money damages that Mary could seek. John Q.'s potential work years until retirement at age 65 numbered 23. When his annual salary during that time was considered, along with normally expected increases of even a minimal amount, the sum was enormous: $450,000. Even when reduced to present value, the amount was great: approximately $200,000 when compounded annually at 6%. He would have to be sure Mary Worker understood that this was the asking sum, that judges and juries often do not award the amount asked, and that adverse parties often will settle only for much less. (Mary already understood that she would not be able to recover twice for the same cause, and that the form she signed accepting workmen's compansation benefits from The Firm provided that the corporation had a right of *subrogation*. That is the right of one person to substitute for or take the place of another with respect to a legal claim.)

REQUEST TO SETTLE

Henry called Mary to inform her that he believed she had a reasonably good case, although he would not and could not guarantee results. Henry suggested the first step should be an attempt to arrive at an amicable settlement without litigation. Mary agreed. Therefore, Henry wrote to Zagger Supply, requesting compensation for John Q.'s death caused by a defective zagger which the company had manufactured and sold to The Firm, Inc.

His letter caused much activity at Zagger Supply. President Will Very took it to the corporation's legal department where he consulted W. E. Just, the attorney in charge. Both then called upon Charles Sell, engineering sales manager, seeking background information. They learned that the new zaggers had been developed after Charles had gone to The Firm's plant to discuss with Sam Scott and Jim Boss zaggers for use on the new chattels. Sell's staff worked on an adaptation of the zagger The Firm usually bought, since the latter wanted the new zaggers to be interchangeable with the old ones on the cypres machines. Sixty dozen had been manufactured for the first order from specifications prepared by the Zagger Supply development engineers. Of these, only half a dozen had been tested prior to shipment. When the static test results coincided with those of the other zaggers manufactured at Zagger Supply, dynamic testing was not considered necessary and was omitted so that the promised delivery dates could be met. Charles also recounted the staff's trip to The Firm the day after John Q. Worker's death.

Will Very walked away from the discussion, saying to Attorney Just:

"Fight it. We won't pay—not a nickel."

W. E. decided it would take a minor miracle to be able to do that, knowing only what he did at the present time. Therefore, he started upon his own investigation. His first step was to request that available fragments of the shattered zagger be sought and sent to Acme Industrial Laboratories for testing. He scheduled interviews with the engineers and production personnel who had worked on The Firm's order; gathered production and quality control reports related to the order; and then scheduled several sessions with cypres engineers to learn all he could about the use of zaggers on those machines.

The report from Acme Laboratories was a blow. It said essentially what Professor Learned's report did.

"If they have this kind of information—and at this time I have no way of knowing that they do—then they have a basis for claiming the zagger was defective. If that's true, our best line of defense would be to deny that death occurred because of a defective zagger," W. E. said as he met with Will Very and Charles Sell several days later. "The zagger might have shattered for a number of reasons. The cypres engineers tell me it's entirely plausible that a zagger could shatter if improperly mounted or if an operator becomes distracted and is careless for a few minutes."

"Can you prove that?"

"Oh, yes. Based on prior defective zagger experience, I'd estimate there's a better than two to one chance of proving that."

"Anything over 50 per cent would be good enough for me," said Will Very. "In fact, that should be enough to cool any desire they may have to sue."

"Perhaps," replied W. E. "We don't know yet how seriously they intend to pursue this, but in view of the lab report I believe we should be prepared in case of follow-up."

"Keep fighting," was Very's reply. "Under no circumstances are we going to pay." (His decision is shown in a flow chart in Figure 4-2.)

Will Very was a determined man, willing to assume the accompanying risks or to do the unusual if he believed it would help him accomplish his purposes. That, W. E. Just believed, was one of the reasons the company had changed to self-insurance for its product liability when rates increased. Many had advised against it, including W. E. Just, even when Will Very had agreed to additional legal staff if increased work resulted. Therefore, W. E. Just realized he would, indeed, have little choice in this matter but "to fight it."

After that conversation Henry Law received a letter from W. E. Just stating that Zagger Supply denied that John Q. Worker's death was caused by a defective zagger manufactured by them. Therefore, they also denied any liability and would make no

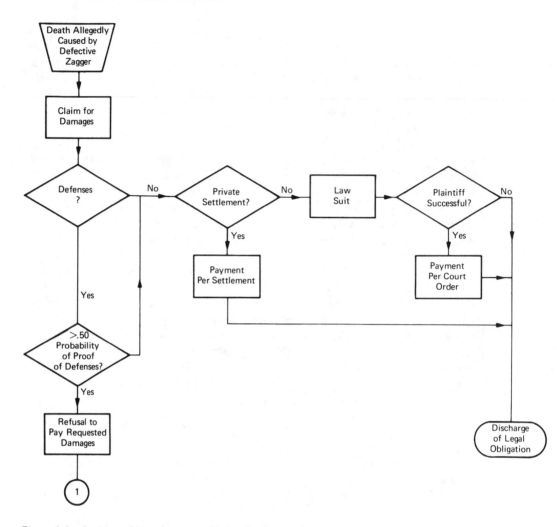

Figure 4-2. Decision of Manufacturer to Refuse Request for Payment to Mary Worker

payment. Attorney Law followed up with a telephone call to W. E. Just, indicating that his client was serious and would maintain suit if necessary. W. E. could only reply that Zagger Supply's position was clear; it continued to deny liability and would defend any legal action brought against it.

DECISION TO BRING CIVIL SUIT

When Henry Law discussed the Zagger Supply response with Mary, the two reviewed the entire situation. Mary then asked Henry to pursue the matter further, and it was agreed that Henry should take the action necessary to institute civil suit against Zagger Supply.

In this way Mary Worker became the plaintiff in a civil action. It would now be up to Henry Law to take the steps necessary to institute a law suit on behalf of Mary Worker. This involved much more than merely walking down to the nearest courthouse and filling out an application or request to begin litigation against Zagger Supply.

Justifiable Action

Henry's mental process at this time consisted of thoughtful review of a number of decisions he made in his earlier determination that Mary Worker had a legal basis for bringing suit. A chain of decisions had led to his conclusion that the John Q. Worker case was *justiciable,* that is, proper for action by the courts. In addition to the existence of a cause of action, he had also decided:

1. There existed a case or controversy;
2. The plaintiff had standing to sue;
3. The defendant was a proper party to the action;
4. The suit would be brought within the time period of the applicable Statute of Limitations.

How did Henry arrive at these determinations? Further inquiry is in order.

Consider first the decision as to case or controversy.[7] Recourse to the courts is possible when there is an actual dispute between adverse parties. The courts do not exist to settle theoretical issues, to determine answers to problems that might arise in the future, to provide a forum for friendly—as contrasted with adversarial—parties, or to pursue an intellectually stimulating question for its own sake. Nor will the courts decide moot questions, those of a kind where a judicial decision would have no legal effect upon an existing controversy.

That there existed a real dispute between Zagger Supply and Mary Worker concerning payment to her for John Q.'s death, there could be no doubt. Determining the existence of a live controversy was one of the easier decisions Henry had had to make.

Henry Law's next decision regarding proper parties was more involved. He knew that Mary as the *plaintiff*—the party bringing the action—must have standing to sue. In other words, she must have been personally wronged in some manner. One of her legally protected interests must have been invaded by the defendant. This requirement prevents an interested but unharmed spectator or bystander from bringing legal action. It also precludes bringing suit for no reason other than mere desire to take legal action against another or to harass him.

Obviously the standing to sue requirement meant that Robert Leader would not have the right to bring suit against Zagger Supply for John Q.'s death, but Mary's position was not quite so obvious.

The person suffering legal injury from the alleged wrong was John Q., now dead and unable to bring suit. Had this occurred in the very early days of the common law, the legal claim for personal injury would have died with John Q. However, modern law has remedied that by passage of death statutes. These take two forms: *survival* acts and *wrongful death* acts. Today each state has enacted either one or both of these death statutes. They commonly provide for two types of action which may be brought following one's death.

A *survival action* is a legal action that the deceased could have brought had he lived and which, as its name indicates, survives his death. It is brought by the deceased's personal representative on behalf of and for the benefit of the decedent's estate. Recoverable damages include compensation for hospital and medical expenses, lost earnings, and pain and suffering sustained by the deceased as a result of injury to him.

A *wrongful death action,* on the other hand, is a legal action brought on behalf of persons dependent upon the deceased to recover for losses they have suffered as a result of his death. Damages are recoverable by them rather than by the estate. Examples include not only funeral expenses but also compensation to a decedent's surviving spouse and children for loss of both financial and nonpecuniary benefits, such as the deceased's services as a spouse and parent as well as the financial support provided by the decedent to the family.

Great State had enacted the two death statutes. They provided that both actions might be brought in the event of death but must be joined for trial so that double recovery would not result. Therefore, Henry Law realized that the Great State statutes conferred upon Mary standing to sue in her capacity as administratrix of John Q.'s estate.[8]

Satisfied that Mary was a proper plaintiff, Henry Law next determined that Zagger Supply was a proper defendant—the party against whom legal action is brought. In referring to §402A of the *Restatement of Torts 2d,* he found that in cases of dangerously defective products which result in physical harm to the user, the seller of the product—if engaged in the business of selling such products—can be held strictly liable. There is no requirement that the user also be the purchaser. While he had previously decided he would prefer to proceed in tort; i.e., *ex delicto,* Henry mentally noted that the supplier of the product would also be a proper defendant if one were to proceed in contract, or *ex contractu.* This was in accordance with the interpretation by the Great State courts of the Uniform Commercial Code. Henry Law had received verification from two sources, Robert Leader and Professor Learned, that Zagger Supply was the manufacturer and supplier of the zagger that had shattered at the time of John Q.'s death. Therefore, he knew that he had no problem with respect to the proper defendant.

The next item for Henry Law's concern was the time period that had elapsed since John Q.'s death. He checked this because of the Statute of Limitations, which sets specific time limits for bringing various kinds of legal actions. The purpose of the statute is to encourage timely suit. Unreasonable delay in instituting legal action makes the rendering of justice difficult. Witnesses may die or move away, those who are still available find it difficult to remember events occurring in the distant past, evidence is lost or destroyed. Therefore, it is a defense to a legal action if it is brought after expiration of the time period provided in the Statute of Limitations.

The Statute of Limitations can be *tolled*; that is, there is a holding action on the time. One event that precipitates this is the official beginning of a law suit. It is not necessary that the legal action be concluded prior to the expiration of the time period set in the statute. There are variations from state to state regarding other situations that will toll the statute and regarding the time limitations. The Great State Statute of Limitations provided that wrongful death actions must be brought within one year and survival actions within two years of the death of the decedent. Since only three months had elapsed since John Q.'s death, Henry Law knew that the law suit would be filed in ample time to meet Statute of Limitations requirements.

Henry Law's determination that there had been a wrong committed for which the law provides a remedy—that there was a cause of action—has already been discussed.

Pleadings

Thus it was that Henry Law concluded that the Mary Worker case was justiciable. He realized his next step would be to initiate the *pleadings.* These are formal, written documents filed with the court prior to trial. They contain statements of the two parties concerning the controversy. The plaintiff actually commerces a civil action by filing the first statement, generally referred to as the *complaint,* with the court. This document identifies the parties, states the nature of the dispute, contains the plaintiff's charges against the defendant, and states the relief sought. The defendant responds to those charges. His reply is commonly referred to as an *answer.* Other statements may follow. Each court system has its own rules of procedure for the preparation of these documents, known as *Rules of Civil Procedure.* These vary from state to state and between the federal and state systems.

Choice of Court

Obviously, Henry would have to know in which court he would file suit before he could know which court's rules of procedure he must follow in his pleadings. That meant making another decision, one that involved answers to these questions:

1. In which level of the court system is it proper to bring this case?
2. Is this case properly brought in the federal or state court system, and, if the state system, which state?
3. Which court has subject matter jurisdiction?
4. Which court has personal jurisdiction, and, can that jurisdiction be perfected?
5. Which is the court with proper venue?

Answers to these questions include concepts that are basic to *due process of law.* That term is used here to refer to fair and orderly legal proceedings which protect the rights and liberty of the persons involved.

Henry's first decision, that of proper level of a court system, was easily made. He knew that the amount of damages to be sought was far in excess of the maximum which the minor judiciary can properly handle. Since this was not an appeal from a decision already rendered by a lower court, he also realized it would not be within the province of an appellate court. Therefore, the proper level would be a trial court.

His next determination would be of a specific trial court. Should it be one in a state or in the federal court system? Henry knew that, as a general rule, courts in both systems have the power to hear and decide cases involving either state or federal law. There is an exception regarding a few special subject matter areas which have been specifically restricted to one system either constitutionally or by statute. In many situations both a state and a federal court can properly hear a case, and in some instances the courts of several states can do so.

As the party initiating legal action, the plaintiff makes the choice of court, or *choice of forum,* as it is called. However, the plaintiff must choose from among those courts which can properly hear the case. It should be noted that in some instances a defendant, after petitioning the court and showing sufficient cause, can have the case removed from a state to a federal court. A defendant can also request a change of venue.

The proper court to hear and decide a case is one that has jurisdiction over the subject matter, jurisdiction over the defendant or property involved, and proper venue. *Jurisdiction* is the power or authority of the court to hear a case. *Venue* refers to geographical location. Hence, change of venue refers to change of location of the trial site.

Jurisdiction

Jurisdiction of the courts can be determined by referring to the sources of judicial power: the constitution (state or federal, depending upon which court system is involved) and legislation enacted pursuant to constitutional provisions. Could litigation in the Mary Worker case properly be brought in a federal trial court? Referring to the United States Constitution and the United States Code, Henry found that the United States District Court has jurisdiction in civil matters as follows:

1. Where the sum in controversy exceeds $10,000 and arises under the Constitution, laws or treaties of the United States;
2. Where the matter involved is one which by federal statute is restricted to the federal courts regardless of the sum involved. Some examples of this are civil rights, bankruptcy, patent and copyright, antitrust, and admiralty cases;
3. Where the sum in controversy exceeds $10,000 and there is diversity of citizenship.[9]

Diversity of citizenship means that the parties are citizens of different states, or that one is a citizen of the United States and the other a citizen of a foreign country. Complete diversity is required. Should there be more than one plaintiff or defendant, it is necessary that all persons on one side be citizens of different states from the states of which the persons on the other side are citizens. For purposes of diversity, a corporation is considered to be citizen of both the state in which it is incorporated and the state in which it has its principal place of business. That meant Zagger Supply was a citizen of only Nearby State.

Therefore, federal jurisdiction existed in the Mary Worker case on the basis of the amount involved and diversity of citizenship. Knowing this, Henry asked himself if the courts of Great State and Nearby State also had jurisdiction.

The Great State Constitution provided for the following special purpose courts:

1. A probate court to handle primarily matters related to the wills and estates of deceased persons;
2. A family court which was concerned with the area of domestic relations;
3. A juvenile court to deal with cases involving youthful offenders;
4. A criminal court to hear criminal cases.

It also provided for a court of common pleas with more general jurisdiction, covering all matters not coming under the aegis of the specialized courts or the minor judiciary. The latter's jurisdiction included civil cases involving not more than $1000.

Consequently, Henry Law realized that the Court of Common Pleas of Great State would have subject matter jurisdiction in the Mary Worker case. He also found that in Nearby State the trial court of general jurisdiction, known as the Circuit Court, had subject matter jurisdiction in civil cases in excess of $500. Thus far, Henry had his choice of the federal, Great State, and Nearby State court systems; all would be proper in the Mary Worker case.

He knew, however, that jurisdiction over subject matter alone is not sufficient. A court must also have jurisdiction over the person of the defendant or the property of the case, depending on whether the action is *in personam* or *in rem*.

In personam jurisdiction is required when the controversy is of such a nature that the plaintiff seeks to have the court render a judgment against a specific person or persons who are the defendants.[10] In an in personam action, the defendant's obligation to do something or to give something is to be decided. The Mary Worker case is an example. In contrast, in rem jurisdiction applies when the plaintiff requests the court to render a judgment affecting an interest in property. An example would be a case in which ownership of a piece of land is the issue to be decided.

A court can acquire in personam or personal jurisdiction over a person if that person is physically present or domiciled within the state in which the court sits.[11] That physical presence in the state may be temporary. It can consist of simply passing through. (Persons entering a state to give testimony in a judicial proceeding or who are brought in by force or trickery do not have jurisdictional presence.) The *World-Wide Volkswagen* decision that follows discusses the "minimum contacts" concept involved in the exercise of in personam jurisdiction over nonresidents.

World-Wide Volkswagen Corp. v. Woodson
444 W.S. 286, 100 S.Ct. 559, 62 L.Ed.2d 490 (1980)

MR. JUSTICE WHITE. The issue before us is whether, consistently with the Due Process Clause of the Fourteenth Amendment, an Oklahoma court may exercise in personam jurisdiction over a nonresident automobile retailer and its wholesale distributor in a products liability action, when the defendants' only connection with Oklahoma is the fact that an automobile sold in New York to New York residents became involved in an accident in Oklahoma. . . .

As has long been settled, and as we reaffirm today, a state court may exercise personal jurisdiction over a nonresident defendant only so long as there exist "minimum contacts" between the defendant and the forum State. . . .

The concept of minimum contacts, in turn, can be seen to perform two related, but distinguishable, functions. It protects the defendant against the burdens of litigating in a distant or inconvenient forum. And it acts to ensure that the States through their courts, do not reach out beyond the limits imposed on them by their status as coequal sovereigns in a federal system.

The protection against inconvenient litigation is typically described in terms of "reasonableness" or "fairness." We have said that the defendant's contacts with the forum State must be such that maintenance of the suit "does not offend 'traditional notions of fair play and substantial justice.'" . . . The relationship between the defendant and the forum must be such that it is reasonable . . . to require the corporation to defend the particular suit which is brought there. . . .

. . . Petitioners carry on no activity whatsoever in Oklahoma. They close no sales and perform no services there. They avail themselves of none of the privileges and benefits of Oklahoma law. They solicit no business there either through salespersons or through advertising reasonably calculated to reach the State. Nor does the record show that they regularly sell cars at wholesale or retail to Oklahoma customers or residents or that they indirectly, through others, serve or seek to serve the Oklahoma market. In short, respondents seek to base jurisdiction on one isolated occurrence and whatever inferences can be drawn therefrom: the fortuitous circumstances that a single Audi automobile, sold in New York to New York residents, happened to suffer an accident while passing through Oklahoma.

It is argued, however, that because an automobile is mobile by its very design and purpose it was "foreseeable" that the Robinson's Audi would cause injury in Oklahoma. Yet "foreseeability" alone has never been a sufficient benchmark for personal jurisdiction under the Due Process Clause. . . .

If foreseeability were the criterion, . . . every seller of chattels would in effect appoint the chattel his agent for service of process. His amenability to suit would travel with the chattel. . . .

When a corporation "purposefully avails itself of the privilege of conducting activities within the forum State," it has clear notice that it is subject to suit there, and can act to alleviate the risk of burdensome litigation by procuring insurance, passing the expected costs on to customers, or, if the risks are too great, severing its connection with the State. Hence if the sale of a product of a manufacturer or distributor such as Audi or Volkswagen is not simply an isolated occurrence, but arises from the efforts of the manufacturer or distributor to serve directly or indirectly, the market for its product in other States, it is not unreasonable to subject it to suit in one of those States if its allegedly defective merchandise has there been the source of injury to its owner or to others. The forum State does not exceed its powers under the Due Process Clause if it asserts personal jurisdiction over a corporation that delivers its products into the stream of commerce with the expectation that they will be purchased by consumers in the forum State. . . .

Because we find that the petitioners have no "contacts, ties, or relations" with the State of Oklahoma, . . . the judgment of the Supreme Court of Oklahoma is Reversed.

Service of Process

As he considered all this, Henry asked himself if it would be possible for the state and federal courts to perfect jurisdiction over Zagger Supply.

To perfect jurisdiction requires that the defendant receive proper notice that a legal action is being brought against him. This is known as *service of process.* Service is accomplished by delivering to the defendant a copy of the plaintiff's complaint, along with a summons ordering him to appear in court. The summons and complaint may be handed to the defendant personally, may be left at his usual place of abode with a person of suitable age and discretion residing there, or may be delivered to an agent authorized to receive service of process. Service upon an officer or agent is made in the case of a corporation, partnership, or association defendant.

A person may voluntarily consent to a court's jurisdiction. Foreign corporations are considered to have done so when they register to do business within a state other than the one in which they were incorporated. Many states have *long arm statutes* which provide for jurisdiction over nonresidents who come into the state and cause injury or loss while there. Most of these statutes include provisions for jurisdiction over nonresident motorists, nonresidents entering into a contract or transacting business within the state, and nonresidents who commit a tort within the state. Many of these statutes state that nonresidents, by coming into the state and engaging in activity there, impliedly give their consent to appointment of a state official, usually the secretary of state, to receive service of process should legal action be filed against them as a result of their activities within the state. Service upon the state's secretary is generally followed by notice to the nonresident by mail. This is referred to as *substitute service.*

In rem jurisdiction exists when the rights in property (a "thing") are to be determined by the court, and the property is located within the geographical boundaries of the court's jurisdiction. If personal service is not possible because the defendant is neither a resident of, nor physically present in, the state, *constructive service* is possible. This may consist of notice of suit by newspaper publication or posting notice on the property itself. In rem jurisdiction will not exist, however, in the absence of requisite "minimum contacts" within the state.

In the Mary Worker case, it was evident to Henry that there would be no problem insofar as in personam jurisdiction was concerned. Zagger Supply was a resident of Nearby State, and personal service was possible there. The firm had registered as a foreign corporation doing business in Great State, and the Great State statute provided for substitute service in that event. Since the Federal Rules of Civil Procedure provide for both personal service and substitute service upon foreign corporations in accordance with state statute, personal jurisdiction over Zagger Supply could also be perfected in a federal action. At this point, Henry found that he had not yet eliminated the federal courts or the courts of either Great State or Nearby State as proper places for entering the Mary Worker suit.

Venue

He thereupon set about determining the question of proper venue. Venue is regulated by statute. With regard to the federal courts, the United States Code provides:

1. In civil actions based only on diversity, action may be brought in the judicial district where all plaintiffs or all defendants reside or in which the claim arose;
2. A corporation may be sued in any judicial district in which it is incorporated or licensed to do business or is doing business.[12]

Since the Mary Worker claim arose in the Great State District and since Zagger Supply was doing business in that same district, a proper location for the trial in the federal court system would be in the United States District Court for the Great State District. At the same time, Zagger Supply was a resident of Nearby State, had been incorporated there, and carried on business there. Consequently, a second proper location for the trial would be in the United States District Court for the Nearby State District.

State venue statutes typically provide that legal action may be brought in the county where the defendant resides or is doing business or in the county where the cause of action arose. These were the Great State and Nearby State provisions. Since Zagger Supply was doing business in Local County of Great State and since the cause of action also arose there, proper venue in the Great State system for the Mary Worker case would be the Common Pleas Court of Local County. In Nearby State, Zagger Supply was a resident of This County. Therefore, proper venue in that system would be in the Circuit Court of This County.

Henry Law concluded that, all other factors being equal, his choice of location would be the Great State District because most of the witnesses—Robert Leader, other employees of The Firm and Local 135 members, as well as Mary Worker herself—resided there. To transport them to Nearby State District would be expensive.

Forum Non Conveniens

Before concluding with venue, Henry Law considered one other matter. That was the doctrine of *forum non conveniens*. This permits a court to dismiss an action when it appears to the satisfaction of the court that the suit might more appropriately be tried elsewhere. Henry also remembered that the United States Code provides that a district court may, in the interest of justice and for the convenience of parties and witnesses, transfer a civil action to another district where it might have been brought.[13] Great State and Nearby State change of venue statutes were typical of those in many states. They provided for relocation under conditions similar to those in the federal law.

Because Henry's reason for preferring Great State over Nearby State was the appropriateness of the place, he concluded that there would be little likelihood of a request for change of venue—and still less for grant of a request for such—if he proceeded in either the Great State District Court or in Local County Common Pleas Court. However, he would wait to make a firm choice until after he reviewed the conflict of laws situation.

Choice of Law

Would a difference in the law that a specific court followed work as an advantage to his client? In a state court, he could expect state procedural and substantive law to be applied. In diversity cases, a federal court must follow the substantive law of the state in which it is sitting, but federal procedure applies. This is known as the "Erie doctrine," since it evolved from the United States Supreme Court decision in *Erie R. Co.* v. *Tompkins,* 304 U.S. 64 (1938). The reason for this rule is to prevent a federal and state court sitting in the same state from reaching different results regarding the same legal question.

Entering into Henry Law's choice of forum was consideration of yet another factor. In the Mary Worker case, most of the events—including John Q.'s death—occurred in Great State. However, the zaggers were manufactured in Nearby State by a Nearby State corporation. Would the laws of Nearby State or Great State apply? Suppose the provisions of Great State law differed from those of Nearby State law. This situation is referred to as *conflict of laws.*

The answer, Henry knew, could be found in that portion of the law referred to as *choice of law.* Each state, either by judicial decision or statute, has provisions specifying which state's laws should be used by its courts in deciding cases that involve events occurring in more than one state. For instance, Great State law provided that in tort cases the law of the place of injury, referred to as *lex loci delicti,* would apply. This meant that since John Q. was injured in Great State, the laws of Great State would be applicable. Henry Law found that Nearby State also followed the lex loci delicti rule. This would mean that even if the case were tried in the Nearby State courts, the court would follow the law of Great State in reaching its decision. That gave Henry more flexibility in his choice of forum than he would have had if the Nearby State choice of law rules had called for application of Nearby State law regarding John Q.'s accident.

Because of differences in state law, the lawyer is sometimes faced with a situation in which there is a conflict in the laws regarding choice of law. For instance, not all states follow the rule of lex loci delicti. There is a trend toward interest analysis and test of significant relationship; that is, which state has the greater interest or concern with the events and the parties involved. There are other variations. In contract cases, for example, the law to be applied may be that of a number of different states. It may be, among others, the law of the state where the action is brought, the state where the contract was made, the state where the contract was to be performed, the state that the parties have specified in the contract itself, or the state where there is the greatest interest and relationship.

When there is a conflict in the laws regarding choice of law, then it is the law of the forum state regarding choice of law that controls. As can be seen, the rules regarding conflict of laws can be quite complicated. They are an important factor in the attorney's selection of the court in which to bring an action. Given a choice of forum, the attorney will ordinarily decide upon the one that will apply laws most favorable to the client's cause.

Henry Law was fortunate in that the rules regarding choice of laws would not limit his choice of forum. His choice of Great State over Nearby State was now firm. He had only one more decision to make regarding the court: would it be federal or state?

Selection of Court Decision

As Henry Law continued this decision-making process, he checked the calendar of both the Common Pleas Court of Local County and the United States District Court for Great State District. He discovered that he could expect almost half the waiting time for trial in that particular federal court since it did not have as great a backlog of cases as did the Local County court. That was the decisive factor as far as he was concerned.

Therefore, and after all those considerations, Henry Law decided to file suit in the United States District Court for the Great State District. Whereupon he brought out his copy of the *Federal Rules of Civil Procedure* (F.R. Civ. P.) for handy reference and proceeded to prepare a complaint in the civil case of *Mary Worker, Administratrix of the Estate of John Q. Worker*, v. *Zagger Supply, Inc.*, a corporation. How he did so is explained in the next chapter.

QUESTIONS

1. Mary's entry into the legal system as the plaintiff in a law suit has been the result of the decisions made by the various persons who have been involved in all of the steps through which she has passed. There is Fred Famous' decision that The Firm would pay her only the amount required by the Great State Workmen's Compensation Act. It is a decision made in full compliance with the law—Fred acted in consultation with the firm's legal counsel—yet it is also an example of the interaction of business and law. Fred himself indicated that the firm's financial condition influenced him in his thinking.

   Would his decision have been different if the company had been in a more affluent state? Had he offered additional payments, would Mary have pursued legal action? Has he really, while acting in full compliance with the law, shifted some of the economic burden and responsibility arising from an employee's death to others in the marketplace? If that is the effect of the statute, should it be amended? Or, is it a proper allocation of economic risks? Is it a result desired by the legislators who enacted the statute?

2. Certainly Henry Law had a great influence upon Mary's entry into the legal system. Not only did legal issues concern him, but his decision was influenced greatly by factual considerations. In his conversations with Mary, he stated that he must have facts and not just suppositions. He also considered mentally the problems involved in meeting the burden of proof.

   What does this suggest regarding the legal system's capabilities for achieving justice for persons who have been wronged but do not have the means of proof? Is there anything that can be done to change that?

3. Henry Law's first approach, once he believed there was a basis for legal action, was to try to effectuate a private, out-of-court settlement. Does this not suggest a "private judicial system"? What are the consequences? Should the legal system tolerate this? Should the law provide for procedures to be followed in private settlements? Why are most disputes settled out of court? Why does the law encourage this kind of settlement?

4. The decision of Zagger Supply to refuse payment for John Q.'s death is apparent from Will Very's first response to Henry Law's letter, "We won't pay." Could he have sustained that position if W. E. Just had been unable to come up with some reasonable defenses? Attorney Just is in the position of having to deal with and defend the company against a *fait accompli*. What does this say about the need for, or advisability of, consultation with the corporate legal staff regarding everyday business transactions? Is this a realistic suggestion?

5. The influence of other persons whose decisions have not been flow charted upon Mary Worker's entry into the legal system must be recognized. For instance, there is Robert Leader's decision to pick up several fragments of the shattered zagger at the time of the accident. There is also his twice-made statement to Mary that he had the fragments if she needed help. Had he not acted in this way, would Mary be starting legal action against Zagger Supply?

6. There is also to be considered the role played by the young woman at the NLSA office who did her best to be of assistance to Mary.

Can you flow chart her actions and decisions in eventually leading Mary to the lawyer referral service? Would you have as much difficulty as Mary Worker had in finding a lawyer? How would you locate one if you needed legal counsel today? If you moved to another area of the country and needed a family doctor, how would you find one? A family lawyer? Should professional codes regulate lawyer and doctor advertising? What is the maximum allowable income and net worth of eligibility for NLSA or the Legal Aid Society in your community? Should these criteria be changed? Do you know of any pre-paid legal services plans? What suggestions do you have for improving the delivery of legal services? Do Mary's experiences indicate that the hurdles for entry into the legal system (1) are too many and too great? (2) are of reasonable difficulty for the purpose of testing one's seriousness of purpose? (3) should be increased or made more difficult in order to eliminate frivolous lawsuits and reduce the caseloads of the courts? What changes would you suggest?

7. The "Erie doctrine" is often advanced as a means of arriving at a similar outcome, whether one is in the state or federal courts. Thus, it is said to be a deterrent to "forum shopping" for the purpose of selecting a court that will apply law more favorable to the plaintiff. Does not the variation in law and the rules regarding choice of law among the states make this very same kind of forum shopping possible? Should it be eliminated? How?

NOTES

[1] 42 U.S.C. § 2996 *et seq.* This refers to Title 42, section 2996 of the *United States Code.*

[2] *Swayne* v. *Connecticut Co.,* 86 Conn. 439, 84 A. 634, 635 (*1913*).

[3] U.C.C. 2–314.

[4] U.C.C. 2–315.

[5] U.C.C. 2–318.

[6] 29 U.S.C. § 655 (a).

[7] Article III, Section 2 of the United States Constitution extends the federal judicial power to "cases" and "controversies."

[8] The personal representative of the deceased when there is no will is referred to as the *administrator* or *administratrix*; if there is a will, that personal representative is known as the *executor* or *executrix.*

[9] Article III, Section 2; 28 U.S.C. § 1331 and 1332.

[10] "Person" includes a corporation, which the law looks upon as an artificial person. The term also includes entities such as partnerships or associations.

[11] Exceptions to this exist by federal statute.

[12] 28 U.S.C. § 1391.

[13] 28 U.S.C. § 1404.

pretrial: development of a case for trial

FIVE

PLEADINGS

Complaint

As Henry Law sat at his desk preparing to draft the complaint, he mentally considered its function.[1] The complaint serves to acquaint the court with the matters in dispute and to give the defendant notice of the claim being asserted by the plaintiff.

Form and content of the complaint would be governed by the Federal Rules. Noting that they were simpler and allowed for greater flexibility than did the Great State rules, Henry found the complaint must have:

1. A short and plain statement of the grounds upon which the court's jurisdiction depends;
2. A short and plain statement of the claim showing that the pleader is entitled to relief;
3. A demand for judgment for the relief (relief in the alternative, or of several different types, may be demanded).

Henry also considered that the action was being brought as both a wrongful death and survival action and on the basis of strict liability in tort for a defective product. As a guide to the content of the complaint, he prepared the worksheet, which appears as Table 5-1. Using it, he was able to complete the complaint, Form 5-1.

Request for Jury Trial

Notice that the last item in the complaint is a request for a jury trial. Henry knew that the Federal Rules provided that a request for a jury trial could be included in the pleadings. Before he took action on this, he telephoned Mary Worker and asked if she would come to his office. There he reviewed with her the contents of the complaint and the steps in the litigation now underway and also asked her wishes about a trial by jury.

"I didn't know there was a choice," she said. "I thought all trials had a jury."

"No," replied Henry Law. "The right to trial by jury in the federal courts in civil matters is guaranteed by the Seventh Amendment to the United States Constitution."

Seventh Amendment

When Mary looked puzzled at this response, he explained that the Constitution is the supreme law of the land. No law that is in conflict with it is valid, nor would any legal procedure which resulted in depriving an individual of a constitutional right be valid. As Mary nodded, indicating understanding, Henry continued. The federal consti-

TABLE 5-1. Henry Law's Guide to Contents of Complaint

NATURE OF SUIT	REFERENCE	CONTENTS OF COMPLAINT

Federal court action Diversity action	F.R.Civ.P. 8(a) 29 U.S.C. § 1331, 1332	Statement of Jurisdiction:
		    citizenship of plaintiff
		    citizenship of defendant (corporate defendant: place of incorporation and principal place of business)
		    over $10,000 in controversy

Strict liability in tort for defective product	F.R.Civ.P. 8(a) § 402A, Restatement of Torts 2d	Statement of claim:
		    defendant sold the product involved
		    defendant is a seller in the business of selling the product involved
		    product was defective at the time of sale
		    product reached user without substantial change
		    plaintiff's decedent was a user
		    product was being used for the purpose and in the manner intended by the seller
		    product was unreasonably dangerous
		    user suffered harm
		    proximate cause

Wrongful death and survival action	F.R.Civ.P. 8(a) Great State Statutes	Prayer for relief:
		    damages–wrongful death
		    damages–survival action
		    capacity of plaintiff re these two actions

Form 5-1. Complaint

DISTRICT COURT OF THE UNITED STATES
FOR THE DISTRICT OF GREAT STATE

MARY WORKER,   :
   Administratrix of the   :
ESTATE OF JOHN Q.   :
   WORKER, deceased,   :
        Plaintiff   :
                :
        v.   :   Civil Action
                :   No. _____
ZAGGER SUPPLY, INC.,   :
   a corporation,   :
        Defendant   :

COMPLAINT

Plaintiff alleges as follows:

COUNT ONE

1. Plaintiff Mary Worker is a citizen of Great State
and is administratrix of the estate of John Q. Worker,
deceased, who was killed on August 26, 19XX in the
accident referred to herein.

2. Defendant Zagger Supply, Inc., is a corporation
incorporated under the laws of Nearby State and having its
principal place of business in Nearby State. Defendant is
engaged in the business of manufacturing and selling
zaggers.

3. The matters in controversy exceed, exclusive of
interest and costs, the sum of $10,000.

4. On or about August 15, 19XX defendant manufactured
and sold to The Firm, Inc., the zagger involved in the
incident referred to herein. The zagger was especially
manufactured and sold by the defendant for the specific
use being made of it at the time of the accident.

5. On August 26, 19XX at approximately 2:00 P.M.,
plaintiff's decedent, John Q. Worker, was killed when the
zagger manufactured and sold by the defendant shattered
with great violence, and a fragment pierced his abdomen
while he was engaged in operating a cypres machine on

which the zagger was being used in the course of his employment and the performance of his duties as a cypres operator at The Firm, Inc. in Big City, Local County, Great State.

6. At the time of the accident, plaintiff's decedent was a user of the zagger and was using it in the manner and for the purpose expected and intended by the defendant.

7. At the time of the accident the zagger existed without substantial change from the condition in which it was manufactured and sold. It was in a defective condition in that it was defectively manufactured and unreasonably dangerous to users. Defendant knew or should have expected that the zagger would reach users without substantial change in the condition in which it was manufactured and sold.

8. Death of plaintiff's decedent and resulting damages were caused by the conduct of the defendant in defectively manufacturing such zagger and selling it in a defective condition unreasonably dangerous to intended users as well as to persons reasonably expected to be within the orbit of such use. Defendant corporation is strictly liable for the death and damages herein set forth.

9. By reason of the aforesaid wrongful acts of the defendant which directly and proximately caused the death of John Q. Worker, plaintiff administratrix claims damages of defendant on behalf of the wife and children of the deceased as follows: (a) for loss to the wife of the society, services, comfort, and companionship of her husband; (b) for loss to the children of the care, companionship, nurture, and parental guidance of their father; (c) for funeral, burial, cemetery, and grave monument expenses.

Wherefore, plaintiff Mary Worker, administratrix of the estate of John Q. Worker, deceased, demands judgment of the defendant Zagger Supply, Inc., a corporation, on behalf of the family of the deceased under the Wrongful Death Act in an amount in excess of the sum of $10,000.

COUNT TWO

10. Plaintiff incorporates herein the allegations made in paragraphs 1 through 8 of this complaint.

11. By reason of the aforesaid wrongful acts of the defendant which directly and proximately caused the death of John Q. Worker, plaintiff administratrix claims damages

of the defendant Zagger Supply, Inc., a corporation, on behalf of the estate as follows: (a) for loss of established earnings and earning power of the deceased for a period of time beginning August 26, 19XX and continuing to the termination of his natural life, which earnings and earning power would have continued but for his death on August 26, 19XX; (b) for expenses incident to the administration of the estate of the deceased; (c) for other expenses caused by the accident.

Wherefore, plaintiff demands judgment of the defendant Zagger Supply, Inc., a corporation, on behalf of the estate of the decedent under the Survival Act in an amount in excess of the sum of $10,000.

A JURY TRIAL IS DEMANDED.

Henry Law
_____
Attorney for Plaintiff
789 Main Street
Big City, Great State

tution, he said, reflects the thoughts of its authors who came to this country steeped in the traditions of the English common law. That included the jury system. It had developed over the centuries following man's early attempts to determine guilt or innocence through trial by ordeal, which was usually by fire or water. Early juries in England consisted of twelve local men (no women, in those days) who served as witnesses and testified as to the events that occurred. The role of the jury as an objective, disinterested group came only later, but did exist at the time the original thirteen colonies were being formed into one nation. The framers of the Constitution considered the jury—a group of one's peers acting as decision makers and interposed between the defendant and the authorities—as one means of preventing possible harassment of citizens by those in power. Because the possibility of abuse was greater in criminal matters than in civil cases, the constitutional provisions for the two kinds of action differ.

The Seventh Amendment provides that the right to trial by jury exists in civil matters over $20, that being a sizable sum of money at the time the Constitution was being written, Henry continued. It also restricts the right to a jury trial in civil cases to those matters where it existed under the common law. That excludes all cases in equity as well as actions at law for which the right to trial by jury had never been provided, such as those for divorce or change of name.

Henry went on to say that Mary could waive the right to trial by jury if she so chose. In the federal court system, the assumption is that a person has waived that right when no request for a jury trial is made. On the other hand, said Henry, the reverse assumption is true in the Great State court system. However, the right to trial by jury would be the same, since provisions of the Great State constitution coincided with those in the federal constitution. Because provisions of the Seventh Amendment have not been made applicable to the states, the right to a jury trial in civil cases in state courts is governed by the provisions of the state constitutions.

At this point Mary asked who made decisions in cases in which there was no jury.

Trier of Fact

Henry replied by describing the jury as the *trier of fact*. The jury is the decision maker regarding factual matters. An example of facts to be decided by a jury would be whether the zagger John Q. had been using at the time of the accident was defective. On the other hand, questions of law are the province of the judge. He explains to the jury any matters of law of which jurors must be aware in their decision making. This is exceedingly important when the jury must apply the law to the facts in a particular case. One example of that would be in a negligence case where the jury, after hearing all of the facts surrounding the event as well as having had negligence defined for them by the judge, would be required to decide if the defendant had been negligent or not. When there is no jury, Henry explained, the judge alone is the decision maker and decides both questions of law and fact.

Mary said it was her opinion that she would benefit more from having a jury—a number of persons who could identify with her and her situation—make the decision in her case. They would be more inclined, she believed, to consider the problems of a working-class family who had lost its husband and father in an industrial accident. A judge she felt, would probably be more interested in points of law.

"I have more faith in a jury," she concluded, "and I really wouldn't feel I had a fair trial without one."

Henry smiled. "Your belief in the jury system is shared by many," he replied. "Observers of Americans have commented that as a nation we regard the jury in much the same esteem as we do the right to vote—as a symbol of the democratic process. People in other countries do not view it in the same manner. In many cases, of course, this is because they have different legal systems. However, the jury system does have its critics. There have been suggestions for change, ranging all the way from dispensing with juries to use of only persons professionally trained as jurors. It is interesting that in one study of jury verdicts in civil matters,[2] judges agreed with the jury's decision in 80 per cent of the cases."

"I'm not interested in being part of the other 20 per cent," was Mary's response.

Preparation of Document

After Mary left his office, Henry gave his secretary a draft of the complaint for typing. While it was being prepared, he glanced at the morning newspaper. There was Will Very's picture on page one. He would be in Big City all week at the meeting of the Zagger Manufacturers Association where he was scheduled to be the principal speaker.

"What incredible luck," thought Henry. "I can have him served personally and will instruct the Clerk of Courts accordingly when I file the complaint."

As he signed the complaint, Henry Law realized that according to the Federal Rules his signature constituted certification by him that he had read the complaint and to the best of his knowledge, information, and belief there was good ground to support it. Thus, the attorney bears responsibility if a false or sham legal action is instituted. In contrast, the Great State rules of procedure required that a complaint be accompanied by an affidavit of the plaintiff swearing to the truth of the statements contained therein. Many other states follow that same practice.

Filing Complaint

Henry Law took two copies of the complaint to the office of the Clerk of Courts for the United States District Court for the Great State District. These he filed with the clerk and paid the filing fee. The clerk gave the case a number and entered the case on the court's *docket*. The docket is the formal record of the court's activities. It contains a record of all action taken on every case to come before it from inception to conclusion.

The clerk also assigned the case to Judge Fairness, since his name appeared on the first assignment card in the torts file. A block of these cards for each category of cases had been prepared in advance by the Clerk of Courts. The cards were numbered consecutively, and each bore the name of a judge. The order in which the judges' names appeared was a well-guarded secret, in keeping with the objective of random assignment of judges to cases. In following this assignment procedure, the Clerk of Courts was complying with the District Court's local procedure. Assignment of a case to a judge to follow from the very beginning to its final conclusion is known as the individual calendar system. This contrasts with the master calendar system, where different aspects of the same case—motions, pretrial conferences, and the trial itself—are handled by the judge assigned to that specific function. This means that several judges may handle portions of one legal action. More efficient disposition of the court's business is claimed by proponents of each system.

One copy of the complaint was retained by the clerk to be placed in a file that would be opened for the Mary Worker case. That file would contain all the important documents related to the case and would be kept in the office of the Clerk of Courts, the court officer responsible for the record-keeping function. The case number and judge's name were stamped on the file jacket, and notice of the assignment was sent to Judge Fairness.

The clerk also issued a summons. Henry delivered it together with the second copy of the complaint to the United States marshal for service on Zagger Supply, the defendant. That summons has been reproduced in Form 5-2.

Service of Process

The marshal, a federal officer whose duties are similar to those of a sheriff and who executes process for the federal courts, found Will Very at the convention.

"Mr. Will Very, president of Zagger Supply, Inc.?" he asked.

"Yes," was the reply. As the marshal handed him the complaint and summons, Will Very added, "What's this?"

"A summons issued by the United States District Court for the Great State Dis-

Form 5-2. Summons

DISTRICT COURT OF THE UNITED STATES
FOR THE DISTRICT OF GREAT STATE
Civil Action, File No. <u>XX-123</u>

MARY WORKER,	:	
Administratrix of the	:	
ESTATE OF JOHN Q.	:	
WORKER, deceased,	:	
Plaintiff	:	
	:	
v.	:	SUMMONS
	:	
ZAGGER SUPPLY, INC.,	:	
a corporation,	:	
Defendant	:	

To the above named Defendant:

You are hereby summond and required to serve upon Henry Law, plaintiff's attorney, whose address is <u>789 Main Street, Big City, Great State,</u> an answer to the complaint which is herewith served upon you, within <u>20</u> days after service of this summons upon you, exclusive of the day of service. If you fail to do so, judgment by default will be taken against you for the relief demanded in the complaint.

SEAL OF THE COURT

<u>*Clark Clerk*</u>
Clerk of Court

Dated: <u>November 21, 19XX</u>

Note: This summons is issued pursuant to Rule 4 of the Federal Rules of Civil Procedure.

---

trict together with a complaint filed in that court in a law suit instituted there against Zagger Supply, Inc. (Showing identification.) As a United States marshal, I am serving you with these papers."

"All right," was Will Very's only reply at that moment.

Service completed, the marshal filled out a "return" form, indicating that he had made service. He returned the form to the Clerk of Courts office where it was placed in the file for the case. Note in Figure 5-1 the activity generated by the complaint prepared by Henry.

Defendant's Reaction

Will Very's immediate reaction was to call W. E. Just and turn the entire matter over to him, repeating his earlier directive to "fight it."

W. E. read through the complaint Will Very forwarded to him. He then asked for the file of information regarding the zagger in the John Q. Worker incident that his paralegal assistant had compiled. A paralegal assistant is a lawyer's aide, much as a nurse is to a medical doctor. The paralegal, although not a lawyer nor a member of the bar, requires special training in legal matters and works directly with, but under the guidance and direction of, the attorney.

In that file was the factual information Attorney Just started to gather at the time he was asked to respond to Henry Law's letter requesting settlement: data regarding

Figure 5-1. Processing of the Complaint

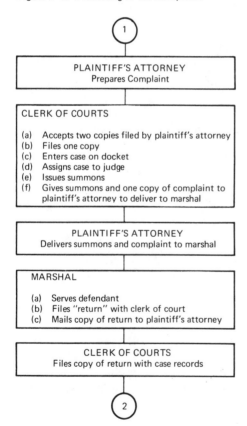

the order and sale of the special zaggers to The Firm, Inc.; the testing done at Zagger Supply prior to shipment of the order; findings by Acme Labs relative to the zagger fragments; statements of cypres engineers that shattering could result from improper mounting or momentary lapse of care; and Charles Sell's report of the accident investigation he conducted.

Third-party defendant   W. E. Just also engaged in researching the law, in the course of which he examined Great State law regarding employer liability in cases of industrial death. He found that there were specific statutory provisions which precluded any employer liability to third parties. He could not, therefore, even consider bringing in The Firm, Inc., as a *third-party defendant* in the case.

Had W. E. been able to do that, Zagger Supply, in addition to being the defendant in the case, would also have been a *third-party plaintiff.* As such, it would have asserted against The Firm a claim for damages arising out of the accident. This would mean that should the jury find that Mary Worker and her family were entitled to recover damages, the possibility existed that The Firm would have to pay some or all of the award. This would have involved questions of whether the two firms were joint *tortfeasors* (a *tortfeasor* being one who commits a tort); of whether there should be *contribution* (a pro-rata distribution of the loss among tortfeasors) or *indemnification* (repayment by the primary tortfeasor to the secondary tortfeasor for the entire loss). The procedure for bringing in a *third-party defendant* is for the defendant, as third-party plaintiff, to have a summons and third-party complaint served on the third-party defendant.

Attorney Just's decision   Unable to proceed in this fashion, Attorney Just made a list of the alternative courses of action open to him. That list appears in Table 5-2. W. E. really had little choice except to file an answer to the complaint. Failure to respond would be in direct contradiction to Will Very's order to "fight it," and he lacked the necessary grounds on which to base any of the listed motions.

Answer

W. E. therefore proceeded with preparation of the answer. In that answer he would respond to each allegation in the complaint. He noted the possible responses and their effect as follows:

1. Admit the allegations in the complaint. Admitted allegations would be considered as proved, and there would be no need to take them up at trial.
2. Deny the allegations in the complaint. This would create "issues" for trial; i.e., matters to be proved at trial.
3. Indicate the defendant presently lacked sufficient information to form a belief as to the truth of the allegations in the complaint. The effect would be the same as that of a denial.
4. Assert affirmative defenses. If these defenses were proved at trial, judgment could be for the defendant even if the plaintiff proved all of his allegations.

5. Assert the plaintiff failed to state a claim for which relief can be granted. If the court agrees with this assertion that there is no basis for any legal action, judgment will be for the defendant. This is similar to a "demurrer" used in some state courts.

After noting those allegations in the complaint to be admitted, those to be denied, and those for which he lacked sufficient information, W. E. was pleased that he could assert an affirmative defense.

Affirmative defense   The Great State Supreme Court in prior defective product cases had stated that "voluntarily and unreasonably proceeding to encounter a known danger, commonly known as assumption of the risk, is a defense as it is in other cases of strict liability." W. E. believed he had sufficient facts to be able to establish this defense. He would cite John Q.'s long experience as a cypres operator which should have made him aware of the hazards involved in working with zaggers. Furthermore, Charles Sell's report of the accident investigation contained pictures taken at the scene. These showed that the guard on John Q.'s machine had not been in its proper position. W. E. knew his case would be much stronger if he could go forward with positive assertions for the defense rather than just make denials of the allegations in the complaint.

TABLE 5–2. Attorney Just's List of Possible Responses to Plaintiff's Complaint

POSSIBLE ACTION	EFFECT OF ACTION
Do Nothing.	Failure to respond will result in judgment (the official decision of a court) against Zagger Supply by default. It indicates the defendant does not wish to contest. The effect is similar to an admission that the allegations made by the plaintiff in the complaint are true. The court will award the relief sought by the plaintiff in the complaint.
File written motions with the court prior to filing an answer:	Motions will precipitate a pretrial hearing before a judge who will determine whether to grant them after hearing arguments from both sides.
Motion requesting court to dismiss the action.	Motion will be granted and action will be dismissed if court finds there is lack of jurisdiction over subject matter, lack of jurisdiction over the defendant, improper venue, insufficiency of process, insufficiency of service of process, failure to state a claim upon which relief can be granted, failure to join an indispensable party.
Motion requesting court to order amendment of complaint.	If the motion is for a more definite statement and is granted, the court will order the plaintiff to amend the complaint to provide information sufficient to enable the defendant to respond.
Motion to strike.	If the motion is to strike and is granted, the court will order that scandalous, impertinent material be stricken from the complaint.
File an answer to the complaint in accordance with time requirements in the summons.	This will move the action closer to trial, although there still exists the possibility of disposition by pretrial motions. The answer may admit, deny, or assert defenses to allegations in the complaint, indicate lack of knowledge sufficient to form a belief as to the truth of the allegations, or enter a counterclaim against the plaintiff.

He also anticipated he would have a strong argument that the plaintiff lacked proof of proximate cause. If so, the plaintiff would be unable to prove a prima facie case. Therefore, W. E. would assert in his answer that the plaintiff failed to state a claim upon which relief can be granted.

Preparation and filing of documents   Having completed the foregoing thought process, W. E. Just prepared two documents. The first was a form stating that he was entering his appearance as legal counsel for the defendant. This served as notification of his association with the case. Since he was a member of the Great State bar, he did not have to secure a local associate counsel as required in the case of out-of-state lawyers. He served one copy on Henry Law by mail and he filed the second with the Clerk of Courts.

Next he prepared the answer. The completed document appears in Form 5-3.

Form 5-3. Answer

DISTRICT COURT OF THE UNITED STATES
FOR THE DISTRICT OF GREAT STATE

MARY WORKER,   :
   Administratrix of the   :
   ESTATE OF JOHN Q.   :
   WORKER, deceased,   :
          Plaintiff   :
                         :

          v.   :   Civil Action
                         :   No. XX-123
ZAGGER SUPPLY, INC.,   :
   a corporation,   :
          Defendant   :

ANSWER

Defendant, a corporation, by its attorneys files the following answer to the plaintiff's complaint:

FIRST DEFENSE

1. Defendant admits the averments in paragraphs 1 and 2 of plaintiff's complaints.
2. Defendant is presently without sufficient information to form a belief as to the truth of the averments in paragraphs 3, 4, 5, and 6 of plaintiff's complaint.
3. Defendant denies the averments in paragraphs 7, 8, and 9 of plaintiff's complaint.

4. In response to averments in paragraph 10 of plaintiff's complaint, defendant incorporates herein and re-iterates paragraphs 1 through 3 of this answer.

5. Defendant denies the averments in paragraph 11 of plaintiff's complaint.

SECOND DEFENSE

6. Plaintiff's complaint fails to state a cause of action upon which recovery can be had by the plaintiff and against the defendant.

THIRD DEFENSE

7. If John Q. Worker's death was caused by defendant's acts as alleged in plaintiff's complaint, John Q. Worker voluntarily assumed the risk.

W. E. Just
_____
Attorney for the Defendant

Zagger Building
That City, Nearby State

CERTIFICATE OF SERVICE

The undersigned hereby certifies that service of the foregoing Defendant's Answer to Plaintiff's Complaint was made on counsel for the plaintiff, Henry Law, 789 Main Street, Big City, Great State, by registered mail return receipt requested.

W. E. Just
_____
W. E. Just

December 3, 19XX

In accordance with the Federal Rules, Attorney Just served one copy of the answer on Henry Law by mail and filed the second copy with the Clerk of Courts. This copy was added to the file of the Mary Worker case.

Henry Law read through the answer when it arrived. He found nothing there that he had not anticipated.

Except in cases in which the court orders a reply to an answer or there is a counterclaim or cross-claim, the complaint and answer constitute the pleadings. That was true in this case. Amendments to the pleadings are permitted. However, at this time neither of the parties in the case had cause to consider amendments.

Judgment on the Pleadings

Another possible step at this stage of the proceedings would be for either of the parties to make a motion for a judgment on the pleadings. This can be done when the pleadings show that both parties agree as to the facts in the matter and the only questions remaining are questions of law. A judge can then make a determination and render a judgment without trial. The reason for this is that, as Henry Law had explained to Mary Worker, questions of law are for the judge while the jury is the trier of fact. A judgment on the pleadings, therefore, will not be granted in cases in which there are genuine issues as to material facts. If the matter in the pleadings is supplemented by other matters, such as information in an affidavit, the motion is treated as one for summary judgment.

However, both parties in this case realized there were definite issues of fact involved. One look at the answer reveals many denials, so that the factual issues are apparent from the face of the document. Therefore, each of the parties now began to concentrate on the next stage in the legal process, discovery.

Historical Perspective

As Henry Law reflected on the present status of the case, he considered the changes that had occurred over the years in the pleading process and in its objectives. He recalled a conversation he had with his secretary, Albert, at the time the complaint for the Mary Worker case was being prepared. With the rough draft in hand prior to typing, Albert had come into his office to ask if Henry did not wish the complaint to state the action was being brought in trespass.

"No," was the response, "notice pleading is sufficient in the federal courts as contrasted with the common law pleading we do in the Great State courts." It was apparent at once that Albert had not understood this reply. Since Albert was also a law student, Henry asked if he would not like to take five minutes for a short discussion of the different kinds of pleadings.

"I believe it will be easier to understand if I can show you how the pleadings evolved historically," Henry began. "As you know, the heritage of the American legal system is the old English common law as distinguished from the civil or code system which exists in most western European nations. The common law emerged following the Norman Conquest during a feudal period when large landholders presided as lords over their manors, and the king reigned supreme over all. The allegiance owed by the lords to the king created a unified organization with central control in the monarch. Many believe that without this social structure an unwritten law based on precedent created by decisions in ad hoc disputes could not have developed."

"Another example of how law and the social order are intertwined?" Albert asked.

"Yes, and the court system and legal procedures that emerged very clearly reflect this. For instance, each lord dispensed justice and presided over the court of his manor. The king, however, was acknowledged as the source of all justice. Disputes between lords or appeals from the decisions of the lords on extraordinary matters were referred to him. As the volume of work increased, he delegated more and more to his subordinates. There eventually emerged a king's court presided over by appointed officials. However, access to that court was only by writ, a written order granting one the privilege of having the court hear his case. Each different type of law suit had its own specific writ. Thus, there evolved a classification system for legal actions. From that emerged the requirement that pleadings had to be prepared according to the form of action or the pigeon hole into which the case was classified. There were a great many of these, some of which are still retained today in states that follow the common law system of pleading. For instance, in Great State we still use:

1. Assumpsit—the form of action for breach of contract;
2. Replevin—the form of action to recover personal property wrongfully taken;
3. Case—the form of action to recover damages for an indirect injury to property;
4. Trespass—the form of action to recover damages caused by injury to the plaintiff. This was originally known as trespass *vi et armis* to distinguish it from other actions of trespass. Many laymen recognize the word only in connection with the tort of trespass."

"You mean, when people talk about trespassing on their neighbor's property—?"

"Yes, there's both a tort of trespass and a common law form of action known as trespass. As I was saying, the early common law had categories of trespass. As you can see, it was a very elaborate classification system. However, that system not only resulted in making pleading a very technical exercise, but was deficient also in that it did not provide a classification for every possible matter for which the citizenry looked to the courts for resolution. For instance, if a person wished a court to order another person to refrain from engaging in certain activity—to secure an injunction—there was no writ for this. Therefore, one had no way of getting the court's help in that situation. In other words, there was no remedy at law.

"The only recourse in that case would be to appeal directly to the king for justice or equity. In the course of time, the king delegated this function to his Chancellor. As the number of such appeals increased, there developed a Court of Chancery. Resort to it was possible only when there was no remedy in a court of law, or when the remedy at law was inadequate. In the case of a breach of contract, for instance, the injured party could recover money damages in a court of law, but only in a court of chancery could he secure an order for specific performance, that is, secure performance according to the contract terms."

"That sounds very much like the actions in equity we have today," said Albert.

"Equitable remedies, such as the injunction and specific performance, aren't granted if there's a remedy at law which is adequate to meet the situation. And I've read some decisions in equity where the judge is referred to as the chancellor."

"That's right," Henry replied. "The courts of chancery eventually became known as courts of equity. There are other practices we still retain in equity. For instance, the Court of Chancery operated much more informally than did a court of law. Writs were not required, and there was no jury. Concern was with 'what ought to be done in order to render justice'."

"All of which is still true."

"Yes, and there also evolved a number of rules, known as equitable maxims. They are still used today as the basis for decisions rendered in actions in equity."

"Some of them come to mind immediately:

He who comes into equity must do so with clean hands.

He who seeks equity must do equity.

Equity will not suffer a right to exist without a remedy.

Equity aids the vigilant.

Equity regards as done that which ought to be done."

"Right," was Henry's response. "The outgrowth of this was the development, side by side, of two court systems: courts of law and courts of chancery. Both the common law system of pleading forms of action as well as the system of separate courts for law and equity were brought to this country by the early English settlers. The one exception occurred in Louisiana, where the French influence resulted in a system of law based upon the civil or code system.

"One of the steps toward change to what we have today occurred around 1848 when code pleading was introduced in New York state. The many different common law forms of action were eliminated and replaced by just one form of civil action at law. This makes it possible for the plaintiff to recover on any legal theory applicable to the facts pleaded and proved. In addition, law and equity were merged so that the same court can hear a case whether it is brought at law or equity."

"In other words, the legal process was simplified by combining the actions at law and then bringing law and equity together in one court."

"Yes. Additional simplification followed. An important development occurred in 1938 when the Federal Rules were adopted. They streamlined the pleading process by providing for notice pleading. That means it is necessary to plead only those circumstances or events necessary to inform the other party of the incident for which he is being sued. The gathering of detailed facts is left for other pretrial activity. The object of pleading is simply to put the other party on notice. In this it differs from both common law and code pleading, where the goal is to formulate the legal issues in the pleadings. As a result, those systems of pleading require that facts be pleaded in support of each of the elements constituting the cause of action.

"Today many of the states have revised their rules of procedure to conform with the federal rules. A few, such as Great State, still follow a revised form of common law pleading. Others, such as Nearby State, use code or fact pleading."

"Hasn't anyone proposed a uniform system? It seems to me that would make things a lot easier," was Albert's response.

"I agree," said Henry. "We have made progress with other uniform laws, the most notable success being the Uniform Commercial Code. That has been adopted by the legislatures of all the states (but only partly in Louisiana). Many believe this result was achieved since the UCC is concerned with sales, secured transactions, commercial paper, investment securities, and other business matters. Businessmen, concerned about the effect of differences in state laws on interstate commercial transactions, were convinced that uniformity was a necessity. Of course, we also have other uniform laws, such as the Uniform Partnership Act, which the majority of the states have adopted. There is also some uniformity which is an indirect result of the 'model acts,' which have been developed by the American Law Institute as guides or patterns which the various state legislatures can follow in enacting legislation. Some similarity is assured when a number of states use the Model Penal Act or the Model Business Corporation Act, for instance, in writing legislation. Additional uniform state laws would truly be a boon and reduce problems arising because of conflict of laws."

"The mention of all those acts makes me realize that we have a great deal of statutory law in our common law system."

"Yes," replied Henry, "but the general policy is still that 'statutes in derogation of the common law' are to be strictly construed. Therefore, while the provisions of a statute may supersede conflicting provisions found in the common law, the latter still prevails when the written law's provisions are not specific."

"So that the common law really fills in any gaps in the statutory law."

At this point their conversation about the historical development of pleadings, common law, equity, and uniform written laws came to an end. Albert commented that the historical perspective increased one's understanding of why certain procedures, such as discovery, are presently in effect.

DISCOVERY

Discovery refers to the process of securing relevant information regarding an impending suit, a process engaged in after completion of the pleadings and prior to trial. Each party to an action may use the mechanisms of discovery to secure all the relevant information possessed by any persons, including the opposing party. Failure to provide requested information can lead to being held in contempt of court. Some matter remains privileged, however, and a protective order may be secured from the court limiting or barring discovery of such material. Examples include matter coming within the attorney-client privilege, the work product of the attorney, and that which would be self-incriminatory in a criminal matter. Protection from discovery of unrelated matter or for harassment purposes is also available. The *Dorsey Trailers* decision which follows provides further details regarding items that may be excluded from discovery.

Ex Parte Dorsey Trailers, Inc.
397 So.2d 98 (Ala.) 1981

Dorsey Trailers, Inc. sought a court order to compel answers to interrogatories by plaintiff, administratrix of estate of deceased who was killed when a steel drum he was cutting with a circular saw exploded.

EMBRY, J. . . .

Generally speaking, the purpose of modern discovery is to assist the administration of justice, to aid a party in preparing and presenting his case or his defense, to advance the function of a trial in ascertaining truth, and to accelerate the disposition of suits. Beyond this, the rules for discovery are designed to eliminate, as far as possible, concealment and surprise in the trial of lawsuits to the end that judgments be rested upon the real merits of cases and not upon the skill and maneuvering of counsel. Stated otherwise, the rules seek to "make a trial less a game of blindman's bluff and more a fair contest with the basic issues and facts disclosed to the fullest practicable extent." . . .

. . . Discovery is not limited to matters competent as evidence at trial. "Relevancy," as used in our discovery rules, means relevant to the subject matter of the action and a reasonable possibility that the information sought will lead to other evidence that will be admissible.

Several of petitioner's interrogatories requested information on the physical, mental and medical history of the deceased, including such pertinent matters as visual impairment. Petitioner contends this information, in conjunction with questions about the deceased's educational background and work history, is relevant to the ability of the deceased to perceive and appreciate the danger of his task and to read and understand any warning labels which may have been on the drum. Plaintiff's response to these interrogatories was "not answered on advice of counsel" . . .

Given the purpose and broad scope of discovery, petitioner was clearly entitled to the information concerning the physical, mental and medical background of the deceased. It is not the prerogative of a party answering interrogatories to refuse to answer because of his opinion regarding the usefulness of the information sought or its relative benefit or harm to the parties involved. . . .

Available information which an answering party is under a duty to disclose also includes facts discovered and opinions held by his own expert witnesses. . . .

All told, 37 of the 50 interrogatories propounded by petitioner received responses from plaintiff that the matter had already been covered by the complaint or by deposition, that the question was not answered on advice of counsel, or simply stating the word "answered." A reading of the remaining 13 answers reveals that several are nonresponsive, incomplete or evasive.

Such disregard of the principles of law governing discovery . . . cannot be overlooked by this court. To permit this case to proceed to trial without requiring further answers from plaintiff to petitioner's interrogatories would contravene the purpose of the rules of discovery and might cause petitioner to suffer grave injustice. The bounds of the trial court's discretion to compel or deny discovery are broad. However, in this case those bounds have been overstepped. *Reversed.*

The concept of discovery represents a distinct departure from the old common law and from the impression sometimes created by television courtroom drama, which features the last-minute surprise witness who saves the hero or heroine from certain defeat. It is the purpose of discovery to avoid surprise at trial and to give each party an opportunity to evaluate both their own and the other side's case prior to trial. This enables each to be better prepared and results in improving the quality of the trial process itself. It makes possible collection of information by less formal, less expensive, and less time-consuming methods than characterize the securing of information at the trial itself. Possession of more and better information prior to trial also enables the parties to refine the issues at that point in time. It often leads to pretrial settlement because the parties are each aware of the other's case. Information obtained through discovery may be used at trial in accordance with the provisions of the rules of procedure and the rules of evidence.

Rules 26 through 37 of the Federal Rules of Civil Procedure deal with discovery. Similar rules have been adopted by almost all the states. It was the Federal Rules that both W. E. Just and Henry Law consulted. They also checked the *local rules* of the Great State District Court. Local rules are those prepared by and for use at a particular court. They supplement applicable federal or state rules.

Each attorney now sought information about witnesses, records, or reports that would provide data related to the law suit and that would help him meet his burden of proof. As the plaintiff's advocate, Henry Law was concerned with being able to establish a prima facie case and with being able to rebut any defenses raised by his opponent. W. E. Just, representing the defendant, contemplated how he could not only refute the plaintiff's case but also prove affirmative defenses. Hence each attorney was concerned not just with presentation of his own case, but also with being prepared for what his adversary would do.

The two attorneys mentally asked themselves the same questions:

—What information do I need?
—Who has it?
—Where can it be found?
—How can I get it?

A large data collection process seemed imminent. Where and how would each attorney begin?

Each had his own list of desiderata, a list which would be reviewed and revised as he learned more about what information was available and what his opponent knew. Each prepared his list with the realization he must acquire factual information sufficient to meet his burden of proof. Therefore, it was no haphazard compilation that took place, but rather one accompanied by careful consideration of the pleadings, jurisdictional requirements, and the elements of action brought under §402A, as well as wrongful death and survival action.

Each attorney planned to secure the information he needed by making use of the same means of discovery: interrogatories, depositions, and production of documents. Each also chose to begin his discovery with interrogatories.

Interrogatories

The Federal Rules provide that one party may serve upon any other party written questions (*interrogatories*) to be answered under oath by the party served. It is an inexpensive method of eliciting information from one's opponent. Interrogatories are often used, as was true in the Mary Worker case, as the initial means of discovery for learning names of witnesses and experts, the existence of records and reports, as well as additional sources of information which the other party has. It is then possible to follow up the answers with either additional interrogatories or with other means of discovery.

One advantage of the interrogatory to people answering is that they have time to reflect upon their answers. Help in framing those answers is not precluded. An obvious disadvantage to the questioning party is the inability to follow up an incomplete or evasive answer with another question, as is possible when interrogation is oral. Another limitation is that it is not available for use with witnesses who are not parties to the action.

Interrogatories are prepared by the attorney and are served either by mailing or delivering them to the attorney for the other party. (Should there be more than two parties to an action, all other parties must receive a copy not only of the questions when submitted but also of the answers.) The Great State District local rules provided that the Clerk of Courts receive written notification when and upon whom interrogatories are served, that interrogatories be prepared with space for answers to be inserted following each question, and that at least three copies be served upon the answering party. They further required that when answers have been inserted, one copy of the completed document must be filed with the Clerk of Courts, one copy returned to the discovering party (and to any other parties), and the final copy retained by the party providing the answers. In this way, every party to the action, as well as the court, is aware at all times of the status of the action being taken.

When interrogatories are received by an attorney, the party involved is informed and generally receives assistance from his attorney in preparation of the answers. Both the signature and affidavit of the party to whom the interrogatories have been directed are required on the answers. Objections to questions may be made by the attorney of the party being questioned. In that case, reasons for the objection are stated in lieu of an answer to the question, and the attorney's signature to the objections is required.

Both W. E. Just and Henry Law prepared interrogatories. Because each party's interrogatories were rather extensive, only portions of the one prepared by W. E. Just have been reproduced in Form 5-4 as an illustration.

It was from answers to interrogatories that W. E. Just learned about plaintiff's witnesses, Leader and O'Goode, and of the testing done by Professor Learned. Thus, the use of the interrogatories had been very worthwhile for him. He had no idea what Leader, O'Goode, or Learned knew or would testify to at the trial. Their testimony might aid his case. On the other hand, it might be devastatingly damaging. Therefore, he realized he could not afford to take the chances attendant with not knowing, and decided to take the depositions of all three.

While he made preparations to do this, Henry Law was contemplating the questions for the interrogatories to be directed to Zagger Supply. In the case of corporations (or other forms of organization), interrogatories may be served upon any officer or agent.

Form 5-4. Interrogatory

DISTRICT COURT OF THE UNITED STATES
FOR THE DISTRICT OF GREAT STATE

MARY WORKER,   :
    Administratrix of the   :
    ESTATE OF JOHN Q.   :
    WORKER, deceased,   :
        Plaintiff   :
                                 :
        v.   :   Civil Action
                                 :   No. XX-123
ZAGGER SUPPLY, INC.,   :
    a corporation,   :
        Defendant   :

INTERROGATORY TO PLAINTIFF

Defendant above named pursuant to Rule 33 of the Federal Rules of Civil Procedure demands that the plaintiff, Mary Worker, Administratrix of the Estate of John Q. Worker, deceased, make full and complete answers under oath to the following interrogatories within the time required by the Rules.

1. State names and present addresses of all witnesses to the events immediately preceding alleged accident which are known to plaintiff, plaintiff's attorneys, agents, investigators, or other representatives.

2. State names and present addresses of all witnesses to the alleged accident which are known to plaintiff, plaintiff's attorneys, agents, investigators, or other representatives.

3. State names and present addresses of all witnesses to the events immediately subsequent to the alleged accident which are known to plaintiff, plaintiff's attorneys, agents, investigators, or other representatives.

. . . .

7. Was plaintiff's decedent employed at the time of the alleged accident? If so, state the name and present address of said employer, nature of duties performed for said employer, length of such employment, and amount of

hourly, daily, weekly, or monthly wages or salary
received from said employer.

8. State the total amount of income earned by plaintiff's
decedent for each of the four calendar years immediately
preceding the alleged accident and the year of said
accident.

. . . .

12. State specifically each and every manufacturing
defect referred to in Paragraphs seven and eight of
plaintiff's complaint.

13. State the name and address of each and every
expert whom you have had examine fragments of the zagger
in question and/or similar zaggers and/or who may have
given you an opinion without an examination of the zagger,
setting forth the area of expertise of said expert.

. . . .

The firm must then designate an officer or agent to answer for it. There is a duty to provide all information known to corporate personnel or determinable without undue burden. Henry Law prepared questions concerned with such matters as the manufacture, sale, and testing of the zagger; defendant's awareness of any defect in the zagger; and witnesses, including experts.

Depositions

As might be expected, consultation in connection with answering this set of interrogatories required a great deal of W. E. Just's time. He was happy he had planned for the first taking of *depositions* to occur several weeks in the future, since his notices of intent to depose had crossed Henry Law's interrogatories in the mail. A copy of the notice regarding the Robert Leader deposition appears in Form 5-5. Notice to all parties is required prior to deposition taking and is served upon the party's attorney.

Had Robert Leader been a party to the action, the notice would have been sufficient to require his attendance. Since he was not, W. E. Just requested that a subpoena be served upon Leader. He did this at the time he filed a copy of the notice with the Clerk of Courts. Similar procedure was followed with both O'Goode and Learned, except that a *subpoena duces tecum* was served on the professor. While a subpoena commands the person to whom it is directed to attend and give testimony at the time and place specified, a *subpoena duces tecum* commands that, in addition, the person bring with him documents or materials in his possession. It was the test report prepared by Professor Learned that W. E. Just wished to obtain.

Form 5-5.   Notice of Deposition

DISTRICT COURT OF THE UNITED STATES
FOR THE DISTRICT OF GREAT STATE

MARY WORKER,   :
   Administratrix of the   :
ESTATE OF JOHN Q.   :
   WORKER, deceased,   :
      Plaintiff   :

             :
       v.   :   Civil Action
             :   No. XX-123

ZAGGER SUPPLY, INC.,   :
   a corporation,   :
      Defendant   :

NOTICE OF DEPOSITION

To: Henry Law, Attorney for the Plaintiff

   Take notice that the deposition of Robert Leader will be
taken for the purpose of discovery and for use at trial
pursuant to Rule 26 of the Federal Rules of Civil
Procedure, as amended, before a notary public duly
authorized by law to administer oaths, on Thursday, the
29th day of December, 19XX at 4:00 PM at the offices of
Clyde Partner, Attorney at Law, Lawyers Building, Big
City, Great State, at which time and place you are invited
to appear and take such part as shall be fitting and proper.
   The scope and purpose of this deposition is to inquire
into the facts and circumstances surrounding the accident
in suit, including the identity and whereabouts of other
witnesses.

                  By _*W. E. Just*_
                       Attorney for the Defendant

      The depositions were scheduled to be held in the Big City law offices of Clyde
Partner, who often did legal work for Zagger Supply. Everyone involved except W. E. Just
was located in Big City. In addition to convenience, the location enabled compliance with
the Federal Rules that require that depositions be taken either in the county in which the

deponent can be served (or within 40 miles of the place of service). Local County was where all three deponents lived and worked.

When Timothy O'Goode asked Robert Leader about the subpoena and the deposition, the men discovered their depositions were scheduled two days apart. Both decided they should consult Henry Law. He explained that deposition taking meant they would be questioned by the defendant's attorney after an oath had been administered to them. Henry Law would be present. He would not only have the right to cross-examine but also to raise objections to improper questions. The entire session would be recorded by a court reporter, who would probably also administer the oath. A transcript would be prepared later. Both deponents would be given the opportunity to read it through before signing. The answers given would be important. They could be introduced at the trial itself and used for such purposes as contradicting testimony the men gave at trial. On the other hand, if they could not be present at the trial because of death or serious illness, the deposition—or parts of it—could be read into the trial record.

Timothy asked if Henry Law knew what questions would be asked. Henry's reply was that he did not know the specific questions. His best estimate was that each man could expect to be asked about the following:

1. Details of the accident, including what occurred just before and after;
2. Explanation of the operation of the cypres machine and especially the use of zaggers on the machine.

"In general," he said, "I would say that you can expect questions very similar to the ones I have been asking you in our conversations."

"It sounds just like being on the witness stand," was Robert's comment.

"Yes," Henry agreed, "that's why the oral deposition is so popular as a discovery mechanism. An attorney can learn a lot more through it than he can by using written depositions."

"I thought the written ones are called interrogatories," Robert commented.

"There are differences," was the reply. Henry Law went on to explain that depositions are not restricted to parties but may be taken of any person. In the case of written depositions, the questions are answered before an examining officer who also administers the oath. Cross, redirect, and recross questions may be served later, thus providing some resemblance to the examination possible at the oral deposition taking.

The taking of the depositions of Timothy O'Goode and Robert Leader went very much as Henry Law had predicted. Each lasted approximately an hour. Both men were questioned in detail concerning their recollection of John Q.'s actions: what he did with the zagger, the manner in which he placed it on the machine, how he had checked his machine prior to starting it up, whether the guard was in place, etc. Neither could state definitely that he positively remembered seeing John Q. go through each of the motions involved. However, each said he was confident that John Q., known as a skilled worker who had never had a prior accident, had followed his usual careful pattern of operation. W. E. Just did elicit the fact that there was more than the usual amount of conversation and some air of excitement because of the start of production of the new chattel.

Asked about the new zaggers he had used, Timothy O'Goode testified that he was extremely careful with them. None that he had used had shattered; however, several other cypres operators assigned to production of the new chattel had experienced shattering. The shatterings were not of the violent, explosive type, and no one had been seriously injured. Timothy also stated the new zaggers were not tight fitting and that "you have to be careful to get it on the machine right or the zagger will wobble once you start up the machine."

"And what happens if the zagger wobbles?" W. E. Just wanted to know.

"At high-speed operations, the zaggers shatter," Timothy responded.

Robert testified that he had never been assigned to work on the new chattels.

Following the two depositions, the attorneys began to see their arguments emerging more clearly. Henry Law knew he would have to concentrate on failure of the zagger to meet OSHA standards as proof of a dangerously defective product. W. E. Just was interested in the hubbub surrounding the start of production of the new chattel and John Q.'s knowing use of the zagger without the guard in place on his machine. Each attorney now waited to see what other discovery would reveal.

Just as the depositions of Mary Worker's witnesses proved helpful to W. E. Just, the interrogatories and depositions taken by Henry Law were rewarding to him. Answers to his interrogatories revealed the existence of a number of documents which he believed he should have, such as the report of the testing done at Zagger Supply prior to shipment of the special purpose zaggers, the purchase order and accompanying correspondence for special purpose zaggers for The Firm. Henry also wished to have Professor Learned analyze the fragments in Zagger Supply's possession, and test other zaggers manufactured for The Firm under the special order.

Production of Documents

Consequently, Henry decided to make use of still another form of discovery: request to another party for production of documents and other items in his possession and control. It can also be used to request entry upon the premises of the other party for the purpose of inspection, photographing, sampling, copying, and the like. This mechanism is available only when the item is in the possession of a person who is a party to the action.

A request to the other party is all that is necessary. Therefore, Henry Law prepared the request to produce, portions of which appear in Form 5–6. One copy he mailed to Zagger Supply, the second he filed with the Clerk of Courts.

The Zagger Supply response was prompt and provided Henry with the requested material. Armed with the knowledge acquired in this way, Henry Law embarked upon his own deposition taking.

Additional Depositions

The deposing of Charles Sell revealed that he was thoroughly acquainted with The Firm's operations. He visited frequently with Sam Scott and Jim Boss since Zagger Supply was The Firm's major supplier of zaggers. He acknowledged the special order and admitted there had been dynamic testing of only half a dozen of the special purpose

DISTRICT COURT OF THE UNITED STATES
FOR THE DISTRICT OF GREAT STATE

MARY WORKER,   :
   Administratrix of the   :
   ESTATE OF JOHN Q.   :
   WORKER, deceased,   :
         Plaintiff   :
                           :   Civil Action
          v.   :   No. XX-123
                           :
ZAGGER SUPPLY, INC.,   :
   a corporation,   :
         Defendant   :

REQUEST TO PRODUCE

Plaintiff above named hereby requests pursuant to Rule 34 of the Federal Rules of Civil Procedure that defendant, Zagger Supply, Inc., a corporation,

(1) produce and permit plaintiff to inspect and to copy each of the following documents:

      a. reports of tests conducted by defendant on the special zaggers manufactured for The Firm, Inc., and shipped to them in August, 19XX under special order #98765;

    . . . .

(2) produce and permit plaintiff to inspect and to photograph each of the following objects:

      a. fragments of zagger #XXX secured from The Firm, Inc., the day following the accident in which John Q. Worker was killed;

    . . . .

It is requested that the aforesaid production be made on the day of December 15, 19XX, at two o'clock in the P. M. at the offices of Henry Law, Esq., 789 Main Street, Big City, Great State.

By *Henry Law*
           Attorney for the Plaintiff

           789 Main Street
           Big City, Great State

zaggers. This, he said, was unusual. It occurred because they were behind schedule and the static testing which had been done on all the special-purpose zaggers showed no abnormalities. Henry was interested in pursuing claims made by Zagger Supply in its sales literature regarding bonding defects. Charles Sell testified that Zagger Supply used a patented process in manufacturing zaggers, which resulted in fewer than the industry average number of bonding defects. Their experience record was for such a defect to show up approximately five times in every 10,000 zaggers. The industry statistics, he said, were five in every 1000.

He acknowledged that it would be most unusual for zagger users to test them after purchase. It was the custom in the industry and at The Firm to rely upon manufacturer testing. He also testified that Zagger Supply packed the special-purpose zaggers and delivered them to The Firm's supply department. His investigation following the accident revealed they had been stored under ideal conditions. He admitted to Henry Law that those in the supply department were in substantially the same condition as when shipped.

"Would the zagger John Q. used also have been in substantially the same condition as when shipped?" he was asked.

"Yes," he replied, "unless at the last minute John Q. did something unusual to it or with it."

"Did your investigation reveal any evidence of that?"

His answer was in the negative.

No separate instructions had been prepared regarding use of the special purpose zaggers, he said, since they would not have differed from those for other zaggers. In response to Henry Law's question, he indicated that Zagger Supply normally printed warnings and instructions on its zagger labels. It also cooperated with the Zagger Institute in producing a safety film regarding proper use of zaggers. A copy of the film had been furnished to The Firm and was used by their safety department. Charles said that on several occasions he had been the speaker at safety meetings for cypres operators at The Firm where the film had been shown.

Henry Law mentally debated whether to depose next the Zagger Supply cypres engineer or Sam Scott. It developed that Sam's time commitments resulted in his being scheduled first.

It was a revealing deposition, particularly with regard to the pictures taken after the accident. They showed that there was no guard on John Q.'s machine. Sam stated that guards are bolted to the framework of cypres machines so they cannot be removed easily. However, they must be taken off when a new zagger is installed. He stressed that company safety instructions were explicit in their directive to operators regarding replacement of the guard as soon as a zagger was installed. Asked if the guard could not have been removed after the accident, Sam indicated there had not been sufficient time for anyone to do so before the pictures were taken. He also stated it was his firm conviction that the guard would have been strong enough to stop the flying zagger fragments.

"Even in the case of a shattering of such tremendous force as has been described in this situation?" he was asked. His answer was "yes."

Henry Law asked if fragments could not have come out of the opening in the guard in front where the chattel came in contact with the zagger.

"No one can answer that for sure. It's a 45-degree opening—a small one—some fragments could come out, but they'd have to be small."

"But the more violent the shattering the greater the likelihood that some would come out?"

"Yes."

"And they would come out in the direction in which the machine operator was standing?"

"Yes, provided he was standing in the normal position—directly in front of the machine." In response to Henry's next question, Sam stated that no one had been able to determine just where John Q. had been standing at the time the accident occurred.

"No," Sam replied when asked if he knew of any reason why John Q. would have been in an other-than-normal position.

"And this opening in the guard—its distance from the floor—would you say it would be about waist high for a man of John Q.'s height?"

"Just about—yes."

He testified that the machine setting indicated John Q. had set the speed for that normally expected and anticipated for work on the new chattels.

With regard to the condition of the cypres machine, Sam replied that it had undergone a complete overhaul three days before the accident since it was to be used for the new chattels.

The deposition of Professor Learned was next. W. E. Just received no comfort from learning through interrogatories that Professor Learned was the plaintiff's expert and was expected to testify at trial. Professor Learned was recognized in the industry as the foremost zagger expert in the country, and W. E. Just would rather have had so formidable an authority in his corner than in his opponent's. He realized the vital importance of learning what the Professor knew about the situation by deposing him.

Professor Learned testified that he had examined the zagger fragments, was positively able to identify them as parts of the shattered zagger, and had definite proof of defectiveness in the zagger bonding which was directly atrributable to the manufacturing process. He further stated that the defect was latent but could and should have been discovered through required dynamic testing before the zaggers left the manufacturer, that the reason for the dynamic testing requirement was to prevent just such shattering as had occurred, and that he was not only familiar with the standards of OSHA and the Zagger Institute but had been chairperson of the committee of experts who wrote them. W. E. Just asked Professor Learned about the possibility of shattering from improper placement of a zagger on the cypres machine. Professor Learned replied that a zagger not properly clamped on the machine would begin to wobble.

"And the effect of the wobbling?" W. E. began to ask.

"Sometimes—especially if the machine is just being started up and if it is being operated at a relatively low speed—the zagger will right itself, and—"

"Does wobbling ever lead to shattering?" W. E. wanted to know.

"Yes," said Professor Learned, "if the machine is being operated in excess of the maximum safe speeds for that particular zagger or if the zagger is not of the correct size and cannot be made to fit properly on the machine."

W. E. asked if the shattering of the zagger in this case could have been caused by wobbling. Professor Learned was emphatic in his reply:

"The shattering in this case was caused by a defective zagger."

"You are positive that the bonding defect was the one and only possible cause of the shattering?"

"It is the most probable cause. No one can say with absolute certainty that other defects were not present and did not also contribute to the accident. What one can say with certainty is that some combination of defects, which included the bonding, caused the shattering."

When queried about the guard, the professor's testimony was much more positive than that of Sam Scott. The former was of the opinion that there was no question but that the violence of the shattering had been such that fragments would have been propelled with great force through the guard opening, resulting in the fatal injury to John Q. At this point he became quite didactic and ignored Henry's earlier request that he not volunteer information.

"It is common knowledge in the industry," he said, "that machine operators are at times in a hurry or impatient or even careless. Sometimes they leave guards off their machines; sometimes they do not clamp their zaggers into position firmly. That is why the present zagger standards were put into effect as requirements. We have the technical ability today—through proper testing—to eliminate from use those zaggers that do not have the necessary qualities to withstand use without shattering under such adverse conditions. Testing will reveal defects—bonding, size, others—that lead to violent shattering. Zaggers that do not meet such standards are dangerous to human life. There is no need— no excuse—for a death such as the one in this case."

W. E. blanched, but quickly recovered. "Can you say positively, Professor, that a zagger that has been subjected to the required testing will never shatter?"

"Since the standards went into effect just about a year ago, there has not been a single shattering incident reported with zaggers that have been subjected to the required testing."

When the deposition taking was concluded, W. E. mentally noted that his prior assessment of this witness as formidable had indeed been correct.

Professor Learned's testimony was in part confirmed by the Zagger Supply cypres engineer and the Acme Lab zagger research engineer, whose depositions Henry Law took several weeks later. Differences did exist, however, with regard to their opinions as to the cause of the shattering. The cypres engineer testified that improper placement of the zagger on the machine and failure of the operator to concentrate completely on the job at hand were the most probable causes of the shattering. He also believed that serious injury could and would have been prevented had the guard been in position on John Q.'s machine. The Acme Lab test engineer did not believe that the bonding defect could have resulted in the violent shattering which had characterized this incident. He stated that improper clamping was one of the most common causes of the very explosive type of shattering.

Henry Law also deposed Peter Superior, who seemed reluctant to discuss the accident. His major contribution was his testimony that there had been five additional shatterings involving the new zaggers in the department he had supervised. While none of these had been serious, the number was a distinct increase over a five-year record of only one or two shatterings a year with the regular zaggers. He also admitted to W. E. Just, on cross-examination, that there had been a general atmosphere of exhilaration in the department that day as John Q. started on the new chattels.

Both attorneys carefully studied transcripts of the depositions. A copy had been prepared for each of the parties and one had been filed with the Clerk of Courts.

Request for Admissions

Use of two other possible discovery mechanisms was ruled out by both attorneys. One of those methods is the written request for admission of any matters within the scope of discovery. It may be served by one party upon any other party. Answers are required. However, if the request relates to a matter that is a genuine issue for trial, the matter may either be denied or the reasons for not answering set forth. Both Henry Law and W. E. Just decided they would forego requests for admissions at this stage. Since this was not a law suit where the mental or physical condition of one of the parties was in controversy, the use of either a mental or physical examination as a discovery mechanism was not appropriate.

Narrowing Issues

Studying the information they now possessed, both attorneys gave thoughtful consideration to whether they had all the relevant and necessary facts. Checking their lists of information to be secured, they found that discovery had not only served its purpose of providing necessary information but also of narrowing the issues. Table 5-3 indicates the status of the major facts and questions following discovery. It is clear from the table that, at this point in time, many facts were no longer in dispute. These would be admitted (or stipulated) prior to trial. In fact, that would be one of the items on the agenda for the forthcoming pretrial conference. Use of discovery in the civil process has been flow charted in Figure 5-2.

TABLE 5-3. Status of Issues after Discovery

MATTERS SETTLED AND NOT AT ISSUE	MATTERS STILL AT ISSUE
Questions of jurisdiction	Zagger was dangerously defective
Defendant engaged in business of selling zaggers	Zagger shattered because of defects
Defendant sold zagger involved in accident	Shattering was caused by John Q.'s lack of concentration
Zagger reached user substantially unchanged	Shattering was caused by improper placement on machine
Zagger had bonding defect	Use of a guard would have prevented the injury
Zagger was not subjected to dynamic testing	Dynamic testing would have prevented accident
John Q. was killed when struck by zagger fragments	
John Q. did not have guard in place on machine	
John Q. was a careful and experienced machine operator	
Cypress machine John Q. was using was functioning properly	

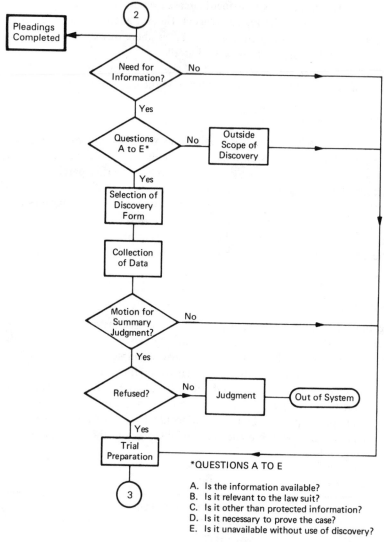

Figure 5-2. Civil Discovery

*QUESTIONS A TO E

A. Is the information available?
B. Is it relevant to the law suit?
C. Is it other than protected information?
D. Is it necessary to prove the case?
E. Is it unavailable without use of discovery?

Both attorneys looked carefully at those matters on which there still was no agreement. Would further discovery lead to information not yet available that would cause the two parties to agree on these items? A glance at the unresolved matters listed in Table 5-3 reveals that they are facts that had been examined and investigated, for which there was information available, but which could be construed as leading to several results. They represent differing conclusions about factual situations, the differences being of a kind at which reasonable persons could arrive. Given the same set of facts and reasonable disagreement concerning the conclusions that can be derived from them, it becomes evident the two parties now need an arbiter—a third party—to settle their differences. And that is precisely the role of the courts.

With both attorneys satisfied that additional fact finding would not yield results of much value, they were ready for the next stage in the civil process: the pretrial conference.

PRETRIAL CONFERENCE

Henry Law called W. E. Just to ask if he were ready for the pretrial conference. When Attorney Just said he was, the two agreed to meet in Henry's office. This was in keeping with the District Court's local rules which required not only that the two attorneys meet but also that each submit a pretrial memorandum to the court in preparation for a pretrial conference with the judge.

Meeting of Attorneys

As the agenda for their meeting, the attorneys followed the format for the pretrial memorandum in the local rules. Therefore their discussion concerned the court's jurisdiction, contentions as to liability, discussion of damages, witnesses to be called by each side and identification of those who would serve as experts, review of the pleadings to determine if amendments were in order, matters to be stipulated, and estimated length of trial.

They agreed to *stipulate,* i.e., admit the truth of those matters no longer in issue. Each man named the witnesses he expected to call at trial. Henry indicated that his would be Mary Worker, Robert Leader, Timothy O'Goode, Professor Learned, Peter Superior, and Sam Scott, although not necessarily in that order.

W. E. Just indicated that he would call as witnesses Charles Sell, the cypres engineer, and the zagger researcher at Acme Labs. The latter two and Professor Learned were designated as expert witnesses. W. E. Just said he would stipulate Professor Learned's knowledge of OSHA and Zagger Institute standards so that it would not be necessary for Henry Law to call other experts regarding those standards.

The attorneys next began to list their exhibits for trial. Henry's list included photographs at the accident scene, parts of the zagger, pictures of zagger fragments, the invoice for the sale of the special purpose zaggers, instructions for the use of zaggers, zagger labels, hospital record and bill, doctor bill, ambulance bill, death certificate, letters of administration, funeral home bill, bill for grave marker, and John Q.'s W2 forms for the past five years, among others. When the total amount of the bills was added to the $250,000 mentioned previously as the present value of John Q.'s anticipated earnings as well as to a sum for loss of the services of a husband and father, the grand total once again came close to $350,000. As they reviewed the sum, Henry said:

"W. E., I called my client last evening to tell her we would be having this conference today. In the course of that conversation, I asked if she wished me to discuss a settlement with you and what terms might be agreeable with her. I am authorized to ask if you are willing to consider settlement at this point."

Henry's offer to settle was based on his thought that W. E. Just might believe he faced some difficulty in defending Zagger Supply's position, and could save that company the added expense of trial.

However, W. E. Just replied: "Since I anticipated you would bring up the matter of settlement, I discussed it with the president of Zagger Supply. After careful consideration, our position is that we will see you in court."

"That being so, let's see if we can estimate the number of trial days that will be needed for this case. Then we can both get busy drawing up the pretrial memoranda." They decided that three to four days would be necessary for the trial.

The next day Henry Law called Mary Worker to report that no settlement had been effected and that it looked very much as if none ever would be. He explained that the next step would be for each of the attorneys to prepare and file with the Clerk of Courts (as well as with each other) a pretrial memorandum. After that, they would be notified by the Clerk when to appear before Judge Fairness for a pretrial conference. When Mary asked what that involved, Henry explained.

Conference with Judge

The pretrial conference, he said, is a meeting of the attorneys for the parties with the judge prior to trial. Its object is to discuss the case and its impending litigation informally. Some refer to it as a time for "clearing the decks" for trial, because it is a time for simplifying the issues, obtaining admissions in order to avoid unnecessary proof at trial, limiting the number of expert witnesses to be called at trial, and perhaps amending the pleadings. It is available in the federal and in most of the state court systems.

The Federal Rules make the pretrial conference discretionary with the court. Some state and local rules, however, make it mandatory. Procedure varies. Generally, the conference is not held until after the discovery has been completed and shortly before trial. There is no requirement, however, regarding the time nor is there a limit in the Federal Rules on the number of pretrial conferences. Some complex law suits necessitate several.

Henry Law went on to say that some districts hold pretrial conferences in open court; others, in the judge's chambers. Some are very formal in approach; others, informal. Some have a court reporter present; others do not. In some cases, local rules require that the attorneys meet with each other first, prepare pretrial memoranda for the court, and only then confer with the judge. Henry explained that this was true in Great State. In other jurisdictions just one conference of the attorneys with the judge is held.

However, in all cases stipulations and statements made by counsel at the pretrial conference are binding. Following the conference, the judge enters an order relating the action taken. This controls subsequent events.

Henry added that such requirements mean the attorneys for both parties are well prepared for trial. A study of the use of the pretrial conference showed that it resulted in improving the quality of the trial process because of better lawyer preparation.[3] That same study refuted claims that the pretrial conference would effect a reduction in court congestion and delay by increasing the number of pretrial settlements and by saving the judges' time. In fact, the study revealed that use of the conference requires additional judge time to be devoted to a case. In other words, Henry concluded, the study showed that the pretrial conference improves quality rather than quantity.

Mary's only comment was that she hoped that better quality would redound to her benefit.

The pretrial conference went much as expected. Judge Fairness welcomed the attorneys into his chambers. A court reporter, the judge's law clerk, and W. E. Just's paralegal aide were the only others present.

"Let's see what we have here--a product liability case, isn't it?" said the judge. It was apparent throughout the entire discussion that he had done his "homework"—read the entire file of the Mary Worker case and was familiar with its contents.

His agenda included the following: a review of the pretrial memorandum prepared by each attorney; a request to Henry Law for a short statement of the substance of the plaintiff's case; a similar request to W. E. Just regarding the defendant's case; a determination from the attorneys that the pleadings were in order and required no amendment; discussion with the attorneys regarding the exhibits each would place in evidence at trial; determination from each attorney of the witnesses—with identification of those who would serve as experts—he would call at trial; and an estimate of the number of days required for trial. The topics for discussion were similar to those covered by the two attorneys in their prior conference. The only new developments consisted of an agreement by W. E. Just to limit the number of cypres engineers he would call as experts to one, and an attempt by the judge to effect a settlement. The latter was to no avail.

Motion for Summary Judgment

Neither attorney presented a motion for summary judgment, although it may be made at this point in the civil process. This motion requests the court to render judgment based on the facts in the pleadings plus those added by discovery and those contained in any affidavits filed with the court. In the sense that it encompasses information beyond that contained in the pleadings, the motion differs from one for judgment on the pleadings.

A motion for summary judgment is properly granted only when the facts are not in dispute and questions of law alone remain to be decided. In the Mary Worker case, not only did facts still remain in dispute, but they were the extremely vital ones. One such question concerned the cause of the shattering of the zagger. Both attorneys, realizing such factual determination was a jury matter and an issue for trial, decided against a motion for summary judgment at this time.

Because both attorneys and the judge had been so well prepared, the conference did not last much more than an hour and a half. At the conclusion, the judge dictated an order embodying the general content and coverage of the conference:

1. Contentions of the plaintiff and defendant;
2. A statement of the facts about which both parties agreed;
3. The issues of fact remaining;
4. The issues of law involved;
5. A list of exhibits for trial;
6. A list of expert witnesses to be called;
7. Estimated length of the trial;
8. A statement that the case was ready to be placed on the trial list.

One copy of the order would be filed with the Clerk of Courts, and each attorney would receive one copy. The judge requested each attorney to prepare and submit to him, with a copy to the opposing attorney, a brief of the legal issues involved in the case and to do this prior to the first day of trial.

It is possible to look at the steps involved in that pretrial conference stage in Figure 5-3.

With the Mary Worker case now on the trial list, each attorney awaited notification of that important date as he prepared his brief. Henry Law's emphasized strict liability for death caused by a dangerously defective zagger, one which did not conform with safety standards and which was being used properly by an experienced cypres operator. On the other hand, W. E. Just's brief concentrated on inability of the plaintiff to establish proximate cause as well as assumption of the risk by an expert cypres machine operator who knowingly used a zagger without a guard after having improperly clamped it to the machine and while failing to give his work his undivided concentration.

The pretrial stages had now been completed.

Calendaring

Since the District Court used the individual calendar system, placing the Mary Worker case on the trial list meant, in effect, putting it on Judge Fairness' calendar. He was responsible for all actions and phases of the cases assigned to him, and he arranged his calendar to provide time for jury and nonjury trials while reserving time to fit in such other matters as pretrial conferences and hearings on motions and petitions for injunctions. As he reviewed his calendar with his secretary, he discovered that the trial could be scheduled to begin in three weeks. Centralized notification of lawyers and witnesses of the date of trial was through the Clerk of Courts office. Record of the status of all cases was kept by a calendar control clerk. With each judge controlling his own calendar, there were times when conflicts could arise if, for instance, two cases involving the same lawyer were scheduled for the same date. This system was in contrast with that in effect in Great State courts, where a master calendar control system was in effect. There, a case was put on the trial list after it had been certified as ready for trial following the pretrial conference. Notification of readiness was then sent to the master calendar control office, presided over by the calendar control judge. There the case was placed in a pool of all cases ready for trial and awaited its turn to be scheduled. Great State had been researching the use of electronic data processing and application of queueing theory to this scheduling process.

Policy decisions regarding calendaring, since they bear a direct relation to adjudication, are made by the court's judges. Execution of such policy, however, is often the function of a court executive or court administrator. Similar to the executive in a business firm, a court administrator is responsible for such "behind the scenes" managerial functions as accounting and budgeting, personnel practices, purchasing, space allocation and acquisition, public relations, data processing functions, and calendaring. Therefore, it was not unusual that the calendar control clerk in the District Court reported to the court executive who, in turn, reported directly to the chief judge of the court.

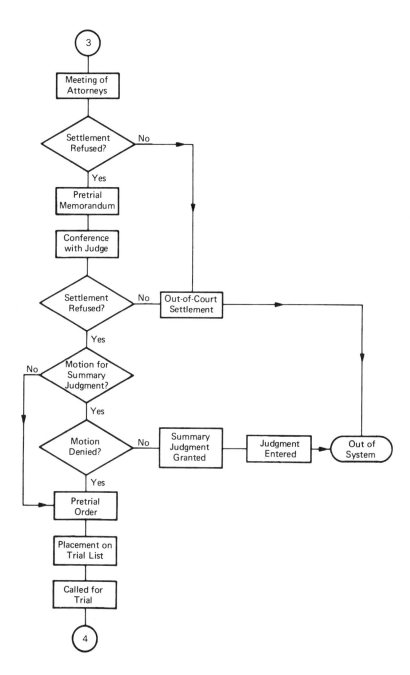

Figure 5-3. Pretrial Conference

Thus it was that the Mary Worker trial was scheduled to begin on February 28, and notification was sent to all concerned. The attorneys met with their witnesses to review the facts and prepare for trial, and Judge Fairness' law clerk research the law regarding defective products. The first day of trial would soon be at hand.

QUESTIONS

1. Consider the number of times attempts have been made to settle this case without going to trial. Why have they not been successful? Have reasons for not settling become more or less substantial as the case has progressed through various stages? With court dockets already crowded, is this the kind of matter that should go to trial or be settled through some alternative method? What method would you suggest?

2. Concentration has been on the legal aspects of this case. Have you found any social, moral, ethical issues involved? What are they? Any questions of public policy?

3. Discovery is often referred to as a fact-finding process. Has the case taken on any new aspects as a result of discovery? Has discovery changed the view of the case you held previously? If so, in what ways?

4. Is the pretrial conference a valuable step in the legal process? Why? What was accomplished through the conference in the Mary Worker case? Is there any danger that by the time a case comes to trial the attorneys will have worked with the facts so often that a sense of carelessness can develop from overfamiliarity?

5. What do the statistics regarding civil litigation in your state reveal about the number of civil jury v. nonjury trials? The waiting period between readiness for trial and date a trial is called? Who is responsible for the lapse of time between the readiness date and the day the trial actually commences?

6. Consider the functions performed by the office of the Clerk of Courts. Is it merely a record-keeping function? What influence, if any, can it have upon litigation? What differences, if any, exist among the roles played by Attorney Just's paralegal aide and Henry Law's secretary? What part in the legal process is played by these "behind the scenes" personnel, such as paralegals, secretaries, clerks in the Clerk of Courts office? What understanding of the legal system should they possess to perform their jobs well?

7. Should the issues for trial be arrived at in the pleadings? Is leaving that process for discovery simply a matter of putting the matter off for a later date? Can you see any reasons for postponing it to the later stage?

8. Consider the content of the complaint and the answer. Do you find them understandable? written in "legalese?"

9. What do the number and kind of decisions made by Henry Law prior to filing the complaint say about the role of the lawyer in the legal process?

NOTES

[1] In some jurisdictions the complaint is known as the declaration, the petition, or the bill.

[2] Kalven, Harry, Jr. and Hans Zeisel, *The American Jury* (Boston: Little Brown & Company, 1966).

[3] Rosenberg, Maurice, *The Pre-Trial Conference and Effective Justice* (New York: Columbia University Press, 1964).

trial:
argument
and adjudication

SIX

On the morning of the first day of trial, Mary Worker met Henry Law at his office and together the two went to the federal courthouse in Big City. As they entered the courtroom of Judge Fairness, Mary looked around. This was the first time she had ever been in that court. Since they were the first persons there, Henry explained the physical arrangements to her.

THE COURTROOM

The immediate focus of attention of anyone entering the room was the judge's bench, loftily centered at the very front. The witness stand was to the left of it at a slightly lower level. At the extreme left was the jury box. Directly in front of the judge's bench was a long table. This, Henry explained, would be shared by the court reporter, the court clerk, and the judge's law clerk. To the right of the judge's bench was the chair for the bailiff, sometimes known as the tipstaff. The bailiff's duties, Henry said, included announcing the opening and closing of court sessions, escorting the jury, and serving as a general aide to court.

Mary and Henry took places at a long double table in the center of the room, below the judge's bench and in front of the railing which separated the seating area for members of the general public from the rest of the courtroom. Henry informed Mary that W. E. Just and representatives of Zagger Supply would be seated on the other side of the table, directly across from them. He also said that most courtrooms are arranged in a somewhat similar manner, although some of the more recently built courthouses have courtrooms "in the round." Proponents of the latter arrangement, he explained, claim that it brings judge, jury, witnesses, and attorneys much closer to each other physically, thus facilitating communication.

LAWYER TO LAWYER

It was not long until W. E. Just and his paralegal assistant arrived. Mary was surprised, almost disheartened, to find that Henry was both friendly and cordial in greeting them. Noticing her concern, Henry thought that a comparison with professional baseball or football players might be helpful in explaining lawyers' relationships with each other. While playing, he told her, professional athletes put all of their energy, effort, and talent into winning for their team or their side. However, it is not uncommon to find they are sometimes close friends off the field with these same athletes who are their opponents on the playing field. So it can be with lawyers, too, he said. Advocates for opposing sides do not necessarily carry that adversarial relationship over into their private and personal lives.

JURY SELECTION

In the meantime, elsewhere in the courthouse, a number of other persons who would play an important role in the trial had already gathered in the jury assembly room. They had been selected randomly from voter lists for the district served by the court, in accordance with the provisions of the Federal Jury Selection and Service Act.[1] Voter lists are used to secure a fair cross-section of the community.

The United States Supreme Court has held that a "jury of one's peers" does not require that a jury consist of persons whose characteristics are identical with those of the parties to the law suit. Instead, the requirement is that there be equal opportunity and possibility for representation of all segments of the community on the *jury panel.*[2] The jury panel is the larger group from which members of the trial jury are chosen. Systematic exclusion from juries of groups of people such as women or blacks results in jury panels that are not representative of the community, and therefore is not permitted.[3]

Determinants of qualification for jury duty, as set forth in the Federal Jury Selection and Service Act, are: age, citizenship, residence in the district, literacy, mental and physical health, and absence of a criminal record. These criteria were selected in order to prevent disqualification of persons for purely subjective reasons and to eliminate insofar as possible opportunities for the creation of the *blue ribbon juries* sometimes alleged in the past to be characteristic of the juries in the federal courts. A blue ribbon jury is one on which the proportion of managerial and professional persons to all others is much greater than it is in the general population.

Under the act, persons excluded from jury service because of occupation include the police, firefighters, soldiers, and public officers. Others who may be excused upon request include mothers with young children, clergy, physicians, lawyers, and dentists. A statute similar to the federal act has been proposed for uniform adoption by the states.

Jury Array

Responsibility for jury selection in this court rested with the court executive and was implemented by the clerk of courts office. In some jurisdictions a jury commissioner assists the clerk. This court had used the computer for a random generation of names from the voter lists. Other courts place the names of all persons on the voter lists in a master jury wheel and draw names from it manually. This list of names drawn was referred to as the *jury array*. It was subject to challenge by a showing that selection had not been made in accordance with the law.

Once the array had been determined, a qualification form was mailed to every person on the list. Each reply was checked to see if the individual met the requirements for jury duty. If so, that person's name was placed in the "qualified" jury pool. As the need for jurors was anticipated, names were randomly selected from that pool. Notices to report to the jury assembly room on a specified date were mailed to the persons whose names had been drawn. They would constitute the *general jury panel*. Requests for excuse from jury duty were referred to a judge who decided if they were valid.

These steps in selection of the general jury panel have been shown in a flow chart in Figure 6-1. Notice that the chart shows that discharge from jury duty may result from either excuse or disqualification.

Trial Panel

When prospective jurors reported to the assembly room, they were welcomed, informed about courthouse facilities and the role of jurors, and given a juror's handbook to study and a juror's identification button to wear. They were instructed to wait in the juror assembly area until a call came for a trial panel. When it did, the names of twenty of the assembled persons were drawn from a jury wheel. This group was then escorted to a courtroom where selection of the jury for a specific trial would be made. If the need arose, additional groups would be sent in order for sufficient persons to be secured to serve on the trial jury, or *petit jury*. The procedures followed by this court in the selection of persons for jury duty do not differ markedly from those followed elsewhere.

Jury Size

The traditional petit jury consisted of twelve persons. Today many courts use as few as six persons for reasons of economy and efficiency. When the constitutionality of juries consisting of fewer than twelve persons was challenged, the United States Supreme Court ruled that the guarantee of trial by jury in the federal constitution does

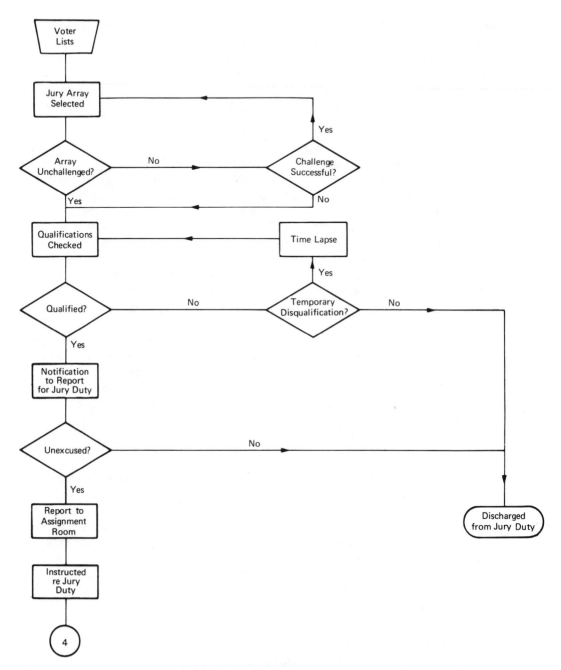

Figure 6-1. Selection of Jury Panel

not have a number requirement.[4] Therefore, one's right to trial by jury is not infringed if there are fewer than twelve *veniremen* or jurors. The local rules of the district court for the Great State district provided for juries of six with two alternates.

Thus it was that a group of prospective jurors was sent to Judge Fairness' courtroom where the parties, the witnesses scheduled for the first day of trial, the judge's law clerk, the court reporter, and the court clerk were assembled. In some courts, the jury for civil trials is selected near or in the juror assembly room and a judge's presence is not required. That was not true in this court, however. Once all necessary persons were present in the courtroom, Judge Fairness entered. Having identified the case about to be tried, he called for selection of the jury to begin.

Challenges

Henry Law had explained to Mary Worker beforehand that both he and W. E. Just would have a list of the general jury panel showing names, addresses, and occupations. Each attorney checked this list as the clerk now called the names of the twenty members of the trial panel. Mary anticipated that the attorneys would make two kinds of challenges to having specific persons from this panel serve on the jury for her lawsuit. Each successful challenge would mean that the individual would be dismissed from participation on the jury in this trial.

Challenges for cause in an unlimited number are possible by each attorney. These challenges must be based upon a good and sufficient reason, such as a prospective juror's being related to or employed by one of the parties or attorneys. Discovery of such matters is by *voir dire* or questioning of the jury panel. Judge Fairness handled the voir dire himself. Both attorneys were permitted to submit to the judge beforehand questions to be used in the voir dire. In some courts, the questioning is done by both the attorneys and the judge. In this case the voir dire resulted in the dismissal for cause of the following members of the jury panel: Clyde Partner's secretary; a shipping clerk employed by The Firm; Will Very's cousin, the publicity director for the Zagger Institute; a local television newscaster, who covered and reported the John Q. Worker accident for his station; a Big City industrial equipment broker, who at times dealt in Zagger Supply products; Professor Learned's laboratory assistant; and the wife of the ambulance driver who had been called to the accident scene.

Both attorneys also made use of the *peremptory* challenge. This is, in effect, a rather arbitrary challenge since no reason need be given to exclude a particular person from the jury. Peremptory challenges are limited in number by the rules of civil procedure. Much has been said and written about the importance of selecting jurors with whom rapport can be established. In fact, it is sometimes said that juries "try the attorneys." Henry Law included in his peremptory challenges the owner of a small business and a salesperson for a railway equipment firm. As he told Mary later, he believed that because of their occupations these individuals might tend to be sympathetic with the defendant's cause. W. E. Just's challenges included a widowed housewife and a union steward.

Final Choice

Those finally selected for the jury were:

1. Geraldine Horne, age 26, a saxophone player and member of a quintet which played regularly in a local lounge;

2. Adam Frank, age 52, bookkeeper;
3. Kathleen Logan, age 62, a part-time computer programmer;
4. Martin Lee, age 31, a salesperson at a Big City haberdashery;
5. Nancy Perkins, age 44, a telephone operator;
6. Sam Wells, age 52, a truck driver.

Rosemarie Friday, 21, a waitress, and Joseph Patrick, 33, a janitor, were selected as alternate jurors. They would sit in the jury box during the trial. Should any of the six regular jurors become ill or incapacitated and unable to take part in the deliberations for a verdict, the alternates would replace them. If not, the two would be dismissed and sent home when the jury retired to begin its deliberations.

The panel members who had not been selected for the jury were thanked by Judge Fairness and escorted back to the jury assembly room to await consideration for membership on other juries. Those not selected for any jury would be paid the $30-per-day federal jury fee and sent home. All of this is shown in Figure 6-2 which flow charts selection of the trial jury.

Opening Statements

The jury having been selected and sworn, it was now time for opening statements by the two attorneys. This stage of the trial provides counsel for each party with the opportunity to talk briefly with the jury about the case as well as about the evidence to be offered and the witnesses to be called. The jury is given a preview and has some idea of what to expect next. Opening statements are not considered evidence, since they are made by attorneys who are advocates and not witnesses. As the party bringing the case, the plaintiff is first. Therefore, Henry began his statement to the jury.

He did so by identifying the parties and their attorneys. He also told the jury about the various steps in a trial. Following that, he became specific about the Mary Worker case. The lawsuit, Henry said, arose from an accident in which John Q. Worker, a cypres machine operator, was killed when a fragment from a shattering zagger pierced his abdomen. Henry explained that the zagger had shattered while being used by John Q. in the course of his employment. The suit, Henry went on, was being brought by John Q.'s widow to recover from the manufacturer of the zagger for the loss to herself and her family of a husband and father. Henry told the jury he would present witnesses who would testify that the zagger was dangerously defective and was the cause of John Q.'s death. There would also be testimony, he added, that the zagger was being used for its intended purpose at the time of the accident by a careful and skilled machinist, and that testing by the manufacturer prior to shipment could have prevented the accident. The evidence would show, he concluded, that the zagger manufacturer's actions were the cause of the accident and John Q.'s death. Finally, he asked that they listen carefully to the testimony that would follow the opening statements.

W. E. Just followed with his opening statement to the jury. He identified himself as the counsel for Zagger Supply, told the jury he would have the opportunity to cross-examine each of Henry's witnesses after that person had testified and said he would

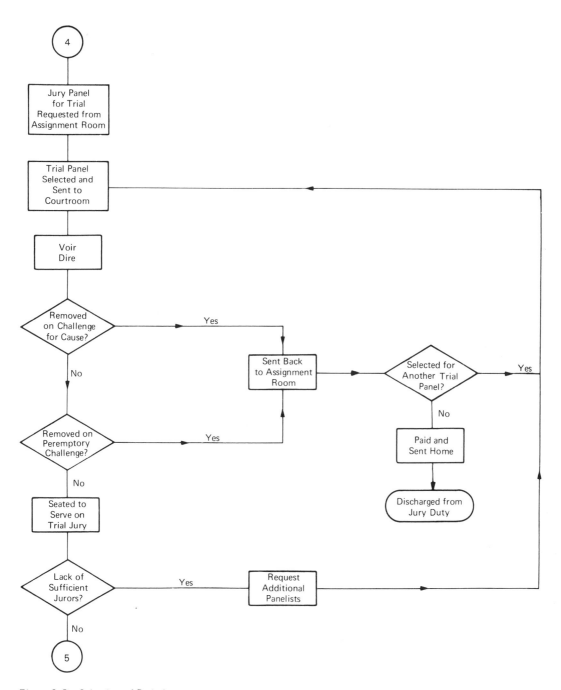

Figure 6-2. Selection of Petit Jury

present the case for the defense when Henry had completed the plaintiff's case. He also said he would present witnesses who would testify that the zagger shattered as it did for reasons other than any defect, that John Q. had used the zagger without a guard on his machine—in such a manner that he knowingly and voluntarily assumed the risk of the accident that resulted. He ended by saying that the evidence would show that his client was not responsible for the accident.

As they spoke, Mary noticed the court reporter busily recording everything that was said, the judge's law clerk making notations, the judge listening to each attorney's statements and from time to time referring to documents related to the case, the clerk busy with papers connected with the trial, and the jury listening with apparent interest. She noticed, too, that so far everything had proceeded much as Henry Law had said it would.

PLAINTIFF'S CASE IN CHIEF

Preparation

The opening statements to the jury completed, Judge Fairness asked Henry if the plaintiff was ready with his first witness.

The examination of each witness called to testify at a trial is conducted in accordance with the following steps:

1. *Direct Examination.* This consists of questioning by the attorney for the party who calls the witness. The objective is to establish the facts or claim of that party.
2. *Cross-examination.* This involves questioning by the opposing counsel and is optional. It offers the opportunity to attack both the credibility and the testimony of the opponent's witness. Cross-examination is generally limited to matters covered on direct examination.
3. *Redirect Examination.* Optional requestioning is possible by the attorney who conducted the direct examination. This is generally used to "rehabilitate" the witness following cross-examination; that is, to recapture the witness' lost credibility. The subject matter is usually limited to answering that which was brought out on cross-examination.
4. *Recross-examination.* The opposing counsel has the option of requestioning following the redirect examination. The limits generally imposed are to new matter brought out on redirect.

This process of witness examination is flow charted in Figure 6–3.

Henry Law had devoted his attention prior to trial to the matter of who would be called as witnesses and the order in which they would be called. Details of the accident and related events would have to be told to a jury, unacquainted with any of the facts, in a manner that they could follow, and that at the same time would be as beneficial as

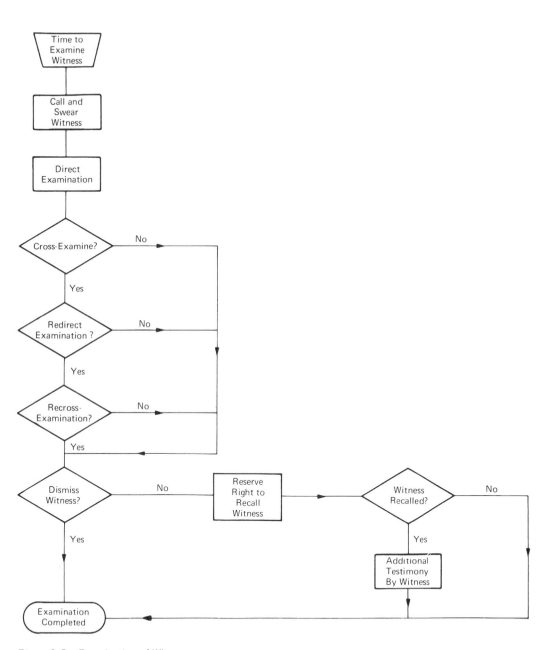

Figure 6-3. Examination of Witnesses

possible to Mary's case. Henry reasoned, therefore, that the most understandable sequence for a jury would be to discuss first the accident, then the defect, and finally the damages.

As to the persons who would serve as witnesses, he could select only from those persons with first-hand knowledge of the facts about which he needed testimony. This was because of the *rules of evidence,* which require that witnesses have personal knowledge regarding that to which they testify. Rules of evidence are those that regulate the admission of proof at the trial of a lawsuit. Uniform Rules of Evidence have been proposed but not adopted; however, the rules tend to be very similar from state to state. For the federal courts, of course, the rules are uniform.

The rules of evidence have been developed from experience in the conduct of trials over the centuries. They are a good example of procedural law, knowledge of which is important to the attorney.

As Henry considered possible witnesses, he naturally looked for persons who would provide testimony favorable to his client. When there was more than one person with the requisite first-hand knowledge, he would choose that person or persons whose manner and appearance would be most convincing to the jury and who would be least likely to damage his client's case on cross-examination.

Henry knew of three witnesses to the accident: Robert Leader, Timothy O'Goode, and Peter Superior. Robert had observed more of the occurrences immediately prior to, during, and immediately following the accident than the other two had. Therefore, he alone would be able to testify regarding certain details. Timothy, as the only one of the three who had worked on production of the new chattels, could testify regarding his experience with the special zaggers. Peter also could make a unique contribution with testimony regarding the five shattering incidents involving the special zaggers, which had taken place in the department he supervised. Therefore, Henry decided he needed all three as witnesses.

Henry realized that for the jury to comprehend the defective qualities of the new zaggers, they would first have to learn about the operation of a cypres machine and how zaggers are used on them. In addition, they must be informed about the order, design, and manufacture of the special zaggers. As the most articulate of these three witnesses and also the most experienced cypres operator, Robert Leader was Henry's choice to provide the jury with a nontechnical explanation of the machine's operation.

For first-hand knowledge of the special zagger order, however, Sam Scott would have to be called. He also qualified to explain differences between the two types of zaggers and could testify regarding the function of the guard on the machine.

Henry planned to rely upon Professor Learned for most of the testimony regarding defectiveness of the zagger and lack of proper testing. In fact, Henry believed the outcome of the trial would be influenced greatly by this man's testimony, not only because of his impressive qualifications and reputation but also because he was an experienced expert witness. As an expert, he could be asked *hypothetical questions;* i.e., those in which the witness is asked to assume a given set of facts and to render an opinion about the result or outcome. The rules of evidence require that witnesses testify as to facts, not conclusions or opinions. An exception is made in the case of *expert witnesses;*

that is, witnesses who by reason of experience, training, or education have special knowledge about matters before the court. They are permitted to give opinions in their area of expertise.

Henry realized it was vital to his client's case to have testimony concerning the results that would follow or could be expected to follow if there were bonding or size defects in a zagger. The same necessity prevailed, in his estimation, regarding the effects or absence of the guard. For that reason, Henry planned to present evidence to qualify not only Professor Learned, but also Sam Scott, as expert witnesses.

Finally, testimony regarding damages was necessary. For this, Henry would call Mary to explain what the loss of John Q. had meant to her and her children.

It should be mentioned that Henry had explored what might be added to the plaintiff's case as a result of the OSHA inspection made at The Firm. He found nothing relevant to his purposes that he had not already considered and included in his preparation. He therefore concluded that delving further into that matter would provide no enhancement for his case. He also decided that W. E. Just would conclude similarly with regard to the defendant's case. In this he was correct.

This, then, had been Henry Law's thought process in arriving at decisions regarding witnesses, most of which had been made prior to the pretrial conference. Except for Peter Superior and Sam Scott, Henry telephoned prospective witnesses and arranged to meet with each in preparation for trial. He explained the procedures in testifying, reviewed with them prior statements they had made, told them what he believed they could expect on cross-examination, and answered questions of concern to them about the trial process. Such witness preparation is entirely proper. It is a necessary part of the trial lawyer's job. Contrary to the opinion of some, it is a legitimate task for the trial attorney to permit witnesses to "refresh their recollection" by permitting them to reread memoranda or statements they have previously prepared. The rules of evidence give recognition to the fact that memories dim with time. Witnesses are permitted to refer to their own writings even while testifying provided all the evidentiary requirements for doing so are met. In no instance, however, is the attorney permitted to suggest to witnesses that they tell anything other than the truth—the whole truth. To do so would be to commit the crime of subornation of perjury.

In the case of Peter and Sam, subpoenas were issued. Previously, when these two men had been subpoenaed for the taking of depositions, they had consulted Leo Lex about the legal ramifications. Following that, Sam Scott called Henry to inform him that both could be present at the time set for the deposition taking. He also indicated The Firm's position was that it would cooperate in the legal process. It would not obstruct justice. However, it did not desire to become the legal antagonist of Zagger Supply with whom it wished to maintain friendly business relations. The two companies, he said, had always been able to settle any problems or differences they might have had between themselves out of court. It was their hope to continue to do so.

When this second subpoena arrived, Sam again called Henry. He asked if he could expect to testify regarding the same matters about which he had been questioned in connection with the deposition. He was informed that this was so. The conversation then turned to the possible use of visual aids for the purpose of making Sam's technical explanations more comprehensible to nonengineers who, in all probability, would constitute the majority of the jury. The two agreed that both a regular and special zagger as well as models of the cypres machine and the new chattel would be appropriate. Such objects are often referred to as *demonstrative evidence,* and may be passed from hand to hand by jurors who have the right to examine them. Henry planned to introduce these objects into evidence at appropriate times during Sam's testimony.

All this preparation having taken place, Robert Leader now took his place in the witness box after having been sworn to tell the truth by the clerk.

The Case in Chief

Anxious at first, Robert soon settled back and responded well to Henry's questions. His testimony contained no surprises. It duplicated information he had provided previously in his deposition and in conversation with Henry Law. However, one incident that occurred during his direct examination is noteworthy.

After the usual preliminary questions dealing with identification, Henry questioned Robert about his twenty years of experience as a cypres machine operator at The Firm, Inc., where he worked at the machine immediately to the right of the one which John Q. had operated. Following that, Robert testified that he had been chairperson of the safety committee of Local 135 for ten years prior to becoming local president. This evidence occurred after Judge Fairness overruled W. E. Just's objection that Robert's union activities were not relevant.

A fundamental requirement for the admission of evidence is that it relate to the matters at issue in the trial, that it have a bearing on the truth of the facts in dispute. The purpose of this rule of evidence is to restrict testimony to trial matters. This is to prevent prolonging the trial and confusing jurors by introducing into evidence extraneous matters.

Henry's response to W. E.'s objection was to ask if counsel could approach the bench. Such a request is, in effect, one for a private conversation between judge and attorneys. Henry's purpose in doing so was to make an *offer of proof,* that is, state to the judge what he expected to show by the answer of the witness. Such an offer is made out of the hearing of the jurors. The reason is to prevent their being influenced by having heard it, should the evidence be ruled inadmissible.

Juries and court watchers are often bewildered, and some jury members are even resentful, when conversations between counsel and judge take place out of their hearing. It is not that the case is being tried in private between judge and attorneys. Instead, the discussion generally involves resolution of such questions as admissibility of evidence or proper trial procedure. In this case, when Judge Fairness heard that Henry wished to establish Robert's experience with a safety committee to lay a foundation for his further testimony regarding zagger safety, he permitted pursuit of the line of questioning.

Both attorneys noted that Robert's description of the accident provoked response from the jury. Geraldine Horne for the first time sat upright in her chair; Mrs. Logan winced; Mr. Frank leaned forward; Jurors Perkins and Wells moved to the edge of their chairs; and Mr. Lee stared intently at the witness. Obviously, an impact had been made.

W. E. Just, on cross-examination, was able to reduce that impact somewhat. In answer to defense counsel's questions, Robert admitted he could not state positively that he had seen John Q. go through each of the motions necessary in properly checking and placing the zagger on the cypres machine. Nor could he state positively that he had seen John Q. replace the guard. Robert also admitted that he had never used any of the new zaggers and that he had never personally examined them.

That brought to a close the first day of trial. Before court began the next morning, Henry checked to see that the visual aids for Sam Scott's testimony were on hand.

In order to qualify Sam as an expert in cypres and zagger safety, Henry questioned him about his engineering school background and his twelve years of experience in the cypres industry. Sam's testimony included an explanation to the jury that production of the new chattel required zaggers of a different size, shape, and hardness from those regularly used by The Firm.

When the special order for zaggers became the topic, the actual order was introduced into evidence. The fact that the original, rather than just a copy, was placed in evidence, was owing to the *best evidence* rule. This requires that proof of the contents of a writing be made by producing that writing itself. Where the terms of that writing are material, the original document must be produced except for good cause. The reason for this rule is apparent. Production of a writing results in much greater accuracy regarding its contents than can be expected from oral testimony based on memory. The requirement of an original eliminates the possibility for error or change connected with the copying process. Authentication of written documents is a usual prerequisite to their admission into evidence.

A related rule of evidence is the *parol evidence rule.* This does not permit oral (parol) testimony regarding variation or alteration of the terms of a written contract if the parties regard their writing as the final expression of their intentions. There are exceptions, such as in the case of fraud or typographical error.

"Your purchase order to Zagger Supply for the special zaggers specified they must comply with OSHA standards, did it not?" Henry asked Sam.

W. E. Just objected that Henry was leading the witness. *Leading questions* are those that suggest or contain an answer. They are not permitted on direct examination because they make it possible for the attorney, rather than the witness, to do the actual testifying by the way the lawyer frames his questions. However, such questions generally are permitted on cross-examination.

W. E. Just's objection was made at the time Henry asked the question. Objections must be made immediately when grounds for inadmissibility are apparent. Failure to object at the time an offer of evidence is made is a waiver of any complaint against its admission. If the attorney could wait until the trial had ended, the evidence would have been heard and taken into consideration by the jury and could constitute such error as to necessitate a new trial. In many jurisdictions, objections must be accompanied by a statement of reasons. These are noted on the trial record. The record stands and other reasons cannot be added at a later time, for example, when appeal might be contemplated.

In this case, Judge Fairness sustained W. E. Just's objection. Henry then reworded the question to ask Sam to describe the zaggers covered by the purchase order.

Sam referred to specifications on the order itself. Henry then requested Sam to read directly from the purchase order. The words were clear: the order was for zaggers that would "meet the standards promulgated by OSHA and the Zagger Institute."

Additional testimony by Sam regarding guards on the cypres machines, inspection of zaggers after purchase, and safety requirements at The Firm was much the same as that given at the taking of his deposition.

On cross-examination, Sam admitted that The Firm purchased primarily from Zagger Supply because of the quality and safety of its zaggers as compared with competitive brands. He also admitted that the zagger shattering record at The Firm was far below industry-wide figures for similar operations. He attributed this to the patented manufacturing process used by Zagger Supply. W. E. elicited from him the information that safety training programs at The Firm, which John Q. had attended several times, stressed the legal requirement in Great State for operation of a cypres machine only with the guard in place.

Timothy O'Goode was Henry's next witness. He testified that he had operated the cypres machine to the left of John Q.'s for the past ten years and that he had been selected to replace John Q. in the first production run of the new chattels. He duplicated testimony given at his deposition, stating that he complied with the directive to use special zaggers only when threatened with the loss of his job and that he had filed a complaint with the union because of fear for his safety in working with new zaggers.

When he said his fellow workers reported that technicians employed at Zagger Supply had told them the new zaggers were not safe, W. E. Just objected to this as hearsay. The need for such prompt objection by Attorney Just to hearsay testimony is treated in the *Newman* decision which follows.

Newman v. *Los Angeles Transit Lines*
262 P.2d 95 (District Court of Appeals, California, 1953)

Action by street car passenger against transit corporation for injuries allegedly sustained in fall caused by jerking of streetcar while passenger was alighting therefrom. The Superior Court of Los Angeles County entered judgment based upon a unanimous verdict rejecting plaintiff's suit for damages for personal injuries, and passenger appealed.

MOORE, Presiding Justice. . . . since the sufficiency of the evidence to support the verdict is not in question, the assignments of error will be discussed in the order presented.

The first assignment is the court's overruling appellant's general objection to the following question propounded to her on cross-examination: "Mrs. Newman, have you ever had a feeling of having a persecution complex?" To which she answered: "I don't." It is not improper to develop any feeling of antagonism or animosity of a witness toward a party. But if such ruling had been error, it could have caused no prejudice since the answer was favorable to appellant. . . .

She complains of the court's adverse ruling on her general objection to the question: "Have you ever accused anybody of spying on you continuously?" She answered that "all kinds of attempts at frameups. . . ." The answer revealed the workings of her mind as intended by the inquisitor. With her own statement about frame-ups against her before the jury, they were more nearly able to weigh her testimony. By means of developing the situation of appellant with respect to her adversary, her interest, her motives, her inclination and prejudices, her powers of discernment and description, the cross-examiner placed the witness in her true light before the jury. Her answer showed that by reason of her suspicions she had created a steel barrier of hate against her adversary. It is a rule of universal application that a witness may be required to answer any question which tends to test his accuracy, veracity or credibility and especially in the case of a party to the action where he appears as a witness. . . . Great latitude should be allowed in developing the existence of bias. . . . Liberal cross-examination is the rule. . . . But appellant made no specific objection to the question asked her. An adverse ruling upon a general objection is never the basis for a reversal except in those instances where the testimony elicited is not admissible upon any ground whatsoever. . . .

Appellant complains that an extraneous, immaterial issue was injected by respondent's asking her: "Is Communism behind this? . . . . Not only was no objection made to such question, nor motion made to forbid their repetition, but appellant appears to have relished the inquiry as another opportunity for denouncing the motorman and all who were opposing her lawsuit. . . .

Appellant contends that it was error for the court over her objection to permit "a demonstration of the mechanical operation of the steps on the streetcar No. 1536; that it was three years after the alleged accident and with a different and skilled operator. . . ."

Whether the court should grant the application for a view of a mechanical device whose operation was allegedly the cause of an accident is peculiarly within the discretion of the court. . . . No proof was made that the car used for the demonstration or that the manner of opening the doors was at all different from the condition of the device three years before. No other objection can on appeal be considered. . . .

Appellant assigns as error the conduct of the trial judge in "permitting two jurors to sleep during most of the trial." There is no record to support such assignment. Not an objection was made; not a request by appellant for the court to reprove somnolescent jurors. . . . But if two jurors had slept throughout the trial, no prejudice was suffered. The jury returned a unanimous verdict, whereas the law required only three-fourths of the jury to return a valid verdict. . . . Finally, not only is there no proof of the presence of the sleeping jurors, but at no time did the trial judge observe such phenomenon.

Appellant asserts that she was excluded from the view of the demonstration of the streetcar doors and steps and also that at the demonstration respondent's witnesses were allowed to make statements in the hearing of the jury. In support thereof she claims further that the reporter's transcript is incorrect in its report of the events that transpired.

The transcript, once settled and approved, cannot be impeached by charges contained in a brief. . . . Inasmuch as error is not to be presumed, but must affirmatively appear in the record, it must be held that the criticized acts did not occur. No objection is found in the record to any ruling of the court and there is no evidence that appellant was excluded from the demonstration or that it was suggested. The presumption is that the incidents of the trial occurred as reported.

Error is assigned in that appellant witness, Mrs. Suchman, was not permitted to testify after having been sworn. After respondent had rested, appellant called in rebuttal Mrs. Provin. The latter testified concerning the behavior of appellant after December 19, 1948. Thereupon, it was stipulated that the testimony of Mrs. Suchman would be substantially the same as that of Mrs. Provin. Since the need for the lady's testimony had disappeared, counsel for appellant did not call her. By reason of the fact that an attorney is agent of his client and is empowered to conduct the cause during its pendency, . . . his agreements with reference to calling or excusing a witness are binding upon his client. . . .

Assignment is made that the court admitted the "hearsay" testimony of witnesses Lacy and Spencer. . . . The complaint is too late. No objection was made during the entire examination of these gentlemen. Therefore, error cannot be effectively asserted in the absence of objection to the introduction of the evidence. . . . Having failed to object at the trial, objection to evidence cannot for the first time be interposed in the appellate court.

Because the deposition of witness Prutsman gave two different times of day for the arrival of car No. 1536, appellant charges error in the court's receiving same. Such deposition was read into evidence by appellant's counsel, not by respondent. An appellant cannot base his appeal on the admission of testimony which was read to the jury by his own counsel. . . . Moreover, inconsistencies do not render testimony inadmissible. Such matters are to be resolved by the trial court. . . .

The court gave the following instruction:

"If, prior to the trial, the deposition of a party to the action was taken, and if all or part of it was read into evidence, and if, in said deposition she made contradictory statement or statements in conflict with her testimony here in court, you may consider such conflicts, and any explanation given therefore, in testing her credibility, in like manner as if all such testimony were given orally at the trial. The deposition, too, was given under oath. Also, if any statement in a party's deposition constituted an admission against interest, it may be considered in determining the truth or falsity thereof as well as in judging her credibility."

Notwithstanding that correctness of the foregoing is not questioned, appellant claims it is prejudicial error because it "singles out the plaintiff for the giving of the instruction and does not make it a general instruction applicable to all persons . . ." The fact is that it concerns and is limited to "the deposition of a party to the action." Appellant is the only party who gave a deposition. The instructions which preceded . . . were general and applied to witnesses as well as to depositions of witnesses, setting forth the rules that in judging credibility, a witness is presumed to speak the truth; that such presumption may be overcome by contradictory evidence, by the manner of testifying, by the character of his testimony or by evidence that pertains to his motives; that a witness false in one part of his testimony is to be disregarded in others; the jury may reject the whole testimony of a witness who has wilfully testified falsely on a material point, unless, from all the evidence, the jury believes that the probability of truth favors his testimony in other particulars; that the jury are not to discount testimony received by way of deposition for the sole reason that it was in the form of deposition; that it is entitled to the same rebuttable presumption of verity and the same judgment of the jury with reference to its weight as that of any witness appearing on the stand. By reason of such instructions having preceded . . . it cannot be reasonably asserted that appellant was singled out as the only one whose credibility was to be tested and determined by the jury. Appellant would reverse the rule and weight and consider any one instruction separately from all others instead of reading it in its context. . . ."

As to the use of Mrs. Newman's deposition, only two short questions were read from it to contradict the testimony she had just given on the stand. Such was proper practice as an aid to the jury's better understanding of the lady's testimony.

In her reply brief, appellant presents for the first time the question of error of the trial court's failure to instruct the jury on the doctrine of last clear chance. Questions presented in this matter will not ordinarily be considered by the appellate court in the absence of meritorious reason for the delay. But the court may nevertheless examine such matters, and may allow an appellant to discuss new points in a final brief upon application showing a reason such as sickness, inadvertence, or excusable neglect. . . . Appellant has made no such application and in fact failed to mention that this question was raised for the first time in her reply brief.

Appellant does admit that no such instruction was requested. Assuming that such an instruction would have been proper, the rule is that the failure of a trial court to give an instruction may not be reviewed on appeal unless the record specifies the instruction and shows that it was requested and refused. . . . It was not error for the trial court to fail to give the instruction in question on its own motion.

Judgment affirmed.

To return to W. E. Just's objection:

Judge Fairness sustained the objection and instructed the jury to disregard the statement. One of the more complex rules of evidence, the *hearsay rule,* excludes evidence that consists of what another person has said or written outside of the court when it is offered for the purpose of establishing the truth of what was said or written. The reason is that the person responsible for the out-of-court statement cannot be cross-examined regarding it to check its reliability. There are many exceptions to the hearsay rule, including spontaneous exclamations made at the time an event occurs (sometimes referred to as *res gestae*), admissions made by the other party, and entries made in the regular course of business in books of account.

On cross-examination, Timothy admitted he experienced no shattering incidents with new zaggers, that he had been able to cope with any clamping problems by using extra care in adjusting and placing the new zaggers on the machine. He did this, he testified, to prevent wobbling which could cause shattering at high speeds.

The direct examination of Peter Superior yielded no new information. On cross-examination, W. E. Just asked if he had used the special zagger during the preproduction trial period when Zagger Supply was working with personnel of The Firm in the design of the new zagger. His answer was in the affirmative. Asked if he had used them following the accident, he again answered "yes." He testified that he had demonstrated their use to Timothy O'Goode. W. E. Just then asked if he had experienced difficulties with shattering, fit, or anything else in their use. This time his answer was negative.

On redirect examination, Peter admitted to Henry that the only special zaggers he had used were those that had been prepared on prototypes. He had never used any from the manufacturing lot represented by the special order, not even in his demonstration for Timothy O'Goode.

Professor Learned's trial testimony was repetitious of his deposition testimony. He told again of the bonding defects in the zagger fragments, how the defects could have been discovered by dynamic testing, and how they would cause shattering when the zagger was revolved at more than 2000 rpm. He maintained the position he had taken earlier at the deposition, that a guard could not have prevented the fatal injuries when there was such a violent and explosive shattering. He also reiterated his earlier contention that the accident would not have occurred had proper testing been done.

When W. E. asked him on cross-examination if improper mounting or clamping of a zagger could lead to wobbling and then shattering, his answer was the same as in his deposition. The defense attorney, however, did not allow that to go unchallenged. He referred to articles and pronouncements by others whom the professor acknowledged to be experts, and then asked if it was not true that Professor Learned's view was neither the prevailing nor the accepted one in the industry.

"It is the correct one," was the response; "popularity is not pertinent."

Repressing a smile, Henry on redirect asked about shattering caused by wobbling when zaggers were used at speeds in excess of those for which they had been tested. This meant, said Professor Learned, that the shattering was the result of improper speed and had nothing to do with improper mounting or clamping. When Henry asked if the zagger could have shattered following wobbling because of an incorrect size, the professor said it had been impossible to reconstruct the zagger from the fragments. Thus, taking measurements had been impossible. However, he added, if there had been a size defect, this would only bear out his conclusion that it was a defective zagger that was responsible for John Q.'s death.

On recross, W. E. asked if the professor meant to infer that a difference in size between regular and special zaggers constituted a defect.

"No," was the response. "There is a defect only when a discrepancy in size prevents a proper fit on the machine, and testing will reveal this."

With that, W. E. said: "Thank you, Professor Learned, that is all."

Henry called Mary Worker next. She testified regarding John Q.'s job, his salary, their children, his activities with and contributions to his family, estate expenses, personal and financial loss to the family resulting from his death. W. E. Just followed his pretrial plan to forego cross-examination of Mary.

With that, Henry rested.

W. E. Just then moved for a *directed verdict* for the defendant. Such a motion, in effect, asks the judge to take the case away from the jury. The judge has the power to do so, provided the evidence is such that reasonable persons could not find for a party other than the one in whose favor the verdict has been directed. If Judge Fairness were to grant this motion, further evidence would not be put forth. Instead, the judge would instruct the jury to retire and return a verdict for the defendant in accordance with his directions. Judge Fairness, however, denied the motion. In his mind there was no question that the plaintiff had met its burden of proof, clinching it, in his opinion, with Professor Learned's testimony.

In some state court systems and in federal nonjury trials, the proper motion at this time would have been for dismissal for failure to prove a prima facie case. It is sometimes referred to as a motion for a *nonsuit*. Such a motion is granted if the judge determines as a matter of law that the plaintiff has not presented sufficient evidence to prove his cause of action. While it is more usual to find the defense making the motion for a directed verdict or for a nonsuit after the plaintiff has rested, it is possible for the plaintiff to make these motions. If the plaintiff's motion were for a directed verdict, the motion would be granted only if reasonable persons could not find for the defendant. That would mean the plaintiff's case in chief had been so strong it was clear—even prior to the presentation of evidence by the defense—that it could not be rebutted. In those states where the plaintiff can move for a voluntary nonsuit, he does so when he finds his case has been so weak that it is to his advantage to seek dismissal without prejudice so that he can proceed at another time more effectively. This motion will not be granted if there has been lack of due diligence by counsel, since the effect of granting such a motion is that the matter is not *res judicata*. *Res judicata* means that the case has been adjudicated and may not be brought again.

DEFENDANT'S CASE IN DEFENSE

Since W. E. Just's motion for a directed verdict was not granted, it was now time for the defendant to present his case in defense. Trial procedure in this country gives the defendant the opportunity to present evidence to rebut the plaintiff's claim and in support of any affirmative defenses put forward. This follows the plaintiff's case in chief. Both the plaintiff and defendant follow the same process of examination with witnesses.

Preparation

W. E. Just's preparation for the case in defense required consideration of how best to controvert what he anticipated the plaintiff would present in the case in chief. One of W. E.'s first decisions was whether he should call any witnesses. In many cases the defense relies entirely on the weaknesses and limitations of the plaintiff's case in chief and on the doubts that can be cast upon credibility through cross-examination. Knowing that the plaintiff had evidence of a man's death and of a shattered zagger, W. E. decided that he could not rely upon inadequacy of the plaintiff's case. His decision, therefore, was to present a case in defense and, in accord with Will Very's wishes, to make the defense as strong as possible. Having made that decision, W. E. Just now had to consider how to present his case. He decided to call three witnesses: Charles Sell, the cypres engineer, and the zagger research engineer from Acme Labs. Charles Sell was an important witness since he could refute implications of a size defect and had first-hand knowledge of John Q.'s difficulty in working with the special zagger. He also had statistical data that W. E. Just hoped might have the effect of downplaying the lack of dynamic testing. The cypres engineer's contribution concerned John Q.'s failure to use a guard. However, it was the Acme Labs researcher who held what W. E. considered to be the key item for the defense: evidence that the Zagger Supply process precluded violent shattering when there were bonding defects. These were the major defenses planned by W. E. He hoped they would be strong enough to overcome two major but undeniable factors unfavorable to the defendant: the bonding defect and lack of dynamic testing.

W. E. Just's next decision concerned the order in which he would call his witnesses. He realized that by the time they took the stand the jury would already have heard the plaintiff's case. That meant they not only would have some familiarity with the occurrences, but also would have begun to form impressions about those events. Therefore, he believed the greatest impact would be made by building up to and ending with the witness who offered the strongest defense testimony, which would be the Acme Laboratories research engineer. W. E. also considered the fact that Charles Sell's testimony would lay the foundation for what the cypres engineer had to say. Therefore, he decided to call Charles Sell, the cypres engineer, and the Acme Labs engineer, in that order.

In preparing his witnesses for trial, W. E. was asked by the Acme Labs researcher about the possibility of videotaping his testimony beforehand. Attorney Just explained that the videotaping of testimony of witnesses (especially those called as experts), and presenting it on the screen in court, is practiced in some but not all jurisdictions. Some courts restrict its use to situations in which the witness will be unable to appear personally or is in such poor health as to be in danger of death before the trial. He added that some advocate a change to totally prerecorded videotaped testimony, filmed beforehand, at times and places that suit the convenience of witnesses and counsel. Others, he said, believe that taping denies the jury the opportunity to observe witnesses firsthand, can create distortions through such photographic effects as closeups, and destroys the psychological effect upon a witness of having to appear in person before judge and jury. The conversation turned to televising of the actual trial for public broadcast and information. W. E. explained that this does not occur often. The presence of the camera and camera crew in the courtroom can be distracting to those involved in the case. He commented on the need for dignity and restraint in a court of law, so that a trial does not become a "three-ring circus."

However, the time for planning was now at an end. It was now time for W. E. to call his first witness. The trial had already reached the last stage depicted in Figure 6-4, having progressed through all of the preceding stages shown in the flow chart.

Case in Defense

Charles Sell, as the first witness for the defense, testified that he and other company design engineers working on the development of the special zagger had visited The Firm at least a dozen times testing prototypes. The latter had been used in trial runs of the new chattels on The Firm's cypres machines. Not only he and his engineers, but also Sam Scott, Jim Boss, and Peter Superior, had used the prototypes—all without incident. He further testified that John Q. had worked with this group during their last four sessions. John Q. had experienced difficulty in placing the special zagger prototype on the cypres machine and getting it clamped in place securely. In answer to Attorney Just's questions, Charles said that John Q. had been the only one in that group to have such trouble. Extra time had been spent working with John Q. until he appeared to have mastered the technique. Charles also testified that Timothy O'Goode, whom he was asked to train on the day after the accident, was able to adjust to the special zaggers immediately and without any of the difficulties John Q. had experienced.

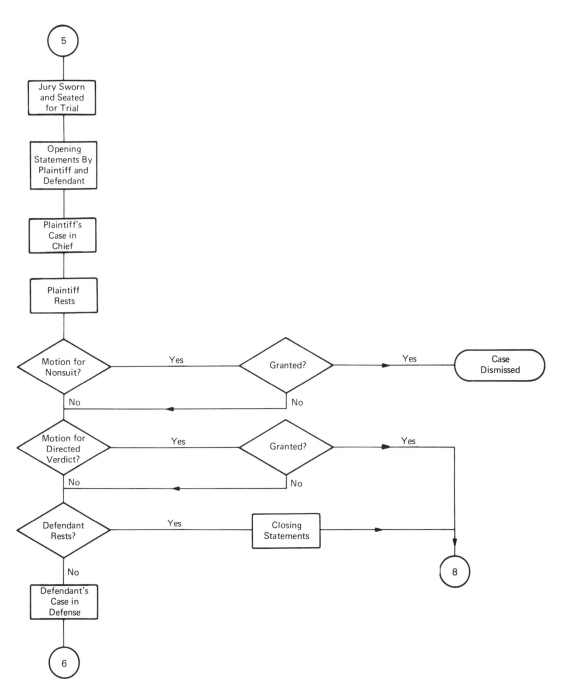

Figure 6-4. Trial: From Opening to Defendant's Case in Defense

Sell explained that a different clamping technique was necessary with the special zaggers. This resulted from the fact that a variation in zagger size was required for work on the new chattels. In response to W. E.'s question, Charles characterized the size differential as a necessary adjustment in design, not an imperfection.

On cross-examination, Charles admitted to Henry Law that the order for special zaggers specified conformity with OSHA standards, that dynamic testing was required to meet those standards, and that only six of the special zaggers shipped had been subjected to dynamic testing. Henry then elicited from him confirmation of the fact that size as well as bonding defects could be detected by such testing, and that the reason for the testing requirement was prevention of shattering accidents. After that, Henry led an uncomfortable Charles through questioning that clearly indicated that Charles could not state with absolute certainty that the special zaggers—except for the six—would not cause shattering due to defects detectable by dynamic testing.

W. E. set out on redirect to "rehabilitate" his witness. Responding to questioning, Charles testified that each of the special zaggers shipped had been subjected to static testing, that this reveals ninety-five percent of the defective zaggers manufactured by the special patented Zagger Supply process, that the patented process resulted in bonding defects in approximately five out of every ten thousand zaggers manufactured, as contrasted with industry figures of five out of each thousand, that this meant dynamic testing was useful in finding defects in Zagger Supply products for only $\frac{1}{400}$ of one percent of the zaggers that they produced. He also testified that The Firm's order for special zaggers had gone through exactly the same production process as the prototypes, and that the latter had been tested and retested to an extent far beyond legal requirements and industry standards.

On recross, Henry Law asked if $\frac{1}{400}$ of one percent did not mean that there was an expectation of twenty-five defective zaggers in every one million produced. Charles Sell answered in the affirmative. Henry asked if it did not then follow that failure to use dynamic testing by a firm, such as Zagger Supply, which manufactured over one million zaggers in a year could cause twenty-five deaths annually due to shattering. W. E. Just was on his feet immediately, objecting strenuously to this question, pointing out that it was argumentative, conclusory, and based on an unproved assumption (that shattering inevitably caused and resulted in death). Judge Fairness sustained the objection. He instructed the jury to disregard it and Henry to withdraw it. Even so, W. E. Just was concerned that the jury had heard the damaging remarks. Could the jurors really mentally disregard it, he asked himself. If Henry had intentionally asked an improper question for the express purpose of having the jury hear it, he would have acted unethically. Henry's apology for the question, however, seemed to be sincere and to indicate it had not been an intentional attempt to illicitly influence the jury.

W. E. Just's second witness, the cypres engineer, qualified as an expert through undergraduate and graduate study in cypres engineering and twenty years of experience as a cypres engineer. The last ten of these were with Zagger Supply, where his primary duties were design of zaggers for use on the cypres machines of that firm's customers. He confirmed Charles Sell's testimony about development of the special zagger, the prototype, and the training of John Q. He also testified regarding his part in the investigation of the accident. In viewing the accident scene and enlargements of the pictures taken immediately after the accident, he noted at all times the absence of the guard on John Q.'s machine. This, he said, was significant since improper placement of a zagger on a cypres machine makes it difficult to fit the guard in place. One of the reasons, he stated, for construction of cypres machine guards in such a manner is to encourage proper mounting of the zagger on the machine. He confirmed that wobbling results when there is improper placement of the zagger on the machine. Asked for his opinion of the cause of the accident, he said that based on the absence of the guard and John Q.'s past difficulty in placement of the zagger on the machine, he believed the accident was caused by wobbling resulting from insecure clamping and improper mounting of the zagger on the machine.

On cross-examination, he did admit to Henry that "I cannot say it would never be impossible" for small zagger fragments to pass through the opening in the guard. When Henry asked if he knew, either directly or indirectly, of any cases of shattering where there was wobbling following improper clamping of a zagger which had been subjected to dynamic testing, his response was:

"No, there have been no reported shatterings with dynamically tested zaggers."

He would not agree with Henry, however, that this proved Professor Learned's contention that improper mounting could not, of itself, be the cause of shattering. He stated that, in his opinion, insufficient time had elapsed since the testing requirement went into effect to have the necessary experience to make such a statement or to prove that the testing would eliminate all shatterings.

Henry then asked if a bonding defect alone could not cause shattering. The engineer replied that a bonding defect could not, in his opinion, have caused the accident which occurred to John Q. Henry responded that that was not what he had asked. He then restated his query as to whether a bonding defect could result in shattering. When the reply was "Yes," Henry Law prevented the engineer's obvious desire to elaborate and explain further.

He simply said:

"Thank you. That is all."

W. E. Just followed up on redirect by asking if, in the engineer's opinion, the violent shattering which had occurred in this case could have resulted from a bonding defect. The answer was: "No. The Zagger Supply process prevents explosive shattering."

The research engineer from Acme Labs qualified as an expert with graduate study in both the cypres and zagger areas and sixteen years of experience in researching the causes of zagger shattering. W. E. Just was careful to point out for the jury the credentials of his witnesses as one means of counteracting the impact of Professor Learned's appearance for the plaintiff.

The Acme Labs researcher testified that he had performed tests on the zagger fragments involved in the John Q. Worker accident at the request of Zagger Supply. He had found bonding defects in the zagger, but he believed that these could not have caused the accident. He testified that the violent shattering that had occurred could have been caused only by wobbling of the zagger while it was being operated at high speeds—in excess of 2000 rpm. This conclusion, he said, was based upon his research studies regarding zagger shatterings that included testing of over one thousand shattered zaggers over a five-year period. These tests included every shattered zagger manufactured by the patented Zagger Supply process, as well as hundreds of shattered zaggers of other manufacturers. His research revealed that the Zagger Supply process resulted in fewer bonding defects. Furthermore, those Zagger Supply products which did have bonding defects did not shatter with an explosive force or in the violent manner connected with the John Q. Worker incident.

Henry followed up, on cross-examination, by asking if the wobbling to which the witness had referred could not have been caused by a size defect in the zagger.

"I have no basis for stating that the zagger was defective with regard to size," was the reply.

He did admit that a size defect could cause wobbling and also acknowledged that size defects commonly accompany bonding defects.

Henry continued, asking if dynamic testing could not have been a factor in the infrequent explosive shatterings of Zagger Supply products. The witness acknowledged that it might have been, since Zagger Supply had voluntarily been doing such testing on random production runs even before the testing was made a requirement.

Continuing with the cross-examination, Henry wanted to know if the research work and testing of zagger fragments at Acme Labs had not been paid for by Zagger Supply and other zagger manufacturers. The answer was that each firm paid for the research it wished to have done.

W. E. Just did not like that last question or its implications. Therefore, on redirect examination he re-established through questioning that Acme Labs, as an independent entity, provided its clientele with an impartial, disinterested means of research regarding their products.

"Has the independence and objectivity of the work done at Acme Labs ever received public recognition?" he asked.

"Yes," answered the engineer, who testified further that the latest such recognition was in an article in the July 19XX issue of the *Zagger Journal*.

"And," asked W. E. Just, "who was the author of that article?"

"Professor Ira Learned," was the reply.

"That is all."

W. E. Just turned to Henry, who, realizing what had happened to his attempt to discredit the testimony of the last witness, had no wish to engage in recross-examination.

With that, W. E. Just rested.

It was now Henry Law who made a motion for a directed verdict. It was denied. Judge Fairness could find no reason to grant such a motion. In his mind, the evidence was sufficiently contradictory to require submission of the case to the jury.

PLAINTIFF'S EVIDENCE IN REBUTTAL

At this point, Henry had to decide if he wished to present plaintiff's *evidence in rebuttal*. After the defendant rests, the plaintiff has the option of calling new witnesses or recalling those who had testified previously. He is, however, limited to refuting evidence introduced by the defendant. The same process is followed with witnesses as for the case in chief. At the conclusion, the plaintiff's attorney announces that he closes. (One of the issues dealt with by the court in the *Newman* decision found earlier in this chapter had to do with witnesses in rebuttal.)

Henry decided to forego this stage. He believed that the defense had introduced no evidence that he had not anticipated and already refuted through his earlier witnesses. Any plaintiff's evidence, in his opinion, would now be mere repetition of matters presented in the case in chief.

DEFENDANT'S EVIDENCE IN REJOINDER

Henry's decision eliminated another trial stage: the defendant's *evidence in rejoinder.* If the plaintiff on rebuttal brings up new points, the defendant has the option of calling witnesses in rejoinder to those matters. He follows the same procedure as with prior witnesses. The defense counsel indicates that he closes at the conclusion of this stage. These proceedings that would have been possible in the trial following the defendant's case have been shown in a flow chart in Figure 6-5. Note the consequences of these occurrences.

CLOSING ARGUMENTS

After each attorney has closed his case, final or closing arguments follow. Each attorney is given the opportunity to review for the jury (or the judge in nonjury trials) important evidence and to state again the arguments and contentions in favor of his client. As with the opening statements, these do not constitute evidence. Generally the plaintiff, who is given the first word in the opening statements, is given the last word in the closing arguments. These are sometimes referred to as *closing statements,* the term used in Figure 6-6, which brings the charting of trial stages up to that point.

Defendant's Close

W. E. Just believed he had an advantage in being able to follow the testimony of defense witnesses with his closing argument to the jury. He felt this would serve as a reinforcement for what the jury had just heard. He told the jurors that the real question in this trial was not whether there was a bonding defect in the zagger, but whether the defectiveness of the product had been the cause of John Q.'s death. He reminded them that they had heard from an expert in zagger shatter research, one with vast experience regarding shattering accidents. The same expert, he said, had stated under oath that in his opinion the bonding defect could not have caused the kind of explosive shattering that resulted in John Q.'s death. According to that expert, the bonding defect alone could have caused no more than a mild shattering. He also recalled the testimony about insufficient time having elapsed since inception of the testing requirement to prove that it could completely eliminate shatterings.

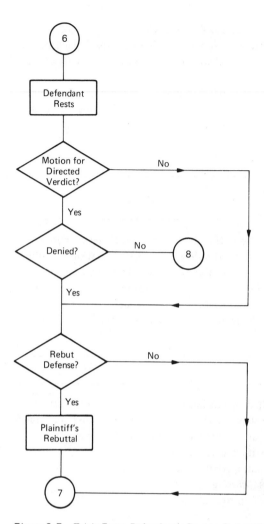

Figure 6-5. Trial: From Defendant's Rest to Plaintiff's Rebuttal

Attorney Just reminded the jurors that they had heard testimony not only from the cypres engineers, but also from plaintiff's witnesses who were cypres operators, about the importance of proper placement and clamping of the zagger on the machine, the wobbling resulting from an improper clamping, and the fact that this wobbling when combined with high speeds caused violent shattering. He reminded them of accident pictures they had been shown, pictures which revealed that John Q. did not have the guard in position. He recalled that there was testimony by the cypres engineer that improper placement of the zagger on the machine makes it difficult to position the guard in place. In addition, there was testimony that John Q. had experienced difficulty during training sessions with properly mounting the zagger on his machine. He reminded them that size differences were necessary adjustments in design, not defects. W. E. suggested to the jury

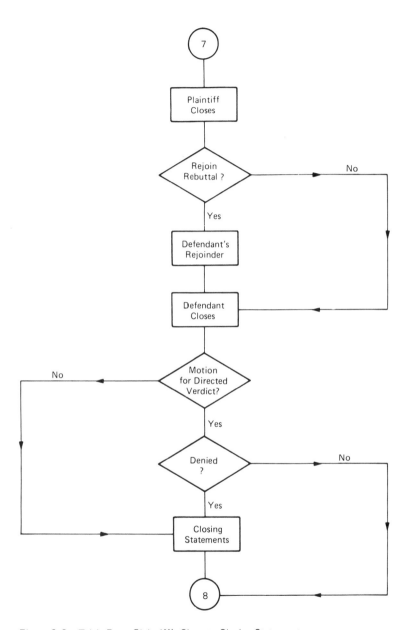

Figure 6–6.   Trial: From Plaintiff's Close to Closing Statements

there had been sufficient evidence presented to show it was not any defect in the zagger, but rather improper placement of the zagger on the machine–operator failure–which had caused the accident resulting in John Q.'s death.

He reminded them that John Q. was an experienced operator, one who knew he was working with a potentially hazardous instrument. Yet John Q. worked without a guard. Further, there was testimony of a general air of exuberance in the plant that day, a factor that could have precluded John Q.'s full concentration on the job at hand. Finally, he suggested that after careful consideration of all this evidence they, the jurors, would find it indicated very clearly that the defendant should prevail for two reasons: first, John Q.'s accident and resulting death had not been caused by any defect in the zagger; second, John Q. had knowingly and voluntarily assumed any and all risks attached to use of the zagger on the cypres machine.

Plaintiff's Close

It was now Henry Law's turn. He began by stating that this was, indeed, a case of a defective product that had caused a working man's death. He told the jury that John Q. was not the bumbling, incompetent, careless operator his opponent attempted to portray. Instead, John Q. was known to his fellow workers as an extremely careful and skilled worker. In fact, his superiors testified that they had selected him to be the first cypres operator to work on the new chattels for that very reason. He reminded the jurors that this man had not had a prior accident in his twenty-three years with The Firm. If John Q. had some difficulty in working with the new zagger, wouldn't any reasonable person consider this natural on a first attempt? Perhaps it was due to size differences, he suggested, and noted that Professor Learned had testified regarding them.

Henry reminded the jury there had been five other accidents with the special zaggers. "Why?" he asked. Answering his own question, Henry said it was because those zaggers did not meet federal safety standards—legal requirements that had been adopted for the very purpose of preventing accidents such as this one which had resulted in the death of an experienced employee. He reminded the jurors that the foremost zagger authority in the country, one of the authors of those standards, had testified as to the reasons for promulgating them. That same authority had tested fragments from the shattered zagger and formed the opinion that test-detectable defects had caused the accident.

Finally, he urged the jury to consider all the testimony carefully. He asked that the jury members use their experience in living and their common sense in determining the truth and arriving at a verdict. As a final word he added:

"I am sure you will find that the correct resolution of this issue must be in the plaintiff's favor."

JUDGE'S CHARGE TO THE JURY

At this point in a jury trial, it is the judge's turn to talk with the jury. This stage is referred to as the *charge to the jury* or *jury instructions* since the judge explains the applicable law. The judge may review some of the testimony and in some courts, including the federal system, has the right to comment on it.

Requested and Pattern Instructions

Each attorney may present to the judge matters to be included in the jury instructions. The requested instructions are often submitted in writing to the judge. Some courts have *pattern instructions;* that is, model jury charges prepared by committees of judges and lawyers. Some jurisdictions require use of the pattern instructions exactly as prepared, while others consider them to be guidelines only. Proponents of pattern instructions assert that not only is there a saving of judicial time, but also greater accuracy, impartiality, and uniformity in jury instructions when patterns are used. Critics allege that pattern instructions, when available, tend to be given verbatim and decrease the probability of instructions' being adapted to fit the case at hand.

Both Henry and W. E. submitted to Judge Fairness requested points for inclusion in the instructions to the jury. After studying them, the judge decided not to use any of them. He believed that Henry's points for charge would lead the jurors to feel they must find for the plaintiff automatically if the defendant had violated OSHA standards. On the other hand, he thought that W. E.'s points would burden the plaintiff with an almost impossible standard of proof of causation. Judge Fairness desired the instructions he used to be not only a correct statement of the applicable law but also to be as objective as possible. He conferred with the two attorneys regarding their requests for instruction. He did this prior to the closing arguments and in his chambers, off the record, and out of the jury's hearing.

Effectiveness of Instruction

The instructions he finally prepared and delivered consisted of twenty-four pages of double-spaced material. There has been much discussion of jury instructions. Some allege the instructions are confusing to the jury, worded in legal terminology not easily comprehended by the lay person, so lengthy and detailed that a jury cannot be expected to remember even the major points. Still others point out that the law is explained to the jury only after the jurors have heard all the evidence, the implication being that the jury could listen more effectively to testimony if instructed at the outset of the trial. On the other hand, some point out that earlier instructions would influence or prejudice the jury and could cause jurors to mentally discard important matters. Still others lament the fact that some judges have been known to read jury instructions in a rapid monotone, so that even the most conscientious of jurors finds it hopeless to follow. Judge Fairness, however, did not do this.

Jury Charge

The judge began by telling the jury members that they would be the sole judges of the facts. He explained they must pass on the credibility of witnesses, should not be influenced by any sympathy or prejudice they might feel regarding the parties, must base their verdict entirely on the evidence, i.e., testimony of witnesses, documents and exhibits admitted into evidence.

He then reviewed some of the facts of the case. Judge Fairness said that there was no dispute about the fact that the shattering accident had occurred, that John Q. had been killed, that the special zagger had been manufactured and sold by the defendant, that a bonding defect existed, that the required dynamic testing had not been done, and that the guard had not been in place on John Q.'s machine. Both the testing and the guard matters, he said, represented failure by the respective parties to comply with legal requirements. He explained that the plaintiff contended that defects in the zagger caused the shattering that resulted in John Q.'s death. On the other hand, he said, the defendant contended that death was caused not by any defect in the product but by the deceased's actions in connection with placing the zagger on the machine and then using it without a guard.

He explained to the jury the five questions the jurors would be required to answer. Those questions are listed in Table 6-1.

Judge Fairness then went on to explain strict liability in tort for a defective product, quoting to the jury from §402A. He described proximate cause as "that cause which, in a natural and continuous sequence, unbroken by any intervening cause, produces the result complained of and without which the result would not have occurred—in other words, a substantial contributing factor in bringing about the result complained of."

He told the jury that the mere happening of an accident did not in and of itself raise a presumption that anyone was liable as a matter of law, that the plaintiff had the burden of establishing by a preponderance of the evidence that there had been a defective product and that it was a proximate cause of John Q.'s death. He said if the jurors did not find this to be so, they need proceed no further. Their verdict would be for the defendant. On the other hand, if they found in the affirmative, they must determine whether John Q. had voluntarily undertaken the task at hand knowing the risks involved and proceeding regardless of those risks. He explained that this constituted a complete defense. Therefore, if they found this to be so, they need go no further. If not, they must proceed to the final two questions. He reviewed for them the bills for estate expenses that had been entered into evidence and also discussed John Q.'s age, salary, and

TABLE 6-1. Questions Submitted to Jury in Mary Worker Case

1. Was the accident that occurred on August 28, 19XX and which resulted in the fatal injuries to John Q. Worker caused by a defective zagger which he was using at the time?

   Answer YES or NO _____

2. Was that defective condition in existence when the zagger was sold by Zagger Supply, Inc.?

   Answer YES or NO _____

3. Did John Q. Worker use the special zagger knowing the risks involved and voluntarily assuming those risks?

   Answer YES or NO _____

4. What were the damages sustained by the estate of John Q. Worker as a result of his death?

   $ _____

5. What were the damages sustained by the family of John Q. Worker as a result of his death?

   $ _____

expected work life. Turning to counsel, he asked if they had any points they believed the court should have covered and did not. If so, he asked them to state those now.

Henry Law requested a side bar conference to be recorded by the court reporter. He and W. E. Just both objected to the court's denial of their requests for items to be included in the charge. Judge Fairness again refused, stating his reasons. The attorneys wanted this on the record, since errors in jury instructions can constitute the basis for an appeal.

The judge then turned to the jury. He told the jurors he had concluded the charge and that it was now time for them to retire and deliberate.

He reminded them again that a unanimous verdict was necessary. He excused jurors seven and eight and thanked them for their services. He also asked if counsel objected to having the exhibits which had been admitted into evidence go out with the jury. There was no objection. The jury retired.

Verdicts

Judge Fairness had given the jury five questions to answer. This is referred to as a special verdict. In the federal courts, the judge has discretion to request either a general or special verdict. A *general verdict* is one that requires the jury to decide in favor of one of the parties and, if damages have been sought, to indicate the sum of money to be awarded. A *special verdict* is one that requires answers to specific interrogatories, such as those given to the jury in this case. Advocates of the special verdict maintain that it has the advantage of providing rationale in support of the jury's decision. This is, of course, lacking in a general verdict. The federal rules also give the judge discretion to request a combined special and general verdict; that is, answers to specific questions as well as indication of the party in whose favor the jury finds.

Problems have arisen in cases in which juries returned answers to special interrogatories that were inconsistent with each other or with the general verdict on the combined ballot. In such cases, the judge may enter judgment based upon consistencies found within the special interrogatories, may send the matter back to the jury, or may order a new trial.

Note that Judge Fairness also instructed the jury to return a unanimous verdict. The federal rules provide that the parties may stipulate that the finding of a stated majority shall be taken as the verdict. That was not done in this case, because W. E. Just would not agree to it. Some states provide for less than a unanimous verdict in their rules of procedure.

JURY DELIBERATIONS AND VERDICT

Following Judge Fairness' charge, the jury was escorted from the courtroom to a conference room where the jury members would deliberate in private. No other persons, including court officials, are permitted in the jury room during this process. All contact with the outside is through the *tipstaff,* who is summoned to notify the judge once the jury reaches a verdict. If the jurors find the need for additional instruction, they may send a message to the judge, who can provide such information to them in open court. Transcripts of depositions or of the testimony during the trial itself are not available to them. In many states they are not permitted to take notes during the trial. Therefore, their deliberations are based upon their recollection of the testimony given during the trial. They normally have available in the jury room materials that have been entered into evidence. Exceptions are possible where undue influence might result.

Inside the jury room, the chairperson, Nancy Perkins, suggested that they might begin by voting on the five questions they had to answer. Adam Frank said he would prefer to vote later, after they had an opportunity to discuss some of the testimony.

"Especially," he added, "what the professor and the engineers had to say about what caused the accident. If I believe the professor, it's the company's fault this man was killed, and his widow should win this case. But, if I believe the engineers, then it's his own fault he was killed. I don't know what to believe. It's confusing."

"There's no problem," said Sam Wells. "Here's a working man who was killed on the job, and his widow is suing the big corporation that manufactured the zagger he was using which exploded. Any zagger that explodes isn't safe to use. That corporation knows it. They even skipped the tests they're supposed to do."

"That's right," Kathleen Logan interrupted. "They broke the law."

"But why did he use it—and without a guard? He broke the law, too," said Nancy Perkins.

"What chance did he have?" was Geraldine Horne's response. "You heard what that younger man said about being forced to use it or lose his job."

"Right," said Sam. "It's just the same with the truck I drive. I tell the foreman the tires are bald and he says, 'Use it; use it; they're not that bad.' They wait for a major breakdown before they take it out of service. It costs less. These big companies are all the same. You want a job, you do what they say."

"But surely not something that would kill a man," said Nancy.

"What do they care?" asked Sam. "All they're interested in is how much money they'll make. And if a man gets killed, they go out and hire some engineer who says it's the man's own fault."

"But I thought that last engineer made a lot of sense," said Adam.

"Of course," said Sam. "Why do you think they hired him? They're not going to put someone on the stand who'll say it's all their fault."

"I feel so sorry for that Mrs. Worker," said Kathleen Logan. "With five children to raise. It's such a pity."

"What's worse is that this never should have happened. When a man has to use a zagger in his work, he should be given one that won't explode." Martin Lee spoke for the first time.

"Well, a man should have safe equipment to work with, I agree," said Adam.

"You're right," replied Sam. "And when he gets killed because he doesn't have it, the company ought to pay. They can afford it."

"Of course," said Geraldine. "Besides, they're insured. Everyone knows that. The insurance company will pay."

"That's the wrong attitude," said Adam. "That's why insurance costs so much these days."

Because it appeared that the two were going to debate the insurance issue, Nancy interrupted to ask if they were ready to vote. Adam still hesitated, but the others said they had made their decision. Finally, Kathleen suggested that they take a first vote to see how close they were to agreement. They could always continue their discussion if the vote indicated it was necessary. That sounded reasonable, and Adam acquiesced.

Nancy read from the verdict ballot the first question, which asked if the accident had been caused by a dangerously defective zagger. They were surprised to find that all had voted in the affirmative. The second question, which asked if the defect existed at the time the zagger was sold, also received a unanimous vote of "yes." It was the third question, which was concerned with whether John Q. had assumed the risk, on which they did not agree. Adam and Nancy voted yes.

"We have to be unanimous," said Nancy.

"Yes," said Martin. "The last jury I was on was a hung jury." In answer to Sam's query he added, "That means the jury's deadlocked. When we reported that to the judge, he declared a mistrial and the same case was tried all over again with another jury."

Kathleen interrupted, addressing Nancy and Adam: "I don't see how you can think a man would intentionally do something that would kill him. That's just like committing suicide."

"But he wasn't using the guard," said Nancy.

"That was probably accidental. We all do things like that at one time or another."

"Even so, that means he caused the accident himself," Nancy replied.

"Read the question again," said Geraldine. "It says he knew the risks and voluntarily assumed them. That's different from being careless."

Nancy reread the question aloud:

"Did John Q. Worker use the special zagger knowing the risks involved and voluntarily assuming those risks?"

"You're right," she said. "I'll change my vote."

"And so will I," said Adam.

In this way they arrived at unanimity on the third question. The two remaining questions dealt with damages. To arrive at the sum to be awarded, they added the bills that had been introduced into evidence and arrived at $4,891.23. It was not quite so easy for them to determine the damages to be awarded for the family. They computed John Q.'s expected salary for the next twenty-three years, but Kathleen was vehement in wanting to add an additional amount as compensation for his unexpected death. This provoked a heated discussion, and they finally agreed on the sum of $300,000.

It had taken them approximately two and a half hours. Nancy completed the verdict ballot, they all signed it, and then summoned the tipstaff to announce they had reached a verdict.

When they returned to the courtroom, the members of the jury were asked if they had reached a verdict. Nancy answered for them that they had. The verdict was read from the ballot by the clerk. W. E. Just asked that the jury be polled. The judge honored that request, and each juror affirmed the verdict. It was apparent that there had been no "sleeping jurors" in this trial, unlike the allegation in the *Newman* case found earlier in this chapter.

Although the work of the jury was completed and the members could be dismissed, the Mary Worker case was far from being over. The next chapter begins with the post-verdict events and then goes on to describe the appeal.

QUESTIONS

1. An interesting aspect of the Mary Worker case involves the fact that Judge Fairness, although privately believing differing conclusions are possible, upholds the jury verdict for the plaintiff. Why did he do so? Should he have granted a new trial? W. E.'s request for a directed verdict? Is W. E. correct in his contention that causation has not been proved? Why?

2. Have the parties in this case each received a fair trial? Has each received justice? Does a losing party ever feel that justice was done?

3. Considering all the evidence, was either party all right or all wrong? Do you believe this is typical? If so, how can a jury arrive at a decision?

4. What is your reaction to the events that took place in the jury deliberation room? Did this jury adequately tackle the task before it? Did the members discuss the real issues in the case? Give reasons for your answer. Has its verdict been unduly influenced by matters extraneous to the trial? If so, what are they? Have you ever served on a jury? How does your experience compare with that reported here? Does this jury's action have any implications for education for jury service? for professional juries? If so, what are they?

5. A judge's power to enter a judgment n.o.v. gives him yet another opportunity to take a verdict away from a jury. What other opportunities does he have for doing so? Does this give him too much discretionary power? Is it necessary power? Is there any control over its possible abuse? If so, what is that?

6. Considering the total effort that has gone into this case so far and anticipating that which is yet to come, do you believe this is a matter which should be resolvable in some other way? How? Should there be a "no-fault" products liability law? Why?

7. Does Zagger Supply really have a good cause to appeal this case? What hope do you believe they might have for success? Would you have appealed? Why? Having the benefit of hindsight, what do you believe W. E. Just could have done differently that might have won the case for the defendant?

8. The rules of evidence were a factor during the trial several times. In each instance, did the rules help in securing a fair trial for both parties? In what way? Does your exposure to just a few of the rules of evidence give any clue as to the amount of procedural law that must be almost second nature to the trial lawyer? Does it imply anything for those who sometimes wish to serve as their own lawyer? Can you see any difference in the work of a trial lawyer and the attorney who does not engage in trial work?

9. What has been the role of Judge Fairness in this trial? Has he given any direction to it? If so, in what way?

NOTES

[1] 28 U.S.C. §1861 *et seq.*

[2] *Fay* v. *New York,* 332 U.S. 261 (1947); *Apodaca* v. *Oregon,* 406 U.S. 404 (1970).

[3] *Taylor* v. *Louisiana,* 419 U.S. 522 (1975); *Peters* v. *Kiff,* 407 U.S. 493 (1972).

[4] *Colgrove* v. *Battin,* 413 U.S. 149 (1973).

post-verdict
motions
and appeal

SEVEN

POST-VERDICT MOTIONS
AND JUDGMENT

The saga of the Mary Worker case continued after the jury's verdict was in. Henry Law, as might be expected, was eager for the court to enter judgment in accordance with the verdict. *Judgment* is the decree and order of the court, indicating the successful party and stating the relief to which that party is entitled. The judgment is the official decision of the court. It may or may not coincide with the verdict.

The federal rules provide that, in addition to the damages recovered, costs may be allowed to the prevailing party. Costs refer to fees paid to the court and do not include attorney's fees. (Other countries provide that the losing party must pay for the counsel fees of the successful party.)

W. E. Just, on the other hand, would forego no opportunity to win the case. He indicated to the judge that he would file a written motion with the court to have the verdict set aside. This motion is for a *judgment n.o.v. (non obstante verdicto)*, that is, judgment notwithstanding the verdict. The motion is properly granted if reasonable persons could not differ on the fact that the jury returned a verdict against the weight of the evidence. This motion is often joined with one for a new trial. Granting a new trial requires a showing of cause, such as error committed during the course of the trial, or some new evidence. It is not intended to provide a losing party with the opportunity to bring a second lawsuit against the same party for the same claim. That would be a violation of the principle of *res judicata,* which, translated, literally means "the matter has been decided." This doctrine is based upon the premise that an individual should be given a fair opportunity to have the controversy decided by a court. Once that occurs, there must be an end to litigation. If not, the same parties would be able to retry the same case *ad infinitum.* The exception occurs when there has been error, in which case there is the right to appeal.

Since the federal rules provide that the motion for judgment n.o.v. must be made no later than ten days after entry of judgment, W. E. Just wasted no time. He set to work immediately after deciding he would ask in the alternative for a new trial. The possible outcomes of such motions are shown in Figure 7-1, which flow charts steps in the trial beginning with the jury instructions. Note the difference in motions possible when there is a jury trial as compared with a nonjury trial. The latter are shown in Figure 7-2.

In support of his motions, W. E. Just gave the following rationale:

1. The plaintiff failed to meet his burden of proving (a) that a defect in the product was the proximate cause of the accident; (b) that the product at the time of the accident was being used as intended, i.e., properly mounted and clamped on a machine with a guard. Therefore, the court erred in permitting the case to go to the jury, or in not properly instructing the jury regarding these matters.
2. The verdict was clearly against the weight of the evidence. The evidence was uncontradicted that the plaintiff's deceased operated the cypres machine without a guard; thus he knowingly and voluntarily exposed himself to a clear danger and assumed the risk of so acting.
3. The damages awarded were excessive.

W. E. filed these motions with the clerk of court. When such motions are made and granted following entry of judgment, that judgment may be reopened and either a new judgment entered or a new trial ordered. Henry Law, who had to tell Mary Worker she would not receive immediate payment of the sum voted by the jury and that there was the prospect of a reversal of that verdict as a result of a post-trial motion, also received a copy of the motions Attorney Just had filed. He prepared replies asking that the motions not be granted.

Judge Fairness, the trial still vivid in his memory, decided the jury's verdict would stand, entered judgment in accordance with it, and denied the defendant's motion. The reasons he gave were as follows:

1. There was sufficient evidence from Professor Learned from which a jury could reasonably conclude that the defective zagger was the cause of the accident.

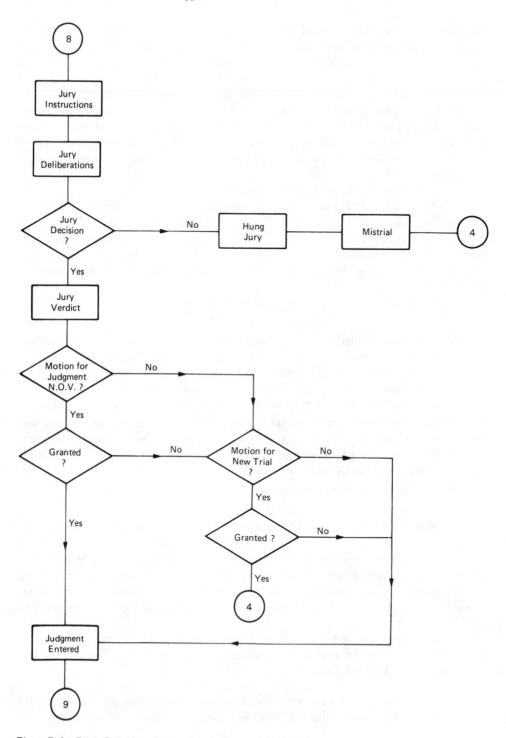

Figure 7–1. Trial: From Jury Instructions to Entry of Judgment

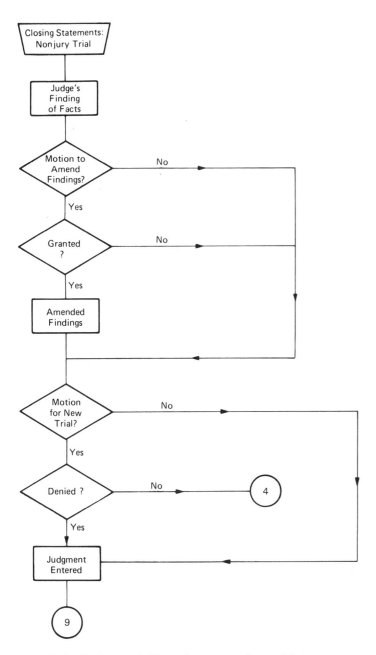

Figure 7-2. Nonjury Trial: Closing Statement to Entry of Judgment

2. The evidence was uncontradicted that the zagger was being used at the time of the accident for the purpose for which it was intended, i.e., on The Firm's cypres machine in the production of new chattels. Testimony of defendant's experts indicated that lack of a guard and improper mounting were conditions not only reasonably foreseeable but actually known to the defendant to exist at times in general usage. Therefore, the defendant could not claim that these conditions were outside the sphere of intended use.

3. Whether the plaintiff's deceased had voluntarily exposed himself to a clear and known danger was a conclusion of fact, to be determined by the jury from all the testimony and not just those portions cited in the defendant's brief. There having been contradictory evidence by plaintiff's and defendant's experts, different conclusions could reasonably be reached as to whether the danger was clear and known to the plaintiff's deceased.

4. The sums awarded as damages were consistent with the testimony of Mary Worker, both for estate expenses and her late husband's expected life earnings.

Only to his wife did Judge Fairness reveal that he believed reasonable persons could have arrived at different conclusions in this case.

With entry of the judgment in favor of Mary Worker, the case would be concluded, as shown in Figure 7-3, when the defendant made payment in accordance with that judgment. This is known as *satisfaction of the judgment.* However, Zagger Supply had no desire to make payment at this point. Instead, Will Very was adamant about pursuing the matter further. Since W. E. Just believed there was sufficient cause to allege error, the defense would pursue the alternate course shown in Figure 7-3 by appealing to a higher court. Will Very had this reaction:

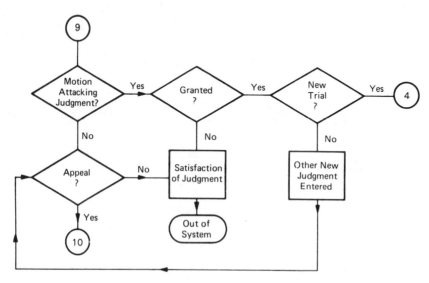

Figure 7-3. Post-Judgment Action

"Over a quarter of a million dollars! When a man didn't use enough care to place the guard in position on his cypres machine! If every careless cypres operator who gets hurt while using our zaggers is going to be able to recover from us, we'll be out of business by the end of this year. Appeal? There's absolutely no question about it. We can't afford not to appeal."

DECISION TO APPEAL

Very's decision was a business judgment, one that W. E. Just privately predicted even before he approached the firm's president about proceeding on appeal. In fact, W. E. did not request a meeting with the president until he had mentally considered these matters with regard to appeal:

1. Is there a legal basis for appeal?
2. What are the possibilities for success?
3. What costs will be involved?
4. What is in my client's best interests?

An *appellant* (the party bringing an appeal) cannot seek reversal of a lower court's decision upon a ground not raised in the trial court, as noted in the *Sturm* decision which follows.

Sturm v. *Chicago & N.W. RY. Co.*

157 F.2d 407 (8th Cir., 1946)

[Appeal from the District Court of the United States for the District of Minnesota.]

PER CURIAM. Gustav C. Sturm (who will be referred to as plaintiff), while employed by the defendant Railway Company (appellee) as a brakeman in Chicago, Illinois, fell from the top of a box car and was injured. He brought this action under the Federal Employer's Liability Act, 45 U.S.C.A. §51–60, to recover damages for his injuries. In his complaint the plaintiff charged that the Railway Company was negligent in failing to equip the car from which he fell with an efficient hand brake as required by the Federal Safety Appliance Act of 1910, §2, 45 U.S.C.A. §11, and that his injuries were the proximate result of such negligence. The Railway Company denied that the brake was inefficient and that its alleged failure to operate properly caused the plaintiff's injuries. The issues were tried to a jury. The evidence of the plaintiff tended to prove that the brake was inefficient and inoperative and that his injuries were due to its failure to operate. The evidence of the defendant tended to show that the brake was efficient and that the plaintiff's injuries could not have resulted from a defect in the brake. Neither party moved for a directed verdict at the close of the evidence. The issues were submitted to the jury. There were no requests for instructions. No exceptions were taken to the trial court's charge. The jury returned a verdict for the defendant, upon which a judgment was entered. The plaintiff has appealed from the judgment.

It is obvious that this appeal presents no question which is reviewable by this court. No ruling of the trial court is challenged. The question of the sufficiency of the evidence to support the verdict is not subject to review, since that question was not presented to the trial court by a motion for a directed verdict or any other equivalent action. . . . This court is without power to retry this case. It cannot concern itself with the credibility of witnesses or the weight of evidence. . . . The verdict of the jury, whether right or wrong, was completely determinative of the issues of fact tried and submitted.

The judgment is affirmed.

W. E. Just had already laid the foundation for appeal in his motions for a directed verdict, for judgment n.o.v., and for a new trial. In each instance, he had raised legal issues and alleged error by the trial court. Thus, he was satisfied that the legal basis for appeal existed. Furthermore, he believed he had sufficient, relevant, Great State precedent in support of his contentions to convince the appellate court of the legal soundness of the appellant's position.

As a lawyer, W. E. did not share the widely held, erroneous belief of many lay persons that there is an automatic right of appeal granted by the federal constitution. Nor do many persons understand that an appellate court's review of facts is much more limited than is its review of the legal issues. Details regarding the limits and possible results of an appeal are shown in Table 7–1. All these matters were considered by Attorney Just in weighing the wisdom of proceeding with an appeal.

Costs, W. E. believed, would not be as significant a factor in Zagger Supply's decision to appeal as they would be if Mary Worker were making the decision. Although not all trial lawyers also handle appeals, W. E. did. Since he was salaried, no additional counsel fees would be incurred. Court costs are recoverable by a successful appellant from the appellee (his opponent). However, when he compared court costs with the economic benefits that would result if the appeal were a success, W. E. believed the best interests of his client indicated appeal should be undertaken.

W. E. discussed all of this with Will Very, since it is the client and not the attorney who makes the decision regarding appeal. Not only was Will positive about his wishes, but he also added:

"Call Charles Sell and tell him I want him to take all the time necessary to prepare and appear in court with you on this."

Then W. E. found it necessary to explain that there is neither a jury nor witnesses in an appellate court. Instead, the attorneys for both sides present their arguments orally before a panel of judges. The oral arguments supplement written materials. These include a record of what transpired in the lower court as well as each counsel's *brief* or written rationale, which must be submitted to the court prior to the date of argument. This is to give the judges an opportunity to review the materials prior to that day. W. E. characterized appeal as a review, rather than a retrial.

"It's a battle for the lawyers, is that it?" Will Very asked. W. E. acknowledged then that the president understood.

TABLE 7-1. The Right of Appeal in Civil Matters

SOURCE OF THE RIGHT	ACTIONS FROM WHICH APPEAL MAY BE TAKEN	CONSIDERATIONS UPON APPEAL

1. Right exists in the state courts as provided in state constitutions and state statutes.
2. Right is provided in the federal courts although NOT required by the federal constitution (nor considered to be a requirement of due process).
	1. From final judgment of a lower court
	2. From certain interlocutory* (not final) orders; e.g.,
	  a. where an injunction is involved.
	  b. when the trial judge certifies a question of law to the appellate court.
		1. Evidence is viewed in a light most favorable to the party prevailing in the lower court.
		2. Generally no review of error induced or invited by actions of appealing party.
		3. Generally no review of error to which objection was not raised in lower court.

LIMITS OF THE RIGHT	RESTRICTIONS ON MATTERS REVIEWED ON APPEAL	POSSIBLE RESULTS OF APPEAL
1. Usually limited to one appeal to an intermediate appellate court. 2. Additional appeal generally discretionary with the highest court of appeals.	1. Normally limited to review of errors of law. 2. Generally limited to prejudicial (as opposed to harmless) error; i.e., error resulting in miscarriage of justice. 3. Usually no review of facts unless there is NO substantial evidence to support findings of fact made by judge or jury.	1. Action of lower court affirmed. 2. Decision of lower court reversed. 3. Case remanded (sent back) to the lower court with directions as to action to be taken by lower court, such as new trial. 4. In cases of discretionary appeal, denial of petition for review.

*An interlocutory order is not a final decision of the whole controversy; it settles only some point or matter intervening between the commencement and the end of a lawsuit.

NOTE: Appeal in civil cases is distinguished from appeal in criminal matters. The latter are affected by the constitutional provision regarding double jeopardy which normally precludes appeal by the prosecution.

INITIATING APPEAL

Following this conference, W. E. took the first step necessary to initiate an appeal. He filed notice of appeal in the Office of the Clerk of the same United States District Court in which the trial had been held. A copy of that notice appears as Form 7-1. At the same time he filed a bond as security. This had the effect of staying execution or enforcement of the trial court's judgment against Zagger Supply, pending outcome of the appeal.

A copy of the notice of appeal was sent to Henry Law by the clerk of courts as official notification. The clerk also recorded all of these transactions on the court's docket. W. E. was happy that he had been able to meet the deadline for filing notice of appeal, which was thirty days following entry of judgment. Note that this appeal was in

Form 7-1. Notice of Appeal

DISTRICT COURT OF THE UNITED STATES
FOR THE DISTRICT OF GREAT STATE

MARY WORKER,	:	Civil Action
Administratrix of the	:	XX-123
ESTATE OF JOHN Q.	:	
WORKER, deceased,	:	
Plaintiff	:	
	:	
v.	:	Notice of Appeal
	:	
ZAGGER SUPPLY, INC.,	:	
a corporation,	:	
Defendant	:	

Notice is hereby given that Zagger Supply, Inc., corporate defendant above named, hereby appeals to the
United States Court of Appeals for the Y Circuit from the
final judgment entered in this action on the sixteenth day
of March, 19XY.

W. E. Just

W. E. Just, Attorney for
Zagger Supply, Inc.
Zagger Building
That City, Nearby State

accord with what is sometimes referred to as the "final judgment" rule. This requires that
final judgment be entered before an appeal can be made. However, there are exceptions
for situations in which delay of appeal would be harmful or wasteful. Appeal prior to
final judgment is referred to as an *interlocutory* appeal.

While he was at the district court, W. E. ordered from the court reporter a transcript of the entire trial in order to complete the record of the case on file in the clerk
of courts office. (He also ordered a copy for his own use in preparing for the appeal.)
That record, consisting of the original papers and exhibits filed in the district court, the
transcript of the proceedings, and a certified copy of the docket entries prepared by the
clerk of the district court, would have to be transmitted to the clerk of the Court of Ap-

peals of the Y Circuit. Responsibility for actual forwarding of the record rested with the clerk of the district court, but it was W. E.'s responsibility to request that it be sent.

Selection of the Y Circuit Court of Appeals represented the only possible course of action. The sole question that had to be resolved was which was the proper appellate court for review of a case tried in the federal district court for the Great State District. Direct appeal from a federal district court to the United States Supreme Court is possible in only a few situations. As shown in Table 7-2, one example is a final judgment which holds an act of congress unconstitutional in a civil action to which the United States is a party. The Mary Worker case, however, did not qualify for direct review by the United States Supreme Court. Therefore, review of her case would be by an intermediate federal court of appeals, one for that circuit covering the Great State district. That was the Y Circuit. Oral arguments would be held in the federal court house located in Center City, Great State.

Mary Worker's first official word regarding the appeal came from Henry Law, who telephoned her when he received the copy of the notice of appeal. She had experienced a sense of victory when the jury's verdict was read in open court and again when Henry informed her that Judge Fairness had entered judgment in accordance with that verdict. It was a distinct letdown to hear now that her legal battle was far from being over, that the possibility existed that she could lose on appeal everything she had gained as an outcome of the trial. She felt she had no choice but to continue to fight. Although Henry explained to her that he had limited appellate experience, she asked him to stay with the case.

In the meantime, W. E. had forwarded the docket fee to the clerk of the court of appeals so that the appeal could be entered on that court's docket. It would be listed under the title given to the action in the district court. (Not all appellate courts follow this practice; some list the appeal as the appellant v. appellee.) Soon after that, the record was transmitted from the lower court. The clerk sent notice to both W. E. and Henry of the date on which that record was filed. W. E. now had forty days in which to prepare and file his brief.

TABLE 7-2. Appeal to the United States Supreme Court

FROM THE FEDERAL COURT SYSTEM	FROM THE STATE COURT SYSTEMS

Review of decisions of the lower federal courts:
1. Review from federal courts of appeal
  a. by certification by the court of appeals of a question of law,
  b. by appeal by a party relying on a state statute held unconstitutional by the court of appeals,
  c. by writ of *certiorari* granted by the Court upon petition of a party to the case.
2. Direct appeal from federal district courts only in limited cases specified by Congress.
	Review of final judgment of the highest court in a state:
	1. By appeal:
	  a. if a United States statute or treaty is involved and the state court has held it invalid,
	  b. if a state court has upheld a state statute which is alleged to be in violation of the constitution, treaties, or statutes of the United States.
	2. By writ of *certiorari*
	  a. in any of the situations listed above,
	  b. if any right, privilege, or immunity is claimed under the constitution, treaties, or statutes of the United States.

APPELLATE BRIEFS

The brief is an exceedingly important document in the appeal process. It contains the legal arguments upon which a party bases contention that the lower court's decision should either be reversed or upheld. Some appeals are decided on the basis of the contents of the brief, since oral arguments may be dispensed with either at the request of the parties or by the court on its own motion. The panel assigned to decide a case on appeal may consist of three, five, seven, or nine judges, depending upon the court and the case. In the federal court of appeals, panels of three are common. In unusual situations a court may sit *en banc,* which means that a panel consisting of all the judges of that court will hear the case.

Multiple copies of the brief are required to be filed with the clerk of courts, so that each judge will receive his own copy. The brief contains each attorney's statement of the questions to be decided by the court on review, the action the attorney wishes the court to take, and—most importantly—the reasons to support his position. That rationale generally includes reference to authoritative sources, such as the precedent of prior court decisions, statutes, and legal treatises. Therefore, finding relevant authoritative support for his position is vital in the attorney's legal research.

Copies of the appellant's brief must be served on the appellee who is given thirty days in which to prepare and file copies of his own brief with the clerk of the court of appeals. An appellant has the option of filing another brief in reply to that of the appellee.

Failure of either party to file a brief can be disastrous to his cause. If the appellant fails to file within the time provided, the appellee may move for dismissal of the appeal. If the appellee fails to file his brief, he cannot take part in the oral argument before the court except by special permission. This is indicated in Figure 7-4, which shows procedure prior to the appellate decision in a flow chart.

With all this in mind, W. E. began work on the appellant's brief. The required contents included:

1. A statement of the legal issues to be presented to the court for review.
2. A brief history of the case: the facts, the proceedings, and disposition by the trial court.
3. Appellant's argument: contentions as well as supporting rationale.
4. A statement of the relief sought on appeal.

W. E.'s brief necessarily contained many matters already known to the reader. Therefore, discussion is limited to the legal issues and points of argument he presented for review.

In asking the court to reverse the judgment of the lower court, W. E. raised the following issues, which he charged constituted reversible error:

1. In a case brought in strict liability in tort for an allegedly defective product, the court erred in refusing to grant appellant's motion for a directed verdict:

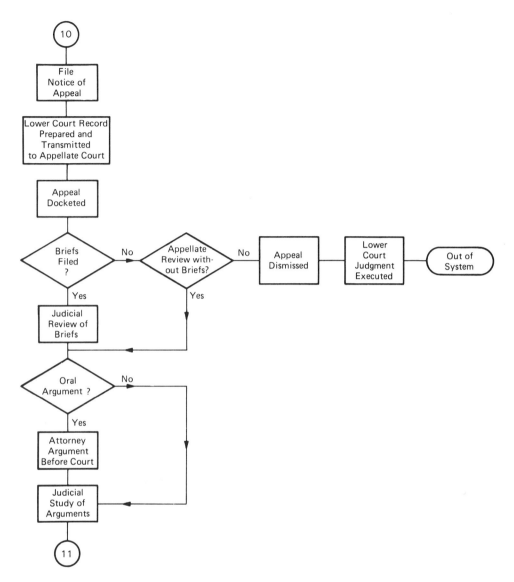

Figure 7-4. Procedure on Appeal Prior to Appellate Decision

    (a) when the appellee failed to prove that a defective and unreasonably danger-
ous condition of the product manufactured by the appellant was the proximate cause of the accident and injury and death to appellant's decedent;

    (b) when there was uncontradicted testimony clearly showing appellee's dece-
dent voluntarily proceeded, with full knowledge of the risks involved, to
expose himself to a clear and known danger.

  2. The court erred in failing to give sufficient and proper instructions to the jury:

(a) in not explaining that in order for the appellee to meet his burden of proof as to causation, he must not only prove which defect caused the accident but must also eliminate such other causes of the accident as fairly arose from the evidence;

(b) in not explaining that the appellee decedent's voluntary actions in exposing himself to a clear and known danger constituted assumption of the risk and thus denied to the appellee any right of recovery.

3. In light of both of the above and a jury verdict that was clearly against the weight of the evidence, the court erred in refusing to order a judgment n.o.v. for the appellant or, in the alternative, a new trial.

In support of his contention that the appellee had not met his burden of proof regarding causation, W. E. referred to *Carlin* v. *Goodbar,* 248 G.S. 334, 19XW,* which involved a service station operator who sought to recover from the manufacturer after a snow tire exploded while the operator was working with it. The court said in this 402A case that the operator "had the burden of proving that there was a defect in the tire, that the defect existed when the tire left the manufacturer's hands, that the defect was unreasonably dangerous to the user, and that there was a causal connection between the defect and the explosion." W. E. charged that Mary Worker had failed with respect to the latter two required proofs. Referring to specific pages of the trial transcript, W. E. noted that Professor Learned had admitted under cross-examination that he could not state positively that the bonding defect in the zagger was the only possible cause of the shattering. W. E. also pointed to explanation by appellant's witnesses as to why the bonding defect could not have caused the accident and their testimony advancing other possible reasons for the shattering. He urged that the trial judge had erred in failing to instruct the jury properly with regard to causation or, in the alternative, in failing to grant a directed verdict for the defendant.

In connection with the issue of assumption of the risk, W. E. referred to the Great State statute requiring that cypres machines be operated only with the guard properly positioned. He called attention to the picture exhibits as well as to specific pages of the transcript to show that the testimony had been uncontradicted regarding John Q.'s failure to have the guard in place. As support for his contention that failure to use the guard constituted assumption of the risk, W. E. referred to the case of *Farmer* v. *Glass Crushers, Inc.,* 256 G.S. 156, 19XX, involving an experienced operator of a glass-crushing machine. That operator was injured when, instead of using the long-handled device provided for such purposes, he reached with his hand into the machine to dislodge glass that had jammed. The lower court entered judgment for the plaintiff in accordance with the jury's verdict. The Great State Supreme Court reversed, ruling as a matter of law that the plaintiff's actions constituted voluntary assumption of a known risk. W. E. noted the similarities between that glass worker's actions and John Q.'s failure to use a guard. He alleged that Judge Fairness had erred in instructing the jury, by failing to charge that if the jurors found that John Q. had been an experienced worker, trained in safety procedures, who had operated his machine without the guard in place, then they must find that there was no right to recover.

*Years are indicated as –XV or –XW, etc., to show their occurrence prior to the year 19XX; as –XY, etc., to show occurrence thereafter.

Henry's brief, submitted in reply, asked that the appellate court affirm the lower court's judgment. He noted Professor Learned's testimony that the injury could have been prevented by the required testing. Thus, he urged, there had been proof that the accident was caused by a test-detectable defective zagger. He contended that the appellant's attempt to explain the accident as operator failure was not only rebutted by the appellee's expert witness but further denigrated by the very proponents of that explanation under cross-examination. He noted, too, that the appellant had not only stipulated as to the expertness of the appellee's witness but also to his recognition as the foremost zagger authority in the country. Therefore, he concluded, there was ample evidence of causation upon which to send the matter to the jury.

Henry contended that not only proximate cause but also assumption of the risk were jury questions and that both had been properly submitted to them. He called attention to the Great State Supreme Court decision in *Franke* v. *James Machinery*, 234 G.S. 922, 19XV, a case involving industrial machinery shown to be defective in certain respects. In that case testimony involving a defective condition was admitted as circumstantial evidence as to the cause of injury. The question of proximate cause was submitted to the jury. The Great State Supreme Court upheld this action of the lower court. Henry contended that the decision as to whether a defense had been refuted was for the jury.

With regard to the assumption of the risk issue, Henry charged that the *Glass Crushers* case had important factual differences from the instant case. He agreed the *Glass Crushers* decision stood for the proposition that an experienced worker who reached into moving machinery with his hand had voluntarily assumed the risk, but he noted that there had been no allegations of defective functioning or manufacture of the equipment in that case. The allegations of defectiveness were of design in not providing a shield to prevent insertion of an employee's hand into the moving mechanism. That, he said, was quite different from the instant case in which John Q. had been working with zaggers, which, even the appellant had admitted, contained bonding defects. Therefore, he concluded, the *Glass Crushers* case must be considered inappropriate as precedent for this appeal.

He urged that W. E.'s concept of what constituted voluntary assumption of the risk in cases of strict liability for defective products did not coincide with that of §402A of the *Restatement of Torts* 2d as adopted by the courts of Great State. Henry argued that voluntary assumption of the risk referred to the situation in which an individual had knowledge of a product's defect, realized that using it in its defective state would be unreasonably dangerous, and then proceeded to do so regardless of the hazards involved. He noted that John Q. could not have knowingly assumed the risk of the bonding defect, since it was latent.

JUDICIAL ACTION

Only the two briefs were filed. The case was assigned to Judges Quest, Looke, and Search, who first read the list of legal issues involved as well as the summary of the arguments of both the appellant and the appellee. All three recognized that issues of substance were raised. Therefore, the appeal was neither frivolous nor subject to dismissal. They read further, then checked the decisions cited as precedent by both parties. The judges' law clerks gave assistance in this research. Two judges sent for the trial record to reread Judge Fairness' charge to the jury and the testimony of the expert witnesses.

Judge Quest believed he could reach a decision from the written materials, but the others had questions they wished to pursue with counsel at oral argument. A hearing date was set by the clerk of courts, who also informed all the parties of the time and place.

ORAL ARGUMENT

When Henry called Mary to tell her the date for oral argument had been set, she asked for additional information about what would transpire at that time. In his explanation, Henry told her that each side would have thirty minutes for argument. The appellant was entitled to both open and close the argument; he would begin with a brief review of the case and would then launch into the legal arguments. Henry also explained that the lawyers could expect to be interrupted at any point by judges who had questions. He also said that sometimes the arguments seem rather technical to the lay person.

What was most important to Mary was that no decision would be announced that day. Instead, the judges would restudy the matter after hearing the oral arguments. Their opinion would not be forthcoming for several weeks. This caused Mary to decide that, although this was an event of great importance to her, she would not make the trip to Center City to observe the arguments.

And that was how it came to be that on June 4, 19XY five individuals—three judges and two lawyers—participating in one hour of legal arguments in an appellate courtroom were the determining forces of Mary Worker's case.

The oral arguments took an interesting turn, with each judge seeming to focus on one particular issue. W. E. had not gone far in his presentation to the court and was contending that the appellee had failed to prove proximate cause when he was interrupted by Judge Quest.

"Tell me, counselor, just what is the standard of proof you allege the appellee should have met? Is the interpretation of Great State law that you are urging upon this court one that would require a standard of proof beyond a reasonable doubt?"

"No," replied W. E., but went on to urge that, "when the appellant's expert witnesses have shown that the reasons alleged by the appellee for the accident could not have caused it, then I submit causation has not been proved and, further, that the weight of the evidence—the preponderance—is contrary to a jury verdict in favor of the appellee."

Judge Quest followed up on this when it was Henry's turn. He asked Henry to answer W. E.'s contention that the weight of the evidence regarding causation was clearly in favor of the appellant. Henry replied that the jury, making its own decisions as to credibility of experts, as well as other witnesses, apparently did not agree with appellant's counsel that the latter's expert witnesses had refuted the appellee's proof of causation but believed, instead, that the weight of the evidence was in favor of the appellee. He reiterated that there had been ample evidence submitted by the appellee to enable the jury to reasonably arrive at that conclusion.

When W. E. began his discussion of assumption of the risk, Judge Looke asked him about the interpretation of the *Glass Crusher* decision in Henry's brief and why that did not make it an inappropriate precedent for this case. W. E. replied that John Q. was an experienced employee whose accident had been caused by his own action in failing to use a guard and not by the defect in the product he was using. That, he said, made the two cases similar. Later during the argument, Henry insisted that since the zagger had a defect—one admitted to exist by the appellant—the cases differed.

Judge Looke pursued with W. E. the matter of John Q.'s actions. Where in the record, he wanted to know, was there testimony that John Q. had intentionally used the machine without a guard; where had there been testimony to prove that John Q.'s actions were anything more than mere inadvertence at the most. W. E. replied that removing the guard was certainly deliberate and required conscious action. Pressed by the judge, however, he had to admit there had been no testimony that failure to replace the guard had been deliberate. When Henry's turn came, he contended that any failure by John Q. to use required safety measures must be construed to be, at the most, momentary lapse of attention. He quoted *Cross* v. *Book Binders,* 248 G.S. 15, 19XW, where momentary lapse of attention by a machine operator was not accepted as a defense in a 402A case, the court noting that it did not constitute voluntary assumption of the risk.

Judge Search asked W. E. to defend his contention that the zagger had not been used for the purpose for which it was intended. Didn't the record indicate, he wanted to know, that the appellant realized that operators at times used zaggers improperly mounted and without a guard on cypres machines? Therefore, weren't such uses foreseeable?

W. E. responded that failure to use a guard was a violation of Great State law. He urged that illegal usage was certainly not one intended by the manufacturer. Henry, on the other hand, contended that foreseeability of such uses was evident from the very requirement of dynamic testing.

The hearing ended when time expired. Both attorneys went home to await the court's decision, as eager to know the outcome as their clients were.

JUDGES' CONFERENCE

At a conference held a week later, the three judges discussed the Mary Worker case, together with others that had been argued that week. In the meantime, they reread selected portions of the record and briefs, rechecked the cases cited as precedent, and engaged in other necessary research.

"I have reread Judge Fairness' charge at least three times," said Judge Quest, "and I can find no error in it."

"I agree," said Judge Looke. "Nor can I find any legal basis for disturbing the jury's verdict. Resolution of the conflicting evidence regarding cause of the accident was clearly a jury function, and it was properly submitted to them. Furthermore, there was sufficient evidence from Professor Learned from which the jurors could reasonably arrive at the conclusion they did. I hasten to add that I agree with their decision that the cypres operator's actions did not constitute voluntary assumption of the risk. There was no evidence that he acted other than inadvertently."

"Gentlemen," said Judge Search, "we are in agreement in one respect. We all find that we should affirm the lower court's decision. However, I find this is just one more of a long line of product liability cases in which we are left with a gnawing impression that a panel of professionals, knowledgeable about zaggers and cypres machines, would be the logical persons to resolve these technical disputes. Furthermore, this is another case involving state law that comes into the federal courts as a diversity action, proceeding to clog our calendars, and requiring that we interpret the law of a specific state. It is time to speak out, to urge not only that different procedures be adopted for product liability cases involving technical testimony, but also that diversity actions be removed from the jurisdiction of the federal courts. Therefore, I intend to write a concurring opinion stating these views, even if the two of you elect to issue no more than a 'judgment affirmed' announcement."

Judge Search was referring to the fact that when appellate courts reach a decision in what they consider to be a clear-cut affirmation of a lower court's decision, involving no new law, they seldom write an explanatory opinion. Instead, they merely issue an announcement affirming the lower court's decision. To do otherwise would result in filling the appropriate *Reporter* with duplication.

Both Judges Quest and Looke said they would prefer the short statement of affirmation. However, they would read the Search concurring opinion before deciding if they wished to join in it. As it turned out, neither wished to be associated with it. Thus it was Judge Search who made the Mary Worker appeal famous. While the decision itself was unspectacular, the concurring opinion was quoted by the Chief Justice of the United States, denounced and exalted in numerous law review articles, read and studied by lawyers, judges, and law students so that the Mary Worker case was known to almost all of them.

The appellate decision was a unanimous one. While unanimity is not required, a majority of the judges hearing an appeal must agree upon the disposition to be made of it. At times an appellate judge may agree with the final result reached by colleagues, but not with the reasons they have set forth. The judge may then decide to write a concurring opinion, so that his views will be publicly known. On the other hand, an appellate judge who disagrees with the majority may write a dissenting opinion. In the regular reading of dissenting opinions of a particular court, trends are often discernible. Certainly added insight into the thinking of the court is provided.

In the Mary Worker appeal, the actions of the lower court were affirmed. Had the appellate court found that the trial judge had committed prejudicial error (either during the trial or, later, in denying the defense motions for judgment n.o.v. and a new trial) or that there had been no evidence from which the jury could reasonably have reached the verdict it did, then the decision would have been to reverse. Prejudicial error is that which results in a miscarriage of justice. Harmless error does not occasion reversal. There can be partial as well as complete reversal or affirmation. Appellate courts frequently remand—that is, send back—a case to the lower court with specific directions, such as ordering a new trial. Such was the result in the *Ferraro* v. *Ford Motor Company* decision which follows.

Ferraro v. *Ford Motor Company*
423 Pa. 324, 223 A.2d 746 (1966)

EAGEN, JUSTICE. William G. Ferraro instituted this action in trespass to recover damages for loss resulting from a unique automobile accident. The named defendants were the Ford Motor Company (Ford) and the Toohey Motor Company (Toohey). Since Toohey, a corporation, had been dissolved, service was never effected on this defendant. Ford was properly served, and the action proceeded against it alone.

After trial, the jury awarded the plaintiff the sum of $107,851. Ford filed motions for a new trial and judgment notwithstanding the verdict. The lower court granted the latter motion and directed the entry of judgment for the defendant. After judgment was so entered, the plaintiff, Ferraro, appealed.

The record discloses the following: Ferraro, a contractor, purchased a new Ford dump truck, for use in the operation of his business, from Toohey, an authorized Ford dealer. . . . He used and operated the truck . . . for a period in excess of two months (and a total of approximately 500 miles . . .), when the accident involved occurred. . . . as Ferraro was engaged in operating the truck on a public highway and executing an extreme left-hand turn at an intersection, the left front wheel locked in the turned position. Ferraro attempted to apply the brake when his foot accidentally bumped the gas accelerator pedal, dislodging it from the ball socket underneath and causing the motor to race. The truck shot forward, left the highway, hit a house, and as a result, Ferraro was seriously injured.

In his testimony Ferraro admitted that on two occasions prior to the day of the accident, he experienced similar instances of the front wheel locking as he executed a turn with the truck; . . . He also admitted experiencing trouble with the accelerator pedal dislodging before the day of the accident. This could be corrected temporarily by manually readjusting the ball under the pedal.

As a result of these known malfunctions, Ferraro brought the truck to the Toohey garage on at least three separate occasions before the day of the accident and complained about its condition. . . . On each occasion he was reassured by employees of Toohey and told that the malfunctions were not serious, dangerous or sufficient to worry about; that the worst he could do would be to rub a little rubber off the tire and once it rubs off, "You're all right"; that Toohey didn't want him bringing the truck to the garage every week and to wait until he had more mileage on the truck and then bring it back for a thorough check and repairs. On these occasions Toohey did nothing to correct the locking problem, but an employee did show Ferraro how to install the displacement-prone ball underneath the gas pedal.

The lower court concluded that Ferraro was grossly negligent in continuing to operate the truck for a period of about six weeks after knowing the existence of the malfunctions and the fact that they were not permanently remedied.

In *Webb* v. *Zern,* . . . this Court recently adopted Restatement (Second), Torts §402A

(1965), as the law of this Commonwealth in tort actions involving the liability of those who sell products in a defective condition. The question was not reached or ruled upon therein, as to whether or not contributory negligence or assumption of risk by the buyer would constitute a defense in such actions. After studied consideration, it appears to us that if the buyer knows of the defect and *voluntarily* and *unreasonably* proceeds to use the product or encounter a known danger, this should preclude recovery and constitute a complete defense to the action even in cases of strict liability. . . .

Therefore, the crucial issue in this case in determining if Ferraro's own actions preclude recovery is, whether or not, in view of his knowledge, he continued to use the truck and unreasonably encounter a known danger. Our conclusion is that this cannot be said as a matter of law, under the circumstances established by the record. . . .

In the present case the essential facts are not disputed; however, crucial inferences proceeding from these facts are rationally susceptible to opposing interpretations. . . .

Rather we do believe, that, under the circumstances, reasonable men could honestly differ as to what impact, if any, the dealer's assurance would or should have had on the mind of a reasonably prudent automobile driver. Hence a jury question was presented. We will, therefore, reverse the entry of judgment n.o.v.

While the lower court did not dispose of the new trial motion, since it granted judgment n.o.v., it did strongly manifest its thinking in this regard. It said in part: "The verdict for Ferraro against the Ford Motor Company in the amount of $107,851.00 was startlingly excessive. It shocked the conscience of the court. It would be an injustice to allow the verdict to stand. The court would have felt impelled to grant the motion for a new trial because of the excessiveness of the verdict and other grounds. It cannot be rectified by a remittitur." We do not regard this view of the lower court as either arbitrary or a clear abuse of discretion.

Judgment reversed and new trial ordered.

In any case, appellate decisions are transmitted to the lower court so that appropriate implementation or execution may be taken.

The procedures involved in the appellate decision have been shown in a flow chart in Figure 7–5.

REACTION TO APPELLATE OPINION

When the opinion was finally prepared, it was filed with the clerk of the court of appeals who sent copies immediately to Judge Fairness and to both Henry and W. E. The latter discussed the outcome with Will Very. His first reaction was to appeal further—to the United States Supreme Court. However, W. E. explained that they had already had one review in an appellate court. Their recourse to the United States Supreme Court would have to be by writ of *certiorari*, best described as a request that the high court review a case that is within its discretionary province. He explained that review by the highest court in the land is a matter of right if an appellate court holds a state statute

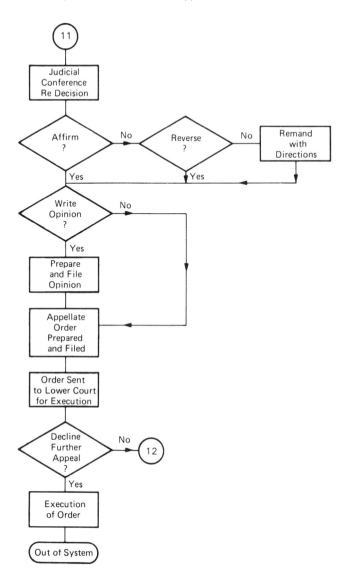

Figure 7–5. Procedure re Appellate Decision

to be unconstitutional or contrary to federal law, or if a state supreme court holds a federal law to be unconstitutional. None of these had occurred in this case. One other means of access to the high court, he said, takes place when a court of appeals certifies a question of law to that court. After discussion, Will reluctantly agreed to consider the litigation to be at an end. The procedures that would have been involved have been flow charted in Figure 7-6. Payment of the judgment to Mary Worker was another matter. Will Very reluctantly ordered payment, thus satisfying the judgment, and then reconsidered the matter of self-insurance.

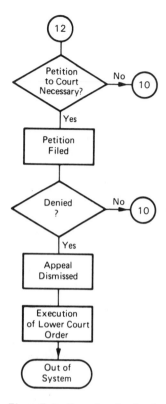

Figure 7-6. Procedure for Further Appeal

For Mary Worker, the news was a joy which diminished only when the financial realities became evident. The total jury award was for $304,891.23. Her contract with Henry Law called for counsel fees of 50 percent if the case were appealed. Therefore, calculation of the monetary return by her was as follows:

Jury verdict	$304,891.23
Less counsel fee	152,445.61
	$152,445.62
Less fees and expenses	3,402.35
Net return to Mary Worker	$149,043.27

Then Henry Law explained that there was still the matter of complying with the provisions of the subrogation agreement with the workmen's compensation carrier for The Firm. (Great State law provided that such carriers must assume a pro-rata share of the expenses and counsel fees, based on benefit to them from the litigation.)

Like all lower court judges, Judge Fairness was interested in learning what the higher court said regarding his decision in the Mary Worker case. Appellate review, in reality, is an evaluation of a trial judge's work by a group of judges. There is a modicum of truth in the old saying that the lower courts try the case but the appellate courts try the trial judges.

After the opinion had been printed and all the documents and records were gathered together in the case file in the office of the clerk of the court of appeals, the latter completed the docket entry showing that the case had been affirmed on appeal and arranged for permanent storage of the entire file. In the district court, the clerk not only noted the affirmation on appeal on the docket for the case, but also satisfaction of the judgment after payment into court was made by Zagger Supply. Had Zagger Supply not paid, then Mary could have requested the court's assistance in enforcement of the judgment. In that case, the clerk of courts would have directed an order to the sheriff instructing the latter to seize such Zagger Supply property as approximately equaled in value the amount of the judgment, sell it, and turn proceeds equivalent to the judgment over to Mary. Any remainder would be returned to the owner of the sold property. As should be obvious from this, it is possible to secure judgment against another party and then find that the latter is without sufficient assets to make payment. While there is an extended time period during which one has the right to collect, some judgment creditors never become able to make satisfaction in full.

This, then, marked the official end of the Mary Worker case. It was now *res judicata*. As a civil case, pursued through both trial and appellate stages, it provides a background for comparison with the criminal case which follows.

QUESTIONS

1. How do you reconcile the concept of appellate review of a lower court's judgment with the statement made by the appellate judge in this case about a "gnawing impression" that a panel of professionals would be the logical decision makers? Shouldn't the appellate court have reversed on those grounds?

2. What actually happens on appeal? Has the appellate court fulfilled its function in this case? Is the appellate decision here one that might be included among the "hard cases that make bad law"? Consider the arguments put forth by both sides. Were they sound? Was the court's decision reasonable and logical? Why? Was the position of the appellant influenced by the desire of the corporate president for appeal?

3. Do you believe that the decision to appeal in this case was a wise one? Why? Did W. E. make the best use of the opportunity? Should he have sought certiorari in the United States Supreme Court? What would have been his chances for success?

4. Consider the appellate procedure. Is it consistent with the concept of review? Does it make review possible? How could it be improved?

5. Should the right of appeal be extended so that it is an automatic right? What protections does a client have if his counsel fails to raise objections leading to the right to have error corrected (assuming that there was error in the lower court) on appeal? Why do parties and witnesses play so insignificant a role in the appellate process? Should it be changed to provide more participation by them?

6. Now that you have had the opportunity to follow a civil case from its inception through appeal, a relevant question is whether there can truly be said to be a civil "system"? Are the characteristics of a system, as explained in Chapter 2, present? Explain. If so, are any subsystems present within it? What are they? If it is a nonsystem, what is lacking?

7. Are there overall goals for the civil process? Who sets them? Who determines the priorities? Are these consistent with those society or the general public expects of the process? What does society expect of it? How is this determined? Are there any conflicting objectives pursued independently by various elements within the process? Give examples. In what ways, if any, does this interfere with attainment of expected objectives? Is there any method for measuring the effectiveness of the "system"? What is it? Is it pursued formally or informally? What feedback is there? Is any action taken with regard to it?

8. Is the civil process composed of such steps and procedures as best effectuate desired goals and objectives? Explain. What improvements do you suggest? How is input of information made into the civil process? Is this done effectively? Can it be improved? Is information available to those who need it for decision-making purposes? Give examples. Who defines the problems to be resolved within the civil process? How is this done? Can it be improved? How? Who are the decision makers within the process? Are they primarily persons within or persons from outside the "system"? Is their approach to problem solving an interdisciplinary one? Does it consider the total environment? Does it focus narrowly on one approach? Explain these answers.

9. Who manages the "system"? Can you suggest alternative models for the present civil process that would more effectively attain desired goals? Does attainment of those goals involve changes without the process as well as within it? rather than within it? In what areas?

10. Do you see the civil process as a part or "subsystem" of some larger system? What is it? Where is the place of the civil process within it?

entry into
the system:
control subsystem
and entry
into the court
subsystem

EIGHT

Harvey Worker would have been surprised had he known that executives at The Firm were aware that cypres parts were missing. He would have been even more surprised had he known that he was under surveillance in connection with their disappearance.

It had all started about a year ago when Harvey, shortly after his father's death, dropped out of college and went to work at The Firm. A cypres buff, he soon discovered that the supply room at The Firm stocked in great quantity the very kind of pieces he used in his basement workshop. One day he unobtrusively slipped into his pocket a small but expensive piece he needed at home. Apparently its disappearance went unnoticed. Questions were asked of employees in the department when the third and fourth pieces he took were found to be missing. After that, Harvey worked out a method of changing inventory and production requisition records so that he was able to take additional pieces apparently without his being detected or their being missed. When he found that some of his former college classmates were willing to pay for parts that he offered them at bargain prices, Harvey increased the number and frequency of his takings.

INVESTIGATION

In fact, discrepancies between parts actually on hand and the number which should have been on hand were noted when Chester, Porter, and Adams, CPAs, conducted the annual audit at The Firm. When they suggested the possibility of employee theft to Fred Famous, he was at first incredulous. Shown the figures which revealed that over $8,000 in parts were unaccounted for, he assigned to Al Chase, manager of security at The Firm, responsibility for investigative work to uncover the source of the loss. It was Al who persuaded a reluctant Fred that Big City police should be notified about the missing parts and provided with their serial numbers. Al knew that once Big City detectives were alerted, he would have their assistance and cooperation in his investigation. He also hired a young private detective named Ed Under to work in the plant. Ed made it a point to become friendly with everyone, including Harvey. When he learned that Harvey's hobby was working with cypres, he watched intently for signs that Harvey might be involved in some way in the disappearance of the parts. He was, however, exceedingly careful to avoid any form of conduct which might later involve him in some form of criminal activity.

Criminal Involvement

Ed realized he must not induce, counsel, plan with, nor aid and abet Harvey in theft of cypres parts. His instructions were that he could not participate in any activity that would ordinarily lead to criminal charges. These charges might be either solicitation or conspiracy, or acting as an accessory. Further, if he induced Harvey to steal and, in so doing, could be said to have acted on behalf of an officer of the law, then he would have created a defense for Harvey through entrapment. These forms of involvement in criminal activity, other than as the principal perpetrator of the crime, are defined and further distinguished in Table 8–1. Their legal effect is also shown.

Surveillance

Realizing all of this, Ed continued to observe, listen, and report his findings. In the meantime, Al Chase's early decision to involve Big City police bore fruit. Detective Sergeant Dick Find called Al to report than an employee of The Firm named Harvey Worker had been identified as the source of the stolen cypres parts, which had been found in the apartment of a fence when the latter was arrested for receiving stolen goods. While it was now known that Harvey was involved, there was still no evidence as to whether he was working alone or with others. Therefore, Ed Under was assigned to center his surveillance on Harvey. That paid off.

One afternoon Ed saw Harvey unlatch a side entrance door soon after it had been secured by one of the plant guards on his regular rounds just prior to closing time. Ed notified Al. Plans were made. Al would watch the side entrance that evening. Ed would be inside the building in a spot where he could see the supply room without being observed himself. Uncertain of what to expect, they agreed that Ed would signal Al to come to the supply room or to call the police if either seemed advisable.

TABLE 8-1. Forms of Involvement in Criminal Activity Other Than as Principal Perpetrator

INVOLVEMENT	CHARACTERISTICS AND DEFINITION	LEGAL EFFECT
Entrapment	Entrapment occurs when a law enforcement officer, for the purpose of instituting criminal prosecution, induces a person to commit a crime that the person did not contemplate committing. It is distinguished from the situation in which the criminal intent is already present in the accused's mind, and he is simply furnished with an opportunity to do what he already intended to do. A private citizen acting for, on behalf of, or by direction of an officer of the law may be treated as a law enforcement officer in a situation that might involve entrapment.	Entrapment can be raised as defense by the person charged with committing the crime.
Solicitation	Solicitation consists of hiring, procuring, or counseling another person to commit a crime, even if that crime is not committed. In some states it is necessary that the crime involved be a felony.	Solicitation is a crime in and of itself.
Conspiracy	Conspiracy occurs when two or more persons combine or agree to do an unlawful act or to do a lawful act by unlawful means. The wrong associated with conspiracy exists in the agreement or the forming of a scheme between the parties. Conspiracy exists even if the crime planned is not committed.	Conspiracy is a crime in and of itself.
Accessory	An accessory is one who aids and abets another in criminal activity. He need not actually be present at the scene of the crime. It is sufficient if he advises, counsels, or otherwise acts to forward the crime or assists the criminal in preventing or hindering his being apprehended. This may occur before or after the fact. A crime must have been committed for there to be an accessory.	Acting as an accessory is a criminal offense if the actual crime is committed.

The Incident

When Harvey appeared alone that evening, Al was surprised. Surprise, however, did not deter him from calling the Big City police when signaled by Ed. Responding to a call reporting burglary in progress at The Firm, the police were met at the entrance by Al. He led them to the supply room, where they found Harvey in the act of taking cypres parts from the shelves. He had a large plastic bag with him into which he was placing those parts.

While many of the events of that evening were a confused blur in his mind, Harvey found that some stood out prominently. He remembered how, while busily engaging in selecting the parts he wanted, he had turned around and was unexpectedly greeted by two uniformed policemen, Al Chase, and Ed Under. How well he remembered these words:

"Harvey Worker, you're under arrest."

He recalled being read "his rights" and being patted down. In his opinion, this had included some unnecessary roughing up. He was then taken from the building to Big City police headquarters. Except for sounds emitted by the police car radio, the ride there had been an unpleasantly silent one. His mind reeled with the thought that he had been arrested.

Arrest was something he had not anticipated. Harvey was apprehensive. He did not know why various procedures were being followed and assumed the worst. At this point, some discussion of arrest law should contribute to a better understanding of Harvey's experiences that evening.

ARREST

Arrest occurs when a person is taken into custody to answer for the commission of an offense. Most arrests, as in Harvey's case, are made by law enforcement officers. They may enlist the aid of private persons in effecting arrest. State laws vary, regarding the conditions under which a private citizen has the right to make an arrest. Great State law provided that a private citizen is privileged to arrest, without a warrant, when a felony has actually been committed or is being committed, and the citizen has reasonable grounds to suspect that the person to be arrested has committed it. A private citizen must turn the arrested person over to authorities without unnecessary delay. Both the private citizen and the police can incur civil liability for false arrest or for the use of excess force in making an arrest.

Great State law provided that a police officer is justified in using as much physical force as necessary to effect arrest or to defend himself or others from bodily harm while making the arrest. It further provided that the individual being arrested does not have the right to use force in resisting the officer, even if the arrest is unlawful. In these respects, Great State law was similar to that of most states.

So, too, were the Great State statutory provisions that permitted a law enforcement officer to arrest without a warrant for a crime committed in his presence or for a felony committed out of his presence when he had reasonable grounds to believe that the individual had committed the felony. An arrest warrant was necessary in other cases.

Arrest Warrant

An *arrest warrant* is a court order which commands that the individual named by it be taken into custody and brought before the court. It is issued by a judicial authority, usually a magistrate. The warrant is directed to a law enforcement officer or another person authorized by law to execute it.

Application for an arrest warrant is in the form of a complaint, which accuses an individual of actions in violation of the law. The person filing the complaint is generally a police officer but may be a private citizen. The complainant must provide facts. Conjecture or suspicion will not suffice. The facts must be given either under oath or by affirmation. When the accuser lacks personal knowledge, the facts stated may be on the basis of information and belief. In that case, the accuser must show that the information has been received from a trustworthy and reliable source.

If, on the basis of the information provided, the magistrate finds probable cause to believe that the offense has been committed and that the accused has committed it, the warrant will be issued. Probable cause is more than mere suspicion. However, it does not require the degree of certainty that would be necessary to justify a conviction.

When issuance of a warrant is denied, further investigation may lead to the ability to correct the deficiencies that existed in the original application. A warrant may then be issued on the basis of a second application. These decisions involved in securing and issuing an arrest warrant are shown in a flow chart in Figure 8-1.

An improperly issued warrant can result in an illegal arrest. In such cases, the accused can still be brought to trial. However, any evidence obtained as a result of the unlawful arrest must be excluded.

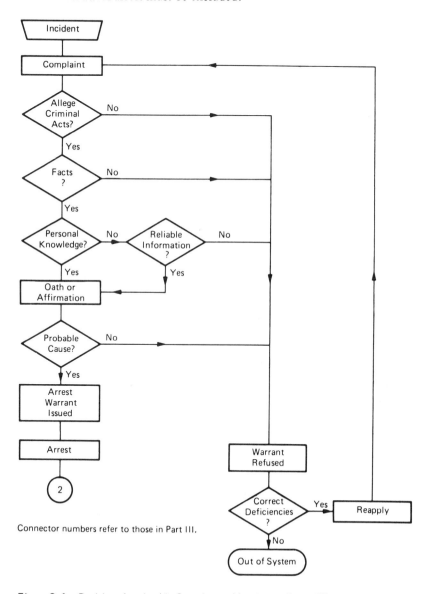

Connector numbers refer to those in Part III.

Figure 8-1.   Decisions Involved in Securing and Issuing an Arrest Warrant

In some states and according to the Federal Rules of Criminal Procedure, when a person arrested without a warrant is brought before a magistrate, a complaint must be filed.[1] As we will see later, this was done in Harvey's case.

Constitutional Considerations

When arrested, a person is no longer free. The person has been deprived of his liberty. This gives rise to constitutional considerations. As a result, the procedure surrounding arrest is complicated.

The predominant constitutional considerations at this stage of the criminal process are provisions of the Fourth, Fifth, and Sixth Amendments of the United States Constitution: the right provided by the Fourth Amendment against unreasonable search and seizure; the privilege provided by the Fifth Amendment against compulsory self-incrimination; and the right provided by the Sixth Amendment to the assistance of legal counsel. These provisions of the federal constitution have been held by the United States Supreme Court to be applicable to the states.[2] This means that the relevant provision of the federal constitution is binding upon the states in their actions. The result is that neither in a federal nor in a state action can a person be deprived of these particular rights. The basis for making these rights applicable to the states is the Fourteenth Amendment, which states that "no state shall . . . deprive any person of life, liberty, or property without due process of law." The rights made applicable to the states may be said to have been incorporated in the Fourteenth Amendment and to be part of the due process required by it. In addition, almost every state constitution has counterparts of these provisions of the Fourth, Fifth, and Sixth Amendments. Those three amendments read as follows:

FOURTH AMENDMENT

The right of the people to be secure in their persons, houses, papers, and effects, against unreasonable searches and seizures, shall not be violated, and no Warrants shall issue, but upon probable cause, supported by Oath or affirmation, and particularly describing the place to be searched, and the persons or things to be seized.

FIFTH AMENDMENT

No person shall be held to answer for a capital, or otherwise infamous crime, unless on a presentment or indictment of the Grand Jury, except in cases arising in the land or naval forces, or in the Militia, when in actual service in time of War or public danger; nor shall any person be subject for the same offence to be twice put in jeopardy of life or limb; nor shall be compelled in any criminal case to be a witness against himself, nor be deprived of life, liberty, or property, without due process of law; nor shall private property be taken for public use, without just compensation.

SIXTH AMENDMENT

In all criminal prosecutions, the accused shall enjoy the right to a speedy and public trial, by an impartial jury of the State and district wherein the crime shall have been committed, which district shall have been previously ascertained by law, and to be informed of the nature and cause of the accusation; to be confronted with the witnesses against him; to have compulsory process for obtaining witnesses in his favor, and to have the assistance of counsel for his defense.

The procedures and practices followed in the criminal process must be such that they do not deny an accused these constitutional rights. Evidence obtained in a manner that violates these rights of an accused can be subject to the *exclusionary rule.* That means it must be suppressed or excluded; it is not admissible against the accused as evidence of guilt. However, it has been held admissible for impeachment purposes and before the grand jury.[3] The exclusionary rule leads to motions by defense counsel for suppression of evidence. When suppression motions are granted, the prosecution is often left without sufficient admissible evidence to prove its case. In this way, the exclusionary rule can serve as a deterrent to unconstitutional practices. It should be of interest to note the care exercised by all concerned to protect Harvey's constitutional rights.

At the same time, it is important to remember that a whole body of law has developed in connection with constitutional criminal procedure, only the more significant aspects of which are highlighted in this account of Harvey's experiences. Much of this law is embodied in the case law made by the courts in their interpretation of constitutional provisions. As such, it reflects the dynamic and changing characteristics of case law as well as development in connection with ad-hoc factual situations. Constitutional interpretation by the United States Supreme Court, in the opinion of many, is dramatically revealing of the impact of social forces upon the law. Had Harvey Worker's arrest taken place fifty years earlier, there would have been no "Miranda requirements," as described in the following pages.

Search and Seizure

The pat down search made by police at the time of Harvey's arrest brings into focus provisions of the Fourth Amendment. The general rule is that searches and seizures made without a warrant (or with one improperly issued) are illegal.[4] There are exceptions to the warrant requirement, the most important of which is search incident to lawful arrest.[5] This was the issue in the *Robinson* case which follows.

United States v. *Robinson*
414 U.S. 218, 94 S.Ct. 467, 38 L.Ed. 2d 427 (1973)

Respondent Robinson was arrested by Police Officer Jenks who had reason to believe that respondent was operating a motor vehicle after the revocation of his operator's permit. During a pat down, Jenks felt an object in the left breast pocket of the heavy coat respondent was wearing and pulled out a crumpled up cigarette package. It contained capsules of white powder, which later analysis proved to be heroin. The heroin was admitted into evidence at respondent's trial, which resulted in his conviction for possession and facilitation of concealment of heroin. The court of appeals reversed, holding that the heroin introduced in evidence against respondent had been obtained as a result of a search which violated the Fourth Amendment to the United States Constitution. Respondent concedes that Jenks had probable cause to arrest respondent and that he effected a full custody arrest.

MR. JUSTICE REHNQUIST. . . . We conclude that the search conducted by Jenks in this case did not offend the limits imposed by the Fourth Amendment, and we therefore reverse the judgment of the court of appeals.

It is well settled that a search incident to a lawful arrest is a traditional exception to the warrant requirement of the Fourth Amendment. This general exception has historically been formulated in two distinct propositions. The first is that a search may be made of the person of the arrestee by virtue of the lawful arrest. The second is that a search may be made of the area within the control of the arrestee. . . .

. . . The authority to search the person incident to a lawful custodial arrest, while based upon the need to disarm and to discover evidence, does not depend on what a court may later decide was the probability in a particular arrest situation that weapons or evidence would in fact be found upon the person of the suspect. A custodial arrest of a suspect based on probable cause is a reasonable intrusion under the Fourth Amendment; that intrusion being lawful, a search incident to the arrest requires no additional justification. It is the fact of the lawful arrest which establishes the authority to search, and we hold that in the case of a lawful custodial arrest a full search of the person is not only an exception to the warrant requirement of the Fourth Amendment but is also a "reasonable" search under that Amendment. . . . Having in the course of a lawful search come upon the crumpled package of cigarettes, he [Jenks] was entitled to seize them as "fruits, instrumentalities, or contraband"; probative of criminal conduct. . . .

A law enforcement officer has the right to search the person being arrested in order to find concealed weapons, to prevent destruction of evidence which that individual may have in possession, and to deprive the individual of means of escape. The officer may also search the area within the arrestee's immediate control; i.e., the area from which the arrestee might gain possession of a weapon or destructible evidence.[6] This explains the pat down at the time of Harvey's arrest. A warrantless search also meets constitutional standards when it occurs after the appropriate individual voluntarily consents to the search.[7] The United States Supreme Court has also recognized as constitutional warrantless searches that are reasonable under exceptionally compelling circumstances, such as those involved in the "hot pursuit" of a suspect or when contraband is being transported in a moving vehicle.[8]

Distinction is made between the *search and seizure* referred to in the Constitution, and the practice often referred to as *stop and frisk*. A *stop* does not involve taking the individual into custody. Therefore, it is less than an arrest or a seizure. A *frisk* is a superficial pat down, generally for weapons, and is less than a search.

With respect to the right of the police to stop and frisk, the United States Supreme Court has said that when a police officer observes unusual conduct which leads him to reasonably conclude, in the light of his experience, that criminal activity may be afoot and that the person involved may be armed and presently dangerous; when, in the course of investigating this behavior, he identifies himself as a policeman and makes reasonable inquiries; and when nothing in the initial stages of the encounter serves to dispel reasonable fear for his own or other's safety, the officer is entitled, for the protection of himself and others in the area, to conduct a carefully limited search of the outer clothing of such a person in an attempt to discover weapons that might be used to assault him.[9]

Miranda Requirements

The reading of "his rights" to Harvey at the time of his arrest was only the first of a number of times that he was informed of his constitutional rights. This practice flows from the United States Supreme Court decision in *Miranda* v. *Arizona,* 384 U.S. 436 (1966). That decision sets forth specific instructions regarding treatment of an accused to assure protection of constitutional rights, especially those arising from provisions of the Fifth and Sixth Amendments. The five protective measures outlined by the Court are as follows:

1. If a person in custody is to be subjected to interrogation, he must first be informed in clear and unequivocal terms that he has the right to remain silent.
2. The warning of the right to remain silent must be accompanied by an explanation that anything said can and will be used against the individual in court.
3. An individual held for interrogation must be clearly informed that he has the right to consult with a lawyer and to have the lawyer with him during interrogation.
4. It is necessary to warn the individual not only that he has the right to consult with an attorney, but also that if he is indigent a lawyer will be appointed to represent him.
5. If the individual indicates in any manner at any time prior to or during questioning that he wishes to remain silent, the interrogation must cease.

These protective measures are required when an individual is interrogated "while in custody at the station or otherwise deprived of his freedom of action in any way."[10] They apply with respect to an accused or a suspect, to one who will be in jeopardy of criminal prosecution. Two exceptions to this requirement have been recognized by the United States Supreme Court. They are "inevitable discovery," where the police would have found the evidence anyway, and cases of "overriding public safety."[11] Questioning of a person who is merely an innocent onlooker or witness does not impose the same obligation.

The Miranda requirements apply to custodial interrogations by law enforcement officers or persons acting on their behalf. Thus, one must distinguish situations in which private citizens act in a purely private capacity. Incriminating statements made by an accused to persons such as friends, family, or employers who are not acting for or on behalf of the police are not excludable because Miranda requirements were not met. And this is so whether those incriminating statements were volunteered or in answer to questioning.

Furthermore, the Miranda decision does not prohibit waiver of his rights by an accused. It does, however, require that any such waiver be knowing, intelligent, and voluntary. The Court stressed that the prosecution would have to bear the "heavy burden" of proving that the waiver was so. As a result, the police and judiciary normally follow the practice of asking a person who waives his rights if he is acting on his own volition and with full understanding. This is then made a part of the record. The *Neville* decision which follows provides a good example of the type of situations that can arise involving the Fifth Amendment privilege against self-incrimination.

South Dakota v. Mason Henry Neville
  459 U.S. 553, 103 S.Ct. 916, 74 L.Ed.2d 748 (1983)

JUSTICE O'CONNOR. *Schmerber* v. *California,* 384 U.S. 757 . . . (1966), held that a State could force a defendant to submit to a blood-alcohol test without violating the defendant's Fifth Amendment right against self-incrimination. We now address a question left open in *Schmerber,* and hold that the admission into evidence of a defendant's refusal to submit to such a test likewise does not offend the right against self-incrimination.

Two Madison, South Dakota police officers stopped respondent's car after they saw him fail to stop at a stop sign. The officers asked respondent for his driver's license and asked him to get out of the car. As he left the car, respondent staggered and fell against the car to support himself. The officers smelled alcohol on his breath. Respondent did not have a driver's license, and informed the officers that it was revoked after a previous driving-while-intoxicated conviction. The officers asked respondent to touch his finger to his nose and to walk a straight line. When respondent failed these field sobriety tests, he was placed under arrest and read his *Miranda* rights. Respondent acknowledged that he understood his rights and agreed to talk without a lawyer present. . . . Reading from the printed card, the officers then asked respondent to submit to a blood-alcohol test and warned him that he could lose his license if he refused. Respondent refused to take the test, stating "I'm too drunk, I won't pass the test." The officers again read the request to submit to a test, and then took respondent to the police station, where they read the request to submit a third time. Respondent continued to refuse to take the test, again saying he was too drunk to pass it. . . .

South Dakota law specifically declares that refusal to submit to a blood-alcohol test "may be admissible into evidence at the trial." . . . Nevertheless, respondent sought to suppress all evidence of his refusal to take the blood-alcohol test. The circuit court granted the suppression motion. . . . The South Dakota Supreme Court affirmed the suppression of the act of refusal on the grounds that . . . the introduction of this evidence, violated the federal . . . privilege against self-incrimination. . . .

Since other jurisdictions have found no Fifth Amendment violation from the admission of evidence of refusal to submit to blood-alcohol tests, we granted certiorari to resolve the conflict. . . .

"The Court has held repeatedly that the Fifth Amendment is limited to prohibiting the use of 'physical or moral compulsion' exerted on the person asserting the privilege." This coercion requirement comes directly from the constitutional language directing that no person "shall be *compelled* in any criminal case to be a witness against himself." . . .

Here, the state did not directly compel respondent to refuse the test, for it gave him the choice of submitting to the test or refusing. . . .

The values behind the Fifth Amendment are not hindered when the state offers a suspect the choice of submitting to the blood-alcohol test or having his refusal used against him. The simple blood-alcohol test is so safe, painless, and commonplace, . . . that respondent concedes, as he must, that the state could legitimately compel the suspect, against his will, to accede to the test. Given, then, that the offer of taking a blood-alcohol test is clearly legitimate, the action becomes no *less* legitimate when the State offers a second option of refusing the test, with the attendant penalties for making that choice. Nor is this a case where the State has subtly coerced respondent into choosing the option it had no right to compel, rather than offering a true choice. To the contrary, the State wants respondent to choose to take the test, for the inference of intoxication arising from a positive blood-alcohol test is far stronger than that arising from a refusal to take the test. . . .

We hold, therefore, that a refusal to take a blood-alcohol test, after a police officer has lawfully requested it, is not an act coerced by the officer, and thus is not protected by the privilege against self-incrimination. . . .

While the State did not actually warn respondent that the test results could be used against him, we hold that such failure to warn was not the sort of implicit promise to forego use of evidence that would unfairly "trick" respondent if the evidence were later offered against him at trial. We therefore conclude that the use of evidence of refusal after these warnings comported with the fundamental fairness required by Due Process.

Citation and Summons

Arrest was the means by which Harvey entered the criminal system. As shown in Figure 8-2, it is not the only mode of entry. The initiating action may be the issuance of a citation or a summons. These are orders directing the accused to appear before the proper authority at a specified time and date to answer the charges against him. As noted on the summons in Form 8-1, failure to appear as ordered can result in the issuance of an arrest warrant. Some jurisdictions use the citation procedure, rather than arrest, for the less serious offenses. A citation is issued by the police. A summons, on the other hand, is generally issued by a magistrate after a complaint alleging criminal activity has been filed. Although the complaint is usually filed by the police, a private citizen may also do so. Some jurisdictions require a magistrate to send all private complaints to the district attorney for a determination as to whether probable cause exists to have either a summons or an arrest warrant issued. Which of the two is issued generally depends upon the offense involved. Private complaints may also be lodged directly with the district attorney. The citation and summons procedures are shown in a flow chart in Figure 8-3.

Having looked at some aspects of the initial stages of the criminal process, let us return to the activities in which Harvey Worker was involved.

Booking and Custodial Interrogation

Following Harvey's ride to police headquarters, the administrative process known as *booking* occurred. This consists of preparation of the official arrest records. Harvey's name, address, and age were recorded along with the offenses with which he was

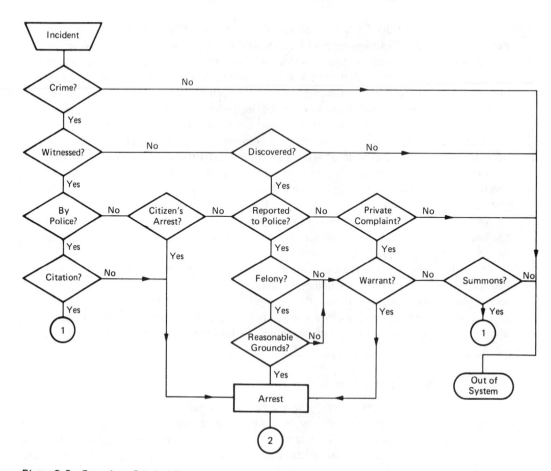

Figure 8–2. Entry Into Criminal System

charged, and the time and place of their occurrence. He was being held on two counts, burglary and theft. The Great State Criminal Code defined the two crimes as follows:

> Section 3502. A person is guilty of **burglary** if he enters a building or occupied structure with intent to commit a crime therein, unless the premises are at the time open to the public or the actor is licensed or privileged to enter.
>
> Section 3921. A person is guilty of **theft** if he unlawfully takes, or exercises unlawful control over, movable property of another with intent to deprive him thereof.

Burglary was classified as a felony, as was theft when it involved property worth more than $2000.

   The arresting officers prepared a detailed report of the circumstances surrounding the arrest. Record was also made of the plastic bag full of parts which had been taken up at the scene by the police. The parts were appropriately tagged and labeled.

   Harvey was thoroughly searched and given a receipt for his car keys, wallet, and

Form 8-1. Summons

SUMMONS

STATE OF GREAT STATE   :
                            :   SS
COUNTY OF _____   :

TO _____
        Defendant

    You are notified that _____
                                Affiant
of _____ has filed a
            Address
complaint, a copy of which is hereto attached, charging
that on _____ 19 ___ , you committed the
offense of _____ .
    You are commanded therefore to appear before the
undersigned at ____ M, on _____
                                Date
at _____ in _____
            Place
for a preliminary hearing upon said charges according to
law and if you fail to appear at the time and place mentioned, a warrant will be issued for your arrest. You have
the right to be represented by a lawyer.

                    _____ (SEAL)
                        Issuing Authority

                        _____
                        Magisterial District

Date _____ 19 _____

---

the other personal belongings taken from him. For identification purposes, he was finger-printed and photographed. Informed that he could notify one person, he called Mary Worker, his mother. She, in turn, called Henry Law. Both started for police headquarters.

  In the meanwhile, police began a check to determine if Harvey had a prior record of arrests or if there were warrants outstanding against him. They also verified The Firm's previous report of theft of cypres parts.

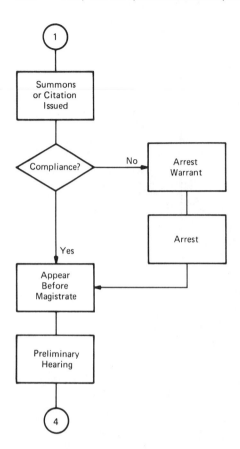

Figure 8-3. Entry Into Criminal System by Summons or Citation

At the same time, Detective Find and his partner, Hubert Seek, took Harvey to an interrogation room. After reading him his rights and the charges against him, they asked if he understood these. He replied that he did. He also said that he did not want a lawyer. Under questioning, he informed the detectives that he had been stealing cypres parts for almost a year, that he was working alone, that he sold most of the parts he stole, and that he had an unsold supply at home in his basement workshop. When Detective Find asked Harvey if he would be willing to tape record a statement to that effect, Harvey replied that he would. As the taping began, Detective Find asked Harvey for his name, if he understood the charges against him, and if he understood his rights. Both the charges and his rights were read again to Harvey in connection with the question. When he had completed his statement, Harvey was asked if it had been voluntarily given without either coercion or threat by the police, if it had been given without promise of clemency, and if he had been treated well. His answer to all of these questions was in the affirmative. That completed, Harvey was told he would shortly be taken to a magistrate for what was referred to as an *initial appearance.* In response to Harvey's question, Detective Find told him this was essentially a hearing to determine if he could be released on

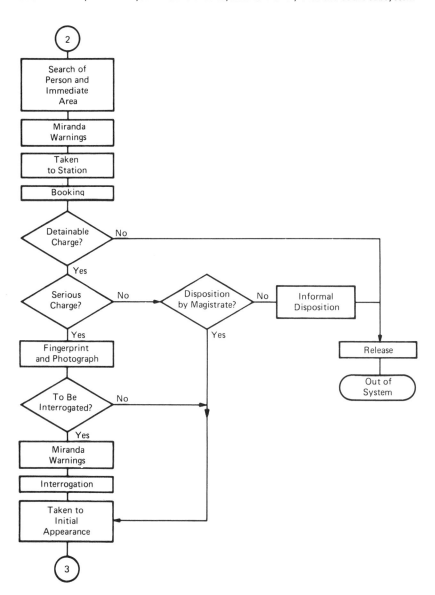

Figure 8-4. From Arrest to Initial Appearance

bail. As Harvey waited for police to make the necessary arrangements, both his mother and Henry Law arrived.

Mary and Henry were distressed when they learned of the serious charges on which Harvey was being held. The Great State Criminal Code provided for a maximum of twenty years imprisonment and fine of not more than $25,000 for a conviction of burglary; and a maximum of seven years imprisonment and fine of not more than $15,000 for a conviction of theft when the value of the property stolen was more than $2000.

Henry asked why Harvey had confessed.

"They caught me in the act," was all Harvey could say.

Soon all left for the magistrate's office. Henry inquired about the time at which each event occurred that evening. He determined that Harvey's arrest at The Firm took place somewhere between 7:15 and 7:30, Harvey arrived at police headquarters at approximately 8:20, and it was around 10:00 when the initial appearance began. Henry's concern with time was because the Great State Rules of Criminal Procedure provided that "when a defendant has been arrested without a warrant, he shall be taken without unnecessary delay before the proper authority where a complaint shall be filed against him and the initial appearance shall begin immediately." Had there been unnecessary delay? That would become an issue later. This Great State procedural rule made possible compliance with the requirements of the Fourth Amendment, as interpreted by the United States Supreme Court, that a judicial determination of probable cause is a prerequisite to extended restraint on liberty following arrest.[12]

Events following Harvey's arrest are shown in Figure 8–4. Note the possibilities for exercise of police discretion at the time of booking. It exists at many other stages of the criminal process and is a controversial issue. The police have an obligation to enforce the law, but can or should it be an automatic process, devoid of discretion?

INITIAL APPEARANCE

Magistrate Joseph Mann's office and courtroom were in another wing of the same building in which police headquarters were located. Detective Find filed the complaint shown in Form 8-2 with the magistrate, and took an oath as to the truth of its contents. In it, Harvey was accused of burglary and theft. Magistrate Mann was satisfied that there had in fact been probable cause for Harvey's arrest. When the complaint had been executed, the magistrate noted Henry's appearance as counsel for the accused and continued the proceedings. Magistrate Mann realized that he would be making a determination regarding bail and also that the initial appearance served to provide the accused with notice of the charges against him. The Great State Rules of Criminal Procedure stated specifically that the judicial authority at the initial appearance "shall not question the defendant respecting the offense charged." Turning to Harvey, therefore, he:

1. Informed him of the charges against him and gave him a copy of the complaint. Harvey indicated that he understood the charges;

2. Informed him of "his rights." Harvey indicated he understood them;

3. Informed him of his right to have a preliminary hearing on the charges against him and that, unless he waived that right, the hearing would be held on May 26 at one o'clock in the afternoon in the Big City Magistrate's Court. After consultation with Henry, Harvey indicated he understood this and would not at this time waive the right to the preliminary hearing;

4. Informed him that until the hearing he could be released on bail; otherwise, he would be committed to the county jail until the time of the preliminary hearing.

Form 8-2. Criminal Complaint

STATE OF GREAT STATE v. Harvey Worker
                                                Defendant

Big City, Great State   Address:
Magisterial District 1   200 Ninth St., Big City

I, the undersigned, do hereby state under oath (affirmation):
    (1) My name is   Detective Sgt. Richard Find   and
I live at   Police Station #1, Big City, Great State;
    (2) I accuse   Harvey Worker   who lives at
600 Fifth Street, Big City with violating the penal laws of
the State of Great State;
    (3) The date when the accused committed the
offense was on   Tuesday   ,   May 20   ,   19XX; and   on or
about June 14, 19WX; October 11, 19WX; January 20, 19XX;
April 3, 19XX.
    (4) The place where the offense was committed was
in the County of   Local   ;
    (5) The acts committed by the accused were:
Burglary and Theft   On May 20, 19XX, defendant unlawfully and feloniously did willfully and maliciously enter a
building located at the Terminal St. Extension, belonging
to The Firm, with intent to commit a felony therein and,
being therein, did feloniously and burglarously steal, exercise unlawful control over, take and carry away personal property of The Firm consisting of cypres parts
numbering two dozen and valued at $2400 with intent of
depriving the owner thereof and converting it to a use
other than that of the owner and without his consent. All
of the above in violation of Sections 3502 and 3921 of the
Great State Criminal Code. And defendant did further,
on prior dates listed above, at all such times, unlawfully and feloniously take and carry away personal
property of The Firm consisting of cypres parts
valued in all in excess of $10,000 with intent of de-
priving the owner thereof and converting it to a use
other than that of the owner and without his consent in
violation of Section 3921 of the Great State Criminal
Code.
    (6) I ask that the accused be required to answer the
charges I have made; and
    (7) I swear to (or affirm) the within complaint upon

my knowledge, information and belief, and sign it on
May 20 , 19XX before   *Joseph Mann*
whose office is that of Magistrate .

_____
Signature of Affiant

STATE OF GREAT STATE   :
                         :   SS
COUNTY OF LOCAL   :

Personally appeared before me on _____ May 20 _____ ,
19XX, the affiant above named who, being duly sworn
(affirmed) according to law, signed the complaint in my
presence and deposed and said that the facts set forth therein
are true and correct to the best of his knowledge, information and belief.

_____(SEAL)
Issuing Authority

Bail

The purpose of bail is to assure than an accused, if not detained in jail, will
appear for court at the proper time. To guarantee this, money or other property is posted
as security with the understanding that it will be returned when the accused appears as
required. It is, of course, forfeited if he does not. The word *bail,* when used as a verb,
refers to the act of procuring the accused's release by posting security. Used as a noun,
it refers to the guarantee of the accused's appearance or to the sum of money required
as security.

Many accused persons do not have the personal resources to provide the necessary security. They, therefore, seek others who can post that security for them. Those
who do so are referred to as the *surety* since they serve to assure appearance of the accused in court. The United States Supreme Court has held that a surety is authorized to
retrieve a defendant who fails to appear.[13]

Individuals who are in the business of acting as sureties are known as professional *bail bondsmen.* Their fee is usually from ten to fifteen percent of the amount required for release of the accused on bail. The term *bondsman* derives from the fact that
the document signed by the accused and his surety guaranteeing the accused's appearance
is referred to as a bail *bond.*

The bail system has often been a hardship on an indigent accused. Unable either to post security himself or to find a surety who will do so, he is detained in jail until time for his appearance in court. Because of that, such alternatives as ROR, nominal bail, and court-administered bail systems have been given attention recently.

ROR, or *release on one's own recognizance,* means that the accused is released on his promise that he will appear in court. No security is required. ROR is limited to cases involving the less serious crimes and to persons with indicia that they will appear as required. These include residence in the area, family and other ties to the community, history of employment, and the absence of prior conviction for serious crime. The appearance record for persons on ROR has been good but not perfect.

Nominal bail may be used as an alternative to ROR in cases in which it is desirable to have a surety. A deposit of $1 is required and a bond is executed. The surety incurs no financial liability but acts to ensure the accused's appearance.

Court-administered bail systems enable an accused to procure a bond at low cost through the court. Security, usually around ten percent of the total amount of bail, is deposited with the clerk of courts. As with the nominal bond, a responsible party must be named as surety. When the accused appears as scheduled, his deposit is refunded except for a small fee to cover the cost of administering the system. This may be as low as $10 or may be a percentage, usually ten percent, of the deposit.

The setting of bail is usually the function of a judicial officer. In some cases, it may be set by the police following arrest. In cases in which the accused represents a potential hazard to society if released, sound judgment dictates that bail be denied. Some state laws prohibit a magistrate from releasing on bail persons accused of murder or voluntary manslaughter. When persons released from custody fail to appear as required, necessary warrants may be issued to bring the defendant before the court.

A decision regarding release of the accused on bail is made several times during the criminal process. That decision is shown in a flow chart in Figure 8-5, which also shows the course of events resulting from that decision.

In Harvey's case, Henry urged the magistrate to give consideration to ROR since Harvey had no prior criminal record, lived in Big City with his mother, and had been regularly employed. The magistrate declined to do so because of the seriousness of the charges against him. He did agree that Harvey was a sufficiently good bail risk so as not to require the setting of bail in a large amount. Therefore, he decided upon nominal bail since there would be a surety. Mary agreed to serve as such. After the bond was executed, the initial appearance came to an end. Harvey was free until the preliminary hearing.

The proceedings at the initial appearance are shown in a flow chart in Figure 8-6. The initial appearance need not occur in cases when entry into the system has been by other means than arrest. This is for two reasons: (1) the accused is informed in writing of the charges against him since they appear on the citation or summons that he receives; (2) because he has not been taken into custody, there is no need to consider bail, nor is there need for judicial determination of probable cause for restraint of liberty. Both of these may be considerations at the hearing at which the accused has been directed to appear.

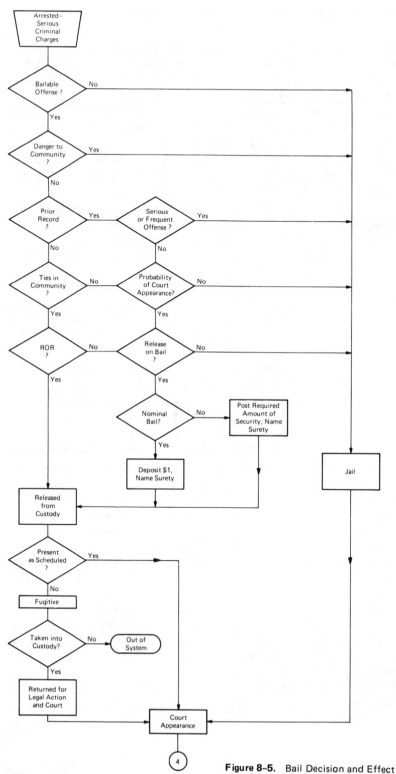

Figure 8-5. Bail Decision and Effect

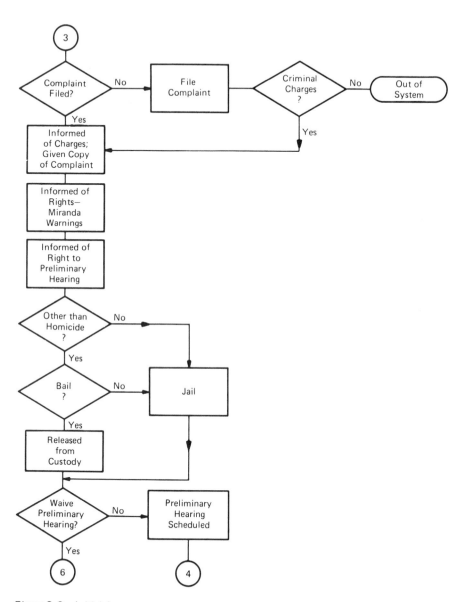

Figure 8-6. Initial Appearance

IN THE MEANTIME

While Harvey's initial appearance was in progress, other events related to the case were taking place. In his confession, Harvey had admitted that stolen parts were stored in his basement workshop at home. As the fruit of prior thefts, they were of concern to the police not only as evidence but also that they might be returned to their rightful owner. If Harvey were released on bail after his initial appearance that evening, as they fully expected, the possibility existed that he would hide, destroy, or otherwise dispose of the parts. Therefore, they felt a sense of urgency about getting those parts into police custody before Harvey returned home. To do this, a search warrant would be needed.

Search Warrant

In Great State, searches conducted after 11:00 PM were considered to be night time searches. A magistrate could authorize them only under certain conditions. Therefore, the first action following Harvey's confession was to prepare an application for a search warrant which Detective Seek would take to Magistrate Dixon, whose office was located on the way to the Worker home. Arrangements were also made for Detective Seek to meet, after the warrant was issued, four officers who would assist in the search. Provided no complications occurred, police expected to be at the Worker home before 10:00 PM. Since they knew where the parts were stored, an hour seemed to be ample time for their search.

The application that Detective Seek presented to Magistrate Dixon is shown in Form 8-3. In applying for a search warrant, the police officer must file with the appropriate judicial authority a deposition or affidavit showing probable cause to believe that illegal goods are located in a certain place. *Illegal goods* may consist of contraband or the fruits of a crime; items criminally possessed, such as drugs; property that is, has been, or will be used in the commission of a crime; goods that are evidence that a crime has been committed. The same requirements that apply to an arrest warrant exist with regard to facts, personal knowledge, and probable cause.

Form 8-3. Application for Search Warrant

STATE OF GREAT STATE   :

                                           :   SS

COUNTY OF ____Local____   :

APPLICATION FOR SEARCH WARRANT

____Hubert J. Seek____ of ____Big City Police Department____
        Name   Police Department

being duly sworn (or affirmed) according to law, deposes
and says that he has probable cause to believe that certain
property is evidence of or the fruit of a crime or is contra-

band or is unlawfully possessed or is otherwise subject to seizure, and is located at particular premises, as described below:

IDENTIFY ITEMS TO BE SEARCHED FOR AND SEIZED (be as specific as possible)

Cypres parts

DESCRIPTION OF PREMISES TO BE SEARCHED (e.g., street or other address, including apartment number, or specific description of vehicle, safe deposit box, etc.):

Dwelling house at 600 Fifth Street, Big City, Great State, including workshop and basement at said premises.

NAME OF OWNER, OCCUPANT OR POSSESSOR OF SAID PREMISES (give alias or description if name is unknown):

Owner of premises is Mary Worker, who occupies said premises with Harvey Worker, her son, and her other children, names unknown.

CRIME WHICH HAS BEEN OR IS BEING COMMITTED (describe conduct or specify statute):

Theft of cypres parts from The Firm, in violation of Section 3921 of Great State Criminal Code

PROBABLE CAUSE BELIEF IS BASED ON THE FOLLOWING FACTS AND CIRCUMSTANCES (Special instructions: 1 — If information was obtained from another person, e.g., an informant, a private citizen, or fellow officer, state specifically what information was received, and how and when such information was obtained. State also the factual basis for believing such other person to be reliable.

2 — If surveillance was made, state what information was obtained by such surveillance, by whom it was obtained, and state date, time and place of such surveillance.

3 — State other pertinent facts within personal knowledge of affiant.

4 — If "nighttime" search is requested (i.e., 11:00 p.m. to 6:00 a.m.) state additional reasonable cause for seeking permission to search in night time.

5 — State reasons for believing that the items are located at the premises specified above.

6 — State reasons for believing that the items are subject to seizure.

7 — State any additional information considered pertinent to justify this application.):

On May 20, 19XX Big City Police Officers Teresa Copp and

Vincent Polise arrested Harvey Worker whose address is 600 Fifth Street, Big City, charging burglary and theft, upon finding him at approximately 7:30 P.M. in the closed factory building of The Firm, Terminal Street Extension, Big City, taking cypres parts from the shelves in the factory supply room and placing them in a plastic bag belonging to said Harvey Worker. Following arrest, Harvey Worker gave a statement (copy attached) to Big City Detectives Hurbert Seek and Richard Find at approx- imately 9:40 P.M. at Big City Central Police Headquarters, in which he confessed to burglary and theft of cypres parts from The Firm and stated that these stolen parts are presently stored in the basement workshop in his home at 600 Fifth Street, Big City. Cypres parts have been reported stolen by The Firm in reports filed with Big City Police on June 14, 19XW, October 11, 19XW, January 20, 19XX, and April 3, 19XX; copies attached.

Hurbert Seek

Signature of Affiant

SEAL:

89   *10*

Badge Number   District/Unit

Magesterial District __14__

Office Address:

Sworn to and subscribed before me this __20__ day of __May__, 19XX.

204 Fifth Street
Big City, Great State

Anthony Dixon

Signature of Issuing Authority

Date Commission Expires:

December 31, 19XX

In this situation, Magistrate Dixon was satisfied that probable cause did exist and issued the warrant shown in Form 8-4.

A search warrant is a written order issued by a judicial officer in the name of the state. It is directed to an officer of the law. It commands the officer to search specified persons or premises, or both, for specific property alleged to be illegal goods and to bring the goods, when found, before the issuing authority. It may also include a provision to bring along the persons occupying the searched premises in order that they may be dealt with according to law.

Form 8-4. Search Warrant

STATE OF GREAT STATE   :
                        :   SS
COUNTY OF ___Local___

SEARCH WARRANT

TO LAW ENFORCEMENT OFFICER:

WHEREAS, facts have been sworn to or affirmed before me by written affidavit(s) attached hereto from which I have found probable cause, I do authorize you to search the following described premises or person: Dwelling house at 600 Fifth Street, Big City, Great State, including workshop and basement at said premises And to seize, secure, inventory, and make return according to the Great State Rules of Criminal Procedure the following items:

Cypres parts as described on reverse side.

As soon as practicable but in no event later than ___May 21___ , 19XX, and only during the daytime hours 6:00 a.m. to 11:00 p.m.

SEAL: Issued under my and this __20th__
                         day of ___May___ , 19XX, at
                         __9:45__ P. M. o'clock. (Time
                         of issuance must be specified.)

Magisterial District __14__   *Anthony Dixon*
Office Address: Signature of Issuing Authority
204 Fifth Street
Big City, Great State
Date Commission Expires:
December 31, 19XX

Entry to Search

While the warrant provides the police officer with the right to search specific premises, the officer cannot execute that search until first securing entry. Federal and many state statutes provide that in the absence of exigent circumstances, a law enforcement officer does not have the right of forcible entry. Prior to entry, there must be notice of identity and purpose, and then wait of a reasonable time for a response from the occupants. If not admitted after a reasonable period, as much physical force to effect entry as necessary may be used. Evidence secured as a result of an illegal entry is subject to the exclusionary rule.[14]

Detective Seek and the accompanying police officers arrived at the Worker home shortly before ten o'clock, while Mary was at police headquarters with Harvey. Betsy Worker, at home with her younger brothers and sisters, heard a loud knock followed by the words: "Police. Search Warrant. Open Up." Looking out the window, she saw that indeed there were uniformed police standing at the door. She opened it. Detective Seek showed her identification as well as the search warrant. Although she was a high school senior, she did not understand what a search warrant was and said so. After Detective Seek explained, she took the police to the basement where they soon discovered cypres parts neatly stored in an unlocked cabinet. They gathered these up, prepared a receipt for the parts which they gave to Betsy, and left.

Reports

One copy of the receipt and a copy of the police report of the search were delivered to the magistrate. This was in compliance with the warrant, which required that the police officer executing it make a return and deliver to the magistrate an inventory of all property seized. After reports had also been filed at police headquarters, the seized parts would be checked against the list of stolen items reported by The Firm. Al Chase would later be called to identify them.

DENIAL OF JUSTICE?

Mary and Harvey learned of the search when they arrived home.

"Henry didn't tell us about this," Mary said. She was referring to the conversation she and Harvey had had with Henry following the initial appearance.

They had been confused by what had occurred. Both had previously appeared before a magistrate for traffic violations. In each instance, they had been found guilty by the magistrate and a fine had been imposed. They had expected much the same procedure to be followed this evening and were greatly surprised that Harvey had not been given an opportunity to speak in his own behalf. In fact, both were greatly concerned about this. They asked if there had been a denial of justice.

"No," said Henry.

Petty Offenses

He explained that the criminal process is shortened in cases involving offenses of a less serious nature than a misdemeanor. These are sometimes referred to as *petty* or *summary* offenses, and include minor traffic violations. A magistrate has jurisdiction to make final disposition, from which there is a right of appeal, at the preliminary hearing in cases involving those offenses and some misdemeanors. At that time, he may accept a guilty plea, hold a trial to determine guilt or innocence, and impose a fine or jail sentence if the accused is found to be guilty.

With the serious crimes, Henry said, such disposition is reserved for the trial court, a court of record. In Local County, this would be the Criminal Court. Harvey's case would be heard in the state rather than the federal court system. Both crimes, burglary and theft, were state offenses.

The process followed in the magisterial court when there is final disposition of a case at the preliminary hearing has been flow charted in Figure 8-7. Note that appeal from the judgment of the magistrate is to the criminal court. There the case is heard *de novo;* that is, afresh or anew.

An initial appearance is often not necessary in these cases, because they involve the type of offense for which a citation or summons may be used. When an appearance is necessary, it may be scheduled to immediately precede the preliminary hearing. This is seldom done with cases involving serious offenses, which Henry termed the *court cases.*

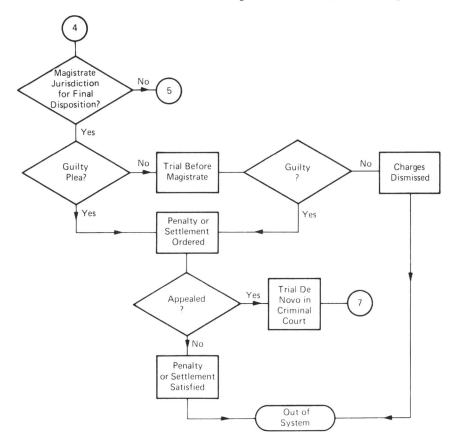

Figure 8-7. Judgment by Magistrate in Criminal Case

Court Cases

The Great State Rules of Criminal Procedure required that the preliminary hearing in court cases be held within three to ten days following the initial appearance. The purpose of the preliminary hearing, Henry continued, is to determine if probable cause exists to believe that a crime has been committed and the accused committed it. That is not the same, he hastened to add, as determining the accused's guilt beyond a reasonable doubt, which is the standard required for a guilty verdict at trial. The object of the hearing, he said, is to determine whether reasonable grounds exist for holding the accused for the next step in the criminal process. If not, the charges against him are dismissed; but if grounds do exist, he is "bound over for the grand jury."

Thus, Henry continued, for *court cases* the preliminary hearing is a screening device to determine if the accused should be held for the next step in the criminal process. For the less serious cases, the preliminary hearing is the stage at which final disposition is made.

In answer to Harvey's question about different procedures followed in Nearby State, Henry explained that not only is there variation among the states, but federal criminal procedure can differ from state procedure. The same variation exists with regard to terminology, he said. However, as he told Harvey, Great State criminal procedure was in most respects not unlike that of many states.

That, in essence, had been the extent of their conversation. No mention had been made of any search. One reason was that Henry was not yet aware of all the facts. Actually, it was only after they arrived home that evening that Mary Worker learned all of the details.

THE NEXT DAY

The next day, as might be expected, Harvey's employment at The Firm was terminated, effective immediately. Fred Famous was adamant that preventive measures be taken so that a similar occurrence would be less likely in the future. Jim Boss was assigned responsibility for implementing new methods of internal control as suggested by Chester, Porter, and Adams. Improvement of security was deemed necessary, and Al Chase was so informed. Fred Famous, although originally reluctant to involve the police, now believed there would be some deterrent effect flowing from the criminal prosecution. Others would realize that there would be no private resolution of such matters at The Firm, he told himself. He became so adamant that subsequent efforts by Harvey—at the urging of both Mary and Henry—to effect rapprochement and attempt to work out some method of restitution, were to no avail.

Defense Counsel

Harvey spent the next afternoon conferring with Henry Law. Although Mary Worker had enlisted Henry's aid the previous evening, Henry had not been retained for Harvey's defense. That, however, was merely because of the pressures of time. As Harvey told his mother, Henry was definitely his choice of advocate.

The Worker family did not qualify as indigents and therefore could not avail themselves of court-appointed counsel. In Local County that would have involved a lawyer from the Public Defender's office, a tax-supported office. The application for securing such assistance appears in Form 8-5.

Form 8-5. Application for Appointment of Legal Counsel

STATE OF GREAT STATE   Charge _____

            V.   No. _____ Term _____

_____

APPLICATION FORM FOR THE ASSIGNMENT
OF COUNSEL

    The applicant _____ residing at
_____ shows that:

    1. I am a defendant in the above entitled criminal cause of action alleging that I did commit the crime of
_____ at the _____ of _____
in the County of _____ and State of Great State,
on the _____ day of _____ , 19 ___.

    2. I am unable to obtain funds from anyone, including my family and associates, by way of compensation for counsel and represent that the answers to the following questions are true to the best of my information and belief:

      a. Do you have any money? _____ If so, how much?
        (1) On the person $ _____
        (2) In the bank $ _____
        (3) At home $ _____
        (4) In custody of the Warden $ _____
        (5) Elsewhere $ _____
      b. Do you own an automobile? _____
        (1) Year and Make _____
        (2) Cost $ _____
        (3) I owe $ _____ to _____
        (4) It is now at
      c. Do you own any real estate? _____ If so,
        give location: _____
      d. Do you own any other property or do you have
        any other assets? _____ If yes, furnish
        description thereof and specify its present

---

location: _____

e. Does anyone owe you money? _____ If yes, give the person's name and address and the amount he owes you: _____

f. If married, what is the name, age, and address of your spouse? _____
   (1) When did you last live with your spouse?
   (2) Does your spouse work?
   (3) What is the name and address of your spouse's employer? _____

g. Do you have any children? _____ If yes, give names, ages, and addresses: _____

h. What is your home address? _____

i. Where did you last work? _____

j. What is your social security number?_____

k. What salary or wages were you receiving?
   $ _____ per _____

l. What was the total amount of your income during the past 12 months? $ _____

m. Is there a job waiting for you? _____ If yes, specify what and where: _____

4. Line out a or b, whichever does NOT apply:

a. I am presently in jail and unable to obtain bail.

b. I am presently released from jail on bail in the amount of $ _____ . The cost of such bail was defrayed and paid by _____ , in the sum of $ _____ .

5. I have not previously been represented by an attorney in any case in court except: (give name of attorney, name of case in which you were represented and state whether or not your attorney was paid in this case and by whom.) _____

WHEREFORE, petitioner prays:

That this Honorable Court assign counsel to represent (him) (her) in the above entitled criminal cause of action without fee or cost to the defendant.

_____

STATE OF GREAT STATE   :

                        :   SS

County of _____   :

_____ , being

duly sworn according to law upon (his) (her) oath, deposes and says:

    1. I am the petitioner in the above entitled action.

    2. I have read the foregoing petition and know the contents thereof and the same are true to my own knowledge, except as to matters therein stated to be alleged as to persons other than myself, and, as to those matters I believe it to be true.

    3. This affidavit is made to inform the Court as to my status of indigency and to induce the Court to assign counsel to me as an indigent defendant for my defense against the criminal charges that have been made against me.

    4. In making this affidavit I am aware that perjury is a felony and that the punishment is a fine of not more than $3,000 or imprisonment for not more than seven years or both.

_____

Signature of Defendant

Right to Counsel

Harvey felt some sense of relief in knowing that now he had legal counsel. The United States Supreme Court has held that the right to representation by legal counsel exists at "every stage of a criminal proceeding where substantial rights of a criminal accused may be affected."[15] Examples of such stages, referred to as *critical stages,* include custodial interrogation, the preliminary hearing, the entry of a guilty plea, as well as the trial itself.[16] The right to counsel applies with regard to all criminal cases, even those for petty offenses where a sentence involving loss of liberty may be imposed, and it does not preclude self-representation.[17]

Attorney-Client Privilege

After agreeing to defend him, Henry explained to Harvey how necessary it was that he confide in his attorney and provide him with the entire truth.

"What you tell me confidentially in the course of my professional relationship with you is privileged information. It is a privilege which you, as the client, have the right to assert so that the information cannot be used against you. You can, of course, waive the privilege. However, the reason for its existence is to encourage and enable individuals to confide in their attorneys so that the latter can do the best possible job for their clients."

Advice and Plans

Henry was frank in telling Harvey that his chances were not good in view of his being caught in the act and his confession. Henry asked a great many questions about Harvey's treatment by the police and the circumstances surrounding his confession. In addition, the two discussed the preliminary hearing. Henry indicated that Harvey would not be required to plead. His best advice at this point, he said, would be for Harvey to exercise his right to remain silent. In response to Henry's question, Harvey said that he did not wish to waive the preliminary hearing. This would be the first event in the criminal process for which he was prepared and knew beforehand what to expect. Henry decided to make use of the opportunity he would have of hearing first-hand from the state the evidence against Harvey. He planned to tape the preliminary hearing.

PRELIMINARY HEARING

At the preliminary hearing, the magistrate began by once again informing Harvey of his rights and the charges against him. Henry's presence as his legal counsel was noted. The witnesses against him, Detectives Find and Seek and the arresting officers, were placed under oath and then questioned by the magistrate. No representative from the Local County District Attorney's office was present. Henry introduced no evidence on behalf of the defense, although he did cross-examine about Miranda warnings at the time of arrest and interrogation. The magistrate decided that since Harvey had been arrested in the very act of burglarizing and stealing parts, there was indeed probable cause to hold him for the grand jury. He continued bail as it had been set at the initial appearance. That meant Harvey was once again free, awaiting further action.

The flow chart of the preliminary hearing appears in Figure 8-8. Following the hearing, the magistrate sent to the clerk of the criminal court a transcript of the hearing, the complaint filed against Harvey along with Detective Find's affidavit, the copy of the bail bond on which Harvey had been released, and a copy of the search warrant and return. In the clerk's office the case was assigned a number, 1246 of 19XX, and two additional copies of the file materials were made. The district attorney's office and the public defender's office picked up, on a daily basis, files of cases bound over for court at preliminary hearings. In Local County the majority of criminal defendants received the legal assistance of the public defender's office. Since Henry had entered his appearance as Harvey's counsel, the file for the Harvey Worker case had been marked to show private defense by Henry Law.

Decision making crucial to Harvey's future would now take place in the district attorney's office, and will be discussed in the next chapter.

QUESTIONS

1. Three groups of persons have made decisions which have had a major effect upon Harvey's life: executives at The Firm, members of the Big City police, and members of the minor judiciary in Big City. It was Fred Famous' decision which triggered events leading

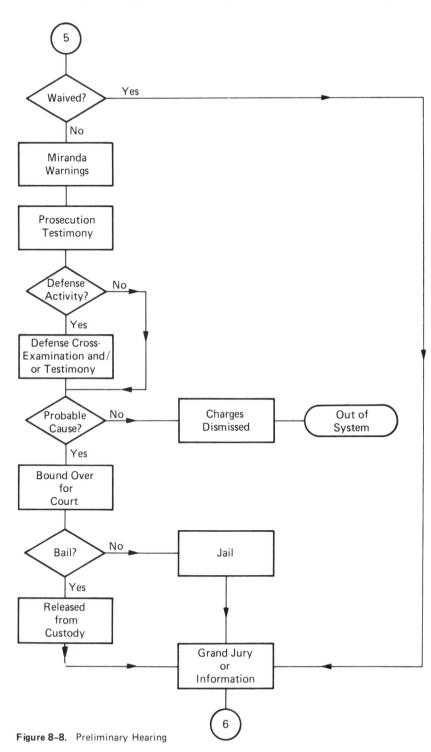

Figure 8-8. Preliminary Hearing

ultimately to Harvey's arrest. Why was Fred reluctant at first to file a report with the police about stolen parts? Should businesses handle employee theft privately by simply firing the individuals involved? Is that consistent with the concept of crime? Should "white collar crime" be treated differently from other crime? Should restitution be required in cases of theft? If so, should there also be prosecution? Do you agree with Fred Famous' later thoughts that this incident will have a deterrent effect upon others?

2. How much discretion were the police really able to exercise in Harvey's case? Cite specific instances. Consider the decision making required of a police officer called to the scene of a crime, remembering that he must give thought to at least the following matters and often must do so within seconds:

(a) Safety—what dangers exist in this situation? What measures can I take in my own defense? in defense of others? How much force may I use? May I call upon bystanders for assistance if I need it?

(b) Crime—does the incident involve criminal activity? If so, what crime or crimes? Are these felonies, misdemeanors, or summary offenses? May I arrest in this situation? If so, under what conditions? Do I need a warrant? What facts must I have in order to get a warrant? Do I have time to get a warrant? Is this a crime for which a citation is issued? What must I include on the form so that it does not lack legal effectiveness? Is this a crime for which I must apply to the magistrate for a summons? If so, what information must I have to present to him? What are my chances for success in getting one? If I arrest, may I search this person? how thoroughly? his surroundings? to what extent? May I enter the premises? under what conditions? What procedures must I follow before entering? Do I need a search warrant? If so, do I have sufficient facts to show probable cause? Will the evidence be destroyed and the individual gone before I can get one?

(c) Constitutional rights—is this a situation where Miranda warnings must be given? If I question the suspect, search him or the premises, or effect entry to the premises, will the evidence I secure be subject to exclusion?

Can you add to this list? What other jobs of which you know require such crucial decisions with split second timing under tense and often dangerous conditions?

3. Did you find any instances where Harvey's constitutional rights were denied him? Cite the specific instances.

4. Do you agree with the decisions of the magistrate regarding bail for Harvey? Why?—Regarding probable cause for the issuance of the search warrant?—For holding Harvey for court at the preliminary hearing? Why?

5. Should the state go to the trouble and expense of taking Harvey through all the steps in the criminal process when he is "obviously guilty" and has already confessed? Why not just sentence him now? Why would Henry Law defend an "obviously guilty" man? Should an accused have to pay for private defense counsel when the public defender's office is operated with tax monies? Is Harvey "obviously guilty"? Why?

6. The criminal process has been described as a screening device. What kind of screening took place in this case?—At what points?

7. The police and other law enforcement agencies are often referred to as the control subsystem within the total criminal system. In the Harvey Worker case, what aspects of control did you find in the police participation? Prevention of crime is considered by many to be an important—if not the most important—function of control. Could the police have prevented Harvey's criminal activity? Was there a natural transition from the control subsystem to the court subsystem? How much "control" has the court subsystem over the control subsystem and the manner in which the latter operates? What relation, if any, exists between this and the court's function in interpreting the Constitution? What examples, if any, have you seen that illustrate the primacy of the federal constitution?

8. What differences have you seen so far between the criminal process and the civil process? Can you think of reasons which explain why these differences exist?

NOTES

[1] Fed. R. Crim. P. 5 (a).

[2] *Malloy* v. *Hogan*, 378 U.S. 1 (1964); *Mapp* v. *Ohio*, 367 U.S. 643 (1961); *Gideon* v. *Wainwright*, 372 U.S. 335 (1963).

[3] *Harris* v. *New York*, 401 U.S. 222 (1971); *United States* v. *Calandra*, 414 U.S. 338 (1974).

[4] *Katz* v. *United States*, 389 U.S. 347 (1967); *Coolidge* v. *New Hampshire*, 403 U.S. 443 (1971); *Chambers* v. *Maroney*, 399 U.S. 42 (1970).

[5] *United States* v. *Robinson*, 414 U.S. 218 (1973); *Illinois* v. *Lafayette*, 77 L.Ed.2d 65 (1983).

[6] *Chimel* v. *California*, 395 U.S. 752 (1969).

[7] *Davis* v. *United States*, 328 U.S. 582 (1946); *Zap* v. *United States*, 328 U.S. 624 (1946); *United States* v. *Matlock*, 415 U.S. 164 (1974).

[8] *Warden* v. *Hayden*, 387 U.S. 294 (1967); *Carroll* v. *United States*, 267 U.S. 132 (1925); *Arkansas* v. *Sanders*, 99 S.Ct. 2586 (1979).

[9] *Terry* v. *Ohio*, 392 U.S. 1 (1968).

[10] *Miranda* v. *Arizona*, 384 U.S. 436 (1966).

[11] *Nix* v. *Williams*, 81 L.Ed.2d 377 (1984); *New York* v. *Quarles*, 81 L.Ed.2d 550 (1984).

[12] *Gerstein* v. *Pugh*, 420 U.S. 103 (1975).

[13] *Frisbie* v. *Collins*, 342 U.S. 519, rehearing denied 343 U.S. 937 (1952).

[14] *Ker* v. *California*, 374 U.S. 23 (1963).

[15] *Mempa* v. *Ray*, 389 U.S. 128 (1967).

[16] *Escobedo* v. *Illinois*, 378 U.S. 478 (1964); *Miranda* v. *Arizona*, 384 U.S. 436 (1966); *Coleman* v. *Alabama*, 399 U.S. 1 (1970); *Gideon* v. *Wainwright*, 372 U.S. 335 (1963).

[17] *Argersinger* v. *Hamlin*, 407 U.S. 25 (1972); *Faretta* v. *California*, 422 U.S. 806 (1975).

initial
processing
phase:
court subsystem

NINE

Jim Solicitor was a young assistant district attorney in Local County. It was his job to review the cases that had been bound over for the grand jury at preliminary hearings. On this June third morning he became intrigued as he read the file on the Harvey Worker case. He remembered having processed a case not too long ago involving a fence charged with receiving stolen cypres parts. Some college students who had been buying parts from the fence had been incensed when the stolen goods were traced to them and they were asked to return them. Could Harvey Worker have been the fence's supplier?

This recent local activity in stolen cypres parts was something new. The parts were expensive and small. This made them desirable as well as easy to steal. Interest in cypressing had increased recently, especially on college campuses. Was Local County now seeing the start of a wave of theft of cypres parts? Did this rash of thefts warrant stern measures designed to discourage any further development? Could it possibly be that this young man was part of some larger operation, as yet unknown?

Jim decided that he would like to know more about this case than appeared on paper. A telephone call to Detective Find revealed that both he and Detective Seek were out on assignment. Jim left a message, requesting that his call be returned.

As an assistant district attorney, Jim Solicitor was one of fifty-two lawyers on the staff of the Local County public prosecutor. As has already been seen, public prosecutors exist at the federal, state, and local levels. Their positions are usually that of attorney general or district attorney. Because crimes are acts done in violation of the duties one owes to the community, the law provides that the offender shall make satisfaction to the public when that duty is breached. Therefore, legal action in criminal cases is brought by the government, and not by private plaintiffs, as in the case of civil actions. Proceeding against a person in a criminal case is referred to as *prosecution*. The attorneys who bring these actions are known as *prosecutors*.

In Local County, the district attorney's office served a large metropolitan area. In contrast with more sparsely populated areas where there is often only a part-time district attorney, Local County required a staff of lawyers. Some engaged in trial work; others, in appellate work; and some, such as Jim, in such out-of-court activities as case review and preparation.

PROSECUTOR DISCRETION

Jim studied the materials in the Harvey Worker file. His was a screening function, and the decision of whether or not to send a case to the grand jury was entrusted to him. He also decided upon alternative dispositions of cases such as diversion to rehabilitative programs.

Nolle Prosequi

One of the discretionary powers of the public prosecutor is that of *nolle prosequi* (often used in abbreviated form, *nol pros* or *nolle pros*). Nolle prosequi is the authority not to proceed any further with the action, even though there is sufficient evidence that the accused has committed a crime. Although this power of the prosecutor has been the subject of much critical comment, it has been upheld by the United States Supreme Court.[1] It permits selective enforcement, as well as prosecution, for less than the full extent possible under the law.

The cases that often prompt a prosecutor to exercise his discretion to nolle pros include those in which an accused has cooperated in the apprehension or conviction of others, those in which victims are reluctant to testify, those in which there is insufficient admissible evidence, and those in which the prosecutor believes that diversion of the accused to a program of rehabilitation will accomplish more for that individual and for society than prosecution will. Among rehabilitative programs are those for alcoholism, drug addiction, and mental illness. Great State also had a program for persons with no prior convictions who were accused of nonviolent crime of a less serious nature. It was referred to as *accelerated rehabilitation,* since the accused could be placed on probation without being convicted and sentenced. A closer look at it should provide a better understanding of these diversionary programs.

The district attorney could request that an individual be placed into the accelerated rehabilitation program by filing a motion with the criminal court. A hearing on the motion was required to be held in open court, and the defendant, his attorney, and any victims notified of the time and place. Determination of whether or not the accused would be accepted into the program was made by the criminal court judge who presided at the hearing. Acceptance resulted in placement of the accused under the supervision of a probation officer for a designated period of time. If the accused successfully completed the program of probation, the charges against him were dismissed. If he failed to live up to any of the conditions imposed, he was eliminated from the program. When that occurred, the district attorney sent the case to the grand jury, as he also did in those cases in which the accused was not accepted into the program. The purpose of accelerated rehabilitation was to encourage first offenders to make a fresh, new start under supervision and to free other facilities of the criminal system for use with habitual and violent criminals.

Because Harvey was charged with felonies, he would not be eligible in Great State for accelerated rehabilitation. Nor were other rehabilitation programs appropriate in his case. Jim Solicitor studied the file again. If he agreed with the magistrate's decision that probable cause existed, this case would go to the grand jury.

Decision to Prosecute

The grand jury was created to protect the innocent from the harassment of trial when there are not reasonable grounds to believe that the person has committed a crime. It serves as an impartial buffer between the accused and the public prosecutor. Its function is to determine if probable cause exists to bring the accused to trial for the crime (or crimes) with which he is charged. This is the same decision that the magistrate makes at the preliminary hearing. Note that it is also the same decision that Jim Solicitor was making in his review of cases. In this way, the grand jury and magistrate can act as a check on the prosecutor's decision. In all, Great State procedure resulted in three different and independent determinations of probable cause to prosecute before an accused was brought to trial. In some states this determination occurs only twice because either the preliminary hearing or the grand jury is omitted. In still others, the prosecutor makes the sole determination. This is often restricted to cases involving the less serious crimes.

CHARGING ALTERNATIVES

Table 9-1 shows the screening and charging phases of the criminal process. It gives some indication of the wide variety of procedures followed in the various states. The United States Supreme Court has indicated there is no single preferred pretrial procedure.[2]

The Court has permitted the states the option of using either a grand jury *indictment* or a prosecutor's *information* as the instrument for formally charging an accused with crime.[3] The provision of the Fifth Amendment of the United States Constitution that "no person shall be held to answer for a capital, or otherwise infamous crime, unless on a presentment or indictment of a Grand Jury," has not been made applicable to the states. However, it does apply to federal prosecutions. As noted in Table 9-1, the Federal

TABLE 9-1. Screening and Charging Phases of the Criminal Process

STEPS	VARIATIONS IN PRACTICE IN DIFFERENT JURISDICTIONS		
	Information	Indictment	Information or Indictment*
1. Screening by prosecutor prior to formal charging.	1. Screening by prosecutor.	1. Screening by prosecutor.	1. Screening by prosecutor.
2. Alternate methods of formal charging.	2. Preliminary hearing.	2. Grand Jury.	2. Preliminary hearing.
	3. Information filed.	3. Indictment.	3. Information OR Grand Jury and Indictment.
EITHER	OR	OR	
	1. Screening by prosecutor.	1. Screening by prosecutor.	OR
Information prepared and filed by prosecutor after determination of probable cause by magistrate at preliminary hearing.	2. Information filed.	2. Preliminary hearing.	1. Preliminary hearing.
		3. Grand Jury.	2. Screening by prosecutor.
		4. Indictment.	3. Information OR Grand Jury and Indictment.
		OR	
OR		1. Preliminary hearing.	
		2. Screening by prosecutor.	
Indictment issued by grand jury after finding by them of probable cause.		3. Grand Jury.	
		4. Indictment.	

*In some states an option is available in each county regarding the charging instrument. Rule 7 of the Federal Rules of Criminal Procedure provides as follows with regard to charging instruments:

OFFENSE	CHARGING INSTRUMENT
Punishable by death.	Indictment.
Punishable by imprisonment for more than one year.	Indictment or by information if indictment is waived.
All others.	Indictment or information.

Rules of Criminal Procedure require an indictment in cases involving crimes punishable by death.

An *indictment* is a written accusation by a grand jury charging that there is probable cause to believe, based on evidence presented to it, that the person or persons named in it have committed the criminal offenses specified. The document itself is sometimes referred to as the *bill of indictment*. Note that it merely charges the person with crime. It does not represent a finding of guilt beyond a reasonable doubt. An *information,* on the other hand, is a document drafted by a prosecutor who charges an accused with a crime. It may follow testing for probable cause before a magistrate at a preliminary hearing. Use of the information eliminates the need for a charging grand jury.

GRAND JURY

Grand juries can have both an investigative and a charging function. Generally, special grand juries are convened to carry out investigatory work. They may bring charges on their own when they uncover criminal activity.

The grand jury has substantial powers. It may compel the production of evidence or the testimony of witnesses.[4] The exclusionary rule is not applicable.[5] Miranda warnings need not be given.[6] Immunity may be granted to witnesses in order to secure needed testimony that would incriminate the witness.[7] The *United States* v. *Mandujano* decision which follows deals with these issues.

Unites States v. *Mandujano*
   425 U.S. 564, 96 S.Ct. 1768, 48 L.Ed. 2d 212 (1976)

MR. CHIEF JUSTICE BURGER. This case presents the question whether the warnings called for by *Miranda* v. *Arizona,* 384 U.S. 436 (1966), must be given to a grand jury witness who is called to testify about criminal activities in which he may have been personally involved; and, whether absent such warnings, false statements made to the grand jury must be suppressed in a prosecution for perjury based on those statements. . . .

The grand jury is an integral part of our constitutional heritage which was brought to this country with the common law. The Framers, most of them trained in the English law and traditions, accepted the grand jury as a basic guarantee of individual liberty; notwithstanding periodic criticism, much of which is superficial, overlooking relevant history, the grand jury continues to function as a barrier to reckless or unfounded charges. . . . Its historic office has been to provide a shield against arbitrary or oppressive action, by insuring that serious criminal accusations will be brought only upon the considered judgment of a representative body of citizens acting under oath and under judicial instruction and guidance. . . .

. . . the law vests the grand jury with substantial powers, . . . Indispensable to the exercise of its power is the authority to compel the attendance and the testimony of witnesses, . . . and to require the production of evidence, . . .

When called by the grand jury, witnesses are thus legally bound to give testimony. . . . The grand jury's authority to compel testimony is not, of course, without limits. The same Amendment that establishes the grand jury also guarantees that "no person . . . shall be compelled in any criminal case to be a witness against himself. . . ."

Under settled principles, the Fifth Amendment does not confer an absolute right to decline to respond in a grand jury inquiry . . . The privilege cannot, for example, be asserted by a witness to protect others from possible criminal prosecution. . . . Nor can it be invoked simply to protect the witness' interest in privacy. . . .

. . . Moreover, the Court has expressly recognized that "[T]he obligation to appear is no different for a person who may himself be the subject of the grand jury inquiry."

Accordingly, the witness, though possibly engaged in some criminal enterprise, can be required to answer before a grand jury, so long as there is no compulsion to answer questions that are self-incriminating; the witness can, of course, stand on the privilege, . . .

The witness must invoke the privilege, however, as the "Constitution does not forbid the asking of criminative questions." . . .

. . . If in fact "there is reasonable ground to apprehend danger to the witness from his being compelled to answer," . . . the prosecutor must then determine whether the answer is of such overriding importance as to justify a grant of immunity to the witness.

If immunity is sought by the prosecutor and granted by the presiding judge, the witness can then be compelled to answer, on pain of contempt, even though the testimony would implicate the witness in criminal activity. . . .

In this constitutional process of securing a witness' testimony, perjury simply has no place whatever. Perjured testimony is an obvious and flagrant affront to the basic concepts of judicial proceedings. . . .

. . . [O]ur cases have consistently—indeed without exception—allowed sanctions for false statements or perjury; they have done so even in instances where the perjurer complained that the Government exceeded its constitutional powers in making the inquiry. . . .

. . . [Miranda] warnings were aimed at the evils seen by the Court as endemic to police interrogation of a person in custody. . . . But the Miranda Court simply did not perceive judicial inquiries and custodial interrogation as equivalents; . . .

. . . Indeed, the Court's opinion in Miranda reveals a focus on what was seen by the Court as police "coercion" derived from "factual studies [relating to] police violence and the 'third degree,' . . . physical brutality—beating, hanging, whipping—and to sustained and protracted questioning incommunicado in order to extort confessions. . . ." *Miranda, supra.* at 445–446. To extend these concepts to questioning before a grand jury inquiring into criminal activity under the guidance of a judge is an extravagant expansion never remotely contemplated by this Court in Miranda. . . .

. . . To extend the concepts of Miranda, . . . would require that the witness be told that there was an absolute right to silence, and obviously any such warning would be incorrect, for there is no such right before a grand jury. Under Miranda, a person in police custody has, of course, an absolute right to decline to answer any question, incriminating or innocuous . . . whereas a grand jury witness, on the contrary, has an absolute duty to answer all questions, subject only to a valid Fifth Amendment claim. And even when the grand jury witness asserts the privilege, questioning need not cease, except as to the particular subject to which the privilege has been addressed. . . .

. . . A witness "before a grand jury cannot insist, as a matter of constitutional right, on being represented by counsel. . . ." . . . Under settled principles the witness may not insist upon the presence of his attorney in the grand jury room. . . .

Grand jurors serve to hear presentations regarding not just one case, but many cases, over a period of time referred to as a term. This may be as long as eighteen months in some jurisdictions.

The circumstances surrounding Harvey Worker's arrest left no doubt in Jim Solicitor's mind that there was probable cause to prosecute. Following his conversation with Detective Find, he scheduled Harvey's case for the grand jury, the charges being burglary and theft. This prosecutor's screening decision and its possible consequences have been flow charted in Figure 9-1.

Subpoenas were issued for the appearance of witnesses. A copy of a grand jury subpoena appears as Form 9-1. Notice was sent to Harvey in accordance with Great State requirements that an accused be notified at least ten days prior to presentation of his case to the grand jury. This was to inform him of action being taken against him, not to ensure or even request his presence. Neither a defendant nor his attorney is permitted to be present during presentations by witnesses against him to the grand jury.

Harvey did have the right to waive grand jury proceedings. In Great State, waiver of the grand jury was permitted in all cases except those involving murder or voluntary manslaughter. Both the defendant and his attorney were required to sign a waiver statement on the bill of indictment. Harvey, however, did not choose to exercise his right of

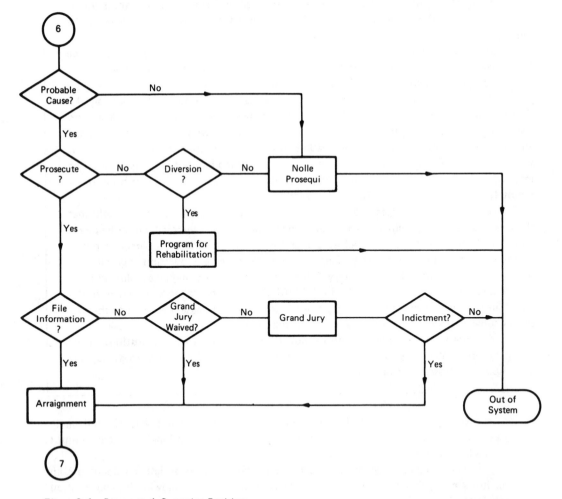

Figure 9-1. Prosecutor's Screening Decision

Form 9-1. Subpoena for Grand Jury Witness

COURT OF LOCAL COUNTY
CRIMINAL DIVISION

STATE OF GREAT STATE   :   CHARGE:
V.   :
Harvey Worker   :   Burglary and Theft

GRAND JURY SUBPOENA

You are ordered to appear before the Grand Jury, Third
Floor, Local County Court House, 1 Courthouse Square,
Big City, Great State, on _____June_____ ___17___ , 19XX , at
___9:30___ , ___A. M.___ , to testify in the above case.
Failure to do so may subject you to fine and/or
imprisonment.

Date: ___June 4, 19XX___

Attest: *Connie Scribe*   *S. Jean Ruhle*
Clerk of Courts   President Judge

---

waiver. He considered the possibility that a grand jury might not find probable cause in his case.

Juror Selection

Grand jurors are selected from voter lists, just as are members of petit juries. The number of persons on a grand jury is not the same in all states. Great State required not less than 16 nor more than 23 persons on a grand jury. Great State further required that a list of persons selected for grand jury service be posted in the offices of the clerk of courts and the district attorney. An accused held for court, his attorney, and the district attorney had the right to challenge the array on the basis that the grand jury had not been selected according to law. If sustained, the challenge resulted in dismissal of that grand jury, and selection of another was begun. Individual members of the grand jury could be challenged for cause. This could result in discharge of a juror or jurors, in which case replacements would be selected. All challenges were required to be in writing. There was, however, no right to voir dire. Henry examined the grand jury list but filed no challenge.

Members of the grand jury are sworn to secrecy, and their sessions are held in private. Their work is not done in a typical trial setting presided over by a judge. In addition to jurors, the only persons permitted to be present are the witness who is testifying, the prosecuting attorney, a court reporter in cases in which a transcript is permitted to be made of the proceedings, and an interpreter if one is required. The prosecutor calls witnesses against the defendant. The oath is administered to those witnesses by the grand jury foreperson. In many jurisdictions only prosecution testimony is heard; there is no evidence in defense.

Indictment

When the presentations are finished, the jury retires to deliberate in private. If the members decide to approve the charges against the accused, the foreperson signs the bill of indictment, which has been prepared beforehand by the district attorney's office. The signed bill is sometimes referred to as a *true bill.* A copy of the one in the Harvey Worker case appears as Form 9-2. A unanimous decision is not required to indict. In Great State, the minimum vote necessary for indictment was 12. The foreperson reports the decisions of the grand jury in open court at least once a day in the presence of all members of that grand jury. Great State required that a copy of the indictment be sent to the defendant. A copy was also sent to the clerk of courts where it served as the triggering document for scheduling the next step in the criminal process, the arraignment.

Form 9-2.   Bill of Indictment

COURT OF LOCAL COUNTY
CRIMINAL DIVISION

STATE OF GREAT STATE   :
       V.   :   Criminal Action No.
    Harvey Worker   :   __1246__ of 19XX

            The Grand Jury of __Local__ __County__ by this indictment charges that, on or about __May 20__ , 19XX, in said county, __Harvey Worker__ did __willfully,__ unlawfully, feloniously, and maliciously enter a building belonging to The Firm, and located at the Terminal Street Extension in Big City with intent to commit a felony therein and, being therein, feloniously and burglarously did steal, take, exercise unlawful control over, and carry away property of The Firm consisting of two dozen cypres parts valued at $2400.   The Grand Jury does further charge that Harvey Worker on the day and year aforesaid unlawfully and feloniously did then and there steal, take, exercise unlawful control over and carry away those certain goods and property as set forth above, with intent of depriving

the owner thereof and of converting it to a use other than
that of the owner and without his consent.

        The Grand Jury does further charge
that Harvey Worker on or about June 14, 19XW, and on or
about October 11, 19XW, and on or about January 20, 19XX,
and on or about April 3, 19XX did at all such times unlawfully and feloniously steal, take, exercise unlawful control
over, and carry away personal property of The Firm consisting of cypres parts valued in all in excess of $10,000
with intent of depriving the owner thereof and converting
it to a use other than that of the owner and without his consent.

        All of which is against the peace and
dignity of the State of Great State and in violation of
Sections 3502 and 3921, Great State Criminal Code.

Ray Jacob

                Foreperson

James Bethann

by *James Solicitor*

   Attorney for the State

WITNESSES:

Teresa Copp

Vincent Police

Hurbert Seek

Richard Find

Note: Notice of time, date, and place of arraignment on
reverse side.

If a grand jury decides to dismiss charges against the accused, the bill of indictment is marked "not found" or "not a true bill" and is said to be ignored. When that occurs, any bail is refunded. If a defendant has been confined to jail, he is released from custody. In Great State, the district attorney could not resubmit a dismissed case to another grand jury unless the criminal court granted permission to do so. Request was made to the court by a motion of the prosecutor.

Grand juries in Local County approved 94 percent of the bills of indictment presented to them during the calendar year 19XX. To those who asserted that this was proof that the grand jury was merely a rubber stamp for the prosecutor, Jim Solicitor replied that it was more a reflection of efficient screening prior to grand jury action. There were those who responded by asking if there really was a need, under these conditions, for a grand jury.

In Harvey's case, the grand jury members, after hearing Detectives Find and Seek and the two arresting officers, agreed unanimously and without hesitation that Harvey should be indicted. Had Harvey's case occurred in a jurisdiction where the charging instrument was an information rather than an indictment, a similar document would have been prepared by the district attorney and filed with the criminal court without any grand jury action.

Information Compared

Arraignment follows the filing of an information just as it does an indictment. At least half of the states do not use the indictment process. There are some that allege that the grand jury is a cumbersome, costly, and outmoded procedure, whose functions are better served through a preliminary hearing. A comparison of characteristics of the two is revealing:

PRELIMINARY HEARING	GRAND JURY
1. Determination of probable cause.	1. Determination of probable cause.

2. Decision by magistrate
   [one person
   [a professional.
	2. Decision by grand jurors
	   [a group
	   [laypersons.

3. Prosecution testimony.	3. Prosecution testimony.
4. Public.	4. Secret.
5. Accused present.	5. Accused not present.
6. Right of accused to assistance of counsel.	6. No right to counsel for accused.
7. Right of accused to cross-examine.	7. No right to cross-examine by accused.
8. Defense testimony permitted.	8. No defense testimony.
9. Accused's counsel may record.	9. No recording by accused.
10. Transcript required.	10. Transcript often not permitted.
11. Waiverable (with exceptions).	11. Waiverable (with exceptions).

12. Miranda warnings required.	12. No Miranda warnings required.
13. Suppression of illegally secured evidence.	13. Exclusionary rule not applicable.
14. Self-incriminating testimony not required.	14. Grant of immunity possible to secure incriminating testimony.

In Great State, the district attorney had yet another opportunity to exercise his discretion. He could file postindictment motions requesting that the defendant be accepted for accelerated rehabilitation or for nolle prosequi. Neither of these was considered in Harvey's case.

RIGHT TO SPEEDY TRIAL

The copy of the indictment sent to Harvey contained a notice of the time and place for which his arraignment had been scheduled. Time was important, since Great State had adopted a statute which required that the trial of criminal cases must begin no later than 180 days after a criminal complaint has been filed. At the federal level, the Speedy Trial Act generally requires that an accused be brought to trial within 100 days from the date of his arrest, with a maximum time schedule as follows:[8]

Arrest to indictment or information . . . . 30 days

Indictment or information to arraignment . . . . 10 days

Arraignment to trial . . . . 60 days

These laws were enacted for the purpose of furthering the Sixth Amendment right to a speedy trial, a right that has been made applicable to the states by the United States Supreme Court.[9] The legislation is the result of public and legislative concern about the effect of a backlog of criminal cases in the courts. This is of vital significance to those accused who are unable to obtain bail and must await trial while in custody.

PLEA ALTERNATIVES

Harvey asked many questions of Henry Law concerning the forthcoming arraignment. When he learned that he would be called upon to plead to the charges, Harvey asked for advice.

"I can explain the alternatives to you and the consequences of each," said Henry, "but the final decision must be yours."

The two explored the possible pleas: guilty, not guilty, nolo contendere, and silence. A plea of *guilty,* Henry said, would mean that Harvey would forego trial and would be sentenced. It was the equivalent of being found guilty by a jury, he added. A *not guilty* plea, on the other hand, would mean that Harvey would go to trial. He would have the right to a trial by jury but could waive the jury if he so chose. A plea of *nolo contendere* could be entered with consent of the court. It meant that Harvey did not intend to contest the charges. One effect was the same as if he had pleaded guilty: sentencing would result. However, the plea could not be used against Harvey later should a civil suit be brought against him for the same wrong. Finally, there was silence, which meant that the accused stood mute before the court. In that case, Henry explained, the judge was required to consider the silence of the accused as the equivalent of a not guilty plea.

"It's really a choice between guilty and not guilty, isn't it?" asked Harvey.

Henry nodded affirmatively.

"With a not guilty plea, I still have a chance. With a guilty plea, I have none," Harvey commented.

Henry suggested that they take a realistic look at Harvey's chances should he go to trial. He reminded Harvey that the district attorney had witnesses who saw Harvey in the plant stealing parts; that the police had in their possession stolen goods that had been recovered from his home workshop; and that they also had a tape recording of his confession. That, Henry added, would establish a very tight case against Harvey. Henry also noted that there was not much to be offered in defense.

DEFENSE CONSIDERATIONS

Henry had considered the position of the defense for some time. Defense counsel in a criminal action looks for measures that can result in either exculpating the defendant or mitigating the seriousness of the offense. Some measures were obviously not appropriate in this case. For instance, it was out of the question for Harvey to claim either that he did not unlawfully enter the building on the night in question or that, while there, he did not take cypres parts belonging to The Firm. This was not a case in which an alibi could be introduced.

Criminal Act and Intent

But Henry asked, did the fact that the acts took place mean that a crime or crimes had been committed? The Great State Criminal Code retained the common law concept that a crime requires both an act and an evil intention. (Exceptions to that did exist. By statutory provision certain acts were in and of themselves offenses against the Great State Criminal Code, regardless of criminal intent. In common parlance these acts are referred to as crimes, although scholars question if they are "true crimes.") Therefore, Henry mentally considered if there had been present the two elements necessary to the commission of crime:

1. the *actus reus*—criminal acts or deeds;
2. the *mens rea* and criminal intent—the mental intent.

The actus reus, or the guilty act, generally differs from crime to crime. The acts or deeds that constituted the two crimes with which Harvey had been charged were to be found in Sections 3502 and 3921 of the Great State Criminal Code. Referring to the Code, Henry once again quickly went down the list of items that made up each crime:

Burglary: entered a building,
building not open to public,
no license or privilege to enter,
intent to commit a crime therein.

Theft: unlawfully,
take and exercise control over,
movable property of another,
intent to deprive owner of the property.

Henry asked himself if each existed in Harvey's situation. He found that he had no choice but to say "yes" with regard to each item, whether it represented an act or an intent.

A wrongful or blameworthy mental state is required for crime in general. Some crimes, such as burglary and theft, require an additional mental element. For them, the specific intent is as much an element of the offense as the act itself, and proof of general malice will not suffice. The terms *criminal intent* and *mens rea* are at times used interchangeably. However, some writers have pointed out that the first term properly refers to a general guilty or evil state of mind, whereas the latter includes many different ones for the many different offenses.

Henry asked himself about his client's mental capacity at the time the acts were committed. Harvey had been neither drugged nor intoxicated. Nor was he mentally impaired. He had acted consciously, understanding what he was doing and knowing that it was wrong. Furthermore, Henry could not find that Harvey had acted under duress, out of fear, or because of threats. Instead, he had acted voluntarily. He had fully intended to do exactly what he did, having been compelled in no way to do so. Henry concluded that both the requisite criminal act and mental intent had been present. In addition, insanity and duress, which can serve as defenses in some criminal matters, were inapplicable. Also inapplicable were such affirmative defenses as entrapment, consent, and self-defense.

Burden of Proof

Henry considered other defense matters. Since this was a criminal action, the prosecution had the burden of proving the defendant's guilt beyond a reasonable doubt. Would the district attorney be able to do so? If he could not, Henry's task would be easy. He would simply move at the close of the prosecution's case for a judgment of acquittal because of the state's failure to establish a prima facie case. What evidence, he asked himself, did the district attorney have? He came up with this list:

—eyewitnesses to the burglary and theft: two police officers, Ed Under and Al Chase;

—cypres parts in Harvey's plastic bag recovered at the burglary scene;

—other cypres parts which had been recovered from Harvey's basement;

—Harvey's confession to the police;

—witnesses who had purchased cypres parts from Harvey at extremely low prices.

With regard to burglary and theft on the night of May 20, the eyewitnesses and the plastic bag of cypres parts could well serve to prove the *corpus delicti,* that is, the body of the crime (*not* the body of a homicide victim, as is commonly assumed). Furthermore, Henry believed this was competent evidence, not subject to the exclusionary rule.

Proof of the other thefts was another matter. There were witnesses who could testify to purchasing cypres parts from Harvey at extremely low prices, but none knew the source of the parts he sold. Furthermore, Henry believed he could create doubt in the minds of the jurors as to the credibility of the fence, should the latter be called as a witness. Much more damaging evidence existed in Harvey's confession and the cypres parts recovered from his basement workshop with the search warrant.

Suppressible Evidence

However, Henry believed that the confession might be subject to suppression. It had been secured during a delay between Harvey's arrest and the initial appearance. If that had been an unnecessary delay, it violated Rule 118 of the Great State Rules of Criminal Procedure. And in *Great State* v. *Futch,* 447 G.S. 389 (19XR), the Great State Supreme Court had held that a confession resulting from such violations of Rule 118 was excludable along with all evidence flowing from the confession.

"If I can convince the court that the delay was unnecessary," Henry said to himself, "suppression of the confession and the seized cypres parts should leave the prosecution unable to meet the burden of proving beyond a reasonable doubt the thefts prior to May 20. Then, even if Harvey is convicted on the charges stemming from the May 20 incident, the sentence should be lighter." That made suppression worth striving for, Henry decided. If he wished to have evidence excluded, he would have to file a motion for suppression with the court prior to trial. A hearing would be held before one of the criminal court judges, who would then decide whether or not the facts warranted granting the motion.

As Henry thought more about it, he decided there could be additional arguments raised in support of Harvey's confession. Harvey had been apprehensive and fearful at the time of his confession; he had just been "roughed up" at the scene of his arrest. Could he, under those circumstances, have made a truly voluntary statement?

"I should be able to prepare a persuasive argument," Henry thought.

Other Defenses

However, he did not end his consideration of the defense there. He carefully reexamined the documents related to the case, such as the criminal complaint and the indictment. A defense might emerge from them. For example, there might be error intrinsic to a document, such as an indictment which did not charge a crime. Or, there might have been an indictment for charges on which the defendant had previously been acquitted or convicted. In that case, the defense could file a motion to quash the indictment on the grounds that it was in violation of the Fifth Amendment protection against double jeopardy, that is, being placed in jeopardy twice for the same offense. This provision has been held applicable to the states by the United States Supreme Court.[10] If granted, such a motion would remove the accused from the criminal system. Double jeopardy, it should be noted here, means that one must twice actually be in jeopardy. A prior invalid legal action, such as one in a court lacking jurisdiction, does not constitute a jeopardy. It should also be noted that a defendant, by his actions, may waive the bar of jeopardy. Instances when this may occur include those when he asks for a new trial or appeals his verdict.[11] However, in Harvey's case, these were not applicable.

Henry next determined that the Statute of Limitations could not be raised as a defense. The time limit for the initiation of prosecution for burglary and theft in Great State was four years.

Nor did problems of jurisdiction exist. The case was before the criminal division of the state trial court in Local County. No federal offense had been committed. Therefore, the action properly belonged in the state court system. Great State law, like that of many other states, provided that any person who committed a crime "in whole or in part" within the territorial limits of that state could be convicted there of crime. So long as the suspect was arrested within the state, no problem arose in bringing him before its courts. However, when the accused fled beyond the state's borders, *extradition* became necessary. Extradition is a formal process by which a person is transferred from one state to another to be tried on criminal charges pending against him in that second state. He has the opportunity for a hearing to show cause why he should not be extradited. However, this was not the situation in Harvey's case.

No venue problem existed. Proper venue in criminal cases generally is the county in which the crime was committed. Nor had the publicity been so great in Harvey's case as to cause Henry to believe that Harvey would not receive a fair trial in Local County. Therefore, no request for change of venue was contemplated.

GUILTY PLEA?

Henry conveyed his assessment of the defense to Harvey explaining that the suppression motion represented just about the only possibility. Furthermore, he could not guarantee that it would be granted. Even if it were, it would help only with respect to the thefts prior to the time of the burglary.

"In this country, one is presumed to be innocent until proven guilty." Henry added, "However, that does not mean that persons who perpetrate criminal acts should expect that they will not be proven guilty. To think so would be foolhardy and unrealistic."

"Why bother with a defense, then?" Harvey wanted to know.

Henry explained that defense counsel can act to protect the defendant's rights and to see that the defendant is accorded due process at all times.

Realizing that Henry was not holding out a great deal of hope, Harvey asked:

"Suppose I plead guilty. What kind of sentence do you think I'd get then?"

Bargaining

Henry said he would talk with the prosecutor's office about this. There were mitigating factors: this was a first offense, and about half of the stolen parts had been recovered and would be returned to The Firm. Henry sought out the assistant district attorney to whom Harvey's case had been assigned for trial. That was Bob Barrister. The latter had reviewed the materials in the Harvey Worker file. He remarked to Henry that it seemed rather clear that the defense had little to offer. However, were Henry's client to plead guilty, the prosecutor's office could forego the time, expense, and work involved in having to prove guilt beyond a reasonable doubt. In view of this and of Harvey's lack of prior convictions, he was prepared to recommend probation at the time of sentencing if a guilty plea were entered. Henry indicated that he would discuss this offer with his client.

Henry and Bob had been involved in a practice known as *plea bargaining*. This occurs when the prosecutor and defense counsel (and, at times, the defendant also) engage in negotiations about the plea, the charges, and the sentence recommendation. The usual outcome is a reduction in charges or a promise by the prosecutor to recommend a more lenient sentence in return for the defendant's plea of guilty.

The vast majority of criminal cases in this country are resolved by a guilty plea. While this has been attributed to good police work and efficient pretrial screening, many believe that plea bargaining is the most important reason for it. At the same time, many critics of plea bargaining allege that it leads to guilty pleas by innocent persons who are frightened and distrustful of the consequences of going to trial. Still others have contended that justice is not something that can be negotiated and have recommended that plea bargaining be completely abolished. On the other hand, there are those who claim that plea bargaining is a necessity if the courts are to be able to cope with the multitude of criminal cases coming before them. The United States Supreme Court has recognized that plea bargaining is a phase of the criminal process, and in the following *Santobello* v. *New York* opinion, even stated that "properly administered" plea bargaining should be encouraged.

Santobello v. *New York*

404 U.S. 257, 92 S.Ct. 495, 30 L.Ed. 2d 427 (1971)

Santobello entered a guilty plea to a lesser charge as a result of bargaining between defense counsel and the prosecutor. The latter agreed to make no recommendation as to sentence, but at the time of sentencing had been replaced by another prosecutor who recommended imposition of the maximum sentence on the reduced charge. Over defense counsel's objections, the judge imposed the maximum sentence. It was upheld in the state appellate courts.

MR. CHIEF JUSTICE BURGER. We granted *certiorari* in this case to determine whether the State's failure to keep a commitment concerning the sentence recommendation on a guilty plea required a new trial. . . .

. . . The disposition of criminal charges by agreement between the prosecutor and the accused, sometimes loosely called "plea bargaining," is an essential component of the administration of justice. Properly administered, it is to be encouraged. If every criminal charge were subjected to a full-scale trial, the States and the Federal Government would need to multiply by many times the number of judges and court facilities.

Disposition of charges after plea discussions is not only an essential part of the process but a highly desirable part for many reasons. It leads to prompt and largely final disposition of most criminal cases; it avoids much of the corrosive impact of enforced idleness during pretrial confinement for those who are denied release pending trial; it protects the public from those accused persons who are prone to continue criminal conduct even while on pretrial release; and by shortening the time between charge and disposition, it enhances whatever may be the rehabilitative prospects of the guilty when they are ultimately imprisoned. . . .

This phase of the process of criminal justice and the adjudicative element inherent in accepting a plea of guilty, must be attended by safeguards to insure the defendant what is reasonably due in the circumstances. Those circumstances will vary, but a constant factor is that when a plea rests in any significant degree on a promise or agreement of the prosecutor, so that it can be said to be part of the inducement or consideration, such promise must be fulfilled.

On this record, the petitioner "bargained" and negotiated for a particular plea in order to secure dismissal of more serious charges, . . . It is now conceded that the promise to abstain from a recommendation was made, . . . That the breach of agreement was inadvertent does not lessen its impact.

The judgment is vacated and the case is remanded for reconsideration not inconsistent with this opinion.

The Great State Rules of Criminal Procedure set forth the following specific requirements regarding plea bargaining:

1. The trial judge is not permitted to participate in the plea negotiations.
2. Counsel for both sides are required to state on the record in open court in the presence of the defendant the terms of the agreement.
3. The judge is required to conduct an inquiry of the defendant to determine if he understands and concurs in the agreement.
4. The judge is permitted to accept the agreement if he is satisfied that the guilty plea is understandingly and voluntarily offered.
5. The judge is not required to be bound by the plea agreement unless he accepts it. If he does not, the accused must be permitted to withdraw the guilty plea.

These rules were developed to eliminate secret deals and to assure, insofar as possible, the voluntariness of confessions of guilt.

Decision

Henry took Bob Barrister's offer back to Harvey. The two discussed it. Henry asked Harvey to consider it very carefully. In answer to Harvey's question, he said that a guilty plea could be entered at the forthcoming arraignment, at a later date prior to trial and after a decision had been rendered by the court regarding the suppression motion, or even during the trial. While Harvey relished the thought of release on probation, he realized there could be no guarantee of this. He also decided that he preferred to try every possible avenue of defense before he would plead guilty. The list of pros and cons he considered in arriving at a decision not to accept the prosecution's offer at least for the present is shown below:

PLEAD GUILTY	PLEAD NOT GUILTY
1. Quick disposition.	1. Longer time required.
2. No trial.	2. Must stand trial.
3. Less legal fees to be paid.	3. Greater legal fees.
4. Probability of leniency in sentencing.	4. Uncertainty as to leniency.
5. Criminal record.	5. Uncertainty as to criminal record.
6. No chance for acquittal.	6. Chance for acquittal.
	7. Henry's a good lawyer, interested in me, will do his utmost.

The final decision had not been easy. Henry had suggested taking time to reconsider "carefully and realistically" after the first indication of similar intention. He pointed to Harvey's commission of the acts, as well as the paucity of defenses. In a telephone conversation one day Mary explained to Henry that neither she nor Harvey would ever feel satisfied if they did not exhaust every possibility. The death of John Q. had resulted in a severe and detrimental impact upon Harvey's life, including his dropping out of college, and "now this," she said. Therefore, she had determined to provide him with every opportunity and all the support she could, not only now but "all the way through an appeal, if that becomes necessary."

ARRAIGNMENT

As scheduled, Harvey appeared with Henry before Judge Joseph Roe in the Local County Criminal Court at ten o'clock on the morning of July 3, 19XX, for arraignment. Bob Barrister was present representing the district attorney's office. In Great State, arraignment was required to be held in open court at least ten days prior to trial. Harvey was read the charges against him which appeared in the indictment. At this point, he would have been given a copy of the document had he not already received one. He was again advised of his rights. Because the arraignment is considered a critical stage in the criminal process, note was made of the fact that he was present and represented by legal counsel. When the judge asked how he wished to plead, he answered:

"Not guilty."

Record of Plea

The case was set for trial. Harvey indicated he wished to have a jury trial. The judge reviewed his bail and continued it as it had been set at the initial appearance. A transcript of the arraignment was filed with the clerk of court's office. Notice to set a trial date was sent to the deputy court administrator in charge of the criminal trial list.

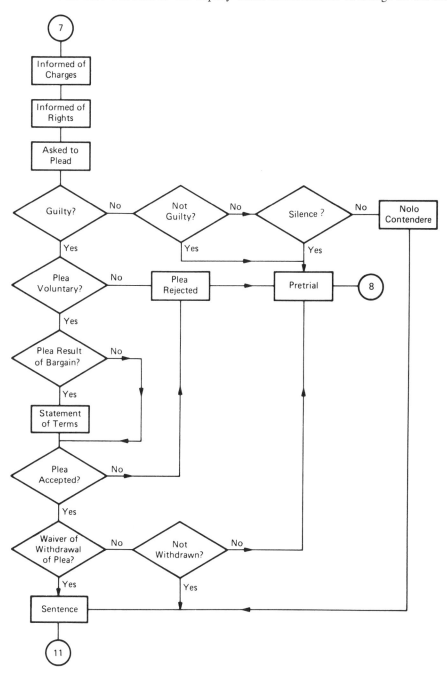

Figure 9–2. Arraignment

Voluntariness of Plea

Had Harvey pleaded guilty, the judge would have exerted effort to determine the voluntariness of that plea. Coerced confessions clearly violate the Fifth Amendment privilege against compulsory self-incrimination. Before accepting a plea of guilty, therefore, the judge's concern is that the accused is entering that plea knowingly and of his own accord. One test frequently used to determine this is to elicit answers to questions such as these:

—Do you understand the nature of the charges to which you are pleading?

—What is the factual basis for your plea? What, in fact, did you do?

—Do you understand that you have the right to trial by jury?

—Do you understand that you are presumed innocent until found guilty?

—Do you know the range of sentences for the offense for which you are charged?

—Do you know that the judge is not bound by the terms of any plea bargain unless the judge accepts the agreement?

If the judge were satisfied that the plea had been voluntarily given, he could either impose sentence then or schedule sentencing for a later date. Prior to sentencing, withdrawal of a guilty plea is possible with leave of court.

The arraignment process is shown in a flow chart in Figure 9-2.

DISCOVERY

Henry now engaged in trial preparation. Since this was a criminal case, the extent of discovery in civil actions was not applicable. Great State Rules of Criminal Procedure provided, in general, that the prosecution must provide the defense with substantial, material evidence in its possession. However, the prosecutor was not required to turn over the complete file on the case. Deposition taking was limited to that of prospective witnesses whose testimony was considered to be material and who would be unable to attend the trial. The United States Supreme Court has held that a prosecutor has a constitutional duty to provide material exculpatory evidence to the defense, whether or not a request is made.[12]

Many commentators have taken issue with limitations on criminal discovery. Because of the privilege against self-incrimination, some restrictions that would not exist in a civil case appear to be necessary.

MOTION TO SUPPRESS

The court granted Henry's motion to secure a copy of the tape recorded confession which Harvey had given to the police. Henry's next step was to prepare an application for the suppression of evidence, a copy of which appears as Form 9-3. Note that he based his re-

Form 9-3. Aplication to Suppress Evidence

COURT OF LOCAL COUNTY
CRIMINAL DIVISION

STATE OF GREAT STATE   :
        V.   :   No. 1246 of 19XX
HARVEY WORKER   :   Burglary and Theft

APPLICATION TO SUPPRESS EVIDENCE AND
CONFESSIONS AND/OR ADMISSIONS

And now this tenth day of July 19XX comes the above
defendant by his attorney pursuant to Great State R. Crim.
Pro. 232, 324, and 2001 and respectfully represents as
follows:

    1. This matter was set for trial following arraign-
ment before Judge Joseph Roe on July 3.

    2. Defendant was arrested on May 20, 19XX for the
above mentioned charges.

    3. Defendant believes there will be introduced into
evidence at the time of the trial of this case certain
written, taped, and/or oral statements and/or admissions
which may amount to a confession or which may contain
admissions implicating the defendant in the subject case.

    4. That said incriminating statements were made
while defendant was being held at Central Police Headquarters in Big City and in fact in police custody.

    5. That said incriminating statements were made by
defendant without the presence of legal counsel to advise
him.

    6. That the circumstances warranted the defendant
being warned of his constitutional rights enunciated in the
Fourth, Fifth, Sixth, and Fourteenth Amendments of the
United States Constitution and in the case of *Miranda* v.
Arizona, 384 U.S. 436 (1966).

    7. That even assuming defendant was warned of
said constitutional rights before giving a statement, he did
not intelligently waive those rights because of the over-
bearing nature of the circumstances in which he found
himself because authorities pressed for answers to
questions and overbore his will to resist making a statement.

    8. That the statements above mentioned were not

voluntarily and intelligently and knowingly given to the police but were the product of undue pressure, influence, coercion, design, and/or trickery, all of which prompted defendant in making the statements.

All of which above described violates the Fourth, Fifth, Sixth, and Fourteenth Amendments to the Constitution of the United States and the case law made pursuant thereto.

9. That subsequent to arrest, certain cypres parts were seized from the premises at 600 Fifth Street in Big City pursuant to a search warrant executed and issued on the basis of the information illegally and unconstitutionally secured from the defendant as described above and are therefore "fruit of the poisonous tree."

10. That defendant's detention at Central Police Headquarters was prolonged following the completion of booking procedures and the defendant's initial appearance before a magistrate was delayed by the police for the purpose of the above described interrogation of the defendant.

11. That such delay in the initial appearance is in violation of Great State R. Crim. Pro. 118.

12. That all evidence obtained as a result of such unnecessary delay in violation of Rule 118 is inadmissible, *Great State* v. *Futch,* 447 G.S. 389 (19XR).

Whereupon defendant requests a rule to issue upon the State to show cause why all the evidence seized and the written, taped, and/or oral statements given and the evidence which flows therefrom should not be suppressed.

Respectfully submitted,

Henry Law
Attorney for the Defendant

quest for suppression upon the delay between arrest and initial appearance and also upon an allegation that Harvey's confession was the product of undue pressure and coercion.

A copy of the application was filed with the clerk of courts and another with the district attorney. Bob Barrister prepared a request to the court to deny the application. A copy of this appears as Form 9-4. Not only did he contend that any delay following Harvey's arrest was necessary and reasonable, but he also stated that according to Harvey's own admission there had been no undue influence exerted upon him to confess.

Notice, too, that Bob concluded by requesting that a hearing on the application be scheduled for as soon as possible in order not to delay the date of trial.

The Great State Criminal Court followed a master calendar plan instead of the individual calendar system. Therefore, different aspects of any one case might be assigned to different judges. For instance, all pretrial applications, petitions, and motions were assigned to the administrative judge. It was in this way that the hearing on Henry's suppression motion came to be scheduled before Judge Homer Grant.

Form 9–4. State's Request for Denial

COURT OF LOCAL COUNTY
CRIMINAL DIVISION

STATE OF GREAT STATE   :
                V.   :   No. 1246 of 19XX
HARVEY WORKER   :   Burglary and Theft

STATE'S REQUEST FOR DENIAL OF DEFENDANT'S
APPLICATION TO SUPPRESS EVIDENCE
AND CONFESSIONS AND/OR ADMISSIONS

And now this fourteenth day of July comes James Bethann, District Attorney, by Assistant District Attorney, Robert Barrister, and in answer to Defendant's Aplication to Suppress Evidence and Confessions and/or Admissions respectfully shows:

1. Defendant was arrested on May 20, 19XX at 7:30 p. m. at The Firm's factory and transported immediately to Central Police Headquarters in Big City, arriving there at 8:20 p. m. Booking, fingerprinting, and photographing followed. At 9:10 p. m. defendant began a statement to the police which was concluded at 9:40 p. m. Defendant's initial appearance before the magistrate began at 10:00 p. m.

2. The time between arrest and initial appearance is fully accounted for and was consumed by the above described necessary police procedures. There was no unnecessary delay, in terms of the requirements of Great State R. Crim. Pro. 118, between the time of arrest and initial appearance.

3. Limited police interrogation of an arrestee is permissible under *Great State* v. *Futch,* 447 G. S. 389 (19XR) where at 392 the Court quoted from *Adams* v. *United States,* 399 F. 2d 574, 579 (D. C' Cir., 1968) as follows:

"Necessary delay can reasonably relate to time to administratively process an accused with booking, fingerprinting and other steps and sometimes even to make same (sic) limited preliminary investigation into his connection with the crime for which he was arrested, especially when it is directed to possible exculpation of the one arrested."

4. Defendant was warned of his constitutional rights at the time of his arrest, at the time he was booked, prior to police interrogation, and again immediately before he provided his taped statement to the police.

5. Defendant is 20 years of age, has attended college for one year, understands and speaks the English language well, and is fully capable of understanding and comprehending the meaning of statements of his constitutional rights.

6. By defendant's own admission, recorded on his taped statement, he was neither coerced, tricked, threatened, subjected to physical harm, made any promises of deals, nor was he in any other way influenced or pressured to give his statement to the police.

7. By defendant's own admission, recorded on his taped statement, he voluntarily and knowingly waived his right to remain silent and to have legal counsel present during the time he gave his statement to the police.

8. Seizure of cypres parts was made at the defendant's home pursuant to a legally issued and executed search warrant and in full accord with defendant's constitutional rights.

For all these reasons, the State requests that defendant's application to suppress evidence and confessions and/or admissions should be denied.

The State further requests that a hearing on the matter of the defendant's application be held at the earliest possible date in order not to delay the date of trial.

James Bethann

James Bethann, District Attorney

Robert Berrister

Assistant District Attorney

Suppression Hearing

A private hearing was required because the issue of the inadmissibility of a confession would be considered. Were the contents of the confession to be revealed in a public hearing, a grant of the motion to suppress the confession would be of little value! The only persons permitted to be present included Harvey, Henry, Bob Barrister, court officers, and the witness testifying. Other witnesses waited in the hall until called. The judge heard from Harvey (who, as Henry explained beforehand, did not in that way waive his right to remain silent at trial), Detectives Find and Seek, Al Chase and Ed Under, and the two arresting officers. He also listened to the tape recorded confession.

At one point during the hearing the judge himself undertook questioning of Harvey regarding the circumstances surrounding his confession. Portions of that examination follow:

JUDGE: Did you know you had the right to have a lawyer present?

HARVEY: Yes.

J: How did you know?

H: The police told me.

J: When did they tell you that?

H: Several times.

J: When would that have been?

H: When I was arrested . . . out at The Firm, when they brought me to the police station, when the detectives took me into the interrogation room where I made the statement, before I made the tape recording.

J: At all of these times?

H: Yes.

J: Did the police tell you anything else at these times?

H: Yes.

J: What was that?

H: That I could remain silent, that anything I said would be held against me.

J: Did they say anything more about a lawyer?

H: Yes.

J: And what was that?

H: If I wanted one and couldn't get one, they'd get one for me.

J: And what did you say about a lawyer?

H: That I didn't want one.

J: That you didn't want one? Why was that?

H: I didn't think then that he could do me any good.

J: Was that because the police advised you of that?

H: No. That was what I thought then. I know better now.

J: Did the police advise you either way: that you needed a lawyer or that you didn't need one?

H: No. They just told me I could have one if I wanted one.

J: And you said?

H: I didn't want one.

J: Did the police force you or in any way threaten you to say that?

H: No.

J: Were you tricked into saying that?

H: I didn't know then that a lawyer could help me.

J: Does that mean you know that now?

H: Yes.

J: How did you learn that?

H: I have a lawyer, and he helps me. He explains things. He tells me what's going to happen. I know what to expect.

J: And you didn't then?

H: No. I thought they'd probably just lock me in jail.

J: What else did you think would happen to you?

H: I didn't know.

J: Well, did you think, for instance, the police might abuse you?—Beat you?

H: No.

J: Did they mistreat you at any time?

H: I was roughed up when I was arrested.

J: By the police?

H: Yes.

J: The arresting officers?

H: Yes.

J: What did they do to you?

H: Kicked me in the shins and punched me in the ribs when they were patting me down.

J: Did you require medical attention?

H: No.

J: Did you consult a physician?

H: No.

J: Why not?

H: I didn't need one.

J: Why not?

H: I knew it would get better by itself.

J: How serious was it? Did you, for instance, have bruises, marks, welts, or discolorations on your body from the blows?

H: No.

J: Were you incapacitated in any way?

H: No.

J: What discomfort, if any, did you suffer from the roughing up?

H: It hurt.

J: At the time?

H: Yes.

J: Did the pain continue?

H: Yes.

J: For how long?

H: I don't know.

J: Were you still feeling pain at the time you arrived at the police station?

H: Yes.

J: Did it continue?

H: Yes.

J: For how long?

H: I don't remember.

J: Did you tell the police at the station you were in pain?

H: No.

J: Why not?

H: I guess I was too frightened.

J: Did any other police officer, at any time, either rough you up or in any way beat, hit, or otherwise cause physical harm to you?

H: No.

J: Did any of them threaten to do so?

H: No.

Motion Denied

Several days later, the judge issued an order denying the relief requested. At the same time, he filed a statement of findings of fact and conclusions of law with regard to the defendant's application to suppress evidence. Pertinent portions of that document, later quoted to the appellate court, were as follows:

FINDINGS OF FACT

1. Defendant was arrested without a warrant by police officers who, responding to a call reporting burglary in progress at The Firm, found defendant in The Firm's building after business hours and in the process of removing parts from shelves where they were stored and placing them in a plastic bag.

2. Defendant was given Miranda warnings by the police at the time of his arrest, at the time of booking, and again before his statement to the police regarding his participation in the felonies.

3. Defendant is 20 years of age, has completed one year of college, understands and uses the English language well.

4. Defendant admits he understood he had the right to legal counsel and to remain silent when questioned by the police and further admits that he waived those rights.

5. Defendant admits he was neither threatened nor physically abused by the police at the time he gave them his confession, nor was he made any promises or special deals in return for his confession.

6. While there is some discrepancy in the testimony as to whether defendant was "roughed up" physically at the time of his arrest, defendant neither required

medical attention nor suffered any bruises, marks, or discoloration as a result of the alleged treatment.

7. Defendant was arrested at approximately 7:30 PM at The Firm's factory; was transported to central police headquarters where he arrived at 8:20 PM; was booked, fingerprinted, and photographed; gave a statement to the police beginning at 9:10 PM and concluding at 9:40 PM; appeared before a magistrate for his initial appearance beginning at 10:00 PM.

CONCLUSIONS OF LAW

1. Defendant's warrantless arrest was legal, having been made by police who witnessed the defendant in the act of theft and had probable cause to believe he had also committed burglary.

2. The lapse of time between arrest and initial appearance did not constitute unnecessary delay, nor was it unreasonable, in terms of the requirements of Rule 118 of the Great State Rules of Criminal Procedure. The time having been used for necessary police procedures, the initial appearance began within a period that fully complied with the requirements of Rule 118.

3. Defendant's confession was voluntary, having been made after he had been fully informed of his rights and had knowingly and voluntarily waived his right to remain silent and to have counsel present.

4. The search and seizure of cypres parts at defendant's home was valid, since it was conducted pursuant to a search warrant issued and based upon probable cause.

5. The application of defendant to suppress the evidence should be denied.

PRETRIAL PLANNING

Defense Plans

Harvey was disappointed but still determined to go to trial. He and Henry discussed the course of action to be taken should Harvey be found guilty. Henry noted that his first act would be to urge leniency in sentencing. He believed the mitigating factors of a first offense and partial restitution made it likely this would be granted. In addition, Henry planned to quote to the court from the Model Penal Code, which recommends probation unless imprisonment is necessary for "protection of the public." Finally, he and Harvey decided that any other action following that would have to remain indefinite, pending outcome of the trial.

One decision Henry made about this time concerned whether or not Harvey should take the stand in his own defense. Henry concluded that it would be to Harvey's advantage to exercise his privilege against self-incrimination by not testifying. By taking the stand, he would become subject to cross-examination by the prosecution whose skillful questioning could lead Harvey to fatal admissions. Henry also planned to call charac-

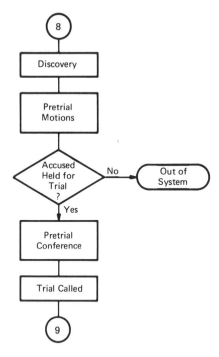

Figure 9-3. Pretrial Procedures Following Arraignment

ter witnesses. He and Harvey decided upon the dean of the college Harvey had attended as well as Harvey's former summer employer.

Pretrial Conference

A pretrial conference could be ordered by the court in criminal cases in Great State. This was generally reserved for complicated cases. None was requested in this case. Many persons have advocated an omnibus pretrial hearing for criminal cases, at which time all pretrial motions would be made and means of discovery would be open to both sides. In addition to suppression motions, other possible pretrial motions include those:

1. to nolle prosequi;
2. to disqualify a judge;
3. to request a psychiatric examination of the accused;
4. to request a pretrial conference;
5. to request a change of venue;
6. to quash the indictment;
7. to request a bill of particulars (in effect, a means of discovery, since it is a request for information).

Proponents of the omnibus hearing claim it will enable defense counsel to make more intelligent recommendations to their clients regarding guilty pleas, going to trial, and taking the stand in their own defense.

Prosecutor's Preparation

While the defense was thus at work, Bob Barrister also took steps in connection with the Harvey Worker case. He caused subpoenas to be issued to ensure attendance at the trial of these witnesses: the two arresting officers, Detectives Find and Seek, Ed Under, Al Chase, and two of Harvey's former customers. He also made sure that the tape recording of Harvey's confession was in good condition. He planned to play it for the jury.

The pretrial procedure from arraignment to the trial has been sketched in Figure 9-3.

TRIAL SCHEDULING

At this point the district attorney's office sent to the court administrator's office a list of cases ready for trial. Harvey Worker's case was among them. It was placed on the trial list. Great State rules required that the trial list be called ten days prior to trial. Written notice to both the defendant and his surety was also required. Accordingly, all parties involved were notified that the trial of Harvey Worker on charges of burglary and theft was scheduled for August 28, 19XX before Judge Shirley Wolfe. Cases came to trial more slowly in the summer months in Local County because of court employee vacations.

And so, almost 100 days following his arrest, Harvey Worker would come to trial. That trial is described in the next chapter.

QUESTIONS

1. The chances for Harvey's acquittal appear to be slim, but he has not changed his mind about pleading guilty. Do you agree with him in this decision? Did Henry make the best use of the negotiations with the prosecutor? Would accepting his offer have been of any advantage to Harvey? any disadvantage? Do you agree with those who advocate elimination of plea bargaining?

2. Does Henry's suppression motion have merit? Or, is it really a desperate attempt to take some defensive action in a case in which there is very little hope?

3. In comparing the indictment and the information as charging instruments, have you reached an opinion as to which represents the better procedure? Can the grand jury ever be replaced? Is the preliminary hearing a suitable replacement? The preliminary hearing has been compared in function with the summary judgment and the demurrer in the civil process. Do you agree? Are all the screening steps in the criminal process necessary? Do you find any duplication of effort? Where?

4. In this case there has been considerable pretrial activity, none of which involved The Firm, which was the entity actually suffering a loss because of the crime. What happened to its participation in this process? Should it be excluded? Do you agree that the limited discovery in the criminal process should be changed? Why?

5. Is the discretionary power of the prosecutor one that should be curbed? How? Why? Has it any value? Is it any greater than the discretion available to the police? Is the discretionary power of the prosecutor one that allows him to ignore the social policy established on behalf of the public by the legislature through enactment of the criminal code? Does the fact that many public prosecutors are elected officials have any bearing on your answer? Are rehabilitation programs into which some criminal cases are diverted an indication that some acts which are classed as criminal should not be so considered? Does it have any other implications? What are they?

6. What advantages would accrue if the charging procedure in the various states were to be made uniform? Which procedure would you advocate for that? Do you agree with charges that provisions of speedy trial laws tend to overdo speed? Are such laws really an overreaction to publicity about court congestion? Reaction by whom?

7. Because of specialization in both the Local County prosecutor's office and in the criminal court of Local County, more than one prosecuting attorney and more than one judge will have been involved in this case. What benefits do you see to this? Any disadvantages? To whom?

8. The criminal process, including those phases which occur between the initial appearance and trial, has been subject to much criticism. What recommendations do you have for improvement? What practices would you change? How can change within the criminal system be effectuated?

NOTES

[1] *Oyler* v. *Boles,* 368 U.S. 448 (1962).

[2] *Gerstein* v. *Pugh,* 420 U.S. 103 (1975). Note that the Court also said: "We do not imply that the accused is entitled to judicial oversight or review of the decision to prosecute. Instead we adhere to the Court's prior holding that a judicial hearing is not prerequisite to prosecution by information."

[3] *Hurtado* v. *California,* 110 U.S. 516 (1884).

[4] *United States* v. *Calandra,* 414 U.S. 338 (1974).

[5] *Ibid.*

[6] *United States* v. *Mandujano,* 425 U.S. 564 (1976).

[7] *Kastigar* v. *United States,* 406 U.S. 441 (1972).

[8] 18 U.S.C. §3161, P.L. 93–619, 88 Stat. 2067.

[9] *Klopfer* v. *North Carolina,* 386 U.S. 213 (1967).

[10] *Benton* v. *Maryland,* 395 U.S. 784 (1969).

[11] *United States* v. *Tateo,* 377 U.S. 463 (1964).

[12] *United States* v. *Agurs,* 427 U.S. 97 (1976).

trial, sentencing, and appeal: court subsystem and exit to corrections subsystem

TEN

"All rise."

The words were familiar to Mary Worker, who sat in the front row of the observer's section in the courtroom as Judge Shirley Wolfe entered. The trial of Harvey Worker was about to begin.

TRIAL

At the defendant's table, Harvey had been engaged in earnest conversation with Henry Law. Their concern was with the selection of the jury, which was about to take place now that the judge had directed that the Harvey Worker trial begin. A group of fifty prospective jurors sat in the courtroom.

According to Great State Rules of Criminal Procedure, Harvey could have agreed to a jury of fewer than twelve, the minimum number being six. Since the prospect of clemency seemed greater to Harvey with larger numbers, he had not done so. Consequently, the clerk drew the names of fourteen persons from the jury wheel. They took seats in the jury box as their names were called.

Jury Selection

In his pretrial conversations with Harvey, Henry had expressed the opinion that careful selection of a jury was vital. Therefore, Harvey listened with interest to the questioning that took place as the voir dire progressed.

"Would you be inclined to give more weight to the testimony of a police officer than you would any other witness?"

When one prospective juror raised her hand in affirmative response to that question, Henry was quick to react.

"Call another," he said.

Thereupon the woman was asked to step down from the jury box. The clerk drew the name of another person from the wheel, and that individual took the seat that had just been vacated in the jury box. Voir dire continued.

"Do you or does anyone in your family know Harvey Worker? know any member of his family?"

"Have you read, seen, or heard any news or other items regarding this defendant, who is charged with burglary and theft at The Firm?"

"Do you know anyone seated at counsel table or anyone in the district attorney's office?"

The questioning went on, challenging for cause. Then, both Bob and Henry exhausted the peremptory challenges. At last twelve jurors and two alternates were selected.

Bob Barrister had excluded college students and younger persons, while Henry had eliminated business proprietors, such as the owner of a gasoline station and of a dairy store. The result was that the jury had no members under age 25. Eight of the 12 were women, as were the two alternates. The juror's occupations were diverse. Two were housewives. There was also a taxi driver, a meteorologist, an unemployed photographer, a highway construction worker, a plumber, a chemist, a lumber salesperson, a public relations writer, a barber, and an auto mechanic. Both alternates were housewives.

Harvey studied their faces. His immediate future was in their hands. Mary, too, studied the jury. She and Harvey had discussed the possible outcomes of a jury trial versus a *bench trial;* i.e., trial by a judge without a jury. Henry had told them that most criminal defendants do not elect to go to trial, and of those who do, most do not choose to exercise their right to trial by jury. He had explained that the right to trial by an impartial jury in criminal prosecution is guaranteed by the Sixth Amendment of the United States Constitution.[1] The United States Supreme Court has made this provision applicable to the states.[2] It pertains to prosecutions for serious crimes, as distinguished from petty offenses. (Offenses which carry a potential sentence of more than six months have been termed "serious" by the Court.[3]) This constitutional right to trial by an impartial jury is discussed in the *Duncan* v. *Louisiana* opinion which follows.

Duncan v. Louisiana

391 U.S. 145, 88 S.Ct. 1444, 20 L.Ed. 2d 491 (1968)

Appellant was convicted of a misdemeanor, punishable by two years imprisonment and a $300 fine. Trial by jury was sought but the request denied because the Louisiana Constitution provided for jury trials only in cases in which capital punishment or imprisonment at hard labor might be imposed. Appellant was convicted and sentenced to serve 60 days in the parish prison and pay a fine of $150.

MR. JUSTICE WHITE . . . Because we believe that trial by jury in criminal cases is fundamental to the American scheme of justice, we hold that the Fourteenth Amendment guarantees a right of jury trial in all criminal cases which—were they to be tried in a federal court—would come within the Sixth Amendment's guarantee. . . .

The guarantee of jury trial in the Federal and State Constitutions reflects a profound judgment about the way in which law should be enforced and justice administered. A right to jury trial is granted to criminal defendants in order to prevent oppression by the Government.

Those who wrote our constitutions knew from history and experience that it was necessary to protect against unfounded criminal charges brought to eliminate enemies and against judges too responsive to the voice of higher authority. The framers of the constitutions strove to create an independent judiciary but insisted upon further protection against arbitrary action. Providing an accused with the right to be tried by a jury of his peers gave him an inestimable safeguard against the corrupt or overzealous prosecutor and against the compliant, biased, or eccentric judge. If the defendant preferred the common-sense judgment of a jury to the more tutored but perhaps less sympathetic reaction of the single judge, he was to have it. Beyond this, the jury trial provisions in the Federal and State Constitutions reflect a fundamental decision about the exercise of official power—a reluctance to entrust plenary powers over the life and liberty of the citizen to one judge or to a group of judges. Fear of unchecked power, so typical of our State and Federal Governments in other respects, found expression in the criminal law in this insistence upon community participation in the determination of guilt or innocence. The deep commitment of the Nation to the right of jury trial in serious criminal cases as a defense against arbitrary law enforcement qualifies for protection under the Due Process Clause of the Fourteenth Amendment, and must therefore be respected by the States.

Of course jury trial has "its weaknesses and the potential for misuse." We are aware of the long debate, especially in this century, among those who write about the administration of justice, as to the wisdom of permitting untrained laymen to determine the facts in civil and criminal proceedings. . . . At the heart of the dispute have been express or implicit assertions that juries are incapable of adequately understanding evidence or determining issues of fact, and that they are unpredictable, quixotic, and little better than a role of the dice. Yet, the most recent and exhaustive study of the jury in criminal cases concluded that juries do understand the evidence and come to sound conclusions in most of the cases presented to them and that when juries differ with the result at which the judge would have arrived, it is usually because they are serving some of the very purposes for which they were created and for which they are now employed.

. . . in the late 18th century in America crimes triable without a jury were for the most part punishable by no more than a six-month prison term, although there appear to have been exceptions to this rule. We need not, however, settle in this case the exact location of the line between petty offenses and serious crimes. It is sufficient for our purposes to hold that a crime punishable by two years in prison is, based on past and contemporary standards in this country, a serious crime and not a petty offense. Consequently, appellant was entitled to a jury trial and it was error to deny it . . .

Harvey had decided at the time of his arraignment that he would not waive this right. Influenced perhaps by his mother's experience in a civil suit, he was inclined to believe that his chances for success were greater with a jury.

Note that Harvey was in the courtroom from the very beginning of the trial, exercising his constitutional right as a criminal defendant to be present at every stage of the trial—an issue discussed in the *Illinois* v. *Allen* opinion which follows.

Illinois v. *Allen*
397 U.S. 337, 90 S.Ct. 1057, 25 L.Ed. 2d 353 (1970)

Allen was convicted of armed robbery. Following unsuccessful appeal of his conviction to the Illinois Supreme Court, he petitioned for a writ of habeas corpus in federal court alleging that he had been wrongfully deprived of his constitutional right to remain present throughout his trial. During that trial, he had repeatedly interrupted the proceedings with loud talking, argued with the judge in abusive language, and at one point threatened the judge's life. Allen was removed from the courtroom twice and was permitted to return upon his promise to conduct himself properly. He was absent during part of the selection of the jury and during presentation of the prosecution's case, except for several instances of identification. The District Court found no constitutional violation and declined to issue the writ. The Court of Appeals reversed, ruled that a criminal defendant has an absolute right to be present at all stages of the proceedings even if it means that the trial judge must resort to shackling and gagging to restrain the defendant. The Supreme Court granted certiorari.

MR. JUSTICE BLACK . . . The Confrontation Clause of the Sixth Amendment to the United States Constitution provides that "In all criminal prosecutions, the accused shall enjoy the right . . . to be confronted with the witnesses against him . . . ." We have held that the Fourteenth Amendment makes the guarantees of this clause obligatory upon the States . . . One of the most basic of the rights guaranteed by the Confrontation Clause is the accused's right to be present in the courtroom at every stage of his trial . . . .

. . . Although mindful that courts must indulge every reasonable presumption against the loss of constitutional rights, . . . we explicitly hold today that a defendant can lose his right to be present at trial if, after he has been warned by the judge that he will be removed if he continues his disruptive behavior, he nevertheless insists on conducting himself in a manner so disorderly, disruptive, and disrespectful of the court that his trial cannot be carried on with him in the courtroom. Once lost, the right to be present can, of course, be reclaimed as soon as the defendant is willing to conduct himself consistently with the decorum and respect inherent in the concept of courts and judicial proceedings.

It is essential to the proper administration of criminal justice that dignity, order, and decorum be the hallmarks of all court proceedings in our country. The flagrant disregard in the courtroom of elementary standards of proper conduct should not and cannot be tolerated. We believe trial judges confronted with disruptive, contumacious, stubbornly defiant defendants must be given sufficient discretion to meet the circumstances of each case. No one formula for maintaining the appropriate courtroom atmosphere will be best in all situations. We think there are at least three constitutionally permissible ways for a trial judge to handle an obstreperous defendant like Allen: (1) bind and gag him, thereby keeping him present; (2) cite him for contempt; (3) take him out of the courtroom until he promises to conduct himself properly . . . .

It is not pleasant to hold that the respondent Allen was properly banished from the court for a part of his own trial. But our courts, palladiums of liberty as they are, cannot be treated disrespectfully with impunity. Nor can the accused be permitted by his disruptive conduct indefinitely to avoid being tried on the charges brought against him. It would degrade our country and our judicial system to permit our courts to be bullied, insulted, and humiliated and their orderly progress thwarted and obstructed by defendants brought before them charged with crimes. As guardians of the public welfare, our state and federal judicial systems strive to administer equal justice to the rich and the poor, the good and the bad, the native and foreign born of every race, nationality, and religion. Being manned by humans, the courts are not perfect and are bound to make some errors. But, if our courts are to remain what the Founders intended, the citadels of justice, their proceedings cannot and must not be infected with the sort of scurrilous, abusive language and conduct paraded before the Illinois trial judge in this case. The record shows that the Illinois judge at all times conducted himself with that dignity, decorum, and patience that befits a judge. Even in the holding that the trial judge had erred, the Court of Appeals praised his "commendable patience under severe provocation." . . .
Reversed.

Judge's Remarks

After the jury had been impaneled and sworn, the judge asked the clerk to read the indictment. She then addressed the jury, telling them that the defendant had pleaded "not guilty" to the charges they had just heard. She stressed the importance of remembering that a person is presumed innocent until proven guilty. That was why, she said, during the trial that followed, the district attorney would have the burden of proving the defendant's guilt beyond a reasonable doubt. The defense, she added, had no obligation to present evidence. However, should the defense desire, it could present its evidence after the prosecution rested.

She outlined trial procedure briefly. The judge told the jurors that the district attorney would talk with them briefly about the case and would then call witnesses to testify. Next, the defense would have the option of presenting evidence. When all testimony had been heard, the jury would hear closing arguments from the attorneys. After that, she would explain the applicable principles of law to the jury. They would then retire to deliberate.

She asked them to listen carefully and not to discuss the case with anyone. Their primary function, she explained, was a finding of the facts in the case since "a trial is a search for the truth of the matter. You, the jury, will be the ones who say in the end what actually happened at times and places that are important to the ultimate decision in this case of the guilt or innocence of the defendant on the charges you are considering."

Trial Procedure

As Henry had explained to Mary earlier, trial proceedings in civil and criminal cases and in the different jurisdictions tend to follow much the same order. He cautioned, however, that some variations do exist. He also told her that generally the rules of evidence were much the same for civil and criminal cases, with statutory and constitutional considerations accounting for most of the differences.

Therefore, following her conversation with Henry, Mary anticipated the following:

1. Opening statement by the district attorney. (In some states opening remarks by defense counsel would follow. In Great State, however, these were deferred until the state rested.)
2. Evidence by the state.
3. Opening statement by defense counsel.
4. Evidence by the defense.
5. Rebuttal testimony, if any, first by the state and then by the defense.
6. Closing statements to the jury, first by the defense and then by the district attorney.
7. Judge's charge to the jury with instructions on those matters of law which are at issue in the case. The judge could also review testimony. (The judge's right to comment on the evidence varies greatly among the different jurisdictions. In some states, the judge may also give the jury instructions on the law before evidence is entered.)

Prosecution's Case in Chief

Bob Barrister began his opening statement to the jury by reminding them this was a case involving burglary and theft. The witnesses he would call, he said, included two police officers who had arrested the defendant on the evening of May 20. They would testify that they had found him in the factory building of The Firm taking cypres parts. Other witnesses, he went on, included two employees of The Firm. One would testify that he had observed the defendant enter the building that evening; the other, that he had seen the defendant take cypres parts from the shelves in the supply room. Finally, Bob continued, there would be testimony by two Big City police detectives who had investigated the case and two persons who had purchased cypres parts from the defendant. His statement was, essentially, a preview of the prosecution's case.

At this time, Bob Barrister called as his first witness police officer Teresa Copp. The witnesses had been sequestered; that is, placed out in the hall to await their turn to testify. Therefore, the tipstaff now escorted Officer Copp into the courtroom.

Most of the testimony during the trial duplicated the recital of events thus far and will not be repeated here. Instead, the description is limited to new matter.

On cross-examination, the arresting police officers told Henry that they remembered that Harvey had been cooperative. Furthermore, they insisted that, if it were true that Harvey had received blows to the ribs and had been kicked in the shins, it would only have been because such force was needed at the time. Detectives Find and Seek described Harvey as no more frightened than many other first-time offenders and insisted that he had been made aware of his rights at all times. When Henry asked Al Chase why he did not attempt to prevent the burglary by locking the side entrance at The Firm following Ed Under's report to him, Al stated it would have hampered his inquiry into the persons involved in the thefts occurring at The Firm as well as their *modus operandi* (manner of operation). All of the prosecution evidence came in, but not without real effort by Henry to keep it out. At one point a sharp exchange developed between Henry and the judge during a side bar conference regarding suppression of evidence. It came after Henry had repeatedly objected to the introduction into evidence of Harvey's confession, photographs of cypres parts seized from the Worker home, and testimony about Harvey's admissions concerning his long period of theft. Finally, the judge asked both attorneys to approach the bench. In rather certain terms she told Henry she had already ruled on his objections, that the objections were being duly noted on the record and thus would be preserved in case of appeal, that she had granted his motion to incorporate by reference into the trial record material from the suppression hearing, that he had introduced no new or additional reasons for the exclusion of evidence other than those already ruled upon at the suppression hearing, that the purpose of suppression hearings was to dispose of such matters prior to trial and to avoid repetition of the very same matters during the trial, that she had studied the record of the suppression hearing and given careful consideration to all the arguments he had made at that time, and that she would find additional objections which were repetitions of those on which there had already been a ruling to be a form of harassment and delay. Henry's annoyance at this point matched hers. He remarked that, if she continued, he would move for a mistrial, adding that "it is obvious Your Honor got out on the wrong side of bed this morning." Her response was that such frivolous remarks were unworthy of counsel. It was Bob Barrister who brought a close to the incident by suggesting a fifteen-minute recess. That recess helped to cool tempers and when the trial continued it did so without further similar incident.

Defense Demurrer

When the prosecution rested, Henry moved to demur to the evidence. This is the counterpart of the defendant's motion for a nonsuit in a civil action. It requires the court to consider the evidence presented by the prosecution. If the motion is granted, the defendant is discharged without any deliberation by the jury. If the motion is denied, the case proceeds as if the demurrer had not been made. It tests, in effect, the sufficiency of the evidence against the defendant. Judge Wolfe did not consider long. In her mind there had been more than sufficient evidence to indicate that Harvey had been engaged in criminal activity. Therefore, she overruled the demurrer and ordered the trial to continue, asking Henry if the defense wished to present any evidence.

Defense

In his opening statement to the jury, Henry said that they had already heard from investigating police detectives that Harvey was a frighened young man, not a hardened criminal. He reminded them that not just guilty persons are brought to trial. He also said the defense would present witnesses who would testify to Harvey's good character and reputation, as well as the effect upon him of his father's untimely death. The testimony of both character witnesses, the dean and Harvey's former employer, confirmed Henry's statement. At the conclusion of his case, Henry moved that the court direct a verdict of acquittal. Judge Wolfe refused to do so. It was her opinion that there had been ample evidence by the prosecution, uncontradicted by the defense, to establish a prima facie case.

Closing Arguments

In his closing statements, Bob Barrister concentrated on the testimony by prosecution witnesses that Harvey had actually committed those acts that constituted burglary and theft. He added that no refutation of this had been made by the defense. He also told the jury that personal grief or hardship did not justify commission of a crime. Henry, on the other hand, concentrated on Harvey's apprehension upon being arrested, his intimidation and treatment by the police, and the pressures exerted upon him to make statements he would not have made of his own free choice.

Judge's Charge to Jury

In her charges to the jury, the judge asked the jurors to remember that statements by counsel were not evidence. She reminded them again of the presumption of innocence until proven guilty and that the standard of proof was beyond a reasonable doubt. Judge Wolfe defined both burglary and theft. She explained that a defendant in a criminal case has a right not to take the stand and not to testify; furthermore, when he does not do so, this cannot be held against him nor should it be considered by the jury as either proof or indication of guilt. She also told them that a unanimous verdict would be necessary and that they must return a separate verdict on each count. (The unanimous verdict was a Great State requirement. The United States Supreme Court has held that unanimous verdicts in criminal cases are not always necessary to meet due process requirements of the Federal Constitution.[4])

Jury Deliberations and Verdict

The jury began deliberations by discussing the case. It soon became obvious that there was agreement that Harvey had committed the acts of which he was accused. Although they believed this was serious criminality, they did not view him as a hardened criminal. However, they were of the opinion that he might become one if sent to the kind of prisons about which they had read. Since they had received no instructions from the judge about sentencing, they sent a note with the tipstaff to the judge asking for further instructions. Reassembled in the courtroom, they learned that their only decision was to be whether Harvey was guilty or not guilty of burglary and theft. Sentencing, said the judge, was her function. Although she did not say so, in only a few states is there jury sentencing in noncapital cases. Retiring again, the jury took a vote and unanimously found Harvey guilty on all counts. Their foreperson then prepared the verdict slip, shown as Form 10-1, and the jury returned to the courtroom. After the verdict was announced, Henry asked that the jury be polled. They were found to be in agreement. The jurors were then dismissed.

Form 10-1. Verdict Slip

COURT OF LOCAL COUNTY
CRIMINAL DIVISION

STATE OF GREAT STATE   :
          V.   :
    Harvey Worker   :

Criminal Action
No. _1246_ of _19XX_

VERDICT

This day, _____August 29_____ 19_XX_ , we the jurors selected to serve in the above described case find the defendant, Harvey Worker, on the

first count: burglary   _Guilty_

second count: theft   _Guilty_

third count: theft   _Guilty_

                        Eve Juror
                        Foreperson

Instructions: When the jury has reached a unanimous verdict on the counts submitted, the foreperson shall enter in the blank space opposite each count "guilty" or "not guilty" as the jury has unanimously determined. The foreperson shall then sign the verdict slip.

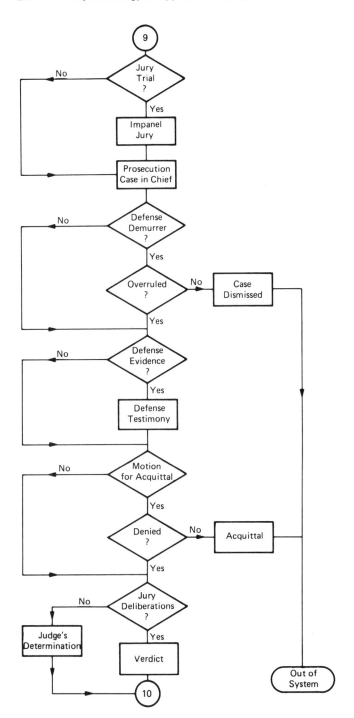

Figure 10-1. The Criminal Trial

TABLE 10–1. Postconviction Remedies of Defendant

IN THE TRIAL COURT

---

1. POST-TRIAL MOTIONS
   A. In Arrest of — Counterpart of judgment n.o.v. in civil cases.
      Judgment   Grounds include insufficient evidence, court lack of jurisdiction, error intrinsic on the record such as an indictment which charges no crime.
   B. New Trial   — Grounds include improper admission of evidence, error in charge to jury, verdict contrary to court's instructions.

   Trial court's denial of post-trial motions is appealable.

2. POSTCONVICTION HEARING STATUTE REMEDIES
   By statute (Postconviction Hearing Statute) in Great State, one basic procedure exists for relief from convictions obtained and sentences imposed without due process of law. This procedure encompasses all prior procedures including Coram nobis and habeas corpus.*

   Trial court's denial of relief is appealable.

IN THE APPELLATE COURTS

---

3. APPEAL
   A. Review of Final Judgment — Direct appeal from judgment of sentence.
      (Judgment of Sentence)   A matter of right in Great State by statutory provision.
   B. Review of Interlocutory   — Available in Great State where necessary to safeguard basic rights.
      Order
   C. Review of Denial of   — See above.
      Post-trial Relief

IN THE FEDERAL COURTS

---

4. FEDERAL HABEAS CORPUS
   In cases of a state conviction, recourse to the federal courts is possible if state remedies are unavailable and if federal constitutional rights have been violated. Arises from Article I, §9, cl. 2 of United States Constitution. Denial of writ is appealable.

BY EXECUTIVE GRACE

---

5. EXECUTIVE ORDERS
   A. Pardon   — Relieves offender from further punishment; removes all legal disabilities resulting from conviction.
   B. Commutation of Sentence — Reduces severity or penalty.

   Both of these are matters of privilege rather than of right. In Great State, they may be granted by the governor upon favorable recommendation of the Great State Board of Pardons. This is by state constitutional provision.

---

*Coram nobis is a civil writ for the purpose of review of a criminal judgment in the trial court; it is similar in many ways to a motion for a new trial. A writ of habeas corpus seeks the release of a person in custody; it is not limited to post conviction stages but may be invoked at any stage of the criminal proceedings.

Judge Wolfe asked Harvey to come forward. As he stood before her, she informed him that he had been found guilty of the felonies of burglary and theft. She advised him of his right to file postverdict motions for a new trial or in arrest of judgment. This, she said, must be done within seven days and Harvey would have the right to the services of counsel in doing so. Asked if he had any questions, Harvey indicated he did not. Henry requested that sentencing be stayed until he had an opportunity to file post verdict motions. The judge granted that request. She also continued Harvey's nominal bail. As Mary, Harvey, and Henry left the courthouse, Henry noted that although the trial, which is flow charted in Figure 10-1, was over, the case was far from being over. Henry had explained that there were many forms of post conviction relief, as shown in Table 10-1.

Form 10-2. Motion for New Trial and in Arrest of Judgment

COURT OF LOCAL COUNTY
CRIMINAL DIVISION

STATE OF GREAT STATE   :
           V.   :
Harvey Worker

Criminal Action No.
__1246__ of 19__XX__

Motion for New Trial and In Arrest of Judgment

        And now this fourth day of September, 19XX comes defendant by his attorney and respectfully requests a new trial and in arrest of judgment for the following reasons:

1. The verdict is against the law.
2. The verdict is against the evidence.
3. The verdict is against the law and the evidence.
4. The court erred in failing to grant the motion to suppress.
5. The defendant was denied a fair and impartial trial because of prejudicial remarks of the Court.

Respectfully submitted,

Henry Law
Counsel for the Defendant

Post-Trial Motions

Within the time requirements, Henry filed a motion for a new trial and in arrest of judgment. A copy of this motion appears as Form 10-2. Judge Wolfe asked that a brief be filed by both parties prior to a hearing on the motion to be held before a panel of three judges of the criminal court. Henry's brief alleged that the verdict was based on evidence unlawfully admitted at the trial. He reiterated arguments made at the time of the suppression motion. In addition, he charged that the trial judge had prejudiced the case against the defendant by her remarks to defense counsel. The contentions in the reply brief prepared by Bob Barrister were similar to those made by the prosecution at the time of the pretrial motion to suppress. He denied the court's remarks were prejudicial. The hearing on the motions was held before Judges Wolfe, Grant, and Roe. It resulted in denial of the motions for the same reasons as had been articulated by Judge Grant in his statement of facts and conclusions of law and, as added reason, that remarks at a side bar could not be prejudicial. The postverdict motions have been flow charted in Figure 10-2.

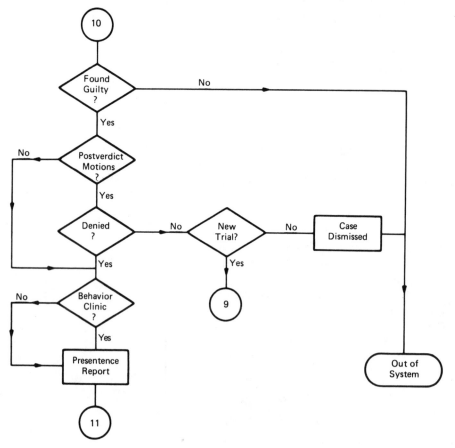

Figure 10-2. Postverdict Motions in Criminal Cases

SENTENCING

Great State required that, absent extenuating circumstances, sentencing be done by the judge who presided at the criminal trial. Therefore, following denial of the post verdict motions, Judge Wolfe requested that a presentence report be prepared by the county probation office. Sentencing would occur after she had received and studied that report. Had this been a case of murder, voluntary manslaughter, or one involving a sex offense, she would have requested a psychiatric examination and report by the county behavior clinic. She could still do so in this case, should the probation officer's report indicate a need for it. In the meantime, the judge continued nominal bail.

Presentence Investigation and Report

Probation officer Maria Will did extensive interviewing. She talked with the police; with Jim Solicitor, Bob Barrister, and Henry Law; with Jim Boss and Peter Superior, both of whom had supervised Harvey's work at The Firm; with Harvey and Mary; with Harvey's high school principal and the dean of the college he had attended; with his former summer employer. She learned a great deal about him.

In Great State, the probation officer's presentence report was confidential and could be disclosed only to the sentencing judge. The district attorney and defense counsel had the right of inspection. They also had the right to comment to the judge on the report and to point out any inaccuracies it might contain. By order of the sentencing judge, a copy could be made available to professionals with a legitimate interest in the case, for example, a psychiatrist appointed to assist the court in sentencing, a correctional institution, or the department of probation or parole. The desirability of confidentiality of presentence reports is still an unresolved and controversial issue.

In Harvey's case, the report indicated that he had a very stable and satisfactory home situation and had been known to be reliable and trustworthy, normally industrious, and a reasonably good student and employee. All who knew him at the time detected a change after his father's death, but did not consider it abnormal under the circumstances. His supervisors at The Firm said that he had worked hard and displayed great interest and enthusiasm for his work. In fact, they still found it hard to believe that Harvey had been the person who had been doing the stealing. Most of his young friends were of good character. However, the probation officer expressed concern about his association with a small group of students who had introduced him to the fence. She concluded her report by expressing the opinion that this young man was not disposed to a life of crime and that he had learned a very difficult lesson through this experience. She recommended that, as one means of rehabilitation, he be given an opportunity to make restitution and that discontinued association with the one group be made a condition precedent to his release into the community. Judge Wolfe considered the report, together with a request from Henry for leniency. The latter emphasized that this was a first offense, that partial restitution was already possible, and voiced a conviction that rehabilitation would be enhanced if Harvey could be placed on probation and given an opportunity to work in the community rather than be sentenced to prison. He also cited the Model Penal Code's recommendations.

Judge's Considerations

In arriving at her decision, Judge Wolfe considered the following factors to be significant:

FACTORS FAVORING LENIENCY	FACTORS NEGATING LENIENCY
1. First-time offender.	1. Seriousness of offenses—felonies.
2. Healthy home environment.	2. Defendant's continued and increased participation in theft over a long time.
3. History of prior acceptable behavior.	
4. Temporary emotional crisis following father's death.	3. Associations with some persons of questionable character.
	4. Need to prevent recurrence.

Of those factors, Judge Wolfe's greatest concern was with deterring Harvey from engaging in criminal activity in the future. His continued participation in theft and his undesirable associations caused her to look for some means of providing Harvey with professional assistance to prevent his becoming a *recidivist;* i.e., a habitual criminal. In determining just what those measures might be, she also considered

1. The options open to her in sentencing according to Great State law;
2. The conditions and programs available in local and state facilities.

The Great State Criminal Code imposed upon a judge maximum but not minimum limitations for sentences. Those for burglary and theft were reported in the previous chapter. No fixed sentences were provided for felonies. In most jurisdictions, judges are given some sentencing discretion.[5] Wide differences do exist, however, with regard to the degree of discretion granted and the situations in which it may be exercised. As with opportunities for exercise of discretion by the police and the prosecutor, the discretionary power of the judge has been subject to much criticism. Some of the options and choices available to Judge Wolfe in Harvey's case included:

1. Fine or restitution;
2. Incarceration in jail or prison;
3. Diversion program, such as halfway house or work release;
4. Split sentence;
5. Suspended sentence or probation;
6. Fixed or indeterminate sentence.

The discretionary power of the judge is discussed in more detail in the *Commonwealth* v. *Martin* decision which follows.

Commonwealth v. *Martin*
   (Pa.) 351 A.2d 650 (1976)

Appellants (six) attack their sentences on the ground they were imposed in accordance with a presentence agreement among three judges of the trial court to impose sentence of three to ten years imprisonment plus fine for the sale of heroin, without giving consideration to defendants' individual characteristics. There was no evidence of a conspiracy among appellants, and no claim that identical sentences were imposed because of any conspiracy.

MR. JUSTICE ROBERTS . . . The record amply demonstrates that the three judges had agreed in advance that the sentence to be imposed for a sale of heroin was to be three to ten years imprisonment plus a fine, and all of the sentences were to run consecutively. In no case was a presentence report ordered. No meaningful inquiry was made into the appellants' backgrounds, individual characteristics, relative culpability or prospects for rehabilitation, despite clear evidence that the appellants' offenses were committed in varying circumstances. In short, all appellants' sentences were based on an abstract predetermination of the sentence to be imposed for the particular offense, without regard to the individual circumstances of particular cases. . . .

. . . At one time, sentencing by a court after a finding of guilt was purely ceremonial, since there was but one penalty at law for any given crime. However, during the nineteenth century, when incarceration became the primary mode of punishment, the practice of discretionary sentencing began. At first this took the form of executive pardons, and the judge's duty remained only to apply the sentence mandated by law. However, discretionary sentencing soon became an integral part of judicial procedure; the sentencing court had increasing discretion in its choice of sentence. This development reflected the move toward individualized sentencing, which attempted to rehabilitate, as well as punish, the offender.

The indeterminate sentence won early recognition in Pennsylvania. . . . The Legislature reinforced these provisions by allowing suspension of sentence and probation, at the sentencing court's discretion, in all but the most serious crimes. . . .

. . . Pennsylvania's procedure of indeterminate sentencing carries with it an implicit adoption of the philosophy of individual sentencing. This necessitates the granting of broad discretion to the trial judge, who must determine, among the sentencing alternatives and the range of permissible penalties, the proper sentence to be imposed. The importance of this discretion cannot be overemphasized; many commentators argue that it is one of the most important, and most easily abused, powers vested in the trial court today . . . .

The procedures employed by the sentencing court in the appeals before us today ignore the basic premises of Pennsylvania sentencing. Here . . . the nature of the criminal act was used as the sole basis for the determination of the length of sentence, and all sentences of imprisonment were to run consecutively. Thus the court failed to exercise its broad discretion in accordance with the applicable statutory requirements.

The sentence must be imposed for the miminum amount of confinement that is consistent with the protection of the public, the gravity of the offense, and the rehabilitative needs of the defendant. . . . At least two facts are crucial to such determination—the particular circumstances of the offense and the character of the defendant. . . . We hold that regardless of whether a presentence report is ordered, the sentencing court must at least consider these two factors in its sentencing determination. Failure to give such individualized consideration requires that these sentences be vacated . . . .

In these cases the court did not order any pre-sentence reports although it was authorized to do so . . . . Normally such reports should be used, although they are sometimes unnecessary because other sources of information are available. However, presentence reports are of obvious importance to the sentencing court. . . .

The ABA Project on Minimum Standards of Justice, Standards Relating to Probation §2.1 (Approved Draft, 1970), recommends that a pre-sentence report is peculiarly necessary in any of the following circumstances: 1) where incarceration for one year or more is a possible disposition; 2) where the defendant is less than twenty-one years old; and 3) where the defendant is a first offender. These situations require the utmost care in sentence determination . . . . Judgments of sentence vacated and cases remanded for sentencing.

Restitution

In deciding upon a sentence, Judge Wolfe's major concern was what would redound to the greatest good for Harvey. She viewed a fine as a means of punishment that, if it created a financial obligation Harvey was unable to meet, could encourage him to further theft in order to pay the fine. At the same time, Judge Wolfe looked with favor upon the idea of restitution. It provided compensation to the victim of the crime by the perpetrator of that crime. Judge Wolfe considered this to be not only just, but also a deterrent to further crime. If she could determine that Harvey would be able to meet the financial burden of restitution, she would not reject restitution in connection with the thefts. However, there was also the matter of sentencing for the burglary.

Incarceration

Incarceration would have the effect of depriving Harvey of his home and family life. At the same time, it would remove him from the community and from present undesirable associations he had there. If Harvey were to be sentenced to a detention facility, Judge Wolfe determined it must be to a rehabilitative facility. She shared the jury's concern about the effect of imprisonment upon Harvey as she mentally considered the possibility of incarceration in jail or prison.

Jails and Prisons

A distinction is usually made between those correctional institutions termed jails and those referred to as prisons or penitentiaries. *Jail* refers to a facility, generally operated by city or county authorities, where persons are detained while awaiting trial. It also houses persons who are serving short sentences, usually a term of less than one year. The concept of jail generally refers to a place of confinement rather than a place of punishment. On the other hand, a *prison* is a facility housing persons convicted of the more serious crimes who are serving longer sentences. Prisons are generally state or federally operated. There are also military prisons. Jails are usually found within the community, often at its center, while prisons are most likely to be located in outlying areas. Programs of education, vocational training, counseling, and other forms of rehabilitation are more frequently found in prisons than in jails. Quality of these programs varies greatly.

The Local County Jail in Big City was overcrowded, understaffed, inadequately funded, dirty, and lacking recreational or educational programs. Judge Wolfe was keenly aware of all of this. In fact, one of the reasons she had continued Harvey's nominal bail was to avoid sending him to that jail. She believed that the jail environment would have had a pernicious influence upon Harvey. On the other hand, a new Great State prison facility located in Little Town had good programs of counseling, therapy, education, recreation, vocational training, as well as a work release program, which she considered would be beneficial in Harvey's case. Residents of the facility who qualified were released during the day to work at regular jobs in the community and returned to the institution at night. Part of their wages could be used in making restitution.

Halfway Houses

While the judge was favorably inclined toward this program for Harvey, she was not inclined to send him to a halfway house located in Big City. More like a home than a prison, it had space for fifteen persons. They were confined there overnight and during weekends but left during the day to go to work, to school, or for treatment. Both a counselor and a case worker were available to the residents. Judge Wolfe believed there was an advantage to this noninstitutional atmosphere. At the same time, she knew that better counseling services existed at the Little Town facility. She believed the halfway house was better suited to assisting persons who had been confined to prison to return to life in the community, although she knew that in certain cases some of her fellow judges had been sentencing there directly.

Probation and Suspended Sentence

Judge Wolfe weighed the possible effect upon Harvey of institutional life over permitting him to live at home as a result of either a suspended sentence or probation. Were she to sentence Harvey to probation, incarceration would be suspended and he would be placed under the supervision of a probation officer. Certain conditions would also be imposed for his continued freedom from institutionalization. Those conditions generally include restriction on travel outside the state, abstinence from alcohol and other drugs, and continued employment. A suspended sentence, on the other hand, would mean that she would impose sentence, but Harvey, instead of being incarcerated, would be released immediately without supervision. Judge Wolfe believed that Harvey's long period of theft indicated that he needed supervision. Probation would place him right back in the community with those acquaintances whose influences had led him toward crime rather than away from it. She kept coming back to the Little Town facility in her mind as the most desirable alternative.

Fixed and Indeterminate Sentence

She discarded the possibility of a split sentence—that is, a jail (rather than prison) term followed by probation. It would have all of the characteristics of jail and probation, neither of which she found suitable for Harvey. The only undecided matter now was whether to impose a sentence for a fixed or an indeterminate time. An indeterminate sentence is one in which the individual is to be incarcerated for a period of time extending somewhere between a minimum and a maximum period, the least possible minimum being one day and the greatest possible maximum being life. This is sometimes referred to as a *completely indeterminate* sentence, and the term *partially indeterminate* is used to designate a sentence with a specified period of time, such as three to five years. Judge Wolfe was not so positive about Harvey's future conduct as to feel she could pinpoint a precise and fixed time in which he would definitely be rehabilitated. Therefore, she was inclined to set a maximum term with a recommendation that he be considered for parole at the end of a designated minimum term. Generally, when there is no judicial recommendation regarding eligibility for parole, such eligibility, by statutory provision, occurs after one-third of the sentence has been served.

Parole

Parole is distinguished from probation, in that *probation* means serving a term in the community without going to a correctional institution, whereas *parole* means release to the community following a period of confinement in an institution. Just as with probation, parole involves release under supervision. Usually certain conditions are imposed for continued parole. Complete discharge from the criminal system follows at the end of the term to which one has been sentenced. Release on parole is a privilege, not a right, and the decision to parole an individual is influenced not only by the judge's recommendation at the time of sentencing, but also by the inmate's behavior and experiences during institutionalization. These sentencing alternatives have been illustrated in a flow chart in Figure 10-3.

Judge's Decision

Judge Wolfe thought that the Little Town personnel would have sufficient opportunity to observe Harvey in one year to make some valid judgment as to his future conduct. Were he placed in a work release program, she believed he could earn enough within that time to make complete financial restitution. She thought he might be ready for parole at the end of one year. However, were he not, continued confinement and treatment would be required. She believed than an additional two years would provide more than ample time for the counseling and therapy that would be necessary. She therefore settled upon a minimum of one and a maximum of three years.

In this way she arrived at the decision to sentence Harvey to the following concurrent sentences:

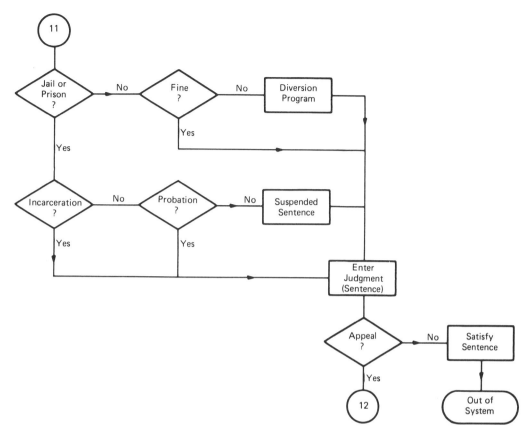

Figure 10–3. Sentencing Decision

1. For theft: restitution to be made to The Firm, with credit given for those cypres parts recovered and returned. (The net effect was that Harvey would owe approximately $4700.)

2. For burglary: detention for a minimum of one and a maximum of three years in the Little Town Correction Center, with a recommendation that Harvey be placed in a work release program with portions of his earnings designated for restitution, and that he be considered for parole at the end of the first year.

Judge Wolfe would later discover that this decision, to which she had devoted so much careful thought, pleased very few people. Harvey, Mary, and Henry considered it to be unjustly severe and harsh. They had hoped for probation. On the other hand, although The Firm eventually received complete restitution, Fred Famous publicly stated that one to three years was a real indication that the courts were "soft on criminals." That same feeling was shared by Detective Find and police officer Teresa Copp, who noted that a sentence of twenty years was possible for burglary under the Great State Criminal Code. When Judge Wolfe ran for re-election the following year, Harvey's sentence was listed in a newspaper editorial as one example of sentencing disparities. It was compared with the twenty-year term given by Judge Wolfe to a bank burglar who had stolen $4000, but Judge Wolfe noticed that the editorial did not state that this was the bank burglar's fifth conviction for burglary.

Sentencing

Having determined what sentence she would impose, Judge Wolfe set a time for sentencing two days later. Harvey, Henry, and Bob Barrister were notified. Some delay occurred at the start of the sentencing session, because Harvey, who had gone out for a cup of coffee, was late in returning. The Sixth Amendment of the United States Constitution provides that "in all criminal prosecutions, the accused shall enjoy the right . . . to be confronted with witnesses against him . . . ," and the United States Supreme Court has held that the right of confrontation is applicable to the states.[6] The right of confrontation cannot exist unless the accused is present at those proceedings which constitute criminal prosecution. That includes the preliminary hearing, the arraignment, every stage of the trial when his substantial rights may be affected by the proceedings against him, and the imposition of sentence. The right may be waived. In some cases, a defendant may lose the right through continued disruptive behavior in the courtroom.[7] In Great State, the Rules of Criminal Procedure were specific in stating not only that the defendant must be present during criminal prosecutions, but also that the record of the proceedings must contain a statement to that effect, as well as of representation by counsel.

Note should be made of the fact that the right of confrontation does not apply in the case of investigatory proceedings, such as the grand jury.

When Harvey had returned to the courtroom and the proceedings did get underway, the judge asked Harvey to come forward. She asked if either he or his counsel wished to make a statement. Harvey indicated that Henry would speak for him, and there followed a short request for leniency. The prosecutor had no statement to make.

Judge Wolfe then addressed Harvey. In imposing sentence, she told him of her concern for his future and his rehabilitation, and explained why she had decided upon the particular sentence. She also advised him of his right to appeal, informed him that he must file notice of intent to do so within ten days, and stated that he had the right to the assistance of counsel in doing so.

Henry told the judge that notice of appeal would be filed that very day. He then requested that Harvey be released on bail pending the outcome on appeal. In cases in which the maximum sentence imposed exceeded two years, Great State provided that bail could be granted at the discretion of the judge. Since the bail request followed conviction and sentencing, Judge Wolfe set bail at $30,000. Henry helped Mary to arrange for an eight-percent bond. That meant that Mary would deposit with the clerk of courts $2400, or eight percent of the amount at which bail was set. All but ten percent of this deposit would be returned to her when and if Harvey appeared as required until final disposition of the case. The remaining ten percent would be retained to cover costs of processing the bond. Mary was named in the bond as surety. A copy of the first page of the bail bond appears as Form 10–3. In this way Harvey came to be at liberty once again. Judge Wolfe entered judgment of sentence, which the clerk of courts entered on the court's records.

Form 10–3.   Bail Bond

	Police Case No.	J.P. No.	C.P. Term & No.
CERTIFICATION OF BAIL AND DISCHARGE No.			

State vs. (Defendant Name and Address)	Charges	Date of Charges
	— — — — —	— — — — —

Police I.D. No.	Indictment No.	District of Arrest	NEXT COURT ACTION FOR FURTHER HEARING	
			Date and Time	Date and Time
			— — —	— — — — —
□ ROR (no surety) □ Bail (total amount set, if any):		Nominal Bail $	Location (Room No.)	Location

Conditions of Release (aside from appearing at court when required:)

_____

_____

_____

(attach addendum, if necessary)

_____

Security or Surety (if any):

  □ Cash in full   □ Surety
     amount of bail   Company

  □ Percentage cash   □ Professional
     bail   Bondsman

Money furnished by   □ Realty
  □ Defendant   □ Other:
  □ 3rd Party

_____

Judge or Issuing Authority

_____

TO: □ Detention Center

             □ Other

I hereby certify that sufficient bail has been entered

  □ by the defendant

  □ on behalf of the defendant by:

(Name & Address of Surety)

DISCHARGE THE ABOVE-NAMED DEFENDANT FROM CUSTODY IF DETAINED FOR NO OTHER CAUSE THAN THE ABOVE STATED.

Given under my hand and the Official Seal of this Court, this _____ day of _____ , 19___.

_____

(Clerk of Court or Issuing Authority)

_____

APPEARANCE OR BAIL BOND

THIS BOND IS VALID FOR THE ENTIRE PROCEEDINGS AND UNTIL FULL AND FINAL DISPOSITION OF THE CASE INCLUDING FINAL DISPOSITION OF ANY PETITION FOR WRIT OF CERTIORARI OR APPEAL TIMELY FILED IN THE SUPREME COURT OF THE UNITED STATES.

STATE OF GREAT STATE

Refund of cash bail will be made
within 20 days after final disposition.
Bring Cash Bail Receipt to
    Clerk of Court.

v. _____

APPEAL

In Great State appeal in criminal cases was a matter of right by statutory provision. It is so by constitutional provision in some of the states. Persons convicted and sentenced for felonies in Great State could appeal directly to the state's supreme court. Misdemeanor cases went to an intermediate appellate court. Considering the time table within which the state supreme court had been working recently, Henry calculated it would take about six months at the most to appeal and for an appellate decision to be handed down.

Mary and Harvey had talked with Henry about appeal prior to the time of sentencing. Henry had been authorized to appeal immediately should imprisonment be imposed, and he was now deeply involved in the decision making connected with that appeal.

Issues

As counsel for the appellant, he was the one who would determine the issues to be raised on appeal. As early as the trial, he had been paving the way. He had been very careful to enter objections at appropriate times in order to preserve all rights on appeal. Judge Wolfe might even say that he had been somewhat overeager in this respect.

Preparing his brief for the Great State Supreme Court, Henry asked himself if his client had at any time been denied his legal rights, if he had received a fair and impartial trial, if error that could be the basis for reversal had occurred. He had before him materials which the appellate judges would have available: a transcript of the trial and the suppression hearing; a copy of Judge Grant's findings of fact and conclusions of law; and a copy of Judge Wolfe's order denying his request for an arrest of judgment and new trial.

Three bases for appeal emerged from his reflection, and he made a note of these issues to present to the court:

1. The unnecessary delay between arrest and initial appearance was in violation of Rule 118, making inadmissible all evidence directly related to the delay. Therefore, the trial court erred in refusing to grant defendant's motion to suppress this evidence.

2. Defendant's confession was involuntary, as a result of statements made to the police without the presence of legal counsel while defendant was in a state of apprehension after having been physically "roughed up" at the time of arrest and after having waived his rights without fully comprehending the legal effect

of doing so. Therefore, the confession and all evidence flowing from it were inadmissible, and the trial court erred in refusing to grant the defendant's motion to suppress this evidence.

3. The trial judge's criticism and rebuke of defense counsel in connection with his efforts to have the foregoing evidence suppressed reflected unfavorably upon the defendant, thus prejudicing his case and denying him a fair and impartial trial.

Appellate Briefs

With this as a beginning, he started to work on the appellant's brief, portions of which appear in Form 10-4. He also made arrangements for transfer of the trial court records and docketing of the case with the supreme court. Henry knew he faced an uphill battle and anticipated the arguments that would appear in the brief, which the state, as the appellee, would file in response.

In the district attorney's office, Bob Barrister who engaged in trial, but not appellate, work discussed the case with the assistant district attorney, Mel Advocate, to whom the appeal had been assigned. Selected portions of the brief Mel prepared in reply appear in Form 10-5.[8] Notice the restatement of the questions presented to the court. Note, too, that he has included Judge Grant's findings of fact and conclusions of law in the history of the case. Those findings do not appear in the appellant's brief.

Form 10-4. Appellant's Brief

IN THE SUPREME COURT OF GREAT STATE

STATE OF GREAT STATE,   :
          Appellee   :
          v.   :   **BRIEF FOR APPELLANT**
Harvey Worker,   :
          Appellant   :

Table of Contents

. . . .

Table of Cases

. . . .

Questions Presented for Review

1. Where appellant following warrantless arrest was taken to police headquarters at 8:20 p. m. and where after the administrative chores of booking were completed appellant was interrogated by police until a confession had

---

been obtained resulting in delay of the initial appearance of appellant before a magistrate until 10:00 p. m., is the delay between the time of the appellant's arrest and his initial appearance "unnecessary" and unreasonable within the meaning of the Great State Rules of Criminal Procedure §118 thereby rendering appellant's confession and the evidence flowing from it inadmissible at trial?

2. When appellant has been interrogated by police without the presence of legal counsel and where appellant was in a state of apprehension after having been physically "roughed up" at the time of arrest and neither understood nor appreciated the legal implications of statements made to the police in such circumstances, does the appellant's confession lack the voluntariness required by *Miranda* v. *Arizona,* 384 U. S. 436 (1966), thus making it as well as any evidence flowing from it inadmissible against appellant?

3. When the trial court, in denying defense counsel's motions to suppress evidence, refers to defense counsel's statements as frivolous, does the interjection by the court of such remarks prejudice appellant's case and offend against the fundamental requirements of an unbiased and unprejudiced tribunal thereby denying defendant a fair and impartial trial and thus constituting reversible error?

. . . .

Argument

1. Under the circumstances of the case, delay between the arrest and initial appearance of appellant was unnecessary and unreasonable within the meaning of Great State Rules of Criminal Procedure §118 thus rendering appellant's confession and the evidence flowing from it inadmissible at trial.

The mandate of Great State R. Crim. P. §118 is clear: "When a defendant has been arrested without a warrant, he shall be taken without unnecessary delay before the proper judicial authority where a complaint shall be filed against him." In connection therewith, your honorable court has held: "All evidence obtained during unnecessary delay between arrest and initial appearance is inadmissible except that evidence which has no reasonable relationship to the delay whatsoever." *Great State* v. *Futch,* 447 G. S. 389, 394, 290 Z. 417 (19XR). See also *Great State* v. *Wayman,* 454 G. S. 79, 309 Z. 784 (19XS).

In the instant case, the initial appearance of the appellant before a magistrate was delayed after completion of the administrative processing associated with arrest and booking. This delay, of approximately one hour, was not caused by unavailability of a magistrate. Instead, the time was used for interrogation of appellant by the police without the presence of counsel and while appellant was in a state of apprehension after having been physically "roughed up" by police at arrest and concluded with appellant's inculpatory statement.

Delay for the purpose of obtaining incriminating statements from an arrestee is clearly impermissible under Rule 118 as construed in *Great State* v. *Futch* where at 447 G. S. 392 your honorable court quoted from *Adams* v. *United States,* 399 F. 2d 574, 579 (D. C. Cir., 1968) (concurring opinion) as to what constitutes permissible delay between arrest and initial appearance:

. . . .

The one-hundred minute detention and delay before the initial appearance in the instant case was not consumed solely in "administratively processing the accused" nor was any of it "directed to possible exculpation of the one arrested." Instead, a delay of one hour was used to secure inculpatory statements. Such delay cannot be said to be either necessary or reasonable in terms of Rule 118. Thus it represents a clear violation of the requirements of that rule, and any evidence obtained as a result of the delay must be excluded.

2. . . . .

3. . . . .

Conclusion

For the reasons stated above, appellant submits that the verdict and judgment of the lower court must be reversed.

Respectfully submitted,

Henry Law

Attorney for Appellant

789 Main Street
Big City, Great State

Form 10-5. Appellee's Brief

IN THE SUPREME COURT OF GREAT STATE

STATE OF GREAT STATE,	:	
Appellee	:	
v.	:	BRIEF FOR APPELLEE
HARVEY WORKER,	:	
Appellant	:	

. . . .

Counter Statement of Questions Presented for Review

1. Whether under the facts of this case the delay between the time of appellant's arrest and initial appearance was not unreasonable within the meaning of *Great State* v. *Futch,* 447 G. S. 389, 290 Z. 417 (19XR) and therefore appellant's confession as well as the physical evidence seized subsequent thereto and flowing from such confession was properly admitted into evidence by the trial court.

2. Whether under the facts of this case appellant's confession did meet the standards required by *Miranda* v. *Arizona,* 384 U. S. 436 (1966), and therefore the confession and the evidence flowing from it were properly admitted into evidence by the trial court.

3. Whether the trial court's reprimand of defense counsel at a side bar conference was not prejudicial to appellant's case and thus did not give rise to an unfair trial.

Counter History

. . . .

In denying appellant's motions to suppress, Judge Homer Grant on July 15, 19XX, entered findings of fact and conclusions of law as follows:

. . . .

Argument

1. Under the facts of this case, the delay between the time of appellant's arrest and initial appearance was not unreasonable within the meaning of *Great State* v. *Futch, supra,* and therefore appellant's confession and evidence

flowing from it were properly admitted into evidence by the trial court.

In the instant appeal, the time from arrest to initial appearance was less than two hours. In no case which has come before your honorable court has a time span of such short duration been deemed an unreasonable delay. See *Great State* v. *Wayman,* 454 G. S. 79, 309 Z. 784 (19XS) (involving eighteen hours); *Great State* v. *Dutton,* 453 G. S. 547, 307 Z. 238 (19XS) (involving eight hours); *Great State* v. *Tingle,* 451 G. S. 241, 301 Z. 701 (19XS) (involving twenty-one hours); *Great State* v. *Dixon,* 454 G. S. 444, 311 Z. 613 (19XS) (involving fifteen hours). The first contention of the State, therefore, is that the time period involved in this case cannot be termed an unreasonable delay.

In *Great State* v. *Futch,* your honorable court at 447 G. S. at 392 commented that permissible activity between arrest and initial appearance included not merely booking and administrative procedures but also limited preliminary investigation into the accused's connection with the crime. Given the time constraints in the instant case, no more than such limited investigation could have taken place. Were all police questioning to be forbidden following arrest and prior to initial appearance, law enforcement agencies would be handcuffed in their fight against crime. It follows from the Futch decision that limited questioning by the authorities is permissible, for only after such questioning can it be determined if the material is inculpatory or exculpatory. Therefore, the State submits that all that occurred in the instant case between the time of arrest and the initial appearance falls within the ambit of permissible activity as determined by your honorable court in Futch.

The police in the case at bar did not resort to "awful instruments of the criminal law." They did not use coercive tactics such as administering a polygraph test and then confronting the defendant with the results, nor did they isolate the defendant for a lengthy period. Following his arrest defendant did not make repeated denials of guilt. In *Futch, supra,* the police used the 14-hour delay to put the defendant in a line-up without the benefit of counsel. Conversely, in the case at bar, appellant was at all times advised of his right to counsel.

Therefore, the State submits that the appellant has failed to establish that the confession and evidence flowing from it resulted from unnecessary and unreasonable delay between arrest and initial appearance.

2. . . . .

3. . . . .

Conclusion

For the reasons stated above, the State submits that the verdicts of the lower court were proper and that they be, in all respects, affirmed.

Respectfully submitted,

James Bethann

District Attorney

BY *Mel Advocate*

Assistant District Attorney

Room 705 Local County Courthouse
Big City, Great State

Oral Arguments

The case was marked for oral argument after the justices of the state supreme court reviewed the briefs. They decided they should hear more from both appellant and appellee with regard to the first question presented to them by the appellant. The set of facts contained in it was different from any which had been present in other cases they had decided involving Rule 118. It involved issues which were before the court for the first time: Did "without unnecessary delay" mean immediately? Did the Rule automatically make excludable all confessions obtained between arrest and initial appearance? Was police interrogation permissible under Rule 118 before the initial appearance? Not only would their decision establish a precedent, but their interpretation of Rule 118 could have far-reaching effects upon police practice. The other two questions presented for review were more easily answered. The facts needed to determine voluntariness of the appellant's confession and prejudicial effect, if any, of the court's remarks were provided in the record of the suppression hearing and the trial. Had they been the only questions raised, no oral argument would have been scheduled.

That took place before the seven supreme court justices three weeks later. Henry was especially pleased with a portion of his argument to the court concerning Rule 118:

> The prohibition in Rule 118 against any unnecessary delay between arrest by an
> accusatorial authority and an initial appearance safeguards against unnecessary

abridgement of a citizen's liberty. Such an abridgement would, of course, be unconstitutional. The danger of any such unnecessary and unconstitutional restriction of liberty diminishes significantly when a citizen is brought swiftly before a neutral judicial authority, there to be informed of the charges and provided with an immediate and reasonable opportunity to regain his liberty by the posting of a reasonable bail.

The significance of Rule 118, requiring initial appearance without unnecessary delay, becomes fully apparent when that rule is read together with the requirements of Rule 119. Under Rule 119, at the initial appearance before a neutral authority, the citizen, who is presumed innocent, must be given a copy of the complaint, informed of his rights, and must be provided an immediate and reasonable opportunity to post bail. The fundamental purpose of the initial appearance is, therefore, to guarantee a citizen substantially the same rights to which he is entitled under both the United States and the Great State constitutions.[9]

Henry was aware that most of the justice's questions were directed to him. Some of the dialogue was as follows:

"Is it your contention that Rule 118 precludes any police questioning of an arrestee prior to the initial appearance?" Henry was asked.

"Yes," he replied, "except for securing that information which is necessary for booking purposes."

"Would not such severe limitation on the investigatory powers of the police adversely affect the apprehension of criminals and the solution of crime?"

"There is no limit on the information they can secure or the questioning that can be done of other persons. The arrested person's privilege against compulsory self-incrimination must be protected. It is not protected when the first-time offender, such as the appellant, succumbs to the subtle pressures arising from police questioning following arrest because of the fear engendered by the situation in which he finds himself and the lack of knowledge of police procedures."

At this point, the chief justice asked Mel Advocate:

"And what is your response to that?"

"It would be a strange rule of criminal procedure, indeed, that would not permit the police to accept the confession of a person who has just committed a crime when that confession is voluntarily offered. The purpose of Rule 118, as announced when it was first promulgated, is regulation of police practices. The rule is based on the presumption that reprehensible practices—the third degree, for want of better terminology—are not possible within the time of a reasonable delay. In this way it acts to preclude forced confessions, and it is these involuntary confessions that are the evil sought to be avoided by the Miranda requirements."

Henry thought that one question directed to him regarding the third issue was somewhat revealing:

"How can remarks of the court made at side bar—out of the hearing of the jury —be prejudicial to the defendant's case?"

"In this case it was a rebuke connected with the entrance of objections. In that way it can act to restrict or limit pursuit of the suppression of evidence, to lessen the aggression with which the attorney proceeds, and thus deny the client the full effect of a zealous advocacy."

"A zealous and aggressive advocacy is to be recommended, but should it not also be limited to reasonable bounds?"

"I agree. No excess was present in this case, however." That response brought smiles from everyone.

Postargument Conference

At the conferences of justices following the oral argument, it was soon apparent that Henry's arguments were insufficient, in their opinion, to warrant a reversal. There was agreement that short shrift should be made of the second and third issues—those concerned with the involuntary confession and prejudicial effect of the judge's remarks at side bar. The court found sufficient evidence, "in appellant's own words," as one justice remarked, that Harvey had voluntarily waived his rights and that his confession had been voluntary. Henry's argument that Harvey did not understand all of the legal implications was unpersuasive. As the chief justice remarked:

"Followed to its logical conclusion, that argument would require that only lawyers would be able to waive their rights. And that is clearly inconsistent with the decision in *Miranda* v. *Arizona.*"

They also agreed that the trial judge's statement that defense counsel's motion for a mistrial was frivolous did not prejudice the defendant when the response was given at a side bar conference out of the hearing of the jury. In addition, they were unanimous in their opinion that had it been the intention of the drafters of Rule 118 to require an "immediate" initial appearance, the word "immediate" would have been used rather than "without unnecessary delay." They also believed that the absolute restriction upon police interrogation following arrest which Henry advocated would unreasonably hamper police investigation of crime. Nor was such restriction constitutionally required.

However, the justices did decide there was a need to put in writing further explanation of Rule 118 in order to make clear that limited police questioning following arrest did not constitute "unnecessary delay." They also agreed that they should not set a specified time limit which would automatically become an "unnecessary delay," their thought being that this would vary with the circumstances of each situation. The newest member of the court, Judge Kathleen Cary, was assigned the task of writing the opinion, portions of which appear in Form 10-6.[10]

Filing of Opinion

The appellate procedure culminating in that opinion is shown in a chart in Figure 10-4. A copy of the opinion was filed with the clerk of the supreme court who thereupon sent copies to Mel Advocate, to Henry, and to the Local County Criminal Court where it was forwarded to Judge Wolfe.

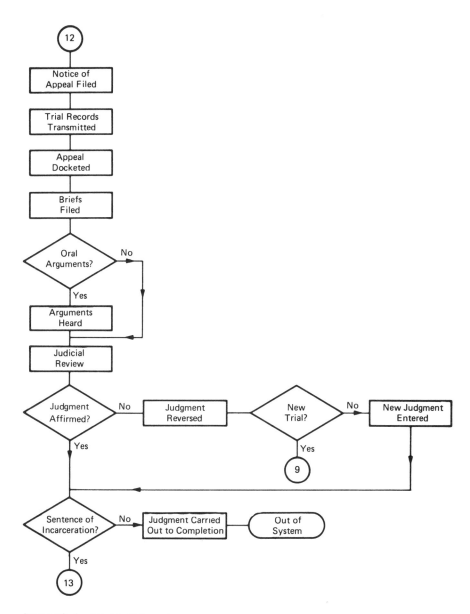

Figure 10-4. Process of Appeal

Form 10–6. Opinion

IN THE SUPREME COURT OF GREAT STATE

STATE OF GREAT STATE, :
              Appellee :
            v.   :   Appeal from No. 1246 of 19XX
HARVEY WORKER,   :   Local County
            Appellant :

CARY, J.   December 12, 19XX

OPINION

The appellant, Harvey Worker, was convicted of burglary and theft on August 29, 19XX following a jury trial. Post-trial motions were denied and the appellant was sentenced to a term of imprisonment not to exceed three years. This appeal followed.

Appellant was arrested without a warrant at approximately 7:30 p. m., ...

. . . .

Appellant contends that his confession was the product of unnecessary delay between his arrest and initial appearance and therefore should have been excluded along with the evidence flowing from it. Prior to trial appellant requested suppression of both his inculpatory statement and the physical evidence. These requests were denied by the trial court.

In *Great State* v. *Futch,* 447 G. S. 389, 290 Z. 417 (19XR) this court adopted the "federal approach" to evidence obtained during unnecessary delay prior to the initial appearance and announced a procedural rule excluding all evidence so obtained from admission at trial. (Congress repudiated this approach by enacting the Omnibus Crime Control and Safe Streets Act of 1968, Act of June 19, 1968, Pub. L. 90–351, 82 Stat. 210, 19 USC §3501.) Like its federal prototypes, *McNabb* v. *United States,* 318 U. S. 332, 63 S. Ct. 608 (1943) and *Mallory* v. *United States,* 354 U. S. 449, 77 S. Ct. 1356 (1957) our decision in *Futch* was not based on constitutional considerations. The exclusionary rule we promulgated was grounded on the Court's supervisory powers over the administration of justice in the courts of this state. The rule is directed entirely to police conduct prior to trial. The threat of exclusion operates to deter dilatory or illegal police conduct.

The instant case does not involve the prolonged questioning and lengthy time lapse which occurred in those prior cases in which this Court has found unreasonable delay between arrest and initial appearance. *Great State* v. *Wayman*, 454 G. S. 79, 309 Z. 784 (19XS). . . .

Nor is there any record of suspect or reprehensible practices commonly known as the "third degree." The time constraints permitted only limited preliminary questioning in addition to booking and other administrative processing. This is permissible under *Futch*. That such questioning result in exculpation is not a requirement. Reasonable limited inquiry by the police is consistent with Rule 118.

We are satisfied that the delay in the instant case was occasioned by proper and necessary steps in the police process and cannot be said to be either unnecessary or unreasonable in light of the requirements of Rule 118. The trial court properly refused suppression of appellant's confession and the physical evidence seized as a result thereto.

Appellant next contends. . . . .

JUDGMENT OF SENTENCE AFFIRMED.

Kathleen Cary / J.

TO CORRECTIONS

Notice was sent to Harvey, the sheriff, and the Little Town Correction Center of orders directing the sheriff to take Harvey into custody and transport him to Little Town to begin his term of imprisonment.

Harvey was at first stunned, then bitter.

"It's all Henry's fault," he told his mother. "He should have made me plead guilty. Then I'd be on probation, not on my way to prison."

Bitterness turned to outrage when a bill for legal services came from Henry's office.

"Why should I pay him?" Harvey asked. "What did he do for me? Just sent me to prison, that's all."

It was Mary who eventually settled matters with Henry. They discussed the fact that Great State, unlike some other states, did not have a procedure for expunging criminal records following imprisonment and successful readjustment to society. The records of ex-offenders in Great State remained on file along with all the information gathered in the criminal process. That meant Harvey would later be looked upon by many as an "ex-con." This could limit his opportunities for employment and even to be licensed and enter certain professions.

Although Harvey said he was "through with lawyers," Mary attempted to persuade Harvey to talk with Henry about some other forms of postconviction relief. That eventually occurred, but not until Harvey had entered upon an entirely new phase of his life, which is discussed in the next chapter.

QUESTIONS

1. Since Harvey's new life is a direct result of the outcome of the trial, it seems appropriate to ask if Harvey's election to go to trial—and to a jury trial—was unrealistic judgment on his part. Should Henry have further encouraged or even insisted that Harvey plead guilty? Do you believe the judge would have placed Harvey on probation if he had pleaded guilty? If so, is he really being punished for having exercised a constitutional right to trial by jury?

2. Would the jury's verdict have been any different had Harvey taken the stand and testified in his own behalf? What would have been the effect of cross-examination? Why did Henry make the motions to demur to the evidence and for a directed verdict for acquittal? Wasn't it just as obvious to him as it was to the judge that they would not be granted? Is this not also true regarding his request for a new trial?

3. What value exists in the presentence report prepared for the judge by the probation officer? Did the judge really make use of it? If so, does this really mean that the person preparing the report, rather than the judge, becomes the real influence in determining sentence? Should this be so?

4. Do you agree with the judge's analysis of the sentencing alternatives and their appropriateness in Harvey's case? What sentence do you believe should have been imposed in Harvey's situation? Why? Nothing is said about the district attorney's reaction to Harvey's sentence. What do you think it was? Why?

5. At each stage of the criminal system through which Harvey has progressed, a different group of people has played significant roles. In the beginning stages, it was the police. Then there were magistrates, then lawyers and judges, and a probation officer. Have you seen any interaction between these different groups of persons? Is there some means of coordination and integration, so that the effect is that of a whole system? Or, do you see these groups as working mostly by themselves, so that the final effect is one of separate and distinct systems loosely tied to each other? What suggestions have you for improvement?

6. What differences did you note between the criminal trial and the civil trial? Are these merely matters of form, or are they of real substance?

7. Can you think of issues which Henry could have raised on appeal but which he did not? Why do you suppose he did not? Should cases like this one be appealed? Why? Do you agree with the appellate court's decision? Why?

8. If you were arrested and interrogated by the police in Great State for three hours before being taken to a magistrate for an initial appearance, would the *Worker* decision be precedent for inclusion or exclusion of any statement you might have made to the police during that time? Based on the *Worker* decision, would you need to know more than just the amount of time that elapsed? Why? Did the court in that decision define "without unnecessary delay?" If not, why not? If yes, what is that definition? When the court determined that Harvey had not been held "without unnecessary delay," was it making new law? In what way? When an appellate court interprets statutory law, does it really make new law? If so, why did this appellate court look to the specific wording of Rule 118? Why did the Great State Supreme Court in *Futch* rely upon a federal court's decision if Great State, rather than federal, law was involved? What effect did the Omnibus Crime Control and Safe Streets Act have on the *Worker* decision? Why would Congress pass such legislation after the United States Supreme Court had already made a contrary decision in both the *McNabb* and *Mallory* cases?

9. Should Harvey Worker seek additional attempts at relief? If so, which of the postconviction forms of relief would be appropriate? What hope of success has he? Should postconviction relief be more limited in cases like Harvey's? Why?

NOTES

[1] In federal cases, Article III, § 2, cl. 3 also applies.

[2] *Duncan* v. *Louisiana*, 391 U.S. 145 (1968).

[3] *Baldwin* v. *New York*, 399 U.S. 66 (1970).

[4] *Johnson* v. *Louisiana*, 406 U.S. 356 (1972), *Apodaca* v. *Oregon*, 406 U.S. 404 (1972).

[5] *Commonwealth* v. *Martin*, (Pa.) 351 A.2d 650 (1976).

[6] *Pointer* v. *Texas*, 380 U.S. 400 (1965).

[7] *Illinois* v. *Allen*, 397 U.S. 337 (1970).

[8] Parts adapted from Brief for Appellate filed in the Supreme Court of Pennsylvania in the case of *Commonwealth* v. *Whitson*, No. 177, March Term, 1974.

[9] Adapted from Opinion of the Court, *Commonwealth* v. *Dixon*, 454 Pa. 444, 311 A.2d 613 (1973).

[10] Parts adapted from *Commonwealth* v. *Whitson*, (Pa.) 334 A.2d 653 (1975).

incarceration and release: corrections subsystem and exit

ELEVEN

Dread. Dejection. Despair. Degradation. All of these words characterized Harvey's feelings at the moment. Handcuffed and accompanied by two constables, he sat in the back of their car on the way to the Great State Correction Center in Little Town, 140 miles away from Big City. Although he didn't know what awaited him there, he was relieved to be out of the Local County jail. A traffic accident involving the sheriff's car had caused an unexpected delay in his transportation to Little Town. He had been taken to the jail to await completion of the arrangements for the trip. The short time he had been there had, without question, been the worst experience of his life. He did not believe he would survive if life at Little Town turned out to be anything like it was in that jail.

JAIL

He had been depressed as he entered the jail, following a tearful goodbye to his family. As electrically-controlled steel doors clanged open and then closed behind him, he was horrified at the unbelievable ugliness of the scene before him. The filth, the stench, and the reverberating animal-like sounds assaulted his entire being. A guard pushed him into a cell with these words:

"Get in there, you . . . punk . . . you."

"This one's for the country club," that guard had said to another. "Judge Wolfe's in a hurry again; doesn't want any of her people here too long. Her orders say he has to be in Little Town by four-thirty today."

Harvey looked around. He did not even wish to sit down. There was no chair, just a cot covered with a torn and dirty mattress. Lice crawled over it. The lighting was extremely poor, but Harvey could distinguish plainly the peeling paint on the walls and the decaying particles of food on the steel bars of the cell door. A toilet and sink were at the other end of the cell. The concrete floor still contained evidence of the vomit of the last occupant. The rancid putridness coming from it together with the all pervasive smell of urine combined to assail Harvey's olfactory sense to a point at which he thought he could no longer breathe. Nor was there any escape from the sounds of cell doors loudly clanging, the screams of a drug user in the process of withdrawal, the senseless mutterings of the individual arrested for intoxication who was in the cell next to him, the incredible sounds coming from the cell across the way where a prisoner battered his head against the wall. As he stood there near the cell door, not knowing where to turn or what to do next, a passing prisoner spat at him.

Harvey found it hard to believe this was real. Was this not cruel and unusual punishment, as prohibited by the Eighth Amendment of the United States Constitution?[1] (This provision has been held applicable to the states by the United States Supreme Court.[2]) How could human beings be expected to live in a place like this? He rejected an offer of lunch. He was filled with revulsion at just the thought of eating in this place. When at last a guard came to take him to the car for the ride to Little Town, he could hardly wait to get to the jail yard so that he could breathe the outdoor air again. He realized that he had been in jail for less than two hours. To him it seemed more like 200 years. The *James* v. *Wallace* decision which follows indicates that his experience was not unique.

James v. *Wallace*
406 F.Supp. 318 (M.D., Ala.) 1976

Consolidated actions were filed by inmates of Alabama penal institutions for declaratory and injunctive relief in respect to alleged deprivation of their Eighth and Fourteenth Amendment rights. The District Court held that action was maintainable as a class action on behalf of all persons presently confined by Alabama Board of Corrections or who might be so confined in the future, . . .

Judgment for plaintiff.

JOHNSON, CHIEF JUDGE . . . this Court has a clear duty to require the defendants in these cases to remedy the massive constitutional infirmities which plague Alabama's prisons. It is with great reluctance that federal courts intervene in the day-to-day operation of state penal systems, . . . a function they are increasingly required to perform. While this Court continues to recognize the broad discretion required for prison officials to maintain orderly and secure institutions, . . . constitutional deprivations of the magnitude presented here simply cannot be countenanced, and this Court is under a duty to, and will, intervene to protect incarcerated citizens from such wholesale infringements of their constitutional rights. . . .

. . . There has been growing recognition by the courts that prisoners retain all rights enjoyed by free citizens except those necessarily lost as an incident of confinement. . . . The Supreme Court recently identified three legitimate functions of a correctional system: deterrence, both specific and general; rehabilitation; and institutional security. . . . *Pell* v. *Procunier,* 417 U.S. 817 (1974). . . .

Prisoners are entitled to be free of conditions which constitute cruel and unusual punishment in violation of the Eighth and Fourteenth Amendments. The content of the Eighth Amendment is not static but "must draw its meaning from the evolving standards of decency that mark the progress of a maturing society." . . . There can be no question that present conditions of confinement in the Alabama penal system violate any current judicial definition of cruel and unusual punishment, a situation evidenced by the defendant's admission that serious Eighth Amendment violations exist. . . .

The conditions in which Alabama prisoners must live, as established by the evidence in these cases, bear no reasonable relationship to legitimate institutional goals. As a whole they create an atmosphere in which inmates are compelled to live in constant fear of violence, in imminent danger to their physical well-being, and without opportunity to seek a more promising future.

The living conditions in Alabama prisons constitute cruel and unusual punishment. Specifically, lack of sanitation throughout the institutions in living areas, infirmaries, and food service—presents an imminent danger to the health of each and every inmate. Prisoners suffer from further physical deterioration because there are no opportunities for exercise and recreation. Treatment for prisoners with physical or emotional problems is totally inadequate. This Court has previously ordered that the penal system provide reasonable medical care for inmates in these institutions. . . .

Prison officials are under a duty to provide inmates reasonable protection from constant threat of violence. . . .

Not only is it cruel and unusual punishment to confine a person in an institution under circumstances which increase the likelihood of future confinement, but these same conditions defeat the goal of rehabilitation which prison officials have set for their institutions. . . .

Prisoners are protected by the Due Process and Equal Protection Clause of the Fourteenth Amendment; therefore, they must be free from arbitrary and capricious treatment by prison officials. . . .

. . . However, a state is not at liberty to afford its citizens only those constitutional rights which fit comfortably within its budget. . . . It is well established beyond doubt that inadequate funding is no answer to the existence of unconstitutional conditions in state penal institutions. . . .

. . . A public official may be held liable where he, in subjective good faith, acts in disregard of a person's clearly established constitutional rights. The court now acts in these cases with a recognition that prisoners are not to be coddled, and prisons are not to be operated as hotels or country clubs. However, this does not mean that responsible state officials can be allowed to operate prison facilities that are barbaric and inhumane. Let the defendant state officials now be placed on notice that failure to comply with the minimum standards set forth in this Court filed with this opinion will necessitate the closing of those several prison facilities herein found to be unfit for human confinement. . . .

[The Court appended "Minimum Constitutional Standards for Inmates of the Alabama Penal System" containing specific standards detailing, among other matters:

1. Number of inmates to be confined to any one institution;

2. Number of prisoners to be confined to a single cell and size of cell;

3. Conditions and length of confinement in isolation;

4. Plan for classification of inmates;

5. Standards for food service;

6. Requirements for protection from violence;

7. Criteria for mental health care;

8. Staff requirements;

9. Standards for educational, vocational, work, and recreational programs;

10. Correspondence and visitation privilege requirements;

11. Standards re living conditions.]

When Harvey talked with the two constables about his experience in the jail, they were not at all surprised. Harvey learned that more than 420 persons were currently housed in the jail, although it had been built over 50 years ago to accommodate no more than 300. One wing was set aside as a women's section, and persons under 16 years of age were taken to a separate juvenile detention facility in Big City. The constables told Harvey of problems at the jail, such as the incidence of homosexual assault and the increasing number of suicides.

They also assured him that Little Town was strikingly different. It was so recently constructed that the buildings still had the smell of new plastering. Although the constables had merely transported prisoners there and had never spent much time inside, they did know it had acquired a reputation for the "country club atmosphere" which was said to exist there. That brought Harvey some sense of relief, enough that he was able to engage in conversation with the constables about their work.

SHERIFF AND CONSTABLES

He learned that the constables in Local County worked under the direction of the sheriff. The latter, an elected official, was the principal law enforcement officer of the county. His principal duties included:

1. Maintaining the county jail and its prisoners;
2. Assisting the county court through the service of process, summoning jurors, conducting judicial sales, executing judgment, providing bailiffs and tipstaffs;
3. Keeping the peace in the unincorporated areas of the county.

The two constables with Harvey told him they were assigned to the county jail and worked principally with prisoners, although on occasion they had assisted sheriff's deputies in effecting arrests and executing search warrants. They discussed a new county regulation which required all sheriff's deputies and constables to be graduates of the Big City police academy. It was not yet clear whether this new ruling would apply only to personnel to be hired in the future or whether it also pertained to those already employed. If the latter, both constables said they would have to find some way to take the course in order to keep their jobs.

MAXIMUM SECURITY FACILITY

A highway sign indicated the exit to Cul deSac just ahead. Harvey learned that the two constables sometimes transported prisoners to the state maximum security prison located there. Their description coincided with the image of prison Harvey had formed from his reading, the movies, and television. They told him how it was surrounded by a 25-foot-high, thick stone wall with 35-foot guard towers manned around the clock by armed sentries. It has a population of about 1500 men. Neither women nor juveniles were sent there, and only infrequently men under the age of 25. The one electric chair still in existence in the state was located there, but it had not been used in the past ten years.

Life in the "pen," as the constables referred to the Cul deSac facility, had been described to them by a prison social worker. Men were confined to steel-barred cells, twenty of which were in a row, with rows six tiers high in each cell block. Prisoners moved from one place to another only in a company and under guard. They were required to march in twos, arms folded, with eyes straight ahead, and in silence. Meals were eaten in the mess hall, where the men filed through a cafeteria-type line, walked to the first unoccupied seat at a long table, and sat eating silently while facing the back of the man in front.

Inmates spent most of the time between the hours of 6:00 p.m. and 6:00 a.m. confined in their cells. Entering another man's cell was not permitted, nor was the passing of articles from one cell to another. Smoking was permitted in cells between the hours of 6:00 a.m. and 10:00 p.m., which were the times for rising and retiring. Men were required to sleep with their feet toward the door and with their head uncovered, their shoes placed at the door and the rest of their clothing on the chair next to the door. Should a man fail to do this, he would be awakened by a guard.

Visiting by family and friends was permitted during scheduled hours on Sundays once a month. A small gymnasium and an outside prison yard provided limited recreational facilities. Fourteen teachers were employed full time at the institution to provide instruction in subjects varying from basic grammar to social studies. The staff also included four psychologists and five social workers. Inmates worked during the day in the prison laundry, bakery, and kitchen. Some were employed in making license plates and brooms.

Discipline was strict. Frequent or serious violation of the rules could result in solitary confinement. This meant the prisoner was kept locked either in his cell or in the "hole" 24 hours a day, placed on a restricted diet, and denied such privileges as visitation and receiving mail.

Harvey learned from the constables that the persons most likely to be sent there were those who represented a grave risk to the safety of the community because they were violently assaultive, had committed atrocious crimes, or were hardened criminals. He also learned that corrections institutions were classified as maximum-, medium-, and minimum-security facilities. The one to which he was being sent was a minimum-security institution. A medium-security facility differed from one of minimum security, he learned, in that the former had guards, was enclosed behind a high fence, generally had cells instead of dormitories, and limited residents to work and study programs within the institution.

STATE CORRECTION CENTER

"Do you have his papers back there?" the driver asked as they approached the highway exit to Little Town. He was referring to records related to Harvey's case, including the judge's order of commitment and the presentence report, which were being sent to the personnel at the Little Town facility.

Harvey's first surprise came as they arrived at the entrance to the Great State Correction Center. To him it looked just like a college campus. There were no guards; there was no entrance check point, no fence. He noted spacious and well-kept grounds, people moving freely about from one building to another, an absence of bars on windows. At the end of a serpentine driveway the car came to a stop outside a building marked "Reception Center."

Intake

The sense of prison returned as Harvey noticed the entrance to the building was electronically controlled. In the office, Paul Grace, intake officer, was expecting them. Harvey's file was turned over to Paul, and he signed the constable's form certifying delivery of the prisoner to the facility, noting time and date. He also made a mental note of what occurred as the constable removed the handcuffs from Harvey. Shaking hands with Harvey, the constable departed with these words:

"Good luck, son."

It was already past mid-afternoon. Paul said they would get Harvey settled and would wait until the next morning for further discussion. Once again Harvey experienced a sense of prison as he was searched and given a change of clothing. He welcomed a shower, feeling clean for the first time since leaving the jail. He was given a booklet containing regulations and information about the Center, and was assigned to a private room. It was small and sparsely furnished, but it was clean. Most importantly to Harvey, it was not a cell with steel bars. Hungry, he hoped that eating arrangements would be comfortable and the food palatable. He found that the dining room was not unlike that in his former college dormitory. There was a cafeteria line, with seating arrangements at round tables for eight. Another young resident recognized that he was new and asked him to join a group of four. Harvey did. He enjoyed the food but was uncomforable with the conversation and with the other residents. He did, however, go with them after dinner to the lounge to watch TV and play ping pong. In a short while, he left for his room. He was physically tired and filled with a great sense of loneliness, of being cut off from the rest of the world. The feeling of being imprisoned remained until he fell asleep.

The following morning Paul Grace met with him and explained that Harvey would remain in the reception center for the next few weeks for an orientation program. Harvey was kept busy. He was given a medical and dental check-up. He seemed to be forever meeting with either counselors, case workers, or psychologists. To him they appeared to be most interested in his year of college, his knowledge of computers, his cypres hobby. He participated in a variety of recreational activities with some of the other residents. However, he did not develop a feeling of ease with them.

Paul Grace presided at a staff meeting for the purpose of discussing Harvey's assignment and program at the Center. Few of the other residents had either a background or interests similar to Harvey's. Therefore, in assigning him to a cottage, the staff decided to place him with other men of his age group. They also agreed that Harvey would probably not be either challenged or happy with the programs currently available at the Center, and so they looked to community resources. A work program in the cypres industry was not available in the locality. However, there did exist opportunity for employment in several firms with computer facilities. Furthermore, the nearby community college offered some cypres engineering and computer science courses in the evenings which should be of interest to Harvey. The staff also agreed that Paul Grace had developed the greatest rapport with Harvey and therefore appeared to be the best person to serve as his counselor.

As the meeting ended, Paul smiled to himself. Great State was currently in the process of converting from the practice of having the sentencing judge specify the prison to which a convicted individual should be sent, to the kind of program which exists in most states, where the judge merely sentences to the state correction system. The convicted individual is then sent to a reception and classification center, such as the one they were presently developing in Little Town. There, following screening and diagnosis by the professional staff, the sentenced individual is assigned to the most appropriate institution or program for corrective treatment. Paul Grace mused that, after weeks of study by a group of professionals, the staff had come up with the same recommendation as Judge Wolfe had.

Rehabilitative Program

Harvey was happy with the news from Paul Grace. Moving to a cottage meant that he would be unrestricted in his movements about the grounds, and that the only locked doors would be those of the cottage at night. That freedom was one he had taken for granted until recently. He was very interested in the possibility of going out to work.

Paul explained that there had been much controversy and resistance, as well as complaint in the small community, over the idea of having "prisoners" employed in local industry. However, he planned to seek out an appropriate job opportunity for Harvey. He also gave Harvey a bulletin listing courses offered at the community college, suggesting that Harvey take a few days to determine courses he might like to take.

Harvey asked if he might have some of his own clothes sent to him from home. Paul recommended that he invite his family to bring them, there being liberal visiting privileges. It was the happiest day Harvey had experienced since he arrived at the Center. He wrote to his mother. He declined a ride to the cottage to which he had been assigned. Although it was on the other end of the grounds, he walked the entire way in the rain.

It was now Paul Grace's turn to experience disappointment and frustration. Several firms whom he contacted about employing Harvey were cordial but insisted they could not afford the employee morale problems and poor public relations that would follow. Others simply refused outright. Gail Earl, who taught computer science at the community college and with whom Paul discussed Harvey's enrollment, provided helpful information. She said that the Planning and Research Division of the Great State Department of Corrections had undertaken a study of juvenile recidivism. The data were being processed at the computer center at the Juvenile Ranch, located twenty miles from Little Town. Since she was one of the consultants for the project, Gail knew that trained personnel were sorely needed.

Paul arranged for Harvey to be interviewed by Michael Patrick, director of the computer center at the Ranch. The Ranch was a medium-security facility for boys aged 13-15 who assisted in the operation of a large dairy farm while institutionalized. The offices of the Juvenile Division of the Great State Department of Corrections occupied one of the buildings on the grounds. There Harvey viewed the computer facilities and talked with Michael Patrick about his background. Michael asked a great many questions about the changes Harvey had made in The Firm's records in his attempt to cover up the theft of the cypres parts.

"I'll try him," Michael told Paul Grace over the telephone. "He knows more about computers than anyone else I have working here. Furthermore, he won't have the temptation he had with the cypres parts. About the only thing he could steal here would be office supplies."

When Paul told Harvey he had been hired, he emphasized that it would be on the condition that he prove himself. He also talked with him about arrangements for transportation to his job and to the classes at the community college two evenings a week in the Correction Center's minibus.

Family Visitation

When Mary Worker came to visit Harvey, she was not only pleased with the news about his job, but also pleasantly surprised at the "unprison-like" characteristics of the Center. Henry Law accompanied her. In the course of their conversation, Harvey asked him about a "postconviction hearing." Residents of his cottage talked about it a great deal. Forms requesting such a hearing were available at the Center.

POSTCONVICTION HEARING

Henry explained that a postconviction hearing is a procedure established to provide relief to persons who have been convicted and sentenced without due process of law. A prisoner in Great State could apply for such relief by sending copies of the completed form, referred to as a petition, to the clerk of the criminal court in which he had been tried. His petition would have to show three things:

1. That he was convicted of a crime;
2. That he was currently imprisoned or on parole or probation in Great State;
3. That his conviction and sentence resulted from one or more unconstitutional legal grounds.

Henry also explained that the petition must conform with the requirements of the Great State Postconviction Hearing Statute. He added that meeting this requirement had become easier since the printed petition form came into use. The form had been designed so that it was easily completed. Forms were made available to inmates of all penal institutions in the state. Henry added that many prisoners prepared the forms themselves, without the assistance of legal counsel. These often failed to meet requirements.

"What happens when a petition is completed and sent to the clerk of courts?" Harvey wanted to know.

Henry said that a copy was received by the judge who had presided at the trial, after the clerk of courts filled in identification numbers of the original proceedings. The judge then reviewed the petition to determine whether it had merit. Should he decide that it did not, he would issue an order dismissing the petition. Otherwise, the judge would direct that the second copy of the petition be sent to the district attorney with a request that the prosecutor show cause why relief should not be granted.

An answer to the petition would then be prepared by the district attorney, who would either admit, deny, or explain the allegations made in the petition. The prisoner who originated the petition received a copy of this answer, as did the judge and any lawyer designated on the petition. The answer was used by the judge to arrive at a second decision. The judge could either dismiss the petition, based on information contained in the answer, or could schedule a hearing at which evidence could be introduced regarding the matters stated in the petition. Following such a hearing, the judge would enter an order either granting appropriate relief or dismissing the petition. The relief granted might consist of discharge of the prisoner, retrial, or resentencing. The judge's order is a final judgment for the purposes of review by an appellate court.

The postconviction relief process appears in a flow chart in Figure 11-1. Henry explained to Harvey that the statute had been enacted to simplify procedure. As a result, the one process replaced several forms for postconviction relief previously used in the state, including *habeas corpus*.

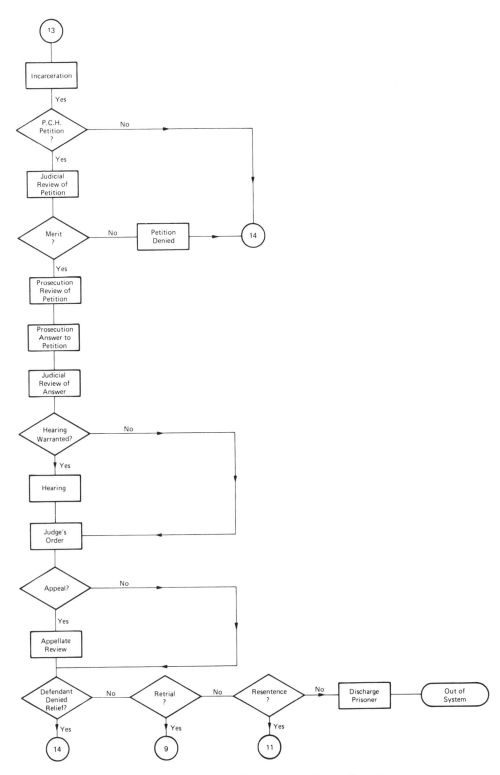

Figure 11-1. The Postconviction Hearing Process

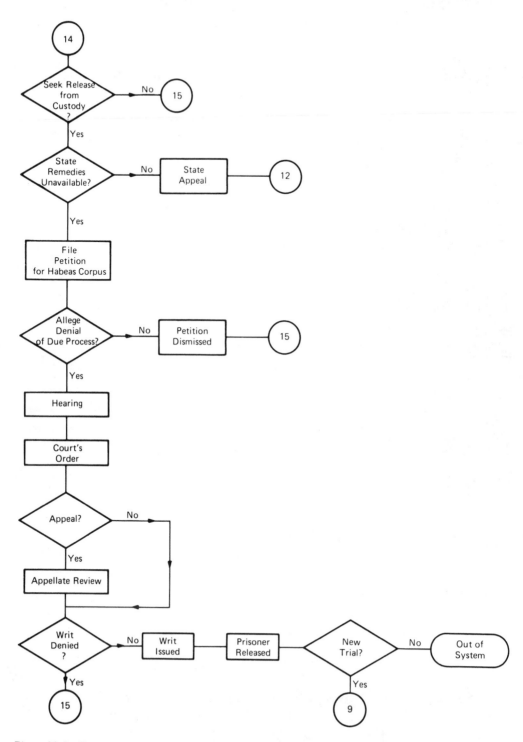

Figure 11-2. Procedure for Federal Writ of Habeas Corpus as Postconviction Relief

HABEAS CORPUS

"Habeas corpus? Tell me about that. There's a lot of talk around here about it, too."

Henry said the literal translation of habeas corpus is "you have the body." A writ is a written court order. Therefore, petitioning the court for a writ of habeas corpus is an application for the release of a person held in custody. It is available at any stage of the criminal process, not just after a person has been imprisoned following sentencing. The issue involved in habeas corpus is not an individual's guilt or innocence, but whether his liberty has been restrained without due process.

Henry went on to say that under the old common law habeas corpus was known as the Great Writ. The United States Constitution provides that the privilege of the writ of habeas corpus shall not be suspended except when the public safety so requires in cases of rebellion or invasion.[3] Under federal statute recourse to the federal system for the writ is possible when, under a judgment of a state court, a person is held "in custody in violation of the Constitution, or laws, or treaties of the United States."[4] However, the federal courts will not intervene where a state has provided an opportunity for full and fair litigation of a defendant's claim.[5] Of course, in the case of federal prisoners, application for habeas corpus is properly made in the federal courts.

If the petition for habeas corpus alleges facts that show deprivation of constitutional rights, a hearing follows. If the allegations are shown to be true, a writ is issued for the release of the individual. Otherwise, the petition is dismissed. As seen in Figure 11-2, which flow charts the process, appeal of the court's decision is possible.

Henry cautioned, however, that discharge of a prisoner under either of these two forms of relief does not automatically guarantee against the possibility of recommitment following retrial, a matter often overlooked by hopeful prisoner applicants because of their misconceptions about the constitutional provision against double jeopardy.

"But why do you ask?" Henry directed the question to Harvey. "Are you interested in further pursuit of your case?"

Harvey was rather emphatic in stating that he did not wish to do so until he saw what happened to his fellow residents as they sought these various forms of relief.

"I have no desire to be a three-time loser," he said.

WORK RELEASE

In the weeks that followed, Harvey began both his job and his classes. He not only enjoyed them, he did well at both. Eventually he was given responsibility for supervision of two teenagers who were residents at the Ranch and who were assigned to work in the computer center several hours each day. He found this to be especially rewarding and developed a fine working relationship with the two young individuals.

For his work at the computer center, Harvey was paid a salary by the State Department of Corrections. His check was made payable to the warden at the center in trust for Harvey. Because he was employed, Harvey was required to make monthly payments to the institution for his maintenance. This amount was deducted from his salary and the remainder deposited in an account held in his name by the warden. Harvey authorized payment of most of that sum for restitution purposes. The small amount remaining was sufficient to cover his personal needs.

JUVENILE PROGRAMS

Through his job-related activities, Harvey gained some insight into the matter of juvenile offenders in Great State. Until now, he had given little thought to the delinquent juvenile. He was greatly impressed with the tremendous emphasis given to programs designed to help young people with their problems, to deter them from criminal activity, and to discourage youthful offenders from becoming recidivists.

Even more, he was surprised to learn that special programs dealing with treatment of juveniles were held for police officers in the state. Those particularly encouraged to attend were members of the smaller police departments which did not have the specially trained youth squads for working with juveniles found in larger cities. Some of the topics discussed at these juvenile programs included:

1. Police reaction at the time of first contact with juveniles, and the impact of the manner in which police respond to the situation upon the young;
2. Dealing with youthful behavior that might be mischievous, insolent, arrogant, or annoying to others, but did not constitute a violation of the law;
3. Handling "status offenders"—that is, youth charged with acts that would not be considered violations of the law were the actor an adult;
4. Police discretion, especially when the offense is of a minor nature and the young person has no prior record of trouble with the law;
5. Community programs and treatment centers to which police might make referral of juveniles.

In addition, statewide standards had been promulgated requiring each police agency to have written policies and guides regarding police discretionary authority at the first contact with a juvenile offender, as well as at the police station. Written procedures related to the taking of a juvenile into custody included the following:

1. Whom to notify and when;
2. Where the child could be detained;
3. Rules covering police interviews and interrogation;
4. Ground rules for police disposition without referral to the juvenile court;
5. When police should refer the child to the juvenile court;
6. Nature of police records and confidentiality of them, including fingerprinting and photographing.

The standards also required each juvenile court jurisdiction to work out procedures with local police governing discretionary diversion authority of police officers. Diversion to community-based programs and agencies outside the juvenile justice system was recommended when the welfare of the child and the safety of the community would not be jeopardized.

From Sam, a 14-year-old resident of the Ranch whom he supervised, Harvey learned a great deal about the juvenile court. Sam was at the Ranch after having been found guilty for the third time of stealing cars.

"But you're not even old enough to get a Great State driver's license," Harvey had said when Sam told him how he came to be at the Ranch.

"Yeah. The judge said something about that, too," Sam replied.

In the course of one of his conversations with Paul Grace, Harvey repeated this short conversation and added that he found it difficult to believe that Sam could be a car thief.

"He's such a decent kid. He's been honest about everything with me. I can de-

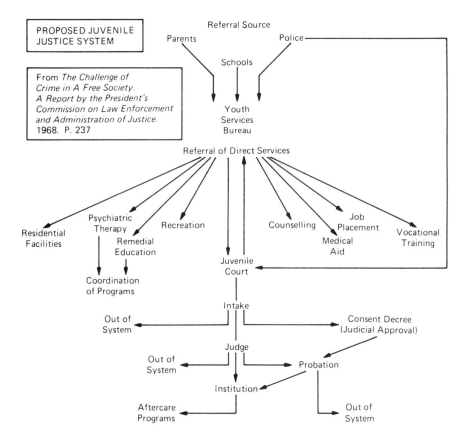

Figure 11–3. Proposed Juvenile Justice System

pend on him. He's very intelligent—learns quickly. He's just not the kind of person you'd expect to be stealing cars."

Harvey was surprised at Paul's answer:

"That's very interesting. Sounds something like what the counselors around here say about you."

That comment made a deep impression upon Harvey. He thought about it over and over again. And each time he did, he asked himself a question that had been on his mind ever since the day he spent in the Local County jail.

"How did I ever get myself into this?" He still could not explain why he had ever started to steal; he only knew he would never do such a thing again.

One day Harvey had occasion to work with the report of the President's Commission on Law Enforcement and Administration of Justice regarding a suggested juvenile justice system.[6] It intrigued him, especially the flow chart of the system recommended by that Commission, which is shown in Figure 11–3. Harvey decided to compare it with the Great State system.

JUVENILE COURT

It was not long before Harvey could say that he was acquainted with the procedure in juvenile courts in Great State from intake to final disposition. With the exception of homicide cases, all persons under the age of 16 accused of criminal activity in Great State were required to be processed through the juvenile system. Harvey learned that youngsters were referred to the juvenile court by the police when diversion to some community agency was not appropriate. In addition to the police, parents and schools frequently made referrals to the court. Neighbors, victims, and social agencies also did so on occasion.

Referrals to the court might originate by an information filed with a district magistrate, by a police arrest report being sent in, by the police bringing the juvenile to the court following an arrest, or by a referral in person or by correspondence from a school, parent, or others.

Referrals came to the Intake Department of the court, which was staffed by officers experienced in working with juveniles. Intake officials reviewed each case, evaluating the situation and circumstances that led to the referral. Their first decision was whether an adjudicatory hearing was warranted. Such a hearing is held before a judge of the juvenile court. Evidence is heard to determine if the facts sustain a finding beyond a reasonable doubt that the youngster is guilty of criminal activity.

In Great State, over 40 percent of all referrals to the juvenile courts were disposed of other than by way of an adjudicatory hearing. In those cases, the usual recourse was diversion to an appropriate community agency. Sometimes this involved finding short-term residences or foster homes for youngsters in order to remove them from an environment which tended to encourage delinquency.

In Great State, each juvenile court jurisdiction was required to have written guidelines and procedures which set forth criteria for screening youngsters out of the juvenile justice system. When a diversion decision was made by the intake officer, with or without consultation with the prosecutor's office, the staff member who made it was required to state in writing the basis for the decision. These written reports were then reviewed periodically by one of the judges of the juvenile court, by the chief administrator of the juvenile probation services, and by the prosecutor's office, in order to insure that diversion programs were being operated as intended. The objective was to provide intake services for screening and referral, to divert as many youngsters as possible from the juvenile justice system, and to reduce detention of youngsters to an absolute minimum.

In cases in which the intake officer decided that an adjudicatory hearing should be held, a petition to the court would be prepared setting forth the charges against the juvenile. This petition was filed with the clerk of the court. A copy was sent to the juvenile and his parents or guardian together with notice of the date and time set for the hearing. (Notification of a juvenile's parent or guardian was automatic with regard to all action taken by the court.) For those cases referred to the juvenile court by an information from a magistrate, no such petition was necessary since the information served in its place.

At the time the petition was prepared, the case was assigned to one of the juvenile probation officers for investigation. He proceeded in much the same way as would an adult probation officer who was preparing a presentence investigatory report for one of the criminal court judges.

When an intake officer decided an adjudicatory hearing should be held, he also decided whether or not a detention hearing was necessary. The purpose of the second hearing was to obtain a judicial determination as to whether the young person should be detained in a juvenile facility or returned home while awaiting the adjudicatory hearing. In some states, this determination is made by an intake or probation officer rather than by a judge as it was in Great State. The usual practice in Great State was to recommend detention only when some alternative disposition was not advisable—in cases, for example, in which the youngster was a threat to self or others, or was a runaway risk, or in which home and family difficulties were the source of his problems.

An adjudicatory hearing can be held only in the juvenile court which has jurisdiction in the case. In Great State, that was the juvenile court in the youngster's home county or in the county where the offense allegedly occurred. In some unusual cases, such as an individual over the age of 14 who was charged with murder, the matter was transferred to the criminal court.

In Great State, the rules of evidence applied at adjudicatory hearings although the atmosphere was more informal than in the criminal court. A juvenile is entitled to due process.[7] He has the right to the assistance of counsel and the right to confront his accusers and to cross-examine them. Because he is also entitled to the privilege against self-incrimination, he must be advised of his constitutional rights as required in *Miranda* v. *Arizona*. Since there were questions as to a juvenile's ability to knowingly and intelligently waive his rights, Great State required that the Miranda warnings be given in the presence of either counsel or a parent or guardian. A further requirement was that the consent of such individuals be secured to waive any rights.

If the evidence did not reveal facts that would sustain a finding beyond a reasonable doubt that the youngster was guilty of unlawful activity, there could be no adjudication of delinquency and the judge would dismiss the case. This would be tantamount to a finding of not guilty in a criminal case. On the other hand, if the evidence led to an adjudication of delinquency, the judge would ask the juvenile probation officer for his report of the social history of the youngster and a recommendation regarding disposition. After receiving that report, the judge made a determination of disposition. His decision was announced either at a separate hearing or immediately following the adjudicatory hearing. The judge might decide upon commitment to a state or private institution or upon probation.

A prevalent belief among Great State juvenile authorities was that probation usually offered the best remedy, with the least risk of damage to the child and at the least expense to the community. Many of the juvenile judges considered a good probation staff as the juvenile court's most effective tool. On the other hand, they also recognized that commitment might be necessary when a juvenile's aggressive actions presented danger to the community, when his family was a threat to the youngster's rehabilitation, or when the juvenile had special needs that could be met only under a closely controlled situation.

Great State provided by statute that a juvenile acquired no civil disabilities, nor was he deemed to have committed a crime as a result of his appearance in juvenile court. A separate docket was kept for the court and withheld from indiscriminate public inspection. The legal records were in the custody of the clerk of courts. The social records were kept by the probation staff. All were required to be held strictly confidential.

Following the judge's disposition of the case and entry of his final order, a juvenile or his parents could request a rehearing. There was a 21-day limit in which this request must be made. If they were still not satisfied after the rehearing, they could appeal to the intermediate appellate court.

This entire process was shown in a flow chart by Harvey. His chart appears in Figure 11-4. In preparing the flow chart, Harvey found that many of the steps were analogous to those through which he had been processed. His interest, however, was not limited to procedure. The information generated by the computerized data system on which he was working also caught his attention.

For instance, he noted the data showed a male, age 12, who had been before the juvenile court nine times: twice for possession and sale of drugs; twice for auto theft; once each for burglary, robbery, assault, disorderly conduct and intoxication; and, finally, for parole violation. Another, age 13, was there for the eighth time: once for assault; once because he had run away from home; once for disorderly conduct and intoxication; three times for retail theft; and twice for other theft. Harvey found this hard to believe. It was even more difficult to reconcile with the existence of extensive and many-faceted programs for youth in the state, coordinated in each county by a youth service bureau. When he talked with Gail Earl about it, she explained that one of the main purposes of the project was to identify factors common to juvenile recidivists and determine causal relationships. Harvey learned that during the past several years, about one-third of the youngsters appearing before the juvenile courts in Great State were there for other than the first time.

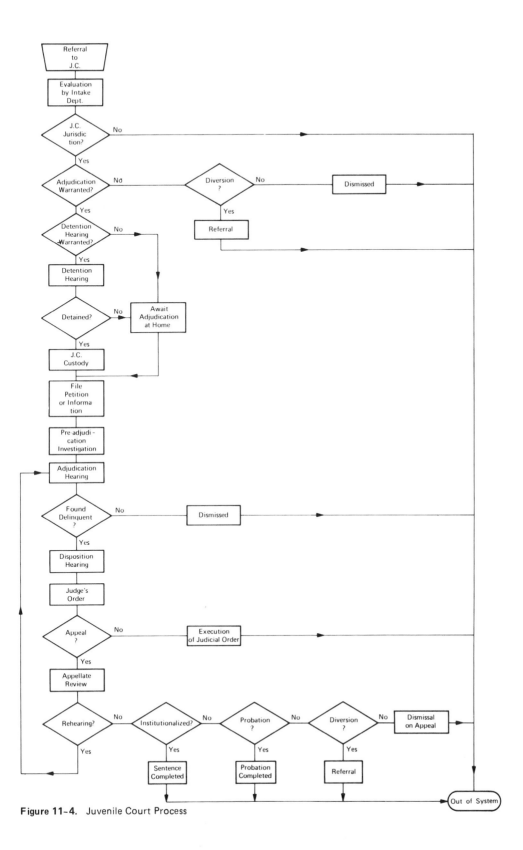

Figure 11-4. Juvenile Court Process

PAROLE

As Paul Grace continued to receive good reports about Harvey's progress—reports that coincided with his own observations—he decided that Harvey should be recommended for parole at the first date on which he would be eligible.

Parole meant that Harvey would be released from prison, subject to supervision by a parole officer, and that during the term of his parole he must meet certain conditions. The conditions imposed in Great State were similar to those found in many other states. The parolee must:

1. Remain employed;
2. Obey the law (conviction of another crime would result in automatic revocation of parole);
3. Refrain from "undesirable associations" (i.e., persons with whom he would be likely to engage in criminal activity);
4. Refrain from the use of narcotics and use alcohol only in moderation;
5. Secure permission from the parole officer to travel out of state, to own and operate a car, to change employment or residence, and to marry;
6. Neither possess nor make use of any weapon.

Parole consists of serving the remainder of one's sentence in the community. As such, it is a controlled transition from prison life to life in society. Since the period immediately following release from prison is crucial for acceptable social adjustment and integration in the community, supervision is an important element.

Such supervision is the function of a parole officer. While his concern is reintegration of the parolee into the community, there are some who view his function as more similar to law enforcement than to social work. In some localities, probation officers also serve as parole officers. Authorities do not all agree that this is in the best interests of either the parolee or the case worker. Parolees are considered to be more difficult to supervise than probationers. The ideal case load for a parole officer, according to many authorities, ranges from 35 to 50 persons. In Great State, parole and probation supervision was separated in larger communities such as Big City. In smaller communities, one person often did both.

Over two-thirds of the persons imprisoned in Great State were eventually released on parole. Few prisoners, except those with minimal sentences such as one year, served their entire term. Persons who had not been returned to prison because of repeated offenses or parole violations generally secured favorable consideration upon application for parole, provided they could present a definite plan of constructive life in the community following release. The Great State statistics compare with those of the nation as a whole, although there is great variation among the different jurisdictions.

Parole is an executive function and is generally granted by an administrative board or agency, as contrasted with probation, which is a function of the courts. As is true in most states, parole in Great State was the responsibility of a parole board. That board consisted of five persons, all of whom worked full time on the task. They were appointed by the governor with the approval of the state legislature. While they had exclusive power over parole and recommitment for parole violations, their jurisdiction did not extend to persons sentenced to death or life imprisonment, to juveniles, or to persons whose sentence was for two years or less. In the latter case, Great State statutory law required that the judge retain complete control. In the case of persons serving indeterminate sentences, the board's jurisdiction did not begin until the minimum term had been served. As noted in the *Morrissey* v. *Brewer* decision which follows, there is no uniform code of procedure for the operation of parole boards.

Morrissey v. *Brewer*
  408 U.S. 471, 92 S.Ct. 2593, 33 L.Ed. 2d 484 (1972)

MR. CHIEF JUSTICE BURGER. Petitioner asserts he received no hearing prior to revocation of his parole . . .

In practice not every violation of parole conditions automatically leads to revocation . . . . Yet revocation of parole is not an unusual phenomenon, affecting only a few parolees. It has been estimated that 35–45 percent of all parolees are subjected to revocation and return to prison. Sometimes revocation occurs when the parolee is accused of another crime; it is often preferred to a new prosecution because of the procedural ease of recommitting the individual on the basis of a lesser showing by the State.

Release of the parolee before the end of his prison sentence is made with the recognition that with many prisoners there is a risk that they will not be able to live in society without committing additional antisocial acts. Given the previous conviction and the proper imposition of conditions, the State has an overwhelming interest in being able to return the individual to imprisonment without the burden of a new adversary criminal trial if in fact he has failed to abide by the conditions of his parole. Yet the State has no interest in revoking parole without some informal procedural guarantee.

In analyzing what is due, we see two important stages in the typical process of parole revocation.

a. *Arrest of Parolee and Preliminary Hearing.* The first stage occurs when the parolee is arrested and detained, usually at the direction of his parole officer. The second occurs when a parole is formally revoked.

In our view due process requires that after the arrest, the determination that reasonable grounds exist for revocation of parole should be made by someone not directly involved in the case. The officer directly involved in making recommendations cannot always have complete objectivity in evaluating them. This independent officer need not be a judicial officer.

It will be sufficient, therefore, in the parole revocation context, if an evaluation of whether reasonable cause exists to believe that conditions of parole have been violated is made by someone such as a parole officer other than the one who has made the report of parole violations or has recommended revocation.

With respect to the preliminary hearing before this officer, the parolee should be given notice that the hearing will take place and that its purpose is to determine whether there is probable cause to believe he has committed a parole violation. The notice should state what parole violations have been alleged. At the hearing the parolee may appear and speak in his own behalf; he may bring letters, documents, or individuals who can give relevant information to the hearing officer. On request of the parolee, persons who have given adverse information on which parole revocation is to be based are to be made available for questioning in his presence. However, if the hearing officer determines that the informer would be subjected to risk of harm if his identity were disclosed, he need not be subjected to confrontation and cross-examination.

The hearing officer shall have the duty of making a summary, or digest, of what transpires at the hearing in terms of the responses of the parolee and the substance of the documents or evidence given in support of parole revocation and of the parolee's position. Based on the information before him, the officer should determine whether there is probable cause to hold the parolee for the final decision of the parole board on revocation. Such a determination would be sufficient to warrant the parolee's continued detention and return to the state correctional institution pending the final decision. No interest would be served by formalism in this process; informality will not lessen the utility of this inquiry in reducing the risk of error.

b. *The Revocation Hearing.* There must also be an opportunity for a hearing if it is desired by the parolee, prior to the final decision on revocation by the parole authority. This hearing must be the basis for more than determining probable cause; it must lead to a final evaluation of any contested relevant facts and consideration of whether the facts as determined warrant revocation. The parolee must have an opportunity to be heard and to show, if he can, that he did not violate the conditions, or, if he did, that circumstances in mitigation suggest the violation does not warrant revocation. The revocation hearing must be tendered within a reasonable time after the parolee is taken into custody. A lapse of two months, as the State suggests occurs in some cases, would not appear to be unreasonable.

We cannot write a code of procedure; that is the responsibility of each state. Most states have done so by legislation, others by judicial decision usually on due process grounds. Our task is limited to deciding the minimum requirements of due process. They include a) written notice of the claimed violations of parole; b) disclosure to the parolee of evidence against him; c) opportunity to be heard in person and to present witnesses and documentary evidence; d) the right to confront and cross-examine adverse witnesses (unless the hearing officer specifically finds good cause for not allowing confrontation); e) a "neutral and detached" hearing body such as a traditional parole board, members of which need not be judicial officers or lawyers; and f) a written statement by the fact finders as to the evidence relied on and reasons for revoking parole. We emphasize there is no thought to equate this second stage of parole revocation to a criminal prosecution in any sense; it is a narrow inquiry; the process should be flexible enough to consider evidence including letters, affidavits, and other material that would not be admissible in an adversary criminal trial.

We do not reach or decide the question of whether the parolee is entitled to the assistance of retained counsel or to appointed counsel if he is indigent. . . .

In Great State, the date of eligibility for parole might be fixed by the sentencing judge, as Judge Wolfe had done with Harvey. In other cases, statutory provisions required that one-third of the sentence must be served before a prisoner could be considered for parole. This is a frequent, although not universal, requirement.

Parole decisions in Great State were completely within the board's discretion and not reviewable in any court. Factors considered by the board when it received an application for parole included:

1. Prior history of the offender;
2. Sentence served;
3. Readiness and suitability for release;
4. Need for supervision and assistance in the community;
5. Reaction of the community to the offender's release.

The board held periodic interviews with all prisoners under its jurisdiction. The first time members met with a prisoner was two months prior to expiration of the minimum sentence or date of eligibility for parole. These were informal sessions held at the prison. Prisoners were given an opportunity to express themselves and to state reasons why they should be released on parole. The third week of each month the board also interviewed family, friends, or attorneys who wished to provide information regarding any of the parole applicants. Prison counselors assisted by advising the prisoner and his family with regard to procuring a job on release, and finding a home and community environment conducive to rehabilitation.

Therefore, in anticipation of helping Harvey with the preparation of his parole application, Paul Grace consulted Gail Earl and Michael Patrick concerning Harvey's prospects for employment in the computer field in Big City, should he be released on parole. Following some checking with colleagues in Big City, Gail reported that Harvey would not have an easy time finding a job there. Unfavorable economic conditions made job opportunities scarce. In addition, many firms refused outright to employ a person with a criminal record, especially for work in computer centers where there could be access to sensitive information. Mike said he didn't know about Big City, but he would be more than happy to continue Harvey's employment at the Ranch.

In conversation with Paul, Harvey said he would not be reluctant to start a new life in another town, especially if it were Little Town. Paul therefore investigated living arrangements. One of the employees at the Ranch offered to rent a small apartment over his garage. Harvey liked the idea. As a result, in his application for parole he indicated that his future plans included continued employment at the Ranch, continued part-time attendance at the community college, and renting the apartment in Little Town.

When the time came for his parole hearing, Harvey met with the entire board. They had available the complete institutional file compiled regarding Harvey, the presentence investigative report prepared for Judge Wolfe, and records of his employment and course work while at the Center. They asked a great many questions about his desire to remain in Little Town. While several were hesitant about continued removal of Harvey from his family, the majority found Paul's recommendations to be most persuasive. Great

State did not follow the practice of having legal counsel present to represent prisoners at parole hearings. While there has been much discussion of the advantages and disadvantages of this, there is no constitutional right to counsel at the hearing, since it is not a hearing of an adversarial nature and parole is not a right.

In informing Harvey that his request would be granted, the board members stressed that parole is not a pardon. The latter is an act of forgiveness and remission of punishment which frees the individual from responsibility to the state with respect to the remainder of his sentence. They told him that, instead, his maximum term would remain unaffected during the time he was on parole. He would not lose credit for the time spent on parole. However, should he commit a new crime and be convicted of that, he faced the loss of all time spent at liberty. It would be added to the maximum term plus the new sentence. Should he violate parole conditions, he would be entitled to a full due process hearing prior to parole revocation, as required by the United States Supreme Court. Harvey mentally determined there would be no violation. Because there were few parolees in the Little Town area, Paul Grace was assigned to serve as his parole officer. That was good news.

Harvey later learned that the Great State parole board was somewhat unusual, in that the board personally informed parole applicants of the parole decision and the reasons for it. In many jurisdictions, the prisoner merely receives written notification of either approval or rejection of his parole application.

RELEASE

Harvey's parole was a success. At the end of two years, when he was released from supervision and his sentence officially came to an end, he continued to live in Little Town and to work at the Ranch. His parole process is shown in a flow chart in Figure 11-5. Although he was happy, his criminal record denied him several opportunities in the years that followed. One such instance was especially frustrating to him. When Michael Patrick was transferred to another location, he recommended Harvey as the person best qualified to succeed him. Harvey was informed he would not be given the job because of his criminal background. Hearing of this, Paul Grace intervened. He argued strongly that the Department of Corrections should be the leader in employing rehabilitated former prisoners. It was to no avail. Although ten years later Harvey did get that very job, he could not help wondering how much his career had been held back as a result of his conviction.

When he spoke of this to Henry Law, whom he consulted in connection with the purchase of a small piece of land, Henry replied:

"Have you ever wondered where you would be if you had never been sent to Little Town?"

To Harvey, that comment had the force of the one made by Paul Grace when Harvey had talked with him about Sam.

Many years later, when Judge Wolfe came to Little Town to speak at a meeting of the civic clubs, Harvey sought her out. She did not remember him. After he had identified himself and told her of his experiences, she said:

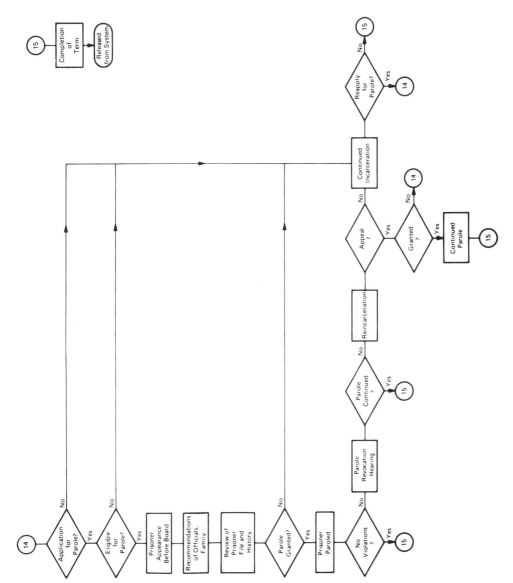

Figure 11-5. Parole Process

"We don't have as many success stories as we should, but yours is certainly one. I am happy to see that the system can work. We desperately need to know why it doesn't more often."

And with these words of Judge Wolfe, the saga of Harvey Worker comes to an end.

QUESTIONS

1. Were Judge Wolfe to consult you regarding suggestions for meeting what she terms a "desperate need," what recommendations would you make?

2. When told of her statement, Henry Law said that, with all due respect, he would have to disagree. It was his thought that the real "desperate need" was to keep people out of the criminal system. Do you agree? What recommendations do you have for accomplishing that?

3. Harvey had been confined in two different correctional institutions, albeit only briefly in one. He also had described for him a third. Which do you think had the greatest effect upon Harvey's rehabilitation? Why? What type of facility produces real correction, that is, rehabilitation? Considering your answer, how do you explain the high recidivism rate in this country? Viewed from the perspective of the juvenile population, what accounts for the reappearance rate in the juvenile court of Great State? What relation, if any, do you see between that and the entire juvenile program in that state as described by Harvey? Should juvenile repeaters continue to be kept out of the criminal system in which adult offenders are processed when their records are similar to the two Harvey reported? Why?

4. What accounts for the fact that Harvey did not become a repeat offender? Had he been rehabilitated prior to release on parole? If so, what contributed the most to that? Should parole be restricted to persons similarly situated? What benefits accrue from parole, to the prisoner or to the community? Why is parole an executive function?

5. Where else in the criminal system did you see the executive branch of the government play a role? In the description of the Great State juvenile justice system, what coordination, if any, did you find between the branches of government? What coordination, if any, did you see between the corrections subsystem and the court subsystem? Do the three—control, courts, and corrections—actually operate as subsystems within the entire criminal system? Is it truly a system?

6. Did you find any examples of the effect of the demands of the public, of society as a whole, upon the criminal system? Where?—Any examples of change within the system as society changes?

7. Can you answer Henry Law's question about what would have happened to Harvey had he not been sent to Little Town?—Or Harvey's question about how he ever got into this? Of all the persons who had some role in affecting Harvey's future, which one do you believe exerted the most influence? Why? How?

8. Compare the criminal and civil processes as "systems." What similarities, what differences do you see?—What relationships to each other?—To some larger system?

NOTES

[1] *James* v. *Wallace*, 406 F. Supp. 318 (M.D., Ala.) 1976. At 328, n. 12 states: "Federal courts in a number of states including Massachusetts . . . Maryland . . . Arkansas . . . and Mississippi . . . recently have had occasion to hold conditions in penal institutions in those states unconstitutional."

[2] *Robinson* v. *California,* 370 U.S. 660 (1962).

[3] Article I, §9, cl. 2.

[4] 28 U.S.C. §2254.

[5] *Stone* v. *Powell,* 428 U.S. 465 (1976).

[6] The President's Commission on Law Enforcement and Administration of Justice, *The Challenge of Crime in a Free Society* (Washington, D.C.: Government Printing Office, 1968).

[7] *In Re Gault,* 387 U.S. 1 (1967).

administrative
process:
occupational safety
and health

TWELVE

On that fateful August day when tragedy struck in the Cypres Department, it was quiet for the remainder of the day as employees, stunned by the death of one of the most popular persons in the department, took the rest of the day off. The atmosphere was even grimmer that evening as most of them congregated in the United Cypres Operators of America building. Initial shock soon gave way to slowly mounting anger among members of the group as they discussed the situation. Timothy O'Goode became one of the most vocal participants in the discussion. "Working on those zaggers is absolutely unsafe, and there is no reason why we should go back and use them as long as the present conditions exist. We must have some rights under that new occupational safety and health act that everybody is talking about." Robert Leader, the President of Local #135, and himself a machine operator who worked right next to John Q. Worker, took the floor. "Yes, I learned something about OSHA at that supervisory development session at Local University. This act, the Occupational Safety and Health Act of 1970, was set up to cover all businesses engaged in or affecting interstate commerce. It was passed to assure safe and healthful working conditions for all workers. Each employer has to provide a safe and healthful set of working conditions either by following the specific standards set up by the government for particular work activities, or through a general duty to provide a work place free from recognized hazards that cause or are likely to cause death or serious physical harm. We can file a complaint." Leader then stated that a state agency would take charge if it were in existence and met the federal requirements for action, but that Great State did not have an agency so qualified, and he would have to go directly to the federal office. He knew there was an area office right in Big City and that he could easily find it in the telephone directory, under the listing "U.S. Department of Labor," under which the Occupational Safety and Health Administration was subsumed. Satisfied that something was going to be done on their behalf, the union members left for their homes.

IMMINENT DANGER

When he returned home, Leader consulted the notes he had made when he attended the supervisory development session dealing with occupational safety and health. One of the first entries in the notes consisted of a discussion on imminent danger situations. The OSHA regulations provide for moves for a voluntary abatement of conditions or practice in which reasonable certainty exists that death or serious physical harm could be expected before regular enforcement procedures would take place.[1] Upon notification the local OSHA office would send out an inspector and, if an imminent danger situation were found, the employer would be asked to abate the situation voluntarily.

After considering the matter, Leader felt sure that this was an imminent danger situation, and that it was his duty to call the local OSHA office first thing in the morning.

Leader's call to OSHA early the next day was transferred by the receptionist to the area director, George Gem, who personally took all the information over the telephone. Gem soon came to the conclusion that this probably was an imminent danger situation, and promised to send one of his compliance officers over for an immediate inspection of the cypres department.

"Can I call my men off the job until this is taken care of?" asked Leader. Gem informed him that there is no right to walk off the job because of potentially unsafe work conditions. If anyone did so, the employer could take disciplinary action. There was a right, however, to refuse in good faith to expose oneself to a situation in which a "reasonable person" would conclude there is a real danger of death or serious injury in the situation, and the employer refused to take steps to eliminate that danger when asked to do so. In addition, the employees would have to be aware of the fact that there was no time for normal enforcement procedures. Since Gem promised to have an inspection made that very morning, Leader did not consider further the possibility of telling the cypres operators to walk off the job.

Tom Newboy was a bit taken aback when, in midmorning, OSHA compliance officer Conrad O'Neil appeared; Newboy had had no advance warning of the visit, but knew enough about OSHA provisions not to question the legality of the inspection. As he rushed out to join O'Neil, Newboy asked his secretary to put in a hurried call to The Firm's legal counsel, Leo Lex, and to alert Fred Famous, the president.

Newboy accompanied O'Neil on his inspection of the cypres department and made notes (just as O'Neil did) on the questioning of workers and other aspects of the inspection. After about an hour of this, O'Neil decided that there was some question about the ability of zaggers to remain intact under present work conditions. O'Neil acknowledged that there was no firm conclusion he could come to at this time, since the question was a very complex scientific one that required further analysis. At this point, however, O'Neil said he felt that suspension of the use of the zaggers in the production process would abate the imminent danger. He asked Newboy to have The Firm do this voluntarily without delay. O'Neil then advised all affected workers of the hazardous situation.

Newboy returned to the president's office with the news. Fred Famous was upset to hear of the abatement request. "If we don't use those zaggers, our whole production schedule gets thrown off. We could really take a bath, financially, on this," roared Famous. He turned to Lex and questioned him about the consequences if The Firm considered the abatement request frivolous and refused to comply. Lex pointed out that OSHA, through its regional solicitor, would apply for an injunction or other appropriate remedy to the local Federal District Court and the Court was likely to act in favor of the petitioner. Under those circumstances, all felt there was little alternative but to comply with the request of the compliance officer for abatement.

"I wonder how they heard about this," asked Fred Famous. Lex reminded Famous that The Firm was obliged to report the fatality to OSHA within 48 hours, in any case. Lex was further concerned that Famous' comments could be interpreted by others as being an attempt to find out who "blew the whistle" and punish that person subtly in the process. However, Lex remembered that anyone who felt discriminated against for reporting to OSHA could file a complaint. Action on that person's behalf by the Secretary of Labor, if favorable to the complainant, would result in penalties for the company in addition to the burden of litigation in the interim.

Leader was pleased with the outcome of the inspection, and felt he had acted properly to act quickly by making the telephone call to OSHA. However, he felt that he should personally follow through in this area of occupational safety. He knew that another inspection by the OSHA office was forthcoming, but he sensed an opportunity to play a more active role. And in any case, he felt that he should have more information about OSHA in order to do his job as president of the union local.

FILING OF COMPLAINT

Two days later Leader drove to the area office of the Occupational Safety and Health Administration, located in the Federal Building in Big City, and asked to see George Gem, the Director, with whom he had spoken on the telephone. Leader asked Gem to provide him with some information as to OSHA procedures. Gem was happy to discuss the basis for OSHA, the reasons for jurisdiction, and the various types of violations.

A *nonserious* violation, Gem said, has a direct relationship to occupational safety and health, but cannot be considered a serious violation. A *serious* violation is present if there is a substantial probability that death or serious physical harm could result from an existing condition, or from one or more practices, means, methods, operations, or processes in use in such a place of employment, unless the employer did not and could not, with the exercise of reasonable diligence, know of the presence of the violation. A *willful* violation occurs when the employer intentionally and knowingly violates the act and is aware of such violation, or is aware that a hazardous condition exists but makes no reasonable effort to eliminate that condition (even though he may not be conscious of violating the act). A *repeated* violation occurs when the same violation is committed by an employer who was cited earlier for a violation. Gem then gave Leader a copy of the form OSHA-7, in which the details of a complaint must be listed. Gem was careful to mention to Leader in this connection that his, Leader's, name would not be revealed to the employer, should he wish to keep this confidential. Gem further indicated that upon receipt of the complaint, the area director would send out a compliance officer, who would do a tour of inspection of the facilities in what was commonly called a "walkaround." If the inspection showed that plant conditions existed that did not comply with the provisions of the act, a citation would be issued for the alleged occupational safety and health violations. "Will you let us know ahead of time when you're inspecting?" said Leader. "Yes, because that would be helpful," came the response. "Representatives of the employees, usually a union officer, can accompany the compliance officer in his walkaround." Gem pointed out further that the employer would get advance warning if such warning would provide quicker abatement of a hazard, or if it would facilitate entry into the plant. Notice could not be given more than 24 hours ahead of the visit, however.

Leader returned to the plant, where he found some production problems because zaggers were not in use. Leader informed the men he met about his session at the OSHA office, and got their suggestions in filling out the complaint form. "I'm going to be the employee representative accompanying the OSHA compliance officer when he conducts his inspection, but I want to get a good idea ahead of time of the unsafe conditions we think exist. There may be other hazards, however, that we will want to point out to the compliance officer. I want to know where these are in the plant, how long they have existed, and the names and job titles of everyone who is exposed to the hazard, as well as whether The Firm has tried to remedy the hazards." Leader then indicated that he probably should have these notes arranged in the order in which the compliance officer would be likely to move through the plant. The most logical and usual route for the officer would be to follow the order of manufacture; that is, he would start where the raw materials enter the plant, and move through the usual manufacturing sequence to the point where the finished products were being shipped to customers. Leader also indicated that the compliance officer would note or comment upon findings in the order in which he proceeded. Having filled in the complaint, Leader rushed back to the OSHA office to deliver it in person, to make sure that as little time was lost as possible.

Early the next morning the telephone rang in the office of Jim Boss, the plant manager for The Firm. At the other end of the line, George Gem told Boss that another complaint had been filed by one of the employees of The Firm, alleging further unsafe conditions that violated the Occupational Safety and Health Act of 1970. Boss was informed that a compliance officer would inspect the premises of The Firm within six hours. This advance notice, although not generally done, was given in this case because it was likely to ensure the presence of appropriate representatives of the company and employees. Gem further stated that such notice is often given if it will facilitate the inspection in any way, or when special preparations are called for, such as in an inspection conducted after regular business hours. Gem then telephoned Robert Leader with the same information.

As soon as he put down the telephone, Jim Boss rushed to the office of the president of The Firm, Fred Famous, with the news. Famous immediately instructed his secretary to call Tom Newboy, the plant engineer Sam Scott, and Leo Lex. As they assembled, each participant was attentive to the information presented by Jim Boss, and each participant recognized the additional burdens upon The Firm. When Boss had finished, Famous turned to Newboy and asked, "The safety program is part of your responsibility, Tom. What's our situation with respect to this whole mess?" "Well, F.F.," responded Newboy, "you know that I've been handling all the safety matters on top of everything else in the personnel area, and it's been quite a struggle. My request for a full slot for a safety director has been in channels here for a long time. We really needed one." Newboy indicated that a better place to start would be for Leo Lex to give a short background on the statute, and what was initially required as the result of an accident (Figure 12-1).

Leo Lex took over and gave the background of the purposes of the law. "The Occupational Safety and Health Act of 1970," he said, "is also known as the Williams-Steiger Act for its two sponsors in the Congress." It was passed "to assure safe and healthful working conditions for working men and women; by authorizing enforcement of the standards developed under the Act; by assisting and encouraging the states in their efforts to assure safe and healthful working conditions; by providing for research, information, education, and training in the field of occupational safety and health; and for other purposes."[2] The two main aspects of the act affecting The Firm (as well as other companies) were the duty to provide a safe working environment, and adherence to standards developed under the Act.

"Standards? What standards?" asked Fred Famous. Leo Lex pointed out that these, like all other information about federal government action, were published in the *Federal Register*. "The Occupational Safety and Health Standards were published in Volume 39, No. 125 of the *Federal Register* on Thursday, June 27, 1974. And they're very precise and specific in most cases," said Lex. "Well, I think our association representatives in Washington should have kept us informed about all this," replied Famous. Tom Newboy mentioned that he had been collecting some information in his office but was a little bit hazy on all the specifics of the standards as they applied to all of the manufacturing operations in The Firm. "We'll have to go over those parts of the standards that refer to zaggers in greater detail." Lex further indicated that the Secretary of Labor, through regional offices of the Department of Labor, was charged with the responsibility for ensuring that the specific standards were met and that the employers discharged their general duty of providing safe working conditions. "The compliance officer will probably tour the plant, this time paying close attention to the specific conditions alleged to be a violation. As you know, we have 48 hours to report a fatality or the hospitalization of five employees, and the compliance officer would have been here anyway." Lex also noted the duty of the company to report and record specific types of injuries. He ob-

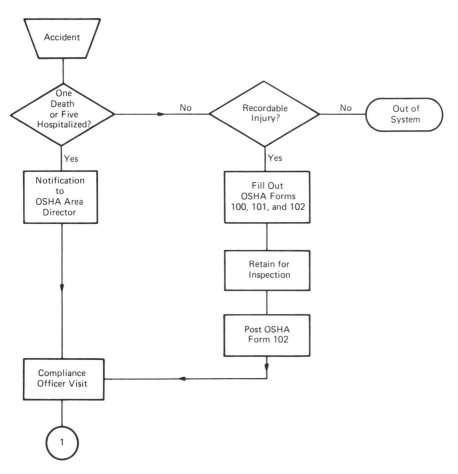

Figure 12-1. Employer Responsibilities in Occupational Injury or Illness

served that the compliance officer could take cognizance of any other unsafe conditions or practices in addition to those mentioned in the complaint. "I already know about imminent danger, but what are these other complaints?" asked Fred Famous. "Well, if he finds that we have violated one or more standards, the officer will point that out and determine the seriousness of the violation." There are four types of violations for which a citation is issued along with a possible penalty. One situation, called a *de minimis* violation, calls for a notice but no citation (see Table 12-1).

A serious violation of OSHA standards is one where the condition involves a "substantial probability of death or serious physical harm involving permanent or prolonged impairment of the body." However, a violation of this category is not determined unless the employer "knew or could have known of the violation." Lex noted that the minimum penalty for this type of violation is $500. A nonserious violation is one that has a direct bearing on the safety or health of workers but would probably not cause death or serious physical harm. The penalty may or may not be assessed in this type of violation.

TABLE 12-1. Determinations in Occupational Injury or Illness
(by Compliance Officer and Area Director)

VIOLATION TYPE	DESCRIPTION	ACTION	PENALTY (POSSIBLE)
Initial Violations			
Imminent Danger	Hazard that can cause death or serious physical harm immediately or before the imminence of the danger can be eliminated through the procedure of the Act.	Citation	Request for voluntary abatement or federal court order to abate
Serious	This violation refers to a substantial probability that death or serious physical harm will result.	Citation	$500 to $1000 for each violation
Nonserious	Violation of a standard would probably not result in death or serious physical harm.	Citation	Up to $1000 for each violation
De minimis	This violation has no direct or immediate relationship to the safety or health of an employee.	Notice	No penalty
Willful or Repeated Violations			
Willful or repeated violation	Employer intentionally or knowingly violates the act and was aware of such violation, or was aware that a hazardous condition existed and made no reason-	Citation	Up to $10,000 fine
Willful or repeated violation resulting in death	able effort to eliminate the condition (even though not conscious of violating the act).	Citation	Up to $10,000 fine and/or 6 months imprisonment

A willful violation occurs when the employer commits a knowing violation of the act, or when there was awareness of the condition with no reasonable effort to eliminate that hazard. In order for this violation to be charged, it must be definitely shown that the employer knowingly permitted the dangerous condition to exist. Penalties of up to $10,000 are provided for this type of violation.

A *repeated* violation exists when the employer was already cited by OSHA for the same violation.

All these situations are in addition to the determination of imminent danger by the OSHA office, a determination already made in the aftermath of the death of John Q. Worker.

"But can the OSHA people just come in like this?" objected Fred Famous. "Don't we have some basic rights that are being violated?" In response, Lex pulled a stack of papers out of his briefcase. He had a copy of a case typical of such situations, he said, and handed it to the president to read.

No. 75-2334

In the Matter of Establishment of: **RESTLAND MEMORIAL PARK**
990 Patton Street
Monroeville, Pa. 15146

(D.C. Civil No. 75-1189)   **Restland Memorial Park, Appellant**

On Appeal From the United States District Court
for the Western District of Pennsylvania
Submitted June 22, 1976
Before: Adams, Hunter and Weis, *Circuit Judges*

Robert E. McKee, Jr., Esq.
Feldstein Bloom Grinberg
Stein & McKee
Pittsburgh, Penna. 15219

Attorneys for Appellant

William J. Kilberg
Solicitor of Labor
Benjamin W. Mintz
Assoc. Solicitor for Occupational
Safety and Health
Michael H. Levin
Counsel for Appellate Litigation
Allen H. Feldman
Asst. Counsel for Appellate Litigation
Sidney M. Nowell
Attorney
U.S. Department of Labor
Washington, D.C.

Counsel for Appellee

OPINION OF THE COURT
(Filed July 30, 1976)

ADAMS, CIRCUIT JUDGE. During the consideration of the bills which ultimately became the Occupational Safety and Health Act of 1970 (OSHA), the intention to make the maximum use of the commerce power was repeatedly expressed by various Congressmen.[1] The Act is by its terms applicable to every "person engaged in business affecting commerce who has employees."[2] In this proceeding, a cemetery company seeks some definition of the scope of the phrase "affecting commerce." The issue is raised by way of an appeal from the district court's denial of a motion to quash a civil search warrant authorizing an inspection of the cemetery's business premises.

I.

Restland Memorial Park, a cemetery, is operated by a corporation whose shares are owned by a husband and wife. These two shareholders and their son comprise three of the four employees of the company. The cemetery is located in Pennsylvania; a very high

---

[1] See *Brennan* v. *OSHRC,* 492 F.2d 1027, 1030 (2d Cir. 1974).
[2] 29 U.S.C. §652(5) (1970).

portion of those buried in it were Pennsylvania residents; its supplies and equipment are purchased from Pennsylvania dealers. The Secretary asserts that the caskets used for the burials in Restland have often been imported into Pennsylvania, that each year several persons who died outside of Pennsylvania are buried there, and that Restland's equipment is operated on public highways.

The operations of the cemetery require the use of a backhoe, mowing machinery, and two trucks. In view of the safety hazards created by such equipment, principally amputations that result from improperly guarded mowers, the agency has assumed the responsibility of inspecting cemeteries, golf courses, and similar establishments. At Restland, however, OSHA's representative was ordered off the premises. The Secretary then sought, and obtained, an inspection warrant. Despite this, his representative was again refused entry.

Before the Secretary could obtain enforcement of his warrant from the district court, Restland petitioned that court to quash the warrant, contending that the operations of the cemetery do not bring it within the jurisdiction of the agency under the interstate commerce clause and the provisions of the Act. The district court denied the petition to quash the warrant and ordered the officials and employees of the corporation to permit an authorized safety officer to enter the premises and conduct a reasonable inspection.

Restland has appealed the decision of the district court. We have jurisdiction under 28 U.S.C. §1291.[3]

II.

Pursuant to his duties under the Act, the Secretary is authorized to enter any place of employment "affecting commerce," and to inspect that place, its structures, and equipment for violations of OSHA standards.[4] *Whether the agency is authorized to enter Restland Memorial Park depends on whether the cemetery is an employer "affecting commerce."* Restland seeks a determination of that issue prior to permitting entry by the Secretary or his representative. This Court, however, is precluded from considering that question at this stage of the proceedings.

The Occupational Safety and Health Act has created a central forum for adjudications in the Occupational Safety and Health Review Commission,[5] which is authorized to pass on all factual and statutory defenses available against the enforcement actions of the Secretary.[6]

---

[3] The present action is independent of, although ancillary to, any enforcement proceeding that may subsequently be pursued under OSHA. The order of the district court refusing to quash the warrant provides "a final and indisputable basis of action as between the [agency] and the [cemetery] . . . ." *ICC* v. *Brimson,* 154 U.S. 447, 487 (1894). The matter reverts to the processes of the Department of Labor, and there is nothing further for the district court to do. See *Cobbledick* v. *United States,* 309 U.S. 323, 329–30 (1940).

[4] 29 U.S.C. §657 (a) (1970).

[5] *Id.* §661. See *Atlantic & Gulf Stevedores* v. *OSHRC,* No. 75–1584 (3d Cir. March 26, 1976); *Frank Irey, Jr., Inc.* v. *OSHRC,* 519 F.2d 1200 (3d Cir. 1974, aff'd en banc 1975), *cert. granted,* 44 U.S.L.W. 3531 (U.S. March 22, 1976) (No. 75–749); *Budd Co.* v. *OSHRC,* 513 F.2d 201 (3d Cir. 1975) (per curiam); *Brennan* v. *OSHRC (Hanovia Lamp Div.),* 502 F.2d 946 (3d Cir. 1974).

[6] 29 U.S.C. § §651 (b) (3); 659 (a), (c) (1970).

The Review Commission would appear competent to consider the scope of the Act's coverage. If a citation is issued, and if the employer chooses to contest the citation, the Secretary is obliged to serve a formal complaint setting forth, *inter alia,* the basis for jurisdiction.[7] The Review Commission must then decide whether the agency has exceeded its jurisdiction by attempting to enforce the Act against an employer who does not affect commerce—an employer such as Restland claims to be. The decision of the Commission would then be subject to review by a Court of Appeals.[8]

Where Congress has designated a specific forum for the review of administrative action, that forum is exclusive, and a concerned party must exhaust his administrative remedies prior to seeking relief from the courts.[9] As the Supreme Court explained in *Myers* v. *Bethlehem Shipbuilding Corp.,* "[N]o one is entitled to judicial relief for a supposed or threatened injury until the prescribed administrative remedy has been exhausted."[10] Given these principles and the structure of the administrative process created by OSHA, this Court has held that the doctrine of exhaustion of administrative remedies applies under that Act.[11]

The doctrine of exhaustion of administrative remedies is well established, and is "required as a matter of preventing premature interference with the agency processes, so that the agency may function efficiently and so that it may have an opportunity to correct its own errors, to afford the parties and the courts the benefit of its experience and expertise, and to compile a record for judicial review."[12] In addition, the doctrine exemplifies judicial recognition of the autonomy of the executive branch, whose dominion the courts will not invade unless the agency has clearly exceeded its jurisdiction.[13]

In the Occupational Safety and Health Act, Congress has delegated to the Secretary of Labor broad jurisdiction under the interstate commerce clause. Because of the policy considerations underlying the doctrine of exhaustion, we conclude that *until Restland has exhausted its administrative remedies, the courts should not consider the question of the Secretary's jurisdiction.* If a citation is issued, appealed from, and then upheld by the Review Commission, Restland may, in its petition for review, present to this Court the matter of the Secretary's jurisdiction under the interstate commerce clause and the Act.[14]

---

[7] 29 C.F.R. § 2200.33 (a) (2) (1) (1975).

[8] 29 U.S.C. § 660 (1970).

[9] *Whitney Nat'l Bank* v. *Bank of New Orleans,* 379 U.S. 411, 422 (1965). See *McKart* v. *United States,* 395 U.S. 185, 193-95 (1969); *Myers* v. *Bethlehem Shipbuilding Corp.,* 303 U.S. 41, 48 (1938).
This is not to say, however, that exhaustion of remedies is required under all circumstances; when not compelled by statute, exhaustion may not be required in every instance. See *United States ex. rel. Sanders* v. *Arnold,* No. 75-1080 (3d Cir. 1976) (Adams, J., dissenting).

[10] 303 U.S. at 50-51.

[11] See *Keystone Roofing & Harold E. Sweeney Corp.* v. *OSHRC,* No. 75-2101 (3d Cir. 1976). See generally cases cited in note 5 *supra.*

[12] *Weinberger* v. *Salfi,* 422 U.S. 749, 765 (1975).

[13] *McKart,* 395 U.S. at 193-94.

[14] Prior judicial intervention would tend to disrupt a statutory scheme which is designed to provide swift issuance of abatement orders to protect employees endangered by the conditions of their work. See 29 U.S.C. § 659 (1970).

> Accordingly, the judgment of the district court will be vacated, and the proceeding remanded with instructions to dismiss for failure to exhaust administrative remedies.
>
> A True Copy:
>
> Testee:
>
> *Clerk of the United States Court of Appeals for the Third Circuit.*

COMPLIANCE OFFICER VISIT

Promptly at 3:00 p.m., Conrad O'Neil appeared at the front gate of The Firm and was immediately directed to the office of Tom Newboy in the Personnel Department. Since both men had met, O'Neil did not have to present his credentials again, but just the copy of the complaint. Newboy read over the complaint with the specific allegations of a violation of safety standards under OSHA. The allegation stated, in effect, that "The Firm permitted unsafe operation of zaggers on the cypres machine in violation of Section 1910.215 of the Occupational Safety and Health Standards."[3] O'Neil also told Newboy that he wished to review the records kept within the past year on accidents and the summary record of accidents. O'Neil reminded Newboy that the company must keep three types of records, among them OSHA Form No. 100 (Form 12-1), the "Log of Occupational Injuries and Illnesses." This form records details on each injury that occurs on the job. O'Neil stated that he would take this opportunity to inspect the entire plant, not just the cypres machine operation. He asked Newboy to call in Robert Leader as the representative of the Union, in order that Leader might accompany them through the plant on the walkaround.

When Leader reached the personnel department office, the trio left to inspect the plant. As Leader had predicted, the compliance officer chose to begin the inspection at the logical beginning point of manufacturing operations, the receiving room for raw materials. Soon after they entered, Leader pointed out some grease spots on an inclined roadway that apparently caused some slippage problems for the fork lift trucks shifting the pallets in the receiving room. Conrad O'Neil hurriedly made some notes covering this possibility. "Wait," said Newboy, "the union representative isn't supposed to butt in on the inspection, he's just supposed to watch." "No, according to the Compliance Operations Manual, he can point out alleged violations or hazards," said O'Neil. Newboy asked, "Are you going to issue a citation?" "The Manual states that I'm not required to respond as to whether a citation will be issued, but I can give some indication whether a hazard exists or not. This looks like an easily abatable hazard; I think the foreman here can correct it immediately." O'Neil jotted down some further thoughts on his inspection sheet.

The inspection proceeded without further incident until the party arrived at the cypres department. Here Leader introduced the compliance officer to several of the employees who were most familiar with the important features of the job situation. Timothy O'Goode, interviewed first, pointed out the safety guard on each one of the

Form 12-1. OSHA Form No. 100

OSHA NO. 100

LOG OF OCCUPATIONAL INJURIES AND ILLNESSES

Form Approved
OMB No. 44R 1453

RECORDABLE CASES: You are required to record information about: every occupational *death*, every nonfatal occupational *illness*; and those nonfatal occupational *injuries* which involve one or more of the following: loss of consciousness, restriction of work or motion, transfer to another job, or medical treatment (other than first aid).
More complete definitions appear on the other side of this form.

CASE OR FILE NUMBER	DATE OF INJURY OR ONSET OF ILLNESS	EMPLOYEE'S NAME (First name or initial, middle initial, last name)	OCCUPATION (Enter regular job title, not activity employee was performing when injured or at onset of illness.)	DEPARTMENT (Enter department in which the employee is regularly employed.)	DESCRIPTION OF INJURY OR ILLNESS Nature of Injury or Illness and Part(s) of Body Affected (Typical entries for this column might be Amputation of 1st joint right forefinger Strain of lower back Contact dermatitis on both hands Electrocution—body)	Injury or Illness Code See codes at bottom of page.	EXTENT OF AND OUTCOME OF CASES					
							DEATHS (Enter date of death.)	LOST WORKDAY CASES			NONFATAL CASES WITHOUT LOST WORKDAYS	TERMINATIONS OR PERMANENT TRANSFERS
								Enter a check if case involved lost workdays.	LOST WORKDAYS		(Enter a check if no entry was made in columns 8 or 9 but the case is recordable, as defined above.)	(Enter a check if the entry in columns 9 or 10 represented a termination or permanent transfer.)
									Enter number of days AWAY FROM WORK due to injury or illness.	Enter number of days of RESTRICTED WORK ACTIVITY due to injury or illness.		
							Mo./day /yr.					
(1)	(2)	(3)	(4)	(5)	(6)	(7)	(8)	(9)	(9A)	(9B)	(10)	(11)
	Mo./day /yr.											

NOTE: This is NOT a report form. Keep in the establishment for 5 years.

Company Name _____
Establishment Name _____
Establishment Address _____

Injury Code
10 All occupational injuries

Illness Codes
21 Occupational skin diseases or disorders
22 Dust diseases of the lungs (pneumoconioses)
23 Respiratory conditions due to toxic agents
24 Poisoning (systemic effects of toxic materials)
25 Disorders due to physical agents other than toxic materials)
26 Disorders associated with repeated trauma
29 All other occupational illnesses

machines, particularly the one that John Q. Worker was attending at the time of the fatal accident. "I believe this is a violation of section 1910.215 of the *Rules and Regulations of the Occupational Safety and Health Standards* covering machine guarding of abrasive wheel machinery," said O'Neil, as he sketched a diagram of the safety guard on the machine and made more notes.[4]

O'Goode then pointed out the exact procedures for unpacking the new zaggers. He demonstrated the technique used by the workers in removing the zaggers and mounting them on the machine. In addition to making notes, O'Neil took out a small camera and began taking photographs from several different angles. "Does the foreman here require the workers to do a ring test on each one of the zaggers before mounting?" asked O'Neil. "No, what's a ring test?" asked O'Goode. The compliance officer explained that when the zagger is removed from the packing, after all the sawdust or packing material is removed, the zagger should be tapped with a nonmetallic instrument to determine whether it gives a clear sound. "Remember that organic bonded zaggers sound a little different from the Vitrified or silicate types," he said. The compliance officer remarked that apparently this procedure was not followed. "I could have you sign a statement to that effect, but since I am interviewing you publicly and others have heard your remark, I don't think that's necessary," he said as he scribbled more notes.

The rest of the tour proceeded without incident, and eventually the inspection was completed. As they returned to the Personnel Department offices, O'Neil mentioned to Newboy that the *Compliance Operations Manual* called for a closing conference after the completion of the inspection.[5] He turned to Leader and said, "We sit down separately with the employer to inform him of all the conditions we feel may be violations of the act." "Do you have a closing conference with the employee representative?" asked Leader. "Generally not, since you have participated in the inspection and already given us your comments. However, if you request a closing conference, we can sit down and describe the general results of the inspection and any alleged violations that could result in a citation." Leader thought for a minute and decided that, together with other employees, he had pretty much pointed out all of the possible violations that they thought existed. He left the room.

O'Neil and Newboy then sat down to go over the list of violations. "This is to give the employer an opportunity to correct the violations as soon as possible," said O'Neil. "Mr. Newboy, what do you think is the length of time it will take to correct these alleged violations? Also, how much do you think it will cost to do so in each case?" O'Neil paid close attention to Newboy's responses, since these would help to determine how long a period would be available for abatement and what penalty would be assessed, if any. O'Neil avoided any specific statement about a citation (except, of course, the reference to the easily correctable hazard he noted), nor would he discuss a length of time for abatement or a specific possible penalty. "Wait until I call in Sam Scott, the plant engineer. He should be able to give a better reading on what it will take to get this done." When Scott arrived he listened intently to the recitation of alleged hazards seen by the compliance officer during the inspection. "We should be able to fix things up to your satisfaction within a week," said Scott. "And I estimate the cost for implementing these changes to be just under $1000."

At that point Conrad O'Neil thanked both men and returned to his office in the Federal Building.

DETERMINATION OF VIOLATION

The next morning Conrad O'Neil sat down with George Gem to discuss his findings. O'Neil knew that he could not issue a citation for a violation and assess a penalty without the direction of the area director to that effect, except in the case of an easily abatable hazard that is noticed, or in the case of what is known as an "instant citation" procedure. Both of these are for minor problems. The director's approval for a citation is needed for serious violations. The two men also knew that they were required to issue a citation promptly following an inspection; this action must follow with "reasonable promptness," a time period that has been interpreted as no more than three days.

O'Neil's notes indicated two violations that he discovered:

1. Violation of §1910.215 (d) (1) in that no "ring" test was made on the zagger prior to mounting on the wheel.
2. Violation of §1910.215 (b), whereby the safety guard mounted above the wheel left more than the maximum exposure permitted by the standards.[6]

O'Neil felt the standards were quite clear on these points and that the events constituted a violation of those standards.

Gem asked O'Neil his opinion of the level of violation. "This is clearly not a de minimis matter—I cleared up one of those on the spot," said O'Neil. He indicated that it was neither a willful nor a repeated violation, since there was no evidence that the employer committed an "intentional and knowing violation of the act or was conscious of that fact, or if not conscious of the act that he was aware that the condition existed and made no reasonable effort to eliminate it." There was no earlier violation so this could not be a repeated one, O'Neil told Gem. He felt this was more than a nonserious violation, since that category indicated no probability of serious injury or death.

O'Neil and Gem then sat down with the OSHA Compliance Manual and found the detailed formulas and factors used in calculating penalties for the violation. They started calculating at a maximum $1000 penalty for each violation. (A penalty adjustment up to a maximum of 50 percent is allowed based upon the history of violations in the past, size of the company, and employer good faith.) The men calculated that The Firm would receive the maximum 50 percent adjustment so that the penalty for each of the two violations was $500, for a total of $1000.

Had the violation been determined by the two men to be not serious, the penalty would have been calculated according to a more complicated formula, which might provide more reductions than the serious penalty. In addition to the same penalty adjustment as serious violations called for, there would be an adjustment with respect to gravity of violation, as well as an abatement credit which would reduce the adjusted penalty up to 50 percent, if the violation were corrected by the employer within the stated time period.

Form 12-2. OSHA-2 (Citation Form)

U.S. DEPARTMENT OF LABOR
OCCUPATIONAL SAFETY AND HEALTH ADMINISTRATION

CITATION and NOTIFICATION OF PENALTY

¹ ISSUANCE DATE	² OSHA NUMBER
³ REGION	⁴ AREA	⁵ PAGE OF

PENALTIES ARE DUE WITHIN 15 DAYS OF RECEIPT OF THIS NOTIFICATION UNLESS CONTESTED (See enclosed Booklet)

This Section May Be Detached Before Posting

OSHA AREA OFFICE MUST DETACH THIS SECTION BEFORE MAILING OR FILING IN CASE FILE

TYPE OF VIOLATION-S	CITATION NO.

INSPECTION DATE:

INSPECTION SITE:

TO:

THE LAW REQUIRES that a copy of this Citation be posted immediately in a prominent place at or near the location of the violation(s) cited below. The Citation must remain posted until the violations cited below have been corrected, or for 3 working days (excluding weekends and Federal holidays) whichever is longer.

This citation describes violations of the Occupational Safety and Health Act of 1970. The penalty(ies) listed below are based on these violations. You must correct the violations referred to in this citation by the dates listed below and pay the penalties proposed, unless within 15 working days (excluding weekends and Federal holidays) from your receipt of this citation and penalty you mail a notice of contest to the U.S. Department of Labor Area Office at the address shown above. (See the enclosed booklet which outlines your responsibilities and courses of action and should be read in conjunction with this form.)

ITEM NUMBER STANDARD, REGULATION OR SECTION OF THE ACT VIOLATED: DESCRIPTION	DATE BY WHICH VIOLATION MUST BE CORRECTED	PENALTY	NBR INST.	REC	MOD

¹⁴ AREA DIRECTOR

NOTICE TO EMPLOYEES — The law gives an employee or his representative the opportunity to object to any abatement date set for a violation if he believes the date to be unreasonable. The contest must be mailed to the U.S. Department of Labor Area Office at the address shown above within 15 working days (excluding weekends and Federal holidays) of the receipt by the employer of this citation and penalty.

EMPLOYER DISCRIMINATION UNLAWFUL — The law prohibits discrimination by an employer against an employee for filing a complaint or for exercising any rights under this Act. An employee who believes that he has been discriminated against may file a complaint no later than 30 days after the discrimination with the U.S. Department of Labor Area Office at the address shown above.

EMPLOYER RESPONSIBILITIES AND COURSES OF ACTION — The enclosed booklet outlines employer responsibilities and courses of action and should be read in conjunction with this notification.

TOTAL PENALTY FOR THIS CITATION
Make check or Money Order Payable To: "DOL OSHA" Indicate OSHA No. on Remittance

TOTAL PENALTY FOR THIS PAGE

CITATION AND NOTIFICATION OF PENALTY

OSHA 2 REV. 5/76

◀ DETACH HERE

The men remembered that a de minimus violation called for no penalty. The willful violation calls for a maximum fine of up to $10,000 for each violation. O'Neil and Gem had never assessed this type of violation and knew that it was very rarely found. This type of violation occurs only where it was clear that an employer permitted the violation intentionally and knowingly, or was aware that a hazardous condition existed and made no reasonable attempt to correct it.

The two OSHA officials then had to decide on the abatement period. It was clear that a long complicated program to eliminate the true hazards was not necessary, and the two men agreed that a period of fifteen (15) days was appropriate.

Gem then had his secretary fill out the citation form, OSHA-2 (Form 12-2). It described the alleged violations and specified conditions of posting. Two copies were sent to the employer, along with a booklet of information which included details about the conditions under which the employer can contest the citation, either in an informal discussion with the area director of the U.S. Department of Labor, or in a formal appeal to the OSHA Review Commission in Washington, D.C. If neither of these steps is taken, the citation is considered a final order of the Review Commission and is not subject to review by any court or agency. An appeal to the OSHA Review Commission must be made within 15 working days and can contest the citation of the violation itself, the penalty assessed, or the abatement period. A contest of the citation by the employer stops the abatement period, which then does not begin to run until a final order of the Commission.

The secretary finished typing up the forms, had them signed by Gem, and sent them off immediately by certified mail to The Firm.

The arrival of the citation at the office of The Firm caused a certain amount of consternation in the offices. Tom Newboy immediately took a copy of OSHA-2 and posted it in a conspicuous place near the site of the fatal accident. Any failure to do so would have incurred the penalties stipulated under the act.

APPEAL

When Newboy returned to his office, there was a message asking him to join the meeting the president was holding with Leo Lex. Fred Famous was visibly upset by the whole situation, as he had always felt himself to be solicitous of the welfare of his employees, and looked upon this citation as impugning his good motives in personnel matters. "I don't think we're getting a fair shake on this," said Famous, "what can we do about it?" Leo Lex outlined the entire procedure from beginning to end (Figure 12-2) and pointed out some immediate steps, such as discussion with the area director, or formal appeal to the Occupational Safety and Health Review Commission. Fred Famous believed that the area director had already made up his mind and that it would be fruitless to have a discussion with him. He asked what the Review Commission was like and what it did.

Lex described the procedure for appeal and identified the composition of the Commission. The OSHA Review Commission is a three-person independent board appointed by the President of the United States to make final determinations on OSHA citations. The Review Commission has the power to "affirm, modify or vacate" the

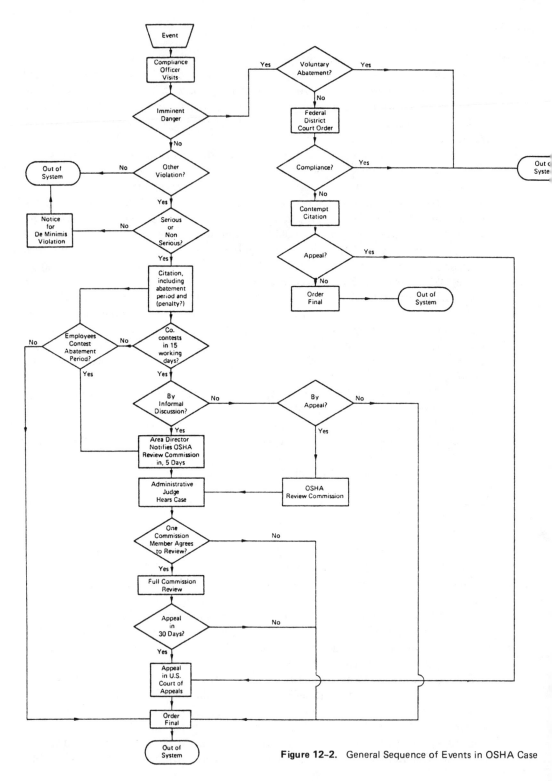

Figure 12-2. General Sequence of Events in OSHA Case

cited violations, penalties, or abatement period orders. Upon appeal, the case is heard by an OSHA Administrative Law Judge in one of nine offices strategically placed throughout the United States. After a hearing on the matter, one of the judges issues a decision. After the decision either the employer or a representative of the employees may request a review by the commission, but a review does not take place unless a commissioner requests a full commission review of the judge's decision within thirty days after that decision has taken place. When the commission hears a case, it must issue a majority decision. If no review is requested the decision becomes a final order of the commission after the end of the thirty day period. At this point an appeal is possible to the United States Court of Appeals in the circuit in which the case arises.

"It is my opinion that we should simply accept the abatement period and pay the fine," said Lex.

"This is an important matter of principle for me and I want you to contest the citation," stormed Fred Famous. Lex then informed him that a copy of the appeal and any supporting documents must be given to the authorized employee representative.

Back in the cypres room the employees gathered around the posted notice and commented in various ways. One of them stated his opinion that the fines for the incident were much too low and insulted the memory of a fine man. There was a suggestion of an appeal by the Union representatives on this matter but Leader informed them that the employees could contest only the matter of the abatement period and not the amount of the fine levied. He further pointed out the fact that the abatement period did not begin to run until the date of the Commission's final order, and he happened to know that there was quite a backlog in these cases. That could mean that the company could have something like six months or more before they were required to institute the changes that would bring the working conditions up to the standards required by the act.

At the direction of Fred Famous, Lex proceeded with the appeal and filed it within the 15-day period required by the statute. Lex also provided a copy of the appeal and all support documents to Leader, the authorized employee representative. This, too, was as mandated by the law. Had he not appealed within the time set, the citation would have become a final order of the Commission and would not have been subject to review.

Two weeks after the appeal was filed a Notice of Hearing was mailed to The Firm. It contained information as to

1. Time, place, and nature of the hearing.
2. The legal authority under which the hearing would be held.
3. Specification of the issues of fact and law.
4. The designation of a hearing examiner appointed under 5 U.S.C. 3105 to preside.

Immediately upon receipt of the notice, Lex began preparing for the hearing.

The case was duly assigned to Mark Sensor, one of the Administrative Law Judges appointed for the specific purpose of hearing appeals from citations under OSHA. The hearing procedure allows for the filing of briefs for the record and presenting evidence, even from the employees' representative. After the hearing Sensor set to work on his decision and issued it within two weeks, a fairly short period in these matters.

No OSHA Commissioner requested a Commission review of the decision within 30 days; the decision, therefore, became a final order of the Commission. Lex told Famous that this was the usual situation as only about 20 percent of the decisions were ever reviewed by the commission. When asked by Famous whether there was any further recourse, Lex noted that the final order of the commission was subject to review by the U.S. Court of Appeals. This review was even rarer, as only about 1 percent of the decisions ever went as far as the Court of Appeals. Lex added that when these appeals are carried that far, the U.S. Department of Justice argues the government's case.

At this point Fred Famous was willing to accept the advice given him earlier by Lex to accept the stipulations of the citation and pay the fine. He directed Lex and Newboy to proceed with action in conformity with the OSHA final order.

QUESTIONS

1. Legislation such as OSHA has what may be inevitable consequences in our society. What impact is likely upon the various constituencies involved?

2. The standards promulgated under OSHA are extensive and specific. What are the advantages of this approach?—Disadvantages?

3. Local OSHA citations become final if no appeal is made within the strict time limit of 15 days. Are there any problems with this? Can you think of ways in which problems, if any, can be overcome?

NOTES

[1] 29 CFR 1903.13
[2] Pub.L 91–596 (29 USC 65) et seq., 84 Stat 1590 et seq.
[3] 29 CFR 1910.215
[4] 29 CFR 1910.215
[5] *Compliance Operations Manual* (Washington, D.C.: U.S. Government Printing Office, (1975).
[6] 29 CFR 1910.215 (b) and (d) (1).

torts

THIRTEEN

A tort in the legal sense is a civil wrong usually arising from an act that harms. The term comes from the Latin *tortus,* or twisted, implying conduct that is not straight or right. A tort has always been difficult to define. Most of the definitions have focused upon what it is not; it has been described as an act that is neither a crime nor a breach of a contract, that provides a basis for legal action.

In this situation the best definition may be an operational one—that is, a definition that points to actual instances of behavior and lets those examples combine to provide the definition. This entire chapter, then, defines a tort.

There are various ways of classifying torts, including the following method based upon the originating act:

1. Intentional;
2. Nonintentional:
   (a) Negligence,
   (b) Strict liability;
3. Combinations of the above.

All torts involve some act (possibly words as well as physical movement) or an omission when there is a duty to act. The act must be shown to cause an injury to a party who can recover monetary damages in a civil legal action as a result.

What makes a great deal of difference in the legal action, however, is the variation between the categories of torts in terms of what is required in developing the cause of action in court. Different standards of care, scope of duty, and burden of proof are present.

INTENTIONAL TORTS

Intentional torts may be subdivided into two categories: torts to the person, and torts to property. Each of the two categories has a variety of examples with some unique elements and each has the same range of variation in terms of the defenses that are possible to raise or any specific privileges that arise in the situation.

Torts to the Person

Torts to the person involve the actual invasion of the life space of an individual or the threat of doing so.

Battery   Battery is an intentional touching without consent. There must be some volitional movement by a person; it must be shown that the actor intended the harmful touching of another or must have known that the harmful effect would follow. If, however, the actor actually intended to touch A but touches B instead, no matter, for courts will apply the "transfer of intent doctrine" to fix liability on the toucher for the battery. Reasonable damages as the result of the injury will be awarded by the court.

Assault   The tort of assault arises from a menacing movement that makes one apprehensive of one's personal safety; assault does not involve a touching although mere words alone will not be enough to constitute an assault. For an assault to take place there must be an intentional act that results in placing a person in apprehension of an immediate offensive or harmful touching. Apprehension is sufficient to show the tort even if the person threatened knows there may be a way out.

These two are conceptual categories under common law. Many jurisdictions combine the two under the term assault.

False imprisonment   A confinement of a person within fixed boundaries for some period of time as a result of an intentional act is the tort of false imprisonment. Confinement by actual or threatened physical force to a person or a member of his family or the exclusion of a person from his home all represent confinement. There may also be confinement through the use of mere words, when there is an assertion of legal authority, as in an arrest. There is no confinement, and therefore no tort, if the person either does not know he is confined or is aware that there is a reasonable means of escape.

Defense of Privileged Invasions

Situations can exist in which invasion of personal interests, even though intentional, are not actionable torts.

Consent   One of the most common of these is when a person consents to an invasion; there may be actual consent or consent may be implied from conduct (apparent consent). A third type of consent may be implied by law as when an operation is necessary for the saving of a person's life if the person is unable to give consent. There is no consent, however, in a situation where the actor goes beyond the act the person understood would take place. Under the doctrine of informed consent, for instance, a physician has a duty to inform the patient completely of the dangers inherent in the treatment. There is no consent, furthermore, if such consent were obtained under duress or fraud.

Self-defense   Reasonable reactions to threats of bodily harm when the force is not likely to cause death or serious bodily injury are available to one acting in self-defense. There is a duty to retreat or try to explain if the threat arises through negligence or mistaken identity.

The use of force likely to cause death or serious bodily harm in self-defense is available to a person who can reasonably believe that he is under immediate threat of death or serious bodily harm. There is, however, a duty to retreat although in some states there is no duty to retreat in one's home or when it would be dangerous to the person. A defense of third persons would generally fall under the same guidelines with the additional factor that there be a socially recognized duty to protect a third person and a belief that the third person is not able to defend himself.

Defense of real or personal property   Unprivileged intrusions upon property may be resisted by force not likely to cause serious bodily harm or death if such force is believed necessary. There must first be a demand, however, that the intruder cease and desist. Deadly force can be used only in defense of a dwelling place and only when there is a threat of serious bodily harm or death to the resident. Mechanical devices such as traps or electric fences may be used in defense of property only when such means are reasonable and customary, adequate warning is given, and an intrusion does in fact threaten serious bodily harm or death to the owner.

Reasonable and nondeadly force can be used to regain personal property unlawfully taken (a pickpocket case) or when someone has been wrongfully dispossessed of his land. When there has been no initial wrongful dispossession redress must be through the courts.

Arrest   The extent of privileged actions in arrest situations depends upon whether a warrant has or has not been issued, whether the actor is an officer of the law or a private citizen, and whether the original act is a felony or a misdemeanor.

There is no tort liability for an arrest under a warrant free of defects that a reasonable man might discover and the person named in the warrant is the person arrested (again within a reasonable range of mistakes). Liability for arrests without a warrant varies. If an officer of the law has a reasonable belief that a felony has been committed he may arrest a person he suspects of committing the felony. A private citizen may make an arrest without a warrant only if a felony has in fact been committed and he has a reasonable belief that the person arrested did commit the felony. Both officers and private citizens are under the same constraints with respect to a misdemeanor. There must have been a misdemeanor committed in their presence and the person arrested must in fact be guilty. Some jurisdictions allow reasonable belief of guilt as grounds for an officer to arrest without liability.

Torts to Property

Invasion of interests in real and personal property are known as trespass or conversion. As with other kinds of torts there are privileged invasions and defenses.

Trespass to realty   Intentional invasion of a right to possession of land by actual entry or failure to leave when required is actionable. Only the lessee may bring an action during the term of the lease.

Of increasing importance is the consideration of rights to air space above the land. Courts vary in the designation of the extent of rights—potential or actual use by the landowner may be the determining factors but legitimate invasions can be privileged (aircraft are being put in this category increasingly often).

Trespass or conversion   Personal property interests may be invaded by dispossession, theft, or destruction of a chattel. Dealing with stolen property or misdelivering it is also basis for a tort action. Recovery in trespass is for damages while conversion actions bring recovery for the value of the chattel plus damages.

Defenses or privileged invasions   One can enter land to recover dispossessed chattels with reasonable nondeadly force (except when it is his own fault). Such action is also privileged if entry is necessary to avert a danger to the public (but not a public nuisance). There is a privilege to enter land to abate a private nuisance if there is first a demand that the nuisance be abated.

NEGLIGENCE

This area of torts provides more legal action than any other; court calenders are often jammed with personal injury suits.

A negligence action looks to four elements that must be present to provide a basis for recovery:

1. Duty to conform to a certain standard of care;

2. Failure to conform to that standard;

3. Causal connection between conduct and injury;

4. Actual damage or loss.

Of all four elements the most complex is the question of the duty owed.

Duty

The duty generally owed by one person to another is the "duty of due care" or what a "reasonable person" may be expected to do. This may, at times, be supplemented by standards imposed by statutes or court decision.

The duty of due care means that which the reasonable individual might objectively follow in the circumstances under study. Conditions do make a difference: the greater the risk involved or skill needed, the higher the standard. Physicians or lawyers, for instance, are expected to follow a higher standard than a layperson in certain circumstances.

There may be duties imposed by statutory or case law that are in addition to the basic duty of due care. Violation of the statute would be negligence *per se,* if the legislature intended the statute to stop those acts committed. Traffic violations may be the basis for negligence per se or the selling of liquor to an intoxicated person may make the seller liable for third party injuries. An employer may be liable for a tortious act committed by an employee in the course of employment (*respondeat superior*). In many states parents are now liable for the torts of their children (where they were not so liable under common law). Bailees for hire are at least liable for exercising due care but may even be strictly liable.

Under certain circumstances there may be a duty of care standard different from or less than the level required of a reasonable individual. Occupiers of land, for instance, may have limited liability. Generally there is no liability to those outside the land except for due care to inspect things like fences or protruding trees. With respect to trespassers, the occupier is under no duty to unknown trespassers; the occupier must exercise due care with respect to all risks for known trespassers and risks of serious bodily harm for constant trespassers (those who are in the habit of doing so). The standard is higher in most jurisdictions with respect to young children who trespass upon land containing an "attractive nuisance." Here the occupier must exercise due care to protect immature infants from artificial conditions with a risk of serious bodily harm.

Businesses must be alert also to the standard of care to be exercised with respect to persons who come onto the business premises for a specific purpose. Such persons are known as "invitees." The duty of the occupier of the premises is to inspect and discover any invitees, any natural or artificial conditions that may cause harm, and warn invitees of these or make the conditions safe.

The *scope* of the duty owed is another difficult problem for the legal system to solve. Much of the activity in negligence cases may revolve around the question—to whom is the duty of care owed. A classic case (*Palsgraf* v. *Long Island R. Company,* 248 N.Y. 339) held that the duty of care extended to only a "foreseeable plaintiff" or one who was in a foreseeable "zone of danger." A much broader view is that the duty of care extends to anyone injured as the proximate result of a breach of duty. This latter view has become the accepted approach in most jurisdictions at the present time.

Determination of duty owed becomes even more difficult in a complex, technologically dependent world, as the following case demonstrates.

Dreisonstok v. Volkswagenwerk, A.G.
489 F. 2d 1066 (1974)

DONALD RUSSELL, Circuit Judge:

The plaintiff, along with her mother, sues a car manufacturer for so-called "enhanced" injuries sustained by her when the Volkswagen microbus in which she was riding crashed into a telephone pole. The microbus had passed the crest of a small hill and was proceeding down the grade at the time of the accident. When the vehicle passed the crest of the hill, the driver noted that his speed was about 40 miles an hour. As the vehicle continued down the hill, the bus began "picking up some speed, a little too much." To reduce his speed, the driver attempted to downshift the vehicle. Because he had some difficulty in locating the gearshift lever, the driver took his "eyes off the road" and in some way "pulled the steering wheel" causing the vehicle to veer "to the right" into "the driveway". The plaintiff screamed, causing the driver to look up. As the driver did, he "saw a telephone pole headed right toward us". He tried to cut back into the road but there "was an oncoming vehicle the other way, so it was either the telephone pole or another vehicle." He chose the telephone pole. The bus hit the pole on its right front. The plaintiff was seated in the center of the seat, next to the driver, with her left leg under her. As a result of the impact, her right leg was caught between the back of the seat and the dashboard of the van and she was apparently thrown forward. She sustained severe injuries to her ankle and femur. She seeks to recover for her injuries, and her mother for medical expenses, from the vehicle manufacturer, contending that the latter was guilty of negligent design in the location of the gearshift in its vehicle and in the want of crashworthiness of its vehicle. The action was tried without a jury. The District Court dismissed the claim relating to the gearshift but concluded that the defendant manufacturer had been guilty of negligence in failing to use due care in the design of its vehicle by providing "sufficient energy-absorbing material or devices or 'crush space,' if you will, so that at 40 miles an hour the integrity of the passenger compartment would not be violated", and that, as a result, the injuries of the plaintiff were enhanced "over and above those injuries which the plaintiff might have incurred." From judgment entered on the basis of that conclusion in favor of the plaintiff and her mother, the defendants have appealed. We reverse.

The correctness of the finding by the District Court that the defendant manufacturer was guilty of negligent design in this case depends on the determination of what extent a car manufacturer owes the duty to design and market a "crashworthy" vehicle, one which, in the event of a collision, resulting accidentally or negligently from the act of another and not from any defect or malfunction of the vehicle itself, protects against unreasonable risk of injury to occupants. The existence and nature of such a duty is a legal issue, for resolution as a matter of law. So much all the authorities agree. There are, however, two fairly definite lines of conflicting authority on whether there is such a duty. One group of which *Evans,** is the leading authority, holds that no such duty rests on the manufacturer, since the "intended use" of an automobile does not extend to collisions. The other, while relieving the manufacturer of any duty to design an accident-proof vehicle, would impose a duty to use reasonable care in the design and manufacture of its product so as "to eliminate any unreasonable risk of foreseeable injury" as a result of a collision, for which the manufacturer may not be responsible. *Larsen* is the primary authority for this rule.

. . .

In arguing in favor of liability, the appellees stress the foreseeability in this mechanical age of automobile collisions, as affirmed in numerous authorities, and would seemingly deduce from this a duty on the car manufacturer to design its vehicle so as to guard against injury from involvement of its vehicle in any anticipated collisions. The mere fact, however, that automobile collisions are frequent enough to be foreseeable is not sufficient in and of itself to create a duty on the part of the manufacturer to design its car to withstand such collisions *under any circumstances.* Foreseeability, it has been many times repeated, is not to be equated with duty; it is, after all, but one factor, albeit an important one, to be weighed in determining the issue of duty. Were foreseeability of collision the absolute litmus test for establishing a duty on the part of the car manufacturer, the obligation of the manufacturer to design a crash-proof car would be absolute, a result that *Larsen* itself specifically repudiates.

The key phrase in the statement of the *Larsen* rule is "*unreasonable risk* of injury in the event of a collision", not foreseeability of collision. The latter circumstance is assumed in collision cases under the *Larsen* principle; it is the element of "unreasonable risk" that is uncertain in such cases and on which the determination of liability or no liability will rest. It would patently be unreasonable "to require the manufacturer to provide for every conceivable use or unuse of a car." Nader & Page, Automobile Design and the Judicial Process, 55 Cal.L.Rev. 645, 646. Liability for negligent design thus "is imposed only when an unreasonable danger is created. Whether or not this has occurred should be determined by general negligence principles, which involve a balancing of the likelihood of harm, and the gravity of harm if it happens against the burden of the precautions which would be effective to avoid the harm." In short, against the likelihood and gravity of harm "must be balanced in every case the utility of the type of conduct in question." The likelihood of harm is tied in with the obviousness of the danger, whether latent or patent, since it is frequently stated "that a design is not unreasonably dangerous because the risk is one which anyone immediately would recognize and avoid." The purposes and intended use of the article is an even more important factor to be considered. After all, it is a commonplace that utility of the design and attractiveness of the style of the car are elements which car manufacturers seek after and by which buyers are influenced in their selections. . . .

In summary, every case such as this involves a delicate balancing of many factors in order to determine whether the manufac-

---

Larsen v. *General Motors Corporation,* (391 F.2d p. 498); *Evans* v. *General Motors Corporation,* (7th Cir. 1966) 359 F.2d 822, 824, cert. denied 385 U.S. 836, 87 S. Ct. 83, 17 L.Ed.2d 70.

turer has used ordinary care in designing a car, which, giving consideration to the market purposes and utility of the vehicle, did not involve unreasonable risk of injury to occupants within the range of its "intended use".

. . .

It, perhaps, may not be amiss to note that there is not substantial evidence to sustain a finding that as a result of the design of the microbus the plaintiff's injuries were enhanced. *Cf., Yetter* v. *Rajeski, supra,* at pp. 108-109 (364 F.Supp.). In fact, the record seems clear that in any event the plaintiff, who had made no endeavor to protect herself with a seat belt, would have received severe injuries, irrespective of the type of vehicle she may have been riding in. There was testimony—which was not seriously questioned—that experiments conducted under the auspices of the Department of Trans-portation indicated that "the average barrier equipment velocity for fatalities, the mean velocity is only 33 miles per hour. . . ." It may be that in every case the injuries may be somewhat different but any "head-on" collision at a speed of 40 miles an hour or more will result in severe injuries to the occupants of a vehicle and, certainly in 1968, no design short of an impractical and exorbitantly expensive tank-like vehicle (*see, Alexander* v. *Seaboard Air Line Railroad Company, supra,* 346 F.Supp. 320) could have protected against such injuries; in fact, it is doubtful that even such a vehicle could have. Can it be said that a manufacturer in 1968 must have, in its design, so built its vehicle as to protect against such an "unreasonable risk of injury"? We think not.

Reversed and remanded with directions to the District Court to enter judgment in favor of the appellants-defendants.

Failure to Conform

A breach of duty occurs when the conduct of a defendant in a negligence action can be shown to fall short of the standard of care required. In some instances the mere fact that an act takes place is evidence enough of the breach of duty. The doctrine of *res ipsa loquitur* (Latin for "the thing speaks for itself") may be invoked for showing breach of duty. This concept of liability, however, requires four specific factors:

1. A device in the prior exclusive control of the defendant;
2. An event that would not have happened in the exercise of due care;
3. No voluntary act by the plaintiff contributing to the event;
4. The event is more readily explained by the defendant than the plaintiff.

Some courts look upon *res ipsa loquitur* as permitting an inference of negligence while other courts view it as a presumption that is rebuttable. In the latter case the burden of proof shifts to the defendant to obtain a satisfactory explanation.

Cause

A further necessary element for the establishment of negligence is to show that the action of the defendant was the actual and proximate cause of the injury. Actual cause is shown if the plaintiff would not have been injured but for the act of the defendant. If acts of a third party combine with those of the defendant and the plaintiff would not have been injured except for the two acts occurring together, both acting parties may still be liable. If either defendant alone is a material factor in causing the injury, both are still liable.

Proximate cause   Demonstrating an act as causing an injury is not enough to establish liability—there must also be a determination that the act was the *proximate* cause of the injury. If there is direct causation (no intervening forces) there is little doubt of proximity even though there may be a long chain of events. It makes no difference that such a sequence may have been entirely unforeseen (although courts sometimes draw the line at some reasonable point).

Intervening acts   Most of the difficulty in determining liability comes when there are intervening forces between the original act of the defendant and the injury sustained by the plaintiff. If the intervening act is a normal or expected one, any aggravation of injury does not usually relieve the defendant of liability. Injury as part of a rescue or poor medical attention might be deemed foreseeable or one of the common risks (determined by the jury). The kinds of intervening forces that relieve the defendant of liability are unforeseeable results or "Acts of God."

Actual Damage or Loss

The last element is, perhaps, the easiest of the four to determine insofar as occurrence is concerned, but it is more difficult to convert damage or injury to a monetary figure. How much is a life, limb, or reputation worth? The need to provide specific answers here taxes the abilities of all involved in the calculation of legal damages.

Defenses in Negligence Actions

If a party is injured under a set of circumstances but understood the dangers to be met and voluntarily undertook them, it may be said that the party expressly or impliedly consented to take the chances involved. This is *assumption of the risk*. Most courts hold, for instance, that spectators at a hockey game assume the risk of flying pucks.

Agreements holding one party free from liability (such as releases or waivers) may be upheld if the bargainers had equal power, but it is thought to be against public policy for disadvantaged parties in bargaining to be bound by such agreements. Even if such agreements are valid they are not so in "willful" or "gross" negligence.

Contributory negligence is conduct of a party that helps to cause his injuries and, as a result, serves as a bar to recovery. The standard of self-care to be met by a plaintiff is that of the reasonable individual, or that behavior required by statute (such as the use of seat belts in an automobile). Contributory negligence alone serves as a defense, unless other factors are present so that contributory negligence would not bar recovery. If the defendant had the *last clear chance* of knowingly avoiding the accident and did not, the plantiff would not be barred, despite his negligence.

There is a trend toward the determination by the court of relative contribution to an accident by the parties. Under the doctrine of *comparative negligence* recovery would be allowed according to the proportion of the contribution to the accident.

STRICT LIABILITY

Legal policy holds that there are some situations in which an injured party must recover, even though there was no intent or negligence on the part of a defendant. Absolute liability exists for the act or omission even if it is otherwise legally and morally correct. Strict liability, in general, requires the same elements as does an action under negligence, with the important addition of the existence of an absolute duty to make a situation safe.

Needless to say, there is good reason for restricting the scope of this category of torts, and courts are reluctant to expand coverage.

Scope of Liability

There is an absolute duty to make an "extra-hazardous" activity safe for "foreseeable" plaintiffs. The danger that comes from the extra-hazardous activity must be foreseen to be the kind of danger that normally arises from it and must be a proximate cause of the accident. While courts will differ on this and other points, there is a tendency to eliminate strict liability for certain activities as they become more common and under control (i.e., blasting) and to expand into newer areas where increased protection is deemed necessary (manufacture of defective equipment).

Types of Situations

Extra-hazardous activities and dangerous animals can be the occasion for determining strict liability. The activities must be such that they are not in common usage in the community and involve a risk of serious harm to persons or property that cannot be eliminated by the use of due care. Different courts have included virtually everything from manufacturing of explosives to fumigating (at one time automobiles and airplanes were included). There is a further trend in holding manufacturers or suppliers of defective products liable in the concomitant move away from the necessity of showing privity between user and manufacturer in order to establish a cause of action. In these new cases, however, a defect must be shown.

Animals with a dangerous propensity (threat to life and limb) and understood as such "by a reasonable individual" make the possessor strictly liable. Watchdogs with dangerous propensities come under the same rule as mechanical devices protecting property (above).

Defenses

Assumption of the risk is a good defense. Teasing an animal or accepting the benefits of a dangerous situation can be said to be good evidence that the party assumed the risk. Contributory negligence is not a defense unless it is the actual cause of the accident.

TORTS WITH MIXED BASIS

An extended list of torts exists that may be actionable on more than one basis. The same tort may be shown to have intentional elements or be based on negligence and/or strict liability.

Defamation

A publication that tends to lower the person in the estimation of a portion of the community or cause others not to associate with him is actionable. The elements of defamation are:

1. Publication (in various forms);
2. Defamatory meaning;
3. Understood to refer to plaintiff in defamatory manner;
4. Damage caused by the act.

This tort is a good example of a mixed basis. Intent or negligence must be shown in publication, but strict liability is the basis for the other elements. It is enough that the matter is defamatory, even though there was no intent that it be so.

Libel is defamation in written or printed form. *Slander* is usually oral in nature although gestures may also be slanderous. Intent to publish defamatory material that is understood to refer to the plaintiff are elements of both libel and slander. The major difference between the two comes in the matter of damages and defenses.

In libel most courts presume general damage from the mere fact of publication but actual (special) damages may also be shown. In slander actual damages must be shown except that certain defamations are actionable *per se*: charges that the person has committed a serious crime, has a loathsome disease, is unchaste (if a woman), conduct incompatible with an office or profession (don't refer to a lawyer as a "shyster").

Truth is a defense to defamation regardless of the motivation of the publisher, but a minority opinion holds that justifiable motives in publishing the truth must be shown. The defense of absolute privilege is available to legislators, top government executives, and participants in judicial processes if statements are relevant to their activity. Utterances within the family are also privileged.

Emotional Distress

Causation of distress may be intentional or through negligence. Intent to cause severe emotional distress that could be foreseen to lead to physical injuries makes a defendant liable. Words or gestures are sufficient. The same result through lack of due care establishes liability.

Invasion of Privacy

While not recognized by all states, a majority of states recognize the right to be left alone or not have one's life exposed to undue public scrutiny. Offensive unauthorized use of a name or picture, divulgence of confidences, and intrusion into personal affairs with reckless disregard can be the basis of this tort. If there is a legitimate public interest in the information the invasion may be privileged; invasion of the private life of a celebrity is not privileged even though his/her public life may be. The case of *Valentine* v. *C.B.S., Inc.* outlines some of the considerations that may be presented for adjudication.

Valentine v. *C.B.S., Inc.*

698 F. 2d 430 (1983)

PER CURIAM:

Bob Dylan and Jacques Levy wrote a song in 1975 called "Hurricane" which gained some measure of popularity. The song depicted the murder trial of prize-fighter Rubin "Hurricane" Carter and mentioned a witness, Patty Valentine. Miss Valentine brought suit for damages alleging common law defamation, invasion of privacy, and unauthorized publication of her name in violation of a Florida statute. The district court granted summary judgment for the defendants on the ground that the facts, about which there was no issue, did not support any of the theories of action. We affirm.

Plaintiff Valentine testified as a witness at the highly publicized 1967 trial of prize-fighter Rubin "Hurricane" Carter and John Artis. Both were convicted of murder. Two other witnesses, Bradley and Bello, later recanted their eyewitness testimony, and a public outcry arose for a new trial. At the height of the controversy about the fairness of the 1967 trial, defendants Bob Dylan and Jacques Levy wrote "Hurricane." Defendant C.B.S. manufactured and distributed a recording of the song, and defendant Warner Bros. Publications published the sheet music.

The song portrays a perceived conspiracy between Bello, Bradley, and the police to unjustly convict Carter. Valentine contends that the defendants defamed her because the song implies she participated in the conspiracy and that defendants maliciously failed to verify the accuracy of the lyrics.

First, we seriously question that the song implies Valentine was a part of the conspiracy. Only three stanzas of the song name Patty Valentine and portray her role as a witness to some of the events occurring the night of the murders. One stanza says Bello and Bradley "baldly lied." Plaintiff pursues the following theory. Stanza four depicts her as agreeing with identification statements by Bello and Bradley. Stanza ten states Bello and Bradley lied. Construing the two stanzas together, it is argued, they imply plaintiff, by nodding her head acquiesced in the lie of the other two witnesses. A review of the entire song makes it clear this interpretation is not reasonably possible. The stanzas actually referring to her all related events occurring the night of the murder. The song does not indicate the alleged conspiracy included Bello and Bradley at that point. The plaintiff's interpretation does not construe the words as the common mind would understand them but is tortured and extreme. *Diplomat Electric, Inc.* v. *Westinghouse Electric Supply Co.*, 378 F.2d 377, 381–82 (5th Cir.1967); *O'Neal* v. *Tribune Co.*, 176 So.2d 535, 548 (Fla.App.1965).

Second, the facts indicate there is no triable issue as to whether the defendants took reasonable precautions to ensure the song's accuracy, particularly in view of their beliefs that Valentine was not part of the conspiracy and that the song did not depict her as being so. Several individuals, including two attorneys, repeatedly reviewed the lyrics. The plaintiff offered nothing to rebut defendant Dylan's deposition testimony that he believed the song did not depict Valentine as a participant in the alleged frame-up. All defendants shared this belief. Nothing in the record contradicts the district court's view in this regard.

Third, a review of the record indicates the plaintiff could not establish the statements were untrue. The record evidence indicates Valentine testified in the 1967 trial that she entered the murder scene from her upstairs room, saw several bodies, screamed aloud, observed a man standing by the door (later identified as Bello), returned to her room upstairs to call the police, and while doing so saw two men running to a car with out-of-state license plates. Cast against this testimony, it is obvious the lyrics are substantially and materially true, *see Hill* v. *Lakeland Ledger Publishing Corp.,* 231 So.2d 254 (Fla.App.1970), and are not reasonably susceptible to a defamatory meaning. *Wolfson* v. *Kirk,* 273 So.2d 774 (Fla.App.1973), *cert. denied,* 279 So.2d 32 (Fla.1973). They indicate only that plaintiff saw the horrifying aftermath of a murder, called the police, and affirmed the description of the getaway car. The district court correctly entered summary judgment on the common law claim.

As to the invasion of privacy claim, under Florida law the publication of facts regarding matters of legitimate public or general interest will not support an invasion of privacy action. *Cason* v. *Baskin,* 155 Fla. 198, 215–16, 20 So.2d 243, 251 (1944). This is so even when a person is an involuntary participant in such matters. *Jacova* v. *Southern Radio & Television Co.,* 83 So.2d 34 (Fla.1955). The lyrics describe Valentine's role as a witness to a murder, clearly an event of legitimate public interest. Plaintiff stipulated that the 1967 trial, including her testimony, received national publicity. The events surrounding Carter's trial and recent retrial continue to be matters of legitimate public interest. The song discloses no private facts but merely details events Valentine previously disclosed through her public trial testimony. The trial court properly entered summary judgment for defendants on the invasion of privacy claims.

Valentine's statutory claim alleges a violation of Fla.Stat.Ann. § 540.08 (West 1972), which prohibits the unauthorized use of a person's name or likeness for commercial, trade, or advertising purposes. The use is actionable under the statute because of the way the defendants associate the individual's name or personality with something else. *Loft* v. *Fuller,* 408 So.2d 619 (Fla.App.1981) (construing § 540.08). The trial court properly held that, as a matter of law, the ballad "Hurricane" did not commercially exploit Valentine's name. The defendants did not use her name to directly promote a product or service. Use of a name is not harmful simply because it is included in a publication and sold for profit. As the court correctly noted, an interpretation that the statute absolutely bars the use of an individual's name without consent for any purpose would raise grave questions as to constitutionality. The court properly construed the statute to avoid confronting the constitutional question. *United States* v. *Clark,* 445 U.S. 23, 100 S.Ct. 895, 63 L.Ed.2d 171 (1980).

Affirmed.

TORTS IN BUSINESS

Virtually any tort can occur in a business setting, but some are more common in that arena. Distinctive elements of commercial transactions lend themselves to certain types of tortious conduct, which deserve mention in this context.

Product Liability

The area of torts that seems to present much concern and possibly the greatest amount of litigation at the present time involves injuries suffered as the result of allegedly defective consumer products. Manufacturers and sellers may be liable to purchasers under the concept of negligence or strict liability, although the legal action may be based upon fraud or misrepresentation. (It must be remembered that non-tort recoveries, such as a breach of warranty, are also available.)

Negligence and strict liability are determined under the conditions expressed above. Suits alleging negligence no longer require privity between producer and plaintiff or seller and user. The rule in matters of negligence is expressed in the *Restatement of Torts* (2d) § 395. The rule expresses the need for the manufacturer "to exercise reasonable care in the manufacture of a chattel which unless carefully made," subjects the manufacturer to liability in the recognition that there is an unreasonable risk of physical harm.

Strict liability is imposed in many states according to the elements outlined in the *Restatement of Torts* (2d) § 402A. Under strict liability, lack of due care, as in negligence, need not be shown. If a seller is in the business of manufacturing or selling a product that left the seller's control in a defective condition with no change in the interim, liability will ensue. Even negligence of the plaintiff is not a defense to the action. The following case opinion includes a discussion of some of the intricacies underlying a matter of strict liability.

Azzarello v. Black Bros. Co., Inc.
480 Pa. 547 (1978)

NIX, Justice.

This appeal raises the question of the appropriate form of jury instruction in products liability cases in this Commonwealth. In the instant case, Azzarello's right hand was pinched between two hard rubber rolls in a coating machine manufactured and sold by the defendant, Black Brothers, Inc. Azzarello brought this suit against Black Brothers Company, Inc., the manufacturer-appellant relying solely on the theory of strict liability under Section 402A of the Restatement Second of Torts.[1] The manufacturer, by joining appellee's employer, Parts Processing, as an additional defendant, injected into appellee's strict liability case the issue of whether the negligence of the employer was the sole or contributing cause of her injuries. Accordingly, the trial court below was faced with the difficult problem of devising instructions

[1] § 402A.

"(1) One who sells any product in a defective condition unreasonably dangerous to the user or consumer or to his property is subject to liability for physical harm thereby caused to the ultimate user or consumer, or to his property, if

    (a) the seller is engaged in the business of selling such a product, and

    (b) it is expected to and does reach the user or consumer without substantial change in the condition in which it is sold.

(2) The rule stated in Subsection (1) applies although

    (a) the seller has exercised all possible care in the preparation and sale of his product, and

    (b) the user or consumer has not bought the product from or entered into any contractual relation with the seller."

Restatement (Second) of Torts, § 402A (1965).

for the jury which required a clear exposition of the law of strict liability upon which appellee exclusively relied, and also explaining with clarity the interrelationship of the more traditional and familiar jury instructions sounding in fault and negligence, necessitated by manufacturer-appellant's theory of the case. In so doing, the trial court repeatedly instructed the jury using the phrase "unreasonably dangerous" taken verbatim from the formulation provided by Restatement Second of Torts.[2]

The trial resulted in a verdict in favor of the manufacturer and against the additional defendant, appellee's employer, in the sum of One Hundred Twenty-Five Thousand Dollars ($125,000.00). The appellee thereupon moved for a new trial asserting *inter alia* that the trial judge incorrectly instructed the jury that the appellee's burden of proof under Section 402A strict liability required a showing that the machine was "unreasonably dangerous."

The motion for a new trial was granted by the court *en banc.* That court held that the opinion announcing the judgment of the Court in the case of *Berkebile* v. *Brantly Helicopter Corp.,* 462 Pa. 83, 337 A.2d 893 (1975) should be followed, and that the use of the phrase "unreasonably dangerous" in the charge required the grant of a new trial.

In granting appellee's motion for a new trial, the court *en banc* found that this issue had not been waived.

. . .

The development of a sophisticated and complex industrial society with its proliferation of new products and vast changes in the private enterprise system has inspired a change in legal philosophy from the principle of caveat emptor which prevailed in the early nineteenth century market place to the view that a supplier of products should be deemed to be "the guarantor of his products' safety" *Salvador* v. *Atlantic Steel Boiler Co.,* 457 Pa. 24, 32, 319 A.2d 903, 907 (1974). The realities of our economic society as it exists today forces the conclusion that the risk of loss for injury resulting from defective products should be borne by the suppliers, principally because they are in a position to absorb the loss by distributing

---

[2] (1) ". . . one who sells any product in a defective condition, unreasonably dangerous to the user, is subject to liability. . . ."

(2) ". . . the plaintiff must prove that the defendant sold the product involved in a defective condition, unreasonably dangerous to the user. . . ."

(3) "By a defective condition is meant that the product at the time it leaves the seller's hands in a condition not contemplated by the ultimate user, which will be unreasonably dangerous to him, and you will hear all during this charge the phrase unreasonably dangerous, and that is the key phrase in this type of case."

(4) "A properly made product is defective if its design is unreasonably dangerous. The prevailing interpretation of defective is that the product does not meet the reasonable expectations of the ordinary consumer as to its safety."

(5) ". . . a manufacturer may be liable under 402A for a design which creates an unreasonable risk of danger to the user. . . . but the design is considered defective only if the design makes the product unreasonably dangerous. Hence, the focal issue in this case is whether or not the absence of infeed guards or the safety devices on the machine, . . . created an unreasonable danger to the operator."

(6) "The focal issue in these cases is whether the absence of safety devices created an unreasonable danger to the operator."

(7) "It is reasonable to require reasonable care to protect even the buyer himself or the user from what may be foreseen as an unreasonable danger to him. Unreasonably dangerous to the user or consumer is the nature of the defective condition. The product must be dangerous to an extent beyond that which would be contemplated by the ordinary consumer who purchases it or uses it with the ordinary knowledge common to the community as to its characteristics. The test of unreasonably dangerous is whether a reasonable manufacturer would continue to market his product in the same condition. . . ."

it as a cost of doing business. In an era of giant corporate structures, utilizing the national media to sell their wares, the original concern for an emerging manufacturing industry has given way to the view that it is now the consumer who must be protected. Courts have increasingly adopted the position that the risk of loss must be placed upon the supplier of the defective product without regard to fault or privity of contract.

While this expansion of the supplier's responsibility for injuries resulting from defects in his product has placed the supplier in the role of a guarantor of his product's safety, it was not intended to make him an insurer of all injuries caused by the product. It is this distinction that rests at the core of the problem raised in this appeal. Although the expansion of the supplier's liability has been developed through a breach of warranty analysis as well as that of tort, the Restatement elected strict liability in tort as an explanation for imposing this liability. We must focus upon two requirements set forth in Section 402A for liability (physical injury)—that the product be "in defective condition" and that it be "unreasonably dangerous." It is the propriety of instructing the jury using the term of "unreasonably dangerous" which forms the basis of appellee's objection to the jury instructions given below.

In an effort to assure that a supplier of chattels would not become an insurer, the authors of the Restatement described the characteristic which would justify the imposition of liability in terms of a "defect." However, this word is not limited to its usual meaning, i.e., a fault, flaw or blemish in its manufacture or fabrication. Rather, the critical factor under this formulation is whether the product is "unreasonably dangerous." Under the Restatement approach a product may be deemed to be "defective" even though it comports in all respects to its intended design. One difficulty arises from the fact that the term, "unreasonably dangerous" tends to suggest considerations which are usually identified with the law of negligence.

. . .

Thus the mere fact that we have approved Section 402A, and even if we agree that the phrase "unreasonably dangerous" serves a useful purpose in predicting liability in this area, it does not follow that this language should be used in framing the issues for the jury's consideration. Should an ill-conceived design which exposes the user to the risk of harm entitle one injured by the product to recover? Should adequate warnings of the dangerous propensities of an article insulate one who suffers injuries from those propensities? When does the utility of a product outweigh the unavoidable danger it may pose? These are questions of law and their resolution depends upon social policy. Restated, the phrases "defective condition" and "unreasonably dangerous" as used in the Restatement formulation are terms of art invoked when *strict liability* is appropriate. It is a judicial function to decide whether, under plaintiff's averment of the facts, recovery would be justified; and only after this judicial determination is made is the cause submitted to the jury to determine whether the facts of the case support the averments of the complaint. They do not fall within the orbit of a factual dispute which is properly assigned to the jury for resolution. A standard suggesting the existence of a "defect" if the article is unreasonably dangerous or not duly safe is inadequate to guide a lay jury in resolving these questions.

. . .

For the term guarantor to have any meaning in this context the supplier must at least provide a product which is designed to make it safe for the intended use. Under this standard, in this type case, the jury may find a defect where the product left the supplier's control lacking any element necessary to make it safe for its intended use or possessing any feature that renders it unsafe for the intended use. It is clear that the term "unreasonably dangerous" has no place in the instructions to a jury as to the question of "defect" in this type of case. We therefore agree with the court en banc that the use of the term "unreasonably dangerous" in the charge was misleading and that the appellee was entitled to a new trial.

Order of the Superior Court affirming the order of the court en banc is

Affirmed.

The concept of strict liability engenders much controversy in society. Under the doctrine, all the risk is placed upon the manufacturer and/or seller, with the result that the enterprise may be saddled with burdens. The risk of loss is placed upon the firm, but at the same time such costs are actually passed on to the customer, in the form of a higher price for the product. There may be little a seller can do, even in good faith, to escape liability.

Concern has now reached the point where there are strenuous lobbying efforts behind a federal bill to establish a uniform system among states regarding a manufacturer's/seller's liability. The legislation proposed in 1984 marks a significant movement from strict liability to more emphasis upon concepts of negligence in product liability suits.

Unfair Trade Practices

Competition among firms or individuals engaged in trade is protected from unfair practices such as trademark infringement, the use of misleading labels, misrepresentation in advertising, and so on. A company that has developed an enterprise based upon the good will of consumers from recognition of its product cannot tolerate other businesses trading upon its good reputation through the use of similar names, labels, advertisements, or other identifications that tend to mislead consumers. A name or symbol that identifies a product or a trademark is protected under the law.

Trade Secrets

Violation of business rights may also include obtaining vital information or process of a competitor by dishonest means. The value of a trade secret lies in the opportunity to gain a competitive advantage through its use, and the unlawful obtaining of it leads to liability in tort.

CONSTRAINTS UPON ACTIONS

In each of the classifications, several other factors must be taken into consideration in order to evaluate an activity and to judge whether it is indeed an actionable wrong.

Sovereign Immunity

The general rule is that a state cannot be sued for tort unless there is a statute that permits an action to be taken. State officers engaged in official acts are not liable for the negligence incurred in pursuing a governmental function. There is no immunity, however, in proprietary functions—that is, activities that can be pursued by private enterprise. Negligence in the operation of a police or fire department or a school district cannot be the basis for a suit; but maintaining highways, parks, airports, or playgrounds has been labeled a proprietary function, and in many states recovery has been allowed for negligence in connection with these activities.

Charitable Immunity

Nonprofit organizations that presumably work for the public welfare (hospitals, schools, etc.) have been held to be immune to tort liability. Increasingly, however, courts have either eliminated this immunity completely or have severely restricted its application.

Wrongful Death and Survival Actions

Under common law, tort actions did not survive the death of the injured party, nor was there a tort action possible for a wrongful death, but at present all jurisdictions have statutes permitting some suits in both these areas. There is, however, a wide variation among the states as to the extent of the right to sue.

Relationships

Persons in the same family generally cannot sue each other in a tort action; this immunity extends to husband, wife, parents, and children. In some cases persons may be liable for the torts of others; parents, in many jurisdictions, are liable for the torts of their children. Under the doctrine of imputed liability, a master may be liable for the tort of a servant.

QUESTIONS

1. Provide some reasons why differences exist in maintaining various actions under tort law.
2. Can the limits to the use of deadly force be justified on a rational basis?
3. Are there any elements in an action alleging negligence that may be harder to prove? Is that made more difficult in an advanced economy?
4. What may be the basis for differences in litigating the two types of defamation?
5. How do standards of proof differ for cases in negligence and those of strict liability?

contracts

FOURTEEN

In the Mary Worker lawsuit against Zagger Supply Company, there was reference earlier to two contracts: Mary's written contract with Henry Law for legal services; and the contract for the sale of zaggers made between Zagger Supply, Inc. and The Firm. This chapter provides a more detailed look at the legal concept of contract.

A contract, in the minds of many people, is identified with a formal written document embodying the legal rights and duties of the parties in an exceedingly complicated transaction. This may be true; yet it is also true that many other contracts arise out of such ordinary occurrences as buying a loaf of bread or a pair of shoes, subscribing to a magazine, having a car repaired, renting a garage for that car, or obtaining employment. Sometimes no writing at all is involved in a contract. Some contracts are completed even without spoken words, the parties understanding one another's intentions from their actions. Such contracts are referred to as *implied in fact,* in contrast to oral and written contracts which are referred to as *express.*

THE LAW OF CONTRACTS

The law of contracts is found mainly in the common law. An exception exists regarding contracts for the sale of goods when provisions of the Uniform Commercial Code are paramount. The Code, a comprehensive act dealing with the law of commercial transactions (as explained in previous chapters), is a prime example of uniform state legislation. Article 2 of the Code, involving sales, brings modern business practices to the law of contracts.

CONTRACT DEFINED

What, then, is a contract? A short, popular definition is that it is an agreement or promise enforceable by law. Perhaps the most frequently used and widely recognized definition is this: "A contract is a promise or a set of promises for the breach of which the law gives a remedy, or the performance of which the law in some way recognizes as a duty." (*Restatement of Contracts §1*)

ELEMENTS OF A CONTRACT

To have a valid contract, certain requirements must be met. There must be:

1. An agreement;
2. Competent parties;
3. True assent;
4. Consideration (as required);
5. Legal subject matter.

If the contract is to be enforceable, it must also be in the form required by law.

The following opinion of the court in *Lucy* v. *Zehmer* discusses agreement and true assent; it also refers to consideration and competent parties.

Lucy v. *Zehmer*
196 Va. 493, 84 S.E.2d 516 (1954)

... This suit was instituted by W. O. Lucy and J. C. Lucy, complainants, against A. H. Zehmer and Ida S. Zehmer, his wife, defendants, to have specific performance of a contract by which it was alleged the Zehmers had sold to W. O. Lucy a tract of land owned by Z. H. Zehmer—known as the Ferguson farm, for $50,000. ...

The instrument sought to be enforced was written by Z. H. Zehmer on Saturday, December 20, 1952, in these words: "We hereby agree to sell to W. O. Lucy ... the Ferguson Farm complete for $50,000, title satisfactory to buyer," and signed by the defendants, A. H. Zehmer and Ida S. Zehmer.

The answer of A. H. Zehmer admitted that at the time mentioned W. O. Lucy offered him $50,000 cash for the farm, but that he, Zehmer, considered that the offer was made in jest; that so thinking, and both he and Lucy having had several drinks, he wrote out "the memorandum" quoted above and induced his wife to sign it; that he did not deliver the memorandum to Lucy, but that Lucy picked it up, read it, put it in his pocket, attempted to offer Zehmer $5 to bind the bargain, which Zehmer refused to accept, and realizing for the first time that Lucy was serious, Zehmer assured him that he had no intention of selling the farm and that the whole matter was a joke. Lucy left the premises insisting that he had purchased the farm.

. . .

The defendants insist that the evidence was ample to support their contention that the writing sought to be enforced was prepared as a bluff or dare to force Lucy to admit that he did not have $50,000; that the whole matter was a joke; that the writing was not delivered to Lucy and no binding contract was ever made between the parties.

. . .

In his testimony Zehmer claimed that he "was high as a Georgia pine," and that the transaction "was just a bunch of two doggoned drunks bluffing to see who could talk the biggest and say the most." That claim is inconsistent with his attempt to testify in great detail as to what was said and what was done. . . . The record is convincing that Zehmer was not intoxicated to the extent of being unable to comprehend the nature and consequences of the instrument he executed, and hence that instrument is not to be invalidated on that ground . . .

. . .

If it be assumed, contrary to what we think the evidence shows, that Zehmer was jesting about selling his farm to Lucy and that the transaction was intended by him to be a joke, nevertheless the evidence shows that Lucy did not so understand it but considered it to be a serious business transaction and the contract to be binding on the Zehmers as well as on himself. . . . Tuesday, he was back at Zehmer's place and there Zehmer told him for the first time, Lucy said, that he wasn't going to sell and he told Zehmer, "You know you sold that place fair and square." . . .

Not only did Lucy actually believe, but the evidence shows he was warranted in believing, that the contract represented a serious business transaction and a good faith sale and purchase of the farm.

. . .

An agreement or mutual assent is of course essential to a valid contract but the law imputes to a person an intention corresponding to the reasonable meaning of his words and acts. If his words and acts, judged by a reasonable standard, manifest an intention to agree, it is immaterial what may be the real but unexpressed state of his mind.

. . .

Whether the writing signed by the defendants and now sought to be enforced by the complainants was the result of a serious offer by Lucy and a serious acceptance by the defendants, or was a serious offer by Lucy and an acceptance in secret jest by the defendants, in either event it constituted a binding contract of sale between the parties . . .

The complainants are entitled to have specific performance of the contract sued on . . .

AGREEMENT

A contract normally begins when two parties, such as Mary Worker and Henry Law, enter into an agreement. Their contract began when Mary first approached Henry about acting as her lawyer. Henry did not immediately consent, but first explained to Mary the legal ramifications of her situation, his fee system, and the possible outcomes of legal action. Henry wanted her to understand what she would be committing herself to if she engaged him as her legal counsel. Only when she indicated that she understood did he give her the written agreement form to sign, after which he also signed. In that way the two reached an agreement. The process is very similar to what occurred when The Firm approached Zagger Supply about development of a new kind of zagger, and then ordered sixty dozen.

In both instances, there was a proposal to make a deal that one party presented to the other. This is referred to as an *offer*. An agreement occurred when the second party acquiesced. That was the *acceptance* of the offer. When an offer has been accepted, there is an *agreement*. At that point a contract comes into being, provided all the other essentials for a contract are present.

Agreements come into being in a variety of ways. There are formal and informal, simple and complex, verbal and nonverbal agreements, to name a few. There may be much preliminary discussion, explanation, negotiation, and bargaining before the acceptable offer is made. Often an offer is changed and superseded by a *counteroffer,* which, in turn, must be accepted for an agreement to result.

Not all proposals are offers. Conditions necessary for an offer include:

1. It must be communicated to the *offeree,* the person to whom the offer is made. (The person making the offer is known as the *offeror.*) A person cannot accept an offer without knowing about it.
2. The offer must be definite enough so that it is possible to determine the nature of the obligation each party will have under the agreement.
3. It must be made with the intention of creating a legally binding obligation.
4. It must be more than just an invitation to do business, such as an advertisement, solicitation, or circulation of price information.

A contract is a voluntary assumption of legal responsibilities. Therefore, an acceptance must consist of some deliberate assent to the offer. There is an old adage that an offer cannot be accepted by "silence." "Silence" does not necessarily mean lack of verbal communication; it also includes lack of any action or activity that would indicate assent to the offer. For instance, the act of shipping goods ordered by a customer constitutes acceptance of the customer's offer to purchase the goods.

Many, if not most, offers require that an acceptance be made in the nature of a promise. When both offer and acceptance are promises—one promise being made in exchange for another promise—the contract is known as *bilateral.* A *unilateral* contract is one where only one party makes a promise. In that case, acceptance of the offer is usually by some action.

Because an acceptance is in response to an offer, both the content and method of acceptance must comply with the terms of the offer. Obviously there can be no agreement if an offeree, attempting to accept an offer to sell 100 widgets at $10 each, indicates to the offeror a willingness to purchase the same widgets at $5 each. The Uniform Commercial Code allows for some flexibility when there are deviations from the offer in the acceptance.[1] Minor, non-crucial deviations are considered to be proposals for additions to the contract when no objection to deviations or change has been stated in the offer, or when no objection to a change is made within a reasonable time after it is received. If this occurs between merchants, the changes become parts of the contract itself. This contrasts with the old common law requirement that an acceptance be a "mirror image" of the offer, and is more in tune with today's business practice.

Just as an offer must be communicated to the offeree, so also must an acceptance be communicated to the offeror. When no method of acceptance is mentioned in the offer, common sense and reasonableness indicate the method of acceptance. For example, a telephoned offer to sell a railroad car full of ripe tomatoes for resale to grocers would not reasonably be accepted by a letter mailed two weeks later! One interesting aspect of communicating the acceptance, known as the "Mail Box Rule," is part of the common law heritage that has been incorporated and even extended in current law. This rule provides that when an offer is either made by mail or requires acceptance by mail, the acceptance takes place at the time a correctly addressed and stamped letter of acceptance is placed in the mail. A contract exists from that moment, even if the acceptance is never received by the offeror. An offeror can protect against such an occurrence by stating in the offer than an acceptance will not take place until received. Today the "Mail Box Rule" has been extended by both court decision and the UCC to proper dispatch of notice of acceptance.[2] However, it still applies *only* to an acceptance.

Usually an offeror can withdraw an offer any time before it has been accepted. One way for an offeree to prevent that from happening is to enter into a contract with the offeror to keep the offer open for a specific length of time. This is known as an *option*. It creates a legally binding obligation to keep the offer open for the time stated. Under the Uniform Commercial Code merchants have a legal obligation to hold a written, signed offer open for the time stated or for a reasonable time, up to a maximum of three months.[3]

Offers may end under a variety of circumstances, such as when:

1. The offeror withdraws or revokes the offer. This must be communicated either directly or indirectly to the offeree.
2. The offeree rejects the offer or makes a counteroffer.
3. The time period stated in the offer or option expires. If no time is stated, then it will be when a reasonable time has elapsed.
4. One of the parties—offeror or offeree—dies or becomes legally disabled.
5. The subject matter of the offer is destroyed through no fault of either party, or the offer becomes illegal as a result of a change in the law.

COMPETENT PARTIES

Because one cannot contract with oneself, two legally competent parties are required for a valid contract. A party need not be a person, however; a party may be an organization, a business entity such as a corporation or a partnership, or a group of persons.

The law protects several classes of people in their contracts. These people include minors, persons of unsound mind, and persons who are intoxicated because of alcohol or drugs. These people can, under certain circumstances, set aside their contracts. Therefore, their contracts are referred to as *voidable*.

A *minor* is a person who has not yet reached the age of legal majority. In most states, that age is 18. A minor is also referred to as an *infant*. With certain exceptions, contracts made by a minor are voidable by him. In most states, this is true even if the infant has not told the truth about his age. In such a situation, however, the other party may have a cause of action based on fraud or misrepresentation.

An infant avoids a contract by indicating his desire to withdraw from the contract. He may do so expressly or through behavior that is inconsistent with keeping the contract. This is referred to as *disaffirming* the contract. A minor has not only the time of his minority in which to disaffirm but also a reasonable time after he has reached the age of majority. With contracts affecting the title to real estate, an infant must wait until he reaches his majority in order to disaffirm.

When a minor decides to disaffirm a contract, he must return to the other party everything that he has received under the contract. If the infant no longer has all of it or if it is in damaged condition, he need return only what he has in its present condition. Generally, that is all the minor must do. Some states, however, require that the infant return the other party to the contract to the position in which that party was before entering into the contract. That condition is referred to as the *status quo ante*.

The minor who disaffirms a contract generally can recover everything that he has provided under the contract or its money value. That applies even to the recovery of property that has been transferred to a third party. However, if the contract disaffirmed was for the sale of goods, the Uniform Commercial Code provides that a good faith purchaser for value (the third party) will acquire good title (UCC2-403).

Contracts entered into by an infant for necessaries are treated differently. A minor has a legal obligation only for the reasonable value of necessaries that have been supplied to him. Were it not for this requirement, it would be extremely difficult for minors to secure the necessaries of life, because many people are very reluctant to contract with minors.

Necessaries are those things that are needed to maintain the minor reasonably according to his socioeconomic status. Obviously, the category includes food, clothing, and shelter not otherwise provided for the infant. What is a necessary may also depend upon the infant's status in life. In some cases, necessaries may include a college education or a car to provide transportation to and from the minor's place of employment.

Usually parents are not responsible for contracts their minor children enter into, unless the infant is acting as the agent of the parent. In that case the contract is that of the parent and not the infant. Parents who have neglected to provide for their children as required by law are liable for necessaries furnished to the children.

In some cases, the party with whom a minor is dealing refuses to enter into a contract unless the infant secures a person of legal age to act as a cosigner. When that occurs, the cosigner becomes legally obligated and bound by the contract, even if the minor avoids the contract.

By statute in some states, an infant cannot avoid certain contracts. Examples are contracts approved by a court, or those made by a minor while operating his own business.

An individual who has reached the age of legal majority may expressly ratify the contracts he made during infancy. Such ratification—frequently in written form—is required in some states. Actions consistent with ratification, such as performance of his part of the contract or acceptance of performance by the other party, are viewed as evidence of an intention to ratify.

Other groups of persons protected under contract law include those who lack full mental capacity at the time of contracting.

As a general rule, contracts made by a person who is insane are viodable by that person. In cases in which a person has been adjudged insane, a guardian is appointed by the court to handle the individual's business affairs. In that situation, the insane person's contracts are void.

In order for his contracts to be voidable, a person must be so impaired mentally that he neither understands that he is entering into a contract nor the consequences of what he is doing. For that reason, contracts made by an insane person during lucid intervals are valid.

Sane persons, who neither know nor can reasonably be expected to know the mental condition of an insane person with whom they contract, have a right to be returned to the status quo ante if the contract is avoided. On the other hand, when a sane person enters into a contract with an individual whom he either knows or should know to be insane, return to the status quo ante is not required.

Persons who regain their full sanity have the option of either ratifying or disaffirming the contracts they made while insane.

Contracts entered into by persons who are so intoxicated that they do not know they are entering into a contract are treated the same as those of insane persons. Upon reaching sobriety, the individual may disaffirm or ratify contracts made while intoxicated.

In some states, the capacity of persons in a drugged condition to enter into valid contracts is limited. At times, there may exist restrictions on the rights of aliens and prisoners to contract. Today there has been a change from the old common law under which a married woman could not contract.

TRUE ASSENT

A contract arises from an agreement to which there has been mutual assent by two competent parties. Sometimes, however, the assent of the parties is not real or genuine. This may occur because there has been mistake, fraud, misrepresentation, duress, or undue influence.

Mistake

A mistake exists when one or both of the parties believe that a material matter relating to the past or present is true when it actually is not. A mistake is *unilateral* when only one of the parties is in error; it is *mutual* or *bilateral* when both parties are. A matter is *material* when it is of such importance or significance to the transaction that a party would not have entered into the contract had he known the truth.

Different kinds of mistakes may occur in connection with a contract. There may be:

1. A unilateral or bilateral mistake;
2. A mistake of fact or a mistake of law;
3. A mistake in preparation of the written document evidencing the contract; a mistake as to expectations; or a mistake of judgment.

The kind of mistake will determine the effect it has upon the agreement.

As a general rule, a unilateral mistake as to a material fact does not affect the validity of the contract. However, if one party either knows or should have known of the other party's erroneous belief, the mistaken party may rescind the contract. To *rescind* is to cancel or avoid, placing the parties in a position of status quo ante. However, relief is generally not available when the mistake results from an individual's own negligence, as when a party either fails to read or carelessly reads a document, and later alleges he did not realize or understand what it was that he signed.

On the other hand, a bilateral mistake regarding a material fact generally results in a void agreement. Examples of the kinds of mutual mistakes of fact which make an agreement void are: error as to the existence of the subject matter of the contract, as to the identity of the subject matter, or as to the possibility of performance.

Mistakes of law generally will not affect enforceability of an agreement. However, some states treat mutual mistakes of law as they do those of fact.

Sometimes mistakes in drafting occur, when the parties prepare a written document with the intention that it shall recite their agreement, but the writing does not conform with the actual agreement. In that case, a court will reform the document so that it does express the intention of the parties.

Errors in judgment or regarding expectations normally have no effect upon the validity of a contract and do not, therefore, form a basis for relief. The courts will not relieve a party of contractual obligations merely because the party has made a "bad deal" or a "bad bargain," or exercised poor business judgment.

Fraud and Misrepresentation

A false representation regarding a present or past material fact upon which the other party to the contract justifiably relies is known as a *misrepresentation* when it is made innocently, without intention to deceive. If the falsehood is made deliberately or with reckless disregard for the truth and with the intention of having the other party rely upon it, there is *fraud*.

Both fraud and misrepresentation require that the falsehood be about a present or past material fact. Predictions about the future are not considered to be statements of fact. Mere expressions of opinion do not form the basis for either fraud or misrepresentation.

In the case of either fraud or misrepresentation, the injured party may rescind the contract. If there is fraud, the injured party may keep the contract and seek damages in a tort action for fraud or deceit. The Uniform Commercial Code provides that both rescission and an action for damages are available to the party injured by fraud in connection with contracts for the sale of goods (UCC 2-721). In the case of other contracts, the individual ordinarily must make a choice of which remedy he wishes to pursue.

Does the concealment of information constitute fraud? In the absence of specific questions, a party is generally not required to volunteer information he possesses even though it be material. However, there is a discernible trend toward requiring a seller to volunteer to a buyer material facts regarding which a buyer would not be likely to inquire. In such cases, concealment constitutes fraud. When parties are in a fiduciary relationship, there is a duty to reveal matters that are to the other party's material interest. Failure to do so is fraud. Fraudulent concealment may also occur when important matter is placed in extremely fine print or under misleading headings on written documents with the expectation and intention that the other party will not read it.

Duress and Undue Influence

When a contract is the result of coercion, whether it be physical or mental, there is no real assent of the parties to the agreement. Therefore, contracts made under duress or unde influence are voidable by the innocent party.

Duress is the wrongful use of force or threat of force with the intention of causing a person to do what he otherwise would not do. Threat and/or physical force are not the only forms of duress. Threat of criminal prosecution, withholding of goods to compel payment of exorbitant sums, and threat of a civil suit which would bring financial ruin may, in some cases, constitute duress. Ordinarily, threat of economic loss is not considered to be duress.

Undue influence arises out of a confidential relationship in which a person in a dominant position takes advantage of the relationship by exerting wrongful pressure upon the other party to enter into a contract for the unjust benefit of the dominating party. Parent and child, or attorney and client, are forms of confidential relationship in which undue influence may develop. In order for undue influence to exist, there must be more than mere persuasion. The person in the weaker position must be deprived of his free will and coerced into a contract which provides unusual or unjust benefit to the dominant party.

Relief is available when by wrongful means a person has been coerced into an unjust or unconscionable contract. In the case of duress, the injured party may either rescind the contract or may seek damages for any amount over a reasonable sum which he has been forced to pay. Where undue influence can be shown, the contract is voidable by the injured party.

CONSIDERATION

One example of a promise which is rarely enforceable at law is a promise to make a gift. A gift is something rendered voluntarily, with no expectation of return or compensation. Lack of consideration is its very essence, and consideration is necessary if the promise is to rise to the status of a contract. While an executory promise which is not supported by consideration will not be enforced, lack of consideration will not cause an executed gift to be rescinded.

Consideration has been defined as the "bargained for exchange." It has also been described as a legal benefit which the promisor exacts and receives for his promise, and a legal detriment to the promisee. *Legal benefit* means something to which the party is not already entitled under the law. A *legal detriment* may consist either of giving up a legal right or of assuming a legal obligation that the individual is not already bound to perform.

Consideration is usually in the form of money or some type of property. It may also take the form of services, conduct, or forbearance. *Forbearance* consists of abstaining from action, such as when one promises not to bring a law suit.

Moral consideration is that which is given because of a moral obligation or out of love, affection, or friendship. An example is the promise of a child to care for his aged parents. Moral consideration is ordinarily unacceptable as consideration to support a contract.

The same is true of *past consideration,* which consists of that which has already been performed. Thus, valuable services rendered by an employee to an employer over the past forty years cannot serve as consideration to support a promise to pay $100 when that promise is made by the employer at the time of the employee's retirement. The forty years of service is past; it was not bargained to be performed in exchange for the $100.

Promises that lack valid consideration include those that are *illusory*. An example would be my promise to buy your car for $9000 if I should ever decide to buy a car. However, requirements contracts and output contracts are enforceable. An agreement to purchase from a particular supplier all of the oil one needs to run a factory for a year is an example of a *requirements contract,* while an agreement to purchase all of the wool produced by a certain manufacturer during one month is an example of an *output contract.*

For reasons of public policy, promises or pledges to contribute to recognized charities are generally enforceable. In some states, however, the promise does not become enforceable until the charity has incurred obligations in reliance upon the subscription.

Adequacy of consideration is not a requirement. The bargained for exchange need not be equal. However, when a great discrepancy in values occurs and is combined with other circumstances that might give rise to an unconscionable transaction or is combined with evidence of fraud or duress, the courts may make inquiry into the matter of adequacy. When identical matter—such as money—is exchanged, equality is required. If consideration of a nominal sum (such as $1) is recited in a written document merely for the sake of giving the appearance of consideration, that will not be considered as valid consideration to support the contract.

Consideration may be furnished by a third party, such as when a wife promises to pay a merchant for a coat purchased by her husband.

The settlement of debts sometimes poses problems of consideration. *Liquidated debts* are those that are fixed or settled. In connection with them, it may happen that a debtor who owes several creditors is hard pressed financially. When two or more (although not necessarily all) of those creditors agree to accept a pro-rata portion of what is owed in full satisfaction of their accounts, there is a *composition of creditors*. Such arrangements are legally enforceable, the consideration for such agreements being the mutual promises of the creditors.

When an honest dispute exists as to whether there is a debt at all or as to the amount of the debt, the debt is referred to as *unliquidated*. Often the parties in such situations are able to work out a settlement to their mutual satisfaction. That kind of compromise is referred to as an *accord and satisfaction*. Consideration is recognized as existing in such an arrangement, since each of the parties has foregone his right to bring legal action concerning the alleged debt.

ILLEGALITY

The law condemns the making and performing of agreements that are illegal. Examples are agreements to commit a crime or a tort, agreements which are prohibited by statute, and agreements which are opposed to public policy.

Effect of Illegality

Ordinarily, illegal agreements are void and will not be enforced by the courts. In fact, the courts will usually do nothing to assist either party to an illegal agreement. Instead, a court will leave the parties where it finds them. Neither party will be aided, either to enforce the illegal promise or to get back that which he gave as part of the agreement. The underlying theory is that such inaction will serve as a deterrent to illegal agreements. An exception occurs when the effect of refusing assistance would be to defeat the very purpose for making the transaction illegal. In such cases, relief may be granted.

Agreement to Accomplish Illegal Purpose

A contract that in an of itself would be perfectly legal may become illegal if it is made to accomplish an illegal purpose. Under normal circumstances, the leasing of a dock would be legal. When its use is sought for the purpose of smuggling, however, the lease can become illegal.

It frequently happens that one of the parties to a contract is ignorant of any unlawful purpose. If he has no such knowledge and does not participate in accomplishment of the illegal act, the courts usually hold that he may bring suit against the other party to enforce the contract provisions. However, if he knows of the unlawful purpose at the time the agreement is made, the entire agreement is illegal (and therefore unenforceable).

Unconscionable Agreements

Agreements that are so grossly unfair to one of the parties as to be oppressive may be said to be unconscionable and this may be the basis for relief by the courts. When a contract has been reduced to a writing which consists of a standard form prepared by a party with greater bargaining and economic power and when the other party has little or no opportunity to go elsewhere or to deal with others in order to satisfy his needs, the contract may be classified as one of *adhesion,* and may be set aside because of unconscionability if greatly oppressive provisions are imposed upon the weaker party. In the case of contracts for the sale of goods, the Uniform Commercial Code specifically provides that the courts may refuse to enforce unconscionable contracts (UCC 2-302).

FORM REQUIRED BY LAW

In order to be enforceable, certain kinds of contracts must ordinarily be evidenced by a writing. This requirement arises from the Statutes of Frauds, which have been adopted by the various states. The purpose of these statutes is to prevent fraud and perjury in the proof of contracts. Although statutory provisions vary from state to state, those types of contracts usually required to be in writing are discussed here.

Contracts that, by their nature, cannot be performed within one year of the date the contract came into being. The decisive question is whether performance is possible within one year.

A collateral or secondary promise made to a creditor to pay or guarantee payment of the debt or obligation of another person should the latter default. Distinction must be made between contracts that are primarily for the benefit of the promisor (these are not required to be in writing) and those in which the promise to pay the debt is ancillary to that of the primary or original contract (these must be written under the statute). Furthermore, the promise must be made to the creditor rather than to the debtor. For example: rich Uncle Joe promises Tom Haberdasher that if Tom will extend credit to Nephew Goerge, Uncle Joe will pay for the clothes George buys if George cannot pay for them. Note that Uncle Joe's promise is ancillary to George's contract to buy clothes. Furthermore, Uncle Joe's promise is not for his own benefit, but for that of George. In addition, Uncle Joe made his promise directly to Tom, not to George. That being the case, Uncle Joe's promise will not be enforceable against him unless it is in writing.

The promise of the executor or administrator of a decedent's estate to pay the debts of the deceased from the personal funds of the executor or administrator, as distinguished from funds of the estate, must be in writing to be enforceable.

Contracts for the transfer of an interest in real property. This includes contracts to sell or to mortgage real estate and those granting easements or leases. In most states, special statutory provisions deal with the writing requirements for the leasing or rental of real property.

Miscellaneous requirements. There may be other writing requirements provided by specific statute. A common example is the need for a written policy in connection with insurance contracts.

UCC Provisions

The Uniform Commercial Code provides that contracts for the sale of goods must be evidenced by a writing when the price is $500 or more, except for the following times:

1. When there has been payment for the goods;
2. When there has been receipt and acceptance of the goods by the buyer;
3. When the goods are to be specially manufactured and are not fit for sale to others, and the seller has made a substantial beginning toward their manufacture or a substantial commitment to the procurement of the necessary raw materials for their manufacture;
4. When existence of a contract is admitted in judicial proceedings (UCC 2-201).

Kind of Writing Required

Requirements concerning the kind of writing necessary under the various statutes vary. Most states provide that a note or memorandum is sufficient. This may consist of several writings. It may be in the form of letters, receipts, telegrams, or a formal contract. Except for contracts for the sale of goods, the writing must contain all of the material terms of the contract: normally, the names of the parties, a description of the subject matter, the price or other consideration, and the terms of payment.

The writing must be signed by the party sought to be charged (or an agent of that party). Unless there is statutory provision to the contrary, the signature may be at any place on the writing. It need not consist of a fully signed name but may take the form of initials. It may be typewritten or stamped. The signature requirement may be satisfied by a mark or symbol.

In the case of contracts for the sale of goods, the Uniform Commercial Code provides that the writing requirement is satisfied if the writing indicates that a contract of sale has been entered into between the parties. However, enforceability is limited to the quantity of goods stated in the writing (UCC 2-201).

Failure to Execute a Writing

Failure to execute the necessary writing is a defense to an action brought either to enforce the contract or to seek damages for failure to perform. Part performance may make the writing unnecessary.

INTERPRETATION OF A WRITING

To ask a court to enforce a contract is to request that it effectuate the intentions of the parties. However, the language, words, and other manifestations of the intent of the parties to a contract are not always clear. Therefore, before a court can enforce a contract, it must first determine what the intentions of the parties are. This process is referred to as *interpretation* of contracts. Over the centuries, the courts have evolved some principles or standards for such interpretation and these are discussed below.

The transaction is viewed as a whole. This is especially important when the contract consists of several writings, or some writing supplemented by oral statements.

Conduct of the parties after execution of the written document is considered. Action of the parties is often revealing of the meaning they place upon the manifestation of their intentions.

The contract is construed strictly against the party preparing the written document, especially when the drafter of the contract is one skilled in preparation of such agreements. This is often the case with insurance policies.

In the absence of circumstances indicating a contrary intention, the following apply:

(a)   the ordinary or plain meaning of a word or words is preferred;

(b)   technical terms are given their technical meaning;

(c)   the usage of a trade, profession, locality, or community will be followed in the contracts of members of such groups.

When a term is missing in a contract, the court will first determine if the silence was intentional. If it was not, custom and prior practice will be referred to in order to determine the missing term.

When several interpretations are possible, a contract will be construed to be legal as opposed to illegal; and as avoiding justice, undue hardship, or unfairness to one or both of the parties.

In case of inconsistencies, typewritten words will be considered to prevail over printed words; written, over typewritten; words, over figures.

Parol Evidence Rule

When the parties have incorporated their intentions in a writing or writings and have come to regard such writing as the final expression of their intentions, then it may not be contradicted by evidence of any prior or contemporaneous oral agreement. Oral evidence may be introduced, however, to explain or clarify the writing. This is known as the *Parol Evidence Rule.*

RIGHTS OF THIRD PARTIES

Third-Party Beneficiaries

In some situations, persons other than the parties to the contract may derive some benefit from it. These are known as *third-party beneficiary* contracts.

When the benefit is a gift to the third person, he is known as the *donee beneficiary.* A common example is life insurance, in which the insurer agrees in consideration for premiums paid by the insured to pay the face amount of the policy to a named beneficiary upon the death of the insured. A donee beneficiary has the right to bring suit on the contract. In fact, the promisee also has a right of action and can recover nominal damages.

In other instances, the benefit to the third party is for the purpose of satisfying a legal obligation owed to that person. In that situation, the third party is known as a *creditor beneficiary*. For instance: A sells to B in return for which B promises to pay A's debt to C. A's purpose in securing B's promise is to confer a benefit upon his creditor, C. C is the creditor beneficiary. As such, C can proceed against either A or B if B does not perform.

A third type of beneficiary is created when a third party obtains a benefit from a contract which was entered into for the benefit of the two contracting parties and without intention to benefit a third person. Such a person is known as an *incidental beneficiary*. Incidental beneficiaries are often created as a result of contracts entered into by government bodies. An example would be in the case of a municipality's contract with a paver for improvement of a street. Persons owning property along that street receive the benefit of the improvements resulting from the contract. An incidental beneficiary has no rights under the contract.

A third party beneficiary acquires only those rights that are granted by the terms of the contract, and is limited to its terms.

Assignment

In the case of some contracts, it may be necessary or desirable to transfer either the rights or duties arising out of the contract. The law permits such transfers when the contract is not personal in nature. Such a transfer is known as an *assignment*.

The person making a transfer under a contract is known as the *assignor*. The person to whom the transfer is made is known as the *assignee*. Except when there is agreement to the contrary, an assignor remains bound by the legal obligations imposed upon him by the original contract. He must perform if the obligor does not. So, too, the rights acquired by an asignee are no greater than those the assignor had under the original contract. An assignee can usually bring legal action in his own name.

Ordinarily, a person can transfer his rights to receive the payment of money or goods under a contract. The securing of another person to perform one's duties under a contract is referred to as a *delegation of duties*. Delegation is permitted if the work to be performed is such that it does not require special skill, training, ability, or personal characteristics. For that reason contracts for personal services, such as those for employment, are not assignable.

An assignment generally requires no special form. It may be oral or written, except for those cases in which, by statutory provision, a specific written form must be executed. One situation in which this frequently occurs is the assignment of wages.

UCC Provisions

In the case of contracts for the sale of goods, the Uniform Commercial Code provides that such contracts may be assigned unless the parties otherwise agree and except when the assignment would materially change the performance of the other party.

Unless the language or circumstances indicate the contrary, it is a delegation of performance of the duties of the assignor and its acceptance by the assignee constitutes a promise by him to perform those duties (UCC 2-210).

CONTRACT TERMINATION

The termination of the legal duties which represent the contractual obligations of the parties is referred to as a *discharge*. Discharge may occur as a result of:

1. *Performance*—that is, carrying out the promises made. This is the usual method of discharge and, when done satisfactorily, gives rise to no cause of action.
2. Failure of a condition to occur. Ordinarily, this discharges the parties of their obligation but does not give rise to a cause of action.
3. *Rescission,* or mutual agreement by the parties to cancel or revoke their contract. When rescission is by mutual agreement, there is no cause of action.
4. *Breach*—that is, failure of one or both of the parties to fulfill their contractual obligations. This gives rise to a cause of action.

Performance: Effect of Conditions

Discharge by *performance* occurs when both parties have satisfied their contractual obligations in accordance with the terms of the agreement. Although the duty to perform is created by and exists from the creation of the contract, the time when performance is required may be conditioned upon the occurrence of a future event. Such a provision in the contract is known as a *condition precedent.* An example is a fire insurance policy, in which the condition precedent to performance is the occurrence of a fire. Note that failure of the condition to occur results in no obligation to perform. When the parties agree that they may be relieved of the duty to perform by some future occurrence, there is a *condition subsequent.* Again, fire insurance provides a good illustration. A frequent policy provision is that no action may be brought against the company unless notice of the fire is given within one year after the loss occurs. Failure to do so within that time would, therefore, be a condition subsequent and would relieve the company of the duty to perform.

It can be seen that the term *condition* in a contract refers to some event or fact, other than just the lapse of time, upon which the obligation to perform depends. Nonoccurrence of a condition discharges the contractual obligation and gives rise neither to breach of contract nor to a cause of action.

Discharge by Performance

Performance may be either satisfactory or substantial. When the parties fulfill the obligations they have promised to undertake, performance is complete. It is *satisfactory* when performance is made as promised. This would be true in the case of payment in full for goods purchased or delivery of goods which meet the specifications required by the order.

When performance unintentionally results in slight deviations from the agreement, or when the finished job is of a quality only slightly below that of satisfactory performance, there is said to be *substantial performance.* If improvement is neither possible nor made to bring the performance up to a state where it can be considered to be satisfactory, the courts will ordinarily require payment of the contract price less a sum for damages in an amount to compensate for the defective condition.

Breach of Contract

When a promisor either fails to perform or performs with major deviations from his promise, there is *breach of contract* and a cause of action is created. A material breach gives the injured party the right either to reject the tendered performance, or to accept it and recover damages.

Impossibility of Performance

A party may be excused from performance of a promise because of impossibility. If the subject matter is destroyed through no fault of either party, the party's obligations cease. For instance, in a contract for the sale of the original copy of the Declaration of Independence, performance would be excused if the original were destroyed by an accidental fire. So, too, the contract of employment of a major league baseball pitcher terminates if the player is killed in an automobile accident.

UCC Provisions

Provisions of the Uniform Commercial Code make possible release of contractual obligations because of "impracticability," a more liberal provision than the impossibility required for release under common law. Hence, in contracts for the sale of goods, the duty to perform may be ended because of the occurrence of a contingency, the nonoccurrence of which was assumed when the contract was made (UCC 2-615). This might be in the nature of a raw material shortage due to war, embargo, unforeseen shutdown of major sources of supply, or major crop failure, which result in marked increases in cost or prevent the securing of supplies.

Mutual Rescission and Waiver

Mutual agreement of the parties to rescind or revoke a contract is valid, since the consideration of each party to such an agreement is the giving up of a legal right under the contract. Not only may the parties mutually agree to cancel or rescind, but one party may voluntarily forego certain of his rights under the contract. Thus, acceptance of incomplete or defective performance without objection is a waiver of the right to strict and satisfactory performance. However, a party cannot first waive his rights and then later bring an action because of failure to receive those same rights. When defective performance occurs, a party's failure to give notice of the defect can sustain a reasonable belief that there has been a waiver and he may be estopped later from asserting any rights. A party may accept a defective performance but reserve his right to seek damages. Such would be the case when a party is in urgent and immediate need of a good. He may accept delivery of material of lower quality than ordered because of that need yet still wish to reserve the right to seek damages. A reservation of right may be oral, but it is preferably written.

UCC Provisions

In the case of contracts for the sale of goods, the Uniform Commercial Code provides in Section 1-107 that "any claim or right arising out of an alleged breach can be discharged in whole or in part without consideration by a written waiver or renunciation signed and delivered by the aggrieved party" (UCC 2-309).

REMEDIES FOR BREACH OF CONTRACT

An injured party who seeks a remedy because of breach of contract must take action within the applicable Statute of Limitations. The time period for this under the Uniform Commercial Code is normally four years after the cause of action accrues (UCC 2-725). In the case of other contracts, the allowable time varies from state to state. A common provision is six years for simple contracts, and 21 years for contracts under seal.

In the case of breach of contract, the remedy at law is for damages. The injured party has a duty to *mitigate damages.* That means he must prevent an increase in damages and cannot act in a manner that would result in their becoming any greater. Nor can he make a profit from the breach. The purpose of damages is to place him in the same position he would have occupied had the contract been satisfactorily performed. Damages are of several kinds: compensatory, consequential, punitive, nominal, liquidated, and unliquidated.

Compensatory damages refer to the sum necessary to make up for the actual loss incurred as a result of the breach. It is the amount the injured party is out as a result of nonperformance. In the case of the sale of property, it is frequently computed as the difference between contract price and market price, calculated so as to enable the injured party to replace the goods through another source of supply.

Consequential damages are those that do not arise directly from the breach but from unusual circumstances attendant the contract. For instance, in a contract to provide air conditioning service for a retailer for whom a faulty mechanism caused an interruption of service, consequential damages resulted when a customer of the store fell and was injured because the defective mechanism leaked, resulting in a slippery surface when water spilled onto the floor.

Punitive damages, also known as *exemplary damages,* are generally not recoverable in a contract situation. An exception occurs when there has been wanton, reckless, and irresponsible action. *Nominal damages* are those for a token amount, such as one dollar, and are awarded if there is no reasonable certainty as to the occurrence of a loss. Such an award would be based on mere speculation. A person, however, may recover for losses that would be sustained in the future if he can prove such losses will occur.

Liquidated damages refer to those which are stated in the contract as due to be paid in case of breach or default. Courts are reluctant to enforce such provisions unless it can be shown that the amount specified is not excessive, that it is reasonable and proportional to the presumed loss, that the contract is such that it would be difficult either to prove damages or that damages anticipated are uncertain, and that the parties intended to liquidate damages in advance. Liquidated damage provisions that require payment of an unreasonable sum or a sum not related to the possible damages to be incurred are looked upon as a penalty and are considered by most courts to be void. When the liquidated damage provisions of a contract are not enforced, compensatory damages will be awarded upon sufficient proof.

When damages are inadequate as a remedy, equitable relief is possible in the form of specific performance. Generally, this is sought when the injured party seeks to have a contract for the sale of realty enforced or seeks enforcement of a contract for the sale of goods that are unique or unusual. Another equitable remedy is an injunction. Frequently this is sought when artists or athletes of great prominence threaten to breach a contract of employment by performing for a third party. An injunction enjoins employment of their talents for any but the party to the original contract.

UCC Provisions

In the case of contracts for the sale of goods, the Uniform Commercial Code provides that the remedies available under the Code are to be liberally administered so that the injured party is put in "as good a position as if the other party had fully performed." Neither consequential nor punitive damages are available unless specifically provided for in the Code (UCC 1-106).

Other remedies under the Code include *rejection* of goods that a buyer receives that do not conform with the goods ordered (UCC 2-601). The seller has the right to *cure;* that is, the right within a reasonable time to make correction of defects in performance of the contract (UCC 2-602). A buyer also has the right to *cover,* which refers to his right to purchase goods in substitution for those a seller has failed to supply under a contract (UCC 2-712).

A seller has the right to *stop delivery* of goods when the buyer either repudiates the contract or fails to make payment due (UCC 2-705). A seller who is in possession of goods that were intended for a buyer who has either breached or repudiated the contract has the right of *resale* (UCC 2-706). All of these are in addition to the remedies of damages and specific performance.

The following opinion of the court in *Lee* v. *Joseph E. Seagram & Sons, Inc.,* discusses both the parol evidence rule and the matter of damages awarded for breach of contract.

Lee v. *Joseph E. Seagram & Sons, Inc.*
552 F. 2d 447 (1977)

This is an appeal by defendant Joseph E. Seagram & Sons, Inc., from a judgment in favor of the plaintiffs on a claim asserting common law breach of an oral contract. . . . The plaintiffs are Harold S. Lee (now deceased) and his two sons, Lester and Eric. . . .

The Lees owned a 50% interest in Capitol City Liquor Company, Inc., a wholesale liquor distributorship located in Washington, D.C. The other 50% was owned by Harold's brother, Henry D. Lee, and his nephew, Arthur Lee. Seagram is a distiller of alcoholic beverages. Capitol City carried numerous Seagram brands and a large portion of its sales were generated by Seagram lines.

. . . In May, 1970, Harold Lee discussed the possible sale of Capitol City with Jack Yogman, then Executive Vice President of Seagram (and now President). Lee offered to sell Capitol City to Seagram but conditioned the offer on Seagram's agreement to relocate Harold and his sons, the 50% owners of Capitol City, in a new distributorship of their own in a different city.

. . . The purchase of the assets of Capitol City was consummated on September 30, 1970 pursuant to a written agreement. The promise to relocate the father and sons thereafter was not reduced to writing.

. . .

The plaintiffs claimed a breach of the oral agreement to relocate Harold Lee's sons, alleging that Seagram had had opportunities to procure another distributorship for the Lees but had refused to do so. The Lees brought this action fifteen months after the sale of the Capitol City distributorship to Seagram. They contended that they had performed their obligation by agreeing to the sale by Capitol City of its assets to Seagram, but that Seagram had failed to perform its obligation under the separate oral contract between the Lees and Seagram. . . .

Appellant urges several grounds for reversal. It contends that, as a matter of law, (1) plaintiffs' proof of the alleged oral agreement is barred by the parol evidence rule; and (2) the oral agreement is too vague and indefinite to be enforceable. Appellant also contends that plaintiffs' proof of damages is speculative and incompetent.

[The District Court,] in a careful analysis of the application of the parol evidence rule, decided that the rule did not bar proof of the oral agreement. We agree.

The District Court . . . treated the issue as whether the written agreement for the sale of assets was an "integrated" agreement not only of all the mutual agreements concerning the sale of Capitol City assets, but also of *all* the mutual agreements of the parties. Finding the language of the sales agreement "somewhat ambiguous," the court decided that the determination of whether the parol evidence rule applies must await the taking of evidence on the issue of whether the sales agreement was intended to be a complete and accurate integration of all of the mutual promises of the parties.

Seagram did not avail itself of this invitation. It failed to call as witnesses any of the three persons who negotiated the sales agreement on behalf of Seagram regarding the intention of the parties to integrate all mutual promises or regarding the failure of the written agreement to contain an integration clause. . . .

The District Court stated the cardinal issue to be whether the parties "intended" the written agreement for the sale of assets to be the complete and accurate integration of all the mutual promises of the parties. If the written contract was not a complete integration, the court held, then the parol evidence rule has no application.

. . . The written agreement does not contain the customary integration clause. . . . The omission may, of course, have been caused by mutual trust and confidence . . .

Nor do we see any contradiction of the terms of the sales agreement . . . The written agreement dealt with the sale of corporate assets, the oral agreement with the relocation of the Lees. Thus, the oral agreement does not vary or contradict the money consideration recited in the contract as flowing to the selling corporation. . . .

III

The jury awarded the two sons and the estate of the father damages in the amount of $407,850. The essence of the court's charge on the subject was that in a contract action the basic principle of damages "is to indemnify a plaintiff for the gains prevented and the losses sustained by a defendant's breach, to leave him no worse but in no better position than he would have been had the breach not occurred." . . .

. . . Plaintiffs' evidence bore directly on the damages sustained by breach of a contract to provide a distributorship of one-half the cost and worth of Capitol City . . . Appellant's contention that plaintiffs should have been required to prove . . . that there was a Seagram distributor actually willing to sell his distributorship to them, is without merit. The oral agreement . . . was for Seagram to *provide* a distributorship for the Lees. . . .

. . . Lost profits can . . . be a proper measure of damages for breach of contract.

Seagram objects to the fact that plaintiffs' proof concerned the profit experience of Capitol City. It suggests that the best way of determining profits would be to consider the profits of an existing distributorship. But it came forward with no such proof . . . Since Seagram's breach has made difficult a more precise proof of damages, it must bear the risk of uncertainty created by its conduct. . . .

Affirmed.

QUESTIONS

1. Considering what you have done so far today and what you are planning to do for the rest of the day, identify any contracts into which you have entered. Are they already executed or executory? How many were oral or implied rather than being written? Has anyone made an offer to you today to enter into a contract? Did you accept and, if so, how did you accept? Was it for a bilateral or unilateral contract?

2. How would you go about withdrawing an oral offer you made this morning to buy a classmate's textbook? What would you say or do? What time frame would be necessary in order for the withdrawal to be effective?

3. Assume you are in business and a young-looking person offers to enter into a contract with you. How would you protect yourself if you do not know that person's age? Why would it be important for you to consider self-protection?

4. Give an example of a situation where a contract would be affected by fraud, by duress. How would you change these examples from fraud to misrepresentation and from duress to undue influence?

5. Why is consideration required for a contract? Can you think of reasons why a "bargained-for exchange" is a necessary element?

6. What is the effect when a contract is oral and the Statute of Frauds requires that it be in writing? What do the courts do in such situations?

7. The remedies for breach of contract under the UCC include "self help" in addition to damages and specific performance. Why do you think these provisions were included in the UCC? Do you see them as an improvement over the right to go to court or do you consider them to be less satisfactory? Why?

NOTES

[1] UCC 2–207
[2] UCC 2–206
[3] UCC 2–205

criminal law

FIFTEEN

This chapter deals with the substantive criminal law. It is that area of law which defines conduct that is criminal and provides for the punishment to be imposed for such conduct. Most criminal law is developed under state statute rather than federal law. The origin of many of the provisions is the law of crimes as developed in the early English common law. Frequently it is in code form, the states having supplemented or modified, and some having replaced, the common law by statute. One crime, treason, is mentioned in the United States Constitution. Similar provisions appear in most state constitutions.

Crimes are public wrongs. A crime is an act or omission which is prohibited by law and for which an offender is prosecuted by the state. Punishment upon conviction may be by fine, imprisonment, or both. It may also be by death, although that is infrequent today.

CLASSIFICATION OF CRIMES

The early common law divided crimes into three major groups according to the gravity of the offense: treason, felonies, and misdemeanors. The classification of a crime is important and can have far-reaching consequences. For instance, today it can be determinative of whether arrest for commission of the act is permissible without a warrant, whether a specific court has jurisdiction over the matter, whether probation or parole will be granted to a person convicted of the act, and whether a convicted person will have the right to serve on a jury or to practice a particular profession.

For procedural purposes, crimes are often divided into major crimes (treason, felonies, and misdemeanors) and petty offenses. The latter are also known as summary offenses since they commonly come within the jurisdiction of a magistrate who has the authority to dispose of the matter summarily.

In the United States today, the most important classification of crime is that of felony and misdemeanor. Felonies are the very serious crimes; misdemeanors, less serious. Under federal law, a felony is any crime for which the penalty is death or imprisonment for more than one year. Federal misdemeanors are those offenses for which the penalty is imprisonment for less than a year.

State criminal codes frequently set up categories related to the sentences for crimes. The classification made by one state in its code is shown in Table 15-1. Note that murder in the first degree has been distinguished from other crimes and placed in a category by itself.

Mala in Se and Mala Prohibita

Crimes are sometimes described as crimes *mala in se,* those consisting of actions that are wrong in themselves or inherently evil, and crimes *mala prohibita,* those consisting of actions that are not inherently evil but are wrong only because they are prohibited by statute. This distinction is used in determining whether certain homicides constitute involuntary manslaughter.

Ordinance Violations

There is some difference of opinion as to whether violations of ordinances enacted by counties, cities, townships, and other municipalities are crimes, even though the penalties include fine and imprisonment. Generally these violations are disposed of by a municipal, city, or police court. The matters involved usually deal with regulation of traffic, garbage, pets, and the like.

Corpus Delicti

An individual's guilt or innocence in connection with a crime becomes relevant only after it has first been established that a crime has been committed. To do this, a prima facie case must be established. Those elements which the prosecution must plead and prove to show that a particular crime has been committed are referred to as the *corpus delicti* of the crime. Each crime has its own distinctive elements. If one or more is missing, the particular crime could not have been committed.

The corpus delicti of each crime consists of a *mens rea,* or criminal state of mind, and an *actus reus,* the commission of some prohibited act.

TABLE 15-1. Categories of Crimes by Sentence

CRIME	SENTENCE	
	Maximum Fine	*Term of Imprisonment*
Murder in the first degree	—	Life (death penalty alternative)
Felony of the first degree	$25,000	More than 10 years
Felony of the second degree	$25,000	Maximum of 10 years
Felony of the third degree	$15,000	Maximum of 7 years
Misdemeanor of the first degree	$10,000	Maximum of 5 years
Misdemeanor of the second degree	$ 5,000	Maximum of 2 years
Misdemeanor of the third degree	$ 2,500	Maximum of 1 year
Summary Offense	$ 300	Maximum of 90 days

Mens Rea

The mens rea is the mental element necessary to a crime. For most crimes, proof of a general mens rea is sufficient. The requirement is that the accused meant to do what he did. (An exception exists in those cases in which negligence is the basis of criminal liability.) Some crimes require, in addition, proof of a specific mens rea, such as a particular intent.

Some statutory violations are labelled criminal although there is no requirement of a mens rea. In the case of these offenses, a person is held strictly liable upon commission of a prohibited act. This occurs most frequently in connection with acts that are against the public welfare, such as the sale of adulterated food. There is a question of whether there can be a "true crime" without a mens rea.

Actus Reus

A crime requires an act; the law does not punish a person for mere thought. The criminal act may be one of commission or omission. If the criminal act is one of omission, it must be of a possible and legally required performance. Failure to meet moral or ethical standards, when there is no legal requirement involved, is not a crime.

Causation

An accused's criminal act must be the legal cause of the injuries for which the state is prosecuting. Essentially, the standards for the requisite, legally recognized causation are the same as those for proximate cause in the law of torts.

Anticipatory Acts as Crimes

Acts which are anticipatory to the commission of a particular crime may be crimes in themselves. These include solicitation, conspiracy, and attempt.

Solicitation occurs when, having the intention that another person commit a crime, an individual entices, encourages, incites, or otherwise induces that person to commit a felony or misdemeanor. It is not necessary that the crime being solicited actually be committed.

Conspiracy is a combination between two or more persons to accomplish a criminal or unlawful act, or to do a lawful act by criminal or unlawful means. The common law crime of conspiracy requires merely the forbidden combination; no additional act is necessary. By statutory provision in some jurisdictions, some overt act in furtherance of the unlawful plan is required.

An attempt to commit a crime can be a crime in itself. The crime of *attempt* requires that there be both an intent to commit a particular crime and an act in pursuance of that intent which goes beyond mere preparation but which falls short of actual commission of the crime. Determination of whether an act has gone sufficiently beyond preparation is often difficult. The intended crime must be legally possible of commission, and there must be apparent ability to commit that crime. Attempt cannot be a crime unless the attempt, if completed, would have constituted a crime.

The opinion of the court in *State* v. *Carbone*, which follows, deals with solicitation.

State v. *Carbone*

10 N.J. 329, 91 A.2d 571 (1952)

. . . [A]ppeal a judgment of conviction against Carbone and Franze [charged with conspiring] to transgress the laws of the State denouncing bookmaking on horse races. . . .

There was evidence tending to show the illegal combination charged, the commission of the overt acts specified and other such acts in the advancement of the undertaking. . . .

At common law, a conspiracy consists not merely in the intention but in the agreement of two or more persons (not being husband and wife) to do an unlawful act, or to do a lawful act by unlawful means. So long as such a design rests in intention only, it is not indictable. When two agree to carry it into effect, the very plot is an act in itself . . . The agreement is an advancement of the intention which each has conceived in his mind; the mind proceeds from a secret intention to the overt act of mutual consultation and agreement. . . . It is not requisite, in order to constitute a conspiracy at common law, that the acts agreed to be done be such as would be criminal if done; it is enough if the acts agreed to be done, although not criminal, be wrongful, i.e., amount to a civil wrong. . . . The gist of the offense of conspiracy lies, not in doing the act, nor effecting the purpose for which the conspiracy is formed, nor in attempting to do them, nor in inciting others to do them, but in the forming of the scheme or agreement between the parties. . . . The offense depends on the unlawful agreement and not on the act which follows it; the latter is not evidence of the former. . . . The combination itself is vicious and gives the public an interest to interfere by indictment. . . . The external or overt act of the crime is concert by which initial consent to a common purpose is exchanged. . . . In order to render one criminally liable for conspiracy at common law, it must be shown that he entered into an agreement as thus defined with one or more persons, whether charged with him in the indictment or not, and whether known or unknown. . . .

But it is not essential that there be direct contact between the parties, or that all enter into the conspiratorial agreement at one and the same time. "It may be that the alleged conspirators have never seen each other, and have never corresponded. One may have never heard the name of the other, and yet by the law they may be parties to the same common criminal agreement." . . . One who joins a conspiracy after its formation is equally guilty with the original conspirators. . . .

When two or more persons have entered into a conspiracy to perpetrate a crime, the acts and declarations of one of the conspirators in furtherance of the common object are deemed in law the facts and declarations of all. . . .

The convictions of both defendants are well grounded in the evidence. . . . Proof of the existence of a conspiracy is generally a "matter of inference deduced from certain criminal acts of the parties accused, done in pursuance of an apparent criminal purpose in common between them." . . . Though the act of conspiracy is the gist of the offense, "it is not necessary to show an actual association or confederacy, but it may be left to reasonable inference." . . .

Judgment affirmed.

Parties to a Crime

Criminal culpability, that is, blame or fault, can rest not only with the person who actually commits the criminal act but also with other persons who aid and abet in any significant way in the commission of the crime. Under the common law, the perpetrator of a felony is a *principal in the first degree.* Persons other than perpetrators who are present at the time of the commission of a felony and who aid and abet in its commission are *principals in the second degree.* Nonperpetrators who aid and abet and who are not present when the felony is committed are *accessories.* They may be designated as accessories before or after the fact. In the case of misdemeanors, all culpable persons are considered to be principals except for accessories after the fact, who are not considered to be parties to the crime at all. Modern criminal statutes tend to treat all parties as principals, whether they be perpetrators or merely aid and abet. In some jurisdictions, the designation "accessory after the fact" has been retained in felony cases to distinguish them from principals.

CRIMINAL RESPONSIBILITY

Capacity of Parties

Responsibility for the consequences of one's actions is basic to the criminal law. Lack of capacity may diminish that responsibility and therefore be a defense to criminal charges.

Insanity   Legal insanity is a defense to criminal charges. A person cannot be convicted of a crime if at the time he committed the offense his mind was so defective he was incapable of forming the requisite criminal intent. The courts, however, are not agreed as to what constitutes insanity.

A person is presumed to be sane at the time of committing an offense. The prosecution must prove the accused's sanity only when insanity is raised as a defense. Substantive criminal law is concerned with sanity or lack thereof at the time of commission of the offense. Procedural questions, however, may arise concerning an accused's mental capacity to stand trial. This can lead to postponement of a trial until a person is determined to be competent.

Intoxication   Involuntary intoxication is generally a defense to criminal charges when the intoxication is to such a degree that the accused cannot be held responsible for his acts. Voluntary intoxication, on the other hand, is generally not a defense to criminal charges. If, however, the crime requires proof of a specific mens rea, evidence of intoxication may be admitted to determine if the accused was capable of the necessary intent. Whether the degree of intoxication was sufficient to prevent formation of the intent is a jury question.

Many jurisdictions apply the same rules regarding intoxication to mental states and conditions resulting from the use of narcotics and dangerous drugs.

Infancy   Under the common law, children are not always considered to be sufficiently mature to form a criminal intent. A child under the age of seven is conclusively presumed to be incapable of committing a crime. In the case of a child aged 7 to 14, presumption of incapability is rebuttable. This means that the prosecution can offer evidence to show the particular child was capable of forming the requisite intent. Without proof that this is so, the child cannot be convicted. Children over 14 are treated as adults. Some states have made statutory changes in these presumptions, generally in the direction of restricting infancy as a defense.

Corporations   In some cases, a corporation may be held criminally liable for crimes committed on its behalf by its employees and agents. There is some question as to whether a corporation can commit a crime requiring a mens rea. Some courts answer this question by imputing the mens rea of the firm's agents or employees to the corporation.

Mistake

Ignorance or mistake of fact may negate criminal intent. The mistake must be genuine and consist of a reasonable belief in facts which, if they did exist, would either make the act an innocent one, justify it, or excuse it. Ignorance or mistake of the law, on the other hand, is seldom an excuse.

Coercion

Coercion or compulsion, consisting of threat of death or serious bodily harm to the accused or a member of his family, may constitute a defense to a crime requiring criminal intent, except under the common law in the case of homicide. Duress does not excuse the killing of another human being.

Self-defense

An individual is justified in using nondeadly force in self-defense if a reasonable person would have been put in apprehension of immediate harm and if the force used was reasonable under the circumstances. *Deadly force* is that which is likely to or does cause death. It is justified in only a few situations. As a general rule, it can be said that deadly force is never justified if nondeadly force will accomplish one's purpose. Deadly force is not justified in the defense of property, even if it is in one's home. Only when an atrocious felony which threatens life or serious bodily harm is being committed may deadly force be used, and then only as a last resort.

In most jurisdictions a person has a duty to retreat as far as possible before one is justified in taking another's life in self-defense or in defense of another person. An exception ordinarily exists in defense of human life in one's home, office, or place of business, provided such force is necessary under the circumstances. One normally has the same rights to use force in defending others as he has in defending himself.

A law enforcement officer may be justified in the use of deadly force to prevent commission of an atrocious felony, but not to prevent commission of a misdemeanor. So, also, deadly force used in making an arrest or to prevent escape can be justified only in felony cases, and then only if there is no other means of apprehending the felon. Some jurisdictions further require that the felony committed be one of violence and surprise. Officers act at their peril if they use deadly force upon mere suspicion that a felony has been committed.

Consent

In the case of some crimes, such as rape, consent of the victim means that there may be no crime at all. Aside from such crimes, consent is not a defense for an act which results in a public injury, such as one which causes breach of the peace or constitutes an affront to public morals.

Entrapment

Entrapment is a valid defense to criminal charges. It consists of conduct by a law enforcement officer which instigates the commission of a crime by another. When the officer merely provides an opportunity for commission of a crime, there is no entrapment.

Statute of Limitations

Expiration of the time period provided by the applicable Statute of Limitations may be a defense in criminal cases, just as it is in civil cases.

CRIMES AGAINST THE PERSON

Homicide

Homicide is the killing of a human being by another human being. Not all homicides are criminal. Homicide that is either justifiable or excusable is noncriminal.

Homicide is *justifiable* when it is commanded or authorized by law, when it is done in the performance of a legal duty or exercise of a legal right where the slayer is not at fault. Examples include execution by court order of a convicted capital offender, necessary killings by police officers in preventing atrocious felonies or in capturing a felon, necessary killings in self defense and in the defense of others.

Homicide is *excusable* when the slayer may be at fault to some extent but not to a degree sufficient to impose criminal sanction. An example of excusable homicide is a killing by a person, such as an infant or insane person, incapable of committing a crime. Homicide may be excusable when a slaying results from an accident or misadventure, such as when a person runs in front of a moving vehicle, the driver of which is unable to avoid hitting and fatally injuring the person.

Killings which are neither justifiable nor excusable are criminal. Criminal homicide may be either murder or manslaughter.

Murder   *Murder* is the unlawful killing of a human being by another with malice aforethought. While the malice cannot be an afterthought, killing on the spur of the moment is not precluded by the requirement of "malice aforethought." *Malice* means a specific intention to act in such a way that death of a human being may result. The requisite intention, sometimes referred to as a "man endangering state of mind," exists when there is:

1. Intent to kill or to inflict great bodily injury, or
2. Intent to act with wanton and willful disregard of unreasonable risk to human life, or
3. Intent to resist lawful arrest with force, or
4. Intent to commit a dangerous felony.

Therefore, malice aforethought may be said to exist in the case of killing by firing a loaded gun into the eyes of another, intending to blind him; by deliberately setting fire to a home with knowledge that persons are asleep therein; by fatal blows to the head received by a law enforcement officer in a struggle with the accused who was resisting arrest being made with legal authority and in a reasonable manner; by actions committed in perpetration of such violent crimes as rape, arson, and robbery. The latter is the basis for the *felony murder rule,* which is that an unlawful killing caused by actions in the attempt or perpetration of another felony inherently dangerous to human life is murder, whether it is intentional or not.

When the person killed is different from the intended victim, the slayer's malice aforethought as to the intended victim is considered to be transferred to the actual victim. This is known as the doctrine of transferred intent. (It is applicable in the case of other crimes, as well.) For instance, when a husband, with intent to kill his wife, fires a gun in her direction but fatally wounds, instead, a neighbor who is standing beside her, he will be deemed to have the requisite malice as to the neighbor.

Unlike the common law, modern statutes recognize degrees of murder. Ordinarily, murder is classified as of the first degree when it is committed by means of poison;

by lying in wait; by any other kind of willful, deliberate, and premeditated killing; or in the commission of such felonies as robbery, rape, arson, burglary, or kidnapping. It is not uncommon to find all other kinds of murder classified as of the second degree.

Manslaughter   *Manslaughter* is the unlawful killing of one human being by another without malice aforethought. Manslaughter may be voluntary or involuntary.

Voluntary manslaughter is an intentional killing, committed without premeditation or malice aforethought in a sudden heat of passion caused by legally adequate provocation by the victim. The provocation must be sufficient to inflame a reasonable person to passion. Words alone are never sufficient, nor ordinarily are insulting gestures, simple assault, or technical battery. On the other hand, seduction of a man's wife or mutual quarrel and combat can constitute adequate provocation.

Heat of passion consists of more than mere anger and is less than insanity. The provocation must so arouse and inflame that the slayer does not know what is being done. At the time of the killing the slayer must still be acting in the heat of passion. If it has cooled to the point where he knows what he is doing, the homicide is murder. Lapse of time is an important, but not the sole, determining factor in deciding whether cooling has taken place.

Causal connection must be shown. The provocation must have caused the heat of passion which caused the homicide.

It is also voluntary manslaughter if a person intentionally kills another, believing unreasonably at the time of the killing that the circumstances are such as to justify the killing.

Involuntary manslaughter is an unintentional and unlawful killing, without malice aforethought. It covers unintentional killings that occur in connection with unlawful, inherently dangerous, mala in se acts, as well as unintentional killings which are the result of criminal negligence. Examples include a killing caused by careless use of a loaded firearm and death of a pedestrian caused by a drunken driver. In the latter case, it should be noted that some jurisdictions have a separate crime, manslaughter committed in the operation of a motor vehicle.

Classification   Murder and manslaughter are felonies, with the exception of involuntary manslaughter which is classified as a misdemeanor in some jurisdictions.

In connection with homicide, much discussion and debate have been focused on the criminal status, if any, in the killing of a fetus that has not yet been "born alive" and the withdrawal of life support systems from persons with "brain death."

Assault and Battery

Battery is the intentional, nonconsensual, unlawful touching of another. There is a battery no matter how slight the injury to the victim. Some jurisdictions require that the touching be a rude, angry, revengeful act, but the more common requirement is simply that the touching be willful.

Assault consists of an attempted battery or placing a person in apprehension of an immediate battery. Unlike battery, assault requires no physical contact. As a general rule, words alone are not sufficient to constitute an assault; the words must be accompanied by some threatening or menacing act.

Both assault and battery are misdemeanors at common law. Modern statutes tend to combine the two into one crime, usually assault. The Pennsylvania criminal code, for instance, provides that "a person is guilty of assault if he:

1. attempts to cause or intentionally, knowingly or recklessly causes bodily injury to another; or

2. negligently causes bodily injury to another with a deadly weapon; or

3. attempts by physical menace to put another in fear of imminent serious bodily injury."

The common law crime of *mayhem,* which consists of removing or permanently disabling some part of a person's body, may be included in statutory assault. Permanent disfigurement is usually also covered by the crime. Statutes usually provide for different types of assault, such as aggravated assault (involving serious bodily harm), assault with a deadly weapon, assault on a police officer, and simple assault. The first three are usually classified as felonies; the latter, a misdemeanor.

Rape

Rape is defined in modern criminal codes as sexual intercourse with another person by forcible compulsion or threat of such or with a person incapable of consent. This crime is sometimes referred to as forcible rape to distinguish is from the crime of statutory rape. Under the old common law definition, rape consisted of unlawful sexual intercourse with a female without her consent.

Statutory rape consists of sexual intercourse with a person under a statutorily specified age (16, for example) whether the person consents or not. It is based on the presumption that a person under that age is incapable of understanding the full implications of giving consent. Mistake as to the age of the person is ordinarily not a defense to statutory rape.

Rape is a felony. Increased attention has been focused in recent years upon treatment of victims of rape.

Other Sex Offenses

State statutes make criminal other offenses related to sexual activity. The trend in recent years has been to remove criminality from sexual acts between consenting adults, except where such acts are performed for money or are incestuous. Criminal sex offenses include involuntary deviate sexual intercourse, indecent exposure, indecent assault, corruption of minors, and prostitution.

Involuntary deviate sexual intercourse is ordinarily a felony. It is involuntary when it is forced, when one of the parties is incapable of giving consent because of age or mental incapacity, or when one of the parties is under a statutorily specified age.

Indecent exposure is generally defined as exhibition of one's genitals under circumstances where such conduct is likely to cause affront or alarm and for the purpose of arousing or gratifying the sexual desires of the exhibitionist or others. Usually it is a misdemeanor.

Indecent assault, also usually a misdemeanor, consists of sexual contact with another person not one's spouse when one knows that the contact is offensive to the other person, or the other person is incapable of appraising the nature of the conduct, or the other person is unaware such contact is being committed, or the other person is not able to resist because of a drugged, intoxicated, or like condition.

Corruption of a minor is generally defined as any act which corrupts the morals or contributes to the sexual delinquency of a minor. It is usually a misdemeanor.

Prostitution consists of engaging in sexual activity as a business. Statutory provisions ordinarily make it a crime not only to engage directly in prostitution but also to promote, compel, procure, encourage, or solicit prostitution. Persons of both sexes can commit prostitution. It is usually a misdemeanor. Prostitution is generally considered to be an offense against public decency rather than a crime against the person; some, in fact, consider is to be a victimless crime.

Kidnapping

Kidnapping, as generally defined by federal and state statute, is the intentional and unlawful confinement or movement from one place to another of a person against his will. It is a felony and may even be a capital offense if there is a ransom demand. The federal crime of kidnapping requires that there be movement across state lines.

Other offenses, related to deprivation of a person's liberty include false imprisonment and interference with custody of children or committed persons. They are usually misdemeanors.

False imprisonment consists of knowingly and unlawfully restraining another so as to interfere substantially with his liberty. *Interference with custody* occurs when a person, not privileged to do so, knowingly or recklessly takes or entices a minor from the custody of the parent or guardian, or a committed person away from lawful custody.

CRIMES AGAINST PROPERTY

Burglary

At common law, *burglary* consists of breaking and entering the dwelling house of another in the night time with the intent to commit a felony. In most jurisdictions today, burglary has been expanded by statute so that it consists of either breaking or unlawful entry; it includes buildings other than dwelling houses; it can occur during the day as well as at night; and it includes the intent to commit any crime, not just a felony.

Burglary is a felony. A closely related offense is *criminal trespass.* It consists of entering or remaining in a building without license or privilege to do so. In some jurisdictions, it is a felony; in others, a misdemeanor.

Larceny or Theft

Common law *larceny* consists of taking and carrying away the personal property of another with the intent to permanently deprive the owner of his property. Two other common law crimes, embezzlement and obtaining property by false pretenses, are closely related to larceny. Common law *embezzlement* consists of unlawful appropriation of another's goods by one who obtained lawful possession of them by virtue of his office or employment. *False pretenses* is the criminal act of obtaining both possession and title to the property of another through false representations.

By statutory change in many jurisdictions, these three common law crimes have been classified as types of theft. *Theft* is ordinarily defined as unlawfully taking or appropriating another's property for one's self or one's benefit. Separate offenses may be designated when the theft is accomplished by other than a taking. For instance, there is *theft by deception*. This occurs when one deprives another of his property by some falsity, including deceiving the other person by false impression or by other fraudulent means.

Theft by extortion is often referred to as blackmail. It consists of obtaining the property of another by threat, intimidation, or fear of accusation or exposure. The threat may be to inflict bodily injury, to publicly expose matters which hold another up to contempt or ridicule, to take or withhold some form of official action, to bring about or to continue a strike or boycott, or to disrupt or injure another's business. *Theft by failure to make required disposition* is committed by a person who obtains property upon agreement or subject to legal obligation to make specified payment or other disposition of that property. The offense occurs when that person intentionally deals with the property as his own and fails to make the required payment or disposition. It is also not uncommon to find theft of services, retail theft (commonly known as shoplifting), unauthorized use of motor vehicles, and theft of trade secrets designated as separate crimes.

Theft may be a felony or misdemeanor. In some states, theft is a felony when the amount involved exceeds $2000 or if a firearm, airplane, or motor vehicle has been stolen. It is also not uncommon for theft to be a felony when property is taken by threat or in breach of a fiduciary obligation. Other thefts are ordinarily misdemeanors.

Receiving and Concealing Stolen Goods

Closely associated with theft is the offense of *receiving and concealing stolen property*. Either receipt or concealment is sufficient to constitute a crime. A person may be the receiver of stolen goods if he exercises dominion and control over the property. It is not necessary that the person actually have the goods in his hands; nor is it necessary that the accused receive the stolen goods directly from the thief. In fact, he need not know the true owner. Furthermore, it is not material that he received them from a person who knows that the property was stolen.

Concealing stolen property does not require that an accused physically hide the goods. All that is necessary is that he aid the thief in doing something with the property to prevent the true owner from using and enjoying his goods or that he assist in securing the goods to the benefit of the thief. This might consist of actions such as removing identification or serial numbers, or painting or otherwise changing the color of the article.

In the absence of express statutory provision, it is unclear whether knowledge that goods were stolen is requisite to the crime or whether mere suspicion is sufficient. The intent required is the same as that for theft: to deprive the true owner of his property.

Many states classify receipt and concealment of stolen goods as a felony when the receiver is in the business of buying and selling stolen property. Whether it is a misdemeanor or felony is ordinarily otherwise determined by the value and kind of property involved.

Robbery

Common law *robbery* is the unlawful taking and carrying away of the personal property of another from his person or in his presence by violence or by threat of violence. Robbery is larceny from the person by force or intimidation. Robbery differs from larceny in two ways:

1. Robbery requires force or threat of force. The slightest force—even a shove or a tug—is sufficient.
2. Robbery requires a taking from a person or in his presence. Any place within his hearing or sight is ordinarily deemed to be sufficient.

Some jurisdictions, by statute, have expanded the concept of robbery so that a person is guilty of the crime if, in the course of committing a theft, he inflicts or threatens another with serious bodily injury or he commits or threatens to commit a serious felony.

Robbery is itself a felony. Different degrees of felony may be designated, based upon whether the theft involved was accompanied by mere threat or by actual physical injury. Armed robbery is ordinarily a very serious felony.

Arson

Common law *arson* consists of the willful and malicious burning of the dwelling house of another, by day or by night. The crime has been expanded by statute to include buildings other than a dwelling house and to include one's own property. In some jurisdictions, the burning of another's personal property, when it is valued at more than a statutorily specified minimum, constitutes arson. In some, arson includes causing an explosion even though there be no burning. It is not uncommon to find a specific statutory crime for the burning of property with the intent to defraud an insurer, regardless of whether that property is owned by the accused or by another.

Arson is a felony. Closely related to arson are crimes, ordinarily classified as felonies, which consist of causing or risking catastrophe by reckless employment of fire, explosives, or other such dangerous means.

The following opinion in *Lear* v. *State* addresses the distinction between robbery and larceny.

Lear v. *State*

39 Ariz. 313, 6 P.2d 426 (1931)

The appellant was convicted of robbery. He appeals and assigns as error the insufficiency of the evidence to sustain the conviction and the giving of erroneous instructions.

The prosecuting witness, George Gross, testified that around 7 o'clock on the morning of August 12, 1931, he opened the Campbell Quality Shop, located in Buckeye, Maricopa county; that just about that time appellant entered the store and inquired about purchasing some shirts and shoes; that in the meantime he had taken a box of currency and a bag of silver out of the store safe; he had placed the currency in the cash register and the bag of silver on the counter; that, while he was in the act of untying or unrolling the bag of silver, and while it was on the counter, appellant grabbed it from his hands and ran out of the back door; that appellant said no word at the time, exhibited no arms, and used no force other than to grab the bag as stated above. Appellant admitted taking the bag of silver and that it contained $33.

It was the contention of appellant at the trial, and is his contention here, that the facts do not show that he committed the crime of robbery. This crime is defined by our statute . . . as follows: "Robbery is the felonious taking of personal property in the possession of another, from his person or immediate presence and against his will, accomplished by means of force or fear. The fear may be either of an unlawful injury to the person or property of the person robbed, or of a relative or member of his family; or of an immediate and unlawful injury to the person or property of any one in the company of the person robbed at the time of the robbery."

The crimes of robbery and larceny are not the same. The former is classified as a crime against the person and the latter as a crime against property. In robbery there is, in addition to a felonious taking, a violent invasion of the person. If the person is not made to surrender the possession of the personal property by means of force or fear, the dominant element of robbery is not present. The mere taking of property in possession of another, from his person or immediate presence and against his will, is not robbery. Such taking must be accomplished by force or fear to constitute robbery.

The element of fear is not in the case. Appellant made no threat or demonstration. He simply grabbed the bag of silver from the hands of the prosecuting witness and ran away with it. There was no pulling or scrambling for possession of the bag. Was the force employed by appellant the kind of force necessary to constitute robbery? We think not. As we read the cases and textwriters, "the force used must be either before, or at the time of the taking, and must be of such a nature as to show that it was intended to overpower the party robbed, and prevent his resisting, and not merely to get possession of the property stolen." . . .

OTHER CRIMES

Many other crimes exist under the common law and by statutory provision. Common law *perjury* is the willful taking of a false oath in a judicial proceeding with regard to a judirial matter. Modern statutes have expanded the crime to include false affidavits under oath, and to almost every kind of governmental proceeding. Generally, falsity of an accused's sworn statements must be established by the evidence of two witnesses. Perjury is normally a felony. *Subornation of perjury* is a separate offense. It consists of procuring another to commit perjury.

Counterfeiting is the unlawful making of false money and has been extended by statute to include any obligation or security of the government.

Bribery is an offer or tender of anything of value to a person who holds public office, or the receipt of anything of value by a public office holder. The intention is that such official be influenced in the performance of his duties. Note that both giving and accepting a bribe is a crime. It is a felony under most statutes.

Forgery is the false making or material alteration of a written instrument, with the intent to defraud. The writing must be one that, if genuine, could be the foundation of a legal liability. Such writings include deeds, wills, checks, and securities. Forgery is ordinarily a statutory felony.

Treason is defined in Article III, §3 of the United States Constitution as levying war against the United States, adhering to this nation's enemies, or giving them aid and comfort.

Other crimes include rioting, disorderly conduct, public intoxication, loitering, harassment, carrying concealed weapons, dealing in the use of dangerous drugs and other controlled substances, furnishing obscene material to minors, cruelty to animals, obstruction of justice, falsifying business records, issuing and negotiating a bad check, fraudulent use of a credit card, and issuing false financial statements. Still other crimes may be found by reference to the criminal codes of the various jurisdictions, and other specific criminal penalties exist in some socio-economic areas discussed in the next chapter. Most of these are business related.

QUESTIONS

1. Why do you think the criminal system holds persons responsible for solicitation, conspiracy, and attempt? Should this be so? If there is no actual crime committed by an individual, is there justice done when that person is held for a crime? Why?

2. Should insanity remain a defense to a crime? Should there be special action taken by the courts with parties who plead insanity? Why?

3. Assault and battery are crimes and also torts. How can the same matter be both? Why would the legal system not classify them as either one or the other?

4. Burglary, robbery, and larceny are all associated in many persons' minds with theft. What is the distinction? Why would they be different crimes instead of simply the one crime of theft?

5. Why do you believe that there is criminal penalty attached to socio-economic laws? Should this not be a civil rather than a criminal matter?

6. The last sentence in the chapter states that most socio-economic crimes are business related. Can you account for this?

economic
regulation

SIXTEEN

Maintenance of the public welfare through administration of social and economic activity is a basic power of governmental entities under constitutions, statutes, and court decisions. A "free enterprise" system is not entirely without controls, although there is a continuing controversy as to the extent to which agents of government ought to be involved in group and individual economic or social activity. Basic policy questions are at the bottom of all discussions of government regulation.

The power to regulate business is a police power to promote the public welfare. The power is restricted by safeguards in the same document in that laws must be uniformly applied to members within the same class and that there be no deprivation, without due process, of life or property (under the Fifth and Fourteenth Amendments of the Constitution). This "Due Process Clause" is seldom a basis these days, however, for striking down state or federal legislation that regulates conditions of work or broader social behavior.

Individual civil as well as economic rights are receiving more attention from governmental agents. The right to privacy, equal opportunity in employment, physical protection in the environment, fair dealing in financial matters or in the market place are all examples of the emphasis put upon individual rights. These rights are being enforced in all spheres of society—in organizations other than business as well as in industrial and commercial entities. Often the regulation of business represents the implementation of individual rights of those persons in contact with the corporation.

ANTITRUST

The regulation of broad and fundamental activity in economic matters represents, at present, the development of some of the longest and most active approaches to control of enterprises. Concern that too few control too many has been present in the thoughts and acts of public servants and private citizens alike. Maintenance of efficient service to society has been the aim of such governmental regulation.

Antitrust Legislation

One of the earliest governmental actions toward regulation of business was the enactment of the Sherman Act of 1890. The Sherman Act is known as the Antitrust Act because it was intended to prevent monopolies or combinations in restraint of trade. Section 1 of the Act provides that "every contract, combination in the form of trust or otherwise, or conspiracy, in restraint of trade or commerce among the several States, or with foreign nations, is hereby declared to be illegal." Section 2 makes it a misdemeanor for any person to "monopolize or attempt to monopolize, or combine or conspire . . . to monopolize" in the same area of trade or commerce as in Section 1 of the Act.

The Sherman Act provides a maximum penalty of $100,000 fine for a person, a million dollars if a corporation and three years imprisonment, or both in a 1974 amendment and other legislation has supplemented it in providing protection from monopolies.

Early judgments by the courts in interpreting the Sherman Act caused later legislation to emerge. The Clayton Act of 1914 and its later amendments tightened some of the provisions of antitrust statutes. Whereas the Sherman Act was interpreted to prohibit actual unreasonable restraint of trade, Section 7 of the Clayton Act now says that a merger of corporations shall be illegal when the effect "may be substantially to lessen competition, or to tend to create a monopoly" (15 USC Section 18). The Clayton Act also prohibits the purchase of stock in one corporation by another when that same result (monopoly and restraint of trade) would be effected.

Further curbs on unfair methods of competition and the establishment of an agency to police such activity came with the enactment of the Federal Trade Commission Act. The Federal Trade Commission (FTC) was intended to monitor adherence to existing laws, but has also determined an extensive number of practices to be in violation of the law. Practices condemned include those such as coercion, disparagement of a competitor, discrimination or boycott, making gifts to obtain benefits, pretended free trial offers or premiums, offers with no intention to deliver, incuding breach of contracts, spying on a competitor, appropriating trademarks or simulating a competitor's goods, using deception in labels or brands, false or misleading advertising, and many other "unfair methods of competition."

Court interpretation of the antitrust statutes over the years has required close attention to detail although results may have varied. The following case illustrates some of the complexities with which the courts have had to deal.

Continental T. V., Inc. v. *GTE Sylvania Inc.*

433 U.S. 36 (1976)

MR. JUSTICE POWELL delivered the opinion of the Court.

Franchise agreements between manufacturers and retailers frequently include provisions barring the retailers from selling franchised products from locations other than those specified in the agreements. This case presents important questions concerning the appropriate antitrust analysis of these restrictions under § 1 of the Sherman Act, 26 Stat. 209, as amended, 15 U.S.C. § 1, and the Court's decision in *United States* v. *Arnold, Schwinn & Co.,* 388 U.S. 365 (1967).

Respondent GTE Sylvania Inc. (Sylvania) manufactures and sells television sets through its Home Entertainment Products Division. Prior to 1962, like most other television manufacturers, Sylvania sold its televisions to independent or company-owned distributors who in turn resold to a large and diverse group of retailers. Prompted by a decline in its market share to a relatively insignificant 1% to 2% of national television sales, Sylvania conducted an intensive reassessment of its marketing strategy, and in 1962 adopted the franchise plan challenged here. Sylvania phased out its whosesale distributors and began to sell its televisions directly to a smaller and more select group of franchised retailers. An acknowledged purpose of the change was to decrease the number of competing Sylvania retailers in the hope of attracting the more aggressive and competent retailers thought necessary to the improvement of the company's market position. To this end, Sylvania limited the number of franchises

granted for any given area and required each franchisee to sell his Sylvania products only from the location or locations at which he was franchised. A franchise did not constitute an exclusive territory, and Sylvania retained sole discretion to increase the number of retailers in an area in light of the success or failure of existing retailers in developing their market. The revised marketing strategy appears to have been successful during the period at issue here, for by 1965 Sylvania's share of national television sales had increased to approximately 5%, and the company ranked as the Nation's eighth largest manufacturer of color television sets.

This suit is the result of the rupture of a franchiser-franchisee relationship that had previously prospered under the revised Sylvania plan. Dissatisfied with its sales in the city of San Francisco, Sylvania decided in the spring of 1965 to franchise Young Brothers, an established San Francisco retailer of televisions, as an additional San Francisco retailer. The proposed location of the new franchise was approximately a mile from a retail outlet operated by petitioner Continental T. V., Inc. (Continental), one of the most successful Sylvania franchisees. Continental protested that the location of the new franchise violated Sylvania's marketing policy, but Sylvania persisted in its plans. Continental then canceled a large Sylvania order and placed a large order with Phillips, one of Sylvania's competitors.

During this same period, Continental expressed a desire to open a store in Sacramento, Cal., a desire Sylvania attributed at least in part to Continental's displeasure over the Young Brothers decision. Sylvania believed that the Sacramento market was adequately served by the existing Sylvania retailers and denied the request. In the face of this denial, Continental advised Sylvania in early September 1965, that it was in the process of moving Sylvania merchandise from its San Jose, Cal., warehouse to a new retail location that it had leased in Sacramento. Two weeks later, allegedly for unrelated reasons, Sylvania's credit department reduced Continental's credit line from $300,000 to $50,000. In response to the reduction in credit and the generally deteriorating relations with Sylvania, Continental withheld all payments owed to John P. Maguire & Co., Inc. (Maguire), the finance company that handled the credit arrangements between Sylvania and its retailers. Shortly thereafter, Sylvania terminated Continental's franchises, and Maguire filed this diversity action in the United States District Court for the Northern District of California seeking recovery of money owed and of secured merchandise held by Continental.

. . .

In answers to special interrogatories, the jury found that Sylvania had engaged "in a contract, combination or conspiracy in restraint of trade in violation of the antitrust laws with respect to location restrictions alone," and assessed Continental's damages at $591,505, which was trebled pursuant to 15 U. S. C. § 15 to produce an award of $1,774,515. App. 498,501.

On appeal, the Court of Appeals for the Ninth Circuit, sitting en banc, reversed by a divided vote.

. . .

The traditional framework of analysis under § 1 of the Sherman Act is familiar and does not require extended discussion. Section 1 prohibits "[e]very contract, combination . . . , or conspiracy, in restraint of trade or commerce." Since the early years of this century a judicial gloss on this statutory language has established the "rule of reason" as the prevailing standard of analysis. *Standard Oil Co.* v. *United States,* 221 U. S. 1 (1911). Under this rule, the factfinder weighs all of the circumstances of a case in deciding whether a restrictive practice should be prohibited as imposing an unreasonable restraint on competition. *Per se* rules of illegality are appropriate only when they relate to conduct that is manifestly anticompetitive. As the Court explained in *Northern Pac. R. Co.* v. *United States,* 356 U. S. 1, 5 (1958), "there are certain agreements or practices which because of their pernicious effect on competition and lack of any redeeming virtue are conclusively presumed to be unreasonable and therefore illegal without elaborate inquiry as to the precise harm they have caused or the business excuse for their use."

In essence, the issue before us is whether *Schwinn's per se* rule can be justified under the demanding standards of *Northern Pac. R. Co.* The Court's refusal to endorse a *per se* rule in *White Motor Co.* was based on its uncertainty as to whether vertical restrictions satisfied those standards. Addressing this question for the first time, the Court stated:

> "We need to know more than we do about the actual impact of these arrangements on competition to decide whether they have such a 'pernicious effect on competition and lack . . . any redeeming virtue' (*Northern Pac. R. Co.* v. *United States, supra,* p. 5) and therefore should be classified as *per se* violations of the Sherman Act." 372 U. S., at 263.

Only four years later the Court in *Schwinn* announced its sweeping *per se* rule without even a reference to *Northern Pac. R. Co.* and with no explanation of its sudden change in position. We turn now to consider *Schwinn* in light of *Northern Pac. R. Co.*

The market impact of vertical restrictions is complex because of their potential for a simultaneous reduction of intrabrand competition and stimulation of interbrand competition. Significantly, the Court in *Schwinn* did not distinguish among the challenged restrictions on the basis of their individual potential for intrabrand harm or interbrand benefit. Restrictions that completely eliminated intrabrand competition among Schwinn distributors were analyzed no differently from those that merely moderated intrabrand competition among retailers. The pivotal factor was the passage of title: All restrictions were held to be *per se* illegal where title had passed, and all were evaluated and sustained under the rule of reason where it had not. The location restriction at issue here would be subject to the same pattern of analysis under *Schwinn.*

It appears that this distinction between sale and nonsale transactions resulted from the Court's effort to accommodate the perceived intrabrand harm and interbrand benefit of vertical restrictions. The *per se* rule for sale transactions reflected the view that vertical restrictions are "so obviously destructive" of intrabrand competition that their use would "open the door to exclusivity of outlets and limitation of territory further than prudence permits." 388 U.S., at 379–380. Conversely, the continued adherence to the traditional rule of reason for nonsale transactions reflected the view that the restrictions have too great a potential for the promotion of interbrand competition to justify complete prohibition.

We conclude that the distinction drawn in *Schwinn* between sale and nonsale transactions is not sufficient to justify the application of a *per se* rule in one situation and a rule of reason in the other. The question remains whether the *per se* rule stated in *Schwinn* should be expanded to include nonsale transactions or abandoned in favor of a return to the rule of reason. We have found no persuasive support for expanding the *per se* rule. As noted above, the *Schwinn* Court recognized the undesirability of "prohibit[ing] all vertical restrictions of territory and all franchising. . . ." 388 U.S. at 379–380. And even Continental does not urge us to hold that all such restrictions are *per se* illegal.

We revert to the standard articulated in *Northern Pac. R. Co.,* and reiterated in *White Motor,* for determining whether vertical restrictions must be "conclusively presumed to be unreasonable and therefore illegal without elaborate inquiry as to the precise harm they have caused or the business excuse for their use." 356 U.S., at 5. Such restrictions, in varying forms, are widely used in our free market economy. As indicated above, there is substantial scholarly and judicial authority supporting their economic utility. There is relatively little authority to the contrary. Certainly, there has been no showing in this case, either generally or with respect to Sylvania's agreements, that vertical restrictions have or are likely to have a "pernicious effect on competition" or that they "lack . . . any redeeming virtue." *Ibid.* Accordingly, we conclude that the *per se* rule stated in *Schwinn* must be overruled. In so holding we do not foreclose the possibility that particular applications of vertical restrictions might justify *per se* prohibition under *Northern Pac. R. Co.* But we do make clear that departure from the rule-of-reason standard must be based upon demonstrable economic effect rather than—as in *Schwinn*—upon formalistic line drawing.

In sum, we conclude that the appropriate

decision is to return to the rule of reason that governed vertical restrictions prior to *Schwinn*. When anticompetitive effects are shown to result from particular vertical restrictions they can be adequately policed under the rule of reason, the standard tradi- tionally applied for the majority of anticompetitive practices challenged under § 1 of the Act. Accordingly, the decision of the Court of Appeals is

Affirmed.

Mergers

A significant aspect of the economy that antitrust laws monitor is the matter of merging of companies and the impact this may have upon society. A merger that may lessen competition substantially or tend to create a monopoly is a violation of Section 7 of the Clayton Act. Note that the focus is on probable future events, rather than on reviewing actual circumstances that have occurred.

There are three major types of mergers. A *horizontal* merger involves similar companies that are in direct competition with each other at the same level or in parallel operations. A *vertical* merger is one that brings together companies at different levels of the economy, such as those in a chain of distribution; companies in seller-buyer relationships are related in this manner. A *conglomerate* merger unites companies in different areas of activity or operations. Sometimes a company will be acquired solely to add a single product to the acquiring company's line. This variation on the conglomerate merger has been called a *product extension* merger.

One important question concerning the horizontal merger is what market is affected by the merging. The market may be a geographic one (how large an area?), or it may be a product field. A market, however, may not be easy to determine. What, for instance, would be the relevant market for wrapping paper, or for Christmas gift paper? The percentage of the market captured by the combined companies would differ, depending upon the categorization in the first place. Courts have determined, moreover, that even a small additional percentage of the relevant market may have anticompetitive results.

A major question concerning vertical mergers is the ability of other firms to compete or enter the field, when certain companies control a significant part of the chain of distribution from manufacturing to the retail outlets. Vertical integration might prevent competing companies from selling their lines in the "captive" stores.

The effects of conglomerate mergers may be more difficult to assess, since they involve firms in different fields. The courts have determined in some cases that there is less competition in a company acquiring a firm in a different industry than if the acquiring firm, or others, would enter the competitive arena on their own with their products.

Further monitoring of mergers is the result of the passage of the Antitrust Improvements Act of 1976, under which firms intending to merge must notify the Justice Department and the FTC of their plans at least thirty days before any action is taken on the merger. This allows the federal officials time to make a more extensive investigation. At the same time, recent Department of Justice guidelines indicate a departure from following rigid terms relating to percentages of market share, and more reliance upon other economic and demographic factors.

Price Discrimination

The Clayton Act drafters included pricing as one further aspect of maintenance of competition in the economy. The act prohibited price discrimination when the intent was to lessen competition or tend to create a monopoly. Differences arising from product quality, quantity of goods, costs of transportation, or bonafide attempts to meet competition are allowable. These exceptions were later reinforced by the Robinson-Patman Act of 1936, which made illegal price discrimination a criminal offense. The act prohibited the granting of promotional and advertising aid by sellers to buyers unless all buyers were included in receiving the same assistance. Sellers are permitted to choose their customers, however, unless the intent of the choice was to restrain trade.

The fixing of prices between parties on the same level in the production or distribution system, *horizontal price-fixing,* is a violation of federal law. *Vertical resale price agreements* had been deemed valid under federal and many state statutes but have been declared invalid. The so-called *Fair Trade* laws enacted by many States during the Big Depression of the 1930s provided for just this maintenance of retail prices because of a feeling that this would support the economic order.

Under the Robinson-Patman Act, a buyer may be liable as well as the seller when price discrimination exists. The seller may have a defense if the differential in price is one that is set to meet competition. If so, there is no liability for the buyer as well, as the case below illustrates.

Great A&P Tea Co. v. *FTC*
440 U.S. 69 (1978)

MR. JUSTICE STEWART delivered the opinion of the Court.

The question presented in this case is whether the petitioner, the Great Atlantic & Pacific Tea Co. (A&P), violated § 2 (f) of the Clayton Act, 38 Stat. 730, as amended by the Robinson-Patman Act, 49 Stat. 1526, 15 U. S. C. § 13 (f), by knowingly inducing or receiving illegal price discriminations from the Borden Co. (Borden).

The alleged violation was reflected in a 1965 agreement between A&P and Borden under which Borden undertook to supply "private label" milk to more than 200 A&P stores in a Chicago area that included portions of Illinois and Indiana. This agreement resulted from an effort by A&P to achieve cost savings by switching from the sale of "brand label" milk (milk sold under the brand name of the supplying dairy) to the sale of "private label" milk (milk sold under the A&P label).

To implement this plan, A&P asked Borden, its longtime supplier, to submit an offer to supply under private label certain of A&P's milk and other dairy product requirements. After prolonged negotiations, Borden offered to grant A&P a discount for switching to private-label milk provided A&P would accept limited delivery service. Borden claimed that this offer would save A&P $410,000 a year compared to what it had been paying for its dairy products. A&P, however, was not satisfied with this offer and solicited offers from other dairies. A competitor of Borden, Bowman Dairy, then submitted an offer which was lower than Borden's.

At this point, A&P's Chicago buyer contacted Borden's chain store sales manager and stated: "I have a bid in my pocket. You [Borden] people are so far out of line it is not even funny. You are not even in the ball park." When the Borden representative asked for more details, he was told nothing except that a $50,000 improvement in Borden's bid "would not be a drop in the bucket."

Borden was thus faced with the problem of deciding whether to rebid. A&P at the time was one of Borden's largest customers in the Chicago area. Moreover, Borden had just invested more than $5 million in a new dairy facility in Illinois. The loss of the A&P account would result in underutilization of this new plant. Under these circumstances, Borden decided to submit a new bid which doubled the estimated annual savings to A&P, from $410,000 to $820,000. In presenting its offer, Borden emphasized to A&P that it needed to keep A&P's business and was making the new offer in order to meet Bowman's bid. A&P then accepted Borden's bid after concluding that it was substantially better than Bowman's.

I

Based on these facts, the Federal Trade Commission filed a three-count complaint against A&P. Count I charged that A&P had violated § 5 of the Federal Trade Commission Act by misleading Borden in the course of negotiations for the private-label contract, in that A&P had failed to inform Borden that its second offer was better than the Bowman bid. Count II, involving the same conduct, charged that A&P had violated

§ 2 (f) of the Clayton Act, as amended by the Robinson-Patman Act, by knowingly inducing or receiving price discriminations from Borden. Count III charged that Borden and A&P had violated § 5 of the Federal Trade Commission Act by combining to stabilize and maintain the retail and wholesale prices of milk and other dairy products.

. . .

A&P filed a petition for review of the Commission's order in the Court of Appeals for the Second Circuit. The court held that substantial evidence supported the findings of the Commission and that as a matter of law A&P could not successfully assert a meeting-competition defense because it, unlike Borden, had known that Borden's offer was better than Bowman's. Finally, the court held that the Commission had correctly determined that A&P had no cost-justification defense. 557 F. 2d 971. Because the judgment of the Court of Appeals raises important issues of federal law, we granted certiorari. 435 U. S. 922.

II

The Robinson-Patman Act was passed in response to the problem perceived in the increased market power and coercive practices of chainstores and other big buyers that threatened the existence of small independent retailers. Notwithstanding this concern with buyers, however, the emphasis of the Act is in § 2 (a), which prohibits price discrimination by sellers. Indeed, the original Patman bill as reported by Committees of both Houses prohibited only seller activity, with no mention of buyer liability. Section 2 (f), making buyers liable for inducing or receiving price discriminations by sellers, was the product of a belated floor amendment near the conclusion of the Senate debates.

As finally enacted, § 2 (f) provides:

"That it shall be unlawful for any person engaged in commerce, in the course of such commerce, knowingly to induce or receive a discrimination in price *which is prohibited by this section.*" (Emphasis added.)

Liability under § 2 (f) thus is limited to situations where the price discrimination is one "which is prohibited by this section." While the phrase "this section" refers to the entire § 2 of the Act, only subsections (a) and (b) dealing with seller liability involve discriminations in price. Under the plain meaning of § 2 (f), therefore, a buyer cannot be liable if a prima facie case could not be established against a seller or if the seller has an affirmative defense. In either situation, there is no price discrimination "prohibited by this section." The legislative history of § 2 (f) fully confirms the conclusion that buyer liability under § 2 (f) is dependent on seller liability under § 2 (a).

. . .

Under the circumstances of this case, Borden did act reasonably and in good faith when it made its second bid. The petitioner, despite its longstanding relationship with Borden, was dissatisfied with Borden's first bid and solicited offers from other dairies.

. . .

Borden was unable to ascertain the details of the Bowman bid. It requested more information about the bid from the petitioner, but this request was refused. It could not then attempt to verify the existence and terms of the competing offer from Bowman without risking Sherman Act liability. *United States* v. *United States Gypsum Co., supra.* Faced with a substantial loss of business and unable to find out the precise details of the competing bid, Borden made another offer stating that it was doing so in order to meet competition. Under these circumstances, the conclusion is virtually inescapable that in making that offer Borden acted in a reasonable and good-faith effort to meet its competition, and therefore was entitled to a meeting-competition defense.

Since Borden had a meeting-competition defense and thus could not be liable under § 2 (b), the petitioner who did no more than accept that offer cannot be liable under § 2 (f).

Accordingly, the judgment is reversed.

It is so ordered.

Other agreements   The Clayton Act prohibits, if in restraint of trade, the imposition of an *exclusive dealer agreement* whereby a dealer must agree not to handle goods of a competitor of the manufacturer. The act also prohibits the use of a *tie-in* sale or lease where the buyer of goods promises to purchase or lease only from the seller. Such provisions are permissible only if their use does not lessen competition or create a monopoly. If, for example, a product can only be served by specific supplies from the seller or a machine could not be run without the materials furnished by the manufacturer, the tie-in restrictions would not be struck down. If there are alternate sources of supply, however, tie-in provisions are in violation of the statute.

It must be added that most States have statutes that prohibit the same activities on the commercial scene. Under tort law, these activities also may be actionable as the tort of unfair competition.

Decisions and Developments

Some anticompetitive methods have been regarded by courts as inherently illegal in impeding competition. This concept is known as the *per se* rule in determining whether or not an activity represents a move to monopolization. Where restrictions must be categorically presumed to be unreasonable and therefore illegal (without elaborate inquiry as to their precise harm to business), or have no redeeming value for their use, they are illegal per se. On the other hand, the court may invoke the *rule of reason* when reviewing a case in controversy, if the factual situation requires that a closer inquiry into the nature of the agreements or their consequences is justified. Final decisions are made on the basis of a cognitive evaluation of circumstances, instead of adhering to a preconceived line establishing an outcome.

Certain areas or activities are exempt from antitrust laws, either by specific statute or by court decision. Labor unions, farm and fishery organizations, certain export marketing associations, firms operating only in intrastate activity, and those responding jointly to threats to the defense of the limited states are exempt. Baseball, the only sport to be favored, is also excluded from the restrictions. In addition, there may be some antitrust immunity for programs that are under direction or control of a state. There may also be some constitutional protection when competitors act together to influence legislation in a legitimate manner.

REGULATION OF TRANSPORTATION AND COMMUNICATION

Control in these areas occurs primarily under federal legislation although state statutes control intrastate activity. The Interstate Commerce Commission Act of 1881 established the governmental commission of the same name and provided a set of regulations covering the transport of goods in commerce throughout the country on freight and passenger lines. Since at that time the primary carriers were the railroads, the impact on them had considerable effect on the economy generally. The growing importance of other carriers either extended ICC regulation or led to the development of other federal and state regulatory agencies. The Federal Aviation Agency (FAA) has regulatory powers in air transportation, although the Department of Transportation (DOT) assumed much of the control of this area after the elimination of the Civil Aeronautics Board (CAB) in 1985. The Federal Communication Commission (FCC) licenses and monitors radio and television broadcasting, and has some control over date transmission by other carriers.

Agencies comparable to the ICC at the state level display a variation in names, although the designation "Public Utility Commission" is common. These agencies may regulate other areas as well as transportation and communication.

FINANCIAL PROTECTION

Development of programs looking to the financial welfare of workers, or the regulation of existing ones, is a major concern of government. Few problems cause as much unease as those faced by the old and out-of-work with limited financial resources.

Unemployment Compensation

Some semblance of financial security for workers when they are without work through no fault of their own is provided by unemployment compensation programs in all states. The Social Security Act of 1935 encouraged states to set up programs and today the federal base is built upon to different levels in each state; requirements with respect to time needed to qualify and the amount of benefits vary.

An unemployed worker who meets the tests of the acts draws payments regardless of need. The programs are financed from the federal unemployment tax, but credit is made for employer payments into a state fund. Actually, all money is deposited into the Federal Unemployment Trust Fund to be drawn upon by states in paying unemployment benefits (and only those benefits). An employer with a good experience rating (the company that has less unemployment and fewer claims) may have the payments reduced.

Social Security

Federal legislation establishing a system of aid and assistance to the needy and elderly came with enactment of the Federal Social Security programs; the most direct federal support comes in the area of Old Age and Survivor's Disability Insurance, most frequently known simply as Social Security. Unemployment compensation, maternal and child care services, and general welfare activity are programs operated by states with the extensive support of the federal government if the state plan is approved.

The Social Security Act of 1935 provided the first income security for a limited number of persons, but the coverage has expanded to the point at which 90 percent of the workers in the country are included. Social Security payments by employees are deducted from their wages, matched by employer contributions and generally deposited in an authorized bank with quarterly reports made to the Internal Revenue Service. Earnings affected by retirement, death, or disability make the worker or his family eligible for monthly payments. A recently enacted *Medicare* program provides hospital and health insurance for those over age 65.

Retirement Plans

Private pension plans are strengthened by provisions of the Internal Revenue Code. Employee contributions to a qualified plan are excluded from taxable income and payments from the annuity fund are taxed to the recipient only when received after retirement. Employer contributions to a retirement fund under a qualified plan may be claimed as tax deductions. A qualified plan is one that meets IRS requirements to assure broad coverage of employees, not just a favored few at a particular managerial level.

Concern aroused by a large number of deficient retirement plans led to the enactment of the Employee Retirement Income Security Act of 1974 (ERISA). The Act imposes strict funding requirements to assure a strong financial base as well as providing a means whereby some equity in annuities earned is available to the employee ("vesting" of benefits). In the past many employees had worked for years and departed with no benefits because they did not reach retirement under the plan. Strong actuarial programs and insurance coverage under the Pension Benefit Guaranty Corporation are requirements of a qualified plan. Vesting is immediate as to the employee's contributions and those from the employer must be fully vested in ten years or a stated gradual vesting over fifteen years.

Civil suits may result in damages for aggrieved parties or an injunction may be sought by private parties or the Secretary of Labor. There are some violations of the act that are criminal in nature.

CONSUMER PROTECTION

Protection of persons in consumer activity, as well as in the general environment, is a valid exercise of police powers under the Constitution of the United States and subsequent federal and state statutes. Health and purity standards received their first important impetus under the Food and Drug Act of 1906 but except for intermittent flurries of regulation in food and drug commerce, little happened in the intervening period. Not until the decade from 1965 to 1975 did the most extensive activity in legislation looking to the preservation of the health of the nation's citizens take place.

Health and Safety

A review of some of the federal statutes may give an idea of the extent of the societal interest. Controls over depressant and stimulant drugs were strengthened in the Drug Abuse Control Amendments of 1965 to the Food, Drug and Cosmetic Act. The Fair Packaging and Labeling Act of 1966 provided further consumer protection in terms of the accuracy and validity of designations external to the product. The Public Health Cigarette Smoking Act of 1969 required the now well-known warning on cigarette packages of the hazard to health as determined by the Surgeon General.

The Consumer Product Safety Act of 1972 established the Consumer Product Safety Commission and charged it with the responsibility of determining safety standards for all consumer products and regulating most aspects of their manufacture and distribution. Manufacturers are required to maintain extensive inspection procedures and to notify the Commission and general public if a product is found to be defective. Products may be removed from the market and each violation may carry with it a penalty of $2000 up to a maximum of half a million dollars.

As in many other areas of law, the interpretation of statutes governing foods and drugs requires a close analysis of the various aspects of a given situation. The following case gives some idea of the elements of a controversy in this area.

United States v. *An Article of Food*
678 F.2d 735 (1982)

CUMMINGS, Chief Judge.

The United States filed its amended complaint in this *in rem* food condemnation case in May 1979. The defendant food comprises numerous cases containing tablets of Aangamik 15, also known as "Calcium Panga-mate," "Pangamic Acid," "Vitamin B-15," "Gluconic 15," "Sport 15," or "the famous Russian formula." Aangamik 15 is produced in Burlington, Vermont by the other defendant and claimant herein, FoodScience Laboratories, Inc., and then shipped to various points around the country. According to the government's complaint, the tablets are an adulterated food under 21 U.S.C. § 342(a)(2)(C) of the Federal Food, Drug and Cosmetic Act in that they contain a food additive — N,N–Dimethylglycine hydrochloride ("DMG") — which allegedly is unsafe under 21 U.S.C. § 348(a).

The government also claimed that the Aangamik 15 is misbranded under 21 U.S.C. § 343(a) because the label describes the article as "Vitamin B-15," although calcium pangamate is neither a vitamin nor a provitamin and since indeed "there is no accepted scientific evidence which establishes any nutritional properties of the substance or has identified a deficiency of calcium pangamate in men or animals. . . ." The government further charged that the substance was misbranded because it is "fabricated from two or more ingredients and its label fails to bear the common or usual name of each such ingredient. . . ." Finally, the government alleged that FoodScience violated 21 U.S.C. § 331(a) by introducing this "adulterated and misbranded" article of food into interstate commerce. The government therefore urged the district court to condemn these cases of Aangamik 15 and to enjoin FoodScience from delivering any more of it into interstate commerce.

FoodScience denied the critical paragraphs of the amended complaint and the six consolidated cases were tried without a jury during the week of December 12, 1979. On October 29, 1980, the district court decided all issues in favor of the government.

. . .

The relevant provisions of the Federal Food, Drug, and Cosmetic Act are straightforward. "A food shall be deemed to be adulterated—. . . if it is, or it bears or contains, any food additive which is unsafe within the meaning of section 348 of this title. . . ." 21 U.S.C. § 342(a)(2)(C). Under

Section 348, a food additive is presumed to be unsafe unless the Secretary of Health and Human Services had promulgated a regulation "prescribing the conditions under which such additive may be safely used" or providing for "investigational use by qualified experts." 21 U.S.C. § 348(a) and (i). The parties stipulated prior to trial that Aangamik 15 is a food and, as noted, that the Secretary has promulgated no exempting regulations regarding the Aangamik 15 component DMG. The remaining question in the determination whether Aangamik 15 is an adulterated food, then, is whether DMG is a "food additive."

The Federal Food, Drug, and Cosmetic Act defines "food additive" as follows:

> The term "food additive" means any substance the intended use of which results or may reasonably be expected to result, directly or indirectly, in its becoming a component or otherwise affecting the characteristics of any food (including any substance intended for use in producing, manufacturing, packing, processing, preparing, treating, packaging, transporting, or holding food; and including any source of radiation intended for any such use), if such substance is not generally recognized, among experts qualified by scientific training and experience to evaluate its safety, as having been adequately shown through scientific procedures (or, in the case of a substance used in food prior to January 1, 1958, through either scientific procedures or experience based on common use in food) to be safe under the conditions of its intended use. . . .

21 U.S.C. § 321(s). The district court found that DMG was not commonly used in food prior to January 1, 1958, and FoodScience has not challenged that finding on appeal. Rather, FoodScience asks us to set aside the district court's findings that under the foregoing definition (1) DMG is an "additive" (a "substance the intended use of which results . . . in its becoming a compo-

nent or otherwise affecting the characteristics of" Aangamik 15), and (2) DMG is not "generally recognized as safe."

. . .

The practical effect of holding that DMG is an additive is to place the burden of showing safety upon FoodScience. In order to avoid the label "food additive," FoodScience must now show that DMG is "generally recognized as safe," whereas if DMG were not an "additive," the Food and Drug Administration would have the burden under 21 U.S.C. § 342 of proving by a preponderance of the evidence that DMG is "injurious to health."

. . .

Finally, the district court enjoined Food-Science pursuant to 21 U.S.C. § 332(a) from introducing Aangamik 15 into interstate commerce in food or drug form. Food-Science complains that the injunction is overbroad because there was no proof that

Aangamik 15 would be unsafe as a drug. However, the district judge provided Food-Science with appropriate escape hatches for marketing the tablets as a drug should the tablets be found safe for drug usage. Specifically, FoodScience has been enjoined regarding Aangamik 15 as a *drug* only.

> Until (1) an approved application filed pursuant to 21 U.S.C. 355(b) is effective with respect to said drug, or (2) a Notice of Claimed Investigational Exemption for such drug, filed by defendants pursuant to 21 U.S.C. 355(i) and 21 CFR 312.1, has been accepted as adequate by the United States Food and Drug Administration.

Any competitive disadvantage that Food-Science may suffer as a result of following the above procedures is more than offset by the need the district court perceived to prevent FoodScience from circumventing the injunction.

Business Practices

Consumer protection in the course of business focuses upon the prohibition of deceptive trade practices or the mandating of sufficient information for the making of an informed decision.

The Federal Trade Commission Act prohibits deceptive or unfair practices with respect to consumers. False or misleading advertising is a frequent target of Federal Trade Commission activity. Other tactics such as "bait and switch," misbranding, using names deceptively similar to other products, and disparagement of the products of others (see below) are also subject to legal action by the commission.

The Consumer Product Warranty Act of 1975 (Magnuson-Moss Warranty—FTC Improvement Act) establishes that written warranties be given in simple and understandable terms and conditions. Informal settlement procedures prior to litigation are also issued by the Federal Trade Commission. Manufacturers need not issue a warranty, but if they do the language must be such as to be understood by the buyer.

If a product costing more than $15 has a warranty, the warranty must be labeled "full" or "limited." A defective product with a full warranty must be repaired or replaced without charge within a reasonable period of time. Limited warranties must be clear in their limitations.

The Consumer Goods Pricing Act of 1975 eliminates the practice of "fair trade" laws in all states still having such laws in effect. The so-called fair trade laws date from the great depression of the 1930s and permitted the manufacturer to fix the price of merchandise at the retail level. Public policy in maintaining a healthy economy was given as the reason for such price-fixing legislation but it did stifle price competition.

The Real Estate Settlement Procedures Act of 1974 requires disclosure of all costs in a real estate transaction. Purchasers or borrowers must be made aware of all closing costs, appraisal fees, title charges, and loan discount "points." A point is a charge by the lender and each point equals one percent of the total sum considered. The complete statement must be given to the buyer/borrower at least the day before the closing.

Other practices prohibited by the act are kickbacks, charging for a service not performed, requiring title insurance from a particular company, and placing of more than one month's advance deposit in escrow for taxes and insurance.

Credit Protection

Various facets of consumer protection in financial matters are embodied in the Consumer Credit Protection Act. The primary feature of the act has become known as the Truth in Lending law (Title I—Consumer Credit Protection Act). The act is intended to provide consumers with extensive knowledge of the costs and conditions of credit in order that they may be able to make better financial plans and decisions. The act mandates that those who extend credit or arrange for it to be extended are required to communicate specific details to the borrower. The finance charge must be stated by the creditor as a dollar amount and in the annual percentage rate. The finance charge, as disclosed, is the sum of all charges—interest, carrying charges, required insurance, or any other charges. The seller must also state the cash price, down payment, difference between the two, amount to be financed, payments, repayment dates, late payment charges, and the finance charge in dollars, as well as percentage rate. How careful a seller must be in practice is demonstrated in the case of *Carney* v. *Worthmore Furniture, Inc.* below.

Carney v. *Worthmore Furniture, Inc.*
561 F.2d 1100 (1977)

PER CURIAM:

Worthmore Furniture, Inc., of Richmond, Virginia, appeals from judgment against it in favor of Surlarnce C. Carney for damages, costs, and attorneys fees upon the finding of the District Court that Worthmore violated the Truth in Lending Act, 15 U.S.C. § 1601 et seq., and Federal Reserve Regulation Z, 12 C.F.R. 226, in connection with the sale to Carney of a food freezer. Specifically, the District Court found that Worthmore, at the time that it entered into a fixed-term consumer credit sales agreement with Carney, failed (1) to include in the disclosed finance charge a mandatory fee for a service policy assuring repair of the freezer for the duration of the credit arrangement and (2) to indicate clearly the proper number and amounts of payments necessary to retire the indebtedness.

The facts, as stipulated in the District Court, are these:

Carney entered into a consumer credit transaction with Worthmore March 7, 1975 involving the purchase of a food freezer. A charge of $50.00 for a freezer service policy was added to the sales price of the freezer and included in the amount financed. Carney was required to purchase this policy, which was to last for fourteen months, the same number of months as the period over which Carney contracted to make payments. The policies in Worthmore's credit sales always last for a period of months equal to the number of months that the customer is obligated to make payments. Although the terms of this policy are nowhere set out in writing, Worthmore does repair or replace defective items during its term (in the instant case complementing a one-year "parts only" manufacturer's warranty on the freezer motor). The cost of the policy is a fixed sum based solely on the type of appliance and not on the length of the repayment period.

. . .

The written agreement between the parties, viewed objectively, required Carney to repay her total indebtedness of $536.12 to Worthmore in fourteen (14) monthly installments of $36.00 each, plus a fourteenth installment of $33.12. This aspect of Carney's obligation was disclosed in a somewhat ambiguous clause in the agreement:

> "Purchaser hereby agrees to pay to [Worthmore Furniture, Inc.] at their offices shown above the "TOTAL OF PAYMENTS" shown above in 13 monthly installments of $36.00 (final payment to be $33.12) . . . ."

Blanks here and in the original are indicated by the underscoring and were filled in by hand. Incidentally, the contract includes no credit property insurance purchased by Carney to cover loss of or damage to the freezer, because Worthmore did not sell or arrange the sale of such insurance for its customers.

Concluding that the cost of the service policy should have been included in the finance charge (an item different from the "amount financed," in which, as stipulated by the parties, this charge was included instead of in the finance charge) and that the

contract's characterization of the repayment plan reasonably could have been read by Carney to require a total of only thirteen (13) payments, the District Court held Worthmore in violation of the Act, awarding double damages in the amount of $204.24, 15 U.S.C. § 1640(a)(1), as well as costs and $300.00 in attorney fees, 15 U.S.C. § 1640(a)(2).

I. The Service Policy

Worthmore contends that the $50.00 freezer service charge was not an incident to the extension of credit and, in any event, was not a finance charge within the intent of the Act.

In this regard 15 U.S.C. § 1605 provides:

> "(a) Except as otherwise provided in this section, the amount of the finance charge in connection with any consumer credit transaction shall be determined as the sum of all charges, payable directly or indirectly by the person to whom the credit is extended, and *imposed* directly or indirectly *by the creditor as an incident to the extension of credit. . . ."* (Accent added.)

Subsection 226.4 of Regulation Z, 12 C.F.R. 226.4, defines the finance charge in language virtually identical to that in the Act.

We are unable to agree with either component of Worthmore's argument. Its claim that the service policy is not an incident to the credit transaction might have more appeal if it were able to offer documented evidence of a substantial cash business in which identical charges for service policies were levied in each sales transaction. *See Manzina v. Publishers Guild, Inc.,* 386 F.Supp. 241 (S.D.N.Y.1974). However, where as here the alleged cash sales are insignificant exceptions to what is apparently a credit sales business, the naked claim that the service policy charge is imposed on cash customers is insufficient to acquit it as not incident to the extension of credit. . . .

Finding that the instant service policy's imposition was inextricably intertwined with Worthmore's interests as a creditor, we decide that the cost of the freezer service policy was a finance charge of the type defined at 15 U.S.C. § 1605(a)(5), supra. Worthmore's failure to include this cost in the finance charge disclosure, 15 U.S.C. § 1638(a)(6), and the associated annual percentage rate, 15 U.S.C. 1638(a)(7), was a violation of the Act rendering Worthmore liable for damages in Federal court, 15 U.S.C. § 1640(a), (e).

II. The Number of Payments

Our affirmance on the issue of the freezer service policy charge makes it unnecessary to address the second issue, as the Act authorizes but one recovery for a given credit transaction regardless of the number of infractions compounded in it. . . .

Affirmed.

The Consumer Credit Protection Act includes provisions covering the issuance and use of credit cards. The act prohibits issuance of a credit card without an application for it. The cardholder must be notified of the rights and obligations surrounding the use of the card and be provided with a simple method of notification of loss or theft of the card. In the case of unauthorized use of the card, the act limits the liability of the cardholder to fifty dollars.

Other provisions of the act relate to real property transactions. The giver of a mortgage or lien on a home has a three day period during which the deal can be rescinded; the creditor is required to give written notice of the availability of the right to cancel.

The Consumer Credit Protection Act also places a limit on the percentage of wages that may be garnished as the result of debt delinquency. The act also prohibits an employer from discharging the wage earner as the result of the garnishment.

The Fair Credit Billing Act of 1974 is an amendment to the Truth in Lending Law, which gives consumers additional rights in credit card usage. The right to assert claims against the issuer in the case of a dispute concerning the product is a substantial gain for the consumer. Other rights in a dispute with respect to billing are additional features.

The Equal Credit Opportunity Act of 1975 attempts to put women seeking credit on an equal basis with men. Discrimination on the basis of sex or marital status in the giving of credit is prohibited.

Credit Reporting and Collection

The amount of information being collected on private individuals without their knowledge or control has aroused widespread concern. A major legislative response in the credit area was the enactment of the Fair Credit Reporting Act (Title VI of the Consumer Credit Protection Act).

The act provides an opportunity for a party to become aware of most of the information collected in a report. Ordinarily the report is assembled as the result of investigations connected with applications for credit or employment. Inquiries as to personal character or general reputation often descended into collecting gossip or inaccurate information. The subject of the report has the right under certain conditions to inspect his/her file and have the credit agency check the accuracy of the material. Disputed points may be responded to with a short statement to be placed in the file by the person and included in all future reports. Obsolete information must be removed on request (usually information over seven years is considered to be obsolete).

Usually the individual is entitled to be informed of the conduct of an investigative report, and may request to be informed, in addition to the content of the report, of the names of persons or organizations to whom the report is being sent.

Access to the reports is limited by the act. There may be consent by the subject of the file, of course. Businesses with a bona fide need for the information may obtain it, or access may be gained by court order.

The Fair Debt Collection Practices Act proscribes certain activities in debt collection that have caused concern in the past. The Act is intended to eliminate unfair practices—those that are deceptive, abusive, or that may be considered improper threats and harassment. The statute is specific in outlining prohibited actions. Federal courts have jurisdiction under the act regardless of the amount in controversy (i.e., the sum in question need not be in excess of $10,000).

The case included below outlines many of the methods proscribed by the Fair Debt Collection Practices Act.

Rutyna v. *Collection Accounts Terminal, Inc.*
478 F.Supp. 980 (1979)

McMILLEN, District Judge.

This is an action for violations of the Fair Debt Collection Practices Act, 15 U.S.C. § 1692 *et seq.* (the F.D.C.P.A.). The F.D.C.P.A. was enacted by Congress to eliminate abusive, deceptive, and unfair debt collection practices and became effective on March 20, 1978. This court has subject-matter jurisdiction, without regard to the amount in controversy, under § 1692k(d) of the Act.

The facts of this case are undisputed, except where noted herein. Plaintiff is a 60 year old widow and Social Security retiree. She suffers from high blood pressure and epilepsy. In December 1976 and January 1977, she incurred a debt for medical services performed by a doctor with Cabrini Hospital Medical Group. Her belief was that

medicare or other, private, medical insurance had paid in full this debt for medical treatment. She contends that in July 1978, an agent of defendant telephoned her and informed her of an alleged outstanding debt for $56.00 to Cabrini Hospital Medical Group. When she denied the existence of this debt, the voice on the telephone responded, "you owe it, you don't want to pay, so we're going to have to do something about it." In its brief, defendant denies that it ever telephoned the plaintiff but states that plaintiff did telephone defendant on several occasions. There is no evidentiary support in the record for defendant's contention.

On or about August 10, 1978, plaintiff received a letter from defendant which supplies the basis for her complaint. It stated:

You have shown that you are unwilling to work out a friendly settlement with us to clear the above debt.

Our field investigator has now been instructed to make an investigation in your neighborhood and to personally call on your employer.

The immediate payment of the full amount, or a personal visit to this office, will spare you this embarrassment.

The top of the letter notes the creditor's name and the amount of the alleged debt. The letter was signed by a "collection agent." It is attached as exhibit B to the plaintiff's memorandum. The envelope containing that letter presented a return address that included defendant's full name: Collection Accounts Terminal, Inc.

Upon receiving this letter from defendant, plaintiff alleges that she became very nervous, upset, and worried, specifically that defendant would cause her embarrassment by informing her neighbors of the debt and about her medical problems. In its brief, defendant states its lack of knowledge concerning plaintiff's reaction to the letter.

Plaintiff wishes to reserve certain of her F.D.C.P.A. allegations for trial should this court deny her summary judgment motion. But three of her alleged violations regarding defendant's liability are ripe for disposition by summary judgment. If plaintiff prevails, a hearing will be appropriate to determine a damage award. § 1692k provides for actual and statutory damages, and a reasonable attorney's fee.

(1) Harassment or abuse (§ 1692d). The first sentence of § 1692d provides: "A debt collector may not engage in any conduct the natural consequence of which is to harass, oppress, or abuse any person in connection with the collection of a debt." This section then lists six specifically prohibited types of conduct, without limiting the general application of the foregoing sentence. The legis-

lative history makes clear that this generality was intended:

> In addition to these specific prohibitions, this bill prohibits in general terms any harassing, unfair or deceptive collection practice. This will enable the courts, where appropriate, to proscribe other improper conduct which is not specifically addressed. 1977 *U.S. Code Cong. & Admin. News* at p. 1698.

Plaintiff does not allege conduct which falls within one of the specific prohibitions contained in § 1692d, but we find that defendant's letter to plaintiff does violate this general standard.

Without doubt defendant's letter has the natural (and intended) consequence of harassing, oppressing, and abusing the recipient. The tone of the letter is one of intimidation, and was intended as such in order to effect a collection. The threat of an investigation and resulting embarrassment to the alleged debtor is clear and the actual effect on the recipient is irrelevant. The egregiousness of the violation is a factor to be considered in awarding statutory damages (§ 1692k(b)(1)). Defendant's violation of § 1692d is clear.

(2) Deception and improper threats (§ 1692e). § 1692e bars a debt collector from using any "false, deceptive, or misleading representation or means in connection with the collection of any debt." Sixteen specific practices are listed in this provision, without limiting the application of this general standard. § 1692e(5) bars a threat "to take any action that cannot legally be taken or that is not intended to be taken." Defendant also violated this provision.

Defendant's letter threatened embarrassing contacts with plaintiff's employer and neighbors. This constitutes a false representation of the actions that defendant could legally take. § 1692c(b) prohibits communication by the debt collector with third parties (with certain limited exceptions not here relevant). Plaintiff's neighbors and employer could not legally be contacted by defendant in connection with this debt. The letter falsely represents, or deceives the recipient, to the contrary. This is a deceptive means employed by defendant in connection with its debt collection. Defendant violated § 1692e(5) in its threat to take such illegal action.

(3) Unfair practice/return address (§ 1692f(8)). The envelope received by plaintiff bore a return address, which began "COLLECTION ACCOUNTS TERMINAL, INC." § 1692f bars unfair or unconscionable means to collect or attempt to collect any debt. § 1692f specifically bars:

> (8) Using any language or symbol, other than the debt collector's address, on any envelope when communicating with a consumer by use of the mails or by telegram, except that a debt collector may use his business name if such name does not indicate that he is in the debt collection business.

Defendant's return address violated this provision, because its business name does indicate that it is in the debt collection business. The purpose of this specific provision is apparently to prevent embarrassment resulting from a conspicuous name on the envelope, indicating that the contents pertain to debt collection.

On the subject of the return address on the envelope, defendant cites § 1692k(c), which provides:

> A debt collector may not be held liable in any action brought under this subchapter if the debt collector shows by a preponderance of the evidence that the violation was not intentional and resulted from a bona fide error notwithstanding the maintenance of procedures reasonably adapted to avoid any such error.

Defendant states that it was "unaware that the return address could be considered a violation of any statute." Memorandum in opposition, at 4. No affidavit is offered. § 1692k(c) is designed to protect the defendant who intended to prevent the conduct which constitutes a violation of this Act but who failed even though he maintained procedures reasonably adapted to avoid such an error. Defendant here obviously *intended* the conduct which violates the Act in respect to the return address, but it simply failed to acquaint itself with the pertinent law. This is similar to a provision in the Truth in Lending Act, providing a defense by establishing the facts, not by claiming ignorance of the law. *Haynes* v. *Logan Furniture Mart, Inc.,* 503 F.2d 1161 (7th Cir. 1974).

IT IS THEREFORE ORDERED, ADJUDGED AND DECREED that judgment is entered in favor of plaintiff on the issue of liability.

SECURITIES REGULATION

One of the most significant vehicles for the financing of business operations is the sale of *debt* or *equity* interests in the corporate entity. Debt financing calls for repayment, with interest, of the loan that is evidenced by a *bond* or similar debt instrument. Equity interest is in the form of *stock* ownership that represents an undivided share of the corporation and entitles the shareholder to participate in a distribution of profits as dividends.

Equity and debt instruments are the major forms of securities but the concept covers many more agreements. Early federal regulation, the Securities Act of 1933, defined securities as:

> Any note, stock, Treasury stock, bond, debenture evidence of indebtedness, certificate of interest in participation in any profit-sharing agreement, collateral-trust certificate, preorganization certificate or subscription, transferable share, investment contract, voting trust certificate, certificate of deposit for a security, fractional undivided interest, in oil, gas, or other mineral rights, or, in general, any interest or instrument known as a "security," or any certificate of interest of participation in, temporary or interim certificate for, receipt for, guarantee of, or warrant or right to subscribe to or purchase any of the foregoing.

Although this definition may appear to be rather complete, courts have identified still other interests as securities. A general characteristic of a security may be that it is an interest in a venture with others whereby an investment is made with the expectation of a gain from the efforts of others.

The two major acts in securities regulation at the federal level are the Securities Act of 1933 and the Securities Exchange Act of 1934. The Securities and Exchange Commission (SEC) was formed to regulate the trade in securities by the Act of 1933. Each of the fifty states also has statutes that provide similar regulation within their borders.

The Securities Act of 1933

In the aftermath of the collapse of the stock market in 1929 and the ensuing great depression, emphasis was placed upon development of protection for investors. The 1933 Act established the SEC and gave it powers to require registration of securities prior to offerings to the public, and to monitor other aspects of the placements.

A detailed statement called a *prospectus,* with information about the security and plans for use of funds, must be provided to prospective investors and presented to the SEC along with a more detailed listing of promoters or issuers. The SEC does not have the power to rule on the merits of the offering, and the prospectus must state that the SEC has neither approved nor disapproved the securities; but the commission may require the addition of warnings such as the speculative nature of the offerings. The emphasis of the Act is upon disclosure, so that investors may make a better decision and avoid deceptive practices.

The Securities Act of 1933 enables a person to sue upon a showing of mistatements or omissions and a loss of funds as a result (Section 11). The issuer has absolute liability for any misstatements and other parties such as lawyers or accountants are liable as well unless they can show due diligence in their actions. In this instance the aggrieved party can prevail upon presentation of less evidence than is required for common law fraud.

Certain securities are exempt under the 1933 act. Securities offered only to individuals residing within a state, an *intrastate offering,* are exempt from registration under the 1933 act, as are *private placements,* those not offered to the public at large but limited to institutional investors such as pension funds.

The Securities Exchange Act of 1934

Further protection for investors came with the enactment of the Securities Exchange Act of 1934, which regulates the activity of securities markets, professionals, and corporate insiders, and monitors the trading of securities after issue. The Act of 1934 extended the requirement of registration to all securities listed on the stock exchanges and those trades *over the counter* (OTC), if there are more than 500 shareholders or the company has assets in excess of one million dollars.

Regular reporting by companies is a significant requirement under the act. Monthly (8-K reports), quarterly (10-Q), and annual (10-K) reports are mandated, again, for the promulgation of information which may be of importance to investors in their decision making. Insiders—i.e., officers, directors, or those owning ten percent or more of stock in the company—are required to report any sales or purchases of stock. No profits may be earned within six months of such transactions. If takeover attempts are envisioned and tender offers are made to stockholders, an amendment to the 1934 act (the Williams Act of 1968) mandates the registration with the SEC of the proposals.

Misstatements by those involved in corporate activities may affect the price of securities. Optimistic claims may cause prices to rise, while pessimistic information may have the opposite effect. As with the 1933 act, the 1934 act attempts to protect against misstatements, mismanagement, and fraud. The act states that the use of "any manipulative or deceptive device or contrivance in contravention of such rules and regulations as the Commission may prescribe" in the transfer of securities is unlawful. This protection under Section 10(b) of the 1934 act is framed broadly, but court decisions have found liability only where *scienter,* or the intent to deceive, has been present. It thus differs from the absolute liability for misstatements provided in the 1933 act.

In the following case the court deals with the allegation of fraud in the registration of securities. Note the comparison of the two acts under which litigation is possible.

Herman & MacLean v. *Huddleston*
103 S.Ct. 683 (1983)

Justice MARSHALL delivered the opinion of the Court.

These consolidated cases raise two unresolved questions concerning Section 10(b) of the Securities Exchange Act of 1934, 15 U.S.C. § 78j(b). The first is whether purchasers of registered securities who allege they were defrauded by misrepresentations in a registration statement may maintain an action under Section 10(b) notwithstanding the express remedy for misstatements and omissions in registration statements provided by Section 11 of the Securities Act of 1933, 15 U.S.C. § 77k. The second question is whether persons seeking recovery under Section 10(b) must prove their cause of action by clear and convincing evidence rather than by a preponderance of the evidence.

I

In 1969 Texas International Speedway, Inc. ("TIS"), filed a registration statement and prospectus with the Securities and Exchange Commission offering a total of $4,398,900 in securities to the public. The proceeds of the sale were to be used to finance the construction of an automobile speedway. The entire issue was sold on the offering date, October 30, 1969. TIS did not meet with success, however, and the corporation filed a petition for bankruptcy on November 30, 1970.

In 1972 plaintiffs Huddleston and Bradley instituted a class action in the United States District Court for the Southern District of Texas on behalf of themselves and other purchasers of TIS securities. The complaint alleged violations of Section 10(b) of the Securities Exchange Act of 1934 ("the 1934 Act") and SEC Rule 10b-5 promulgated thereunder, 17 CFR 240.10b-5. Plaintiffs sued most of the participants in the offering, including the accounting firm, Herman & MacLean, which had issued an opinion concerning certain financial statements and a pro forma balance sheet that were contained in the registration statement and prospectus. Plaintiffs claimed that the defendants had engaged in a fraudulent scheme to misrepresent or conceal material facts regarding the financial condition of TIS, including the costs incurred in building the speedway.

After a three-week trial, the District Judge submitted the case to the jury on special interrogatories relating to liability. The judge instructed the jury that liability could be found only if the defendants acted with scienter. The judge also instructed the jury to determine whether plaintiffs had proven their cause of action by a preponderance of the evidence. After the jury rendered a verdict in favor of the plaintiffs on the submitted issues, the judge concluded that Herman & MacLean and others had violated Section 10(b) and Rule 10b-5 by making fraudulent misrepresentations in the TIS registration statement. The court then determined the amount of damages and entered judgment for the plaintiffs.

On appeal, the United States Court of Appeals for the Fifth Circuit held that a cause of action may be maintained under Section 10(b) of the 1934 Act for fraudulent misrepresentations and omissions even when that conduct might also be actionable under Section 11 of the Securities Act of 1933 ("the 1933 Act").

. . .

II

The Securities Act of 1933 and the Securities Exchange Act of 1934 "constitute interrelated components of the federal regulatory scheme governing transactions in securities." *Ernst & Ernst* v. *Hochfelder,* 425 U.S. 185, 206, 96 S.Ct. 1375, 1387, 47 L.Ed. 2d 668 (1976). The Acts created several express private rights of action, one of which is contained in Section 11 of the 1933 Act. In addition to the private actions created explicitly by the 1933 and 1934 Acts, federal courts have implied private remedies under other provisions of the two laws. Most significantly for present purposes, a private right of action under Section 10(b) of the 1934 Act and Rule 10b-5 has been consistently recognized for more than 35 years. The existence of this implied remedy is simply beyond peradventure.

The issue in this case is whether a party should be barred from invoking this established remedy for fraud because the allegedly fraudulent conduct would apparently also provide the basis for a damage action under Section 11 of the 1933 Act. The resolution of this issue turns on the fact that the two provisions involve distinct causes of action and were intended to address different types of wrongdoing.

Section 11 of the 1933 Act allows purchasers of a registered security to sue certain enumerated parties in a registered offering when false or misleading information is included in a registration statement. The section was designed to assure compliance with the disclosure provisions of the Act by imposing a stringent standard of liability on the parties who play a direct role in a registered offering. If a plaintiff purchased a security issued pursuant to a registration statement, he need only show a material misstatement or omission to establish his *prima facie* case. Liability against the issuer of a security is virtually absolute, even for innocent misstatements. Other defendants bear the burden of demonstrating due diligence. See 15 U.S.C. § 77k(b).

Although limited in scope, Section 11 places a relatively minimal burden on a plaintiff. In contrast, Section 10(b) is a "catchall" antifraud provision, but it requires a plaintiff to carry a heavier burden to establish a cause of action. While a Section 11 action must be brought by a purchaser of a registered security, must be based on misstatements or omissions in a registration statement, and can only be brought against certain parties, a Section 10(b) action can be brought by a purchaser or seller of *"any* security" against *"any* person" who has used *"any* manipulative or deceptive device or contrivance" in connection with the purchase or sale of a security. 15 U.S.C. § 78j (emphasis added). However, a Section 10(b) plaintiff carries a heavier burden than a Section 11 plaintiff. Most significantly, he must prove that the defendant acted with scienter, *i.e.,* with intent to deceive, manipulate, or defraud.

Since Section 11 and Section 10(b) address different types of wrongdoing, we see no reason to carve out an exception to Section 10(b) for fraud occurring in a registration statement just because the same conduct may also be actionable under Section 11. Exempting such conduct from liability under Section 10(b) would conflict with the basic purpose of the 1933 Act: to provide greater protection to purchasers of registered securities. It would be anomalous indeed if the special protection afforded to purchasers in a registered offering by the 1933 Act were deemed to deprive such purchasers of the protections against manipulation and deception that Section 10(b) makes available to all persons who deal in securities.

. . .

A cumulative construction of the securities laws also furthers their broad remedial purposes. In enacting the 1934 Act, Congress stated that its purpose was "to impose requirements necessary to make [securities] regulation and control reasonably complete and effective." 15 U.S.C. § 78b. In furtherance of that objective, Section 10(b) makes it unlawful to use *"any* manipulative or deceptive device or contrivance" in connection with the purchase or sale of any security. The effectiveness of the broad proscription against fraud in Section 10(b) would be undermined if its scope were restricted by the existence of an express remedy under Section 11. Yet we have repeatedly recognized that securities laws combating fraud should be construed "not technically and restrictively, but flexibly to effectuate [their] remedial purposes." *SEC* v. *Capital Gains Research Bureau,* 375 U.S. 180, 195, 84 S.Ct. 275, 284, 11 L.Ed.2d 237 (1963). Accord: *Superintendent of Insurance* v. *Bankers Life & Cas. Co.,* 404 U.S. 6, 12, 92 S.Ct. 165, 169, 30 L.Ed.2d 128 (1971); *Affiliated Ute Citizens* v. *United States,* 406 U.S. 128, 151, 92 S.Ct. 1456, 1471, 31 L.Ed.2d 741 (1972). We therefore reject an interpretation of the securities laws that displaces an action under Section 10(b). Accordingly, we hold that the availability of an express remedy under Section 11 of the 1933 Act does not preclude defrauded purchasers of registered securities from maintaining an action under Section 10(b) of the 1934 Act. To this extent the judgment of the court of appeals is affirmed.

. . .

BUSINESS PROTECTION

Business activity enjoys some benefits of regulation or access to courts when rights are threatened. The due process clause of the Constitution provides fundamental protection of persons and property. This may be said to be extended by specific statutes establishing rights in material or intellectual products, and in the right to be free of economic interference.

Rights to Intellectual Products

In order to promote economic activity for the general welfare of the nation, the federal government established, at a very early stage of the development of the United States, a system of protection of rights to inventions and literary or artistic works.

A *patent* represents an exclusive right to make and sell an invention for a set period of time. Patents are issued only on new and useful inventions, improvements, or designs not known in the trade or in use for more than a year prior to application. Infringement is the making of a device that produces the same result as the patented one. A patent holder can sue the infringer for damages and loss of profits.

A *copyright* enables the holder to maintain an exclusive right to publish and sell a literary, musical, and artistic work, or photographs and drawings for a time limit represented by the life of the author plus fifty years. The Copyright Act, under the amendments of 1976, provides for a limited amount of copying for spontaneous educational purposes, but not for the monetary profit of the copier. Infringement calls for actual or statutory damages.

A *trademark* is a distinctive mark, design, or picture by which consumers can identify a product or service. The Lanham Act of 1946 established a Principal Register for the registration of trademarks. Rights to trademarks rest with the developer.

Rights Under Tort Law

Interference with the business activities of another may provide a basis for legal action under the law of torts. This general offense may come about in many different ways—one may disparage the goods of another, interfere in contractual relationships, infringe upon patents, copyrights, and trademarks, or engage in unfair competition. Some of these torts may be actionable under federal and state statutes as well. Review of the more general invasions of property rights such as *deceit, conversion,* and *trespass* is also appropriate in so far as they relate to business activity.

QUESTIONS

1. How do the various antitrust statutes differ? How are mergers addressed by those statutes?
2. Differentiate between the "per se rule" and the "rule of reason."
3. Have there been periods in the history of the United States when protection of health and safety has been an especially acute topic of legislation?

4. What does the Consumer Protection Act cover?
5. What major differences exist between the Securities Act of 1933 and the Securities Exchange Act of 1934?

law
of employment

SEVENTEEN

The importance of what one does for a living is so great that the person is often considered isomorphic with the job or profession. When an individual is asked who he or she is, the answer most frequently is something like "lawyer," "physician," "engineer," etc. It is easy to see, therefore, that the opportunity to obtain and maintain a position and the group supports in such situations represent a significant area for the application of rules of law. Although many persons are professionals or are otherwise self-employed, a major portion of economic activity takes place in organizations; therefore, the employer-employee relationship is the crucial area for study.

BACKGROUND

Attitudes toward collective action in labor matters were generally negative in the United States until relatively recent times. While viable unions existed from 1878 (the founding of the Knights of Labor), it was only during the years of the Great Depression that union activity received significant governmental support. The National Labor Relations Act of 1935 (Wagner Act) introduced collective bargaining on the industrial scene. That legislation marked the real emergence of a union presence although the earlier Norris-LaGuardia

Act of 1932 limiting the use of injunctions in labor disputes paved the way. During World War II unions grew to a position thought by many to be too powerful, so the pendulum swung the other way in the enactment of the Taft-Hartley Act, the Labor Management Relations Act of 1947. This legislation imposed controls on unions that made the give-and-take somewhat more even. More overall monitoring by government agencies on the industrial front was achieved through legislation in 1959, the Labor Management Reporting and Disclosure Act (Landrum-Griffin Act).

Conditions in the working environment also received closer scrutiny from Congress, even though it took some time to take positive action. Long after the evils of child labor were exposed by crusading journalists and others, the Fair Labor Standards Act of 1938, which covers business in interstate commerce was enacted. In addition to prohibiting child labor, the act established a basic living wage and a limit to forty hours of the work week at regular pay with additional compensation thereafter. The minimum wage has been raised several times in the years after (from forty cents an hour in 1938 to over three dollars at present).

While safe working conditions have been the concern of government regulators down through the years, the extensive general legislation in this area is very recent in the form of the Occupational Safety and Health Act of 1970. Specific and stringent criteria for conditions of the work place are outlined with concomitant measures for enforcement.

Prohibition against discrimination in employment practices on the basis of sex, race, religion, or national origin was firmed up in the Civil Rights Act of 1964. This federal legislation has been followed by similar enactments at the state level throughout the country.

LABOR-MANAGEMENT RELATIONS

The relationship of employer and employee is undoubtedly the most important in business and industry. In the past half-century this relationship has shown significant changes; representation by labor unions has grown in intensity and importance, and the body of labor law has expanded commensurately.

The National Labor Relations Act (Wagner Act) in 1935 established the right of employees to form a union and have it represent them in collective bargaining with an employer. In 1947 Congress passed the Labor Management Relations Act (Taft-Hartley) Act amending many of the provisions of the earlier act. Another twelve years later the Labor-Management Reporting and Disclosure Act of 1959 (Landrum-Griffin Act) provided additional controls over labor and management activity.

While these three are the major pieces of federal labor legislation, other statutes have been enacted to supplement them. The Norris-LaGuardia Act (1932) is best known for limiting injunctions by employers in labor disputes. The Railway Labor Act (1926) is an example of legislation similar to all of the above but with specific reference to a particular industry. In addition, many states have adopted labor statutes to cover intrastate activity, particularly in establishing the basic right of employees to organize and utilize other benefits similar to the Wagner Act.

The National Labor Relations Act created the National Labor Relations Board (NLRB) in order to assure the right of self-organization and bargaining representation of employees through the establishment of rules and regulations pursuant to the act, and to monitor the labor activities under it.

Union Representation

The National Labor Relations Act and the Railway Labor Act were enacted to encourage democratic association among employees for the establishment of better working conditions and minimizing labor unrest. The acts ensure the right of representation in bargaining by a union chosen by the majority in an appropriate employee unit.

The first step in the representation process comes when a petitioning group presents satisfactory evidence to the NLRB that at least thirty percent of the target group have indicated support of the request for an election. Signed and dated "authorization cards" are required.

After the petition is filed with the NLRB the Board determines whether it has jurisdiction, the bargaining unit is appropriate, and the requisite thirty percent of that unit have signed cards. If so it will conduct the election. If a majority of employees votes to be represented by a union the board certifies that union as the bargaining agent.

The union, as sole representative of the employees, engages in collective bargaining with the employer in order to establish the contract under which the workers will function on the job. Both sides are under an obligation to bargain in good faith (although there is no duty to reach an agreement). No other representation is permitted by law in bargaining for a contract with the employer. Not all employees are required to be union members, but the union is the representative of all employees, union members or not, and must represent all fairly and without discrimination. All matters under the contract are handled by the union representative.

Union representation has various forms. A *closed shop* is one in which the employer agrees with a union that no one will be employed who is not a member of that particular union. The Taft-Hartley Act of 1947 prohibited a closed shop but permitted a *union shop.* In this situation an employer is free to hire, but after a period of not more than thirty days the new employee must join a union in order to retain his job. A third variation is the *agency shop,* in which nonunion persons may be employed but must pay the union a sum equaling the union dues. State laws may govern with respect to the legality of the agency shop.

The employer is prohibited from contracting with an employee that he or she will not join any union under penalty of discharge. This was known as the *yellow-dog* contract.

It is an unfair labor practice for the employer to interfere with unionization or to discriminate against any employee because of union activity. The right to comment on the issues, however, is ensured by the Taft-Hartley Act. Views, arguments, and opinions are not an unfair labor practice as long as these expressions do not represent force, threats of reprisals, or promises of benefits.

It is an unfair labor practice for the union as well to interfere with the organization by employees of a union. To stop work or to try to persuade others to do so, to cause an employer to discriminate against employees for their attempts to work on behalf of other unions or for no union at all, is prohibited.

In some instances unfair labor practices by an employer have been easy to identify, as the following case demonstrates.

J. P. Stevens & Co. v. N. L. R. B.

417 F.2d 533 (1969)

JOHN R. BROWN, Chief Judge:

Only three things distinguish this case from the run-of-the-mill §§ 8(a) (1), 8 (a) (3) labor cases. The first is the tenacity with which the Employer persists in the exercise of deep seated anti-union convictions. The second is the succession of formal cases culminating in the present one bearing five service stripes in which, except for minor variations, the Board's findings of spectacular Employer violations of §§ 8 (a) (1), 8(a) (3) and 8(a) (5) of the Act have been upheld by three Courts of Appeals. The third is the Board's efforts to devise some character of remedy which has at least some prospects of keeping the recalcitrant Employer's intransigence within the bounds of vigorous but lawful opposition to Union attempts to organize units in a multistate industrial complex.

As *Stevens V* this case, joining the list of predecessors, has a like outcome. We enforce.

The Board concluded that Stevens had violated § 8(a) (1) and (3) by discriminatorily discharging four employees, engaging in surveillance of Union activity, interrogating employees about Union activity, and making threats of discharging employees for Union activity and threats of closing plants if the Union was recognized.

To the usual, traditional requirement of reinstatement and back pay for the § 8(a) (3) discharges and cease and desist order of § 8(a) (1) violations with posting for a specific period, the Board's order additionally required that (1) the notice to employees be read to the assembled employees on shift-time, (2) it be mailed to the employees' homes, (3) the Union, upon request, be given access for one year to the company bulletin boards and (4) the Union be furnished a list of the names and addresses of all Stevens employees working in the plants where the violations occurred.

We focus on requirements of the order (d)(e)(f), and (g) since the § 8(a) (1) and (3) violations warrant no detailed treatment. In the first place, with no real concession at all, Stevens has apparently abandoned its attack on the record support for the findings of coercive surveillance of Union activity, interrogation and threats, which are classic, albeit crude, unlawful labor practices.

Although Stevens does claim that there is not substantial evidence to support the finding that the four employees were discriminatorily discharged, our examination of the record convinces us that in these run-of-the-mill incidents on which the Board, not the Court, has to pass upon the credibility of the witnesses, we cannot say the findings are unsupported by substantial evidence on the record as a whole.

Stevens has been engaged in a massive multistate campaign to prevent unionization of its Southern plants. This campaign has involved numerous flagrant unfair labor practices including coercive interrogation, surveillance, threat of plant closings, and economic reprisals for Union activity. Moreover, the threats have been made good by extensive discriminatory discharges. As a result of these practices, several unfair charges have been brought before the Labor Board . . . and, except for slight variations, the orders of the Board have been enforced by two other Circuit Courts of Appeal in *Stevens I, II, and III and IV.* . . . As the Fourth Circuit said in assessing the company's conduct in *Stevens III and IV,* "the Board properly took into consideration the unfair labor practices that *Stevens I* and II, disclosed, and we, in turn, cannot ignore this evidence. Maphis Chapman Corp. v. NLRB, 368 F. 2d 208, 303 (4th Cir. 1966)". *Stevens III and IV* at 1019 of 406 F. 2d. Nor can we, in our subsequent turn, ignore the unfair labor practices disclosed in *Stevens III and IV.* To these we add the incidents and violations found by the Board to have occurred in the Georgia plants. Thus we assay the order in this atmosphere of persistent, long continued, flagrant violations occurring after and in spite of repeated declarations of illegality by Board and reviewing Courts.

. . . In order to enable employees to enjoy these rights, especially in lawful efforts to organize for collective representation, there are many instances in which the inescapably negative cease and desist order will not suffice. Nor is the reinstatement with backpay order universally and fully effective. In the first place, this merely assuages the direct economic injury suffered by the victims of unlawful discrimination, except to hold out some hope that the incidents will not recur because each will be met by this mild sanction, the backpay order's impact on the efforts of the remaining employees to organize is at best uncertain.

. . .

As the leitmotif in this opus in a major or minor key is the necessity that, within permissible limits, the remedy be tuned to the exigencies of the case, we would emphasize as do all the cases approving adaptability that this opinion does not stand as a precedent . . . in any particular case. It all depends.

We deny the petition for review and grant the cross-petition to enforce.

A later challenge to representation may be made by filing a *decertification* petition with the NLRB, again with signatures of thirty percent of the unit required. A decertification election follows.

Labor and Management Practices

Union tactics in obtaining a favorable end result include strikes, picketing, and boycotts. A strike is a group effort in stopping work, while picketing is the stationing of persons outside the workplace in order to inform others of the nature of the dispute. A boycott is an effort to persuade others not to labor for or use the services and products of the employer.

When employees picket or boycott at the workplace of the employer, their activity is called a *primary* boycott or picketing; when employees extend the scope of their operations to other employers involved in business with their employer, the action is known as a *secondary* boycott or picketing. Secondary boycotts are generally considered to be unfair labor practices.

As the following case illustrates, a secondary boycott may be constrained and have penalties assessed, even when the basic intent involves strong feelings of equity or patriotism.

Intern. Longshoreman's, Etc. v. *Allied Intern.*
102 S.Ct. 1656 (1982)

Justice POWELL delivered the opinion of the Court.

The question for our decision is whether a refusal by an American longshoremen's union to unload cargoes shipped from the Soviet Union is an illegal secondary boycott under § 8(b)(4), U.S.C. § 158(b)(4), of the National Labor Relations Act (NLRA), as amended, 29 U.S.C. § 158(b)(4).

I

On January 9, 1980, Thomas Gleason, President of the International Longshoremen's Association (ILA), ordered ILA members to stop handling cargoes arriving from or destined for the Soviet Union. Gleason took this action to protest the Russian invasion of Afghanistan. In obedience to the order, longshoremen up and down the East and Gulf Coasts refused to service ships carrying Russian cargoes.

Respondent Allied International, Inc. (Allied) is an American company that imports Russian wood products for resale in the United States. Allied contracts with Waterman Steamship Lines (Waterman), an American corporation operating ships of United States registry, for shipment of the wood from Leningrad to ports on the East and Gulf coasts of the United States. Waterman, in turn, employs the stevedoring company of John T. Clark & Son of Boston, Inc. (Clark) to unload its ships docking in Boston. Under the terms of the collective bargaining agreement between ILA Local 799 and the Boston Shipping Association, of which Clark is a member, Clark obtains its longshoring employees through the union hiring hall.

As a result of the boycott, Allied's shipments were disrupted completely. Ultimately, Allied was forced to renegotiate its Russian contracts, substantially reducing its purchases and jeopardizing its ability to supply its own customers. App. 24a-28a. On March 31, 1980, after union officials informed Allied that ILA members would continue to refuse to unload any Russian cargo, Allied brought this action in the United States District Court for the District of Massachusetts. Claiming that the boycott violated the prohibition against secondary boycotts, in § 8(b)(4), 29 U.S.C. § 158(b)(4), of the National Labor Relations Act, Allied sued for damages under § 303 of the Labor Management Relations Act (LMRA), 29 U.S.C. § 187, which creates a private damages remedy for the victims of secondary boycotts. At about the same time, Allied filed an unfair labor practice charge with the National Labor Relations Board under § 10(b) of the National Labor Relations Act, 29 U.S.C. § 160(b).

Finding that Allied had not alleged a violation of § 8(b)(4)(B), the District Court dismissed Allied's complaint. *Allied Int'l, Inc.* v. *International Longshoremen's Assn.,* 492 F.Supp. 334 (D.Mass.1980). The court characterized the ILA boycott as a purely political, primary boycott of Russian goods. So described the boycott was not within the scope of § 8(b)(4).

The Court of Appeals for the First Circuit reversed the dismissal of Allied's complaint and remanded for further proceedings. 640 F.2d 1368 (1981). As an initial matter, and in agreement with the District Court, the court found that the effects of the ILA boycott were "in commerce" within the meaning of the National Labor Relations Act as interpreted by a long line of decisions of this Court. The court held further that the ILA boycott, as described in Allied's averments, was within § 8(b)(4)'s prohibition of secondary boycotts, despite its political purpose, and that resort to such behavior was not protected activity under the First Amendment.

. . .

II

Our starting point in a case of this kind must be the language of the statute. By its exact terms the secondary boycott provisions of § 8(b)(4)(B) of the NLRA would appear to be aimed precisely at the sort of activity alleged in this case. Section 8(b)(4)(B) governs activities designed to influence individuals employed by "any person engaged in commerce or in an industry affecting commerce." Certainly Allied, Waterman, and Clark were engaged "in commerce," and Allied alleges that the effect of the ILA action was to obstruct commerce up and down the East and Gulf coasts. Just as plainly, it would appear that the ILA boycott fell within § 8(b)(4)(B)'s prohibition of secondary boycotts. Allied alleges that by inducing members of the union to refuse to handle Russian cargoes, the ILA boycott was designed to force Allied, Waterman, and Clark "to cease doing business" with one another and "to cease using, selling, handling, transporting, or otherwise dealing in" Russian products.

. . .

The secondary boycott provisions in § 8(b)(4)(B) prohibit a union from inducing employees to refuse to handle goods with the object of forcing any person to cease doing business with any other person. By its terms the statutory prohibition applies to the undisputed facts of this case. The ILA has no dispute with Allied, Waterman, or Clark. It does not seek any labor objective from these employers. Its sole complaint is with the foreign and military policy of the Soviet Union. As understandable and even commendable as the ILA's ultimate objectives may be, the certain effect of its action is to impose a heavy burden on neutral employers. And it is just such a burden, as well as widening of industrial strife, that the secondary boycott provisions were designed to prevent. As the NLR explained in ruling upon the regional director's complaint against the ILA:

> "It is difficult to imagine a situation that falls more squarely within the scope of Section 8(b)(4) than the one before us today. Here, the Union's sole dispute is with the USSR over its invasion of Afghanistan. Allied, Waterman, and Clark have nothing to do with this dispute. Yet the Union's actions in furtherance of its disagreement with Soviet foreign policy have brought direct economic pressure on all three parties and have resulted in a substantial cessation of business. Thus, the conduct alleged in this case is precisely the type Congress intended the National Labor Relations Act to regulate." 257 N.L.R.B. No. 151, at 14 (footnotes omitted).

Nor can it be argued that the ILA's action was outside of the prohibition on secondary boycotts because its object was not to halt business between Allied, Clark, and Waterman with respect to Russian goods, but simply to free ILA members from the morally repugnant duty of handling Russian goods. Such an argument misses the point. Undoubtedly many secondary boycotts have the object of freeing employees from handling goods from an objectionable source. Nonetheless, when a purely secondary boycott "reasonably can be expected to threaten neutral parties with ruin or substantial loss," *NLRB* v. *Retail Store Employees,* 447 U.S. 607, 614, 100 S.Ct. 2372, 2377, 65 L.Ed.2d 377 (1980), the pressure on secondary parties must be viewed as at least one of the objects of the boycott or the statutory prohibition would be rendered meaningless. The union must take responsibility for the "foreseeable consequences" of its conduct. *Id.,* at 614, n. 9, 100 S.Ct. at 2377, n. 9; see *NLRB* v. *Operating Engineers,* 400 U.S. 297, 304–305, 91 S.Ct. 402, 407–408, (1971). Here the union was fully aware of the losses it was inflicting upon Allied. It is undisputed that Allied officials endeavored to persuade ILA leaders to allow it to fulfill its Russian contracts. On the basis of the record before it, the Court of Appeals correctly concluded that Allied had alleged a violation of § 8(b)(4).

Neither is it a defense to the application of § 8(b)(4) that the reason for the ILA boycott was not a labor dispute with a primary employer but a political dispute with a foreign nation. Section 8(b)(4) contains no such limitation. In the plainest of language it prohibits "forcing . . . any person to cease . . . handling . . . the products of any other producer . . . or to cease doing business with any other person." The legislative history does not indicate that political disputes should be excluded from the scope of § 8(b)(4). The prohibition was drafted broadly to protect neutral parties, "the help- less victims of quarrels that do not concern them at all." H.R. Report No. 245, 80th Cong., 1st Sess. 23 (1947). Despite criticism from President Truman as well as from some legislators that the secondary boycott provision was too sweeping, the Congress refused to narrow its scope. Recognizing that "[i]lle- gal boycotts take many forms," *id.,* at 315, Congress intended its prohibition to reach broadly.

. . .

We would create a large and undefinable exception to the statute if we accepted the argument that "political" boycotts are exempt from the secondary boycott provi- sion. The distinction between labor and po- litical objectives would be difficult to draw in many cases. In the absence of any limiting language in the statute or legislative history, we find no reason to conclude that Congress intended such a potentially expansive excep- tion to a statutory provision purposefully drafted in broadest terms.

We agree with the Court of Appeals that it is "more rather than less objectionable that a national labor union has chosen to marshal against neutral parties the consider- able powers derived by its locals and itself under the federal labor laws in aid of a ran- dom political objective far removed from what has traditionally been thought to be the realm of legitimate union activity." 640 F.2d, at 1378. In light of the statutory lan- guage and purpose, we decline to create a far-reaching exemption from the statutory provision for "political" secondary boycotts.

. . .

There are many ways in which a union and its individual members may express their opposition to Russian foreign policy without infringing upon the rights of others.

The judgment of the Court of Appeals is

Affirmed.

The NLRB classifies strikes into three broad categories:

1. Economic strike;
2. Employer unfair labor practice strike;
3. Union unfair labor practice strike.

The economic strike takes place through demands for improvement in wages, hours, and working conditions. An employer unfair labor practice strike is one protesting against employer tactics, such as refusal to bargain collectively or discrimination against union members. Union unfair labor practice strikes are those that are either unprotected or pro-scribed by law. Violation of no-strike agreement, forcing an employer to stop dealing with another person, forcing an employer to join an employer organization, or requiring recognition after another union has obtained bargaining rights, are all examples of strike activity that is prohibited.

A *jurisdictional* strike occurs in a dispute between two or more unions, each of which claims exclusive or unique rights from the employer, as when each of two trades feels its workers are the ones to do a certain job. A *wildcat* strike is one where the union disclaims responsibility as this kind of strike purportedly arises on a spontaneous basis.

Other work stoppages can occur within the workplace. Employees may conduct a *sitdown* strike where they remain on the job but no work is done. A *slowdown* strike is similar, except that work continues but the pace is reduced so that there is little output.

There are various other practices to ensure the security of union members or extraordinarily favorable work conditions. Make-work practices, or *featherbedding,* may restrict the level of output on the job or require the hiring of additional workers to do a job. Make-work practices are generally valid, except that where pay is exacted for services not performed there is a violation of the act. Wasteful and duplicative idiosyncrasies of a trade are not considered violations.

Further efforts to assure union security such as excessive initiation fees and dues (so that the number of available workers will be reduced) are violations of the statute.

Employers, on the other hand, have used *lockouts,* a closing of the workplace, as a weapon in a labor dispute. Court injunctions have been useful in limiting the scope of the union activity to legally recognized methods in a strike and picketing. The Norris-La Guardia Act prohibited the granting of injunctions where no damage to property was involved although the NLRB may obtain an injunction to stop unfair labor practices.

The NLRB also serves as a quasi-judicial agency of the federal government in determinations of the validity of labor practices under the National Labor Relations Act and its amendments.

Whenever an unfair labor practice is alleged, the NLRB will issue a complaint, notifying the party of the allegations and giving notice of a hearing. The board, after the hearing, makes findings of fact and conclusions of law. It either dismisses the complaint or takes such actions as would effectuate the policies of the Act. The action may range from stopping an unfair labor practice, to the more positive reinstatement or reimburse-ment of an aggrieved employee.

Appeals from NLRB decisions may be made to the U.S. Court of Appeals. It is important to note that in this area of activity, as in most others, there are often state statutes that provide for civil, criminal, or administrative agency remedies. If the state and federal laws are in conflict, however, the federal law pre-empts the state statutes.

Duties of Unions

Concern with union conduct of members' interests led to specific action in the Taft-Hartley Act (1947) but more so in the Landrum-Griffin Act, the Labor-Management Reporting and Disclosure Act of 1959. The 1947 amendments prohibited the imposition of excessive and discriminatory dues or fees or to have dues deducted by the employer unless authorized by each member. Campaign contributions from dues are also prohibited. Detailed reports, with copies to members, are to be sent to the Secretary of Labor.

The Act of 1959 imposed still other duties upon unions and their officers. Unions are required to adopt constitutions and bylaws and file them with the secretary along with detailed financial statements. The right of union members is guaranteed with respect to information on financial matters, voting, the contract, and other specific matters. Persons convicted of major crimes are barred as officers or employees for a specific time, and communists are barred from office. Controls are imposed upon union officials and assets to prevent theft or embezzlement. Loans to officers and employees are limited and all officers with interests that may conflict with union activities are required to file a report.

CONDITIONS OF EMPLOYMENT

Concern for conditions of work, from the right to consideration for employment, later organizational activity on the job, and safety at work, has an extensive history. Equal opportunity for employment, standards for hours and wages, compensation under unemployment or as the result of injury, are some of the major areas covered by federal or state legislation.

Wages and Hours

The Fair Labor Standards Act of 1938 sets minimum wages for workers in interstate commerce and industry. The act, known by many as the Wage and Hours Act, also regulates the hours worked and stipulates that work over 40 hours in a week must be paid at time-and-a-half for overtime. Similar special provisions cover employees of railroads which limit the number of hours worked while moving trains or engaged in duties relating to that activity, such as handling communication.

Contractors for materials and services to the United States government are further regulated by several acts. The Public Contracts Act (Walsh-Healey) provides that contracts with the federal government for more than $10,000 meet all wage and hour standards of the act or those set by the Secretary of Labor. The Public Works Contracts Act (Davis-Bacon) requires contractors in building for the United States to pay the prevailing wages determined by the Secretary of Labor. In addition employers are prohibited from requiring employees to return or "kickback" any part of their wages.

Equal Opportunity

The *Equal Pay Act of 1963* began a long series of related acts by mandating equal pay for equal work by men and women. The most extensive legislation, however, came the next year in Title VII of the *Civil Rights Act of 1964* which (as amended) requires that the employer not discriminate in privileges, terms, and conditions of employment on the basis of race, religion, sex, or national origin. The *Age Discrimination in Employment Act of 1967* added the prohibition with respect to age, forbidding discrimination against job applicants between ages 40 and 65. Further legislation came in the *Equal Employment Opportunity Act of 1972,* amending the 1964 Act and in *Executive Order 11246,* which regulates contractors doing business with the federal government.

The Civil Rights Act of 1964, Title VII, as amended by the Equal Employment Opportunity Act of 1972 prohibits discrimination because of race, color, religion, sex, or national origin. The act makes it unlawful for an employer to discriminate on the above basis in:

1. Failing or refusing to hire or discharge any individual or discriminate with respect to compensation or conditions of employment;
2. Limiting or classifying an employee in any way adversely affecting status.

Employment agencies may not refer or refuse to refer on the basis of the demographic variables mentioned above.

It is also an unlawful employment practice for a labor organization to discriminate, as above, by:

1. Expelling or excluding from membership;
2. Limiting, segregating, or classifying its members in any way that deprives or limits employment opportunities;
3. Causing an employer to discriminate.

Any further activity in apprentice or training programs that discriminates is also unlawful. Advertising or printing of notices contrary to the provisions of Title VII is prohibited as is any discrimination arising because a person has filed a complaint or assisted in an investigation of a matter arising under this title.

Certain activities are not considered to be violations of the act. Different standards of compensation are permitted when they relate to performance measures of quality and quantity pursuant to a true seniority system, or work at different locations, provided that there is no intent to discriminate.

Administering and acting on the results of professionally developed tests are not unlawful if acted upon or developed with no intent to discriminate. The tests must be "job related," and the resulting use must not be discriminatory. The lack of intent to discriminate is not enough; there must also be an actual nondiscriminatory effect (see *Griggs* v. *Duke Power Co.,* 401 U.S. 424(1971), below).

A further exception is where religion, sex, or national origin is a real occupational qualification reasonably necessary in the operation of the business. The exception is being narrowly construed and, as the Act indicates, there is no exception on the basis of race or color.

Griggs v. *Duke Power Co.*
  401 U.S. 424(1971)

MR. CHIEF JUSTICE BURGER delivered the opinion of the Court.

We granted the writ in this case to resolve the question whether an employer is prohibited by the Civil Rights Act of 1964, Title VII, from requiring a high school education or passing of a standardized general intelligence test as a condition of employment in or transfer to jobs when (a) neither standard is shown to be significantly related to successful job performance, (b) both requirements operate to disqualify Negroes at a substantially higher rate than white applicants, and (c) the jobs in question formerly had been filled only by white employees as part of a longstanding practice of giving preference to whites. . . .

The objective of Congress in the enactment of Title VII is plain from the language of the statute. It was to achieve equality of employment opportunities and remove barriers that have operated in the past to favor an identifiable group of white employees over other employees. Under the Act, practices, procedures, or tests neutral on their face, and even neutral in terms of intent, cannot be maintained if they operate to "freeze" the status quo of prior discriminatory employment practices. . . .

In short, the Act does not command that any person be hired simply because he was formerly the subject of discrimination, or because he is a member of a minority group. Discriminatory preference for any group, minority or majority, is precisely and only what Congress has proscribed. What is required by Congress is the removal of artificial, arbitrary, and unnecessary barriers to employment when the barriers operate invidiously to discriminate on the basis of racial or other impermissible classification. . . .

The Act proscribes not only overt discrimination but also practices that are fair in form, but discriminatory in operation. The touchstone is business necessity. If an employment practice which operates to exclude Negroes cannot be shown to be related to job performance, the practice is prohibited.

On the record before us, neither the high school completion requirement nor the general intelligence test is shown to bear a demonstrable relationship to successful performance of the jobs for which it was used. Both were adopted, as the Court of Appeals noted, without meaningful study of their relationship to job-performance ability. Rather, a vice president of the company testified, the requirements were instituted on the Company's judgment that they generally would improve the overall quality of the work force. . . .

The Company's lack of discriminatory intent is suggested by special efforts to help the undereducated employees through Company financing of two-thirds the cost of tuition for high school training. But Congress directed the thrust of the Act to the *consequences* of employment practices, not simply the motivation. More than that, Congress has placed on the employer the burden of showing that any given requirement must have a manifest relationship to the employment in question. . . .

Nothing in the Act precludes the use of testing or measuring procedures; obviously they are useful. What Congress had forbidden is giving these devices and mechanisms controlling force unless they are demonstrably a reasonable measure of job performance. Congress had not commanded that the less qualified be preferred over the better qualified simply because of minority origins. Far from disparaging job qualifications as such, Congress has made such qualifications the controlling factor, so that race, religion, nationality, and sex become irrelevant. What Congress has commanded is that any tests used must measure the person for the job and not the person in the abstract.

The judgment of the Court of Appeals is, as to that portion of the judgment appealed from,

Reversed. . . .

Title VII of the Civil Rights Act of 1964 also established the Equal Employment Opportunity Commission (EEOC) in order to investigate and eliminate discrimination. Where a state agency with comparable powers exists, a complainant must first file a complaint with the state agency. After sixty days or completion of the state proceedings, a complaint may be filed with the EEOC. The commission investigates and, if there is cause to believe discrimination exists, attempts conciliation. Should conciliation fail, the commission is empowered to initiate court actions for the complainant under the Equal Opportunities Act of 1972 which amended Title VII. The EEOC also has the authorization, since 1972, to initiate class action suits and those demonstrating "pattern and practice" in discrimination.

Courts have the power to grant injunctions against discriminatory practices and to issue affirmative orders to reinstate workers, with or without back pay.

Executive Order 11246 goes further in requiring *affirmative action* plans on the part of bidders on federal government contracts. These plans must be specific proposals to achieve equal employment opportunity with analyses of present conditions, goals and commitments, timetables, and data supporting the effort, particularly in those areas targeted by the government for special attention. The Executive Order gives the Secretary of Labor the duty of coordinating the efforts; the Secretary of Labor has established the Office of Federal Contract Compliance (OFCC) to administer all activity under Executive Order 11246. Supervision under the Order is not limited to those of governmental agencies. In the construction industry voluntary local efforts are encouraged, and some are already in effect in major cities. If no such local plan exists, the OFCC has indicated that it will impose the so-called "Philadelphia Plan," which, among other conditions, requires bidders to agree to meet specific established goals and timetables.

Affirmative action plans have been attacked on the basis that such programs themselves discriminate against qualified workers who do not belong to a minority group. The following case addresses those concerns.

Steelworkers v. *Weber*
443 U.S. 193 (1979)

MR. JUSTICE BRENNAN delivered the opinion of the Court.

Challenged here is the legality of an affirmative action plan—collectively bargained by an employer and a union—that reserves for black employees 50% of the openings in an in-plant craft-training program until the percentage of black craftworkers in the plant is commensurate with the percentage of blacks in the local labor force. The question for decision is whether Congress, in Title VII of the Civil Rights Act of 1964, 75 Stat. 253, as amended, 42 U. S. C. § 2000e *et seq.,* left employers and unions in the private sector free to take such race-conscious steps to eliminate manifest racial imbalances in traditionally segregated job categories. We hold that Title VII does not prohibit such race-conscious affirmative action plans.

I

In 1974, petitioner United Steelworkers of America (USWA) and petitioner Kaiser Aluminum & Chemical Corp. (Kaiser) entered into a master collective-bargaining agreement covering terms and conditions of employment at 15 Kaiser plants. The agreement contained, *inter alia,* an affirmative action plan designed to eliminate conspicuous racial imbalances in Kaiser's then almost exclusively white craftwork forces. Black craft-hiring goals were set for each Kaiser plant equal to the percentage of blacks in the respective local labor forces. To enable plants to meet these goals, on-the-job training programs were established to teach unskilled production workers—black and white —the skills necessary to become craftworkers. The plan reserved for black employees 50% of the openings in these newly created in-plant training programs.

. . .

Thereafter one of those white production workers, respondent Brian Weber (hereafter respondent), instituted this class action in the United States District Court for the Eastern District of Louisiana.

The complaint alleged that the filling of craft trainee positions at the Gramercy plant pursuant to the affirmative action program had resulted in junior black employees' receiving training in preference to senior white employees, thus discriminating against respondent and other similarly situated white employees in violation of §§ 703(a) and (d) of Title VII. The District Court held that the plan violated Title VII, entered a judgment in favor of the plaintiff class, and granted a permanent injunction prohibiting Kaiser and the USWA "from denying plaintiffs, Brian F. Weber and all other members of the class, access to on-the-job training programs on the basis of race." App. 171. A divided panel of the Court of Appeals for the Fifth Circuit affirmed, holding that all employment preferences based upon race, including those preferences incidental to bona fide affirmative action plans, violated Title VII's prohibition against racial discrimination in employment. . . .

II

We emphasize at the outset the narrowness of our inquiry. Since the Kaiser-USWA plan does not involve state action, this case does not present an alleged violation of the Equal Protection Clause of the Fourteenth Amendment. Further, since the Kaiser-USWA plan was adopted voluntarily, we are not concerned with what Title VII requires or with what a court might order to remedy a past proved violation of the Act. The only question before us is the narrow statutory issue of whether Title VII *forbids* private employers and unions from voluntarily agreeing upon bona fide affirmative action plans that accord racial preferences in the manner and for the purpose provided in the Kaiser-USWA plan. That question was expressly left open in *McDonald* v. *Santa Fe Trail Transp. Co.,* 427 U.S. 273, 281 n. 8 (1976), which held, in a case not involving affirmative action, that Title VII protects whites as well as blacks from certain forms of racial discrimination.

Respondent argues that Congress intended in Title VII to prohibit all race-conscious affirmative action plans. Respondent's argument rests upon a literal interpretation of §§ 703 (a) and (d) of the Act. Those sections make it unlawful to "discriminate . . . because of . . . race" in hiring and in the selection of apprentices for training programs. Since, the argument runs, *McDonald* v. *Santa Fe Trail Transp. Co., supra,* settled that Title VII forbids discrimination against whites as well as blacks, and since the Kaiser-USWA affirmative action plan operates to discriminate against white employees solely because they are white, it follows that the Kaiser-USWA plan violates Title VII.

Respondent's argument is not without force. But it overlooks the significance of the fact that the Kaiser-USWA plan is an affirmative action plan voluntarily adopted by private parties to eliminate traditional patterns of racial segregation. In this context respondent's reliance upon a literal construction of §§ 703(a) and (d) and upon *McDonald* is misplaced.

. . .

III

We need not today define in detail the line of demarcation between permissible and impermissible affirmative action plans. It suffices to hold that the challenged Kaiser-USWA affirmative action plan falls on the permissible side of the line. The purposes of the plan mirror those of the statute. Both were designed to break down old patterns of racial segregation and hierarchy. Both were structured to "open employment opportunities for Negroes in occupations which have been traditionally closed to them." 110 Cong. Rec. 6548 (1964) (remarks of Sen. Humphrey).

At the same time, the plan does not unnecessarily trammel the interests of the white employees. The plan does not require the discharge of white workers and their replacement with new black hirees. Cf. *McDonald* v. *Santa Fe Trail Transp. Co.,* 427 U.S. 273 (1976). Nor does the plan create an absolute bar to the advancement of white employees; half of those trained in the program will be white. Moreover, the plan is a temporary measure; it is not intended to maintain racial balance, but simply to eliminate a manifest racial imbalance. Preferential selection of craft trainees at the Gramercy plant will end as soon as the percentage of black skilled craftworkers in the Gramercy plant approximates the percentage of blacks in the local labor force. See 415 F. Supp., at 763.

We conclude, therefore, that the adoption of the Kaiser-USWA plan for the Gramercy plant falls within the area of discretion left by Title VII to the private sector voluntarily to adopt affirmative action plans designed to eliminate conspicuous racial imbalance in traditionally segregated job categories. Accordingly, the judgment of the Court of Appeals for the Fifth Circuit is

Reversed.

Work Safety

"Preservation of human resources" and assurance of safe and healthful working conditions was the intent of Congress in enacting the Occupational Safety and Health Act of 1970 (The Williams-Steiger Act). The OSHA law applies to all employers engaged in business affecting commerce. Federal and state employees are not included (but may be covered by other equally effective requirements). Employees in certain occupations are excluded because they have already been covered by earlier specific statutes. Employers have the duty of providing a safe place of work by following the standards promulgated under the act, while employees have the duty to comply with the regulations.

The act established the Occupational Safety and Health Administration in the Department of Labor and a new agency, the Occupational Safety and Health Review Commission, a quasi-judicial board of review.

Any employees who believe immediate danger exists or that physical harm is threatened because of a violation of standards may request an inspection by the Department of Labor. If such inspection reveals a violation, the Department will issue a citation, fix a reasonable time for abatement, and notify the employer of the penalty.

Citations for *serious* violations incur mandatory monetary penalties of up to $1000. Serious violations are those where a substantial probability exists that death or serious physical harm could result. A *willful* violation resulting in an employee death is punishable by fine up to $10,000 or imprisonment for up to six months. A *de minimis* violation having no direct relationship to safety or health receives a notice only.

If the employer wishes to contest the citation or penalty he may request a hearing before the Occupational Safety and Health Commission.

Employers have the further duty of maintaining specific records and making periodic reports of work-related deaths, injuries, and illnesses.

Discharge of or discrimination against any employee who exercises a right under the act is prohibited.

QUESTIONS

1. Can major labor-management legislation be related to broader events on the national scene?
2. Identify unfair labor practices by both unions and employers.
3. Describe the role of the National Labor Relations Board.
4. What acts provide for equal opportunity in employment? What provisions are included?

technology
and
the environment

EIGHTEEN

Advances in material respects have always brought with them certain consequences with substantial impact upon the lives of those affected. Never has this been more the case than in very recent times, in terms of the physical environment of individuals and in the influence of the rapid development of data gathering and usage. In just these two selected areas of everyday existence, one can readily see the pressures for regulatory action.

ENVIRONMENTAL PROTECTION

Concern over the quality of life space has been mounting with the passage of time, reaching high and active levels in the past decade. The response has come in the form of community action on a wide front and extensive legislation at all governmental levels, particularly the federal. The National Environmental Policy Act expresses well the purposes to be met in the legislation:

To declare a national policy which will encourage productive and enjoyable harmony between man and his environment; to promote efforts which will prevent or eliminate damage to the environment and biosphere and stimulate the health and welfare of man; to enrich the understanding of the ecological systems and natural resources important to the Nation; and to establish a Council on Environmental Quality.

The act builds upon this statement of purpose by setting broad policy goals, and determining duties for federal agencies with respect to the environment. The purpose of the Council on Environmental Quality (CEQ) is to gather information, analyze it, issue guidelines, and make recommendations to the President on environmental matters.

Much of the activity as a result of the act comes in the requirement that all federal agencies provide a detailed statement of the environmental impact of all major federal actions or proposals for legislation. The Environmental Impact Study (EIS) has been the source of considerable litigation as agencies and courts have attempted to meet the requirements of an act when the provisions have not always been clear.

In 1970 further administrative and regulatory coordination came with the establishment of the *Environmental Protection Agency* (EPA) under the President's Reorganization Plan No. 3. Regulation of air quality, water pollution, solid waste, radiation, and pesticides was transferred from a wide variety of agencies to the new agency in order to provide more effective administration of laws designed to improve the quality of life.

Water Quality

Regulation of water pollution has a longer history than most other areas. The Water Pollution Control Act of 1948 attempted to bring strong federal controls to what was already being perceived as a major problem (there was very early legislation, the Rivers and Harbors Act of 1899, but it was seldom enforced). Significant amendments that represented a "sweeping" campaign to "prevent, reduce and eliminate water pollution" were passed in 1972. Two major goals of the legislation were the achievement of water clean enough for swimming by 1983 and no discharges of pollutants into the Nation's waters by 1985. All waters are covered, not just interstate ones, and the EPA is empowered to step in speedily if states do not act. An immediate court injunction may be obtained if there is an imminent and substantial danger to public health. The EPA has the power to inspect, and information, except for trade secrets, will be made public. Penalties range from $2500 to $25,000 per day and up to a year in prison for the first offense.

Guidelines for control of water pollution are set out in a form outlined as "best practicable" and "best available," but if these do not meet the standards the state may impose stricter controls.

Federal aid to local governments for sewage facilities is available and small business may obtain loans from the Small Business Administration in order to meet the standards.

Some of the complexities involved in enforcing the Water Pollution Control Act are illustrated by the following case.

Weinberger v. *Romero-Barcelo*
102 S.Ct. 1798 (1982)

WHITE, Justice.

The issue in this case is whether the Federal Water Pollution Control Act (FWPCA or the Act), 86 Stat. 816, 33 U.S.C. § 1251 *et seq.* (1976 ed. and Supp. III), requires a district court to enjoin immediately all discharges of pollutants that do not comply with the Act's permit requirements or whether the district court retains discretion to order other relief to achieve compliance. The Court of Appeals for the First Circuit held that the Act withdrew the courts' equitable discretion. 643 F.2d 835 (1981). We reverse.

I

For many years, the Navy has used Vieques Island, a small island off the Puerto Rico coast, for weapons training. Currently all Atlantic Fleet vessels assigned to the Mediterranean and the Indian Ocean are required to complete their training at Vieques because it permits a full range of exercises under conditions similar to combat. During air-to-ground training, however, pilots sometimes miss land-based targets, and ordnance falls into the sea. That is, accidental bombings of the navigable waters and, occasionally, intentional bombings of water targets occur. The District Court found that these discharges have not harmed the quality of the water.

In 1978, respondents, who include the Governor of Puerto Rico and residents of the island, sued to enjoin the Navy's operations on the island. Their complaint alleged violations of numerous federal environmental statutes and various other acts. After an extensive hearing, the District Court found that under the explicit terms of the Act, the Navy had violated the Act by discharging ordnance into the waters surrounding the island without first obtaining a permit from the Environmental Protection Agency (EPA). 478 F.Supp. 646 (D.P.R. 1979).

Under the FWPCA, the "discharge of any pollutant" requires a National Pollutant Discharge Elimination System (NPDES) permit. 33 U.S.C. § 1311(a), § 1323(a) 1976 ed. and Supp. III). The term "discharge of any pollutant" is defined as

> ". . . any addition of any *pollutant* to the waters of the contiguous zone or the ocean from any *point source* other than a vessel or other floating craft." 33 U.S.C. § 1362(12) (emphasis added).

Pollutant, in turn, means,

> ". . . dredged spoil, solid wastes, incinerator residue, sewage, garbage, sewage sludge, *munitions,* chemical wastes, biological materials, radioactive materials, heat, wrecked or discarded equipment, rock, sand, cellar dirt and industrial, municipal and agricultural waste discharged into water . . ." 33 U.S.C. § 1362(6) (emphasis added).

And, under the Act, a "point source" is

> "any discernible, confined and discrete *conveyance,* including but not limited to any pipe, ditch, channel, tunnel, conduit, well, discrete fissure, container rolling stock, concentrated animal feeding operation, or *vessel* or other *floating craft from which pollutants are or may be discharged.* . . ." 33 U.S.C. § 1362(14) (emphasis added).

Under the FWPCA, the EPA may not issue an NPDES without state certification that the permit conforms to state water quality standards. A state has the authority to deny certification of the permit application or attach conditions to the final permit. 33 U.S.C. § 1341.

As the District Court construed the FWPCA, the release of ordnance from aircraft or from ships into navigable waters is a discharge of pollutants, even though the Environmental Protection Agency, which administers the Act, had not promulgated any regulations setting effluent levels or providing for the issuance of a NPDES permit for this category of pollutants. Recognizing that violations of the Act "must be cured," 478 F.Supp., at 707, the District Court ordered the Navy to apply for a NPDES permit. It refused, however, to enjoin Navy operations pending consideration of the permit application. It explained that the Navy's "technical violations" were not causing any "appreciable harm" to the environment. *Id.,* at 706. "Moreover, because of the importance of the island as a training center, the granting of injunctive relief sought would cause grievous, and perhaps irreparable harm, not only to Defendant Navy, but to the general welfare of this Nation." *Ibid.* The District Court concluded that an injunction was not necessary to ensure suitably prompt compliance by the Navy. To support this conclusion, it emphasized an equity court's traditionally broad discretion in deciding appropriate relief and quoted from the classic description of injunctive relief in *Hecht* v. *Bowles,* 321 U.S. 321, 329–330, 64 S.Ct. 587, 591–592, 88 L.Ed. 754 (1944): "The historic injunctive process was designed to deter, not to punish."

The Court of Appeals for the First Circuit vacated the District Court's order and remanded with instructions that the court order the Navy to cease the violation until it obtained a permit. 643 F.2d 835 (1981). Relying on *TVA* v. *Hill,* 437 U.S. 153, 98 S.Ct. 2279, 57 L.Ed.2d 117 (1978), in which this Court held that an imminent violation of the Endangered Species Act required injunctive relief, the Court of Appeals concluded that the District Court erred in undertaking a traditional balancing of the parties' competing interests. "Whether or not the Navy's activities in fact harm the coastal waters, it has an absolute statutory obligation to stop any discharges of pollutant until the permit procedure has been followed and the Administrator of the Environmental Protection Agency, upon review of the evidence, has granted a permit." 643 F.2d, at 861. The court suggested that if the order would interfere significantly with military preparedness, the Navy should request that the President grant it an exemption from the requirements in the interest of national security."

Because this case posed an important question regarding the power of the federal courts to grant or withhold equitable relief for violations of the FWPCA, we granted certiorari,—U.S.—, 102 S.Ct. 88, 70 L.Ed.2d 81. We now reverse. . . .

. . . We do not read the FWPCA as foreclosing completely the exercise of the court's discretion. Rather than requiring a District Court to issue an injunction for any and all statutory violations, the FWPCA permits the District Court to order that relief it considers necessary to secure prompt compliance with the Act. That relief can include, but is not limited to, an order of immediate cessation.

. . . We reverse and remand to Court of Appeals for proceedings consistent with this opinion.

It is so ordered.

Air Quality

Air pollution controls developed slowly from the mid 1950s, reaching a high level in the Clean Air Act amendments of 1970. The amendments require the EPA administrator to formulate air quality standards, set a timetable for development, and monitor their implementation. The administrator also approves state plans and, while state officials enforce air quality standards within the state, the EPA can play an active role in inspection and in litigation if standards are not met. If an inspection determines that there is noncompliance with an air quality standard, the administrator will issue a notice and, after thirty days, seek relief in a civil action or a restraining order if there is an imminent and substantial danger. Failure to comply with an order or the implementation plan can bring a penalty of up to $25,000 per day or one year in prison, or both.

In the case of *Union Electric Co.* v. *E.P.A.* (below), the court identifies the roles of federal and state agencies and the remedies available to parties to the action.

Union Elec. Co. v. *E. P. A.*
96 S.Ct. 2518 (1976)

Mr. Justice MARSHALL delivered the opinion of the Court.

After the Administrator of the Environmental Protection Agency (EPA) approves a state implementation plan under the Clean Air Act, the plan may be challenged in a court of appeals within 30 days, or after 30 days have run if newly discovered or available information justifies subsequent review. We must decide whether the operator of a regulated emission source, in a petition for review of an EPA-approved state plan filed after the claim that it is economically or technologically infeasible to comply with the plan.

I

We have addressed the history and provisions of the Clean Air Amendments of 1970, Pub.L. 91–604, 84 Stat. 1676, in detail in *Train* v. *Natural Resources Defense Council (NRDC)*, 421 U.S. 60, 95 S.Ct. 1470, 43 L.Ed.2d 731 (1975), and will not repeat that discussion here. Suffice it to say that the Amendments reflect congressional dissatisfaction with the progress of existing air pollution programs and a determination

to "tak[e] a stick to the States," *id.,* at 64, 95 S.Ct., at 1474, in order to guarantee the prompt attainment and maintenance of specified air quality standards. The heart of the Amendments is the requirement that each State formulate, subject to EPA approval, an implementation plan designed to achieve national primary ambient air quality standards—those necessary to protect the public health—"as expeditiously as practicable but . . . in no case later than three years from the date of approval of such plan." § 110(a)(2)(A) of the Clean Air Act, as added, 84 Stat. 1680, 42 U.S.C. § 1857c–5(a)(2)(A). The plan must also provide for the attainment of national secondary ambient air quality standards—those necessary to protect the public welfare—within a "reasonable time." *Ibid.* Each State is given wide discretion in formulating its plan, and the Act provides that the Administrator "shall approve" the proposed plan if it has been adopted after public notice and hearing and if it meets eight specified criteria. § 110(a)(2).

On April 30, 1971, the Administrator promulgated national primary and secondary standards for six air pollutants he found to have an adverse effect on the public health and welfare. 40 CFR pt. 50 (1975). See § 108(a) of the Act, as added, 84 Stat. 1678, 42 U.S.C. § 1857c-3(a). Included among them was sulfur dioxide, at issue here. 40 CFR §§ 50.4-50.5 (1975). After the promulgation of the national standards, the State of Missouri formulated its implementation plan and submitted it for approval. Since sulfur dioxide levels exceeded national primary standards in only one of the State's five air quality regions—the Metropolitan St. Louis Interstate region, 40 CFR § 52.1321 (1975)—the Missouri plan concentrated on a control strategy and regulations to lower emissions in that area. The plan's emission limitations were effective at once, but the State retained authority to grant variances to particular sources that could not immediately comply. Mo.Rev.Stat. § 203.110 (1972). The Administrator approved the plan on May 31, 1972. See 40 CFR § 52.1320 et seq. (1975).

Petitioner is an electric utility company servicing the St. Louis metropolitan area, large portions of Missouri, and parts of Illinois and Iowa. Its three coal-fired generating plants in the metropolitan St. Louis area are subject to the sulfur dioxide restrictions in the Missouri implementation plan. Petitioner did not seek review of the Administrator's approval of the plan within 30 days, as it was entitled to do under § 307(b)(1) of the Act, as added, 84 Stat. 1708, 42 U.S.C. § 1857h-5(b)(1), but rather applied to the appropriate state and county agencies for variances from the emission limitations affecting its three plants. Petitioner received one-year variances, which could be extended upon reapplication. The variances on two of petitioner's three plants had expired and petitioner was applying for extensions when, on May 31, 1974, the Administrator noti-

fied petitioner that sulfur dioxide emissions from its plants violated the emission limitations contained in the Missouri plan. See 40 Fed.Reg. 3566 (1975). Shortly thereafter petitioner filed a petition in the Court of Appeals for the Eighth Circuit for review of the Administrator's 1972 approval of the Missouri implementation plan. . . .

The court held that "only matters which, if known to the Administrator at the time of his action [in approving a state implementation plan], would justify setting aside that action are properly reviewable after the initial 30 day review period." 8 Cir., 515 F.2d 206, 216 (1975). Since, in the court's view, claims of economic and technological infeasibility could not properly provide a basis for the Administrator's rejecting a plan, such claims could not serve—at any time—as the basis for a court's overturning an approved plan. Accordingly, insofar as petitioner's claim of newly discovered or available information was grounded on an assertion of economic and technological infeasibility, the court held itself to be without jurisdiction to consider the petition for review, and so dismissed the petition. In so holding the Court of Appeals considered and rejected the contrary or partially contrary holdings of three other Circuits.

. . .

III

Our conclusion is bolstered by recognition that the Amendments do allow claims of technological and economic infeasibility to be raised in situations where consideration of such claims will not substantially interfere with the primary congressional purpose of prompt attainment of the national air quality standards. Thus, we do not hold that claims of infeasibility are never of relevance in the formulation of an implementation plan or that sources unable to comply with emission limitations must inevitably be shut down.

Perhaps the most important forum for consideration of claims of economic and technological infeasibility is before the state agency formulating the implementation plan. So long as the national standards are met, the State may select whatever mix of control devices it desires, *Train* v. *NRDC, supra,* at 79, 95 S.Ct., at 1481, and industries with particular economic or technological problems may seek special treatment in the plan itself.

. . .

In short, the Amendments offer ample opportunity for consideration of claims of technological and economic infeasibility.

Always, however, care is taken that consideration of such claims will not interfere substantially with the primary goal of prompt attainment of the national standards. Allowing such claims to be raised by appealing the Administrator's approval of an implementation plan, as petitioner suggests, would frustrate congressional intent. . . . Technology forcing is a concept somewhat new to our national experience and it necessarily entails certain risks. But Congress considered those risks in passing the 1970 Amendments and decided that the dangers posed by uncontrolled air pollution made them worth taking. . . .

Affirmed.

Solid Waste

An increase in population and affluence carries with it a commensurate growth of waste products of that society. Agricultural and mineral wastes make up over half the total produced. While wastes from homes and businesses make up a small part of the whole, their impact on individuals is likely to be greater because those wastes build up where people live.

The major legislation in the regulation of solid waste is the *Solid Waste Disposal Act* of 1965 and its major amendments of 1970. It is recognized under the act that this is primarily a state or local problem but the EPA is authorized to provide technical and financial assistance to state and local governments as well as interstate agencies. Research support and training grants are also made available to foster development of new methods of processing, recycling, or disposing of solid wastes.

Noise Control

The adverse effects of "noise pollution" have long been noted. In response to continuing concern over the contribution of excess noise to physical and emotional problems, Congress passed the *Noise Control Act of 1972.* The main thrust of the act is toward the control of noise emission in manufactured items rather than control of noise in the general environment. Manufacturers must meet EPA standards if products are identified as a major source of noise. Distribution of a product that does not meet the standards or removal of a noise control device is prohibited by law. Violation brings a fine of $25,000 per day or one year in prison, or both. Private citizens, as well as the EPA, may bring a civil action to force compleince with the Act.

Chemical and Radiological Control

The primary chemical danger to the quality, or even existence, of life occurs in connection with the widespread use of insecticides. Admittedly, the problem of control is accentuated by the obvious fact that our society has been able to flourish, based to a great extent upon the ability to feed the population at low cost. That outcome has been reached largely through the use of fertilizers to increase yields and pesticides to prevent the ravages of insects.

The Insecticide, Fungicide and Rodenticide Act of 1947 (amended 1973) provided some regulation over the uses of potentially hazardous use of chemicals in pest control. Later the *Environmental Pesticide Control Act* of 1972 added more provisions covering the use of pesticides. The Act requires pesticides to be registered with the EPA and adhere to extensive and specific standards with respect to labeling, effectiveness, and application. The EPA is required to determine whether the pesticide may have "unreasonable adverse effects on the environment" before it may be distributed for general or restricted use. The EPA also has wide authority to inspect, halt sales, order seizure, or suspend registration of a pesticide to prevent an imminent hazard.

Radiation pollution control is exercised under several of the above acts. The Water Pollution Control Act and The Clean Air Act are two of the major pieces of legislation that contain provisions relating to radiation pollution. Coverage extends from problems connected with nuclear facilities, to such simple household products as microwave ovens or color television sets. Major regulatory activity is the province of the Nuclear Regulatory Commission (NRC).

COMPUTERS AND THE LAW

The importance of data gathering and processing is unquestioned in most areas of human activity. Nowhere is it more evident than in the conduct of business or other organizational functioning. The role of computers in society has expanded significantly in the past decade alone and it is certain that there will be even greater expansion of activity in the future.

Proprietary Rights

Benefits of ownership and use accrue to holders of rights in material goods and the intellectual property attached to them. Both computer hardware and software are affected. Protection of proprietary rights in data processing machinery and programs may be gained in several ways. *Patents* and *copyrights* are commonly sought, although an established *trademark* may be maintained, or a chattel as well as a process may be kept as a *trade secret*. In addition, there may be prevention of use by others under the tort doctrine of *unfair competition*.

A patent, the exclusive right to use for 17 years, is granted to the inventor or developer of a product that is original, useful, and not obvious. Patents for hardware have been readily granted once the above criteria have been met, but applications for software patents have been refused as the Patent Office has considered software programs as mental products and, therefore, not patentable. Although prior court decisions have stated that programs covering algorithms or processes are not patentable, a stored program system in a general purpose computer may be patented (see the case of *Diamond* v. *Diehr*, below).

Diamond v. *Diehr*
101 S.Ct. 1048 (1981)

Justice REHNQUIST delivered the opinion of the Court.

We granted certiorari to determine whether a process for curing synthetic rubber which includes in several of its steps the use of a mathematical formula and a programmed digital computer is patentable subject matter under 35 U.S.C. § 101.

The patent application at issue was filed by the respondents on August 6, 1975. The claimed invention is a process for molding raw, uncured synthetic rubber into cured precision products. The process uses a mold for precisely shaping the uncured material under heat and pressure and then curing the synthetic rubber in the mold so that the product will retain its shape and be functionally operative after the molding is completed.

. . .

The patent examiner rejected the respondents' claims on the sole ground that they were drawn to nonstatutory subject matter under 35 U.S.C. § 101. He determined that those steps in respondents' claims that are carried out by a computer under control of a stored program constituted nonstatutory subject matter under this Court's decision in *Gottschalk* v. *Benson,* 409 U.S. 63, 93 S.Ct. 253, 34 L.Ed.2d 273 (1972). The remaining steps—installing rubber in the press and the subsequent closing of the press—were "conventional and necessary to the process and cannot be the basis of patentability." The examiner concluded that respondents' claims defined and sought protection of a computer program for operating a rubber-molding press.

The Patent and Trademark Office Board of Appeals agreed with the examiner, but the Court of Customs and Patent Appeals reversed. *In re Diehr,* 602 F.2d 982 (1979). The court noted that a claim drawn to subject matter otherwise statutory does not become nonstatutory because a computer is involved. The respondents' claims were not directed to a mathematical algorithm or an improved method of calculation but rather recited an improved process for molding rubber articles by solving a practical problem which had risen in the molding of rubber products.

The Commission of Patents and Trademarks sought certiorari arguing that the decision of the Court of Customs and Patent Appeals was inconsistent with prior decisions of this Court. Because of the importance of the question presented, we granted the writ. 445 U.S. 926, 100 S.Ct. 1311, 63 L.Ed.2d 758 (1980).

. . .

Analyzing respondents' claims according to the above statements from our cases, we think that a physical and chemical process for molding precision synthetic rubber products falls within the § 101 categories of possibly patentable subject matter.

. . .

Our conclusion regarding respondents' claims is not altered by the fact that in several steps of the process a mathematical equation and a programmed digital computer are used. This Court has undoubtedly recognized limits to § 101 and every discovery is not embraced within the statutory terms. Excluded from such patent protection are laws of nature, natural phenomena, and abstract ideas. See *Parker* v. *Flook,* 437 U.S. 584, 98 S.Ct. 2522, 57 L.Ed.2d 451 (1978); *Gottschalk* v. *Benson, supra,* at 67, 93 S.Ct., at 255.

. . .

Our recent holdings in *Gottschalk* v. *Benson, supra,* and *Parker* v. *Flook, supra,* both of which are computer-related, stand for no more than these long-established principles. In *Benson,* we held unpatentable claims for an algorithm used to convert binary code decimal numbers to equivalent pure binary numbers. The sole practical application of the algorithm was in connection with the programming of a general purpose digital computer. We defined "algorithm" as a "procedure for solving a given type of mathematical problem," and we concluded that such an algorithm, or mathematical formula, is like a law of nature, which cannot be the subject of a patent.

Parker v. *Flook, supra,* presented a similar situation. The claims were drawn to a method for computing an "alarm limit." An "alarm limit" is simply a number and the Court concluded that the application sought to protect a formula for computing this number. Using this formula, the updated alarm limit could be calculated if several other variables were known. The application, however, did not purport to explain how these other variables were to be determined, nor did it purport "to contain any disclosure relating to the chemical processes at work, the monitoring of process variables, or the means of setting off an alarm or adjusting an alarm system. All that it provides is a formula for computing an

updated alarm limit." 437 U.S., at 586, 98 S.Ct., at 2523.

In contrast, the respondents here do not seek to patent a mathematical formula. Instead, they seek patent protection for a process of curing synthetic rubber. Their process admittedly employs a well-known mathematical equation, but they do not seek to pre-empt the use of that equation. Rather, they seek only to foreclose from others the use of that equation in connection with all of the other steps in their claimed process. These include installing rubber in a press, closing the mold, constantly determing the temperature of the mold, constantly recalculating the appropriate cure time through the use of the formula and a digital computer, and automatically opening the press at the proper time. Obviously, one does not need a "computer" to cure natural or synthetic rubber, but if the computer use incorporated in the process patent significantly lessens the possibility of "overcuring" or "undercuring," the process as a whole does not thereby become unpatentable subject matter.

Our earlier opinions lend support to our present conclusion that a claim drawn to subject matter otherwise statutory does not become nonstatutory simply because it uses a mathematical formula, computer program, or digital computer. In *Gottschalk* v. *Benson,* we noted: "It is said that the decision precludes a patent for any program servicing a computer. We do not so hold." 409 U.S., at 71, 93 S.Ct., at 257. Similarly, in *Parker* v. *Flook,* we stated that "a process is not unpatentable simply because it contains a law of nature or a mathematical algorithm." 437 U.S., at 590, 98 S.Ct., at 2526. It is now commonplace that an *application* of a law of nature or mathematical formula to a known structure or process may well be deserving of patent protection.

. . .

Because we do not view respondents' claims as an attempt to patent a mathematical formula, but rather to be drawn to an industrial process for the molding of rubber products, we affirm the judgment of the Court of Customs and Patent Appeals.

It is so ordered.

Software protection has been more readily obtained by copyright or as a trade secret. Under a statutory copyright, the holder can control the reproduction and distribution of the work for the life of the author plus 50 years. A common law copyright can exist if the author restricts circulation of the work. A trade secret is a formula or process that is confidential and gives the owner an advantage over competitive businesses. If computer programs qualify under state statutes their unavailability to others gives the owner opportunity to sell or lease the programs.

Less likely is protection gained through registration of a trademark for software. A more remote method of protection is offered in litigation for the tort of unfair competition. This tort encompasses action by a competitor using products, built up through one's diligent efforts, in a manner detrimental to the developer. Protection under this concept exists only if state statutes recognize the tort since federal protection is not likely. Federal courts have held that access to products unprotected by patent or copyright should not be prevented, as such action would interfere with the ends sought by the Constitution.

Torts

Breach of duty or improper activity in connection with computer usage may be the basis for legal action in tort. These may be in the nature of intentional acts, negligence, strict liability, or a combination, much in the same way as in other areas of operation.

Intentional torts, an action with deliberate moves to achieve an end result (or a failure to act when required) may have punitive as well as compensatory damages. In one case the court held that reliance on computer data was insufficient action, and a firm was required to interpret the data generated. In this instance employees of the company visited a car buyer, insisting that payments were not made despite evidence presented to the contrary. When the car was repossessed the court awarded punitive in addition to compensatory damages.

Negligence involves a breach of duty causing damages when a reasonable person would have acted in a manner to prevent injury. Failure to act when required may also be the basis for an action in tort. The plaintiff must demonstrate, in the case of a computer-related error, that there was a program error (as opposed to a data or machine error), and that the operator should have performed in proper fashion rather than in the manner that took place. Many states require, as well, that the plaintiff be free of contributory negligence. In a case where a bank's computer program failed to act on a stop order on a check because of a program error, an award to the customer might result.

Strict liability is imposed for defective products without the necessity for the demonstration of fault. The program itself may be considered a product and liability will accrue when it is defective or a defect may occur as the result of a program error. Strict liability has been introduced as well in banking under the Uniform Commercial Code. UCC 4–302 requires that banks pay or return a check by midnight of the banking day following the day it is received. This has been interpreted as imposing strict liability without negligence or even injury to the payee.

Certain other torts may be more likely to occur on the business scene. A salesperson describing a competitor's system falsely may be guilty of the tort of *disparagement*. In order to be actionable the statements must go beyond mere "puffing" or sales talk regarding the product comparison. A positive claim that a competitor's system will not work with a potential customer's system is actionable if in fact that statement is false. If the false statements are made with respect to the salesperson's own product, this is the tort of *misrepresentation*. If, for instance, a company relied to their detriment on fraudulent representation that it was necessary to automate their accounting system, a court could find for the company when the automated system failed to work.

Unfair competition may take place in various ways. Misappropriation of trade secrets, infringement of a patent or copyright, passing off another party's goods or services as one's own, and using trade name rights are some examples, as is interference with a contract and interference with existing or prospective business. In one case the court found that unfair competition existed where an employee of the defendant firm had wrongful access to files in the plaintiff's service bureau.

Privacy

The ability to access through computers a large base of information and many details of individual lives has led to much concern about the uses of the data available. There are, of course, moral and ethical problems involved, as well as the legal ones, and dangers to the maintenance of personal privacy have been the focus of formal and informal attention.

One of the official responses to these concerns was the passage of the Privacy Act of 1974. The act requires federal agencies (except law enforcement units) to publish notices of the existence of files, permit inspection, copying, and allow addition to statements if disputed. There is also a prohibition against release without the person's permission, with exceptions. The act carries with it civil liabilities and criminal penalties for willful failure to conform. Although the provisions of this act apply only to federal agencies, the act includes a prohibition of use of social security numbers by state or local agencies.

Private data banks may be controlled under the provisions of the Fair Credit Reporting Act (Title VI of the Consumer Credit Protection Act). A consumer reporting agency is required to provide an opportunity for inspection of reports and corrections, if needed. The agency is limited in the opportunity to release information; reports are confined to credit transactions, employment purposes, insurance applications, or other legitimate needs where financial responsibility is a critical factor.

The courts have established the right of government agencies to access individual files in private data banks. In one case, an attempt by the IRS to subpoena an individual's record in a private data bank was supported.

United States v. *Davey*
426 F.2d 842 (1970)

LUMBARD, Chief Judge:

Gerald Davey, as President of Credit Data Corporation ("Credit Data") appeals from an order of Judge Ryan granting the enforcement of a summons of the Internal Revenue Service ("IRS") pursuant to 26 U.S.C. §§ 7602 and 7402(b), and ordering that Credit Data supply the information requested upon payment of a fee of not more than 75¢ each for a report or reports. Davey challenged the summary nature of the proceeding and requested a full hearing including discovery on the issues of law raised by his affidavits. We remand for a brief and summary hearing by the district court limited to the question of what is a fair amount of compensation to be paid by the IRS to Credit Data for the reports. On all other points we affirm the order of the district court.

On April 6, 1967, Louis Avitabile was interviewed by a Special Agent of the IRS and more than 14 months later, on June 10, 1968, a summons was issued to Davey requiring him to appear as a witness and to produce all credit information relative to Louis and Emma Avitabile. On August 12, 1968, Davey appeared but declined to testify. Almost 11 months later, July 14, 1969, this proceeding was commenced by an order to show cause, supported by affidavits of three IRS agents and an Assistant United States Attorney. Judge Ryan's endorsement

denying the relief sought by Davey was filed on October 31, 1969, and an order was filed on December 30, 1969. This appeal is taken pursuant to a certificate granted by this court under 28 U.S.C. § 1292(b) on January 23, 1970.

Appellant is President of Credit Data, a large credit organization. Credit Data produces consumer credit reports for subscribers, and by virtue of its large computer network and retrieval system is able to produce credit information for its subscribers on any of approximately 20 million residents of the metropolitan areas of New York City, Los Angeles, and San Francisco in only two minutes time. Subscribers consist of almost all the banks in the New York City area and large department and retail stores, as well as loan and finance companies. The service provided by Credit Data is a valuable one, but the subscribers pay only a nominal fee for each separate report on a consumer. In return for this service, they turn over their entire credit information and sources to Credit Data, each subscriber thereby gaining the use of the information gathered by other sources. In addition, information digested from public sources is fed into Credit Data's computer. In effect, therefore, Credit Data is a large central depository for credit information, and the IRS, rather than being forced to go from bank to bank to secure the necessary information, merely seeks access to those technological advances to which the subscribers themselves have access.

The district court held that the IRS must be given the information sought at a fee of 75¢ per report. There is, however, much dispute as to the value of these reports and there is no indication that the district judge gave full consideration to Davey's claims that a larger sum is needed fully to compensate Credit Data for the production of the reports. Although there was evidence before the district court that subscribers in California during 1968 paid between 40¢ and 63¢ per report, these figures do not reflect any regional differentials in rates, nor any adjustments which have been made due to increasing costs and inflation. There was also evidence that the IRS had obtained similar reports at a charge of $1.00 per report from Credit Data during 1968 and on argument it was stated that the IRS was still willing to pay that rate.

We remand for a brief and summary hearing on the narrow question of the fair value of each report which the IRS seeks to obtain. Credit Data has made extensive allegations that the use of its computer time and equipment has a value in excess of 75¢ per report. The hearing should be brief, for it was indicated at oral argument that a hearing of two days or less would be sufficient for Credit Data to submit expert testimony. The rate paid to subscribers, while some indication of value, is not conclusive, for the subscriber parts with valuable credit information in order to become entitled to use the Credit Data system. However, the IRS, which conceded at oral argument that it should pay some amount, gives no reciprocal consideration for the printed report. This factor may also be weighed by the district court. We mention these facts merely as

illustrations of the areas to be considered and in no way to limit the scope of inquiry which the district court may feel is necessary in order to determine what is fair and reasonable compensation to be paid to Credit Data for supplying a report.

Credit Data urges that a full hearing with discovery should be ordered on several issues of law and fact, among them: (1) whether the summons is burdensome; (2) whether compliance will injure the business; (3) whether the work product of Credit Data should be protected; (4) whether the summons is vague and ambiguous; (5) whether or not Credit Data possesses the information; and (6) whether it is an unreasonable search and seizure. We reject these claims. There was ample evidence from which the district judge could find that the IRS was acting in good faith and that the summons was proper, appropriate and necessary to its investigation of the tax liability of Louis and Emma Avitabile. Foster v. United States, 265 F.2d 183 (2d Cir.), cert. denied, 360 U.S. 912, 79 S.Ct. 1297, 3 L.Ed.2d 1261 (1959). The summons here is reasonable and not out of proportion to the ends sought. United States v. Harrington, 388 F.2d 520 (2d Cir. 1968). The IRS indicated that the information sought would be useful in determining the net worth of the taxpayers in order to verify taxpayers' returns for the years 1963-1966. IRS investigations had revealed that the taxpayers had obtained several loans from Chemical Bank New York Trust Company during 1964-1965, and they also learned that Chemical Bank is a subscriber to the Credit Data system. Therefore, the IRS concluded that there is a strong likelihood that Credit Data has some information concerning the taxpayers.

The government has the right to require the production of relevant information wherever it may be lodged and regardless of the form in which it is kept and the manner in which it may be retrieved, so long as it pays its reasonable share of the costs of retrieval. It is not barred from securing this information by subpoena merely because it does not make the same kind of contribution of information which is required to those who are subscribers entitled to get information upon payment of a small fee.

Although Davey claimed that he would need discovery to aid in developing facts relevant to a hearing on a reasonable fee, Davey is unable to advise us as to any matters concerning which discovery would be necessary. We must leave to the district court the matter of what, if any, discovery is necessary to develop the facts relevant to reasonable fees, consistent with an early, immediate and summary determination. As we have stated already, there was sufficient evidence for the district court to conclude that the investigation was being conducted in good faith for the purpose of determining the taxpayers' net worth and not solely for

a criminal prosecution. See, In re Magnus, Mabee & Reynard, Inc., 311 F.2d 12 (2d Cir. 1962), cert. denied, 373 U.S. 902, 83 S.Ct. 1289, 10 L.Ed.2d 198 (1963).

We take this occasion to stress again the desirability of expediting the resolution of any question concerning the validity of subpoenas and the production of evidence in the district court as well as on the appellate level. These matters should be given precedence over other business and, upon application, an expedited schedule for the hearing of the appeal on typewritten papers will be ordered. It is now more than two years since IRS first sought to secure this information from Credit Data, and five months since the notice of appeal was filed.

We remand for a brief, summary hearing to determine the fair value to be paid by the IRS to Credit Data for the reports sought. On all other points we affirm the order of the district court. The mandate shall issue forthwith.

In all of the instances of data gathering and its use, the basic problem may be in the balancing of interests: an individual's right to privacy versus the need to promote efficient processes in organizations and the society generally, provides situations involving a delicate balance between alternatives available. The maintaining of records and access to information is power—a phenomenon that is not new, of course, but one that has achieved much greater impact with the advent of the fast and efficient processing that computer systems provide.

Administrative Capability

Computer facility in the functioning of organizations and governmental units should provide the basis for better decision making at all levels. From weather forecasting to welfare planning, the swift collection and collation of information provides a superior basis for administration.

In the area of law enforcement, the Federal Bureau of Investigation has set up a computerized network, the National Crime Information Center (NCIC) with terminals in police stations throughout the country. The Law Enforcement Assistance Administration developed the *System for Electronic Analysis and Retrieval of Criminal Histories* (SEARCH), a computerized set of files covering all arrests in the country.

Computers are playing an increasing role in the management of courts. Cases are tracked through the system as assignments of judges, scheduling of cases, deadlines, designations of attorneys, and other vital information is provided to court administrators. Lawyers, too, have availed themselves of computer programs to assist in researching the law and preparing briefs for trial or appeal. LEXIS (by Mead Data Central Corporation) and WESTLAW (by the West Publishing Co.) are two commonly used systems of data retrieval in law. LEXIS provides entire documents, while WESTLAW relies on document summaries.

Computer Crime

As computer usage has increased so has the incidence of infringement of rights of owners. The ability of criminal law concepts based upon common law to address the problems adequately has been limited, primarily because of the difficulty in fitting in novel and innovative methods of storing and transmitting electronic data. Since electrical impulses are clearly not articles or goods there has been some lag in control of activity in this area. Most states have or are in the process, however, of enacting specific statutes proscribing most acts considered to be violative of individual and organizational rights in computers and their products.

Thefts of or damage to physical property, the hardware, provide few difficulties in prosecution, as the basic concepts of criminal law easily cover the instances of violation encountered. It is with cases involving software, the intangible programs, or the output or computer functioning, where the established principles of criminal law have been inadequate to sort out the rights and duties of the parties. However, if a state has statutes protecting trade secrets, software may qualify and be protected. It may be possible to identify the physical representation of a program once it is on tape or disc as the *res* and thus have that tangible article as the item taken under the traditional concept of theft.

Unauthorized access through a remote terminal to access information or to obliterate it has been difficult to prosecute in the past, but more modern statutes have included this and similar acts. Theft of services or obtaining them under false pretenses may be the section of a criminal code relating to such activity, or the code may be even more specific, such as in the fraudulent use of a credit card to access a system.

The federal criminal code contains sections under which computer-related crimes may be prosecuted. Pertinent sections cover fraud in communication channels, transmitting data in detriment of national security, alteration of public records, malicious injury to government property, and other acts. Although the federal statutes cover only acts in which the federal government has jurisdiction, the interstate transmission of data, federal media involvement, access to federal property, or other bases for federal intervention provide much opportunity for action under these sections of the code.

Government Regulation

One of the most visible areas of governmental activity is the monitoring of business relationships in order to maintain antitrust laws. The possibility of monopolization or the lessening of competition is present in this area and may be enhanced by the opportunities afforded by innovation and technological change. For instance, information sent rapidly to many parties could be the basis for a finding that concerted price determination is present. Packaging of hardware, software, and services has been a target of federal regulators, as has been the restriction of peripheral equipment to the maker's products by the incorporation of control mechanisms in the mainframe; similarly, the introduction of low-profit equipment to attack competition in certain markets, or offering long-term leasing plans at lower prices, may cause federal or state intervention.

As the ability to transmit data over long distances and in networks of many users has increased, the attention of government agents has focused more and more upon activity in the area of communications. Regulation in this sphere is primarily the responsibility of the Federal Communications Commission (FCC). The Commission is charged with the responsibility of overseeing common carriers by wire or radio in interstate or international communication. Data transmission by telephone lines, microwave, or domestic satellite represents the various modes available and under regulation. Much of the regulation focuses upon the requirement that common carriers furnish service upon reasonable request and with just and reasonable charges.

QUESTIONS

1. What fundamental action does the National Environmental Policy Act provide for?
2. Describe the roles of state and federal governments in the area of quality of the environment.
3. May an algorithm be patented?
4. How may a computer service company be liable in a tort action?
5. How is privacy of individual data affected by federal legislation?

glossary

A

A Priori: (Latin) in logic, what goes before must necessarily be followed by an effect.

Ab Initio: (Latin) from the beginning.

Abandonment: relinquishing or giving up property or rights.

Abatement: a reduction or diminution of payment, action, or the removal of a nuisance.

Abrogate: to annul or repeal a former law.

Acceptance: act of complying with offer or receiving goods with intention to retain.

Accessory: one who contributes to or helps the principal actor in a criminal act, before or after the fact.

Accommodation Paper: a bill or note to which an accommodation party puts his name, without consideration, in order to benefit another party raising money.

Accomplice: one who knowingly combines with the primary offender in the commission of a crime.

Accord and Satisfaction: an agreement whereby one who has a right against another agrees to accept something different.

Acquittal: a release by jury verdict or judicial decree.

Adjudication: the act of judging claims of parties before the courts.

Administrative Law: that branch of the legal system dealing with executive or quasi-judicial duties delegated to it by the legislative or executive branch.

Administrator: in a general sense, one who manages. In decedents' estates, one who is appointed by the court to administer the estate of the deceased.

Adultery: sexual intercourse between a married person and one who is not married to him/her.

Adverse Possession: to claim title by adverse possession one must be in hostile possession of the land or property for the duration of the period prescribed by law.

Affidavit: a written statement of facts confirmed by oath of the party making it.

Agency: the acting for or representing of another under authority.

Amicus Curiae: (Latin) "friend of the court"; a third party who provides the court with information.

Analysis of Decisions Systems: the approach developed in this text that focuses upon the decision making in steps of an ongoing process.

Apparent Authority: authority conferred by law upon an agent in that the actions of a principal led others to suppose it existed.

Appellant: the initiator of an appeal from a court decision.

Appellate Court: a court to which appeals and reviews may be taken.

Appellee: one against whom an appeal has been taken.

Arbitration: submission of a controversy to a private, selected person for determination.

Arrest: the deprivation of a person's liberty under legal authority.

Arson: malicious burning of a building (in common law, the dwelling of another).

Assault: a threat of bodily injury (under common law). Now may include contact.

Assignment: a transfer of a right in action relating to property or the property itself.

Assumpsit: a form of action alleging a breach of contract.

Assumption of the Risk: may be used as a defense in a negligence action. One who voluntarily assumes the risk cannot claim damages.

Attachment: a writ or process seizing a person's property in order to bring that person before the court or to save the property for debtors.

Authority: legitimate power; power delegated to an agent by a principal in agency.

B

Bail: procuring the release of a person from custody by pledging a later appearance in court.

Bailment: delivery of goods under a contract, to be returned to the bailor after a particular purpose is fulfilled.

Bankruptcy: an election under law by a financially burdened person or his creditors to have a court determine a distribution of assets among creditors and allow the person a new start.

Battery: an unlawful touching of another without consent (under common law).

Bearer: one holding a check, draft, or security payable to the bearer or endorsed in blank.

Bigamy: marrying while a previous marriage still exists.

Bilateral Contract: a contract by which one promise is given in exchange for another.

Bill of Exchange: an unconditional written order by a person to another to pay a sum to order or bearer on demand or at a set time. Also known as a draft.

Bill of Lading: a document from a carrier noting presence of goods and the terms for transportation.

Bill of Sale: a writing by a seller describing a sale of personal property to a buyer.

Binder: a contract of insurance by a memorandum before execution of the written policy.

Blank Indorsement: an indorsement that does not name the person to whom the paper is negotiated.

Blue-Sky Laws: state statutes to protect the public from sellers of worthless securities.

Bona Fide: actual, real, valid, not fraudulent.

Bond: a promise or obligation, generally in writing under seal, by representatives or trustees.

C

Cancellation: changing the legal effect of an instrument or eliminating part of it through an agreement or court decree.

Capital: net assets of a corporation.

Capital Stock: money value of corporate stock outstanding.

Cause of Action: a plaintiff's right to relief and/or damages when an unlawful act of defendant occurs.

Caveat Emptor: Latin for "let the buyer beware."

Caveat Venditor: Latin for "let the seller beware."

Certiorari: an order granting standing in an upper court for review.

Charter: authority from the state to a corporation to initiate its existence, shown by a certificate of incorporation.

Chattel: property, *personal* chattels (objects) or *real* chattels (leases).

Chattel Mortgage: transfer of title to personal property by a debtor to a lender as security for a debt (now a "secured transaction" under the Uniform Commercial Code).

Check: a depositor's order to a bank to pay a sum of money to a party (payee).

Chose in Action: a claim in the form of intangible property such as wages.

Circumstantial Evidence: facts surrounding an incident from which deduction may be made by a trier of fact in a legal action.

Civil Law: the system of law in European countries based upon Roman law; in the Common Law system, that branch of law dealing with controversies concerned with private rights and duties.

Clean Hands: in equity, relief can be denied to one who is guilty of inequitable conduct.

Closed Shop: a place of work where only union members may be offered employment; prohibited by the Taft-Hartley Act.

Code: collection of laws, systematically arranged, enacted by a legislative body.

Codicil: a writing adding to or modifying a will.

Coinsurance: a requirement that the insured maintain a certain amount of insurance or otherwise be liable for losses up to that amount.

Collective Bargaining: the process of determining the conditions of employment through negotiations between representatives of employer and employees.

Collective Bargaining Unit: the unit participating in an election of an individual unit to represent them in collective bargaining.

Collusion: an agreement between two or more persons to defraud others or the courts.

Color of Title: appearance of ownership when in fact no valid title is present.

Commercial Paper: short-term negotiable instruments resulting from commercial transactions, i.e., checks and promissory notes.

Common Carrier: a carrier serving the public generally for compensation.

Common Law: a body of law based upon the following of unwritten customs and usages of the community; used as a designation for the Anglo-American legal system.

Common Stock: stock without priorities in dividends or distribution.

Community Property: cotenancy of husband and wife in property acquired during marriage; applicable in certain states.

Complaint: means of initiating an action in the legal process by a plaintiff.

Composition of Creditors: an agreement among creditors to accept part rather than full payment.

Concurring Opinion: a separate opinion by a judge in which he/she agrees with the result of the majority but expresses other reasons for arriving at that result. (See **Opinion.**)

Confidential Relationship: a relationship which, because of law or actual conditions, imposes a trust upon one for the guidance of another.

Conflict of Laws: substantive law that determines which state law applies when more than one state is involved in a case.

Constitution: the fundamental law of a state, nation, or association establishing its basic framework and organization.

Constructive: adjective that qualifies a situation implied to exist in law if not in fact, as in a *constructive* trust.

Constructive Service: a writ or notice other than delivery to a person named; service such as through delivery by mail or by publication in a newspaper. (See **Service.**)

Contingent Beneficiary: the person receiving the benefit of a life insurance policy when the primary beneficiary predeceases the insured.

Contract: a lawful agreement between competent parties which, if breached, will be the basis for a legal remedy.

Contributory Negligence: negligence contributing to one's injury and barring one from recovering.

Conveyance: transfer of an interest in land.

Cooling-Off Period: a delay of a strike as required by statute.

Copyright: a right granted to an author for exclusivity in publication.

Corporation: an organization, considered a fictitious person, created under authority granted by the state.

Counterclaim: a claim by the defendant in an action brought by the plaintiff.

Covenants of Title: a legal declaration that the seller has valid title or that no other factors will prevent the buyer from full enjoyment of rights to the property.

Creditor Beneficiary: a third-person creditor of a promisee benefited by the performance of a contract by the promisor.

Crime: a violation of law to which the government applies sanction.

Cross Complaint: a complaint made by the defendant against the plaintiff in response to the original complaint.

Cross-Examination: examination of a witness by the attorney for the adverse party.

Cumulative Voting: voting by shareholders for directors of a corporation in which the number of votes an elector may cast equals the number of shares owned times the number of directors to be elected, which votes may be allocated as desired.

Cy-Pres Doctrine: a carrying out of the wishes of the settlor of a trust as close as possible to the intent when the original use is not possible.

D

Damages: a sum of money awarded in redress of a legal wrong.

Deceit: fraudulent misrepresentation.

Decision: judicially, a judgment of a court settling a controversy; in management of systems, a conscious selection among alternatives.

Declaratory Judgment: determination by a court of the rights of the parties without ordering anything to be done.

Decree: judgment of a court of equity.

Deed: an instrument indicating the transfer of title to land from the owner (grantor) to the purchaser (grantee).

De Facto: existing in fact.

Defamation: a publication exposing one to ridicule, contempt, or otherwise injuring a reputation; a term encompassing both libel and slander.

Defendant: the party against whom the law suit is brought.

Deficiency Judgment: judgment for a sum still due the mortgagee after foreclosure of a mortgage.

De Jure: (Latin) existing in law or as of right.

Delegation: transfer of power from one person to another.

De Minimis: Latin for "a trifle" or "of minor interest." Short form of "de minimis non curat lex" or "the law is not concerned with trifles."

Demonstrative Evidence: physical objects or other concrete forms of evidence.

Demurrer: a pleading attacking an adverse pleading as not stating a cause of action; a defense.

Deposition: testimony under oath taken outside of court.

Depositary Bank: first bank to which an item is transferred for collection even though it is also the payor bank (UCC 4-105).

Devise: realty passing under a will or the process of passing under a will.

Directed Verdict: a verdict complying with a direction by the court to a jury to return a verdict in favor of one party in the action.

Director: an individual elected by shareholders of a corporation to direct the activity of the corporation.

Discharge in Bankruptcy: discharge of a debtor from most creditors' claims under an order of the bankruptcy court.

Discharge of Contract: a contract terminated through performance or other action or by operation of law.

Discovery: the use of procedures for determining pertinent facts before trial in order to eliminate surprise.

Dishonor: refusal to accept or pay commercial paper (draft, bill of exchange).

Dismiss: (a pleading) to terminate an action on the basis that plaintiff has not pleaded a cause of action.

Disparagement: false and malicious statements of the quality of goods of another.

Dissenting Opinion: a separate opinion by a judge stating a disagreement with the result reached by the majority along with reasons for the disagreement. (See **Opinion.**)

Dividend: a payment of cash or stocks to shareholders out of surplus of the corporation.

Domestic Bill of Exchange: a draft drawn in one state and payable in that or another state.

Domestic Corporation: a corporation so designated by the state in which it is incorporated.

Domicile: location considered as the home of a person rather than impermanent abode or, in the case of a corporation, the state of incorporation.

Donee Beneficiary: a third person benefiting from the contract as a gift from the promisor.

Double Indemnity: a life insurance provision for payment of double the set amount if death occurs under accidental circumstances.

Double Jeopardy: the protection against double jeopardy refers to the principle that no one can be tried twice for the same offense.

Draft: an unconditional written order by a person to another to pay a sum to bearer or order on demand or at a set time. Also known as a *bill of exchange.*

Due Care: the standard of care to which a reasonable man would adhere in order to avoid harm.

Due Process of Law: the constitutional guarantee that no person would be deprived of life, liberty, or property through arbitrary or unfair procedures.

Duress: action that deprives another of the exercise of free will; it may be the basis for setting aside transactions under it.

Dynamic Model: a model showing activity in an ongoing process.

E

Easement: a right in another's land, such as a right to pass through.

Eleemosynary: charitable or benevolent, usually applied to an organization formed for such purposes.

Embezzlement: unlawful conversion of property entrusted to the violator in a fiduciary manner.

Eminent Domain: the power to take private property, with compensation to the owner, for public purposes.

Empirical: based upon data gathered in an organized manner.

Encumbrance: a charge against property, such as a mortgage or judgment lien, held by another.

Equity: the value of an interest in property; also, the body of law developed in Anglo-American courts as the result of the inadequate rules under common law forms.

Escrow: delivery of property or an instrument to a custodian who is to make final delivery to another upon the fulfillment of a condition.

Estate: a decedent's property at time of death; also, the extent of interest in land, as in *estate in fee simple,* the absolute ownership of land.

Estoppel: a principle barring a person from pursuit of an action or asserting a point of law because it would be unfair to permit it.

Evidence: information presented for determination of fact by a tribunal or trier of fact.

Exception: an objection to an act in the legal process, as in the introduction of improper evidence in court.

Execution: the carrying out of a court judgment.

Executor: one named to administer the will, upon the testator's death.

Exemplary Damages: punitive damages in excess of exact compensation in order to serve as an example.

Exoneration: an agreement that a party will not be liable for a loss, as a surety getting agreement that another party be liable first on a claim.

Expert Witness: one who has superior knowledge through education or experience with regard to a particular subject.

Ex Post Facto: Latin for "after the fact," usually applied to a law that makes illegal an act that was legal when done. Such statutes are prohibited.

Extraordinary Bailment: a bailment imposing special duties upon the bailee, such as a common carrier.

F

Factor: a bailee to whom goods are delivered for sale.

Fair Employment Practice Acts: laws enacted to eliminate discrimination in employment on the basis of certain personal characteristics.

Fair Labor Standards Acts: statutes enacted to eliminate unfair employment conditions relating to hours, pay, and child labor.

Fair Trade Acts: statutes authorizing agreements to maintain retail prices; now generally eliminated.

False Arrest: the unlawful detention of a person under color of law by an agent of the government.

False Imprisonment: the tort of confining a person without proper authority.

Featherbedding: an unfair labor practice wherein payment is demanded for services not performed.

Fee Simple: a full and complete interest in realty.

Fellow Servant Rule: a common law rule barring a suit by an employee against the employer for an injury by a fellow employee.

Felony: a criminal offense so designated and punishable by imprisonment or death.

Fiduciary: a person occupying a position of trust or confidence.

Financial Responsibility Laws: statutes requiring proof of financial responsibility by those involved in automobile accidents.

Firm Offer: an offer held to be open for a specified time.

Fixture: personal property that becomes part of the realty by its attachment to the real estate.

Forbearance: refraining from doing an act.

Foreclosure: enforcing rights under a mortgage by public sale of the mortgaged property.

Foreign Corporation: a corporation incorporated under the laws of another state (other than the one making that designation).

Forgery: a fraudulent making or changing of an instrument that apparently alters the rights of another.

Forum: a court.

Fraud: the making of statements that are or should be known to be false with the intent to cause injury and the achievement of that end.

Full Faith and Credit: the required recognition by one state of the laws and proceedings of other states.

Fungible: the designation of the homogeneous nature of materials, as when one unit of goods is recognized as the equivalent of each other unit.

G

Garnishment: designation in some states for an attachment; a process whereby a person's property is applied to payment of that person's debt to a third person.

General Appearance: act of defendant agreeing to jurisdiction of a court for all purposes.

General Creditor: a creditor with a claim against a debtor that is not secured by a lien on the property or through a judgment.

General Damages: damages that ordinarily follow naturally and reasonably from the injury caused by an act of the defendant.

General Legacy: a legacy to be paid out of assets of a testator without specifying the source of funds.

General Partnership: a partnership managed by all partners as co-owners with unlimited liability.

Goods: movable personal property.

Grand Jury: a jury that considers evidence of a crime and either prepares indictments to bring violators to trial or dismisses cases, now generally being replaced by the process of information.

Grant: a conveyance of real property.

Gratuitous Bailment: a bailment without compensation to the bailee.

Grievance: a dispute in a work situation under a labor contract.

Guaranty: an undertaking to pay the debt of another should the creditor not be able to recover against the debtor after a suit.

H

Habeas Corpus: (Latin), a court order releasing a person held unlawfully.

Hearing: a court proceeding to hear arguments and determine facts.

Hearsay: out of court evidence offered as proof of statements made, generally not admissible.

Heir: person designated by statute to inherit estate not passing under a will.

Holder: person in possession of commercial paper payable to him as payee or indorsee or made payable or indorsed to bearer.

Holder in Due Course: a holder who, under certain circumstances, is given favorable treatment, including rights in the instrument despite certain defenses.

Hung Jury: a petit jury that had been unable to reach a verdict.

I

Implied Contract: a contract deduced from facts or conduct.

Imputed: action by one attributed to another, such as acts of an agent charged to the principal.

Incidental Authority: authority necessarily related to that granted and needed for an agent to act under express authority.

Indemnity: a right to be reimbursed for loss under certain conditions.

Independent Contractor: one who undertakes a task under contract free from control of another party and responsible only for a specified result.

Indeterminate Sentence: a judgment of the court wherein the period of incarceration includes a spread of time between a minimum and a maximum date when a prisoner will be eligible for parole. (See **Sentence**.)

Indictment: an accusation of crime made by a grand jury or by information.

Inheritance: the passing of an interest from a decedent to an heir.

Injunction: a court order in equity that orders persons to refrain from an act.

Insolvency: a condition where assets are exceeded by debts or liabilities.

Intangible Personal Property: a nonphysical interest in personal property such as a claim under a contract or stock in a corporation.

Interlocutory: referring to a step in the legal process that is not final.

Interpleader: an action by a person faced with conflicting claimants in order that the court decide which claim is to prevail.

Inter Se: Latin for "between parties themselves."

Inter Vivos: Latin for a transaction among living persons on matters before their deaths.

Intestate: describing the situation of dying without a will.

Ipso Facto: Latin for "the act in itself."

Irrebuttable Presumption: a position in the law in which contrary facts cannot be put forth.

Irreparable Injury: an injury of such unique nature that it cannot be compensated through money damages or material replacement.

J

Joint and Several: descriptive of a condition under which two or more persons have rights or liabilities alone and together.

Joint Stock Company: an association wherein members' shares are transferable and control is delegated to a board.

Joint Tenancy: an estate held by two or more persons with right of survivorship.

Joint Venture: a combination of two or more persons sharing profits and losses from a single undertaking.

Judgment: a final decision or order of the court at the end of a legal action.

Judgment Note: a promissory note with a clause authorizing the holder to enter judgment against the maker if payment is overdue.

Judgment N.O.V.: (judgment *non obstante veredicto,* or, notwithstanding the verdict)— judgment in favor of one party although the verdict was for the other party.

Judgment on the Pleadings: a judgment that may be entered based on the pleadings because it is clear from them that the petitioner is entitled to the judgment.

Judicial Sale: a sale under order of the court.

Jurisdiction: the power of a court to act in the case of a defendant or to hear particular cases.

Jurisdictional Dispute: a labor dispute between two unions, each of which claims the right to work on the tasks under contention.

Jury: a body of persons charged with determining the factual basis of a legal action and arriving at a verdict.

Justifiable Discharge: the right of an employer to fire an employee for just cause.

L

Laches: a rule in equity that denies equitable relief to one who has waited too long to file an action.

Land: earth and all things attached thereto.

Larceny: The unlawful taking of the personal property of another with the intent of permanently depriving the owner thereof.

Last Clear Chance: the rule in tort law that considers the defendant liable for the injury of a contributorily negligent plaintiff if the defendant could clearly have avoided the accident at the last moment.

Law of the Case: a rule that matters decided in litigation are binding in later phases of the case.

Leading Question: a question that suggests an answer to a witness or assumes a fact in dispute.

Lease: an agreement wherein an owner of property gives possession of it to another for consideration (rent).

Legacy: personal property given by a decedent's will.

Legal Tender: money regarded as lawful payment.

Letters of Administration: a formal writing authorizing a person to act as an administrator of an estate.

Letters Testamentary: a formal writing authorizing the person named as executor/executrix in the will to act accordingly.

Levy: physical or constructive seizure of property pursuant to a judgment of a court.

Lex Loci: Latin for "law of the place." Refers to place where facts for legal action occurred.

Libel: defamation in written or visual form made without legal justification.

License: a privileged entry upon land of another, less than an easement or right to possession. Example: setting up a sign.

Lien: a right or claim against property; for example, one that can arise through the entry of a judgment and levy by a court against the owner.

Life Estate: an estate in property for a lifetime of a person.

Limited Jurisdiction: legal restrictions upon the power of a court to hear and adjudicate cases.

Limited Liability: maximum liability, as in the case of a stockholder whose loss is limited to contributed capital.

Limited Partnership: one in which a partner is limited in loss to his contribution provided he takes no part in management of the partnership.

Liquidated Damages: stipulated sum in an agreement identifying amount of damages in the case of a breach of contract or default.

Liquidation: the conversion of property into money; the process of winding up and settling affairs of a firm.

Lis Pendens: Latin for "pending the suit nothing should be changed," a legal doctrine maintaining that certain pending actions are notice to others that rights are preserved pending the outcome of a legal action.

M

Magistrate: commonly used to refer to a member of the minor judiciary, such as a justice of the peace or the judge in a city or traffic court; a public judicial official who has the power to issue search and arrest warrants, to preside at preliminary arraignments and preliminary hearings and to make final disposition of petty offenses and small civil claims; in a wider sense, the term refers to any public civil official with executive, legislative, or judicial powers.

Majority: the chronological age specified by law at which an individual is no longer presumed to be an infant but is deemed to be capable of managing one's own affairs.

Maker: with regard to promissory notes, that party who promised to pay; the signer of a note; one who executes and signs certain negotiable instruments.

Mala in Se: (Latin) an act which is wrong in itself.

Mala Prohibita: (Latin) an act not wrong in itself but prohibited by law.

Malice: a state of mind in which there is intention to act wrongfully without excuse or justification; more generally, a state of mind indicative of a "hard heart."

Malicious Prosecution: institution of charges against another without probable cause but with malice.

Mandamus: a writ issued by a court ordering a party to do a specific thing.

Manslaughter: the unlawful killing of a human being without malice; the absence of malice distinguishes it from murder.

Marshal: a federal official whose duties in executing the law are similar to those of a sheriff.

Maxim: statements concerning generally accepted rules of law, usually used in connection with "equitable maxims."

Mechanics Lien: a claim against real property created by law to secure payment for material and labor provided in either repair or construction of that property.

Mens Rea: (Latin) the state of mind required if an act is to be criminal, often described as "criminal intent."

Merchant: a person who by occupation buys and sells goods; a person who deals in goods of the kind or by occupation holds himself out as having knowledge or skill peculiar to the practice or goods involved in the transaction (UCC 2-104).

Merchantable: a quality referring to goods sold, indicating they are fit for the ordinary purpose for which such goods are sold and used (UCC 2-314).

Merger: with reference to corporations, an entity resulting from a transfer of the assets of one or more corporations to another, the latter to be the sole organization remaining in existence after the transfer.

Midnight Deadline: midnight of the next banking day following that on which a bank received an item or notice from which the time for taking action begins to run, whichever is later (UCC 4-104).

Minor: person under the age of majority or legal competence; an infant.

Misdemeanor: a crime less serious than a felony.

Misrepresentation: a false or incorrect statement of fact made without intent to deceive.

Mistrial: a trial that is invalid because of some irregularity.

Mitigation of Damages: action by the party injured through breach of contract to prevent increase of the damages due by the offending party.

Model: a representation of reality; a replica.

Monopoly: such control and power as to have the exclusive ability to carry on a particular kind of business; ability to restrain trade, to stifle competition.

Moot: a matter already resolved or for other reason not capable of being settled by action of the court; one for which judicial decision would be merely theoretical, not practical in result.

Mutuality: in connection with contract, the binding of both parties. Mutuality of obligation refers to the duty of each party to a contract to perform in accordance with his promises. Mutuality of assent refers to agreement of both parties to the same thing.

N

Necessary: in connection with minors, such things as are needed, within reason, to provide for a person's maintenance according to station in life.

Negligence: failure to exercise that degree of care which a reasonable person would use under the circumstances.

Negotiation: in connection with commercial paper, transfer in such a manner that the transferee becomes a holder (UCC 3-202).

Negotiable Instrument: commercial paper signed by the maker or drawer, containing an unconditional promise or order to pay a sum certain in money, made payable to order or to bearer, and payable on demand or at a definite time (UCC 3-104).

Nolle Prosequi: (Latin) decision by the government or state's attorney not to proceed with the prosecution.

Nolo Contendere: (Latin) plea of an accused which indicates no contest to a criminal action and on which he or she may be sentenced.

Nominal Damages: the sum recoverable when no actual damages have been sustained, consisting of a paltry sum indicating a technical invasion of legal rights.

Non Obstante Verdicto: (Latin) n.o.v.; judgment notwithstanding the verdict.

Nonsuit: judgment against a plaintiff who is unable to prove a prima facie case or who does not proceed with the trial, leaving the issues unresolved.

Notary Public: a public official who has the authority to administer oaths and attest to certain documents.

Notice: providing information or knowledge of certain facts. It may be either actual or constructive, the latter being knowledge implied by law from the circumstances.

Novation: substitution of one contract or obligation for another; it may be between the same or different parties.

Nuisance: that which is annoying or disturbing and which prevents the reasonable use and enjoyment of one's property or causes discomfort to the person.

O

Obiter Dictum: (Latin) (frequently referred to simply as dictum)—statement or expression by the court in an opinion which is neither necessary nor bears upon resolution of the issues involved in the case.

Objection: in the course of a trial, expression by counsel of disapproval for some matter or method of proceeding, usually accompanied with reasons therefor.

Obligation: this may have many meanings; the term is used to refer to a duty, whether it be moral or ethical or is imposed by law, by promise, or by contract; it also refers to a debt.

Obligee: a person to whom a promise is made; a creditor.

Obligor: a person who makes a promise; a debtor.

Offer: in connection with contracts, a proposal made with the intention that it may be accepted by the person to whom it is made and will lead to a legally binding obligation.

Offeree: a person to whom an offer is made.

Offeror: a person who makes an offer.

Opening Statement: in a trial, statement of counsel to the jury, prior to testimony by witnesses, advising the jurors of the general nature of the trial, the issues, and forthcoming proceedings.

Opinion of a Court or Judge: a statement explaining and giving the legal reasons for a court's decision and upon which its judgment is based. An opinion differs from a decision. The *decision* is the court's judgment; the *opinion* gives reasons for that judgment.

P

Panel: list of names of persons summoned to serve as jurors, either for a particular court or trial.

Pardon: a release, granted to an offender by the governor or president, from all punishment and disabilities connected with a crime.

Pari Delicto: (Latin) equally guilty.

Parol Evidence: oral evidence. The parol evidence rule provides that oral evidence may not be introduced to contradict or modify a written contract that contains the final and complete expression of the agreement of the parties but may be introduced for such limited purposes as explaining the writing.

Parole: release of a prisoner upon condition that he or she comply with certain requirements; failure to meet such condition results in return to incarceration.

Party: person or persons who take part in or engage in a particular transaction, such as a party to a law suit (plaintiff, defendant) or to a negotiable instrument (payee, maker, drawer, drawee).

Partition: a division of property held by joint tenants or tenants in common into portions to be held severally.

Partnership: association of two or more persons to carry on as co-owners a business for profit. (Uniform Partnership Act, §6(1)).

Pat Down: search of a suspect's outer clothing, primarily for weapons.

Payee: one to whom commercial paper is made payable.

Payor Bank: a bank by which an item is payable as drawn or accepted (UCC 4–105).

Per Curiam: (Latin) by the court; with regard to an opinion, one written by the court with a specific author not designated.

Peremptory: absolute. A peremptory challenge is an objection made to having a person serve as a juror, with no reasons having to be given for objecting.

Perjury: a false statement made under oath.

Personalty: personal property; things which are movable, such as chattels and goods.

Personal Representative: the administrator or executor of the estate of a deceased person.

Personal Service: service of process which is actually (as opposed to constructively) delivered to the defendant.

Plaintiff: the party who initiates a law suit.

Plea: the formal reply of a defendant to a charge; an answer in a court proceeding.

Plea Bargaining: negotiations between prosecutor and defendant, often resulting in the accused's entering a plea of guilty in exchange for reduction of charges or recommendation of leniency by the state.

Pleadings: written statements of the parties to a law suit consisting of a claim for relief and such denials and defenses as are submitted in response; the process by which the parties to a law suit arrive at the issues.

Pledge: delivery of goods to a creditor as security for a debt or obligation.

Police Court: a court with jurisdiction over minor offenses.

Polling the Jury: calling the name of each juror for the purpose of determining that juror's verdict.

Possession: exercise of power over property for one's own use and enjoyment; physical custody and control of property.

Prayer: a request that a court grant the relief desired.

Precedent: an already decided case used as authority for deciding a present controversy.

Preliminary Hearing: a hearing, generally presided over by a magistrate, for the purpose of determining if there is probable cause to believe the accused committed a crime and should be held over for trial.

Preponderance: the greater weight; preponderance of the evidence is that which has greater credibility, that which creates the stronger impression and is more convincing.

Presentence Report: a report prepared, generally by a court officer, at the request of a sentencing judge to provide the latter with information to be considered in determining the sentence to be imposed.

Presentment: in criminal procedure, a written statement by a grand jury charging there is reasonable ground for believing a particular person has committed a crime, having the same effect as a bill of indictment.

Pretrial Conference: a meeting, prior to trial, of counsel for both parties with the judge for the purpose of discussing the matters related to the trial.

Prima Facie Case: one which has been established by sufficient evidence but which may be discredited by rebuttal of the opposing party.

Principal: in criminal law, the actor or perpetrator of a crime, also one who aids and abets in perpetration of the crime; in agency, the person for whom another acts.

Privacy: the right to be let alone, to be free from unwarranted intrusion into one's personal affairs.

Privity: in connection with contracts, that relationship which exists between the contracting parties.

Probable Cause: reasonable grounds, such as would warrant a prudent person in believing certain facts are true; it is more than mere suspicion but less than beyond a reasonable doubt.

Probate Court: a court with jurisdiction over the administration of the estates and affairs of deceased persons. To probate a will is to prove a will.

Probation: a sentence served in the community rather than by incarceration.

Procedure: the various steps involved in the conduct of a law suit and in enforcing a legal right. The law of procedure is sometimes referred to as adjective law as distinguished from substantive law.

Process: the method by which a court achieves a result; commonly used to refer to the means of compelling a defendant to appear; an order issued by a court to acquire jurisdiction over a person or his property.

Product Liability: liability of a seller or manufacturer for injury caused by a defect in the goods.

Proof: a conclusion derived from the evidence; establishing the truth of a matter or a fact by means of the evidence.

Promissory Note: a form of commercial paper consisting of the written promise of one person to pay money to another.

Property: all of those interests, rights, and privileges which a person has with regard to a particular thing.

Prosecute: to proceed with criminal charges against a person.

Prosecutor: the person who brings criminal action in the name of the government against another.

Proximate Cause: the natural and foreseeable cause of an injury.

Punitive Damages: damages over and above those necessary to compensate for injury which are imposed as a penalty.

Purchase Money Security Interest: a security interest by the seller to secure the price in whole or in part.

Q

Quantum Meruit: (Latin) obligation imposed by law to prevent injustice.

Quash: to annul, to declare to be void.

Quasi Contract: a legal duty imposed by law, in the absence of a valid contract, in order to prevent injustice.

Quiet Title: a proceeding to establish a person's title in realty wherein a person with an adverse claim is brought into court and required either to prove the claim or to refrain from asserting it.

Quit Claim: a deed containing no warranty by which the grantor transfers to the grantee only that interest which the grantor has in the property.

R

Rape: unlawful sexual intercourse, by force and without consent.

Ratification: approval of a prior act.

Realty: real property; real estate. Land and all that which is permanently affixed to the land, such as buildings.

Reasonable Care: that degree of care exercised by the ordinarily prudent person under similar circumstances.

Rebuttal: evidence offered to overcome, disprove, or contradict the evidence presented by the adverse party.

Recognizance: an obligation owed to a court to do some particular act, such as to appear before the court as required.

Record: in practice, the written notation of a court's action, step by step. As a verb, the term refers to the act of placing a document on file in a public office.

Recorder of Deeds: official charged with the duty of receiving, filing, and preserving deeds, mortgages, and other documents related to realty.

Recross Examination: at trial, that examination of a witness following redirect examination which is made by the attorney representing the opposing party.

Redirect Examination: at trial, that examination which is made of a witness following cross-examination and which is made by the attorney representing the party for whom the witness has been called to testify.

Reformatory: place of incarceration for youthful offenders.

Register of Wills: in some states, the clerk of the probate or orphans court; official charged with receiving, filing, and preserving wills as well as other documents related to the administration of the affairs and estates of deceased persons.

Rejoinder: in a trial, that stage following the plaintiff's rebuttal in which the defendant may present additional evidence.

Release on Own Recognizance (ROR): pretrial release of an accused on his promise to appear for court as required; used as an alternative to bail of a pecuniary nature.

Relief: redress for a wrong; that remedy granted by the court in satisfaction for a harm.

Remand: to send back. With reference to a case, sending it back to the court from which it came for such action as indicated. In a criminal context, to send a prisoner back to jail or prison following a hearing or other action.

Remedy: the action or object sought through legal process as a means of redressing an injury.

Removal: in relation to causes of action, the transfer of a case from one court to another.

Replevin: legal action to recover possession of personal property unlawfully taken.

Reply: in connection with the pleadings, the written response of the plaintiff to the defendant's answer.

Res: Latin for a thing.

Rescission: setting aside; in connection with contracts, the setting aside of a contract so that the effect is as if it had never been made.

Res Gestae: Latin; an exception to the hearsay rule, words or acts which are a part of and uttered or done during the course of a particular event.

Res Ipsa Loquitur: Latin for "the thing speaks for itself."

Res Judicata: Latin for "the thing has been decided." It refers to the fact that a final judgment by a court of proper jurisdiction is conclusive of the matter.

Respondeat Superior: the master is liable for the acts of his servant; the doctrine that an employer is liable for the torts of his agent or servant committed within the scope of employment and during the course of such employment.

Respondent: in equity, a person who replies to another's pleadings; similar to a defendant in a suit at common law.

Restitution: restoring or making good by giving the equivalent for damage or harm done.

Restraining Order: a temporary injunction.

Restrictive Indorsement: an indorsement limiting further transfer of the instrument.

Retainer: payment of a fee to an attorney for the purpose of employment to the extent that the client has the right to expect legal services when such are requested.

Return: act of a sheriff, marshal, or constable in bringing back to court such forms or copies of documents as he or she was obliged to execute or serve, together with a statement of action taken, such as time and method of serving or inability to do so.

Robbery: a crime which consists of taking personal property from another's person and by force or threat of force.

S

Satisfaction: discharge of a legal obligation by performing according to requirements. Satisfaction of a judgment occurs when there is payment made of the sum awarded to a party by the court.

Scienter: with knowledge; commonly used to indicate the defendant's knowledge of the wrongfulness of actions committed.

Seal: a stamp, mark, or impression affixed to an instrument for the purpose of indicating the formal execution of the document.

Security: that which is given to a creditor by a debtor to make sure payment of a debt or obligation, forfeiture of the object to occur upon nonpayment.

Security Interest: an interest in personalty (or fixtures) given to a creditor to insure payment of a debt or obligation.

Sentence: judgment of a court declaring the form of a punishment imposed upon a defendant who has been convicted of a crime.

Servant: an employee; a person hired to work for another and subject to direction and control of that person as distinguished from one who pursues an independent calling.

Service: delivery by a person authorized by the court of a notice or writ for the purpose of providing official notification regarding legal action. Service of process consists of delivery of such notice for the purpose of securing jurisdiction over a defendant.

Settlement: agreement of the parties to a dispute to a particular method or means of disposing of the matter; commonly used to refer to acceptance by an aggrieved party of a sum of money in payment for injuries without going to trial.

Severalty: distinct, separate. Ownership in severalty refers to sole ownership.

Sheriff: a public, elected, county official whose duties include keeping the peace and rendering assistance to the courts in such matters as service of process, conduct of judicial sales, summoning persons for jury duty.

Simulation: a model of a situation too complex for the use of other models to picture reality.

Slander: spoken defamation. Oral false and malicious statements about another which injure his reputation.

Solicitation: in criminal law, enticing another person to commit a crime.

Solicitor: an attorney; used frequently in this country to refer to the attorney who represents some governmental unit.

Solicitor General: an assistant to the United States attorney general who represents the government in cases before the United States Supreme Court and the Court of Claims.

Sovereign Immunity: exemption of a state or nation (and political subdivisions) from legal liability when engaged in governmental functions.

Special Appearance: appearance for a limited purpose only of a person in court by his attorney. This does not result in the court's securing jurisdiction over the person as is true with a general appearance.

Special Indorsement: an indorsement which names the person to whom the instrument is indorsed.

Special Verdict: jury verdict consisting of answers to specific questions put to it, as distinguished from a general finding for one party as is true with a general verdict.

Specific Performance: an equitable remedy in which a court orders that a contract be carried out in accordance with the agreement of the parties.

Stare Decisis: Latin for "to stand by the decision," to follow precedent; use of a prior court decision as a guide in reaching a decision in a similar case.

Static Model: a model that does not reflect changes over time.

Status Quo: the state of things at a particular time; with regard to contracts, the status quo ante refers to the state of things prior to the time of contracting.

Statute: a law enacted by a legislative body, often referred to as "written" law to distinguish it from the common or "unwritten" law.

Statute of Frauds: a statute which requires that certain transactions be written if they are to be enforced, the purpose being to prevent fraud in the form of perjury.

Statute of Limitations: a statute that sets specific time requirements for the bringing of legal action.

Stay: to stop, to hold in abeyance. A stay of execution refers to stopping execution on a judgment. A stay of proceedings refers to a temporary halt in an action, ordinarily to permit time for accomplishment of some act relevant and essential to the suit.

Stipulation: an agreement between counsel for opposing parties regarding some matter related to a legal action.

Stock: with regard to corporations, stock refers to the firm's capital derived from contributions of subscribers upon the sale of shares. It represents the right of ownership in the corporation. Preferred stock is a class of stock to which some priority is attached such as with respect to dividends. Common stock is that class without any preference.

Strict Liability: tort liability which is imposed for harm or injury caused without regard to negligence; commonly in connection with defective products or with the use of dangerous or hazardous activities.

Striking a Jury: selection of jury members from a panel through the process of striking off certain persons until the desired number is reached.

Sua Sponte: (Latin) on one's own, without request.

Subornation of Perjury: a crime committed by securing another to commit perjury.

Subpoena: a court order directing the appearance of a witness in court. A subpoena duces tecum commands a person to bring to court records or instruments which are in his/her possession.

Subrogation: substitution of one person for another in connection with some legal claim, such as an insurer, having made payment for injury to an insured, who substitutes for the insured as the party in a legal action brought against the person or persons who caused the injury.

Substantial Performance: performance of all the major aspects of a contract.

Substantive Law: that part of the positive law which relates to the rights and duties of persons, as distinguished from adjective or procedural law.

Substitute Service: a writ or notice delivered to an agent or person other than the individual named in person. (See **Service**.)

Suit: a legal proceeding in which the plaintiff seeks enforcement of a right of redress for an injury. Ordinarily it refers to a civil action as distinguished from a criminal action. It is frequently used in connection with equity, in distinction to an "action at law."

Summary Judgment: judgment of a court upon motion of one of the parties when there is no issue as to any material fact but only as to law and based upon information contained in pleadings, affidavits, depositions, admissions, and answers to interrogatories.

Summing Up: at trial, summary of the evidence presented to the jury by counsel for each party in their closing statements. The judge sometimes "sums up" evidence in the charge to the jury.

Summons: a writ or court order notifying a party that legal action has been instituted against him/her and requiring an answer to the charges and allegations made.

Supersedeas: a writ or court order to stay the proceedings.

Supervening Cause: a cause, second in time, which acts independently to proximately cause injury or harm.

Suppression Motion: a motion to hold back or prevent revelation of certain matters.

Surety: one who undertakes responsibility for performance of another's obligation in case the obligor does not perform. According to UCC 1–201, a surety includes a guarantor.

Survival Action: a legal action which survives the death of the injured party.

Suspended Sentence: a judgment of the court whereby incarceration is postponed, often permanently. (See **Sentence**.)

System: an orderly and methodic arrangement of parts into a whole in such a combination as to achieve particular objectives or goals.

Surveillance: police investigation by means of observation, sometimes including listening, for the purpose of gathering information about suspected criminal activity.

Synergy: the working together of products or medicines to provide a result greater than would be achieved by simple addition.

T

Tenancy: an interest in realty.

Tenant: one who has an interest in property; commonly used to refer to a lessee.

Tender: to offer to perform an obligation.

Term of Court: that period of time during which a particular court transacts business or holds sessions.

Testament: a will; a declaration of the disposition one wishes to be made of property and effects upon death.

Testamentary: relating to a will.

Testator: one who makes a will. (Testatrix is sometimes used to indicate female gender.)

Testes: (Latin) witnesses.

Testimony: answers to questions provided by witnesses under oath. It is distinguished from evidence in that the latter may consist of more than testimony, documents and exhibits being evidence.

Theft: the crime of larceny; the taking of the personal property of another without his/her consent with the intention of depriving the owner of its use and of appropriating it to one's own benefit.

Title: in connection with property, the combination of legal rights which represent ownership.

Tort: a breach of a duty imposed by law; a private wrong as distinguished from a crime which is looked upon as a public wrong.

Tort Feasor: one who commits a tort.

Trade Acceptance: a bill of exchange drawn by the seller on the buyer of goods.

Treason: a crime involving betrayal of one's country or state.

Trespass: inflicting harm or injury to person or property by the doing of a lawful act in an unlawful manner or the doing of an unlawful act. Frequently used in the sense of the common law trespass *quare clausum fregit,* that is, unlawful entry upon the property of another.

Trial: a legal proceeding in a court with proper jurisdiction in which there is inquiry into and determination of issues of law and fact. A bench trial is one without a jury.

Trier of Fact: generally refers to the jury, although in a bench trial or in equity it refers to the judge.

Trust: the transfer of property by one person to another to be held for the benefit of a third person or the transferor.

Trustee: the person charged with management of another's property.

Trusty: a convict deemed to be reliable.

U

Ultra Vires: (Latin) an act which is beyond the power or authority of a corporation.

Unconscionable: that which shocks the conscience.

Undue Influence: persuasion which overpowers the will of a person to make decisions.

Uniform Laws: laws drafted by the National Conference of Commissioners on Uniform State Laws, many of which have been adopted in the various states. One example is the Uniform Commercial Code.

index